Reading
Problems

Reading Problems

EDITION

Assessment and Teaching Strategies

Joyce Holt Jennings

Northeastern Illinois University

JoAnne Schudt Caldwell

Cardinal Stritch University

Janet W. Lerner

Professor Emeritus, Northeastern Illinois University

Allyn & Bacon

Boston   New York   San Francisco
Mexico City   Montreal   Toronto   London   Madrid   Munich   Paris
Hong Kong   Singapore   Tokyo   Cape Town   Sydney

Executive Editor: Aurora Martínez Ramos
Managing Editor: Barbara Strickland
Series Editorial Assistant: Jacqueline Gillen
Executive Marketing Manager: Krista Clark
Production Editor: Paula Carroll
Editorial Production Service: Marty Tenney,
    Modern Graphics, Inc.

Composition Buyer: Linda Cox
Manufacturing Buyer: Megan Cochran
Electronic Composition: Modern Graphics, Inc.
Interior Design: Geri Davis, The Davis Group
Photo Researcher: Annie Pickert
Cover Designer: Elena Sidorova

For related titles and support materials, visit our online catalog at www.pearsonhighered.com.

Between the time website information is gathered and then published, it is not unusual for some sites to have closed. Also, the transcription of URLs can result in typographical errors. The publisher would appreciate notification where these errors occur so that they may be corrected in subsequent editions.

Library of Congress Cataloging-in-Publication Data

Jennings, Joyce Holt.
  Reading problems : assessment and teaching strategies / Joyce Holt
Jennings, JoAnne Schudt Caldwell, Janet W. Lerner. -- 6th ed.
    p. cm.
  ISBN-13: 978-0-13-700857-5
  ISBN-10: 0-13-700857-0
  1. Reading disability. 2. Reading--Remedial teaching. I. Caldwell,
JoAnne (JoAnne Schudt) II. Lerner, Janet W. III. Title.
  LB1050.5.R53 2010
  372.43--dc22

                                        2009000182

Printed in the United States of America

10 9 8 7 6 5 4 3 2 1 HAM 13 12 11 10 09

Credits appear on page 482, which constitutes an extension of the copyright page.

Allyn & Bacon
is an imprint of

www.pearsonhighered.com

ISBN-13: 978-0-13-700857-5
ISBN-10: 0-13-700857-0

Contents

11   Improving Comprehension of Narrative Text   274

12   Improving Comprehension of Informational Text   308

Preface

This book is concerned with helping the many children, adolescents, and adults who encounter difficulty with reading. Designed as a text for both undergraduate and graduate students, *Reading Problems: Assessment and Teaching Strategies* guides prospective and present teachers in assessing and teaching students struggling with reading and writing.

Reading Problems is a comprehensive survey of teaching strategies, formal and informal assessment, theory, and research. The reader will find information both from the field of reading and from allied fields, such as special education, bilingual education, medical science, and policy studies. Together, these areas provide a coherent framework for helping students with reading problems.

The sixth edition of *Reading Problems* combines new approaches with time-tested ones to provide teachers a wide variety of approaches from which to choose. Recent research has clarified the reading process and substantiated effective instructional strategies. New insights provide a rich source of innovative diagnostic and teaching methods.

Most of all, we want *Reading Problems* to be a valuable resource for teachers. Hundreds of instructional strategies are presented for immediate use by teachers. Many of the strategies are illustrated by "Strategy Snapshots" depicting examples of actual classroom use. These snapshots are from our own experiences in working with students in the Reading Centers at our universities and with teachers and students in schools.

Chapters 1 through 5 present general information about the reading process and students with reading problems, the use of interviews to obtain information about factors related to reading disabilities, and an overview of assessment, including formal and informal assessment with an emphasis on the vast amount of information gained through an informal reading inventory.

Chapter 6 discusses successful reading intervention programs, including group and classroom instructional interventions. Teachers can use this information to choose a program or to think about developing their own intervention plans.

Chapters 7 through 13 provide in-depth information about language processes, including early literacy, word recognition, fluency, vocabulary development, comprehension of narrative and informational text, and writing. Each chapter includes specific tools for assessment in these areas followed by principles of teaching and practical instructional strategies.

Chapter 14 presents guidelines, strategies, and materials that have proven effective for teaching in multicultural, multilingual, and multiage instructional settings. Chapter 15 provides ideas for instructional options for students with special needs.

Chapter 16 discusses current trends in the roles of reading specialists and the collaborative nature of assessment and instruction in schools.

Changes to the Sixth Edition

Key changes in the sixth edition include:

◆ A focus on teaching students with reading problems in general education classes.

◆ Discussion of new regular education laws, No Child Left Behind (NCLB), and NCLB requiring all students to meet statewide standards.

◆ Information that encourages collaboration of general education teachers and reading teachers to work together to help students with reading difficulties.

◆ An emphasis on language and cultural issues because a large portion of schools' population are English Language Learners (ELL) and use a language other than English.

◆ Information on teaching reading to students with special needs since many students with reading problems are those with identified disabilities.

◆ Discussion of both formal and informal assessment procedures that are crucial for students with reading disabilities.

◆ An emphasis on the importance of early literacy development for young children and an understanding of the student's early childhood experiences with reading.

◆ A thorough discussion of specific reading skills including word recognition skills, fluency, vocabulary development, comprehension of narrative text, comprehension of informational text.

Supplements for Instructors and Students

The following supplements comprise an outstanding array of resources that facilitate learning about reading problems. For more information, ask your local Allyn & Bacon Merrill Education representative or contact the Allyn & Bacon Merrill Faculty Field Support Department at 1-800-526-0485. For technology support, please contact technical support directly at 1-800-677-6337 or http://247.pearsoned.com. Many of the supplements can be downloaded from the Instructor Resource Center at www.pearsonhighered.com/irc.

Help your students get better grades and become better teachers.

PEARSON
myeducationlab
Where the Classroom Comes to Life

MyEducationLab (www.myeducationlab.com) is a research-based learning tool that brings teaching to life. Through authentic in-class video footage, interactive simulations, rich case studies, examples of authentic teacher and student work, and more, MyEducationLab prepares you for your teaching career by showing what quality instruction looks like.

MyEducationLab is easy to use! In the textbook, look for the MyEducationLab logo in the margins and follow the simple link instructions to access the multimedia

"Activities and Applications" and "Building Teaching Skills and Dispositions" assignments in MyEducationLab that correspond with the chapter content. "Activities and Applications" exercises offer opportunities to understand content more completely and to practice applying content. "Building Teaching Skills and Dispositions" assignments help students practice and strengthen skills that are essential to quality teaching through analyzing and responding to instructional encounters and artifacts.

MyEducationLab includes:

◆ **Video:** The authentic classroom videos in MyEducationLab show how real teachers handle actual classroom situations.
◆ **Case Studies:** A diverse set of robust cases illustrates the realities of teaching and offers valuable perspectives on common issues and challenges in education.
◆ **Simulations:** Created by the IRIS Center at Vanderbilt University, these interactive simulations give you hands-on practice at adapting instruction for a full spectrum of learners.
◆ **Student & Teacher Artifacts:** Authentic preK-12 student and teacher classroom artifacts are tied to course topics and offer you practice in working with the actual types of materials you will encounter daily as teachers.
◆ **Lesson & Portfolio Builders:** With this effective and easy-to-use tool, you can create, update, and share standards-based lesson plans and portfolios.

Instructor's Manual and Test Bank. For each chapter, the instructor's manual features key points, topics for discussion, activities, assignments, short-answer questions, and multiple-choice questions. It also provides several case studies with accompanying questions. (Available for download from the Instructor Resource Center at www.pearsonhighered.com/irc.)

PowerPoint™ Presentation. Designed for teachers using the text, the PowerPoint™ Presentation consists of a series of slides that can be shown as is or used to make overhead transparencies. The presentation highlights key concepts and major topics for each chapter. (Available for download from the Instructor Resource Center at www.pearsonhighered.com/irc.)

Speak with your Allyn & Bacon Merrill sales representative about obtaining these supplements for your class!

Acknowledgments

Many people have contributed to this book. We wish to thank the reading professionals who deepened and extended our understanding of issues and strategies by taking the time to answer personal inquiries. We thank the graduate students, undergraduate students, and children we have worked with for giving us feedback on instructional strategies. The staff at Allyn and Bacon, including Aurora Martínez Ramos, Barbara Strickland, and Kara Kikel, provided invaluable assistance in developing this manuscript.

Also, we acknowledge the valuable input of the following reviewers of this manuscript: Peter Edwards, Shenandoah University; Jane M. Hunt, Loyola University; Priscilla M. Leggett, Fayetteville State University; Patricia Perkins, Southwest Oklahoma State University; and Terrence V. Strange, Marshall University.

Joyce Holt Jennings
JoAnne Schudt Caldwell
Janet W. Lerner

Reading
Problems

Overview of Reading and Reading Problems

Reading is not an elective in life, but a necessity.

—Jon Scieszka, U.S. National Ambassador for Young People's Literature

Introduction

The purpose of this book is to assist teachers who teach children with reading problems. We provide diagnostic tools and many instructional strategies to help teachers understand reading problems and to instruct students in their struggles to read. To do something well, people must enjoy doing it, and so we offer guides for teachers to inspire a love of reading. We include many references to children's literature and instructional materials that will help students realize the wealth of information and enjoyment that reading offers. Many struggling readers have learned from the strategies presented in this book, and we hope that the students you teach also will benefit from them.

Who has a reading problem? To answer this question, we relate the stories of several students who were brought to our reading center because they were encountering difficulty in reading. Case Snapshot 1.1 describes five students who have reading problems.

There are many consequences for students who encounter reading problems and who have serious difficulty in learning to read. Although students with reading problems are a national concern, each child, adolescent, or adult must face the failure to read as an individual. For many, the situation is heartbreaking. Reading problems can be devastating for students and their families. In school, these children are forced to face their inadequacies day after day. As failing students, they are often rejected by teachers and peers. In their academic classes, students with reading problems are assigned textbooks that they cannot read, and they are given homework they cannot do. A common consequence is that failing students turn to misbehavior, or they may

Strategy Snapshot 1.1

Children with Reading Problems

Jason.   Jason's mother began to suspect that her son was not developing normally during his early years. He was later than other children in sitting by himself, crawling, and walking. He was slow to talk, and his speech was difficult to understand. Jason's concerned parents took several measures to help him, including obtaining speech therapy, participating in a motor training program, and delaying his entrance to school by enrolling him in preschool for an extra year. These steps did not eliminate Jason's problems. At the age of 11, when he was in the fifth grade, Jason entered our reading center. By this time, he was falling behind his classmates, both socially and academically. While the rest of his class read from a literature series, Jason was struggling with the easy-to-read book, *Curious George*.

Diane.   Diane was born to a substance-addicted mother. At age 8, she was brought to our reading center by her grandmother. Diane was identified by her school as a special education student, and she had extreme difficulty reading even the simplest material. Her teachers were confounded and frustrated with her poor achievement in reading and by her lack of self-discipline. They had given up even attempting to teach Diane to read.

Ilya.   Ilya was a child in a family of struggling Russian immigrants. He did not go to kindergarten because his parents were unable to make the necessary arrangements. Ilya seemed to be intelligent and able, but he was not proficient in English. By the time he entered the reading center at the end of first grade, he was half a year behind his classmates.

Gail.   Gail's mother became concerned when her daughter's once-excellent grades began to fall in fourth grade. She was having difficulty in science and social studies. Gail was confused by the difficult words, sentences, and concepts in her textbooks.

Roy.   Roy was an adolescent, who was classified as a special education student by his school. He had many learning problems. Despite his teachers' best efforts, he had entered high school with a second-grade reading level. He came to the reading center when he was unable to pass the written examination for a driver's license. For Roy, coming for assistance was a desperate cry for help before he completed high school.

Reflective Questions
1. In what ways are these five children different?
2. In what ways are these five children similar?

simply give up, displaying a trait called *learned helplessness*. It is not surprising that poor readers often suffer from low self-esteem. As these children mature, they often find that the doors to personal enrichment and career opportunities are closed to them.

Educators, parents, physicians, and psychologists, as well as society in general, share a concern about individuals who do not learn to read. However, the primary responsibility for reading instruction belongs to teaching professionals. The teacher is the coordinator and deliverer of instructional services, the person most able to help poor readers. Throughout our nation, hundreds of thousands of classroom teachers, reading teachers, and special education teachers help these students read better and enjoy reading.

Reading Problems: A National Dilemma

Although teaching is a personal activity, professionals should recognize the overall situation of reading problems in our nation. What are the costs of reading problems from a national perspective?

If children in a modern society do not learn to read, they cannot succeed in life. Without the ability to read, opportunities for academic and occupational success are severely limited. Society suffers when citizens cannot read adequately. People with low reading levels comprise many of the unemployed, high school dropouts, the poor, and those convicted of crimes. The problems of the nation's schools, the growth of poverty, and the loss of family values all show some association with poor reading.

A few generations ago, people managed to get along reasonably well in the business and social worlds without literacy skills, but this is no longer possible in today's world. Students face more mandatory tests required by federal, state, and local laws than ever before. Periods of compulsory education are longer, and students need diplomas and degrees to obtain jobs. These hurdles, as well as the necessity of filling out application forms and taking licensing examinations, make life for the poor reader uncomfortable and, indeed, full of impassable barriers.

It is said that the "Children must learn to read so that later they can *read to learn*." The ability to read is a basic requirement for all academic subjects. Failure in school subjects can often be traced to inadequate reading skills. Poor reading leads to many kinds of problems. Poor readers have fewer opportunities for gainful employment. Youth who drop out of high school have twice the unemployment rate, they have few opportunities for continued training, and they often lack the qualifications for postsecondary school or college (Wagner, Newman, Cameto, Levine, Garza, 2006: Gerber & Brown, 1997).

National Reading Levels

How serious are problems of illiteracy in the United States? National longitudinal studies show that more than 17.5 percent of the nation's school children, about one million children, will encounter reading problems in the crucial first three years of their schooling (Lerner & Johns, 2009; Lyon, 2003; National Reading Panel, 2000). Accumulating evidence shows that many of American school children are not mastering essential reading skills. The National Assessment of Education Progress (NAEP) national tests that follow student learning, show that more than 68 percent of fourth-grade students performed below proficient reading levels. More than 10 percent of fourth-grade children could not even participate in the NAEP test because of their severe reading difficulties. Further, these problems often persisted even in upper grades: 26 percent of eighth graders and 23 percent of eleventh graders read below basic levels. According to the 2007 NAEP, 26 percent of eighth graders are unable to read at even a basic level (Lee, Grigg, & Donahue, 2007). Among 17 year olds, only 33 percent were able to understand complex information, and only 3 percent were reading at the highest level of understanding (Hennessy, Rosenberg, & Tramaglini, 2003; Lyon, 2003; NAEP, 2000; National Reading Panel, 2000; National Institute of Child Health and Human Development, 1999). Moreover, the reading of books is on a decline. Only 57 percent of Americans read a book in 2002 (National Endowment of the Arts, 2004).

Overall, the statistics about illiteracy are dismal. Studies from the National Longitudinal Transition Study (Wagner, et al., 2006; Blackorby & Wagner, 1997) show that:

◆ 85 percent of delinquent children and 75 percent of adult prison inmates are illiterate.

- 90 million adults are, at best, functionally literate.
- The cost to taxpayers of adult illiteracy is $224 billion a year in welfare payments, crime, job incompetence, lost taxes, and remedial education.
- U.S. companies lose nearly $40 billion annually because of illiteracy.
- Adults on the lowest level of the literacy scale comprise 44 percent of the population and are more likely to live in poverty than adults at higher levels of literacy.

Reading Needs in Today's World

In today's world, high technology and automation have spurred a demand for highly trained people. Because jobs rapidly become obsolete, the process of retraining is a necessity. Workers in every occupation will have to retrain themselves to prepare for new jobs many times during their work careers. The ability to read efficiently is a key tool for retraining and maintaining employment.

With fewer jobs available for unskilled and semiskilled workers, they are likely to end up being chronically unemployed. Moreover, the lack of reading skills among large numbers of young adults threatens to divide society deeply between the highly literate and a low-income, low-achieving underclass unequipped for educational and professional advancement.

Need for Early Identification and Instruction

Research shows the importance of identifying young children with reading problems and providing early reading instruction. Seventy-four percent of children who are unsuccessful at reading in third grade are still unsuccessful in ninth grade (Lyon, 2003; National Institute of Child Health and Human Development, 1999). Moreover, many of the reading problems faced by today's adolescents and adults were not resolved during their early childhood years.

Unfortunately, many young children with reading problems are not identified early and thus are not given appropriate instruction. For example, most children with reading and learning disabilities are not identified until ages 9 to 14, after they have actually failed (U.S. Department of Education, 2007). This approach to delay instruction is sometimes referred to as the *wait-and-fail* approach to identification of reading problems.

Some of the major findings of wide-scale research studies in reading development reading disorders and reading instruction are (Lyon, 2003):

- Reading is so critical to success in U.S. society that reading failure not only constitutes an educational problem but also rises to the level of a major public health problem.
- Children most at risk for reading failure are those who enter school with limited exposure to the English language and who have little prior understanding of concepts related to phonemic sensitivity, letter knowledge, print awareness, the purposes of reading, and oral language and verbal skills, including vocabulary.

◆ Early identification of young children with precursors of reading problems and timely intervention are essential to maximizing treatment success in children who are at risk for reading failure.

The toll of reading failure is poignantly revealed by the personal stories from well-known adults who have suffered in a world that requires people to read (see Table 1.1).

TABLE 1.1 *Personal Stories about Reading Disabilities*

I remember vividly the pain and mortification I felt as a boy of 8 when I was assigned to read a short page of scripture with a community vesper services during the summer vacation in Maine—and did a thoroughly miserable job of it.

> Nelson Rockefeller
> 41st Vice President of the United States

I'm not lazy, I'm not stupid, I'm dyslexic. My parents grounded me for weeks at a time because I was in the bottom 3 percent in the country in math. On the SATs, I got 159 out of 800 in math (Smith, 1991).

> Henry Winkler
> Actor, Director, Producer

I got all C's and D's in school and I am mildly dyslexic. But I am very persistent and ambitious. When I applied to college, the admissions officer said I wasn't what they wanted. . . . I think that having dyslexia is a competitive advantage. Dyslexic people are good at setting everything aside to pursue one goal. Ambition beats genius 99 percent of the time (Smith, 1991).

> Jay Leno
> Comedian and Late-Night Talk Show Host

When I was about 7 years old, I had been labeled dyslexic. I'd try to concentrate on what I was reading, then I'd get to the end of the page and have very little memory of anything I'd read. I would go blank, feel anxious, nervous, bored, frustrated, dumb. I would get angry. My legs would actually hurt when I was studying. My head ached. All through school and well into my career I felt like I had a secret.

> Tom Cruise
> Actor
> "My Struggle to Read"

Charles Schwab, the innovative investment broker, struggled with severe reading problems throughout his life. He coped by developing other abilities, the capacity to envision, to anticipate where things are going, and to perceive solutions to business problems. He believed that his reading problem forced him to develop these skills at a higher level than attained by people for whom reading came easily.

> Charles Schwab
> Founder of the Schwab Stock Brokerage Company

Where Do Children with Reading Problems Receive Help?

What kinds of reading assistance are students with reading problems receiving? Most students with reading problems are in *general education classes*. These children may receive some additional special assistance in reading. Some students receive help through school- or state-sponsored reading programs Other students are served through *Title I* programs, which are federal programs that support the teaching of basic skills education for students in low-income schools. About five million children have disabilities and are served though special education programs, under the *Individuals with Disabilities Education Improvement Act* of 2004 (IDEA-2004). Almost 50 percent of students in special education have learning disabilities, and 80 percent of students with learning disabilities have reading problems (Lerner and Johns, 2009). The educational settings for students with learning disabilities include the general education class (47 percent), resource rooms (38 percent), special classes (14 percent), and a small percentage are in other settings (1 percent) (Lerner and Johns, 2009; U.S. Department of Education, 2007). Some students receive reading instruction through private reading education therapists. However, a substantial number of students with reading problems receive no additional help other than general classroom instruction.

Different Models of Reading Assessment and Instruction

In this section, we describe three different models or approaches for providing reading assessment and instruction: (1) response-to-intervention (RTI); (2) the components model of reading (CMR); and (3) differentiated instruction. Each model is described in this section.

Response-to-Intervention

The response-to-intervention (RTI) is a relatively new approach for reading instruction and assessment, as well as in other academic areas. RTI is advocated by the U.S. Department of Education in IDEA-2004 and in the regulations for this law (2006). RTI is an instructional method for *all* students in general education. RTI requires that schools use an *evidenced-based* or *research-based* instructional method that is supported by research. An underlying assumption of RTI is that students will learn to read and reading problems will be resolved by using an evidenced-based method of reading instruction.

Evidenced-based instruction is described in the No Child Left Behind (NCLB) Act (2001) as instructional programs that apply rigorous, systematic, and objective procedures to obtain valid knowledge that is relevant to the development of instruction. According to NCLB, evidenced-based programs have to be objective, valid, reliable, systematic, and research based. However, in an extensive study of evidence-based research in education, Slavin (2008) concluded that evidenced-based research in education, including reading programs that have been used in RTI that were purported to be evidenced-based programs, had serious statistical shortcomings in terms of being evidenced-based programs.

In the classical approach to reading assessment, a diagnosis or evaluation of a student encountering a reading difficulty is the initial step to determine the nature of the student's reading problem. (See Chapter 4 and Chapter 5.) Unlike the classical approach to reading assessment, RTI first provides instruction, and an assessment or evaluation occurs only if the student does not respond successfully to the intervention or instructional method after several levels or tiers of instruction. Each tier of intervention provides increasingly levels of intensity of instruction taught in smaller groups (Gersten & Dimiro, 2006; Fuchs, Mock, Morgan & Young, 2003). The underlying expectation of RTI is that the evidenced-based instruction will reduce the prevalence of reading failure.

There are a number of models or versions of RTI, as well as the suggested number of tiers or levels of instruction for RTI. A common approach, however, is to use three tiers of instruction, which are described here (Division for Learning Disabilities, 2007).

The RTI process begins with Tier 1, which is high-quality instruction (or evidenced-based intervention) that is given to all students in the general education class. Students who do not respond adequately to the high-quality instruction in the general education class go to Tier 2. In Tier 2, students are taught with the evidenced-based program but with increasing intensity, in a smaller group of children, and the use of supplemental programs. Students who do not respond successfully in Tier 2, go to Tier 3. In Tier 3, children are taught with the evidenced-based program with even greater intensity in even smaller groups, and more instructional and behavioral supports (Division for Learning Disabilities, 2007).

Tiers of Intervention.   As noted, the RTI model highlights the concept of tiers of intervention. Different models of RTI use different numbers of tiers (or levels of intervention). Many schools use three tiers of intervention, which are described here (Division for Learning Disabilities, 2007).

◆ **Tier 1.**   Tier 1 intervention is high-quality instruction delivered to *all* students in the general education classroom. High-quality instruction uses a method that is judged to be scientifically based or an evidenced-based program.

◆ **Tier 2.**   Tier 2 is for students who are not progressing (responding) adequately in Tier 1. Students in Tier 2 are given additional high-quality instruction in a smaller group and supplemental instructional programs. Students who respond positively to the intervention in Tier 2 return to the general education class. Students who do not respond to Tier 2 intervention go into Tier 3.

◆ **Tier 3.**   In Tier 3, students are given even more intensive intervention using evidenced-based methods in smaller groups, more instructional and behavioral supports, supplemental instructional programs, and more probes of progress. Students who respond adequately to this intervention go back to Tier 2 and eventually to Tier 1. Students who do not respond adequately may be recommended for a comprehensive evaluation or assessment.

The three tiers of intervention are illustrated in Figure 1.1.

Progress Monitoring in RTI. In the RTI framework, ongoing **progress monitoring** is used to determine whether students are responding to the evidenced-based instructional program. Progress monitoring is a *curriculum-based measure* (CBM) of achievement. Information that is collected through progress monitoring allows teachers to make judgments continuously about the success of the instruction and whether the intervention results in progress for the student or whether it results in no progress (Division for Learning Disabilities, 2007; Stecker, 2007).

Implementing RTI: Standard Protocol and Problem-Solving Protocol. There are two approaches to implementing RTI: (1) In the **standard protocol model** of RTI, the teaching methods are the same for all students and (2) in the **problem-solving model**, the teacher considers the individual needs of each student.

FIGURE 1.1 Tiers of Intervention in Response-to-Intervention (RTI)

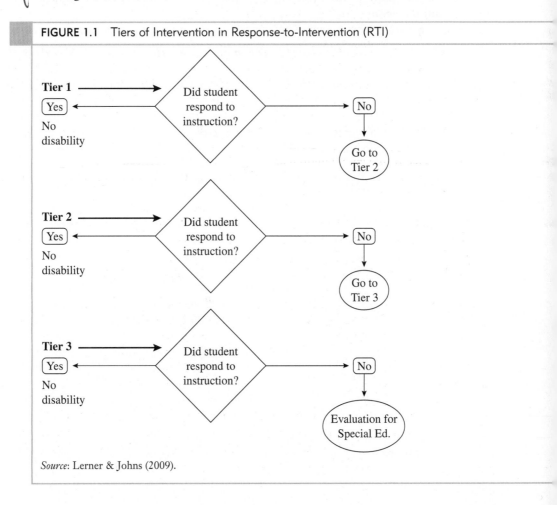

Source: Lerner & Johns (2009).

The Law and RTI. Laws that cover RTI include *the Regulations for the Individuals with Disabilities Education Improvement Act of 2004* (2006) and IDEA (2004). The regulations for this law were published in 2006, and permit schools and states to decide whether they will use RTI or a method that evaluates the student. At the present time, a few states are mandating RTI but most states are not mandating its use (Zirkel & Krohn, 2008).

The Components Model of Reading

Another model of reading instruction and assessment is the *components model of reading* (CMR). This model identifies the components that are involved in reading. Reading instruction then targets the component that is causing the reading difficulty for the student (Aaron, Joshi, Gooden, & Bentum, 2008; Aaron, Joshi & Williams, 1999). As shown in Figure 1.2, the two major components of reading are *word recognition* and *reading comprehension*. Word recognition has the subcomponents of *phonological awareness* and *fluency*. Reading comprehension includes the subcomponents of *vocabulary* and *enjoyment of reading*

Each of these components of reading is discussed in this book (see Table 1.2).

Components of Reading Recommended by the National Reading Panel. Another concept of the essential components of reading was presented in the research of the *National Reading Panel*. The 2000 National Reading Panel was a commission of reading scholars that was assigned by the U.S. Congress to conduct an evidence-based assessment of the research literature on reading and its implications for reading instruction. Finding that over 100,000 research studies on reading had been published since 1966, the National Reading Panel established stringent criteria for the inclusion of research studies in their evidence-based assessment. (More information about their findings is available at the website www.nationalreadingpanel.org.)

FIGURE 1.2 Components of Reading

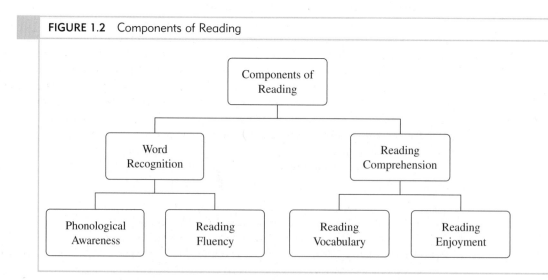

TABLE 1.2 Components of Reading

Component	Chapter
Word Recognition	Chapter 9. Improving Word Recognition Accuracy
Reading Comprehension	Chapter 11. Improving Comprehension of Narrative Text
	Chapter 12. Improving Comprehension of Informational Text
Phonological Awareness	Chapter 7. Early Literacy
Reading Fluency	Chapter 9. Improving Reading Fluency
Reading Vocabulary	Chapter 10. Improving Vocabulary Development and Listening Comprehension
Enjoyment of Reading	Chapter 6. Providing Instruction and Intervention Strategies

The panel concluded that the following reading components of reading were essential for competent effective readers. The National Reading Panel (2000) noted that instructional reading programs have to include these components to be considered as evidenced-based reading programs:

1. Phonemic awareness
2. Phonics
3. Fluency
4. Vocabulary
5. Text comprehension

Differentiated Instruction

Go to MyEducationLab and select the topic *Differentiating Instruction*. Then, go to the Activities and Applications section, watch the video entitled "Teaching to Diverse Learning Styles," and respond to the accompanying questions.

Differentiated instruction is another approach for reading assessment and instruction. Differentiated instruction proposes that teaching should be geared to each student's way of learning and interests. Instead of using a standardized approach for all students, the specific needs and characteristics of each individual student is taken into consideration. According to Mel Levine (2002), one of the biggest mistakes teachers make is to treat everyone equally when it comes to learning. Children process information differently from one another: Some form images, others form words, and still others form sentences. Differentiated instruction takes each student's individual needs into account.

The basic underlying beliefs for differentiated instruction include the following ideas:

◆ No two children are alike.
◆ No two children learn in an identical way.
◆ It is not possible to treat everyone the same when it comes to learning.
◆ An enriched environment for one student is not necessarily an enriched environment for another.

In the general education classroom, there will be differences among students in their prior knowledge about a subject, in the skills they already possess, in their motivation to learn, and in their proficiency with English. When teachers take such differences into account, they can make adaptations to the curriculum and use a variety of teaching and learning strategies. Teachers can provide tasks at varied levels of difficulty, give students varying degrees of support, arrange groups to meet student needs, and vary time allotments for different students (Tomlison, Brimijoin, & Navaez, 2008; Bender, 2006; Tomlinson and McTighe, 2006; Tomlinson & Edison, 2003).

Differentiated instruction offers a way to understand each child. This approach emphasizes that children do not respond to a *one-size-fits-all* curriculum; instead, they need teaching that responds to their personal talents, interests, strengths, proclivities, and cognitive ways of processing information. Children process information differently from one another. Differentiated instruction takes the child's individual needs into account in planning the teaching (see Table 1.3) (Tomlison, 2003).

In many ways, differentiated instruction is similar to basic ideas in teaching special education students, especially students with learning disabilities. Special education seeks to find the way to teach each unique exceptional student. However, differentiated instruction applies to *all* children in the classroom (Bender, 2006; Tomlinson and McTighe, 2006; Tomlison, 2003).

Go to MyEducationLab and select the topic *Formal Assessments*. Then, go to the Activities and Applications section, watch the video entitled "Multiple Intelligences in the Classroom," and respond to the accompanying questions.

Differentiated Instruction for Teaching Reading. *The Access Center: Improving Outcomes for All Students* has a website that focuses on differentiated instruction for teaching reading www.k8accesscenter.org/training_resources/readingdifferentiation. This site suggests that reading implementation looks different for each student and each assignment. In teaching reading, teachers should:

1. ***Use diagnostic assessment to determine an individual student's readiness.*** Informal or formal assessments can be used. For example, the teacher can give a pretest, question students about their background

---

TABLE 1.3   Considering Differentiated Instruction

- ◆ Know the student's interests. Try to use those interests in teaching the student and incorporate them into the curriculum.
- ◆ Know the student's learning preference. How does the student like to learn—visually, auditorily, or by doing things like building something or using art.
- ◆ Know the student's learning pace or rate. Does the student like to do things quickly? Does the student need extra time to process what is being learned?
- ◆ What are the student's personal interests? How can these interests be incorporated into the curriculum?
- ◆ What talents does the student have? Athletics, music, debate, playing chess, art? How can they be brought into curriculum?
- ◆ How is the student's English proficiency? Is the student an English Language Learner (ELL)? Can the student's facility with a native language be used in the learning?

knowledge, or use a KWL chart to discover what the student already **K**nows, what they **W**ant to know, and what they have **L**earned about a topic. (See Chapter 12 for a discussion of K-W-L.)

2. *Determine the student's interest.*   For example, use an interest inventory and/or include students in the planning process. Teachers can ask students to tell what specific interests they have and use these interests to develop lessons.

3. *Identify student styles and environmental preferences.*   Use a learning style inventory. Ask students how they learn best, and observe student activities. To identify environmental preferences, determine if students work best in large or small groups. What environmental factors might inhibit student learning?

How Does a Student Construct Meaning in Reading?

In this section, we discuss the dimensions that contribute to constructing meaning in reading. A physician trying to heal a sick patient must have an understanding of the healthy human body. In the same way, a teacher trying to help a student who has reading problems must understand what good readers do. The findings of studies of the reading process enables teachers to improve their understanding of reading and thus to improve their ability to teach it.

When people read, they actually construct their own meaning of a text; in other words, people create their own mental version of what they read. Three factors contribute to the process of constructing meaning: (1) the reader, (2) the reading material, and (3) the reading situation.

Go to MyEducationLab and select the topic *Comprehension*. Then, go to the Activities and Applications section, watch the video entitled "Checking Comprehension," and respond to the accompanying questions.

Imagine that you are reading a novel. Rather than simply acquiring information, you are actively creating, in your mind, your own personal version of the material you are reading. The version you make is not exactly like what you read on paper. Instead, you, the reader, contribute to the construction of meaning. You visualize the characters and the scenery in a story. In fact, your mind probably even supplies details that are not in the book.

Compare your mental image of a character in a novel with that made by a friend. You will find that no two people's images are ever exactly alike.

Most people have had the rude shock of seeing a movie made from a favorite book and realizing that the actors look nothing like the image they created when they read.

As you read the following selection, you are constructing meaning in your own mind.

The minute she saw the weight register on the scale, she realized she was the winner. She knew exactly how she would spend the prize money.

What meaning do you construct from this passage? Perhaps you "see" a dieter involved in a contest to lose weight and looking forward to buying new clothes. Or you might imagine a farmer getting an award for the largest livestock or pumpkin and planning to spend it on a new tractor or a family vacation. You might imagine a person who caught a large fish, and the money might be reinvested in expensive fishing equipment. Perhaps you thought of even another interpretation. The meaning you construct reflects your background and life experiences.

Students with reading problems are often reluctant to construct their own meaning and interpretation of the text. The fear that they might get something "wrong" prevents them from interpreting the text in an imaginative way. This worry is reinforced when teachers ask large numbers of factual questions, thus giving a perception that reading is a "right" and "wrong" act. Chapter 9 offers several suggestions for fostering personal responses in students when they read. Personal responses help students create their own meaning of the text, resulting in better and deeper comprehension.

In the process of constructing meaning, there are three contributing sources: (1) contributions of the reader, (2) contributions of the written material (or text), and (3) contributions of the reading situation. Figure 1.3 illustrates the contributions of three elements to the construction of meaning.

Contribution of the Reader

The reader forms the cornerstone of reading, because meaning is actually constructed in the reader's mind. The reader activates and controls the reading process. The reader's background, interest, attitude, purpose, and ability dramatically influence the

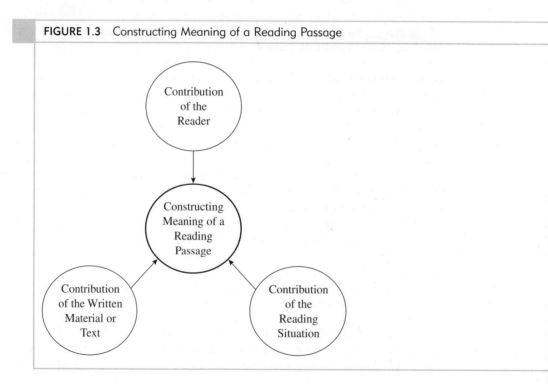

FIGURE 1.3   Constructing Meaning of a Reading Passage

reading process. Reading builds on the reader's *background knowledge*; the richer or more detailed this background is, the richer the reading experience will be. All of us have an easier time reading about familiar topics. A child who has ridden horses is able to understand the terms about horseback riding in the children's book *Black Beauty* (Sewell). This child will have pleasant associations with the book and will find it relatively easy to identify with the problems of the characters. In contrast, a child who brings little background knowledge to *Black Beauty* is likely to have a less-rewarding reading experience.

reasons to build background knowledge

Helping low-achieving students to build their background information is important for two reasons. First, research has shown that these students have less background information than their average-achieving peers. Second is because students with reading problems often have difficulty recognizing words, so they need clues to help them. A good grasp of background information enables the student to use the clue of meaning (or context) when a word cannot be immediately recognized.

Other activities before the reader may be necessary to build background knowledge

The effects of improving background knowledge can be shown through the third-grade reading instruction that was planned for a school with many at-risk children. One reading selection "Through Grandpa's Eyes" (MacLachlan) dealt with the concept of blindness and how blind people can cope through their other senses. Before the children worked with the story, teachers read an encyclopedia article about blindness to them. Next, teachers listed story words that could be identified through other senses, such as marigold and cello; and the children determined how each could be identified, whether by taste, touch, hearing, or smell. After these background knowledge activities, the children's new understanding of blindness and the five senses helped them to comprehend subtle ideas and to recognize words in the story.

Interest is another important way that the reader influences the reading process. Have you ever noticed that many people don't read the sports section of a newspaper until a hometown champion sparks their interest? Interests seem to be particularly important during childhood, as children pursue dozens of series books, such as Baby-Sitter's Club (Martin), or read intensively about a favorite topic, such as dinosaurs. Interest can be a critical factor in helping students with reading problems. Engagement in a subject can keep a struggling reader both absorbed in a book and wanting to read other books. Ten-year-old George, a child in our reading center, refused to read until his tutor discovered his passion for snakes. Suddenly, he was devouring fact books on snakes, snake stories, and snake poems. Throughout this instruction, George was gaining critical practice in reading. He was delighted when his father bought him *Snakes* (Wexo) and *Amazing Poisonous Animals* (Parsons) for Christmas.

Background knowledge and interest are tied together

Of course, interest and background are related. People who are interested in a topic will read about it and, as they read, increase their background information. Therefore, when teachers build their students' interests in what they are reading, they also strengthen their students' reading processes.

The *attitude* of the reader is also an important factor in constructing meaning. One adult reported that she found any article about physics almost impossible to understand because of an unfriendly teacher long ago in a high school physics class. However, she had warm memories of a chemistry teacher who made chemistry very readable. Many students with reading problems are literally afraid of books. Nine-year-old Kenisha experienced a magical feeling of achievement after she overcame her fear of books and read and enjoyed her first hardcover book. For those who teach students with problems, developing positive attitudes toward reading is an extremely important and sometimes challenging task. Many suggestions are given in Chapter 6.

A reader's *purpose* also affects the reading process. Good readers use strategies that fulfill their purposes for reading. Most people use a phone book, for example, simply to locate the number they want. They turn as quickly as possible to the right page, locate the number, and close the book. Unfortunately, many students with reading problems are not this efficient. We still remember a teenager with reading disabilities who was trying to locate the name "Weiss" by starting from page one of a telephone book. When we read to fulfill our purposes, we are doing strategic reading. Strategic reading is difficult for students with reading problems.

The reader's *ability* plays a part in meaning construction. Students with reading problems must often struggle to recognize words and comprehend text. Therefore, they have less energy to pay attention to the meaning of what they are reading.

Contribution of the Written Material

The written material, or text, is a second contribution to the construction of meaning. Without the text, no reading can occur, because the reader uses the material as the input from which to construct meaning. The material sets limits on the construction of meaning that the reader may make. A person reading a manual about health care may decide that some of the author's points are more important than others or may even disagree with some things. However, the reader would probably not think the manual was about using a computer.

Finding the right materials is particularly important for a student who experiences reading difficulties. For one student who had a key interest in snakes, a book about snakes was a key factor in the success of his instruction. Finding books that are interesting yet not too difficult may be a particular challenge.

Students must also learn how to handle many different types of materials. Good readers can often teach themselves to read science texts, computer manuals, and novels strategically. In contrast, readers with problems need direct instruction in the strategies appropriate for different types of reading.

Contribution of the Reading Situation

The reading situation is the third contribution to constructing meaning. One element of the reading situation is the task the reader must accomplish. Imagine that you are leisurely reading, and enjoying, Ernest Hemingway's novel *The Old Man and the Sea*. In fact, you are enjoying this novel despite the fact that it was assigned for an English class. Suddenly, you realize that you have a test on the book tomorrow. The reading situation changes dramatically. You read hurriedly, focusing on getting through the book and trying to understand what it means. In later years, your memory of this novel (or put another way, your construction of meaning) will probably include unpleasant associations of rapid reading and tension.

make reading enjoyable

Students with reading problems often find themselves studying difficult material at a rapid pace to meet classroom demands. They rarely have time to enjoy true leisure reading. Teachers must structure their activities so that these students can read for enjoyment.

The *environment* in which we read is another element of the reading situation. We relax by reading magazines or novels on a couch or in a bed (these situations often result in an even more relaxing nap). Teachers should do all they can to make the environment inviting for students with reading problems. A well-organized, colorful room with beanbag chairs and pillows to curl up with helps students experience reading as pleasurable.

Key Elements of Teaching Reading

In this section, we briefly review some of the key elements of teaching reading. Each of these elements is discussed in greater detail in specific chapters of this book.

Early Literacy

The young child learns many concepts as an emergent reader. In the early stages of literacy development, young children must learn to develop facility with oral language, concepts about print, develop knowledge about the alphabet, develop awareness of phonemic sounds in language, learn letter-sound correspondence, and acquire beginning reading vocabulary. Such knowledge is usually learned in the preschool and kindergarten years, but students with reading problems may still be mastering emergent literacy skills long after these ages. Early literacy is discussed in detail in Chapter 7.

Word Recognition

To read the text, students must recognize the words written on the page. There are several strategies that are used to recognize words, including (1) *phonics* (ability to match letters with their sound equivalents; (2) *structural analysis* (ability to recognize the parts of unknown words; and (3) *context clue* (skills in recognizing clues in the sentences to help recognize a word). Accurate word recognition is often difficult for disabled readers. Word recognition accuracy is discussed in Chapter 8.

Reading Fluency

In addition to recognizing words accurately, students need to read them quickly and fluently, otherwise reading will be labored and not enjoyable, and students will lose meaning. Reading fluency is recognized today as "the missing ingredient" in the instruction for problem readers. Fluency is discussed in Chapter 9.

Reading Comprehension

Comprehension is the essence of the reading act. The many levels of comprehending include drawing on background experiences, literal comprehension, higher-level comprehension, and the ability to study and learn from text.

To comprehend material effectively, readers require some background knowledge. The background that students already have enables them to build bridges to new reading experiences and connect what they read to what they know.

Different levels of comprehension are strongly related.

Literal comprehension, or understanding the information stated directly in the text, is one type of comprehension. However, even here, the good reader picks and chooses, remembering the most important facts.

Higher-level comprehension. Formulating the central thought of a passage is considered part of higher-level comprehension. The main thought constructed is a little different for each of us. We actively participate in the reading process by constructing meaning.

Another form of higher-level thinking consists of the *inferences* or the implied information we draw from the text. The experienced reader will draw many inferences.

Critical or evaluative thinking is also a part of higher-level comprehension. As you read, develop a point of view about whether the ixia plant should be kept on the endangered species list. You evaluate the information in the light of your thinking and experiences.

In school, students are often called on to study (gain information) from their textbooks. Using books, manuals, directions, and many other materials continues throughout adult life. The ability to study is important in school and daily life.

Students with reading problems need work in many areas of comprehension and studying. As mentioned earlier, they do not construct meaning effectively in their minds the way we did when we constructed a central thought for this article.

In addition, low-level readers are particularly at risk in content-area subjects, such as science, social studies, and health. In these areas, the reading is expository, or focuses on giving information rather than telling a story.

This book deals with two types of comprehension. *Narrative comprehension* that involves reading material such as stories and novels is one type of comprehension and is discussed in Chapter 11. *Informational comprehension* involves material that conveys information, such as reading science or social studies books. The comprehension and study of informational materials also is in Chapter 11.

Reading Vocabulary

To read a text effectively, the reader must understand its sentence structures and word meanings, yet readers can certainly read something without understanding every word. In fact, using the comprehension processes, readers are able to increase their vocabulary as they read.

For effective reading, students need a knowledge of word meanings and language. As one reads, the reader also acquires new word meanings and gains experience with language. The more students read, the more word meanings and language they acquire. Thus, teachers need to encourage students with reading problems to read as much as possible.

The language we understand is the natural limit of our reading ability. Meaning vocabulary is an extremely important factor in reading, particularly in the intermediate and upper grades. Students with reading problems lag behind their average-achieving peers in both language development and meaning vocabulary. Many motivating ideas to help build the language and vocabulary of low-achieving readers are provided in Chapter 10.

Reading-Writing Connection

The inclusion of writing as a part of reading may seem strange, yet, as we read, we mentally construct thought. In other words, we compose, or write, in our minds. As we read, we are constructing our own meaning. We are always composing, so reading actually involves "writing."

Reading an article involves composing in our minds. However, when students actually take pencil in hand and write down their thoughts, they learn even more about reading. Trying to spell gives them insights into sound-symbol relationships, or phonics. When students create their own writing, it shows them that somebody actually writes what is read and that they can write too. Thus, students acquire a sense of control over reading. Chapter 13 discusses the reading-writing connection.

Enjoyment and Appreciation

People do what they enjoy and appreciate. For the reading act to be complete, the reader's interest must be engaged. Suggestions for helping students with reading problems enjoy reading are found throughout this book but are particularly concentrated in Chapter 6. Many different strategies and materials are given that you can use to motivate your students.

Summary

Teachers bear the primary responsibility for instructing students who have reading problems. Reading problems are associated with difficulties in life, including poverty, unemployment, and problems with the law. Because they lack skills, individuals with reading problems often are unable to train for jobs in an increasingly technological society.

A substantial portion of the U.S. school population has reading problems. Some students receive help through Title I programs, some students receive special education services through the Individuals with Disabilities Act (IDEA), or through state or locally funded programs. Many students with reading problems, however, receive no special help.

Response-to-Intervention is a relatively new approach to teaching reading and other academic skills in schools. This approach is a tiered approach in which students are taught with evidenced-based materials in Tier 1 (the general education class);

students who do not respond to instruction in Tier 1, go to Tier 2, where evidenced-based instruction in given more intensively and in smaller groups. Students who do not respond well in Tier 2, go to Tier 3. In Tier 3, the evidenced-based program is taught to children with greater intensity and in smaller groups.

The components model of reading (CMR) looks at the components of reading. Children are taught those reading components that they have not mastered.

Differentiated instruction looks at each student in terms of different traits and attributes and teaches each child in the light of the student's strengths and weaknesses.

Reading involves the construction of meaning from text. The construction of meaning depends upon the contribution of the reader, the contribution of the material, and the contribution of the reading situation.

There are several elements that are key in reading. They include early literacy skills, word recognition skills, reading fluency, reading vocabulary, comprehension, the reading-writing connection, and the enjoyment and appreciation of reading.

References

Aaron, P. G., Joshi, M. & Williams, K. A. (1999). Not all reading problems are alike. *Journal of Learning Disabilities, 32*(2), 120–127.

Aaron, P,. & Kotvah, H. (1999). Component model-based remedial treatment of reading difficulties. In I. Lundberg, E. Tonnessen, & I. Austad (Eds.), *Dyslexia: Advances in Theory and Practice* (pp. 221–244). Boston: Kluwer.

Aaron, P., Joshi, R., Gooden, R., & Bentum, K. (2008). Diagnosis and treatment of reading disabilities based on the component model of reading. *Journal of Learning Disabilities, 41*(1), 67–84.

Bender, W. (2006). *Differentiating Instruction for Students with Learning Disabilities*. Arlington, VA: Council for Exceptional Children.

Blackorby, J., & Wagner, M. (1997). The employment outcomes of youth with learning disabilities. In D. Gerber and D. Brown (Eds.), *Learning Disabilities and Employment* (pp. 57–74). Austin, TX: ProEd.

Charles Schwab.   Available at www.schwablearning.org

Division for Learning Disabilities. (2007). *Thinking About Response to Intervention and Learning Disabilities: A Teachers Guide*. Arlington, VA: Council for Exceptional Children.

Fuchs, D., Mock, D., Morgan, P., & Young, C. (2003). Responsiveness to intervention: Definitions, evidence, and implications for the learning disabilities construct. *Learning Disabilities Research & Practice, 18*, 157–171.

Gerber, P., & Brown, D. (1997). *Learning Disabilities and Employment*. Austin, TX: ProEd.

Gersten, R., & J. A. Dimiro. (2006). Rethinking special education for students with reading difficulties. *Reading Research Quarterly, 4(1)*, 99–108.

Hennesy, N., Rosenberg, D., and Tramaglini, S. (2003). A high school model for students with dyslexia: Remediation to accommodation. *Perspectives: The International Dyslexia Association*, 29(2), 38–40.

Lee, J., Grigg, W., & Donahue. (2007). *The Nation's Report Card* NCES-2770-496. Washington, DC: National Center for Educational Statistics, Institute for Education Sciences, U.S. Department of Education.

Lerner, J. W., & Johns, B. (2009). *Learning Disabilities and Related Mild Disabilities: Characteristics, Teaching Strategies, and New Directions*. Florence KY: Cengage Learning.

Levine, M. (2002). *A Mind at a Time*. New York: Simon and Schuster.

Lyon, G. R. (2003). Reading disabilities. What can be done about it? *Perspectives: The International Dyslexia Association*, 29(2), 17–19.

National Assessment of Educational Progress (NAEP). (2003). *The Nation's Report Card. Reading Highlights 2.* Jessup, M. D.: U.S. Department of Education. Available at http://nces.ed.gov/nationsreportcard, accessed January 7, 2006.

National Endowment for the Arts. (2004). *Reading at Risk: A Survey of Literacy Reading in America.* Washington, DC: Author.

National Institute of Child Health and Human Development. (1999). (pp. 1–3). Washington, DC: National Institute of Child Health and Development.

National Reading Association. (2006). *New Roles in Response to Intervention: Creating Success for Schools and Children.* Newark, DE: Author.

National Reading Panel. (2000). *Teaching Children to Read: An Evidenced-Based Assessment of the Scientific Research Literature on Reading and Implications for Reading Instruction.* Washington, DC: National Institute of Child Health and Human Development.

Nelson Rockefeller. *TV Guide*: October 16, 1976.

Slavin, R. (2008). What works? Issues in synthesizing educational program evaluations. *Educational Researcher 57*(1), 5–14.

Smith, S. (1991). *Succeeding Against the Odds: Strategies and Insights from the Learning Disabled Child.* Los Angeles: Jeremy P. Tarcher.

Stecker, P. M. (2007). Tertiary Intervention. *Teaching Exceptional Children, 39*(95), 50–57.

Tom Cruise. "My Struggle to Read." *People*, July 21, 2002, pp. 60–61.

Tomlinson, C., & Edison, C. (2003). *Differentiation in Practice: A Resource Guide for Differentiation.* Alexandria, VA: Association for Curriculum and Development.

Tomlinson, C., & McTighe, J. (2006). *Integrating Differential Instruction and Understanding by Design.* Alexandria, VA: Association and Supervision for Curriculum Development.

Tomlison, C., Brimijoin, K., & Navaez, L. (2008). *Differentiated Schools: Making Revolutionary Changes in Teaching and Learning.* Alexandria, VA: Association for Supervision and Curriculum Development.

U.S. Department of Education. (2007). *To Assure the Free Appropriate Public Education of All Children with Disabilities Act.* Twenty-Seventh Annual Report to Congress on the Implementation of the Individuals with Disabilities Education Act. Washington, DC: U.S. Department of Education.

U.S. Department of Education. Regulations for the Individuals with Disabilities Education Improvement Act. (2006). *Federal Register*, 2006, August 14.

Wagner, M., Newman, L., Cameto, R., Levine, P., & Garza, N. (2006). *An Overview of Findings from Wave 2 of the National Longitudinal Transition Study-2 (NLTS2).* Menlo Park, CA: SRI International.

Zirkel, P., & Krohn, N. (2008). RTI after IDEA: A survey of state laws. *Teaching Exceptional Children, 40*(3), 71–731.

MyEducationLab is a research-based learning tool that brings teaching to life. Go to the Jennings, Caldwell, & Lerner 6th Edition MyEducationLab for Reading Assessment site at www.myeducationlab.com to:

◆ engage in multimedia exercises to help you

build a deeper and more applied understanding of chapter content;

◆ utilize extensive resources including videos from real classrooms, Praxis and licensure preparation, a lesson plan builder, and materials to help you in your teaching career.

Factors Associated with Reading Disability

Introduction

In this chapter, we explore various factors that are associated with difficulty in reading. Reading problems can be rooted in neurological and cognitive factors, associated with environmental factors (factors within the student's home, school, social, or cultural environment), or linked with emotional factors. Reading difficulty is often associated with intelligence and intellectual factors; they can be rooted in language factors and with physical factors. Each of these factors may contribute to an individual student's reading problem, and a combination of the factors can lead to the student's reading difficulty. In this chapter, we explore how each of these factors can affect reading performance. We also examine ways to assess and meet these challenges.

A summary of the factors that are associated to difficulty in reading is shown in Figure 2.1.

Neurological and Cognitive Factors

Experts recognize today that a student's problem in reading can be linked to intrinsic neurological and cognitive factors within the individual student. Every teacher has had experience with a student who struggles with reading difficulty, despite having a dedicated family, a nurturing school environment, average or above intelligence, and many economic advantages.

For more than 100 years, medical researchers have tried to detect those neurological factors within the brain that are related to reading problems. As early as 1896, P. Morgan, a physician, reported on a condition he called "word blindness." Hinshelwood (1917), an ophthalmologist, reported on an otherwise normal teenage

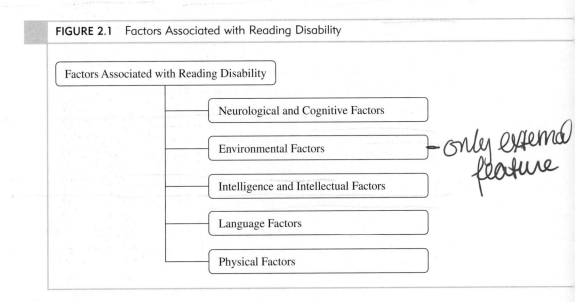

FIGURE 2.1   Factors Associated with Reading Disability

Factors Associated with Reading Disability

- Neurological and Cognitive Factors
- Environmental Factors
- Intelligence and Intellectual Factors
- Language Factors
- Physical Factors

— only external feature

boy who could not learn to read. Other medical researchers reported on similar cases students who had great difficulty learning to read (Critchley, 1970; Orton, 1937). However, it is only recently that researchers have begun to use new technologies to actually study the brain as the individual reads. Using functional magnetic resonance imaging (fMRI) technology, brain research has led to clues about the role of neurological factors that are associated with an individual's reading problem. The brain research shows strong evidence of differences in brain function between poor readers and normal readers (Shaywitz, Morris, & Shaywitz, 2008; Shaywitz, 2003; Shaywitz & Shaywitz, 1998).

The term *dyslexia* is sometimes used to describe individuals with severe reading disabilities, individuals who acquire reading abilities with extreme difficulty. Genetic differences in the brain make learning to read a struggle for children with dyslexia. Luckily, much of our brain development occurs after we're born, when we interact with our environment. This means that teaching techniques can actually retrain the brain, especially when the instruction happens early (Shaywitz, et al., 2008; May, 2006). A fascinating study using research with fMRI scans compared Chinese children and American children with dyslexia. The research shows that dyslexia affects different parts of the brain depending upon whether the child uses an alphabet-based writing system (such as English) or a symbolic writing system (such as Chinese). Learning to read in English, an alphabetic-based writing system requires awareness of the sounds of language (phonemic awareness). In contrast, learning to read in Chinese, a symbol-based writing system requires abilities with pictorial and visual symbols (Hotz, 2008; Siok, Niu, Jin, Perfetti, & Tan, 2008; McGough, 2004).

When we consider neurological or cognitive factors, we take into account the way in which an individual's brain operates during the process of learning to read. The term, *cognitive processing*, refers to the mental activities that an individual uses in learning, such as visual processing, auditory processing, memory abilities, or language-related abilities. Cognitive processing deficits can interfere with the way that students understand information presented to them. For some students with reading disability, cognitive processing deficits can play a major role.

Cognitive processing differences are also recognized in special education law, specifically in the Individuals with Disabilities Education Improvement Act of 2004 (IDEA-2004). Students with learning disabilities are identified as having "disorders in psychological processing." Research shows that poor readers display more differences in cognitive processing than good readers (Lerner & Johns, 2009; Shaywitz, et al., 2008; Lyon, 1997; Stanovich & Siegal, 1994).

Differentiated instruction is an often recommended approach to teaching students in general education. Differentiated instruction reflects a philosophy of teaching that enables the teacher to reach the unique needs of each student, capitalizing on the unique strengths and weakness of each student. That includes the student's individual interests, talents, way of processing information, and other proclivities. The approach of differentiated instruction involves teaching by matching individual student characteristics to instruction. This includes the individual cognitive processing skills of the students (Bender, 2006; Tomlison, 2001).

Environmental Factors

Go to MyEducationLab and select the topic *Causes and Correlates of Reading and Writing Difficulties*. Then, go to the Activities and Applications section, watch the video entitled "The Importance of Culture," and respond to the accompanying questions.

Now consider *environmental* factors that are associated with reading disability. Students live and grow in several different environments, and each environment has a strong impact on student desires and abilities to learn. Environments include the student's home environment, school environment, social environment, and cultural environment. Each of these environments can affect a student's reading. Figure 2.2 illustrates each of these environmental factors and their interaction.

The Home Environment

The home is the child's first environment. The child's home environment can be the foundation for tremendous cognitive growth and development. The child's experiences that occur during the critical first five or six years of life have powerful influences on a child's development.

FIGURE 2.2 Environmental Factors

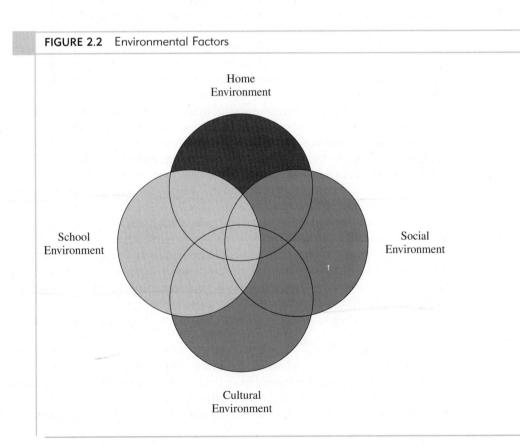

In the home environment, parents can provide emotional well-being as well as intellectual stimulation. For example, a child's early development of self-concept is dependent on the support and encouragement of parents. Studies that compare good and poor readers show that students who experience success are much more likely to have a favorable home environment (Turnbull, Turnbull, & Wehmeyer, 2007).

Parents can also stimulate their child's love for reading. Parents who read to children, take them to libraries, and buy books as presents to teach children to value reading. When children observe parents who are readers, the parents provide a role model for literacy. Further, the parent's role continues to be crucial even after the child enters school.

Youngsters who experience difficulty learning to read need satisfying family relationships. Parents can alleviate some of the psychological and emotional consequences of reading failure by what they do in the home environment. Parents can provide love, acceptance, and other opportunities for success (Turnbull, et al., 2007).

Many children today come from increasingly risk-filled home environments. For example, poverty is a major factor that is related to a child's risk levels in the areas of health, education, emotional welfare, and delinquency (Massinga & Pecora, 2004). According to the U.S. Census Bureau (2007), about 17.4 percent of all children living in the United States are living in poverty.

Homes that are weighed down with poverty, family instability, and neighborhoods where violence is commonplace increase the likelihood that children will be at risk for school failure. On any given night, the number of homeless children is estimated to be at least 500,000 (U.S. Census Bureau, 2007).

Health and emotional problems tend to increase when children live in difficult environments. Poorer mothers are less likely than more affluent mothers to seek prenatal care. Alcohol addiction in parents may affect a child in two ways: the child may be born with fetal alcohol syndrome, and the parent may not have the energy to nurture the child's education.

Children who are hungry or homeless have little energy to focus on school. Their overburdened, often undereducated parents and guardians may lack the time and skills to nurture literacy by sharing books with them, encouraging them to do homework, or communicating with their teachers. Some families are able to rise above their problems and provide warm, nurturing places that support education, but the sad fact remains that children born into poor or unstable families are at risk for educational failure. Thus, many family and home environmental causes combine to produce an increased risk for reading problems.

The School Environment

A substantial portion of a student's waking hours are spent in school, and so the experiences and relationships in the school environment profoundly affect their lives. For the poor reader, school experiences are often unhappy ones. At times, even a well-meaning, stable family may not be able to prepare a child for the school situation.

Even in affluent neighborhoods, teachers are noticing changes in the home environment, such as an increase in family breakups. School problems are multiplied in less-fortunate settings. As family instability increases, teachers in all schools are instructing at-risk children (Lerner & Johns, 2009).

Some school practices can actually contribute to a child's reading problems. For example, in some cases, teachers might give up entirely trying to teaching a child to read, and instead simply read everything to them. During reading time, these children might be expected to sit quietly and do nothing. In such situations, the school system does little to help the child with significant reading problems.

In the school environment, students with reading problems do not read as much as students who are good readers. In an extensive line of research, Allington (1977; 1983; 1984; 1986), Walmsley and Allington (1995), and Stanovich (1986; 1993–1994) compared the time spent and amount of reading in low-achieving and average students. Unskilled readers spent less time reading in school than did average students. Poor readers read only a third as many words as average students in school. Students who already have reading problems are not practicing enough to improve their reading skills (Lerner & Johns, 2009).

Students with reading problems often have unsatisfactory relationships with adults in the schools. Studies show that poor achievers tend to be perceived negatively by teachers, paraprofessionals, and principals. Teachers often identify poor readers as aggressive, lacking self-discipline, and unmotivated. Low achievers receive less praise or acknowledgment from teachers, and they are more likely to be criticized (Wong & Donahue, 2002; Bryan, Sullivan-Burnstein, & Mathur, 1998).

Instruction that does not meet a student's needs can be an important factor in a reading problem. For example, when immature children are given formal reading instruction before they can profit from it, they may become frustrated and develop reading problems. If children do not receive sufficient instruction in critical skills, they may fail in the initial stages of learning to read. For example, research demonstrates that an important link exists between phonemic awareness and early reading. If children do not develop the critical skill of phonemic awareness by first grade, their reading in all of the following grades is affected. Finally, low-achieving students often do not read enough to become better readers (Blachman, Tangel, & Ball, 2004; Lyon, 1998; Johnston & Allington, 1991).

Although students with reading problems are a challenge to teach, they still must be provided with the best instruction possible. Many of the suggestions provided in this book can help youngsters with reading problems break the cycle of reading failure and help them learn to love reading.

The Social Environment

Successful interactions with friends provide students with many satisfactions and opportunities to gain confidence in themselves. Many students with reading problems, however, also have social difficulties. These students have difficulty making friends, interacting with others, and do not understand the nuances of social situation.

A sizable body of evidence shows that social unpopularity tends to accompany school failure. Poor achievers often are rejected or ignored by classmates and are uninvolved in extracurricular activities (Lavoie, 2007; Tur-Kaspa, 2002; Wong & Donahue, 2002; Bryan, et al., 1998; Haager & Vaughn, 1995).

When children develop typically, they learn social skills in a casual and informal manner. Through many incidental experiences, they learn appropriate ways of acting with people, what to say, how to behave, and how to give and take in a social situation. Students with reading and social problems, however, may not be sensitive to social nuances, and they may be unaware of how others interpret their behavior. Further, in contrast to normal achievers, low-achieving students tend to overestimate their own popularity (Bryan, et al., 1998). They seem unable to recognize their own social shortcomings and have difficulty relating to peers in a social setting.

Often students with reading and social problems may be unable to accommodate themselves to another person's point of view. Their chances for successful social interaction with peers are reduced because they fail to consider the needs of other people. See Table 2.1 that offers suggestions for teaching social skills.

Cultural Environment

The number of students in U.S. schools who come from diverse cultural and linguistic populations is rapidly increasing. Many students come from homes in which a language other than English is spoken; these students are *English Language Learners* (ELL). They are not proficient in understanding and using oral English. ELL students are discussed in greater detail in this chapter under the section on language factors.

The population of North America is a composite of hundreds of different ethnic and cultural traditions. In today's society, ever-changing patterns of immigration

---

TABLE 2.1   Strategies for Teaching Social Skills

◆ **Role-Playing.**   Involve the students in role-playing games, in which one person is made to adopt the viewpoint of another person, to improve social relationships.

◆ **Social Autopsies.**   Have students analyze the social dilemmas in which they find themselves. To teach social behavior on the playground, teach it on a playground. To teach appropriate social behavior on the school bus, teaching it on the bus.

◆ **Social Skills Instruction.**   Teach students how to make friends, give compliments, join group activities, and accept thanks.

◆ **Social Stories.**   Social stories are stories about problematic social situations. Social stories offer a way for students to discuss the "how and what" of social situations. For example, a "comic strip" situation might allow students to discuss the "how and what" of a social situation. (See The Gray Center for Social Learning and Understanding at www.thegraycenter.org.)

and movement occur as new groups of people add their cultural riches to the schools. A few decades ago, Americans assumed that everyone would be assimilated into the "melting pot" of the dominant culture. Now we try to value and maintain diverse cultural traditions. One of the greatest challenges schools face is providing an excellent education to students of all cultures, whatever their geographical origin, socioeconomic status, or language.

Because a significant portion of U.S. families live below a specified poverty level, teachers need to be aware of the possible effects of poverty on students' academic performance. A recent study shows that poverty can take a toll on the brain development of children, leading to learning disabilities as well as behavior and emotional problems (Action for Children, 2008). Although individuals with incomes below the poverty level come from diverse backgrounds, they tend to have certain similarities. Parents are likely to have less energy to devote to their children's development if they are necessarily concerned with basic survival needs. Often, children from these families must care for themselves at a young age and may come to school with relatively limited background experiences (Ortiz, 1997). Cultural differences, particularly those arising from a culture of poverty, may lead to intense suspicion and discomfort toward individuals perceived to be in the dominant culture (Lerner & Johns, 2009).

These generalizations do not, of course, hold true for all low-income students. In many poor families, education is cherished, the values of the school are upheld, and family members are encouraged to read and achieve. The opportunity to progress from poverty to economic security is a fundamental promise of democratic nations.

Assessing Environmental Factors

Interviews and questionnaires as tools for gathering information are discussed in Chapter 3. The chapter adds a discussion of systematic behavioral observation, a tool for assessing the environment, and a useful method of assessing student behavior and interaction with many different environments, both social and academic. Even short observations can provide valuable information if they provide objective evidence about behavior.

The key to behavioral observation is to identify and clearly describe the behaviors that are being observed. The observation should not consist of value judgments, such as "Amy caused trouble." Instead, written observation is a careful recording of actual behaviors; for example, "Amy walked up to Maria's desk and tore up Maria's spelling paper." The cumulative records of many observations provide a basis for making diagnostic decisions and planning instruction.

Anecdotal records are a system of observing an individual student over an extended period and describing incidents of particular interest in detail. Many different types of activities can be recorded in the anecdotal record because it is meant to give the "flavor" of a student's activities.

Emotional Factors

Failing readers, particularly if they have a long history of failure, often have accompanying emotional problems that impede reading. Emotional problems tend to increase as a youngster moves up through the elementary years and enters adolescence.

Sometimes it is hard to determine whether a reading problem is the result of an underlying emotional disorder or if emotional problems have developed because of a reading disability. Often a constructive approach is to help the student experience success in reading, and this success, in turn, becomes a kind of therapy. A therapeutic approach to the teaching of reading can build confidence, establish self-esteem, and capture the pupil's interest. However, students with severe emotional disorders may need psychotherapy or counseling (Silver, 2006).

Students react to having reading problems in different ways. Although some failing readers seem to have little evidence of emotional reactions, many display a variety of emotional reactions, as shown in Table 2.2.

Emotional Problems

Assessing Emotional and Behavioral Factors

When teachers are aware of students' emotional responses, they are more effective in teaching them to read. Usually, an informal assessment of emotional factors is sufficient for the purposes of the reading diagnosis.

One helpful informal assessment measure that can be used by a reading teacher is the sentence completion activity. In addition, information from interviews (see Chapter 3) provides useful information about the student's emotional status.

The sentence completion activity is a series of beginning sentence fragments that the student completes, such as "I like _____." In finishing these sentences, students often provide insights into their thoughts and feelings. The activity can be administered orally or in writing. A sample sentence completion form is given in Figure 2.3. In interpreting results, however, bear in mind that it is only an informal measure. Although it may suggest ideas about student attitudes, these hypotheses should be verified through interview, observation, and perhaps the administration of formal measures.

Occasionally, teachers may need to refer a student to mental health specialists (such as psychiatrists, psychologists, or social workers) for further evaluation and possible psychotherapy or counseling. Such referrals are needed when emotional problems are so severe that they interfere with reading progress to the extent that the student achieves little growth over an extended period of instruction.

Intelligence and Intellectual Factors

Intelligence and intellectual factors are often associated with reading disabilities. A student's intelligence may provide an estimate of his or her ability to learn. Teachers

TABLE 2.2 Emotional Reactions to Reading Problems

◆ **Learning Block.**   If learning has been a painful experience, the student may simply block it to keep pain and distress out of the reach of consciousness. Learning blocks can often be overcome when reading is taught in interesting and nonthreatening ways and students begin to enjoy learning.

 Nine-year-old Maria developed an emotional block against books. Whenever the teacher brought out a book her response was, "I told you I can't read a book." To solve this problem, the teacher copied all the words from one picture book and taught them, one word at a time, without showing Maria the source. After all the words were mastered, the teacher presented the book to Maria who, of course, at first refused to read it. However, when the teacher demonstrated that Maria could read any word in the book, she overcame her fear and went on to read that book and others.

◆ **Hostile and Aggressive Behavior.**   Pupils with reading problems may become hostile and overly aggressive to compensate for feelings of inadequacy. Students who appear to be tough, ready to fight, and even delinquent may be seeking a sense of accomplishment that they are unable to find in school. Antisocial behavior can be a manifestation of students' anger and frustration with academics and with the failure of others to understand them. Often such students display less hostility when they are taught in small groups or individually and when their problems receive earnest attention from teachers.

◆ **Learned Helplessness.**   Some disabled readers try to avoid failure by refusing to try. Thus, they avoid stress through withdrawal and apathetic behavior. Such students may become passive and refuse to complete assignments, participate in class discussions, or read. They need to be encouraged to take risks (such as guessing at words they are not sure of) and to learn that a certain amount of failure is an unavoidable and acceptable part of living. When instructing these students, teachers should tell them what they will be learning and why they are learning it. Encouraging and rewarding students for guessing may also be helpful.

 In some cases, poor achievers cannot accept personal responsibility for learning even when they are successful. Attribution theory suggests that such students attribute their success and failure to the teacher who is in charge of the learning situation and has caused the learning to occur (Yasutake & Bryan, 1995). These students need more personal involvement in the learning situation and need to take responsibility for it.

◆ **Low Self-esteem and Depression.**   Understandably, students who have been subjected to continual failure develop a low opinion of themselves. They display a negative self-image, poor ego development, and a lack of confidence. The problem often deepens as students become older and realize that they are not meeting society's expectations (Brooks & Goldstein, 2002; Silver, 1998, 2006; Brooks, 1997).

 A self-defeating "what's the use" attitude may result in overall depression. Such students need to know that they are accepted as they are and that the teacher understands their problems and has confidence that they can learn. Every instructional success must be emphasized for these students.

◆ **Anxiety.**   Anxious students are never sure of their abilities and are afraid of making mistakes and being reprimanded. Stress clouds their lives and drains their energy and ability to concentrate on learning. Anxious students need reassurance that they can learn.

Source: Silver (2006).

FIGURE 2.3 Sample Sentence Completion Form

1. I like _____.
2. Eating _____.
3. I am happiest when _____.
4. School is _____.
5. My greatest fear is _____.
6. I wish I could _____.
7. There are times _____.
8. My mother _____.
9. My father _____.
10. Sometimes I wish _____.
11. I sleep _____.
12. When I dream _____.
13. I want to _____.
14. One thing that bothers me is _____.
15. Sometimes I hope _____.
16. I think I will never _____.
17. Other people are _____.
18. One thing I don't like is _____.
19. I feel sorry for people who _____.
20. My mind _____.
21. Most of the time _____.
22. I try to _____.

have long noted a variation in their student's response to reading instruction: One student grasps the lesson quickly, another student learns the lesson in an unusual or unique way, and a third student has great difficulty catching on. This variation is often attributed to "intelligence."

Definitions of Intelligence

Views about intelligence and its measurement have undergone many changes over the years. As generally used, intelligence refers to an individual's cognitive or thinking abilities or to the child's potential for acquiring school skills. In fact, most intelligence tests have been validated by comparing them with school performance.

A person's intelligence cannot be observed directly, so what is called intelligence is inferred through the student's responses in a test situation. The intelligence quotient (IQ) is a score obtained on an intelligence test, and it is a measure of performance on the intelligent test questions in relation to peers of the same age (see Chapter 5 for a discussion of IQ tests).

Current theories about intelligence suggest that several components make up the factor called intelligence. A student may exhibit a high capacity in one component, such as verbal abilities, and low aptitude in another, such as spatial abilities. Different tests of intelligence are based on different components of intelligence. For example, the Wechsler Intelligence Scale for Children, Fourth Edition (WISC-IV) provides scores on four major components: verbal comprehension, perceptual reasoning, working memory, and processing speed. The Kaufman Assessment Battery for Children, Second Edition (KABC-II) divides intelligence into sequential and simultaneous processing. Another theory of intelligence proposed by Gardner (1999) is that of *multiple intelligences*. Gardner proposes that people have many different intelligences. Gardner suggests eight components of intelligence: linguistic, musical, logical-mathematical, spatial, bodily kinesthetic, sense of self, sense of others, and naturalistic.

Sternberg (1999) suggests that intelligence tests and achievement tests actually measure similar accomplishments. Both are a form of developmental expertise. Moreover, people are constantly in the process of developing expertise as they work in a given domain.

Cultural Bias in the Measurement of Intelligence

Intelligence tests have been criticized because of cultural bias. Studies show that there are race and class differences in IQ scores: Students from middle-class homes tend to score higher than children from lower-class homes. Also, intelligence test items may not match the experiences that minority and lower-class children have in their cultural environment.

In a landmark legal case, *Larry P. v Riles* (1979), the court ruled that IQ testing is racially and culturally discriminatory when used as the sole criterion for placing children in classes for the mentally retarded. The issue of bias in intelligence tests continues to be debated in both the courtroom and academic research.

Using Intelligence Tests to Determine the Existence of a Reading Disability

A reading disability is sometimes measured in terms of the difference between the student's expected reading level (usually a student's grade placement) and the student's actual reading level. Another method uses intelligence test scores to determine whether a student has a reading disability. Using this method, teachers can determine whether a significant discrepancy exists between the student's potential for reading achievement (as measured by an intelligence test) and the student's actual reading performance as measured by a standardized reading achievement test. A large gap, or discrepancy, between reading potential and reading achievement indicates a reading disability, because the student has the potential to read much better.

In calculating a discrepancy, an intelligence test, such as the WISC-IV scale, is used to measure potential and a standardized reading test is used to measure current reading achievement. (The WISC-IV and other tests of intelligence are discussed in Chapter 5.) In calculating a discrepancy, one must (1) determine a reading expectancy level and (2) compare the expected reading level to current reading achievement.

Harris and Sipay (1985) developed a method for calculating a student's reading expectancy age (REA). This method uses a mental age (MA) to calculate whether a reading problem exists. The MA is obtained by multiplying the student's IQ by his or her chronological age (CA) and dividing the product by 100, as in the following formula:

$$MA = \frac{IQ \times CA}{100}$$

Express the MA and CA in tenths rather than years and months.

Once you obtain the MA, you can calculate the reading expectancy age (REA):

$$REA = \frac{2MA + CA}{3}$$

To convert the REA to a *reading expectancy age* (REG), subtract 5.2 from the REA.

For example, Marion is 10.0 years old, and she has an IQ of 120. Her MA is 12.0 years. The REA formula indicates she has a reading expectancy age of 11.3 and a reading expectancy grade of 6.1 (11.3–5.2). If Marion's current level of reading is 3.0, she would have a discrepancy of 3.1 years.

$$REA = \frac{2(12.0) - 10.0}{3} = 11.3$$

REG = 11.3 − 5.2 = 6.1

Reading Expectancy − Reading Achievement = Discrepancy 6.1 − 3.0 = 3.1

Table 2.3, based on the Harris and Sipay formula, helps avoid doing these calculations. If you know the IQ and CA of a student, the reading expectancy grade can then be found by noting the intersection of the CA with IQ. For students over 15 years of age, use 15.0 as the chronological age. If the CA and IQ fall between two values on a table, use the closest value. For convenience, the expectancy grade level, rather than age, is reported directly.

TABLE 2.3   Reading Expectancy Grade Levels

IQ Score

	70	75	80	85	90	95	100	105	110	115	120	125	130	135	140	145
6–0	—	—	—	—	—	—	—	1.0	1.2	1.4	1.6	1.8	2.0	2.2	2.4	2.6
6–3	—	—	—	—	—	—	1.0	1.2	1.5	1.7	1.9	2.1	2.3	2.5	2.7	2.9
6–6	—	—	—	—	—	1.1	1.3	1.5	1.7	2.0	2.2	2.4	2.6	2.8	3.0	3.2
6–9	—	—	—	—	1.1	1.3	1.6	1.8	2.0	2.2	2.4	2.7	2.9	3.1	3.4	3.6
7–0	—	—	—	1.1	1.3	1.6	1.8	2.0	2.3	2.5	2.7	3.0	3.2	3.4	3.7	3.9
7–3	—	—	1.1	1.3	1.6	1.8	2.0	2.3	2.5	2.8	3.0	3.2	3.5	3.7	4.0	4.2
7–6	—	1.0	1.3	1.6	1.8	2.0	2.3	2.6	2.8	3.0	3.3	3.6	3.8	4.0	4.3	4.6
7–9	1.1	1.3	1.5	1.8	2.0	2.3	2.6	2.8	3.1	3.3	3.6	3.8	4.1	4.4	4.6	4.9
8–0	1.2	1.5	1.7	2.0	2.3	2.5	2.8	3.1	3.3	3.6	3.9	4.1	4.4	4.7	4.9	5.2
8–3	1.4	1.7	2.0	2.2	2.5	2.8	3.0	3.3	3.6	3.9	4.2	4.4	4.7	5.1	5.3	5.5
8–6	1.6	1.9	2.2	2.4	2.7	3.0	3.3	3.6	3.9	4.2	4.4	4.7	5.0	5.3	5.6	5.8
8–9	1.8	2.1	2.4	2.7	3.0	3.3	3.6	3.8	4.1	4.4	4.7	5.0	5.3	5.6	5.9	6.2
9–0	2.0	2.3	2.6	2.9	3.2	3.5	3.8	4.1	4.4	4.7	5.0	5.3	5.6	5.9	6.2	6.5
9–3	2.2	2.5	2.8	3.1	3.4	3.7	4.0	4.4	4.7	5.0	5.3	5.6	5.9	6.2	6.5	6.8
9–6	2.4	2.7	3.0	3.4	3.7	4.0	4.3	4.6	4.9	5.2	5.6	5.9	6.2	6.5	6.8	7.2
9–9	2.6	2.9	3.2	3.6	3.9	4.2	4.6	4.9	5.2	5.5	5.8	6.2	6.5	6.8	7.2	7.5
10–0	2.8	3.1	3.5	3.8	4.1	4.5	4.8	5.1	5.5	5.8	6.1	6.5	6.8	7.1	7.5	7.8
10–3	3.0	3.3	3.7	4.0	4.4	4.7	5.0	5.4	5.7	6.1	6.4	6.8	7.1	7.4	7.8	8.1
10–6	3.2	3.6	3.9	4.2	4.6	5.0	5.3	5.6	6.0	6.4	6.7	7.0	7.4	7.8	8.1	8.4
10–9	3.4	3.8	4.1	4.5	4.8	5.2	5.6	5.9	6.3	6.6	7.0	7.3	7.7	8.1	8.4	8.8
11–0	3.6	4.0	4.3	4.7	5.1	5.4	5.8	6.2	6.5	6.9	7.3	7.6	8.0	8.4	8.7	9.1
11–3	3.8	4.2	4.6	4.9	5.3	5.7	6.0	6.4	6.8	7.2	7.6	7.9	8.3	8.7	9.0	9.4
11–6	4.0	4.4	4.8	5.2	5.5	5.9	6.3	6.7	7.1	7.4	7.8	8.2	8.6	9.0	9.4	9.8
11–9	4.2	4.6	5.0	5.4	5.8	6.2	6.6	7.0	7.3	7.7	8.1	8.5	8.9	9.3	9.7	10.1
12–0	4.4	4.8	5.2	5.6	6.0	6.4	6.8	7.2	7.6	8.0	8.4	8.8	9.2	9.6	10.0	10.4
12–3	4.6	5.0	5.4	5.8	6.2	6.6	7.0	7.4	7.9	8.3	8.7	9.1	9.5	9.9	10.3	10.7
12–6	4.8	5.2	5.6	6.0	6.5	6.9	7.3	7.7	8.1	8.6	9.0	9.4	9.8	10.2	10.6	11.0
12–9	5.0	5.4	5.8	6.3	6.7	7.1	7.6	8.0	8.4	8.8	9.2	9.7	10.1	10.5	11.0	11.4
13–0	5.2	5.6	6.1	6.5	6.9	7.4	7.8	8.2	8.7	9.1	9.5	10.0	10.4	10.8	11.3	11.7
13–3	5.4	5.8	6.3	6.7	7.2	7.6	8.0	8.5	8.9	9.4	9.8	10.2	10.7	11.1	11.5	12.0
13–6	5.6	6.0	6.5	7.0	7.4	7.8	8.3	8.8	9.2	9.6	10.1	10.6	11.0	11.4	11.9	12.4
13–9	5.8	6.3	6.7	7.2	7.6	8.1	8.6	9.0	9.5	9.9	10.4	10.8	11.3	11.8	12.2	12.7
14–0	6.0	6.5	6.9	7.4	7.9	8.3	8.8	9.3	9.7	10.2	10.7	11.1	11.6	12.1	12.5	13.0
14–3	6.2	6.7	7.2	7.6	8.1	8.6	9.0	9.5	10.0	10.5	11.0	11.4	11.9	12.4	12.8	13.3
14–6	6.4	6.9	7.4	7.8	8.3	8.8	9.3	9.8	10.3	10.8	11.2	11.7	12.2	12.7	13.2	13.6
14–9	6.6	7.1	7.6	8.1	8.6	9.1	9.6	10.0	10.5	11.0	11.5	12.0	12.8	13.0	13.5	14.0
15–0	6.8	7.3	7.8	8.3	8.8	9.3	9.8	10.3	10.8	11.3	11.8	12.3	12.8	13.3	13.8	14.3

This table gives reading expectancy grade level. If the intelligence score or chronological age falls between two values, use the closest one. For students over 15 years of age, use the 15.0 chronological age value.

Concerns about Using Intelligence Tests to Determine a Reading Disability

Educators have many concerns about using intelligence tests to measure the discrepancy between intellectual ability and achievement as a means of determining a reading (Fletcher, Coulter, Reschly, & Vaughn, 2004). The questions being asked include:

◆ How useful is the IQ score in measuring an individual's intelligence?
◆ Do children who are poor readers have similar characteristics, whether they have a high or a low IQ score?
◆ Are IQ scores good predictors of reading achievement?

Based on these concerns, the most recent special education law, IDEA-2004 permits schools to use another method to determine eligibility for learning disabilities services. Schools can use a response-to-intervention method to determine eligibility for learning disabilities rather than the IQ-Discrepancy formula. (See Chapter 1 for a discussion of response-to-intervention.) When determining whether a child has a learning disability, schools can provide intervention to an at-risk child to determine if the child responds to instruction using scientific, research-based instructional materials.

Language Factors

Language is recognized as one of the greatest of human achievements, more important than all the physical tools invented in the last ten thousand years. Language permits human beings to speak of things unseen, recall the past, and verbalize hopes for the future. People communicate with each other through a communication process. One person sends a message; the other person receives the message (Figure 2.4).

Go to MyEducationLab and select the topic *Causes and Correlates of Reading and Writing Difficulties*. Then, go to the Activities and Applications section, watch the video entitled "Self-Concept Challenge," and respond to the accompanying questions.

Reading is an integral part of the language system of literate societies. The student's ability to express and receive thoughts through oral language provides the foundation for reading; in other words, reading is based on language development. Not surprisingly, some students with reading problems have underlying problems with language. This section describes the many different components of language.

Oral and Written Language

Language is an integrated system linking the oral language forms of listening and talking to the written language forms of reading and writing. As children mature, language plays an increasingly important part in the development of thinking and the ability to grasp meaning. Words become symbols for objects, classes of objects, and ideas.

As children gain competence using language in one form, they also build knowledge and experience with the underlying language system, and this learning carries

FIGURE 2.4   The Communication Process

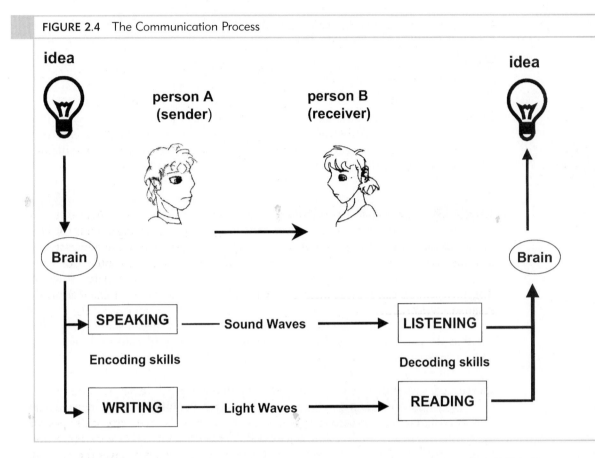

over to learning language in another form. Oral language provides a knowledge base for reading and writing. Similarly, practice in writing improves both reading and oral language. Oral language problems can contribute to reading disability. About 8 percent of children fail to develop speech and language at the expected age (Tallal, Miller, Jenkins, & Merzenich, 1997). Children who have delayed speech and language development often experience problems in reading.

Receptive and Expressive Language

An important distinction needs to be made between *receptive language* (understanding through listening or reading) and *expressive language* (using language in speaking and writing). Usually, people's receptive abilities exceed their expressive ones; that is, they understand more words than they use in speech and can read more words than they can write.

At times a student may appear to have poor language abilities because he or she engages in little conversation or gives one-word replies to questions. However, oral expressive language can be influenced by a student's comfort level. Therefore, teachers must consider the student's language abilities in both receptive and expressive language.

Systems of Oral Language

Linguists identify four different systems involved in oral language: *phonology* (the sounds of language), *morphology* (meaningful elements within words), *syntax* (the grammatical aspects of language), and *semantics* (the vocabulary of language). Students with reading problems may exhibit difficulties in one of these linguistic systems.

◆ *Phonology.*   Phonology refers to the sound system of a language. Oral language consists of a stream of sounds, one after the other. Each individual sound is called a *phoneme*. Important differences exist in the ways speakers of different languages think about phonemes. For example, in English the *b* and *v* sounds are two different phonemes, or sounds. In Spanish, they are simply variations on one phoneme. These differences make the mastery of English difficult for students whose native language is not English, just as Spanish or French is difficult for native English speakers.

Young children may have difficulty producing certain speech sounds. Typically children do not complete full articulation development until about the age of 8. Consonant sounds that are acquired later include r, l, ch, sh, j, th (as in the and thigh), s, z, v, and zh (as in pleasure). Young children who have not mastered these sounds in speech may have difficulty distinguishing them in reading.

Phonological or phonemic awareness is developed as children learn to recognize that words are made up of phonemes, or sounds. This ability is closely related to success in beginning reading (see Chapter 7). *Auditory discrimination*, or the ability to hear distinctions between phonemes (for example, to recognize that big and pig are different), is another problem area for some disabled readers (Wiig & Semel, 1984).

As discussed in Chapter 8, the phonics system in English, which links spoken sounds and written letters, is not completely regular. For example, the letter c represents two different sounds, as in the words city and cat. Although the English alphabet has only 26 letters, the average American English dialect contains 46 sounds.

◆ *Morphology.*   The morphological system refers to meaningful units, or *morphemes*, that form words or word parts. For example, the word walked contains two morphemes: walk and ed, a morpheme that signals the past tense. Other examples of morphemes are s (games) and re (rewind). Many students with reading problems have difficulties recognizing morphemes (Torgesen, 1998). The ability to recognize different morphemes when they appear in print is called structural analysis (see Chapter 9).

◆ *Syntax.*   Syntax, also known as grammar, governs the formation of sentences in a language. For example, in English, a well-formed sentence has a subject and a verb (e.g., Jane walks). Further, sentences are combined by using conjunctions, such as Jane walks and runs.

Children do not acquire syntactic ability passively; rather, they construct syntactic rules for themselves. For example, a young child who says he goed for the past tense of go is using the rule that the past tense is formed by the addition of ed, even though the child is overgeneralizing this rule. Although most basic syntactic structures are acquired by the age of 6, some growth in syntax continues through the age of 10. Development of the ability to understand complex or difficult sentence patterns may continue even throughout the high school years. Because syntactic abilities continue to develop through the school years, teaching sentence comprehension is important to reading instruction. Table 2.4 presents examples of difficult sentence types.

◆ *Semantics.* The semantic system refers to the acquisition of vocabulary or word meanings. Compared with other languages, English has an extremely large vocabulary. The complexity and rich variety of English words makes the mastering of English vocabulary a lifelong task. Because vocabulary is highly related to reading achievement, limited vocabulary development can seriously hamper reading.

Speech Problems and Language Disorders

Reading is an integral part of the language system. Underlying problems with language can affect the ability to read. Two types of language problems are speech problems and language disorders.

TABLE 2.4   Difficult Sentence Types

Category	Example
Passive sentence	Juan was surprise by the teacher.
Out-of-order time sequence	Move a yellow bead, *but first* move a red one.
	Move a yellow bead, *after* you move a red one.
Relative clause construction	Juan, *who is in the second grade*, is learning to read.
	The man, *standing on the corner*, is nice.
Appositives	Mr. Smythe, *the postman*, is very nice.
Complement structure	The fact *that Steve is silly* worries Meg.
	Steve's *being silly* worries Meg.
	Steve asked Meg what was worrying her.
Delayed reference in sentences	Juan promised Meg *to go*.
	Juan asked Leia *what* to feed the doll.
Anophoric, or reference sentences.	Jake saw Melody and *he* said hello.
	Jake saw Melody and said hello.
Sentence connectives	*If you don't* do this, I will go.
	Unless you do this, I will go. I

Speech Problems.   Children display three kinds of speech problems: *articulation problems* (the inaccurate production of sounds), *voice disorders* (improper pitch or intonation), and *stuttering* (breath or rhythm problems). Although low-achieving readers have a somewhat higher incidence of speech problems, these problems do not necessarily lead to reading problems. Nevertheless, students who exhibit speech difficulties should be referred to a speech-language specialist for further evaluation and, if needed, therapy. If a speech problem is noted, hearing acuity should be tested, because sometimes a hearing impairment is the cause of a speech problem. Students with speech problems can be embarrassed when asked to read orally, and therefore oral reading should be avoided for them.

Language Disorders.   Language disorders refer to the slow or atypical development of receptive and expressive oral language. The child with a language delay is slow at talking and poor in vocabulary development and may have difficulty learning to formulate sentences. Language delay is often a forerunner of later difficulty in reading (Torgesen, 1998). If a reading teacher suspects an underlying language disorder, a speech-language specialist can provide further evaluation and treatment.

Rapid Automatized Naming (RAN).   Some children with language delays have difficulty with rapid automatized naming (RAN); that is, they cannot quickly and automatically name objects and are slow with word finding. For example, when given the task of naming pictures as they are shown, these children cannot rapidly produce the names of the pictures. A slowness in word finding and naming is an accurate predictor of later reading disabilities. Slowness in naming is probably due to memory retrieval problems, which make accessing verbal and phonological information difficult (de Jong & Vrielink, 2004; German, 1994).

Problems with naming and slow word retrieval affect adolescents and adults with reading disabilities as well as children. Word-finding problems can be a lifelong source of difficulty in reading, learning, and using expressive language. Tests for assessing word-finding difficulty are the Test of Word Finding, Second Edition (TWF-2), and the Test of Adolescent/Adult Word Finding (TAWF), both from American Guidance Services, Inc.

English Language Learners

English Language Learners (ELL) are students whose native language is not English and are learning English as a second language. Today, one in five students speak a language other than English in his or her home. ELL students often have difficulty with reading because they are not yet proficient with the English language (August & Shannahan, 2006; Genesee, Lindholm-Leary, Saunders, & Christian, 2006).

Chapter 14 covers in greater detail the growing number of students in the United States and Canada who are ELL students and are learning English as a second language. Teaching strategies for instructing ELL students also are explored.

Reading in English poses a serious hurdle for ELL students. They may acquire the ability to use spoken English, but becoming proficient in the written language, reading, and writing often takes many years.

Assessing Language Development

Frequently used formal tests to assess language development are described in depth in Chapter 5. A student's listening level provides an informal estimate of how well that student can understand language. The ability to comprehend oral language through listening is sometimes used as an informal measure of a student's receptive language abilities and reading potential. A high listening level indicates that a student understands language well and has potential to read at a high level. A low listening level indicates that a student needs language development. Chapters 4 and 5 discuss methods for determining a listening level from an informal reading inventory and a standardized test.

Physical Factors

Good health is important to learning. Poor health and/or physical impairments can affect the student's ability to read. This section describes a variety of physical factors that affect reading problems.

Hearing Impairment

Because the ability to acquire reading skills may be severely affected by even moderate or temporary hearing loss, students should be screened for auditory acuity, or the ability to hear sounds. Auditory acuity is different from the ability to work with or distinguish words.

Hearing loss has several causes: childhood diseases, such as scarlet fever, meningitis, mumps, or measles; environmental conditions, such as repeated exposure to loud noises; congenital conditions, such as the malformation of or an injury to the hearing mechanism; temporary or fluctuating conditions, due to allergies, colds, or even a buildup of wax in the ears; maternal prenatal infection, including rubella; middle ear infection or problems; and certain medications, such as aminoglycosides and some diuretics.

Screening for Hearing Impairment.   Auditory acuity is measured in two dimensions: frequency and intensity. *Frequency* refers to the ability to hear different pitches, or vibrations of a specific sound wave. The pitches are actually musical tones; the higher the tone, the higher the frequency. Because different sounds of the spoken language have different frequency levels, a person may be able to hear sounds clearly at one frequency but not at another.

Intensity refers to the loudness of a sound and is measured in decibels; the louder the sound, the higher the intensity, or decibel level. How loud does a sound (or decibel level) have to be before a person should be able to hear it? A person who can hear soft sounds at 0 to 10 decibels has excellent hearing. Students who cannot hear sounds at 30 decibels are likely to encounter some difficulty in learning.

If an auditory screening indicates a hearing problem, students should be referred to an audiologist (a nonmedical specialist in hearing) or to an otologist or an otolaryngologist (medical specialists in hearing). Although the audiometer is a good device for screening, only a specialist trained in measuring and treating hearing difficulties can make a final determination of the extent and nature of a possible hearing impairment.

Alleviating Hearing Problems.   Medical specialists can also take measures to alleviate a student's hearing problem. Sometimes, medication or tubes in a child's ear can alleviate clogged passages and improve hearing. Other children may need to be fitted with hearing aids.

Sometimes students pass the audiometric screening test yet still have hearing problems. One student had a sporadic hearing loss resulting from allergies, but because her visits to the pediatrician came after the allergy season, the hearing problem went undetected for years. Although the hearing problem was eventually cleared up, she missed some important early language growth, and her difficulties in reading continued into the later grades. Thus, if a teacher suspects a hearing loss, the student should be referred to a professional for continued monitoring.

Even moderate loss in the ability to hear may substantially affect the ability to read. A hearing loss impedes communication with teachers and peers, and so the student has difficulty functioning in class. Students may have difficulty learning phonics because they do not hear certain sounds. A low-frequency hearing loss (500–1500 Hz) may cause difficulty with vowel sounds; high-frequency losses (2000–4000 Hz) may cause difficulty with consonant sounds that continue, such as /s/, /z/, /j/, /v/, /th/, /sh/, and /ch/.

The most devastating effect of a hearing loss is that it prevents normal language development. When children cannot hear adequately, they are deprived of the communication necessary for normal language acquisition and growth. Their vocabulary, grammar, and verbal thinking processes often remain poorly developed, and their language skills may be inadequate to acquire higher-level reading skills.

Visual Impairment

The ability to see clearly is obviously critical to the reading process. However, the relationship between reading and vision is complicated. A particular visual impairment may impede reading in one individual, but another person with a similar problem may be able to read effectively.

Types of Vision Problems. Several types of visual impairment are of concern to the reading teacher. These impairments include myopia, hyperopia, astigmatism, binocular vision problems, and color perception.

Myopia or nearsightedness is the inability to see objects at a distance. Myopia is caused by an elongated eyeball that focuses visual images in an improper way. Although the problem of myopia is not highly related to reading difficulty, a student with myopia could have difficulty seeing objects such as writing on the blackboard (Lerner & Johns, 2009). A substantial portion of the population is myopic; the condition often begins between the ages of 9 and 12. Myopia is usually correctable with eyeglasses.

Hyperopia or farsightedness is the inability to see objects clearly at nearpoint (that is, 13 inches or less). In children, it is often caused by an eyeball that is too short to permit focusing. Children are typically hyperopic until they reach the age of 7 or 8; thus, primary-grade textbooks generally contain large print. If hyperopia is a continuing problem, it can be corrected with lenses. Because reading is done at nearpoint, hyperopia can affect the ability to read.

An astigmatism is the blurring of vision because of irregularities in the surface of the cornea. This condition is generally correctable with lenses.

Binocular difficulties refer to the inability to focus both eyes on the same object and is one of the most complicated of visual functions. Both eyes focus together easily on an object that is far away, but as that object moves closer, the eyes must turn inward to maintain their focus. If the eyes cannot focus together, a double image may result. This condition is not tolerated well by the brain, and the image of one eye may be suppressed, possibly leading to a deterioration of that eye. In severe cases, the eyes appear to be crossed. Binocular vision problems may blur vision and also cause the reader to become easily fatigued; thus, they can interfere with reading.

Unfortunately, binocular vision is not as easily correctable as other visual problems. Three strategies used to correct binocular problems are surgery (often used to correct a cross-eyed condition), corrective lenses in eyeglasses, and visual exercises to strengthen eye muscles. Opinions differ among eye specialists about the value of visual exercises as a treatment in overcoming binocular difficulties (Solan, 2004; American Academy of Pediatrics, 1992).

Color perception is also a part of vision. A small portion of the population, usually male, is unable to perceive color. Color blindness, which may be limited to a few colors, is not associated with reading problems. In addition, a set of controversial new treatments focuses on the glare that is experienced by some individuals during reading. This problem is often called scotopic sensitivity. To eliminate this glare, colored overlays or lenses may be provided. Although some have reported decreased problems in reading, this controversial treatment has had somewhat inconsistent results (Fletcher & Martínez, 1994; Ward, 1992). Nevertheless, it remains one treatment option for these visual problems.

Screening for Visual Impairment. Students with reading problems should be screened for possible visual difficulties. An adequate visual screening should at least test nearsightedness, farsightedness, and binocular visual functioning. As with the hearing tests that are used by the reading teacher, visual tests given by schools or teachers are intended only for screening purposes. Students who do poorly on a visual screening test should be referred to an ophthalmologist (a physician who specializes in eye problems) or to an optometrist (a nonmedical eye specialist) for further testing. Vision tests that can easily be administered by a teacher include the Keystone Telebinocular Vision Tests and the Orthorater instruments.

Gender Differences

More boys than girls are identified as having reading disabilities. In fact, about four times more boys are in special reading programs (Shaywitz, 2003), yet research sponsored by the National Institute of Child Health and Human Development (NICHD) shows that as many girls as boys may have reading disabilities, but the girls are not being identified. Girls with reading disability are considered an underserved population (National Reading Panel, 2000).

Several reasons have been suggested for more boys than girls being identified with reading disabilities:

◆ Boys mature physically later than girls. At the age of beginning reading instruction, boys may not have developed certain skills that aid in reading, such as the ability to pay attention and the ability to manage pencils and books.
◆ The school environment may affect boys and girls differently. Most primary grade classrooms in the United States are taught by female teachers, and boys may have more difficulty relating to them. In addition, rewards tend to be given for being neat and quiet in the primary grades, and these qualities are more characteristic of girls than boys.

The fact is that more boys are in special reading classes. Teachers must make these students feel welcome and happy in the reading environment.

Other Physical Problems

Good physical health is also an important basic condition for learning. The pupil who is listless, tires easily, and cannot maintain attention may have an underlying medical problem. Prolonged illness, especially if accompanied by high fevers and long periods of absence from school, can also contribute to a reading problem.

General Health and Nutrition.   Nutrient deficiency in infancy or early childhood has been shown to result in anatomical and biochemical changes in the brain. Early malnutrition impairs growth, both of the body in general and of the central nervous system in particular (Fishbein & Meduski, 1987). Other health concerns include nutrition problems, rheumatic fever, asthma, lack of sleep, biochemical imbalances, and endocrine problems. A general physical examination is often recommended as part of a complete assessment for reading problems.

Injuries and Illnesses that Affect the Brain.   Concussions, or swelling of the brain, can affect cognitive functioning. Concussions are often caused by injuries. If a brain injury results in unconsciousness, a student has experienced a concussion. In addition, some illnesses, such as spinal meningitis and brain tumors, can destroy cognitive functioning.

Summary

A number of different factors are associated with reading disabilities. Experts recognize today that a student's reading problem can be linked to a student's intrinsic neurological and cognitive factors.

Environmental factors include the home, school, cultural, and social environments. The home is the child's first environment, where the critical learning of the early years occurs. The school environment is another important system for the student, one that is often difficult for students with reading problems. Students with reading disabilities tend to have difficulty in their social environments. The cultural environment is another system that affects attitudes and interest in reading. Methods of assessing environmental systems include several systems of observation.

Emotional problems can influence reading achievement. Among the emotional problems exhibited by poor readers are emotional blocks, hostility, aggressiveness, learned helplessness, low self-esteem, depression, and anxiety. Emotional factors may be informally assessed using the sentence-completion activity.

Intelligence refers to the potential for learning. Current views of intelligence divide intelligence into several components. Intelligence tests measure scholastic aptitude. Although much of what is called intelligence is inherited, a child's intelligence can be dramatically influenced by environmental conditions. In general, the child's experiences and environment, including teaching, can make a significant difference.

The child's language is an important factor related to reading performance. Language includes oral language (listening and speaking) and written language (reading and written). The four oral language systems are phonology, morphology, syntax, and semantics or vocabulary. Studies show that some students with reading disabilities have difficulty with one or more of these linguistic systems. Speech problems and language disorders can affect the learning of reading.

Physical factors are also related to reading disability. Hearing impairment, including a mild or temporary hearing loss, can affect language learning and learning to read. The audiometer is used to screen for a hearing loss. Visual impairment is also related to reading disability. Visual problems include myopia, hyperopia, astigmatism, poor binocular vision, and perhaps color sensitivity. Teachers can screen for visual impairment. Other physical factors, such as general health and nutrition or neurological conditions, are related to reading disabilities. Reading difficulties are identified more frequently in boys than girls, however, research shows that girls may have as many reading difficulties but are just not identified.

References

Action for Children. (2008). Child poverty in North Carolina: A preventable epidemic. Raleigh, NC. Action for Children. www.ncchild.org. Accessed April 22, 2008.

Allington, R. L. (1977). If they don't read much, how are they gonna get good? *Journal of Reading, 21,* 57–61.

Allington, R. L. (1983). The reading instruction provided readers of differing abilities. *The Elementary School Journal, 8,* 548–559.

Allington, R. L. (1984). Content coverage and contextual reading in reading groups. *Journal of Reading Behavior, 16,* 85–97.

Allington, R. L. (1986). Policy constraints and effective compensatory reading instruction: A review. In J. Hoffman (Ed.) *Effective teaching of reading. Research and practice* (pp. 261–289). Newark, DE: International Reading Association.

American Academy of Pediatrics. (1992). Learning disabilities, dyslexia, and vision. *American Academy of Pediatrics, 90,* 124–126.

August, D., & Shannahan, T. (Eds.) (2006). *Developing Literacy in Second-Language Learners. Report of the National Literacy Panel on Language-Minority Children and Youth.* Mahwah, NJ: Lawrence Erlbaum Associates.

Bender, W. (2006). *Differentiating Instruction for Students with Learning Disabilities.* Arlington, VA: Council for Exceptional Children.

Blachman, B., Tangel, D., & Ball, E.(2004). Combining phonological awareness and word recognition instruction. *Perspectives: The International Dyslexia Association, 24*(9), 12–14.

Brooks, R. B. (1997). *The Self-Esteem Teacher.* Circle Pines, MN: American Guidance Services.

Bryan, T., Sullivan-Burnstein, K., & Mathur, S. (1998). The influence of affect and social information processing. *Journal of Learning Disabilities,* 31, 418–426.

Critchley, M. (1970). *The Dyslexic Child.* Springfield, IL: Charles C. Thomas.

De Jong, P., & Vrielink, L. (2004). Easy to Measure: Hard to improve (quickly). *Annals of Dyslexia, 54*(1), 39–64.

Fishbein, D., & Meduski, J. (1987). Nutritional biochemistry and behavioral disabilities. *Journal of Learning Disabilities, 20,* 505–520.

Fletcher, J., Coulter, W., Reschly, D., & Vaughn, S. (2004). Alternative approaches to the definition and identifying of learning disabilities: Some questions and answers. *Annals of Dyslexia, 54*(2), 304–321.

Gardner, H. (1999). *Intelligence Reformed: Multiple Intelligences for the Twenty-First Century.* New York: Basic Books.

Genesee, F., Lindholm-Leary, K., Saunders, W., & Christian, D. (2006). *Educating English Language Learners: A Synthesis of Research Evidence.* New York: Cambridge University Press.

German, D. (1994). *Word-finding interactive programs.* Itasca, IL: Riverside Publishing.

Gopnick, A., Melzoff, A., & Kuhl, P. (1999). *The Scientist in the Crib: Minds, Brains, and How Children Learn.* New York: William Morrow.

Haager, D., & Vaughn, S. (1995). Assessment of social competence in students with learning disabilities. In J. Lloyd, E. Kam'enui, & D. Chard. (Eds.), *Issues in Educating Students with Disabilities.* Mahwah, NJ: Erlbaum.

Harris, A., & Sipay, E. (1985*). How to Increase Reading Ability: A Guide to Developmental Reading.* New York: David McKay.

Hinshelwood, J. (1917). *Congenital Word-Blindness.* London: H. K. Lewis.

Hotz, R. L. (2008, May 2). How alphabets shape the brain. *Wall Street Journal, Science.* p. A10.

Larry P. v. Riles 495, F. Supp. 96 (N.D. Cal 1979). aff'd. 1988–84. E.H.I.R D.E.C. 555: 304(9th Cir.) 1984.

Lavoie, R. (2005). *It's So Much Work to Be Your Friend: Helping the Child with Learning Disabilities Find Social Success.* New York: Touchstone Book, Simon and Schuster.

Lavoie, R. (2007). *The Motivation Breakthrough.* New York: Touchstone (Simon & Schuster).

Lerner, J. W., & Johns, B. (2009). *Learning Disabilities and Related Mild Disabilities: Characteristics, Teaching Strategies, and New Directions.* Florence, KY: Cengage Learning.

Lyon, G. R. (1997). Progress and promise in research: Learning disabilities. *Learning Disabilities: A Multidisciplinary Journal, 8,* 1–6.

Massinga. R., & Pecora, P. (2004). Providing better opportunities for older children in the child welfare system. *Futures of Children, 14*(1), 52–54.

May, T. S. (2006). Dissecting dyslexia. *BrainWork.*

McGough, R. (2004, September 2). Dyslexia manifests differently for Chinese readers. *Wall Street Journal,* D4, p. 3.

National Reading Panel. (2000). *Teaching children to read: An evidenced-based assessment of the scientific research literature on reading and its implications for reading instruction: Report of the subgroups* (National Institute of Health Pub. No. 00–4754). Washington, DC: National Institute of Child Health and Human Development.

Ortiz, A. (1997). Learning disabilities occurring concomitantly with linguistic differences. *Journal of Learning Disabilities, 30,* 221–232.

Orton, S. (1937). *Reading, Writing and Speech Problems in Children.* New York: Norton.

Shaywitz, S. (2003). *Overcoming Dyslexia: A New and Complete Science-Based Program for Reading Problems at Any Level.* New York: Alfred A. Knopf.

Shaywitz, S., & Shaywitz, B. (1998). Functional disruption in the organization of the brain in reading for dyslexia. *Proceedings of the National Academy of Sciences, 95,* 5.

Shaywitz, S., Morris, R., & Shaywitz, B. (2008). The education of dyslexic children from childhood to young adulthood. *The Annual Review of Psychology, 50,* 451–475.

Silver, A. (2006). *The Misunderstood Child.* New York: Three Rivers Press.

Siok Wai Ting, Niu Zhendong, Jin Zhen, Perfetti Charles A., & Tan Li Hai. (2008). A structural–functional basis for dyslexia in the cortex of Chinese readers. *Proceedings of the National Academy of Sciences of the USA. 115*(14), 5561–5565.

Slavin, R. (2006). *Educational Psychology: Theory and Practice.* Boston: Allyn & Bacon.

Solan, H. (2004). Learning-related vision problems: How visual processing affects reading efficiency. *Learning Disabilities: A Multidisciplinary Journal, 13*(1), 25–32.

Sousa, D. (2001). *How the Brain Learns.* Thousand Oaks, CA: Corwin Press.

Stanovich, K. E. (1986). Mathew effects in reading. Some consequences of individual differences in the acquisition of literacy. *Reading Research Quarterly, 21,* 360–406.

Stanovich, K. E. (1993–1994). Romance and reality. Distinguished educator series. *The Reading Teacher, 47,* 280–291.

Stanovich, K. E., & Siegel, L. S. (1994). Phenotype performance profile of children with reading disabilities: A regression-based test of the phonological core variable of difference model. *Journal of Educational Psychology, 86,* 24–58.

Sternberg, (1999). Ability and expertise: It's time to replace the current model of intelligence. *American Educator, 23,* 1–30, 50.

Tallal, P., Miller, S., Jenkins, W., & Merzenich, M. (1997). The role of temporal processing in developmental language-based learning disorders: Research and clinical implications. In B. Blachman (Ed.), *Foundations of Reading Acquisition and Dyslexia,* pp. 49–60. Mahwah, NJ: Lawrence Erlbaum.

Tomlison, C. (2001). *How to Differentiate Instruction in Mixed Ability Classrooms.* Alexandria, VA: Association for Curriculum and Development.

Torgesen, J. (1998). Learning disabilities: An historic and conceptual overview. In B. Wong (Ed.). *Learning about Learning Disabilities,* (pp. 3–34). San Diego, CA: Academic Press.

Tur-Kaspa, H. (2002). Social cognition in learning disabilities. In B. Wong and M. Donahue (Eds.), *The Social Dimensions of Learning Disabilities,* pp. 11–32. Mahwah, NJ: Laurence Erlbaum.

Turnbull, A., Turnbull, H., & Wehmeyer, M. (2007). *Exceptional Lives: Special Education in Today's Schools.* Boston: Allyn & Bacon/Merrill.

U.S. Census Bureau. (2007). *Income, Poverty, and Health Insurance Coverage in the United States.* Washington, DC: U.S. Census Bureau.

Walmsley, S., & Allington, R. (1995). Redefining and reforming instructional support programs for at-risk readers. In R. Allington & S. Walmsley (Eds.). *No quick fix: Rethinking literacy programs in America's elementary schools* (pp. 19–44). Newark, DE: International Reading Association.

Whitman, B. Y., (2000). Living with a child with ADHD: Principles of family living, behavior management, and family support. In P. Accardo, T. Blondis, B. Whitman, & M. Stein (Eds.), *Attention Deficits and Hyperactivity in Children and Adults*, pp. 441–460. New York: Marcel Dekker, Inc.

Wiig, E. A., & Semel, E. M. (1984). *Language Assessment and Intervention for the Learning Disabled.* Columbus: OH: Charles E. Merrill.

Wolery, M., & Bailey, D. (2003). Early childhood special education research. *Journal of Early Intervention* *25*(2), 88–99.

Wong, B., & Donahue, M. (2002). *The Social Dimensions of Learning Disabilities: Essays in Honor of Tanis Bryan.* Mahwah, NJ: Lawrence Erlbaum.

Yasutake, D., & Bryan, T. (1995). The influence of affect on the achievement and behavior of students with learning disabilities. *Journal of Learning Disabilities, 28*, 329–334.

MyEducationLab is a research-based learning tool that brings teaching to life. Go to the Jennings, Caldwell, & Lerner 6th Edition MyEducationLab for Reading Assessment site at www.myeducationlab.com to:

◆ engage in multimedia exercises to help you

build a deeper and more applied understanding of chapter content;

◆ utilize extensive resources including videos from real classrooms, Praxis and licensure preparation, a lesson plan builder, and materials to help you in your teaching career.

Obtaining Background Information

Introduction

Accurate assessment helps teachers plan the best possible instruction for students. Chapters 3 through 6 provide information on gathering and analyzing data about students and their reading. Chapter 3 discusses background information while Chapters 4 and 5 concentrate on the assessment of reading abilities. Both kinds of information are essential to good teaching.

This chapter examines ways to obtain a broad understanding of a student's background. Background information is divided into two parts: (1) the student's environments, including home, school, social, and cultural and (2) background factors within the individual, including emotional, potential (intelligence), physical, and language development. Specific methods of gathering information also are discussed.

Background factors can profoundly affect a student's reading. Chapter 1 gave several examples. Some were of students whose environmental backgrounds did not foster reading development: Diane's family could not provide a stable home life; Ilya missed a year of important preparation when he did not attend kindergarten. For other students, problems in reading seem to come from within the individual: Jason's reading problems were related to his physical development.

At times, identified problems can be corrected. For example, a student with visual difficulties may be referred to an eye doctor, receive corrective lenses, and show immediate reading gains.

However, many students face problems that cannot be resolved easily. For example, a teacher has little ability to affect a difficult home situation—but even in that instance, a teacher can make a difference. During a time of family turmoil, a student may need a compassionate, understanding adult. Knowing background information enables teachers to deal sensitively with a fragile human being and to adjust instruction to special needs.

The discussion of background factors in this chapter is oriented to the immediate, practical needs of teachers. More theoretical, research-oriented information is presented in Chapter 2 and in Chapter 15.

When dealing with background factors, teachers must remember that these factors have a complex relationship to reading problems. A factor may coexist with a reading problem but not actually cause that reading problem. For example, some students manage to achieve well in school despite difficult home lives. For other students, however, problems at home may impede learning. Thus, interpreting background information judiciously is important.

Information about the Environment

Students live in several environments: the home, the school, and the social and cultural environment. Each of these environments influences how students think about reading, the desire to learn, and access to reading materials. In addition, these environments interact. For example, a difficult situation at home may contribute to difficulty making friends in the social realm and to trouble in cooperating with teachers at school.

FIGURE 3.1   Collecting Background Information

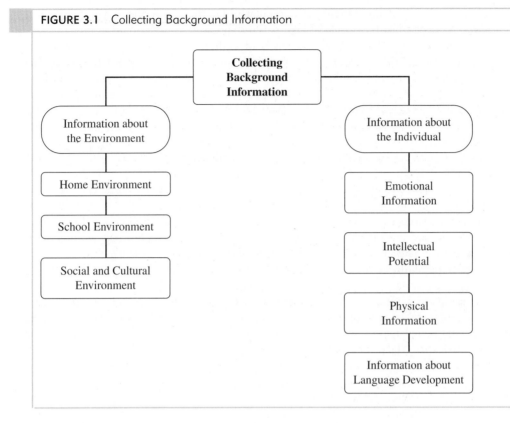

Home Environment

The home exerts a powerful influence on the development of reading and writing. Parents play an important role in modeling the value of literacy and bringing children to books, and the general home situation can influence a student's academic achievement. Events such as divorce or a move to a new neighborhood can affect a student's ability to profit from school reading instruction.

Parents as Models for Literacy.   Parents are a child's earliest and most important literacy role models. If parents read for both recreation and information and provide many reading materials at home, the child learns to value literacy. Parents also stimulate a love of books by reading to their children, taking them to the library, and buying books as gifts. A home environment that is rich in books and in literacy activities fosters success in reading.

A reading teacher can determine whether the home supports and values literacy by interviewing the parents or by asking them to fill out a questionnaire. What information is helpful? Some of the questions to ask parents about their own reading habits are the following: Do they read regularly? Do they subscribe to newspapers and magazines? Do they buy books? Next, parents should be asked about literacy interactions with their child. Do they regularly read to their child? Do they encourage their child to read? Do they take their child to the library or buy books for the child? Do they subscribe to any children's magazines? Do they limit television viewing? Responses to such questions indicate how parents and other family members, including grandparents and older siblings, foster literacy at home.

Information obtained directly from a student can also give insights into how literacy is modeled at home. As you gather information from interviewing and working with your students, you learn whether they have books at home and if reading is done regularly.

What can a reading teacher do if the home does not nurture literacy? Many parents are grateful for teacher suggestions about improving literacy in their homes. Often, the parents of students with reading problems are worried about their child's future and have misgivings about their own parenting skills. A few suggestions often help foster a sense of family security and enhance literacy. For some families, these suggestions reinforce the good things they are doing already:

◆ Provide a good reading-studying environment. Advise parents to provide a quiet, stable, well-lighted place in which their child will study. Supplies (paper and pencils) and reference materials (dictionaries, maps) should be located near this area. Make sure that the television is off during homework or reading time.

◆ Share literacy with the child. When parents read to young children, they promote an interest in reading, foster language development, and share close family experiences. If the child is older, parent and child can share reading time as they each read silently. Students of all ages enjoy reading material that they have mastered to a parent who listens enthusiastically. Encourage parents to take children to a local library and to look for a helpful children's librarian, who will aid them in locating suitable books.

◆ Accept the child as he or she is. Admitting that one's own child has a problem is often difficult. Some parents deny that difficulties exist or hold unrealistic expectations for their child. Children are sensitive to their parents' disappointments. To prevent a reading problem from becoming a family problem, children must know that parents accept and love them as they are.

◆ Help the child to feel secure and confident. Encourage activities that a child does successfully. Playing baseball or basketball, taking cooking lessons, or just being dad's special helper may acquire a special meaning for a child with reading problems.

When parents are unable to provide literacy experiences at home, teachers must nurture a love of literacy during instruction. Classrooms filled with different types of books and magazines, invitingly displayed, show students that literacy is important. Give students time to browse through and share these materials. Teachers can also read to students on a regular basis and ask them to share their own thoughts and feelings about the selections. More suggestions for teachers are given in Chapter 6.

General Home Situation. Children are profoundly affected by what happens to their families. They are often dramatically touched by a move to a new location, divorce or separation of parents, the deaths of relatives, or older siblings leaving home. A child may not be able to pay attention to reading instruction when the father has just moved out or the mother has taken a new job and will no longer be at home after school.

A parent interview is often the means of collecting helpful information about a family. This information includes the names, ages, and occupations of the parents; the number and ages of siblings; names of other family members living in the home; and the members of the nuclear family (parents, siblings) who are not living at home. During this interview, ask parents to share any other information that might help to explain their child's difficulties. Often parental insights give valuable ideas for cooperation between a reading teacher and the family.

Occasionally, the parent interview reveals that a family situation is causing stress for the student and contributing to difficulty in school. Although teachers cannot intervene in a divorce or prevent an impending move to a new neighborhood, they can be sensitive to a student's feelings and emotional needs. At such critical times, the reactions and guidance of an understanding teacher may be more important for the child than direct instruction in reading. Work with Shannon at the reading center illustrates this point. When Shannon's parents separated, she reacted with fits of crying and withdrawal from other children. The teachers realized that certain topics might upset her, so they allowed her to select her own materials for instruction. Shannon avoided books about families. Instead she chose nonsense books such as *Chicken Soup with Rice* (Sendak) and books featuring brave young children, such as *Hatupatu and the Birdwoman* (Cowley) and *Where the Wild Things Are* (Sendak). These selections proved to be key elements in improving her reading.

Teachers can help students cope with difficult home situations by:

◆ Being sensitive. Sensitivity in talking to students and allowing them to express their feelings is extremely important.
◆ Reducing demands. Teachers may want to "go easy" on students for a while by reducing both academic and behavioral demands.
◆ Being aware of the student's living situation. Teachers should be knowledgeable and understanding about the student's living and legal custody arrangements. If parents do not live together, make sure the appropriate parent receives communications. With permission from the custodial parent, both parents may be informed.

School Environment

Many factors in the school environment can influence reading achievement. Information about educational history, school attendance, and instructional methods helps teachers understand the student's problem and forms a basis for cooperation among all the professionals who are helping a student.

Educational History.   By gathering information about a student's educational history, teachers learn what the youngster has already experienced and are able to select new options for instruction. Students differ widely in their educational histories. For some, first grade is the initial instructional experience; others enter first grade with a rich history of preschool and kindergarten. Some students are barely 6 years old when they first encounter formal reading instruction; others are almost 7. Some students have repeated a grade or have received an extra year of kindergarten instruction. Some children have received private tutoring; some have been placed in special school programs.

Educational history may offer some hints about the seriousness of a student's problem. For example, a student who has had many enriching experiences, such as preschool education and previous tutoring, and still has difficulty in reading probably has a serious problem. In contrast, a student who comes with no preschool education or history of special reading help may simply have lacked the opportunities needed for learning to read.

Educational history is gathered from many sources: interviews with parents or guardians and students, teacher interviews and questionnaires, cumulative school records that follow the student from year to year, portfolios, and report cards. If you are not a staff member at the student's school, you must obtain written permission from parents before contacting school personnel.

A complete history of schooling covers several areas:

◆ Ask about preschool experiences, including the length of nursery or preschool education and kindergarten attendance.
◆ Ask about the student's early reading and writing instruction and the age and grade at which such instruction began. Children's early literacy instruction must be considered in conjunction with their age and development (International Reading Association, 2005; Venn & Jahn, 2004; Teale & Yokota, 2000; International Reading Association & National Association for the Education of Young Children, 1998).
◆ Ask if the student has ever repeated a grade; if so, try to determine the cause of retention.
◆ Ask if the student is currently in, or has ever been in, a special school program. Placement in such programs as special education, special reading, or Title I can influence the type of instruction and attention a student receives. If the student is in a special program, is the placement full time or part time? Does the student receive supportive help in a resource room setting or in the regular classroom?
◆ If previous diagnostic work has been done for the student through the school or a private agency, ask the parents to bring in a copy of the findings. You must have written consent from parents or guardians to contact these professionals.

School Attendance.   Absence from school and frequent transfers can be harmful to a student's progress. Some children are absent from school for weeks at a time, missing critical instruction. Other students change schools several times during the year, resulting in abrupt changes in instructional approaches and materials.

Information about school attendance can be obtained from parents, teachers, and cumulative school records. Try to determine how many times the student has been absent in the current school year and in earlier years. Instruction missed in first and second grade seems to have a particularly damaging effect on reading progress. Extended absences are also harmful. Try to determine how long the student has been in a particular school, and how many different schools the student has attended. Ask about the reasons for frequent absences or transfers.

School Instruction.   Reading instruction dramatically affects students' success in reading. Research has shown that a balanced approach to literacy instruction is highly effective (Samuels & Farstrup, 2002; Anderson, Hiebert, Scott, & Wilkinson, 1985). Components of a balanced approach include reading, writing, speaking, and listening presented in a culturally sensitive, multifaceted program that is responsive to individual and developmental needs (Cunningham, Cunningham, Moore, & Moore, 2005). Thus, teachers need a strong repertoire of instructional strategies and approaches in word knowledge, comprehension, and writing. Further, although many students learn word recognition and comprehension strategies through extensive literacy experiences, struggling students may need guided instruction that supports them as they apply strategies (Duffy, 2002; Strickland, Ganske, & Monroe, 2002). Effective instruction for struggling readers must be carefully matched to individual students' needs (Allington, 2005; Duffy, 2001; Short, Kane, & Peeling, 2000).

Struggling readers are often given books that are too hard for them. Because most classrooms use basal programs as the primary instructional material for teaching literacy, it is important to examine the characteristics of these materials (Hiebert & Mesmer, 2006; Hiebert & Martin, 2001). In response to a mandate for more literature-based teaching practices and materials, the basal reading series of one publication contained more difficult words, complex concepts, and longer selections than earlier series (Hoffman, McCarthey, Abbott, Christian, Corman, Curry, et al., 1994). Studies indicated that this series contained more engaging, predictable content than the previous skills-based series. However, many students struggled with the more difficult texts. Analyses of the basal programs indicated that the 1994 programs had little regard for decodability or controlled vocabulary (Hoffman, McCarthey, Elliott, Bayler, Price, Ferree, et al., 1998). In the subsequent revision, the trend shifted back to the more decodable texts for beginning instruction (Hoffman, Sailors, & Patterson, 2002). Yet, if the whole class is using one text, lower-achieving readers may not be able to read the material successfully. Even teachers who organize students into small groups may still have one or two students who struggle with materials that are easy for their classmates. Basal reading programs published in recent years have attempted to provide a comprehensive approach to literacy instruction while providing materials teachers can use to differentiate instruction. These new reading programs integrate the instructional anthology with accompanying sets of leveled books for guided reading instruction (Houghton-Mifflin, 2008; Scott Foresman, 2008; Macmillan/ McGraw-Hill, 2006; Rasinski & Padak, 2004).

Information about a student's first experiences with reading instruction may provide insights into how a problem developed. Was the initial method suited to the student's needs and level of development? Did the reading problem start in first grade, or were the student's early experiences successful? Reading problems that begin in first and second grade often involve word recognition abilities; problems that develop in the intermediate grades (or later) tend to focus on comprehension and language abilities.

Information about school instruction can be obtained from school personnel, parents, and students. The school is a particularly valuable source. For most reading teachers, the school is the primary source of information. It is typically the classroom teacher who approaches the reading teacher with concerns about individual students. Teacher interviews and questionnaires, school records, and information about school-books and assignments all provide insight into instruction. In gathering information from the school, the reading teacher should try to get a full picture of instruction and progress. Is the student receiving specific reading instruction, or is reading and writing instruction addressed within the context of other subjects, such as social studies and science? If reading is taught as a subject, is a reading textbook series used? If so, which one, and at what level is the student placed? If novels and trade books are used, which ones has the student read? Is the class organized into reading groups, or is the whole class instructed together? Are word recognition and comprehension strategies taught explicitly? Are students taught strategies for reading in social studies, health, and science books? Is the class provided time for independent or recreational reading? If so, are books provided at the student's level? Is writing encouraged? How is the student performing in areas such as math, science, social studies, art, and physical education?

The student's own perceptions about reading instruction can also offer valuable insights. Interviews and informal conversations provide information about whether a student likes reading class (or instruction) and whether the books and stories are easy and interesting to read. Ask the student what activities take place during reading instruction. Are stories and novels read orally or silently? We have found that students with reading problems often would like to change something about their instruction. For this reason, the students often are asked, "If you could change one thing about reading class, what would it be?" A student's perceptions of reading can also be revealing. You might ask the student what reading is or what makes a good reader (Johnson, 2005).

Parents' perceptions of the school environment come from their child's comments, homework examples, report cards, and teacher conferences. During an interview, ask the parents to describe the type and amount of homework their child is given. Ask parents if the student brings books home from school to read. Parents often have strong feelings about instructional factors that may have contributed to their child's reading problems. Obtaining this information from parents is important in fostering a cooperative spirit between the school and home.

Sometimes, the information suggests that school factors may have indeed contributed to the reading problem. What can you, as a reading teacher, do? You cannot change the past. Furthermore, assigning blame to a particular school or teacher is not helpful. A classroom teacher may have difficulty responding to the special needs of an individual when coping with a group of 25 to 35 students. A reading teacher can make helpful suggestions to the school and can foster cooperation among all of the professionals who are trying to help the student. For example, one reading teacher suggested the titles of easy books for a low-achieving student to read during recreational reading time in his class. Another reading teacher worked with the classroom teacher to adjust difficult homework assignments for a special-needs student.

In some cases, information about past instruction is helpful in planning an effective current reading program. Ten-year-old Gregg loudly stated that he hated school reading class and "all those hard worksheets." Gregg defined reading as "saying the words right," which explained his lack of interest and enthusiasm for it. To help him overcome negative past experiences, his reading teacher avoided any tasks that resembled rote instruction and emphasized comprehension rather than accurate word pronunciation. Gregg selected the stories that he and his teacher read together. They paused periodically to discuss and predict what might happen next. Because Gregg enjoyed art, the tutor encouraged him to illustrate parts of the story and vocabulary words. At the end of the semester, Gregg proclaimed that these lessons "weren't real reading classes, but I learned to read better."

Social and Cultural Environments

Go to MyEducationLab and select the topic *English Language Learners*. Then, go to the Activities and Applications section, watch the video entitled "Incorporating the Home Experiences of Culturally Diverse Students into the Classroom—Part 1," and respond to the accompanying questions.

Reading is a social process because during reading, an author communicates his or her ideas to the reader. Because of the social nature of reading, a student's relationships with parents, teachers, and peers can affect reading achievement. Social interactions occur through specific personal relationships and through the student's general cultural environment (Gillet & Temple, 2000).

Successful social interactions can provide the student with feelings of high self-esteem and confidence that encourage reading achievement. Unfortunately, many poor readers experience difficulties in social interactions. Students with reading problems often are rejected by their classmates and viewed with disfavor by their teachers. They may be a source of concern to their parents. As a result, poor readers often have difficulty relating to others.

In today's schools, reading instruction tends to be a social experience. Students often read orally in pairs or groups, sharing thoughts and feelings about a novel or working in cooperative groups. These activities can be burdensome to a student who lacks ability in social interactions. Students who are poor readers may withdraw in shame when they have to share their reading. The student's cultural environment may also affect reading progress. Some students are surrounded by peers who do not value literacy. In addition, the student's cultural background may make asking a teacher for

Go to MyEducationLab and select the topic *English Language Learners*. Then, go to the Activities and Applications section, watch the video entitled "Incorporating the Home Experiences of Culturally Diverse Students into the Classroom—Part 2," and respond to the accompanying questions.

help a difficult and uncomfortable experience. When a student's culture does not value academic achievement, instruction can be made relevant by having the student read and write about interesting topics, such as popular TV programs and movies, video games, and favorite musicians or comedians.

Reading teachers should gather background information about both the student's social and cultural environments. Often the parents' description of their child's social interactions is informative. Ask the parents to describe their child's relationships with them and with siblings. Does the student have many friends? Do these friends value education? What is the student's relationship with the teacher and classmates? Does the student willingly join in group activities or prefer to work alone? Is the student shy and withdrawn or outgoing?

Interviewing the student about friends and interests can also be useful. Does the student see reading as something that friends and family value? Does the student spend time with friends? What are the student's interests? Such information provides hints about how to make reading a motivating experience.

At times, the investigation of a student's social relationships indicates cause for concern. However, teachers often find that these relationships improve when academic problems are alleviated. When students read better, their feelings of success make them more confident in social interactions. Thus, by offering good instruction, reading teachers often can affect both a student's achievement and her or his social relationships.

At other times, a teacher's use of a student's interests may draw him or her more comfortably into social interactions. Eamon, the poorest reader in his third-grade class, seldom interacted with his peers. During recess, he stood in the corner of the playground; at lunch, he usually sat and ate alone. To help him, the reading teacher made a point of talking to Eamon alone whenever possible. Discovering that Eamon was passionately interested in snakes and had two pet reptiles at home, she gave him several books about snakes and asked him to bring his pets to school. The eager fascination of the other children motivated Eamon to talk about the care of his pets and how they should be handled. The teacher also read several books about snakes to the class and encouraged Eamon to critique them. Were the facts accurate? Had Eamon ever seen a snake do that? As Eamon became the class snake expert, he gradually increased his willingness to participate in class activities and to seek out the company of his peers.

Carefully planned reading with peers can promote social and reading competence. Jennifer, a sixth-grade student in the reading center, was reading at the third-grade level and had a history of negative social interactions. To improve reading and social skills, Jennifer was paired with Samantha, a fifth-grade student. The two girls read *Charlotte's Web* (White) at home and returned to the reading center to discuss difficult words, the characters in the book, and the plot. Sharing the reading experience helped Jennifer overcome her shyness. Jennifer and Samantha became good friends as they enjoyed the positive social experience of reacting to good children's literature.

Information about the Individual

Many of the factors that contribute to reading problems are found within the individual student. This section discusses information about emotional status, potential (intelligence), physical health, and language development.

Emotional Information

Poor readers often display emotional problems that impede learning. Not surprisingly, many students who have problems in their social environments (discussed in the previous section) also display emotional problems.

For some students, problems with learning to read may result in emotional problems. For example, some children withdraw and refuse even to attempt to read or write. Seven-year-old Carlos eagerly participated in classroom activities that did not involve reading or writing. However, when the teacher asked students to take out their books, Carlos would either put his head down on the desk or turn his chair away from the teacher. To avoid repeated failure, Carlos had decided not to read anymore.

If learning has been a painful experience, some students develop a block against all school activities. Others react by becoming hostile or aggressive. Still others develop self-images of poor readers; because these students believe that they are "dumb," they give up trying to learn. Other students become overcome with anxiety and may start to shake or stutter when asked to read.

For other students, the reading problem may be a result of an underlying emotional problem. For example, some students first develop problems with literacy just as their parents are separating or going through a divorce.

Teachers, parents, and students themselves can all offer insights about emotional factors that may affect reading achievement. The teacher, who sees the child in class, can note reactions to instructional activities. The parents can describe the child at home and with peers. Finally, the perceptions of the student are perhaps the most revealing.

What types of school information are useful in determining a student's emotional state? Knowing whether the student works independently in class is helpful. Does the student cooperate well with others? Does the student pay attention and follow directions? Does the teacher see evidence of emotional outbursts, inappropriate behavior, or depression? Does the student willingly participate in reading activities? How does the student interact with others?

Through parent interviews, the reading teacher can also gain insight into a student's interactions, behavior, and attitudes within the family and with friends. For example, can the child take enough responsibility to do chores and complete work? Does the youngster often withdraw from peer groups? Does the child seem unhappy?

Of course, simply observing and interacting with a student also gives much information. Observation of a student's behaviors and attitudes during reading class can make you aware of that student's emotional state. Finally, as you interact with a student, you will be able to judge the appropriateness of responses.

At times, you may suspect that emotional factors may be affecting reading. However, because a reading teacher is not a psychologist or psychiatrist, directly addressing emotional problems is not appropriate. Rather, a reading teacher may best address these problems by planning sensitive instruction.

Donny, one student in a group of five, was quite hostile during reading instruction. He accused the teacher of liking the other children better and of thinking that he was "dumb." He deliberately dropped books and pencils, loudly complained of a stomachache, and refused to answer questions or read orally. In fact, his behavior totally disrupted group activities. To help Donny, his reading teacher made a special effort to spend some time with him alone. She read orally with Donny, praising him when he was successful and gently helping him when he had difficulties. Donny enjoyed this private attention, away from the possibly negative reactions of others. Slowly, Donny's trust in his teacher developed into an improved self-concept, and he became more cooperative during group reading activities.

Information about Potential (Intelligence)

A student's potential for learning affects his or her ability to read. Potential for learning is often measured by tests of intelligence; however, an individual's total potential cannot be fully captured in a test. This issue is discussed more fully in Chapter 2.

Physical Information

Many physical factors, including hearing problems, vision problems, general health problems, and neurological dysfunction, affect a student's ability to read. This section provides a brief overview of these factors.

Hearing Problems.   A hearing loss, even if it is moderate or temporary, can greatly impede reading instruction. A student who cannot hear the teacher or who cannot differentiate the sounds needed for phonics instruction will often develop reading problems. However, the most serious effect of hearing loss is that it impedes normal language development, which is the basis of reading.

When students cannot hear adequately, all of their communication skills are impaired. The result can be problems with vocabulary, grammar, and verbal thinking skills. Hearing loss is most devastating if it occurs during the language acquisition years (between the ages of 2 and 4).

Because of the importance of adequate hearing, students need to be screened for possible hearing impairment. Often schools do this testing, or preliminary screening may be done by a reading teacher (see Chapter 2).

Additional information can also help pinpoint a hearing problem. The reading teacher can ask the parents if they have observed any speech problems, such as slurred speech or difficulty in making sounds. Has the student suffered frequent ear infections? Does the student turn her or his head to one side while listening? Does the student seem inattentive or ask for information to be repeated? Does the student fail to respond immediately when called? Of course, if you observe such behaviors during your own work with a student, you should immediately request a screening for hearing loss.

What should be done if a teacher suspects a hearing problem? As mentioned, many schools and reading centers have devices for screening students. However, because the testing of hearing is complex and the results may vary from time to time in children, a reading teacher cannot make a definitive diagnosis. Rather, if screening devices or symptoms suggest a hearing loss, the parents or school should be referred to a professional in the field, such as an audiologist.

Teachers can also adjust their instruction to meet the needs of a student with a hearing loss or a suspected hearing loss. Remember to sit close to and face the student directly when speaking. If the student does not respond directly to questions or comments, try to repeat them in a cheerful fashion. Let the student watch you pronounce the words.

Vision Problems.   The ability to see clearly is critical to the reading process. Vision problems may be quite complex, involving difficulties in seeing close up or far away or in focusing both eyes together. In addition, certain students may have difficulties with glare, fluorescent lights, and distinguishing colors. Because vision changes rapidly for children, it should be tested often.

As with possible hearing loss, a reading teacher should try to determine whether the student has a vision problem. School records or parents can provide the results of recent vision screenings. Reading teachers can also administer vision-screening tests (see Chapter 2).

Visual behaviors that indicate problems include:

- ◆ Avoidance of reading and writing
- ◆ Holding a page very close or at an unusual angle
- ◆ Losing one's place while reading
- ◆ Frowning, squinting, or scowling during reading
- ◆ Headaches, rubbing the eyes, or covering one eye

What can a teacher do to help a student with a suspected vision problem? If a screening test or student behaviors indicate a vision problem, the youngster should be referred to a vision professional (optometrist or ophthalmologist) for further testing.

If a reading teacher is dealing with an uncorrected vision problem, certain accommodations will make the student more comfortable. Use books with larger type if they are available. Some computer software allows the teacher to adjust the size of the print. In addition, the teacher may record some of the student's books on audiotape.

General Health Problems. Because learning is an active process, it requires that a student be alert, energetic, and able to concentrate for long periods. Poor physical health can impair the ability to concentrate. Through parent interviews and questionnaires, reading teachers can determine whether the child has any medical conditions that may affect learning or if the child suffers from conditions or takes medications that affect the ability to concentrate.

What can a teacher do when a student suffers from health problems? Sensitivity to the needs of the student is often crucial. Meghan suffered from severe allergies, and the strong medication that she took during certain times of the year tended to make her lethargic. Knowing this situation, her reading teacher praised Meghan for the work she completed and never suggested that Meghan was not trying her best.

Neurological Problems. All learning, including the ability to learn to read, is neurologically based. The reading process demands an intact and well-functioning nervous system; a neurological dysfunction can destroy reading ability.

Children with atypical neurological systems are often "hard-core" disabled readers, who have extreme difficulty learning to read (Vellutino, Scanlon, Sipay, Small, Chen, Pratt, et al., 1996) or are labeled dyslexic (see Chapter 15). Thus, if assessment of a student's reading (as described in the next chapter) suggests a serious reading problem, a teacher might consider the possibility of referring the student for a neurological examination.

To probe further, ask the parents if any other member of the family has experienced a serious reading problem. A history of a difficult pregnancy and delivery may also point to neurological dysfunction. Certain studies suggest that 50 to 70 percent of reading disabilities may be hereditary (Torgesen, 2004). Other signs of possible neurological dysfunction include slow physical development and accidents that have involved damage to the brain.

Evidence indicates that attention deficit hyperactivity disorder (ADHD), a problem that affects the ability to concentrate, is caused by neurological problems (Lerner & Kline, 2006). Students who have ADHD are often prescribed medications, such as Ritalin, to help control their behavior. Finally, many practitioners believe that children with learning disabilities may also have subtle problems in their neurological functioning. Students with learning disabilities are entitled to special services under the provision of the 2004 reauthorization of the Individuals with Disabilities Education Improvement Act (IDEA).

Information on possible neurological problems can be gathered from the parents, school records, and specialists (such as physicians) who have been consulted by the child's parents. If students with suspected neurological problems have been diagnosed as having ADHD or a learning disability, the school will have already gathered much information about these students. For example, thorough testing is required for every special education student to comply with IDEA regulations (see Chapter 15). With parental consent, these records can be released to a reading teacher.

What can be done if a teacher suspects that a student may have a neurological dysfunction? If students need further testing, they should be referred to physicians specializing in pediatrics and neurology or to appropriate professionals in their schools.

However, teachers are still responsible for teaching these students to read. Can they help them? The answer is a resounding yes. At one time, educators believed that very specialized methods were required to teach students with neurological difficulties to read. More recent studies suggest that the same methods that are effective with all students who have reading problems will also work with those who have a neurological dysfunction (Cunningham & Allington, 2006). A reading teacher who concentrates on effective and motivating methods will often help these students make substantial gains. Be aware, however, that students with neurological problems (or suspected neurological problems) may improve at a slower rate and may need longer and more intense instruction than most reading-disabled students.

Information about Language Development

Because reading is language expressed in written form, a student's language development forms the basis for all reading. The ability to express and receive thoughts through language is fundamental to being able to read. A student who is confused about oral language sounds will have difficulty pronouncing written words. A student who does not know many word meanings will gain little information from reading, even if he or she can pronounce all of the words. In other instances, a student's language patterns may be mature but may differ from the language used in school. Many students come to school speaking languages other than English. They need rich experiences in learning English, plus experiences reading in their native languages, to develop high-level comprehension. Students who speak nonstandard dialects may lack both exposure to more standard English language patterns and a feeling of pride and proficiency in their own dialect.

A reading teacher can easily obtain background information about a student's language. Simply listening to or conversing with a student gives many valuable insights. A student who speaks in long sentences, provides full answers to questions, and is able to use many words probably has an excellent language base for reading. Unfortunately, many students with reading problems speak haltingly in short sentences and use just a few words.

Joey, for example, was in kindergarten, yet his language patterns resembled those of a 3- or 4-year-old. He often used his name instead of a pronoun or used pronouns incorrectly. "Joey needs crayons" or "Me need crayons" were typical utterances. Similarly, 8-year-old Paul had difficulty dictating even a single sentence to his reading teacher. In addition to observation, interview questions can reveal much about a student's language. Ask the parents whether their child's language development was slower than that of other children or was within a normal range. Did their child experience any speech difficulties? Has the child had any language or speech therapy? To obtain information about language differences, ask parents what languages are spoken in the home and whether the child knew English when entering school. A history of class placements, including bilingual services or ELL, often gives much information about a student's proficiency in English.

What can be done if a teacher suspects that language problems are affecting a student's reading? At times, evaluation by a language professional (speech therapist or language specialist) may be needed to pinpoint the precise source of the difficulty. However, in many other instances, a reading teacher can foster the development of rich language by employing enjoyable instructional strategies, such as reading language-rich storybooks to the student, encouraging conversation, and developing knowledge of abstract concepts (see Chapter 10).

Twelve-year-old José, a student in the reading center, could speak and understand basic English, but he lacked the English skills to read more sophisticated material. His tutor began by reading selections from the daily newspaper that focused on news about Mexico, his homeland. José enjoyed helping his tutor with the pronunciation of Spanish names. They then discussed what was happening in Mexico and read portions of the articles together several times. Finally José attempted to read articles alone. At one point, he joyfully exclaimed, "That's what NAFTA looks like!" José and his tutor continued this process, moving gradually into other familiar topics such as television and sports. As he did this, José began to locate cognates—words that are the same in Spanish and English—to help his tutor learn Spanish.

Methods of Collecting Information

As shown, a wealth of important background information may be collected about a student with reading difficulties. This information helps teachers understand the factors that contribute to a reading problem. It also aids us in planning effective and motivating instruction.

Generally, background information is collected at the beginning of a teacher's work with a student. The assessment tools most frequently used are (1) interviews and questionnaires, (2) informal talks with the student, parents, and professionals, (3) records of previous testing, school achievement, or report cards, and (4) observation. In the school setting, the classroom teacher usually initiates the process by contacting the reading teacher for help with a student who is struggling in reading and writing. In many reading centers, parents or school literacy specialists may make the initial contact and provide the first source of information. In both situations, it is important for the reading teacher to collect information from the classroom teacher and the parents as well as the student.

Interview and Questionnaire

Interviews and questionnaires with informed and concerned people yield information about the student that cannot be obtained in any other way. In these two formats, those concerned with a student's reading problem are able to state important information frankly and fully.

Interview.   In an interview, a reading teacher follows a prescribed set of questions, asking them orally of the person who is being interviewed. A reading teacher can interview parents, the student, or the classroom teacher. The personal and informal atmosphere of an interview encourages the sharing of valuable information in a sympathetic setting. We interview the parents separately from the student and use different interview forms. A reading teacher who works outside the student's school may get valuable information from interviewing the classroom teachers and other professionals in the school. However, written permission must be obtained from the parents before a student's school may be contacted. Some important procedures ensure a successful interview:

◆ Begin by telling the parents, student, or classroom teacher that this information will be kept confidential.
◆ Strive for an amiable, open atmosphere. Briefly discussing a neutral topic, such as the weather or sports, can reduce initial fears or discomfort about the interview process.
◆ Avoid indicating disapproval of responses.
◆ Follow a directed plan. You should know what questions to ask before the interview begins. These questions should be in front of you so they will not be forgotten.
◆ Take notes, because remembering everything that was said is difficult. Explain why you are taking notes. If the person being interviewed asks about what he or she said, cheerfully read the notes back aloud.
◆ Because of important legal and moral considerations involved in the interview, it must be kept confidential. If you wish to tape the interview, you must ob-

tain written consent from parents, guardians, or the professionals involved. The presence of another individual during the interview also requires consent. Finally, information shared during an interview or any other part of the assessment procedure cannot be released to another agency without parental permission.

Questionnaire.   Like an interview, a questionnaire consists of a group of questions to which parents, a student, or another professional respond. However, the list of questions is responded to in writing. A questionnaire may simply be mailed to the respondent, filled out, and mailed back. Alternatively, it may be filled out in the presence of the reading teacher.

Questionnaires are valuable when a face-to-face interview is not feasible. In the reading center, we often mail questionnaires to the classroom teachers of the students we serve because they have difficulties coming in for interviews. In addition, because questions are responded to independently, the use of a questionnaire enables parents, students, and classroom teachers to formulate thoughtful responses and take the time to gather valuable information about developmental history, school attendance, and grades. However, questionnaires may be unproductive with parents and children who find writing difficult.

Parent Background Information Form.   A sample form for gathering background information from parents is provided on the website for this book. Please feel free to download the document and adapt it for your own context. We suggest that, if possible, this form be used as an interview, rather than as a questionnaire.

Student Background Information Form.   A student information form for younger students that can be used either in an interview or as a questionnaire is provided on the website for this book. A parallel form for older students is also provided. Questions about student interests help to establish rapport with a student and give the teacher information to motivate and personalize reading instruction. You can download the documents and modify questions to suit your locality (for example, adding skiing or surfing).

A final section gives information on how the student thinks about reading (Johnson, 2005). Often, low-achieving students think that reading is just saying words; not surprisingly, they do not focus on meaning. These questions also explore the student's reading strategies. Many students with reading problems will simply "sound it out" as the only strategy they use to cope with an unknown word; they do not realize that meaning can also be used. Other low-achieving students have unrealistic pictures of good readers and believe that such readers know all the words and never make mistakes.

School Information Form.   A form for collecting information from the student's school is provided on the website for this book. Please download the form and add questions that may be pertinent to your setting. If you are working in a setting other than a school, remember that written permission from parents or guardians is needed whenever you contact a student's school.

Informal Talks

In addition to interviews and questionnaires, informal conversations throughout the year can keep providing valuable insights. Twelve-year-old Adam continued to share his frustrations with homework assignments through the school year, thus enabling us to help his classroom teacher modify them.

The parents of another child revealed, over an informal cup of coffee, that he had had extensive difficulties immediately after birth. This information, which was not given in an initial interview, was shared only as the parents became more comfortable with us. The reading teacher or the classroom teacher should be alert to opportunities to gather information through these continuing, informal means. Keeping in touch with parents as instruction continues is important. Equally important is the sharing of information between the classroom teacher and the reading teacher. Informal, but professional interactions between colleagues can often reveal important information and lead to increased effectiveness in providing instruction.

Continued contact with parents provides teachers with valuable information about how students are reacting to instruction, whether they are improving, and if their attitudes toward reading are becoming more positive. Finally, contact helps families to encourage children to read at home.

School Records and Materials

School records, previous diagnostic reports, report cards, and *student portfolios* (organized collections of student's work kept in school) are all valuable sources of information. In addition, cumulative records, which detail a student's progress over a number of years, provide information about the history of a reading problem. Reports, such as an individualized educational program (IEP) prepared for special education students under the provisions of the IDEA, are also valuable sources of information. Reading teachers in schools have access to this information. If you are a reading teacher working in a setting outside of the student's school, ask parents to allow you access to school information because it enables you to gain a more thorough and balanced view of a child's reading problem.

Observation during Reading Lessons

In the discussion of background information, many types of information were presented that could be gathered through direct observation of your student. Direct observation provides insight into students' social interactions and language development. As a reading teacher, you can make observations and enter anecdotal records as you work with a student. However, if possible, observe the student in many different settings. Student reactions and behaviors often vary according to the environment in which they are observed. A student who is quiet and cooperative in individual instruction may be noisy and defiant in a large class. In fact, sometimes a description of one student in these two settings is so different that teachers wonder if the same individual is being observed. To gain a realistic picture of students, observe them in natural settings (at parties, on the playground, in their general education classes) as well as in special reading classes. As a school-based reading teacher or literacy specialist, observations of the student in a variety of learning contexts is crucial to supporting teachers as they plan instruction for the student.

As you make observations, be sure to note them in writing for future reference. Understanding the instructional context is crucial in providing support for classroom teachers. Remember that, even if the student receives supplemental support, the vast majority of instruction for most struggling readers and writers occurs within the general education classroom setting. Thus, an important role of the reading specialist is to provide instructional support to the classroom teacher (Strickland, et al., 2002). Further information about observations is given in Chapter 2.

Summary

This chapter discusses collecting background information on students with reading problems, including information about the environment and the individual. Background factors interact with reading problems in complex ways; a background factor can coexist with a reading problem and yet not cause that problem.

Environmental factors include the home, school, and social and cultural environments. The home influences a child as parents serve as role models for literacy and provide a general environment that nurtures the child. The child's school history, attendance, and school instruction also affect a reading problem. Often, students who have reading problems are not receiving instruction that meets their needs. Students with reading problems also tend to have social difficulties. They may also come from a culture that does not support literacy.

Individual factors include emotional status, potential or intelligence, physical health, and language development. Students with reading problems may have emotional difficulties. Sometimes these emotional problems are alleviated as reading improves. Physical factors include hearing problems, visual problems, general health problems, and neurological problems. Students with ADD and learning disabilities may have subtle neurological problems. Students with reading problems may also have difficulties with language development.

Information may be collected through interviews, written questionnaires, informal talks, school records and materials, and observation.

References

Allington, R. L. (2005). *What Really Matters for Struggling Readers: Designing Research-Based Programs.* Boston: Allyn & Bacon.

Anderson, R. C., Hiebert, E. H., Scott, J. A., & Wilkinson, I. A. G. (1985). *Becoming a Nation of Readers.* Washington, DC: National Institute of Education.

Cunningham, P. M., & Allington, R. L. (2006). *Classrooms that Work: They Can All Read and Write* (4th ed.). New York: Allyn & Bacon.

Cunningham, P. M., Cunningham, J. W., Moore, S. A., & Moore, D. W. (2005). *Reading and Writing in Elementary Classrooms: Research Based K-4 Instruction* (5th ed.). Boston: Allyn and Bacon.

Duffy, A. M. (2001). Balance, literacy acceleration, and responsive teaching in a summer school literacy program for elementary school struggling readers. *Reading Research and Instruction, 40,* 67–100.

Duffy, G. (2002). Direct explanations of strategies. In C. Block and M. Pressley (Eds.), *Comprehension Instruction: Research-Based Best Practices*, pp. 28–41. New York: The Guilford Press.

Gillet, J. W., & Temple, C. (2000). *Understanding Reading Problems: Assessment and Instruction* (5th ed.). New York: Longman.

Hiebert, E. H., & Martin, L. A. (2001). The texts of beginning reading instruction. In S. B. Neuman & D. K. Dickinson (Eds.), *Handbook of Early Literacy Research*, pp. 361–376. New York: Guilford Press.

Hiebert, E. H., & Mesmer, H. A. E. (2006). Perspectives on the difficulty of beginning reading texts. In D. K. Dickinson & S. B. Neuman (Eds.), *Handbook of Early Literacy Research*, Volume 2, pp. 395–409, New York: Guilford Press.

Hoffman, J. V., McCarthey, S. J., Abbott, J., Christain, C., Corman, L., Curry, C., et al. (1994). So what's new in the basals? A focus on first grade. *Journal of Reading Behavior, 26,* 47–73.

Hoffman, J. V., McCarthey, S. J., Elliott, B., Bayler, D. L., Price, D. P., Ferree, A., et al. (1998). The literature based basals in first-grade classrooms: Savior, Satan, or same-old, same-old? *Reading Research Quarterly,* 33, 168–197.

Hoffman, J. V., Sailors, M., & Patterson, E. U. (2002). Decodable tests for beginning reading instruction: The year 2000 basals. Report #1-016. Ann Arbor: University of Michigan, Center for the Improvement of Early Reading Achievement.

Houghton-Mifflin. (2008). *Houghton Mifflin Reading.* Boston: Houghton-Mifflin Publishing.

Individuals with Disabilities Education Improvement Act of (2004), Public Law 108-446.

International Reading Association. (2005). *Literacy Development in the Preschool Years: A Position Statement of the International Reading Association.* Newark, DE: International Reading Association.

International Reading Association & National Association for the Education of Young Children. (1998). *Learning to Read and Write: Developmentally Appropriate Practices for Young Children.*

Johnson, J. C. (2005). What makes a "good reader? Asking student to define "good" readers. *Reading Teacher,* 58, 766–773.

Lerner, J. W., & Kline, F. (2006). *Learning Disabilities and Related Disorders: Characteristics and Teaching Strategies.* Boston: Houghton-Mifflin Co.

Macmillan/McGraw-Hill. (2005). *Treasures Reading Program.* New York: McGraw-Hill Publishing.

Maslin, P. (2007). Comparison of readability and decodability levels across five first grade basal programs. *Reading Improvement, 44*(2), 59.

Rasinski, T., & Padak, N. (2004). Beyond consensus—beyond balance: Toward a comprehensive literacy curriculum. *Reading and Writing Quarterly, 20,* 91–102.

Samuels, S. J., & Farstrup, A. E. (eds.). (2002). *What Research Has to Say About Reading Instruction* (3rd ed.). Newark, DE: International Reading Association.

Scott Foresman. (2008). *Scott Foresman Reading Street.* Boston: Pearson Education.

Short, R. A., Kane, M., & Peeling, T. (2000). Retooling the reading lesson: Matching the right tools to the job. *The Reading Teacher,* 54, 284–295.

Strickland, D. S., Ganske, K., & Monroe, J. K. (2002). *Supporting Struggling Readers and Writers: Strategies for Classroom Intervention.* Newark, DE: International Reading Association.

Teale, W. H., & Yokota, J. (2000). Beginning reading and writing: Perspectives on instruction. In D. S. Strickland and L. M. Morrow (Eds.), *Beginning Reading and Writing.* New York: Teachers College Press.

Torgesen, J. K. (2004). Learning disabilities: An historical and conceptual overview. In B. Y. L. Wong (ed.), *Learning About Learning Disabilities* (3rd ed., pp. 3–34). San Diego, CA: Academic Press.

Vellutino, F. R., Scanlon, D. M., Sipay, E. R., Small, S. G., Chen, R., Pratt, A., et al. (1996). Cognitive profiles of difficult-to-remediate and readily remediated poor readers: Early intervention as a vehicle for distinguishing between cognitive and experiential deficits as basic causes of specific reading disability. *Journal of Educational Psychology,* 88, 601–638.

Venn, E. C., & Jahn, M. D. (2004). *Teaching and Learning in Preschool: Using Individually Appropriate Practices in Early Childhood Literacy Instruction.* Newark, DE: International Reading Association.

MyEducationLab is a research-based learning tool that brings teaching to life. Go to the Jennings, Caldwell, & Lerner 6th Edition MyEducationLab for Reading Assessment site at www.myeducationlab.com to:

- engage in multimedia exercises to help you build a deeper and more applied understanding of chapter content;
- utilize extensive resources including videos from real classrooms, Praxis and licensure preparation, a lesson plan builder, and materials to help you in your teaching career.

Assessing Reading: Formal Measures

Introduction

This chapter presents some of the more frequently used formal measures employed in a comprehensive diagnosis of reading. Chapter 5 presents an in-depth discussion of informal tests as well as the use of the informal reading inventory. Other tools for informal assessment are discussed in Chapters 7 through 13.

Using Both Formal and Informal Assessment

Teachers find that informal and authentic assessment methods provide immediate, usable, and practical information about students. Informal measures, such as informal reading inventories, trial lessons, curriculum-based assessment, and structured observations, are described in Chapter 5. However, for a comprehensive evaluation of a student with reading problems, formal tests offer additional usable information. Formal tests serve several purposes:

◆ They allow teachers to compare a student to others of the same age or grade level.
◆ They provide scores that are more familiar to parents and other professionals, such as psychologists and physicians.
◆ They help teachers make objective decisions about a student's performance.
◆ They fulfill the legal requirements for certain local, state, school, and federal policies.

In fact, a student's performance on a formal test administered schoolwide is often the impetus for a more in-depth diagnosis. Many schools have adopted a *response-to-intervention* process for determining whether a student has a specific learning disability. In this model, a school develops an evaluation plan for a student that includes scientific, research-based intervention. Teachers must carefully document the student's growth; if students do not make adequate progress in response to this intervention, they may be referred for an evaluation for learning disabilities (Lerner & Kline, 2006). The Individuals with Disabilities Education Act (IDEA) was reauthorized in 2004 and specific regulations for identifying students with learning disabilities were enacted in 2006 (U.S. Department of Education, 2006, IDEA, 2004). Under these regulations, criteria used by state and local education agencies to determine whether a student has a learning disability must comply with the following:

◆ The state and local agencies cannot require a severe discrepancy between the student's potential as determined by an intelligence test and the student's achievement level.
◆ The state and local agencies must allow the use of a response-to-intervention process.
◆ The state and local agencies may allow the use of alternative research-based procedures.

Although the evaluation process varies from state to state and district to district, a typical model includes screening, intervention, documentation, and diagnosis. Most models begin with school-wide or system-wide screening with a general achievement test of all students. Based on the results of this screening instrument, the general education teacher provides scientific, research-based teaching and intervention as needed. Student progress is monitored on a continuous basis. Individual students who do not make adequate progress in the general education setting may be referred for further evaluation to determine whether they need more intensive intervention. Progress is continuously monitored and intervention can become progressively intensive as needed. This is usually a cyclical process to provide for systematic assessment to continue to measure students' progress (U.S. Department of Education, 2006).

Although the procedures presented in IDEA and the 2006 regulations focus on students' qualifications for services in special education, reading specialists are often involved in the process. This is especially true of the response-to-intervention model. Reading specialists help teachers analyze the results of the reading achievement tests and provide support in planning appropriate instruction based on the results. They are especially helpful in planning and documenting intervention for students whose achievement levels indicate that they are struggling. The remainder of this chapter will focus on formal assessments that may be used in this process. A more detailed discussion of literacy instruction for students with special needs is provided in Chapter 15.

One of the criticisms of formal tests has been that they lack authenticity, because formal tests tend to assess the reader's proficiency with short passages and isolated words rather than using the types of reading students do in school. However, some formal test publishers are now creating longer, more authentic passages for students to read. One example is the *Iowa Test of Basic Skills* published by Houghton Mifflin. New assessment tools also provide ways to combine formal and informal assessment. The Psychological Corporation has published an *Integrated Assessment System*, which provides formal assessment of a student's reading, writing, and higher level thinking (Harcourt Assessment, 1998). Additional tests are listed and described on the website for this text.

The information in this chapter is intended to serve as a guide to help you choose, administer, and interpret formal tests. For additional information, you can refer to *The Seventeenth Mental Measurements Yearbook* (Geisinger, Spies, Carlson & Plake, 2007), a resource that contains extensive reviews of many different tests. You can also find many reviews of tests online at buros.unl.edu/buros.

Formal tests include a broad class of instruments that are commercially produced, formally printed, and published. They also have specific procedures for administration and scoring. Two types of formal tests are norm-referenced and criterion-referenced tests.

Go to MyEducationLab and select the topic *Formal Assessments.* Then, go to the Activities and Applications section, watch the video entitled "Standardized Tests," and respond to the accompanying questions.

Norm-Referenced Tests

Most formal tests are norm-referenced (also called standardized), which means that they have statistics (or norms) for comparing the performance of a student to a large sample of similar students (the norm sample). Norm-referenced tests are developed carefully using a norm sample, which is a large number of students who are representative of the general population. The test is given to each student in the norm sample, and norms are established to determine, for example, how well the average fourth grader does on the test. These norms permit you, as a teacher, to compare the fourth grader you are testing with the fourth graders in the norm sample. To ensure that your student's scores can be compared with the norm sample, you must strictly follow the procedures for test administration, scoring, and interpretation.

Criterion-Referenced Tests

Some formal tests are criterion referenced. In this type of test, a student's performance is compared to a specific standard or criterion (rather than to the norm sample). This test determines whether a student has mastered certain competencies or skills. For example, can the student recognize -*ing* endings or find the main idea in a paragraph? Criterion-referenced tests are useful because they provide a means of accountability that can be related to the curriculum. For example, a teacher can determine whether a student has mastered the concept of the main idea after it has been taught.

To understand the difference between a norm-referenced and a criterion-referenced test, look at an analogy to another area of learning: swimming. In norm-referenced terms, a child can be tested in swimming and judged to swim as well as the average 9-year-old. In criterion-referenced terms, a child is judged on the basis of certain accomplishments, such as putting his or her face in the water, floating on his or her back, and doing the crawl stroke. In other words, criterion-referenced tests measure mastery rather than grade level, or they describe rather than compare performance.

Bias in Testing

Tests should be fair in representing student performance and should be free of racial or cultural bias. The content of the test should represent the experiences and values of all groups taking the test. For example, a reading test should not contain vocabulary, pictures, or stories that are unfamiliar to certain populations taking the test. As discussed in Chapter 2, formal intelligence tests, in particular, have been subjected to the criticism of cultural bias.

Ethical Considerations

In using formal tests for assessment, professionals must comply with basic professional standards. If professionals from different disciplines are involved in assessment (i.e., educators, psychologists, counselors, social workers, medical specialists), each must abide by the standards of his or her own profession. All must maintain the confidentiality of the student, keep complete records, and follow standard testing criteria.

Scores on Norm-Referenced Tests

The scores on norm-referenced tests indicate how an individual student has performed compared to students of the same grade or age level who are in the norm sample. After a teacher gives a test, the teacher determines a raw score, which is usually the number correct on the test. Raw scores are then converted into derived scores, which can be used for interpreting the student's performance. Derived scores on norm-referenced reading tests can be reported as standard scores, reading grade equivalents, percentiles, normal curve equivalents (NCEs), and stanines.

Many scores on reading and other academic tests are based on a normal distribution curve of scores. Most scores in a normal distribution fall in the middle, creating a "humped curve." However, some high and low scores fall at the upper and lower ends of the curve. In other words, most scores are average, but some are very high or low. The more extreme (high or low) the score, the less frequent it is.

The highest point on the curve is the mean (or average) point. The "area" within each vertical division represents the percent of people in it. The closer to the mean a division is, the more individuals are in it.

Standardized tests are statistically designed so that one-half of the students are below the mean (or average) and one-half are above. Of course, communities want all of their children to score above average. The humorist Garrison Keillor lampoons this notion in his tales of the mythical town of Lake Wobegon, where "all the children are above average."

Standard Scores.   Some formal tests report standard scores, which refer to scores in which the mean and the standard deviation (which is a measure of variation) have been assigned preset values. For example, in the *Wechsler Intelligence Scale for Children* Fourth Edition (*WISC-IV*), the mean is set at 100, and the standard deviation at 15.

Grade Equivalent (GE).   The reading GE indicates how well a student reads in terms of grade level. For example, a score of 4.5 (the fifth month of the fourth grade) indicates that the student correctly answered the same number of questions on this particular test as the average pupil in the fifth month of the fourth grade. Reading GEs do not indicate absolute performance; they indicate how the student performed in relation to the students in the norm sample population.

Percentiles (PR).   Percentiles describe the student's performance in relation to others in the same age group or grade. Percentiles can be understood as a rank within 100, expressed in numbers from 1 to 99. A percentile rank is the percentage of students that scored lower than the student being tested. For example, a percentile score of 57 indicates that this student scored higher than 57 percent of the comparison group and lower than 42 percent. The 50th percentile indicates the median (or middle) score. The highest percentile is 99 and the lowest is 1. Higher percentiles indicate better student performance.

Equal distances in percentiles, however, do not indicate equal differences in raw score points. Because many scores center near the mean, the difference between the 50th and 60th percentiles may be only a few raw score points, whereas the distance between the 18th and 19th percentiles often represents a great many raw score points on the test (Figure 4.1).

   Normal Curve Equivalent (NCE) Scores.   The NCE scores are similar to percentiles in that they have a range from 1 to 99 and a mean of 50. They differ from percentile scores because they have been transformed into equal units of reading achievement. For example, the difference between the 50th and 60th NCE and the 18th and 19th NCE is the same in raw point scores. Figure 4.1 shows the distribution of NCE scores in comparison to percentiles.

Stanines.   The stanine score ranks pupils from 1 to 9. The lowest stanine score is 1, the median stanine is 5, and the highest is 9. Stanine scores are assigned so that the results represent a normal distribution. Thus, in an average class, most students will receive stanine scores of 4, 5, or 6; a few will receive stanine scores of 1 or 9.

   The name stanine is a contraction of "standard nine" and is based on the fact that the score runs from 1 to 9. Stanines are normalized standard scores with a mean of 5 and a standard deviation of 2. Figure 4.1 shows the percentage of students in each stanine and in each 10 NCE units and compares these with percentiles.

Standardization, Validity, and Reliability

Which norm-referenced tests are the best? In judging the value of a norm-referenced test, teachers should consider the test's standardization, validity, and reliability.

FIGURE 4.1   Relations among Stanines, NCEs, and Percentiles

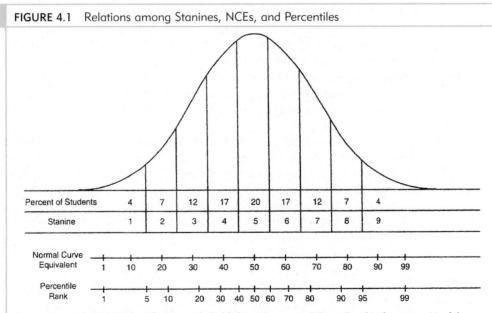

Standardization.   To standardize a test, it is given to a large representative group of students (the norm sample). Based on data derived from this norm sample, inferences are made about other students who take the test. When selecting a test, teachers should consider whether the norm sample was large enough to establish stable performance norms. In addition, the characteristics of the individuals who comprise the norm sample are important. Did the norm sample include representatives of the students who are being tested? If the norm sample group is not considered representative, some school districts develop their own local norms.

Validity.   Validity refers to whether a test measures what it is supposed to measure. Two types of validity are content validity and criterion validity. *Content validity* involves inspecting the test to see whether the items are valid for testing purposes. For example, a valid reading comprehension test would probably contain passages with questions. In contrast, a comprehension test that required the student to match words would have questionable content validity.

   Criterion validity refers to how the test compares with some other aspects of achievement. Most norm-referenced reading tests provide information about the comparison of performance on the reading test with some aspect of school achievement (for example, grade-point average). The comparison is usually done in the form of a statistical correlation. This correlation may range from +1.0 (a high positive correlation) to –1.0 (a very negative correlation). For acceptable criterion validity, the correlation should be positive and high (generally at least 0.70).

Reliability.   Reliability refers to the stability of test scores. If a test is reliable, the person will receive the same score on repeated testings. To be useful for making decisions about an individual, a test must have high reliability. Salvia Ysseldyke, and Bolt, (2006) believe that acceptable reliability for a test depends on the situation. If test scores are reported for groups of students for general administration purposes or screening, a reliability score of about 0.80 is acceptable. For individual decisions about students, such as placement in a Title I class or in special education, the reliability of the test should be 0.90.

   Two forms of reliability are test-retest reliability and internal consistency reliability. In test-retest reliability, the test is given to a group of students two times. Then the scores are correlated to determine whether individual students perform about the same on the first and second administrations. In internal reliability, items within a test are compared with one another. In one form of internal reliability, split-half reliability, a group of students' scores on one-half of the test items is correlated with performance on the items from the other half.

Tests of General Reading Assessment

Tests of general reading assessment are used to evaluate a student's general level of achievement as well as to determine the general areas of reading strengths and weaknesses. Types of tests that are used in the general reading assessment phase include group survey tests, individual survey tests, normed oral reading tests, and diagnostic tests of specific areas.

Group Survey Tests

Survey tests are norm-referenced tests that are used to assess the student's reading level. Both group survey tests and individual survey tests are used for this purpose.

Group survey tests are the most commonly used tests in schools. They are generally used once per year to assess student progress in reading and other academic subjects, to identify those who may have problems, or to evaluate the success of a program. Examples of group survey tests for reading are the *Stanford Achievement Test*, the *Iowa Tests of Basic Skills* (*ITBS*), the *California Reading Test*, the *Gates–MacGinitie Reading Tests*, Fourth Edition, and the *Group Reading Assessment and Diagnostic Evaluation* (*GRADE*). These tests are designed for use with a group of students in a class, but they are also useful for testing individual students. All standardized group reading tests permit teachers to compare a student's score to scores in large norm samples.

A group survey test is actually a series of tests at different levels. The different levels are suitable for students at different grade levels. In addition, each level usually has a few equivalent forms (for example, Form A and Form B). Because the two forms are normed similarly, the scores on the two forms can be compared. If Form A is given during an initial assessment and Form B is given after a period of instruction is completed, the student's progress can be evaluated easily.

Despite their excellent statistical properties, group survey tests have some limitations for use with students with reading problems:

- ◆ Out-of-level tests. Students with reading problems should be given test levels that are appropriate for their reading level but not for their age level. For example, an eighth grader reading at a second-grade level will find the eighth-grade test to be too hard but the second-grade test too "babyish."
- ◆ Inability to measure school-related tasks. Over a period of years, many strides have been made in making these tests better reflect the actual types of reading students do in school. However, the tests continue to measure more discrete tasks, such as reading single words and relatively short passages. For this reason, the teacher must supplement information from standardized tests with informal measures that assess such abilities as reading whole stories and taking notes.
- ◆ Limits of a formal situation. Some students "freeze" on standardized tests. In addition, because they require a standard procedure, formal tests do not allow teachers to observe student performance closely and to probe a student's responses. Informal assessment, with its ability to adjust situations to a student's needs, may give far more information.

The following descriptions of a few tests that are widely used for students with reading problems gives examples of group survey tests that the reading teacher is likely to encounter.

***Stanford Diagnostic Reading Test*, Fourth Edition.**   The *Stanford Diagnostic Reading Test*, Fourth Edition (*SDRT4*) is intended for use with lower achievers and contains more easy items than most survey tests at the same levels. The four levels of the test are red, green, brown, and blue; at each level, the test contains two forms. Phonics abilities are tested at all levels of the test. The red level, for grades 1–2, tests auditory discrimination, basic phonics skills, auditory vocabulary, word recognition, and comprehension. The green level, for grades 3–4, tests auditory discrimination, phonetic analysis, structural analysis, auditory vocabulary, comprehension, and reading rate. The brown level, for grades 5–6, tests phonetic analysis, structural analysis, auditory vocabulary, comprehension, and reading rate. Finally, the blue level, for grades 9–12 and community colleges, tests phonetic analysis, structural analysis, word meaning, word parts, comprehension, reading rate, and scanning and skimming. The test is well standardized and reports many different types of norms for students.

In addition, the SDRT contains a criterion-referenced section called Progress Indicators. All of the test items measuring a certain skill are added together, and a criterion is given for mastery of that skill.

Gates–MacGinitie Reading Tests.   The *Gates–MacGinitie Reading Tests* (GMRT), Fourth Edition, is another standardized reading test often used with low-achieving students. The test comes in five reading levels: prereading level, beginning reading level (grade 1), levels 1 and 2 (primary-level developmental reading skills), levels 3–12 (two tests: vocabulary and comprehension), and adult reading level (two tests: vocabulary and comprehension).

In the vocabulary test, which has a 20-minute time limit, students match isolated words to one of four pictures (at low levels) or one of four synonyms (at higher levels). In the comprehension tests, students read short passages and either match them to one of four pictures (at lower levels) or answer multiple-choice questions (at higher levels). This well-standardized test is used widely in Title I programs.

Group Reading Assessment and Diagnostic Evaluation (GRADE).   The *Group Reading Assessment and Diagnostic Evaluation* (Williams, 2001) was designed to determine what reading skills students have and what skills they need to be taught. It may be used in a group or individually for students ages five through adult. *GRADE* consists of 11 levels. Level P, for use in preschool and kindergarten, includes picture matching, picture differences, verbal concepts, picture categories, matching sounds, rhyming, and listening comprehension. Level K, for use in kindergarten and first grade, includes matching sounds, rhyming, print awareness, letter recognition, word similarities and differences, sound-letter correspondence, word reading, and listening comprehension. Level 1, for use in kindergarten through second grade, and level 2, for use in second grade, includes subtests in reading words, word meaning, sentence comprehension, passage comprehension, and listening comprehension. Level 3, for use in third grade, includes subtests in reading words, vocabulary, sentence comprehension, passage comprehension, and listening comprehension. Levels 4 through 6, for use in the corresponding grade levels, include subtests in vocabulary, sentence comprehension, passage comprehension, and listening comprehension. Level M, for use in Grades five through nine, includes subtests in vocabulary, sentence comprehension, passage comprehension, and listening comprehension. Level H, for use in Grades 9 through 12, includes subtests in vocabulary, sentence comprehension, passage comprehension, and listening comprehension. Level A, for use in Grades 11 through postsecondary, includes subtests in vocabulary, sentence comprehension, passage comprehension, and listening comprehension.

The guidelines for administration include directions for out-of-level testing, as well as guidelines for developmentally appropriate test selection. While reviewers expressed concerns about administering a group test to young children, they found that the content and construction of the *GRADE* provided important diagnostic information seldom found in group tests. The standardization procedures and analysis were also found to be quite good (Fugate, 2003; Waterman, 2003).

Individual Survey Tests

Individual survey tests, which are used widely in assessing students with reading problems, are designed to be administered to a single student. As survey tests, they give general information about reading scores rather than a detailed analysis of reading. In fact, many of these tests also include information about areas such as mathematics and spelling.

Individual survey tests usually consist of one level that is suitable for a wide range of reading abilities. Because an individual survey test might cover Grades 1 through 9, it would be suitable for an older reader who is reading at a primary-grade level. Individual survey tests are usually standardized, so they permit valid comparison with a norm sample.

Through careful observation, the teacher can obtain diagnostic information during the process of giving a survey test. For example, the teacher can note whether the student hesitates or recognizes words instantly and whether the student uses decoding methods.

The actual reading tasks that students perform vary greatly from test to test. Many of the test authors use considerable ingenuity to make their tests brief or to use a multiple-choice format. Unfortunately, such methods may lead to tests that do not measure the authentic ability to read. Before using a test, the teacher should inspect the actual items to determine exactly what they require the student to do. The name of the test, or of its subtests, may not reflect the content.

The most frequently used individual general achievement tests include the *Kaufman Test of Educational Achievement*, Second Edition (*KTEA-II*, Kaufman & Kaufman, 2004c), the *Peabody Individual Achievement Test–Revised/Normative Update* (*PIAT-R/NU*, Markwardt, 1998), the *Wechsler Individual Achievement Test*, Second Edition (*WIAT-II*, 2001), the *Wide Range Achievement Test*, Third Edition (*WRAT-III*, Wilkinson, 1993), and the achievement section of the *Woodcock-Johnson Psychoeducational Battery III* (*WJ-RIII*, Woodcock, McGrew, Mather, & Schrank, 2003).

***Kaufman Test of Educational Achievement,* Second Edition.**   The *Kaufman Test of Educational Achievement,* Second Edition (*KTEA-II*) includes two individual reading subtests in its battery of achievement tests: Reading Decoding and Reading Comprehension. In Reading Decoding, students are asked to identify letters and pronounce words that increase in difficulty; students are not asked to provide meanings of the words. In Reading Comprehension, students are asked to read passages and answer one or two comprehension questions about each passage. The 1998 review conducted by the Institute for Applied Psychometrics also found the *KTEA* to meet the standards established to measure reading achievement. Reviewers indicated that the standardization procedures were well done and that the test was highly reliable (McGrew, 1998). The KTEA-II is considered to be a well-developed, user-friendly instrument for measuring general achievement (Bonner, 2005). Carpenter (2005) describes the second edition as substantially different from the first edition, with considerable improvements. Because the KTEA-II is co-normed with the *Kaufman Assessment Battery for Children,* Second Edition (*KABC-II*), using both instruments to test the same individual allows for comparison of the student's cognitive ability and achievement. (Carpenter, 2005).

Peabody Individual Achievement Test–Revised/Normative Update.   The *Peabody Individual Achievement Test–Revised/Normative Update* (*PIAT–R/NU*) is a battery of achievement tests for students in kindergarten through Grade 12. The battery includes tests in reading, writing, mathematics, and general information, with two reading tests that can be combined into one total score. The two reading subtests are Reading Recognition and Reading Comprehension. At the early levels, the Reading Recognition subtest measures letter identification and beginning sounds in a multiple-choice format. At the next level, students read the word and select the picture (from multiple choices) that represents that word. In later levels, students read lists of words. Students are not asked to provide word meanings. In the Reading Comprehension subtest, students read a single sentence silently and select from among four pictures the one that best represents the meaning of each sentence. The 1999 review conducted by the Institute for Applied Psychometrics found that the *PIAT* is an adequate measure of reading achievement (McGrew, 1998).

***Wechsler Individual Achievement Test,* Second Edition.**   The *Wechsler Individual Achievement Test,* Second Edition (*WIAT-II,* Smith, et al., 2001) measures reading, writing, mathematics, and language for ages 4 through 85 years. Reading is measured by three subtests: Word Reading, Reading Comprehension, and Pseudoword Decoding. In the Word Reading subtest, students are asked to name letters, rhyme words, identify beginning and ending sounds, blend sounds, match sounds with letters and blends, and read isolated words. In the Reading Comprehension subtest, students are asked to match words and pictures as well as answer questions after reading individual sentences and passages. In the Pseudoword Decoding subtest, students are asked to read nonsense words with regular phonics patterns. The *WIAT-II* is designed to provide information that supports educators' decisions about placement, diagnosis, and intervention procedures for students. However, much of this information is based on individual "professional judgment" rather than administration guidelines (Tindal, 2003).

***Wide Range Achievement Test*, Third Edition.**   The *Wide Range Achievement Test*, Third Edition (*WRAT-3*, Wilkinson, 1993) is actually the seventh edition of a battery of screening tests in reading, spelling, and arithmetic first published in 1936. The current edition is designed for use with students ages 5 through 74. The Reading test consists of an isolated word list; the student is asked to identify each word with no meaningful context and is not asked to provide the meaning of the word. In its 1999 review, the Institute for Applied Psychometrics found that the *WRAT-3* did not meet established standards for measuring reading achievement (McGrew, 1998).

Woodcock-Johnson III.   The *Woodcock-Johnson III* (*WJ III*, Woodcock, McGrew, Mather, & Schrank, 2003) was designed to measure overall intellectual ability, specific cognitive abilities, academic aptitude, oral language, and achievement for students ages 2 through adult. The *WJ III* consists of two parts: Tests of Achievement and Tests of Cognitive Abilities. The Tests of Achievement will be discussed here, and the Tests of Cognitive Abilities will be presented later in this chapter.

   The *WJ III* is divided into two batteries: Standard and Extended. The Standard battery measures basic skills, fluency, and application. An expansion of the reading subtests provides information about early reading performance. The *WJ III* includes tests that are organized into six clusters:

- ◆ Reading Clusters measure Broad Reading with tests in letter and word identification, reading fluency, and passage comprehension. Basic Reading Skills are measured through the letter and word identification test as well as tests in word attack. Reading Comprehension includes passage comprehension and reading vocabulary.
- ◆ Oral Language Clusters are part of the standard and extended batteries. Oral Language includes tests in story recall, understanding directions, picture vocabulary, and oral (listening) comprehension. Components include both listening comprehension and oral expression.
- ◆ Math Clusters include Broad Math, which consists of calculations, math fluency, and applied problems; Math Calculation Skills; and Math Reasoning, which includes applied problems and quantitative concepts.
- ◆ Written Language Clusters consist of tests in Broad Written Language, such as spelling, writing fluency, and writing samples. Basic Writing Skills include spelling and editing. Written Expression includes writing fluency and writing samples.
- ◆ Academic Knowledge Cluster measures academic knowledge in science, social studies, and general cultural knowledge.
- ◆ Special Purpose Cluster includes Academic Skills as measured by letter-word identification, calculation, and spelling; Academic Fluency, measured by reading fluency, math fluency, and writing fluency; Academic Applications, measured by passage comprehension, applied problems, and writing samples; and Phoneme/Grapheme Knowledge, measured by tests in word attack and spelling. Total Achievement is measured by letter-word identification, reading fluency, passage comprehension, calculation, math fluency, applied problems, spelling, writing fluency, and writing samples.

When used in conjunction with the Tests of Cognitive Abilities, the tests of Achievement provide a means of comparing students' achievement with their cognitive abilities. This is a valuable tool for members of assessment teams who need to make decisions about students' placements and instructional programs. Although reviewers have expressed concerns about how content validity was determined, they find the test as a whole quite useful for assessment, evaluation, and planning (Cizek, 2003; Sandoval, 2003).

Normed Oral Reading Tests

Normed oral reading tests, like informal reading inventories (see Chapter 5), contain graded passages for oral reading. However, unlike informal reading inventories, these tests include statistical norms. Thus, you have another way to obtain a general reading assessment that compares your student to others in a normed sample.

Several normed tests of oral reading are available through commercial publishers. Examples include the *Gray Oral Reading Test*, Fourth Edition (Wiederholt & Bryant, 2001) and the *Standardized Reading Inventory*, Second Edition (Newcomer, 1999).

***Gray Oral Reading Test*, Fourth Edition.**   The *Gray Oral Reading Test*, Fourth Edition (*GORT4*) was designed to measure oral reading rates, accuracy, fluency, and comprehension for students aged 7 to 18. The test includes two parallel forms, each consisting of 14 stories with five multiple-choice comprehension questions for each story. The authors recommend four specific uses for *GORT4*: to assist in identifying struggling readers, to identify students' specific strengths and weaknesses, to document progress as a result of reading intervention, and to provide research data in measuring reading abilities of school-aged students (Pro-Ed, 2005). While some reviewers caution that the test is highly dependent on the expertise of the administrator, the standardization procedures and norming population meet established criteria for use as a measure of reading performance (Crumpton, 2003; Miller-Whitehead, 2003).

***Standardized Reading Inventory*, Second Edition.**   The *Standardized Reading Inventory*, Second Edition (*SRI-II*) is designed to measure comprehension, word accuracy, and contextual meaning vocabulary for students ages 6 to 14. *SRI-II* consists of five components: Words in Isolation, Passage Comprehension, Word Recognition Accuracy, Vocabulary in Context, and Predictive Comprehension. There are two forms, each consisting of 10 passages. The passages range from Preprimer through eighth-grade reading levels. Although reviewers have found this instrument a valuable tool, they question whether it actually provides more useful information to teachers than informal reading inventories (Solomon, 2001; Stevens, 2001).

Chapter 5 discusses oral reading assessment and the rich diagnostic opportunities oral reading tests provide. The test inventory on the website for this text includes descriptions of several tests of oral reading.

Diagnostic Reading Tests

Diagnostic reading tests yield more specific information than general survey reading tests. These diagnostic tests provide a more detailed analysis of specific reading strengths and weaknesses. Two kinds of tests are described in this section: diagnostic reading batteries and diagnostic tests of specific areas of reading. Both are presented on the website for this text.

Diagnostic Reading Batteries

A diagnostic reading battery consists of a group of subtests, each of which assesses a different component of reading. It offers useful information for obtaining a profile of the student's reading in several areas, such as oral reading, phonics, sight vocabulary, and comprehension. As with all tests, teachers should examine the subtests to make sure that they actually test the skills they describe.

Typically, diagnostic batteries are more suitable for beginning readers. Although they sample several components of reading, they tend to emphasize emergent literacy and word recognition rather than comprehension or word meaning.

Because diagnostic batteries often do not contain extensive reading passages, they should be used in conjunction with other tests of actual reading and comprehension. Sometimes, teachers may administer only the sections of these batteries that are relevant to a particular student, rather than the entire battery. Four widely given diagnostic batteries are the *Woodcock Reading Mastery Test–Revised* (*WRMT–R*), the *WJ III Diagnostic Reading Battery* (*WDRB*), and the *BRIGANCE Comprehensive Inventory of Basic Skills–Revised* (*CIBS–R*). Each of these tests is briefly described in the following sections.

Woodcock Reading Mastery Test–Revised. The *Woodcock Reading Mastery Test–Revised* (*WRMT–R*) is a widely used reading diagnostic test that measures individuals from a beginning reading level through that of an advanced adult. It is available in two forms (Form G and Form H), both of which are accompanied by a comprehensive and well-organized test manual. Form G contains all six subtests, and Form H contains the four reading achievement tests.

In Form H, the four basic reading achievement subtests of the *WRMT–R* are Word Identification, Word Attack, Word Comprehension, and Passage Comprehension. These four subtests may be combined to obtain a full-score reading performance assessment.

In the word identification subtest, the student reads single words aloud. In the word attack subtest, the student sounds out nonsense words. The word comprehension subtest requires the student to perform three separate tasks with vocabulary: providing antonyms, providing synonyms, and completion of analogies for a word (e.g., day is to night as up is to _____). The words used in the word comprehension subtest are divided into general reading, science and mathematics, social studies, and humanities. In the passage comprehension subtest, the student orally fills in a missing word in a paragraph.

Form G also contains two subtests for beginning readers: a visual-auditory test in which children are assessed on their ability to associate words to picturelike symbols and a test of letter identification.

The *WRMT–R* contains many useful features and teacher aids. However, the ability to read in context is measured only in the reading comprehension subtest. Furthermore, this subtest requires only oral reading and, as a response, asks the student to fill in a word. This task is somewhat different from the silent reading and responses to questions that most students are required to do in school.

The *WRMT–R* was renormed in 1998. Reviewers have criticized the renormed version because the same norming population was used for multiple batteries and because the validity and reliability data presented in the *Examiner's Manual* are based on previous norming information (Crocker, 2001; Murray-Ward, 2001). Murray-Ward (2001) expressed concerns that issues and criticisms of previous reviewers had not been addressed because the test was renormed without content revisions. She also expressed concerns about the norming procedures used because of the limited representation of large metropolitan populations or from students with special needs. Of greatest concern is the possibility of overestimating students' reading levels. She recommends that the updated *WRMT–R* be used only in conjunction with other measures of reading.

WJ III Diagnostic Reading Battery. The *WJ III Diagnostic Reading Battery* (*WJ III DRB*, Woodcock, Mather, & Schrank, 2003) is designed to measure specific aspects of reading achievement as well as cognitive abilities related to reading. Results are analyzed both as performance on individual tests and in clusters so that comparisons can be made to provide insight into students' reading difficulties.

The *WJ III DRB* is comprised of 10 tests from Form B of the *WJ III Tests of Achievement and Tests of Cognitive Abilities*. It includes eight clusters that can be used for interpretation of results:

- Brief reading is a screening instrument that measures prereading skills. It was developed to be used with children as young as 3 years, 6 months.
- Broad reading includes tests of reading decoding and comprehension skills.
- Basic reading skills includes tests of reading vocabulary and phonic and structural analysis.
- Reading comprehension includes reading vocabulary and comprehension in passages.
- Phonics knowledge tests sound-symbols correspondence.
- Phonemic awareness tests abilities to analyze and synthesize phonemic information.
- Oral language comprehension tests oral language comprehension for words and passages.
- Total reading provides an overall measure of reading achievement.

The authors of the *WJ III DRB* indicate that this test meets the requirements of the Reading First initiative at both the cluster and test levels. While the *DRB* can provide a good source of information about students' achievement for some components of reading and related skills, some concern has been expressed about the need for further research in its uses as well as additional studies about its validity (Margolis, 2007). Margolis recommends that *DRB* be used in conjunction with other tests that more closely approximate the demands of classroom reading, such as an informal reading assessment. England (2007) suggests that further research is needed to substantiate the authors' assertion that *DRB* provides extensive support for planning and developing instruction as well as a valuable instrument for measuring students' response to intervention. Certainly, teachers and reading specialists would need to determine if the items measure instructionally based reading experiences.

BRIGANCE Diagnostic Comprehensive Inventory of Basic Skills–Revised. The *BRIGANCE Comprehensive Inventory of Basic Skills–Revised* (*CIBS–R*) is another widely used set of diagnostic batteries. The test was revised in 1999 and covers prekindergarten to Grade 9. It is a criterion-referenced test that also provides normed (standardized) information.

The *CIBS–R* has 10 criterion-referenced grade-placement tests. They are listening vocabulary comprehension, listening comprehension, word recognition, oral reading, reading vocabulary comprehension, reading comprehension, spelling, sentence writing, math comprehension skills, and math problem solving.

In addition, the standardized portions of *CIBS–R* are designed to meet state and federal assessment requirements. This portion produces grade and age equivalents, percentiles, and quotients in five areas of achievement: basic reading, reading comprehension, written expression, listening comprehension, and math.

Reviewers of the *CIBS–R* find the criterion-referenced portions of the test helpful because they relate to curriculum. The *CIBS–R* is useful as a diagnostic tool for individual students and for planning instruction related to standards. In their reviews of the test, Cizek (2001) and McLellan (2001) recommend that other measures, such as the *Woodcock-Johnson Psycho-Educational Battery–Revised* be used when norm-referenced results are needed, such as in placement decisions.

Two tests that were specifically developed to measure skills developed in primary grades are the *Dynamic Indicators of Basic Early Literacy Skills*, Sixth Edition (*DIBELS*) and the *Texas Primary Reading Inventory* (*TPRI*). Both of these norm-referenced tests are approved for use in programs funded through the Reading First initiative as part of the No Child Left Behind legislation.

***Dynamic Indicators of Basic Early Literacy Skills*, Sixth Edition.** The *Dynamic Indicators of Basic Early Literacy Skills*, Sixth Edition (*DIBELS*, Good, Kaminski, Moats, Laimon, Smith, & Dill, 2003) measure student performance in seven areas: word-use fluency, initial-sound fluency, letter-naming fluency, phoneme-segmentation fluency, nonsense-word fluency, oral-reading fluency, and retelling fluency. Word-use fluency is measured in kindergarten through Grade 3; initial-sound fluency is measured in kindergarten; letter-naming fluency is measured in kindergarten and early Grade 1; phoneme-segmentation fluency is measured in kindergarten and Grade 1; nonsense-word fluency is measured in kindergarten through early Grade

2; oral-reading fluency is measured in Grades 1 through 3; and retelling fluency is measured in Grades 1 through 3.

DIBELS was reviewed by Brunsman (2005) and Shanahan (2005). Both reviewers questioned the standardization procedures and the validity of the instructional classifications based on the test results. In addition, the scoring was found to be somewhat complicated. Shanahan (2005) also expressed concerns about the lack of vocabulary and comprehension measures. He recommends using DIBELS only in conjunction with other measures.

Texas Primary Reading Inventory.   The *Texas Primary Reading Inventory (TPRI)* measures students' progress in reading fluency in kindergarten through Grade 3. The test consists of two sections: the screening section and the inventory section. The screening section consists of three areas: graphophonemic knowledge in kindergarten and Grade 1, phonemic awareness in kindergarten and Grade 1, and correct identification of isolated words in Grades 1 and 2. The inventory section consists of seven areas: book and print awareness to measure students' knowledge of the function and characteristics of print and print materials in kindergarten, phonemic awareness in kindergarten and Grade 1, listening comprehension in kindergarten and Grade 1, graphophonemic knowledge as measured by letter recognition and sound-symbol relationships in kindergarten and Grade 1, word-building activities in Grade 1 and spelling in Grade 2, reading fluency in Grades 1 and 2, and reading comprehension in Grades 1 and 2. The *TPRI* has not been evaluated for review in the *Mental Measurements Yearbook*.

Diagnostic Tests of Specific Areas

Tests of specific areas concentrate on an in-depth evaluation of a specific area of reading. These tests are particularly useful in gathering detailed information about one area of reading, such as the student's abilities in phonics.

***Test of Reading Comprehension,* Third Edition.**   The *Test of Reading Comprehension,* Third Edition (*TORC-3,* Brown, Hammill, & Wiederholt, 1995) is used to analyze strengths and weaknesses in reading comprehension for students ages 7 through 17. The test consists of eight subtests: four identified as the General Reading Comprehension Core and four identified as Diagnostic Supplements. The General Reading Comprehension Core includes test of General Vocabulary, Syntactic Similarities, Paragraph Reading, and Sentence Sequencing. Scores from these four tests provide a composite Reading Comprehension Quotient. The Diagnostic Supplements include three content area vocabulary tests and a test to measure Reading the Directions of Schoolwork. *TORC* was originally published in 1978; the second edition was published in 1986 as diagnostic tools. *TORC-3* is the first edition to include normative data. In her review of *TORC-3,* Green (1998) indicated that the test would be more useful for middle level and high school students, but would probably not be appropriate for use with primary students, with the exception of some subtests. Perlman (1998) indicated that *TORC-3* might be useful as an individual screening device but would not be useful for program evaluation because of its small norming population.

***Diagnostic Assessment of Reading,* Second Edition.** The *Diagnostic Assessment of Reading* (*DAR*), Second Edition measures students' strengths and weaknesses in nine components of reading and language: print awareness, phonological awareness, letters and sounds, word recognition, word analysis, oral reading accuracy and fluency, silent reading comprehension, spelling, and word meaning (Roswell, Chall, Curtis, & Kearns, 2006). The diagnostic tool is administered individually and can be used from Kindergarten through adulthood. The test is scored as it is administered. Based on the results, schools can purchase *Trial Teaching Strategies* online through the publisher's website at www.riverpub.com/products/tts/index.html. The website provides teachers with access to reading strategies and supporting materials. Reviews for the second edition of the *Diagnostic Assessment of Reading* are in the *Mental Measurements Yearbook*, Eighteenth Edition.

Comprehensive Test of Phonological Processing. The *Comprehensive Test of Phonological Processing* (*CTOPP*, Wagner, Torgesen, & Rashotte, 1999) measures phonological awareness, phonological memory, and naming for students ages 5 to 24. The test consists of two versions. The first version, administered to students ages 5 and 6 includes: Elision, Blending Words, Sound Matching, Memory for Digits, Nonword Repetition, Rapid Color Naming, Rapid Object Naming, and a supplemental subtest for Blending Nonwords. The second version, administered to students ages 7 to 24 includes the previous subtests as well as Rapid Digit Naming, Rapid Letter Naming, and Segmenting Nonwords, with supplemental subtests for Phoneme Reversal and Segmenting Words. The *CTOPP* is intended to be used to identify students who are significantly behind their peers in phonological abilities and to determine their strengths and weaknesses as well as to document their progress in developing those skills through intervention. In reviewing the *CTOPP*, Hurford (2003) and Wright (2003) found the test to be an effective measure of phonological abilities for instructional purposes and program evaluation. However, they recommend the development of alternate forms and further replication studies before the *CTOPP* is used for research purposes.

Measuring Intelligence

Perhaps no concept has provided more controversy in education than the measure of intelligence. Heated public debate periodically erupts on the nature of intelligence, its role in achievement, and the role of culture in intelligence. This important measure is used in making decisions about who is entitled to special education services and, in some instances, who should be classified as reading disabled (see Chapter 15). For this reason, a special section is devoted to the measurement of intelligence.

The full concept of intelligence is much richer than what is actually measured by intelligence tests. Intelligence includes mechanical ability, street knowledge, creativity, and social skills. However, most intelligence (IQ) tests simply predict whether an individual is likely to do well in schoolwork, especially in learning tasks with highly verbal content (Salvia, Ysseldyke, & Bolt, 2006). Therefore, intelligence tests can be best regarded as measures of scholastic aptitude.

An IQ score, in part, reflects a student's background. Intelligence scores are also affected by a student's comfort with the testing situation. Thus, intelligence cannot be measured with absolute accuracy, nor can teachers learn how much a particular student might ultimately achieve. Intelligence tests measure only the current potential for learning; future potential is unknown. In summary, intelligence must be interpreted in a judicious manner.

Teachers should remember that the content of these tests and the validity of their scores have come under serious criticism. An IQ test cannot give a definitive or permanent rating of a student's mental ability. Thus, teachers should be alert to the many other sources of information about students, including behavior in class, independence in living, and interests and accomplishments outside the school setting.

Using Intelligence Test Information in Reading Assessment

The purpose of obtaining information on a student's cognitive abilities and aptitude for learning is to help the teacher better understand the reading problem. The intelligence test information can be used to assess a student's current potential, analyze a student's component cognitive abilities, and observe the student's behavior during the testing situation. Each of these uses is discussed here.

Assessing a Student's Potential.   As described in Chapter 15, information from an intelligence test can help the teacher determine whether a student has the potential to read better than he or she does at present. For example, Ellen's intelligence test score indicated a potential for reading that is much higher than her present reading achievement level. This discrepancy between potential and performance shows she has the cognitive ability to read much better than she does at present. In contrast, Mark's evaluation indicated that although he is reading poorly, he is actually doing fairly well in relation to his potential for learning. Mark, however, will still benefit from reading instruction suited to his individual needs.

When evaluating a student with suspected learning disabilities, federal law, such as the *Individuals with Disabilities in Education Improvement Act of 2004* (*IDEA-2004*) previously required the evaluation team to consider whether the student has a severe discrepancy between the potential for learning and the current level of performance. Specific regulations for identifying students with learning disabilities enacted in 2006 altered this requirement to say that states could not require a severe discrepancy between potential and achievement for determining whether a student has a learning disability. Methods for determining discrepancy are described in more detail in Chapters 2 and 15.

Analyzing a Student's Component Cognitive Abilities.   Intelligence is more than a single general factor. The current theory of intelligence is that intelligence comprises many separate abilities (Moran & Gardner, 2006; Sternberg, 1985, 1999; Gardner, 1983). In addition to providing an overall general score (IQ score), many tests of intelligence contain subtests and subscales that measure different (or component) cognitive functions. These tests help teachers analyze the student's strengths and weaknesses in learning aptitude. Several methods can be used to determine cognitive patterns in students (Lerner & Johns, 2006):

- Comparison of subscales. The subscales contained in some intelligence tests allow comparisons of cognitive abilities. The widely used *Wechsler Intelligence Scales*, including the *Wechsler Intelligence Scale for Children*, Fourth Edition (*WISC-IV*), the *Wechsler Preschool and Primary Scale of Intelligence*, Third Edition (*WPPSI-III*), and the *Wechsler Adult Intelligence Scale*, Fourth Edition (*WAIS-IV*), classify subtests as either verbal tests or performance tests. The *Kaufman Assessment Battery for Children*, Second Edition (*KABC-2*) identifies sequential and simultaneous processing.
- Evidence of subtest scatter and variability. Some intelligence tests, such as the (*WISC-IV*), the *Woodcock-Johnson IV Test of Cognitive Abilities*, and the *Kaufman Assessment Battery for Children*, Second Edition contain subtests that tap differing abilities. A significant scatter among subtest scores, with a student doing well in some subtests and poorly in others, suggests variability in cognitive functioning.
- Clustering of subtest scores to ascertain unique cognitive patterns. Another approach is to regroup or cluster subtest scores to provide a better understanding of the student's strengths or weaknesses in cognitive functioning. Kaufman (1981) used factor analysis to regroup from *WISC-IV* subtests into clusters of verbal comprehension, perceptual organization, and freedom from distractibility. The scoring system of the *Woodcock Johnson IV* enables the tester to group individual subtests to obtain general clusters of cognitive factors, including verbal ability, reasoning, perceptual speed, and memory (Lerner, 2003).

Observing a Student's Behavior.   According to Yogi Berra, "Sometimes you can observe a lot by just watching." Testers have the opportunity to observe students as they take intelligence tests. The tester can observe which activities the student enjoys, which activities are frustrating, and how the student goes about doing tasks. For this reason, examiners watch carefully as students use problem-solving strategies to perform the many different tasks on an intelligence test.

Intelligence Tests that Should Be Administered by Psychologists

Intelligence tests and tests of cognitive abilities provide information about students' aptitude for learning and their specific cognitive characteristics. Most intelligence tests are administered by psychologists. Frequently used intelligence tests administered by psychologists include the *WISC-IV* (Williams, Weiss, & Rolfhus, 2003), the *Stanford-Binet Intelligence Scales*, Fifth Edition (*SB5*, Roid, 2003), and the *KABC-II* (Kaufman & Kaufman, 2004a; Lerner & Johns, 2006).

***Wechsler Intelligence Scale for Children,* Fourth Edition.**   The *WISC-IV* has been redesigned to reflect recent research in intelligence and current neurocognitive models of information processing. The new test includes 10 core subtests and five supplemental subtests to provide four factor-based index scores: Verbal Comprehension Index, Perceptual Reasoning Index, Working Memory Index, and Processing Speed Index. The indices and subtests are organized as follows:

- ◆ Verbal Comprehension Index: Subtests include Similarities, Vocabulary, and Comprehension. Supplemental subtests are Information and Word Reasoning.
- ◆ Perceptual Reasoning Index: Subtests include Block Design, Picture Concepts, and Matrix Reasoning. The supplemental subtest is Picture Completion.
- ◆ Working Memory Index: Subtests include Digit Span and Letter-Number Sequencing. The supplemental subtest is Arithmetic.
- ◆ Processing Speed Index: Subtests include Coding and Symbol Search. The supplemental subtest is Cancellation to measure visual selective attention between structured and unstructured items.

Historically, the Wechsler scales have been widely acclaimed for their usefulness and high quality of their standardization procedures (Braden, 1995; Sandoval, 1995). In his review of the fourth edition, Thompson (2005) finds that the fourth edition has incorporated more current theoretic perspectives and comprises more developmentally appropriate items. He also believes that the newer edition is more user-friendly and yields more useful results. Maller (2005) agrees but raises concerns about gender and ethnic bias among some items.

***Stanford-Binet Intelligence Scales,* Fifth Edition.**   The *SB5* (Roid, 2003) is used to identify gifted individuals as well as those with learning disabilities, mental retardation, attention deficit disorders, speech and language delays, Alzheimer's disease and dementia, traumatic brain injury, and autism. The test is organized into five factors with both verbal and nonverbal subtests to measure each factor:

- ◆ Fluid Reasoning: The nonverbal subtest is Nonverbal Fluid Reasoning, which requires individuals to organize series of objects. The verbal subtest is Verbal Fluid Reasoning, which includes early reasoning activities for Levels 2 and 3, verbal absurdities for Level 4, and verbal analogies for Levels 5 and 6.
- ◆ Knowledge: Nonverbal subtests include Procedural Knowledge for Levels 2 and 3 and Picture Absurdities for Levels 4 through 6. The verbal subtest is a vocabulary measure.
- ◆ Quantitative Reasoning: Both the nonverbal and verbal subtests for quantitative reasoning are administered for Levels 2 through 6.

◆ Visual-Spatial Processing: This factor has been added in the fifth edition. The nonverbal subtests focus on forms for Levels 1 and 2 and form patterns for Levels 3 through 6. The verbal subtests require individuals to perform tasks involving position and direction at Levels 2 through 6.

◆ Working Memory: Nonverbal subtests include Delayed Response at Level 1 and Block Span at Levels 2 through 6. Verbal subtests include Memory for Sentences at Levels 2 through 3 and Last Word at Levels 4 through 6.

The interpretive manual provides guidelines for clustering individuals' cognitive characteristics, which will help users develop profiles useful in educational settings (Kush, 2005). However, limited information is provided about using results to plan and implement intervention (Johnson & D'Amato, 2005). In keeping with its long history of quality, the *SB5* is highly recommended for its reliability and validity as well as its effectiveness as an instrument for making sound educational decisions (Johnson & D'Amato, 2005; Kush, 2005).

Kaufman Assessment Battery for Children, **Second Edition.** The *KABC-II* (Kaufman & Kaufman, 2004) is designed to help educators identify cognitive strengths and weaknesses of students ages 3 through 18. It consists of five scales and 20 subtests:

◆ Simultaneous/Visual Processing measures students' abilities to consider several pieces of information to solve a problem. Core subtests include Conceptual Thinking, Triangles, Face Recognition, Pattern Reasoning, Block Counting, Story Completion, and Rover (in which students determine the shortest path for a dog to move on a checkerboard grid toward a bone). The supplementary test is Gestalt Closure, a test using incomplete pictures for students to identify images.

◆ Sequential Processing/Short-Term Memory tests a student's ability to solve problems by remembering and using ordered series of images or ideas. This task is closely related to spelling and math. The core subtest administered to children at age 3 is Word Order. Supplementary subtests administered at age 3 are Number Recall and Hand Movements. Core subtests for ages 4 through 18 include Word Order and Number Recall. Hand Movements is used as a supplementary test for these ages.

◆ Planning/Fluid Reasoning is a new scale presented in the second edition. It measures a student's ability to verbalize a solution to a problem presented nonverbally. Subtests include Pattern Reasoning, in which students select a picture or geometric design to complete a series of pictures that forms a pattern, and Story Completion for students ages 7 through 18. For ages 5 and 6, these subtests are part of the Simultaneous/Visual Processing Scale.

◆ Learning Ability/Long-Term Storage and Retrieval measures students' abilities to complete both immediate-recall and delayed-recall learning tasks. Atlantis is a core subtest for all ages. In this test, students are taught nonsense names for colorful pictures of sea plants and animals. Then students are shown another picture with the same characters and are asked to point to the correct character as it is named by the examiner. In Atlantis Delayed, a supplementary subtest for ages 6 through 18, students are asked to point to named characters after a period of time has passed. Rebus is a core subtest for ages 4 through 18. In Rebus, students learn words associated with simple line drawings. Then the drawings are presented in a series that forms a meaningful phrase, and students are asked to "read" the phrase. Rebus Delayed is a supplementary subtest for ages 6 through 18.

◆ Knowledge/Crystallized Ability assesses knowledge of words and facts presented with both verbal and pictorial stimuli and requiring either verbal or pointing responses. The Riddles subtest is a core subtest for all ages. Early items present students with sets of pictures. The examiner reads a two- to three-clue riddle, and the student points to the picture that answers the riddle. In later items, the examiner reads the choices and the student selects the answer to the riddle from the choices read. The Expressive Vocabulary subtest is a core subtest for ages 3 through 6 and supplementary for ages 7 through 18. In the Expressive Vocabulary Test, students are shown a picture of an object and must name the object. The Verbal Knowledge subtest is a core subtest for ages 7 through 18 and supplementary for ages 3 through 6. In this subtest, the student is shown six images; the examiner says a vocabulary word or gives a general information prompt and the student points to the picture that represents the answer. No oral response is required.

One advantage to the *KABC-II* is that it is co-normed with the *Kaufman Test of Education Achievement*, Second Edition (*KTEA-II*). Thus, if a district or state requires a comparison between a student's academic potential and achievement, the information would be readily available (www.agsnet.com, 2005). The authors also indicate that the *KABC* and *KABC-II* tests are less culturally biased than other intelligence tests. Reviewers acknowledge that there is slightly less difference in scores across ethnic groups but argue that the differences may not be significant (Braden & Ouzts, 2005). Other than the claims of less cultural bias, Braden and Ouzts found that the standardization procedures were acceptable for validity and reliability. Thorndike (2005) found that the test did not clearly distinguish between students with disabilities and the norm group. Braden and Ouzts (2005) question the test's usefulness for guiding interventions due to the lack of interpretive support.

Intelligence Tests that Can Be Administered by Teachers and Reading Specialists

With training, classroom teachers can administer some tests, such as the Tests of Cognitive Ability from the *Woodcock-Johnson III Norming Update*, the *Kaufman Brief Intelligence Test*, Second Edition, and the *Slosson Intelligence Test–Revised* (Lerner, 2006).

***Kaufman Brief Intelligence Test*, Second Edition.** The *Kaufman Brief Intelligence Test*, Second Edition (*KBIT-2*, Kaufman & Kaufman, 2004b) is a brief screening instrument of verbal and nonverbal ability. It can be used by teachers to obtain quick estimates of students' intelligence levels, to compare a student's verbal and nonverbal intelligence, to screen students to recommend them for special programs, or to reevaluate students who previously participated in a thorough cognitive assessment. The *KBIT-2* is comprised of two scales: Crystallized/Verbal with subtests in Verbal Knowledge, including both receptive and expressive vocabulary items, and riddles and a Fluid/Nonverbal scale with a Matrices subtest. The *KBIT-2* is co-normed with the *Kaufman Test of Educational Achievement*, Second Edition, *Brief Form*. This co-norming allows teachers and other educators to make rough comparisons between students' potential and achievement levels just as the links between the *KABC-II* and the *KTEA-II* provide more in-depth comparisons between ability and achievement (www.agsnet.com, 2004). Reviews of the *KBIT-2* are generally positive. Shaw (2007) found that the changes and updates, while minor, were improvements over the first edition. Madle (2007) concurred that the test was well-developed and easy to administer. However, he cautions that the *KBIT-2* does tend to yield slightly lower IQ scores than Wechsler scales. He also expressed concerns about the use of the test with non-English speakers because this population was not represented in the norming sample.

***Slosson Intelligence Test, Revised,* Third Edition.** The *Slosson Intelligence Test, Revised*, Third Edition (*SIT-R3*), (Slosson, Nicholson, & Hibpshman, 2002) is a quick individual screening test of Crystallized Verbal intelligence for both children and adults. The authors indicate that the *SIT-R3* can be readily adapted for use with students who are visually impaired (www.slosson.com, 2005). Reviews of the *SIT-R3* are not available. It should be noted that reviewers of the 1991 edition expressed concerns about whether the norming population truly reflected U.S. Census data. Although the reviewers acknowledged that the results were highly correlated with previous forms of the *WISC*, they caution users about accuracy of the information for older students and adults, and they recommend the use of components of the *WISC* or the *KBIT* to better match the results of more comprehensive measures used for placement or instructional decisions (Kamphaus, 1995; Watson, 1995).

Woodcock-Johnson III Tests of Cognitive Abilities. The *Woodcock-Johnson III Tests of Cognitive Abilities* (*WJ III*, Woodcock, McGrew, Mather, & Schrank, 2003) is the second set of batteries of the *Woodcock-Johnson III*. The Tests of Cognitive Abilities are comprised of a Standard Battery and an Extended Battery, each consisting of 10 tests. The tests are arranged to tap abilities in seven cognitive areas:

◆ Comprehension-Knowledge includes Verbal Comprehension and General Verbal Knowledge, which is new to the edition. These tests yield important information for reading teachers and specialists because they are related to language development and verbal background information.
◆ Long-Term Retrieval includes Visual-Auditory Learning and Retrieval Fluency. There is also a delayed test of Visual-Auditory Learning that is not considered part of the factor or cognitive performance clusters.

- ◆ Visual-Spatial Thinking includes Spatial Relations and Picture Recognition. There is also a Planning test that is not considered part of the factor or clusters.
- ◆ Auditory Processing includes Sound Blending, and Auditory Attention. A word finding test of Incomplete Words that is not considered part of the factor or clusters. This factor is closely associated with phonemic awareness and sound discrimination.
- ◆ Fluid Reasoning includes Concept Formation and Analysis-Synthesis. The previously mentioned Planning test is also associated with spatial scanning and sequential reasoning but is not considered part of this factor or the clusters.
- ◆ Processing Speed includes Visual Matching as well as two new tests, Decision Speed and Rapid Picture Naming. Another test new to the third edition but not considered part of the factor or cognitive performance clusters is the Pair Cancellation Test.
- ◆ Short-Term Memory includes Numbers Reversed and Memory for Words. New to the third edition but not considered part of the factor or clusters is a test of Auditory Working Memory.

When used in conjunction with the Tests of Achievement, the Tests of Cognitive Abilities provide a means of comparing students' achievement with their cognitive abilities. This is a valuable tool for members of assessment teams who need to make decisions about students' placements and instructional programs. When used alone, the Tests of Cognitive Abilities can provide insight into students' processing abilities for verbal information (www.riverpub.com, 2005). Although reviewers have expressed concerns about how content validity was determined, they find the test as a whole quite useful for assessment, evaluation, and planning (Cizek, 2003; Sandoval, 2003).

Interpreting Intelligence Test Scores

Modern intelligence scores are reported as deviation scores, as a student's score is compared with the scores of a norm group. The IQ score is based on the concept of a normal curve, as shown in Figure 4.1. An IQ of 100 is designated as the mean for each age group. As shown in Figure 4.1, approximately 34 percent of the population will fall within one standard deviation below the mean, and 34 percent of the population will fall within one standard deviation above the mean.

To illustrate (Figure 4.1) one standard deviation on the *WISC-IV* is 15 points. Therefore, 34 percent of the population will score between 85 and 100, and 34 percent of the population will score between 100 and 115.

Intelligence ranges for the *WISC-IV* can be interpreted as presented in Table 4.1.

Teachers may find these interpretations useful for reporting the results of this IQ test to parents. If tests other than the *WISC-IV* are used, the test manual should be consulted for the IQ range for those tests. Although almost all IQs have means of 100, some variations in the standard deviations are reported.

TABLE 4.1 Intelligence Ranges as Determined by *WISC-IV*

IQ Range	Interpretation
130 and above	Very Superior
120–129	Superior
110–119	High Average (bright)
90–109	Average
80–89	Low Average (dull)
70–79	Borderline
69 and below	Mentally Deficient

Summary

Formal tests should be administered according to prescribed procedures. Some are norm referenced and compare students to a norm sample. Others are criterion referenced and determine whether a student has achieved mastery. Formal tests that compare students to others of the same grade and age are familiar to professionals, permit objective decision making, and are required by some laws.

Scores on norm-referenced tests derive standard scores from raw scores generally by using means and standard deviations. Scores include reading grade scores, percentiles, normal curve equivalents (NCEs), and stanines. Normed tests should have an adequate standardization sample, good validity (testing what is supposed to be tested), and reliability (stability of scores).

Tests of general reading assessment include survey tests (both group and individual), normed oral reading tests, and literacy tests. Diagnostic reading tests include batteries of specific skills and tests of individual areas.

Intelligence tests can be used to estimate a student's potential for school achievement, although the results can change with appropriate conditions. Patterns of scores and behavior during testing also give insight into learning. Widely used intelligence tests include the *Wechsler Intelligence Scale for Children*, Fourth Edition, *Woodcock-Johnson III*, *Kaufman Assessment Battery for Children*, Second Edition (and short form), and the *Slosson Intelligence Test*, Third Edition, *Revised*. Scores on an IQ test are distributed on a normal curve distribution.

Of special interest to assessment teams and reading specialists are tests that provide for systematic assessment to measure students' progress. This information is crucial in making placement decisions, planning for appropriate instructional intervention, and measuring response to intervention.

References

Berra, Y., & Kaplan, D. (2008). *You Can Observe a lot by Watching: What I've Learned about Teamwork from the Yankees and Life.* Hoboken, NJ: John Wiley and Sons.

Bonner, M. (2005). Review of Kaufman Test of Educational Achievement (2nd ed.). In R. A. Spies & B. S. Plake (Eds.), *The Sixteenth Mental Measurements Yearbook*. Lincoln, NE: Buros Institute of Mental Measurements.

Braden, J. P. (1995). Review of Wechsler Intelligence Scale for Children (3rd ed.). In B. S. Plake & J. C. Impara (Eds.), *The Twelfth Mental Measurements Yearbook*. Lincoln, NE: Buros Institute of Mental Measurements.

Braden, J. P., & Ouzts, S. M. (2005). Review of Kaufman Assessment Battery for Children (2nd ed.). In R. A. Spies & B. S. Plake (Eds.), *The Sixteenth Mental Measurements Yearbook*. Lincoln, NE: Buros Institute of Mental Measurements.

Brown, V. L., Hammill, D. D., & Wiederholt, J. L. (1995). *Test of Reading Comprehension*, (3rd ed.). Austin, TX: Pro-Ed Inc.

Brunsman, B. A. (2005). Review of Dynamic Indicators of Basic Early Literacy. In R. A. Spies & B. S. Plake (Eds.), *The sixteenth mental measurements yearbook*. Lincoln, NE: Buros Institute of Mental Measurements.

Carpenter, C. D. (2005). Review of Kaufman Test of Educational Achievement (2nd ed.). In R. A. Spies & B. S. Plake (Eds.), *The Sixteenth Mental Measurements Yearbook*. Lincoln, NE: Buros Institute of Mental Measurements.

Cizek, G. J. (2001). Review of Brigance Diagnostic Comprehensive Inventory of Basic Skills, Revised. In B. S. Plake & J. C. Impara (Eds.), *The Fourteenth Mental Measurements Yearbook*. Lincoln, NE: Buros Institute of Mental Measurements.

Cizek, G. J. (2003). Review of Woodcock-Johnson III. In B. S. Plake & J. C. Impara (Eds.), *The Fourteenth Mental Measurements Yearbook*. Lincoln, NE: Buros Institute of Mental Measurements.

Crocker, L. (2001). Review of Woodcock Reading Master Tests–Revised (1998 Normative Update). In B. S. Plake & J. C. Impara (Eds.), *The Fourteenth Mental Measurements Yearbook*. Lincoln, NE: Buros Institute of Mental Measurements.

Crumpton, N. L. (2003). Review of Gray Oral Reading Test (4th ed.). In B. S. Plake & J. C. Impara (Eds.), *The Fourteenth Mental Measurements Yearbook*. Lincoln, NE: Buros Institute of Mental Measurements.

England, C. (2007). Review of Woodcock-Johnson III Diagnostic Reading Battery. In K. F. Geisinger, R. A. Spies, J. F. Carlson, & B. S. Plake (Eds.), *The Seventeenth Mental Measurements Yearbook*. Lincoln, NE: Buros Institute of Mental Measurements.

Fletcher, J. (1998). IQ discrepancy: An inadequate and iatrogenic conceptual model of learning disabilities. *Perspectives: The International Dyslexia Association, 24*, 10–11.

Fletcher, J., Francis, D., Shaywitz, S., Lyon, G., Foorman, B., Stubbing, K., & Shaywitz, B. (1998). Intelligence testing and the discrepancy model for children with learning disabilities. *Learning Disabilities Research and Practice, 13*, 186–203.

Fugate, M. H. (2003). Review of Group Reading Assessment and Diagnostic Evaluation. In B. S. Plake, J. C. Impara, & R. A. Spies (Eds.), *The Fifteenth Mental Measurements Yearbook*. Lincoln, NE: Buros Institute of Mental Measurements.

Gardner, H. (1983). *Frames of Mind: The Theory of Multiple Intelligences*. New York: Harper and Row.

Geisenger, K. F., Spies, R. A., Carlson, J. F., & Plake, B. S. (Eds.). *The Seventh Mental Measurement Yearbook* (2007). Lincoln, NE: University of Nebraska Press.

Green, F. J. (1998). Review of Test of Reading Comprehension (3rd ed.). In J. C. Impara & B. S. Plake (Eds.), *The Thirteenth Mental Measurements Yearbook*. Lincoln, NE: Buros Institute of Mental Measurements.

Hurford, D. P. (2003). Review of Comprehensive Test of Phonological Processing. In B. S. Plake, J. C. Impara, & R. A. Spies (Eds.), *The Fifteenth Mental Measurements Yearbook*. Lincoln, NE: The Buros Institute of Mental Measurements.

Individuals with Disabilities Education Act of (2004), Public Law 108-446.

Johnson, J. A., & D'Amato, R. C. (2005). Review of Stanford-Binet Intelligence Scales (5th ed.). In R. A. Spies & B. S. Plake (eds.), *The Sixteenth Mental Measurements Yearbook*. Lincoln, NE: Buros Institute of Mental Measurements.

Kamphaus, R. W. (1995). Review of Slosson Intelligence Test-Revised (3rd ed.). In J. C. Conoley & J. C. Impara (Eds.) *The Twelfth Mental Measurements Yearbook*. Lincoln, NE: Buros Institute of Mental Measurements.

Kaufman, A. S. (1981). The WISC and learning disabilities assessment: State of the art. *Journal of Learning Disabilities, 14*, 520–526.

Kaufman, A. S., & Kaufman, N. L. (2004a). *KABC-II: Kaufman Assessment Battery for Children* (2nd ed.). Circle Pines, MN: American Guidance Service, Inc.

Kaufman, A. S., & Kaufman, N. L. (2004b). *KBIT-2: Kaufman Brief Intelligence Test* (2nd ed.). Circle Pines, MN: American Guidance Service, Inc.

Kaufman, A. S., & Kaufman, N. L. (2004c). *KTEA-II: Kaufman Test of Educational Achievement* (2nd ed.). Circle Pines, MN: American Guidance Service, Inc.

Keillor, G. (2008). News from Lake Wobegon. *A Prairie Home Companion*. National Public Radio.

Kush, J. C. (2005). Review of Stanford-Binet Intelligence Scales (5th ed.). In R. A. Spies & B. S. Plake (Eds.), *The Sixteenth Mental Measurements Yearbook*. Lincoln, NE: Buros Institute of Mental Measurements.

LaBerge, D., & Samuels, S. M. (1974). Toward a theory of automatic information processing in reading. *Cognitive Psychology, 6*, 293–323.

Lerner, J. W. (2003). *Learning Disabilities: Theories, Diagnosis, and Teaching Strategies* (9th ed.). Boston: Houghton Mifflin Co.

Lerner, J. W., & Johns, B. (2008). *Learning Disabilities and Related Mild Disabilities: Characteristics, Teaching Strategies, and New Directions*. Boston: Wadsworth Publishing.

Madle, R. A. (2007). Review of Kaufman Brief Intelligence Test (2nd ed.). In K. F. Geisinger, R. A. Spies, J. F. Carlson, & B. S. Plake (Eds.). *The Seventeenth Mental Measurements Yearbook*. Lincoln, NE: Buros Institute of Mental Measurements.

Maller, S. J. (2005). Review of Wechsler Intelligence Scale for Children (4th ed.). In R. A. Spies & B. S. Plake (Eds.), *The Sixteenth Mental Measurements Yearbook*. Lincoln, NE: Buros Institute of Mental Measurements.

Margolis, H. (2007). Review of Woodcock-Johnson III Diagnostic Reading Battery. In K. F. Geisinger, R. A. Spies, J. F. Carlson, & B. S. Plake (Eds.). *The Seventeenth Mental Measurements Yearbook*. Lincoln, NE: Buros Institute of Mental Measurements.

McGrew, K. S. (1998). The measurement of reading achievement by different individually administered standardized reading tests: Apples and apples, or apples and oranges? In C. E. Snow, S. M. Burns, & P. E. Griffin (Eds.), *Preventing Reading Difficulties in Young Children*. Washington, DC: National Academy Press.

McLellan, M. J. (2001). Review of Brigance Diagnostic Comprehensive Inventory of Basic Skills–Revised. In B. S. Plake & J. C. Impara (Eds.), *The Fourteenth Mental Measurements Yearbook*. Lincoln, NE: Buros Institute of Mental Measurements.

Miller-Whitehead, M. (2003). Review. In B. S. Plake & J. C. Impara (Eds.), *The Fourteenth Mental Measurements Yearbook*. Lincoln, NE: Buros Institute of Mental Measurements.

Moran, S., & Gardner, H. (2006). Extraordinary cognitive achievements: A developmental and systems analysis. In W. Damon (Series Ed.) and D. Kuhn & R. S. Sidgler (Vol. Eds.) *Handbook of Child Psychology: Vol. 2, Cognition, Perception, and Language* (6th ed.) pp. 905–949. New York: Wiley.

Murray-Ward, M. (2001). Review of Gray Oral Reading Test (4th ed.). In B. S. Plake & J. C. Impara (Eds.), *The Fourteenth Mental Measurements Yearbook*. Lincoln, NE: Buros Institute of Mental Measurements.

Newcomer, P. L. (1999). *Standardized Reading Inventory* (2nd ed.). Austin, TX: Pro-Ed, Inc.

Perlman, C. (1998). Review of Test of Reading Comprehension (3rd ed.). In J. C. Impara & B. S. Plake (Eds.), *The Thirteenth Mental Measurements Yearbook*. Lincoln, NE: Buros Institute of Mental Measurements.

Roid, G. H. (2003). *Stanford-Binet Intelligence Scales* (5th ed.). Rolling Meadows, IL: Riverside Publishing.

Roswell, F. G., Chall, J. S., Curtis, M. E., & Kearns, G. (2006). *Diagnostic Assessments of Reading* (2nd ed.). Itasca, IL: Riverside Publishing.

Salvia, J., Ysseldyke, J. E., & Bolt, S. (2006). *Assessment in Special and Inclusive Education* (10th ed.). Boston: Houghton Mifflin.

Sandoval, J. (2003). Review of Woodcock-Johnson III. In B. S. Plake, J. C. Impara, & R. A. Spies (Eds.), *The Fifteenth Mental Measurements Yearbook*. Lincoln, NE: Buros Institute of Mental Measurements.

Sandoval, J. (1995). Review of Wechsler Intelligence Scale for children (3rd ed.). In J. C. Conoley & J. C. Impara (Eds.), *The Twelfth Mental Measurements Yearbook*. Lincoln, NE: Buros Institute of Mental Measurements.

Shanahan, T. (2005). Review of Dynamic Indicators of Basic Early Literacy. In R. A. Spies & B. S. Plake (Eds.), *The Sixteenth Mental Measurements Yearbook*. Lincoln, NE: Buros Institute of Mental Measurements.

Shaw, S. R. (2007). Review of Kaufman Brief Intelligence Test (2nd ed.). In K. F. Geisinger, R. A. Spies, J. F. Carlson, & B. S. Plake (Eds.). *The Seventeenth Mental Measurements Yearbook*. Lincoln, NE: Buros Institute of Mental Measurements.

Slosson, R. L., Nicholson, C. L., & Hibpshman, T. H. (2002). *Slosson Intelligence Test* (3rd ed.). East Aurora, NY: Slosson Educational Publications, Inc.

Smith, D. R. et al. (2001). *Wechsler Individual Achievement Test* (2nd ed.). San Antonio: The Psychological Corporation, A Harcourt Assessment Company.

Solomon, A. (2001). Review of Standardized Reading Inventory (2nd ed.). In B. S. Plake & J. C. Impara (Eds.), *The Fourteenth Mental Measurements Yearbook*. Lincoln, NE: Buros Institute of Mental Measurements

Spache, G. D. (1981). *Diagnosing and Correcting Reading Disabilities*. Boston: Allyn and Bacon.

Spies, R. A., Plake, B. S., Geisinger, K. F., & Carlson J. F. (Eds.). (2007). *The Seventeenth Mental Measurements Yearbook*. Lincoln, NE: Buros Institute of Mental Measurements.

Stanovich, K. E. (1986). Matthew effects in reading. Some consequences of individual differences in the acquisition of literacy. *Reading Research Quarterly*, 21, 360–406.

Sternberg, R. J. (1999). Ability and expertise: It's time to replace the current model of intelligence. *American Educator*, 23, 1–30, 50.

Sternberg, R. J. (1985). *Beyond IQ: A Triarchic Theory of Human Intelligence*. New York: Cambridge University Press.

Stevens, B. A. (2001). Review of Standardized Reading Inventory (2nd ed.). In B. S. Plake & J. C. Impara (Eds.), *The Fourteenth Mental Measurements Yearbook*. Lincoln, NE: Buros Institute of Mental Measurements.

Thompson, B. (2005). Review of Wechsler Intelligence Scale for Children (4th ed.). In R. A. Spies & B. S. Plake (Eds.), *The Sixteenth Mental Measurements Yearbook*. Lincoln, NE: Buros Institute of Mental Measurements.

Thorndike, R. M. (2005). Review of Kaufman Assessment Battery for Children (2nd ed.). In R. A. Spies & B. S. Plake (Eds.), *The Sixteen Mental Measurements Yearbook*. Lincoln, NE: Buros Institute of Mental Measurements.

Tindal, G. (2003). Review of Wechsler Individual Achievement Test (2nd ed.) Education. In B. S. Plake, J. C. Impara, & R. A. Spies (Eds.), *The Fifteenth Mental Measurements Yearbook*. Lincoln, NE: Buros Institute of Mental Measurements.

U.S. Department of Education. (2006 August 14). 34 CFR Parts 300 & 301: Assistance to states for the education of children with disabilities and preschool grants for children with disabilities. *Federal Register*, Part II.

Wagner, R. K., Torgesen, J. K., & Rashotte, C. A. (1999). *Comprehensive Test of Phonological Processing*. Austin, TX: ProEd, Inc.

Waterman, B. B. (2003). Review of Group Reading Assessment and Diagnostic Evaluation. In B. S. Plake, J. C. Impara & R. A. Spies (Eds.), *The Fourteenth Mental Measurements Yearbook*. Lincoln, NE: Buros Institute of Mental Measurements.

Watson, T. S. (1995). Review of Slosson Intelligence Test-Revised (3rd ed.). In J. C. Conoley & J. C. Impara (Eds.), *The twelfth mental measurements yearbook*. Lincoln, NE: Buros Institute of Mental Measurements.

Wiederholt, J. L., & Bryant, B. R. (2001). *Gray Oral Reading Tests* (4th ed.). Austin, TX: ProEd Inc.

Wilkinson, G. S. (1993). *Wide Range Achievement Test* (3rd ed.). Wilmington, DE: Wide Range, Inc.

Williams, P. E., Weiss, L. G., & Rolfhus, E. L. (2003). Wechsler Intelligence Scale for Children (4th ed.). San Antonio, TX: The Psychological Corporation.

Woodcock, R. W., McGrew, K. S., Mather, N., & Schrank, F. A. (2003). *Woodcock-Johnson Psychoeducational Battery* (3rd ed.). Itasca, IL: Riverside Publishing.

Wright, C. R. (2003). Review of Comprehensive Test of Phonological Processing. In B. S. Plake, J. C. Impara, & R. A. Spies (Eds.), *The Fourteenth Mental Measurements Yearbook*. Lincoln, NE: Buros Institute of Mental Measurements.

MyEducationLab is a research-based learning tool that brings teaching to life. Go to the Jennings, Caldwell, & Lerner 6th Edition MyEducationLab for Reading Assessment site at www.myeducationlab.com to:

◆ engage in multimedia exercises to help you build a deeper and more applied understanding of chapter content;

◆ utilize extensive resources including videos from real classrooms, Praxis and licensure preparation, a lesson plan builder, and materials to help you in your teaching career.

Using an Informal Reading Inventory for Assessment

Introduction

This chapter describes the process of assessing a student's reading performance using an informal reading inventory. It begins by presenting two general questions that are critical to assessment of literacy progress. The chapter focuses on the informal reading inventory, a fundamental tool that gives many insights into a student's reading. It describes how to administer and score this instrument. Other tools for informal assessment are discussed in Chapters 7 through 13.

General Assessment Questions: An Overview

The process of assessing reading involves more than giving tests. In fact, a good reading teacher uses tests, background information, and observation to formulate answers to questions about a student's progress as a reader. Reading assessment thus represents a thoughtful synthesis and interpretation of all the information that is collected about a student.

Assessing a student's reading achievement involves answering three general questions: (1) Does the student have a reading problem; (2) how severe is it?; and (3) what is the general area of the reading problem? You can answer these questions by observing and working with a student and by administering a variety of assessment tools. Often, an informal reading inventory can answer both questions as well as provide much additional information about a student.

Does the Student Have a Reading Problem and How Severe Is It?

To determine the existence and severity of a reading problem, a teacher needs to determine at what level a student is reading and to compare this level with the level at which that student should be reading. Thus, compare

- ◆ The student's current reading level to
- ◆ The student's appropriate reading level

By appropriate level, experts mean the books and stories that are used in the student's classroom, both for reading and for content area instruction (math, social studies, science). Usually, appropriate materials mean those at a student's grade level. However, if the student's class is reading at a higher level, then appropriate materials are at that higher level.

However, the opposite is not true. Children who are experiencing problems in school are often placed in special classes where they read materials well below their grade level. For example, a fourth grader might be in a special class that is reading second-grade material. In this case, second-grade text is *not* an appropriate level; the appropriate level for this student would be the fourth-grade level, the actual grade placement.

A student who can read at an appropriate level with acceptable word recognition and comprehension does not have a reading problem. However, a student who cannot read appropriate materials has a reading problem; the next step is to determine the severity of that problem. The difference between the student's grade placement and the grade placement of the texts he or she can read shows us how severe the reading problem is.

How does a teacher know whether a student's problem can be classified as severe? Guidelines provided by Spache (1981), presented in Table 5.1, compare a student's current grade placement to the student's reading level. As you can see, the younger the student, the less difference is needed to define a reading problem as severe.

Using these criteria, a student who is placed in fourth grade but is reading at the second-grade level would have a reading problem that is severe. A fourth-grade student reading at the third-grade level would have a reading problem, but not a severe one. A fourth-grade student reading at the fourth-grade level would not have a reading problem.

The severity of the student's reading problem helps determine what type of special instruction is most effective. Students with severe reading problems may require long and intensive intervention in daily classes with individual instruction. In contrast, students with less-severe problems may blossom in small group settings that meet once or twice a week.

What Is the General Area of the Reading Problem?

As discussed in Chapter 1, reading consists of many different components, or areas. Problems with reading fall into several general areas:

- ◆ Emergent literacy
- ◆ Word recognition accuracy
- ◆ Reading fluency
- ◆ Comprehension
- ◆ Language and meaning vocabulary

TABLE 5.1 Criteria for Determining a Severe Reading Problem

Student's Grade Placement	Difference between Grade Placement and Reading Level
Grades 1, 2, 3	One year or more
Grades 4, 5, 6	Two years or more
Grades 7 and above	Three years or more

Source: Spache (1981).

Some students may have problems in only one of these general areas. Other students may have problems in a combination of areas. Deciding the general area of a student's reading problem is important, because this information helps you, as a reading teacher, deliver the most effective instruction.

Problems with Emergent Literacy. Emergent literacy refers to the understandings and skills that underlie reading. These skills include the knowledge that print stands for meaning, the recognition of alphabet letters, and the ability to discriminate letter sounds. Although most students have acquired emergent literacy skills by the time they enter first grade, some students with reading problems continue to lack them long after formal reading instruction has begun.

Problems with Word Recognition Accuracy. Many students with reading problems cannot recognize words accurately. They lack strategies for identifying unfamiliar words. For example, trying to read a passage about farms, 9-year-old Carlos pronounced the word *farm* as *from*, *form*, and *for*.

Without accurate word identification, a student cannot comprehend a passage. For example, Carlos's summary of the farm passage was "They—the kids—were going someplace."

Problems with Reading Fluency. In addition to recognizing words accurately, readers need to identify them quickly. Words that we recognize instantly, without any need for analysis, are often called *sight vocabulary*. When we read fluently, we read text without stopping to analyze words. Fluency is important because human beings have limited memories. If we direct all our attention to figuring out the words, we will have difficulties understanding what the author is saying because we will have no resources to devote to comprehension (National Reading Panel, 2000; LaBerge & Samuels, 1974). Only if we recognize words quickly can we devote attention to comprehension. One student, Sofia, did a flawless oral reading of a story about Johnny Appleseed. However, because she labored over many words, she read slowly and without expression. As a result, she could answer only 3 of 10 comprehension questions.

Go to MyEducationLab and select the topic *Informal Assessments*. Then, go to the Activities and Applications section, watch the video entitled "Informal Reading Inventory," and respond to the accompanying questions.

Problems with Comprehension. Many students have problems comprehending what they read. At times, youngsters do not actively construct meaning but simply read to pronounce words or answer questions; thus, they are not reading to comprehend. Comprehension occurs at different levels. Literal comprehension includes understanding content that is explicitly stated in the text. Higher-level comprehension includes organizing what is read, drawing inferences, and thinking critically.

However, at times, poor understanding of text may be rooted in causes other than comprehension. For example, a student who lacks adequate word recognition may not be able to comprehend material. Sofia, mentioned previously, could not comprehend material because she lacked reading fluency. Similarly, apparent problems in reading comprehension may actually be caused by underlying problems in understanding language and word meanings.

Students need comprehension strategies when they read storylike or narrative text. Learning from informational text, or studying, is also part of comprehension;

many students with reading problems do not know how to summarize, take notes, or prepare for multiple-choice and essay examinations.

Go to MyEducationLab and select the topic *Instructional Decision Making*. Then, go to the Activities and Applications section, read the case study entitled "Comprehension and Vocabulary," and respond to the accompanying questions.

Problems with Language and Meaning Vocabulary. Because reading is a language process, the ability to read cannot exceed the language we can understand and the word meanings we already know. Students who can pronounce words as they read but cannot understand them are not really reading. Aushabell, a second-grade student, had recently arrived from Turkey. She could read orally with amazing accuracy. However, she had little idea of what she was reading, because she lacked an understanding of such common English words as *mother, school, run,* and *night.* Many other students may speak English fluently but lack the rich language patterns and meaning vocabulary needed to read more sophisticated stories, novels, and textbooks. In fact, problems with underlying language and word meaning have been recognized as an extremely important factor in reading disabilities for intermediate and upper-grade students beyond third grade (National Reading Panel, 2000; Stanovich, 1986).

Overview of Informal Assessment Measures

Informal assessments are instruments that can be modified to suit the needs of students and the information teachers want to gather. The three key differences between formal and informal measures are:

◆ Student scores on informal measures are not based upon comparison to the scores of a norm group; that is, the average score of the norm group is not used as a reference point for a student's score.

◆ Informal measures are flexible and teachers are free to make modifications in procedures, adapting them to serve specific needs. On the other hand, formal measures are standardized and the administration process must remain the same across all students. Informal measures often represent a more authentic task.

◆ Authentic assessments are measures that are similar to actual reading tasks. In such measures, students read longer selections, summarize them, and answer questions just as they would in a typical classroom or when reading for their own information or enjoyment. In contrast to this, many formal tests only measure the student's ability to read short passages and answer multiple-choice questions.

Go to MyEducationLab and select the topic *Informal Assessments*. Then, go to the Activities and Applications section, watch the video entitled "Performance Assessment," and respond to the accompanying questions.

To summarize, informal measures allow teachers the flexibility to adapt assessment so that it gives maximum information about how students, materials, and classroom situations interact to affect a reading problem. In this way, teachers can best determine how students can meet the demands of school reading.

Informal Reading Inventory

The informal reading inventory (IRI) is one informal assessment instrument that is widely used in reading assessment. The IRI is one of the best tools for observing and analyzing reading performance and for gathering information about how a student uses a wide range of reading strategies.

The IRI is administered to students individually. In an IRI, a student reads graded passages orally and/or silently and answers questions about them. As a student reads, the teacher records performance in word recognition and comprehension. Generally, IRIs contain passages at the preprimer, primer, first-grade, and all other grade levels through the eighth grade. Some IRIs contain high school passages. In addition, many inventories contain graded word lists, which are used to help select appropriate passage levels for students to read.

Passages in IRIs are representative of textbooks at different grade levels. Thus, a teacher can see how a student functions with classroom-like materials (Johnson, Kress, & Pikulski, 1987). Because it is classroom based, the information gained from an IRI is often more useful and realistic than the results of a standardized test. An IRI is also effective for assessing both short-term and long-term growth (Leslie & Caldwell, 2005; Leslie & Allen, 1999; Caldwell, Fromm, & O'Connor, 1997–1998).

A teacher can use an IRI to assess student reading achievement at different times during the school year. After a student has participated in an intervention program, an IRI can be used to measure the student's reading growth.

There are many different types of IRIs. A IRI is included on the website for this book. Whatever IRI you choose, remember that it is an informal measure you can adapt for different purposes and needs.

Obtaining Answers to General Assessment Questions

The IRI helps teachers obtain information on the three general assessment questions presented in the beginning of this chapter: (1) Does the student have a reading problem? (2) How severe is it? (3) What is the general area of the student's reading problem?

To answer the first question, the reading teacher determines an *instructional* reading level for the student. At this level, the student can read with instructional support, such as that provided in a typical classroom. The reading teacher then compares the instructional level on the IRI to the level of reading appropriate for the student. This comparison shows the existence and the severity of the reading problem. For example, a student who has an instructional level of fifth grade on the IRI and is in fifth grade does not have a reading problem. On the other hand, a fifth-grade student who has an instructional level of first grade has a severe reading problem.

The IRI can also help reveal the general area of the reading problem. Through listening to a student read orally, the teacher can determine whether the student's problem is word recognition or reading fluency. By asking questions and having students retell passages that have been read, the teacher can assess comprehension. By having the student listen to a passage and respond to questions, the teacher can determine whether language and meaning vocabulary are problems.

Finally, because the IRI is an individual test, a teacher has opportunities during its administration to make diagnostic observations that answer many different questions. Does the student read better orally or silently? Become easily frustrated? Point to each word or regularly lose the place in reading? Does the student have particular difficulty with drawing conclusions in material? The IRI is a rich source of these and many other insights.

However, like all other assessment tools, IRIs have some limitations. For example, examiners, especially untrained ones, can miss some problems with oral reading (Pikulski & Shanahan, 1982). In addition, a student's performance on a passage may be affected by the amount of personal interest in the subject, background knowledge, and text organization (Leslie & Caldwell, 2005; Caldwell, 1985; Lipson, Cox, Iwankowski, & Simon, 1984). Finally, the shortness of IRI selections (often a few hundred words) may not allow teachers to determine how well a student reads a multipage selection.

To obtain the greatest assessment value, teachers need to prepare carefully for administering an IRI. They need to use professional observation and judgment in effectively translating IRI results into instructional decisions.

Administering and Scoring the Informal Reading Inventory

Each published IRI comes with directions for administration that may vary in detail from other IRIs. All IRIs have some common features, however, and the directions given in this chapter are based on these similarities (See Table 5.2).

The IRI consists of a series of graded reading selections followed by questions. Some IRIs, such as the one provided on the website for this book, also contain graded word lists. The teacher can use these lists to decide which passage to administer first. The student reads passages (orally or silently) at different grade levels and stops when the material becomes too difficult. After the student reads each passage, the teacher asks comprehension questions. For passages read orally, the teacher records reading errors, or *miscues*, which are deviations from what is written. The teacher also records the time needed to read the passage and student responses to the questions. For passages read silently, the teacher records the time needed for reading and the responses to questions. In addition, the teacher may wish to ask students to retell a selection in their own words.

Go to MyEducationLab and select the topic *Informal Assessments.* Then, go to the Activities and Applications section, watch the video entitled "Administering an Informal Reading Inventory," and respond to the accompanying questions.

The percentage of reading miscues determines word recognition accuracy. The time needed for reading, which determines reading fluency, may also be used to judge passages. The responses to questions determine the comprehension score. In turn, word recognition and comprehension scores determine three reading levels for the student:

- *Independent:* the level at which a student can read without teacher guidance. Use this level for recreational reading.
- *Instructional:* the level at which a student can read with teacher support. Use this level for reading instruction.
- *Frustrational:* the level that is too hard for the student. Avoid this level or, if the student must read text at this level, read it to him or her.

TABLE 5.2	Procedure for Informal Reading Inventory Administration		
Administer word lists.	Determine percentage of words read correctly on each list. Stop when student scores below 60 percent.	Use word list performance to select a beginning point for passage administration. Begin at a level where the student scores 90 percent on word list.
Administer passages in oral or reading format.	Record reading errors and determine independent, instructional, and/or frustration levels for word identification.	Record time needed to read each passage.
	Ask questions about the text and determine independent, instructional, and/or frustration levels for comprehension.	
	Stop when material becomes too difficult.	
Administer passages in silent reading format.	Ask questions and determine independent, instructional, and/or frustration levels for comprehension.	Record time needed to read each passage.
	Stop when material becomes too difficult.	

Each level is expressed as a grade level (from preprimer through eighth grade). Teachers can use these three levels to determine the severity of a reading problem as well as to select reading materials for various purposes.

Materials and General Preparation.   To give an IRI, select a period of about an hour to work with an individual student. For younger students and students who are extremely nervous, you may want to divide the testing into two periods.

Materials you will need usually include:

◆ Student copy of the IRI word lists and passages
◆ Protocol (or teacher copy) of word lists and passages
◆ Stopwatch or watch with a second hand
◆ Tape recorder and audiotape
◆ Clipboard

Seat the student across from you and hand him or her the student copy of the passage to read. The student copy contains only the passage, without the questions. Record oral reading miscues and responses to questions on a teacher copy, referred to as a *protocol*. The protocol also contains questions to ask the student. Place the proto-col on a clipboard for ease in handling.

Even experienced examiners find that taping the entire session is helpful so that they can refer to it later. Explain to the student that you are taping because you can't remember everything. Then place the tape recorder off to one side to reduce its intru-sion into your testing situation. Because using the tape recorder often makes students nervous, you might ask your student to state his or her name and the date and then play these back to test the tape recorder.

If you wish to record the speed of your student's reading, you will need a stop-watch. Again, explain what you are doing, allow your student to handle the stopwatch for a short time, and then place it off to one side.

To help prepare a student for the IRI, explain that he or she will read passages both orally and silently and answer questions after each passage. Finally, tell the stu-dent that the material will become progressively more difficult.

Administering Word Lists.   Many IRIs provide a set of graded word lists. A stu-dent's performance on reading these word lists provides a quick way to determine which passage in the IRI the student should read first. Word lists generally start at the preprimer level and continue through the sixth-grade level. Each level usually has 20 to 25 words.

Students usually begin by reading the easiest list. As your youngster reads from the student's copy, record the responses on your teacher's copy. If the student recog-nizes a word *instantly*, mark a "+" in the timed column. If the student must analyze the word, mark a "+" in the untimed column. Administer the graded word lists until the student scores below 60 percent on any list (for example, misses 11 or more words out of 25 on the timed words or 8 or more out of 20). Begin the oral reading passages at the highest level on which the student scores at least 90 percent (no more than two miscues). If students score low on the word lists, begin testing at the preprimer level or eliminate the IRI and use emergent literacy assessments (see Chapter 7).

For example, fourth-grade Reyna's scores on the IRI word lists follow:

Preprimer: 90%   Grade 2: 80%

Primer: 100%   Grade 3: 55%

Grade 1: 80%

The primer level is the highest level at which Reyna scored 90 percent or above. Therefore, the teacher should begin testing Reyna at the primer level.

In addition to determining which passage to administer first, a student's per-formance on word lists can provide important diagnostic information about word recognition abilities. By looking at incorrect responses on a word list, you can gain insights about how a student analyzes words. You can see, for example, whether stu-dents are matching letters and sounds (phonics). You can also determine if they use structural analysis, such as examining prefixes and suffixes. Figure 5.1 shows Reyna's responses to the second-grade word list. If you look at Reyna's incorrect responses,

FIGURE 5.1   Reyna's Scored IRI Word List, Level 2

	Target Word	Timed Presentation	Untimed Presentation	Knew in Context (in oral passage) + or -
		Student's Attempt		
Oral Passages	camp	+		
	year	+		
	spend	+		
	whole	what	when	
	week	will	+	
	packed	pick	+	
	clothes	clap	+	
	dressed	dr...	drossed	
	brushed	+		
	teeth	test	tooth	
	kitchen	+		
	eggs	+		
	toast	test	+	
	seemed	s...	+	
	forever	+		
	hundreds	+		
	shorts	+		
	shirts	shark	shirk	
	tent	+		
	knew	k...	know	
Silent Passages	teacher	+		
	world	work	+	
	playground	+		
	classroom	+		
	card	+		
Results		# Correct	Multiplied by 4	% Correct
Timed Presentation		14	x 4	56
Untimed Presentation		6	x 4	24
Total		20	x 4	80

you can see that she is able to use sounds (such as *t*, *dr*, *wh*) at the beginnings of words but does not always use correct vowels and ending sounds. This information provides the reading teacher with suggestions of phonics strategies that need to be taught.

Some children score much lower on word lists than they do when reading a selection. This situation suggests that the student is using the context of the passage as an aid to word recognition. Although this strategy is normal for beginning readers, older and skilled readers do not use context for word pronunciation, and poor readers often overuse it (Stanovich, 1993–1994; 1991).

Administering Reading Passages.   If you have given a word list, you will know the passage level to administer first. If not, start at a level that you think will be easy for the student. Sometimes information from other testing or classroom performance can suggest a beginning passage level. Remember that beginning too low is better than beginning too high. Students who have difficulty on the first IRI passage they read often become nervous. If you find that the first passage you have chosen is too challenging, stop the reading and immediately move down to an easier level.

Most IRIs provide passages for both oral and silent reading. Administer all of the oral passages first then administer the silent passages and obtain reading levels for this mode. (For an alternative plan, see the section in this chapter on Special Issues and Options in Using IRIs.)

The following steps are appropriate for administering passages for many other published IRIs:

1. Before reading, orally give the student a brief introduction to the topic: For example, say, "This story is about a girl who wanted to become a champion skater."
2. Ask a background question to determine how familiar the student is with the topic: "What do you know about championship skating?" Answers to such questions allow you to determine whether problems with reading might be due to lack of background knowledge. (The IRI on the website provides instructions and background questions.)
3. Hand the student copy to the student to read. State that you will ask questions after reading is completed. Have the student read orally (for oral passages) or silently (for silent passages). If the passage is to be read orally, tell the student that you will not be able to help with words and that he or she can say "pass" if a word cannot be figured out. (See Special Issues and Options in Using IRIs later in this chapter for a discussion of teacher aid.) If the passage is to be read silently, ask your student to look up immediately when finished so that you can record the time correctly.
4. For oral reading, record any differences between the text and the student's reading on your protocol. If you want to record reading speed, time the student with a stopwatch.
5. After the student finishes, take away the passage and ask the comprehension questions. If you want additional information, you may also ask the student to retell the passage in his or her own words.

6. Continue testing until you have determined the independent, instructional, and frustrational levels for your student. For example, if a student scores at an independent level for third grade, have the student read the fourth-grade passage. Continue moving up until you reach the student's frustrational level. If a student scores at a frustrational level on the first passage read, move down until you reach the independent level. The next section explains how to determine these levels.

Reading Levels Obtained from the IRI. Using an IRI, a reading teacher can determine the student's independent, instructional, and frustrational reading levels. The instructional level is particularly critical because the severity of a student's reading problem is determined by *comparing the instructional level with the level at which the student should be reading* (usually the student's grade placement). For example, if a student's IRI instructional level is third grade but he is in a sixth-grade class, he would have a severe reading problem.

How do we calculate reading levels? As stated earlier, reading levels on an IRI are determined by performance on the passages, not scores on the word lists.

The level of an orally read passage is based on (1) the word recognition accuracy score for the passage and (2) the comprehension score. The level of a silently read passage is based on the comprehension score.

The word recognition score comes from the number of miscues, or errors, that the student makes while orally reading a passage. The comprehension score comes from the number of correct responses on the comprehension questions. Table 5.3 lists the criteria suggested for the different IRI levels.

Scoring Word Recognition Accuracy. A word recognition score is obtained from the student's oral reading of passages. To obtain this score, you must code and score this oral reading.

Your first step is to code the oral reading. As the student reads, you need to mark all miscues using a standard system so that you can later determine exactly what the student said. Commercial IRIs generally provide their own coding systems. Teachers who construct their own IRIs or use the one provided with this book should use the coding system presented in Figure 5.2.

Omissions, additions, substitutions, and reversals usually count as word recognition errors. You might, in addition, want to *record* repetitions, hesitations, omissions

TABLE 5.3 IRI Passage Criteria for Three Reading Levels

Reading Level	*Word Recognition Accuracy (%)*		*Comprehension (%)*
Independent	98–100	and	90–100
Instructional	95–97	and	70–89
Frustrational	Less than 95	or	Less than 70

FIGURE 5.2   Coding System for Scoring IRI Passage Miscues

1. *Omissions:* Circle.
   □ on ⟨the⟩ table

2. *Insertions:* Insert the added word above a caret.
   □ on the ^big^ table

3. *Substitutions, mispronunciations:* Underline the word in the text and write the word that the student said above the word in text.
   □ on the ~~table~~ ᵗᵃᵇˡᵉᵗ

4. *Reversals:* Same as substitutions.

5. *Repetitions:* Draw a line with an arrow below the words.
   □ on the table
   ←———┘

6. *Words pronounced correctly but with hesitations:* Write an *H* over the word.
   □ on the taᴴble

7. *Lack of punctuation:* Circle ignored punctuation.
   □ I saw Mary⊙ She was happy.

8. *Student corrections:* Cross out any previous responses and mark with *SC*.
   SC
   □ on the ~~tablet~~ table

---

of punctuation, and spontaneous corrections of errors. Because these four things do not usually alter the meaning of text, experts do not recommend counting them as errors (McKenna, 1983). However, they can provide additional information about a student's word recognition strategies.

After coding the oral reading, you need to score it. The easiest and most reliable way to score the oral reading is to assign one point to each omission, addition, substitution, and reversal (Leslie & Caldwell, 2005). Extensive field testing (Leslie & Caldwell, 2005) indicate that this scoring system places students at appropriate instructional levels. However, some alternatives for scoring miscues are discussed in the section Special Issues and Options in Using IRIs.

Certain scoring problems may arise during an IRI. Some propose solutions to some of these based on field testing by Leslie & Caldwell (2005)

◆ If a student repeatedly mispronounces the same word, count it as incorrect each time. If a student were reading an assignment in school, each mispronunciation would affect comprehension.

◆ If a student omits an entire line or phrase, count it as one miscue. In this situation, the student simply lost his or her place.

◆ Proper names are difficult for students because they often do not follow regular phonics patterns. Do not count a mispronunciation of a proper name as incorrect unless it changes the sex of the character. For example, do not count the substitution of *Mary* for *Maria*. However, do count the substitution of *Mark* for *Maria*. Sometimes students use a nonword to pronounce a proper name such as *Manee* for *Maria*. If the student says this consistently throughout the passage, do not count it as an error. If, however, the student pronounces it differently on other occasions, count it as incorrect each time. Follow these guidelines for names of places.

◆ Miscues that reflect a student's speech patterns should never count as errors. In other words, mispronunciations resulting from dialect differences, speaking English as a second language, immature speech patterns, or speech impediments do not count as errors. For example, a student who speaks a dialect other than standard English might pronounce the word *tests* as *tes*, both in speaking and in reading an IRI passage. In such miscues, readers are simply recoding the written word into their own pronunciation. Pupils should never be penalized for such recoding.

After you have counted all of the errors on an individual passage, total them. Then compute the percentage of words read correctly in the passage. In the coded and scored passage in Figure 5.3, the student had four errors, and 92 correct words in the total 96 words. The percentage correct is 96 percent, an instructional level.

$$\frac{92 \text{ Words Correct}}{96 \text{ Total Words}} \times 100 = 96\%$$

To make this process easier, use Table 5.4. Simply find the intersection between the number of words in the passage and the error count. For example, if the passage contains 103 words and the error count is nine, then the percentage correct is 91, a frustrational level.

After you have determined a percentage of words read correctly, translate this percentage score into a level (independent, instructional, or frustrational) by using Table 5.3.

Grading Comprehension. After the student reads each passage, the teacher asks questions to check comprehension. If the student's answer is incorrect, the teacher writes the exact student response; if the response is correct, simply mark a +. The teacher obtains a percentage score: for example, if the student answers three of four comprehension questions correctly, the comprehension score would be 75 percent on that selection. Table 5.5 provides the percentage of correct scores for different numbers of comprehension questions. Translate the percentage score on comprehension into a level (independent, instructional, or frustrational) from Table 5.3.

FIGURE 5.3   Student's Coded Oral Reading of a Primer-Level IRI Passage

Nick's Trip to the Lake

Once
Nick and his dad like animals. <u>One</u> (day) Nick and his dad went to the lake. They

went to see the animals. They sat next to the lake. They were very still.

out   *Then*
Then Nick saw a big duck. He saw the duck swim‸to a big rock in the lake‸Some-

thing made the duck fly away fast.

Nick asked his dad, "Why did the duck fly away?"

Nick's dad said, "Look over there." He showed Nick something in the lake. Nick
H
thought he would see something big.

SC
What a surprise to see a little green ~~frog~~!

Scoring System

Omissions: ⬭   Repetitions: ◀———┘

Insertions: ‸   Hesitations: H

Substitutions: Write the word and underline   Student corrections: SC

Words in passage	96	
Errors	4	
Oral Reading Accuracy Score	96%	

Determining Passage Levels.   Once you have scored both word recognition accuracy and comprehension, you are ready to determine a *total level for that passage*. For a silent passage, a student has only one score that determines passage level: the comprehension score. Leslie, for example, read a fourth-grade passage silently and achieved at an instructional level for comprehension. Therefore, her level for that passage was instructional.

However, if a student has read a passage orally, the teacher has both a word recognition accuracy score and a comprehension score to determine whether the passage is at a student's independent, instructional, or frustrational level. If a student achieves the same level for both word recognition accuracy and comprehension, determining the level is easy. For example, on a second-grade passage, Leslie achieved at an independent level for both word recognition and comprehension. Therefore, the second-grade passage was at an independent level.

TABLE 5.4   Percentages for Word Recognition Accuracy Scores (*Each Number Indicates Percentage Correct*)

Number of Words in Passage — *Number of Errors*

Words in Passage	1	2	3	4	5	6	7	8	9	10	11	12	13	14	15	16	17	18	19	20	21	22	23	24	25	26
28–32	97	93	90	87	83	80	77	73	70	67	63	60	57	53	50	47	43	40	37	33	30	27	23	20	17	13
33–37	97	94	92	89	86	83	80	77	74	72	69	66	63	60	57	54	52	49	46	43	40	37	34	32	29	26
38–42	98	95	93	90	88	85	82	80	78	75	72	70	68	65	62	60	58	55	52	50	48	45	42	40	38	35
43–47	98	96	93	91	89	87	84	82	80	78	76	73	71	69	67	64	62	60	58	56	53	51	49	47	44	42
48–52	98	96	94	92	90	88	86	84	82	80	78	76	74	72	70	68	66	64	62	60	58	56	54	52	50	48
53–57	98	96	95	93	91	89	87	86	84	82	80	78	77	76	73	71	69	67	66	64	62	60	58	56	55	53
58–62	98	97	95	93	92	90	88	87	85	83	82	80	78	77	75	73	72	70	68	67	65	63	62	60	58	57
63–67	98	97	95	94	92	91	89	88	86	85	83	82	80	78	77	75	74	72	71	69	68	66	65	63	62	60
68–72	99	97	95	94	93	92	90	89	87	86	84	83	82	80	79	77	76	74	73	72	70	69	67	66	64	63
73–77	99	97	96	94	93	92	91	89	87	86	85	84	83	81	80	79	77	76	75	73	72	71	69	68	67	65
78–82	99	98	96	95	94	92	91	90	89	88	86	85	84	82	81	80	79	78	76	75	74	72	71	70	69	68
83–87	99	98	96	95	94	93	92	91	89	88	87	86	85	84	82	81	80	79	78	76	75	74	73	72	71	69
88–92	99	98	97	96	94	93	92	91	90	89	88	87	86	84	83	82	81	80	79	78	77	76	74	73	72	71
93–97	99	98	97	96	95	94	93	92	91	89	88	87	86	85	84	83	82	81	80	79	78	77	76	75	74	73
98–102	99	98	97	96	95	94	93	92	91	90	89	88	87	86	85	84	83	82	81	80	79	78	77	76	75	74
103–107	99	98	97	96	95	94	93	92	91	90	90	89	88	87	86	85	84	83	82	81	80	79	78	77	76	75
108–112	99	98	97	96	95	94	93	92	91	91	90	89	88	87	86	85	85	84	83	82	81	80	79	78	77	76
113–117	99	98	97	97	96	95	94	93	92	91	90	90	89	88	87	86	85	84	84	83	82	81	80	79	78	77
118–122	99	98	98	97	96	95	94	93	92	92	91	90	89	88	88	87	86	85	84	83	82	82	81	80	79	79
123–127	99	98	98	97	96	95	94	94	93	92	91	90	90	89	88	88	87	86	85	84	83	82	82	81	80	79
128–132	99	98	98	97	96	95	95	94	93	92	92	91	90	89	88	88	87	86	85	85	84	83	82	82	81	80
133–137	99	99	98	97	96	96	95	94	93	93	92	91	90	90	89	88	87	87	86	85	84	84	83	82	81	81
138–142	99	99	98	97	96	96	95	94	94	93	92	91	91	90	89	89	88	87	86	85	85	84	84	83	82	81
143–147	99	99	98	97	97	96	95	95	94	93	92	92	91	90	90	89	88	88	87	86	86	85	84	83	83	82
148–152	99	99	98	97	97	96	95	95	94	93	92	92	91	91	90	89	89	88	87	87	86	86	85	84	83	83
153–157	99	99	98	97	97	96	95	95	94	94	93	92	92	91	90	90	89	88	88	87	86	86	85	85	84	83
158–162	99	99	98	98	97	96	96	95	94	94	93	92	92	91	91	90	89	89	88	88	87	86	86	85	84	84
163–167	99	99	98	98	97	96	96	95	95	94	93	93	92	92	91	90	90	89	88	88	87	87	86	85	85	84
168–172	99	99	98	98	97	96	96	95	95	94	94	93	93	92	91	91	90	89	89	88	88	87	86	86	85	85
173–177	99	99	98	98	97	97	96	95	95	94	94	93	93	92	91	91	90	90	89	89	88	87	87	86	86	85
178–182	99	99	98	98	97	97	96	96	95	94	94	93	93	92	92	91	91	90	89	89	88	88	87	87	86	86
183–187	99	99	98	98	97	97	96	96	95	95	94	94	93	92	92	91	91	90	90	89	89	88	88	87	87	86
188–192	99	99	98	98	97	97	96	96	95	95	94	94	93	93	92	92	91	91	90	89	89	88	88	87	87	86
193–197	99	99	98	98	97	97	96	96	95	95	94	94	93	93	92	92	91	91	90	90	89	89	88	88	87	87
198–202	100	99	98	98	98	97	96	96	96	95	94	94	93	93	92	92	91	91	90	90	89	89	88	88	87	87
203–207	100	99	99	98	98	97	97	96	96	95	95	94	94	93	93	92	92	91	91	90	90	89	89	88	88	87
208–212	100	99	99	98	98	97	97	96	96	95	95	94	94	93	93	92	92	91	91	90	90	90	89	89	88	88
213–217	100	99	99	98	98	97	97	96	96	95	95	94	94	93	93	93	92	92	91	91	90	90	89	89	88	88
218–222	100	99	99	98	98	97	97	96	96	96	95	95	94	94	93	93	92	92	91	91	90	90	90	89	89	88
223–227	100	99	99	98	98	97	97	96	96	96	95	95	94	94	93	93	92	92	92	91	91	90	90	89	89	88
228–232	100	99	99	98	98	97	97	97	96	96	95	95	95	94	94	94	93	93	92	92	91	91	90	90	90	89
233–237	100	99	99	98	98	98	97	97	96	96	96	95	95	95	94	94	93	93	92	92	92	91	91	90	90	89
238–242	100	99	99	98	98	98	97	97	96	96	96	95	95	94	94	94	93	93	92	92	92	91	91	90	90	89

TABLE 5.5 Percentages for Comprehension Scores (*Each Number Indicates a Percentage-Correct Score*)

Number of Correct Responses

		1	2	3	4	5	6	7	8	9	10	11	12
	1	100											
	2	50	100										
	3	33	67	100									
	4	25	50	75	100								
Number of Questions	5	20	40	60	80	100							
	6	17	33	50	67	83	100						
	7	14	26	43	57	71	86	100					
	8	12	25	38	50	62	75	88	100				
	9	11	22	33	44	56	67	78	89	100			
	10	10	20	30	40	50	60	70	80	90	100		
	11	9	18	27	36	45	55	64	73	82	91	100	
	12	8	17	25	33	42	50	58	67	75	83	92	100

However, students sometimes have different levels for word recognition accuracy and comprehension. In this case, use the lower level to determine passage level. For example, on a third-grade passage, Leslie achieved at an instructional level for word recognition accuracy but an independent level for comprehension. Therefore, the third-grade passage was at an instructional level. Table 5.6 helps you to assign levels to oral passages.

At times, a student may achieve at the independent or instructional levels on two (or even more) passages. For example, a student reading oral passages might achieve an instructional score on the primer, first-grade, and second-grade passages. If this situation happens, the *highest* level is the instructional level. In this case, the instructional level is second grade.

TABLE 5.6 Criteria for Assigning Levels to Oral Reading Passages

Comprehension	*Word Recognition*	*Passage Level*
Independent	Independent	Independent
Independent	Instructional	Instructional
Independent	Frustrational	Frustrational
Instructional	Instructional	Instructional
Instructional	Independent	Instructional
Instructional	Frustrational	Frustrational
Frustrational	Frustrational	Frustrational
Frustrational	Independent	Frustrational
Frustrational	Instructional	Frustrational

Combining Oral and Silent Levels into One Overall Level. Determine the levels for oral reading and then determine the levels for silent reading. Students often perform differently on oral and silent reading and so may achieve different levels for each one. However, to make instructional decisions, you should combine your results for both modes of reading.

To combine oral and silent levels, first put the level of each oral and silent passage side by side according to grade level. Then, if the two levels are different, choose the *lower* level for the total reading level.

For example, Leslie, who is in the fifth grade, achieved these levels on *orally* read passages:

Grade 2—Independent
Grade 3—Instructional
Grade 4—Frustrational

In this case, Leslie's *oral reading levels*, which are quite easy to determine, are:

Grade 2—Oral Independent Reading Level
Grade 3—Oral Instructional Reading Level
Grade 4—Oral Frustrational Reading Level

On *silently* read passages, Leslie received these levels:

Grade 2—Independent
Grade 3—Independent
Grade 4—Instructional
Grade 5—Frustrational

Based on these passages, Leslie's *silent reading* levels are:

Grade 3—Silent Independent Level
Grade 4—Silent Instructional Level
Grade 5—Silent Frustrational Level

To determine Leslie's *combined* reading levels, place the results from each silent and oral passage side by side and then choose the lower level.

Oral Reading Passages	*Silent Reading Passages*	*Combined Level*
2 Independent	2 Independent	2 Independent
3 Instructional	3 Independent	3 Instructional
4 Frustrational	4 Instructional	4 Frustrational
5 (not given)	5 Frustrational	

Based on this information, Leslie's total reading levels are:

Grade 2—Combined Independent Reading Level
Grade 3—Combined Instructional Reading Level
Grade 4—Combined Frustrational Reading Level

Assigning a combined reading level is helpful in situations where you need a general level for assigning school materials. For example, because Leslie's combined reading is instructional at the third-grade level, she should be reading a third-grade book.

Interpreting the Scores of the IRI

The IRI is a rich source of information about a student's reading, and it can provide detailed answers to the two diagnostic questions asked earlier in this chapter: (1) Does the student have a reading problem and how severe is it? and (2) What is the general area of the reading problem? Answering these two questions requires adding some procedures to ones already given. These procedures provide options for enriching the information obtained from an IRI.

How Severe Is the Student's Reading Problem?   To estimate the severity of a reading problem, the teacher should examine the gap between a student's highest instructional level on the IRI and the level of text that would be appropriate for that student.

Let's consider the case of Subash, a sixth grader whose IRI summary is presented in Table 5.7. His teacher reported that Subash's class is reading sixth-grade material. On the IRI, Subash's combined independent level is 2. Because he scored at an instructional level on both Grades 3 and 4, his instructional level is the higher level (4). His frustrational level is 5. The gap between Subash's appropriate reading level (6) and his highest instructional level on the IRI (4) indicates that he has a severe reading problem, according to the criteria by Spache (1981) mentioned earlier in Table 5.1.

We now move to the second diagnostic question: determining the general area(s) of the reading problem. To answer this question, we will consider the areas one by one.

What Is the Nature of Word Recognition Accuracy?   The student's word recognition accuracy score is generally based on passages because reading a passage is a more authentic task than reading a word list. However, the teacher should be aware that certain things, such as context of the passage, the familiarity of the topic, and the presence of pictures, may inflate a student's score (Leslie & Caldwell, 2005). Rhyme or repetition of phrases in the passage can also aid word recognition. If time permits, the teacher should verify the word recognition level with another passage at the same level. A word recognition accuracy score below the third-grade level on IRI passages is one sign that the primary nature of the reading difficulty is word recognition.

TABLE 5.7   IRI Summary for Subash

Level	Word Recognition Accuracy Level	Comp Level	Passage Level	Comp & Passage Level	Passage Level	Passage Level
	Oral Passages			Silent Passages	Combined Reading	Listening
Preprimer	—	—	—	—	—	—
Primer	—	—	—	—	—	—
1	—	—	—	—	—	—
2	Ind	Ind	Ind	Ind	Ind	—
3	Ind	Ins	Ins	Ins	Ins	—
4	Ind	Ins	Ins	Ins	Ins	—
5	Ind	Frus	Frus	Frus	Frus	Ind
6	—	—	—	—	—	Ins
7	—	—	—	—	—	Frus
8	—	—	—	—	—	—

Judging a student's word recognition accuracy also involves determining the strategies the student uses to recognize words. Only by knowing the tools that students use to identify words can the teacher help them develop missing skills. Miscues, which are mismatches between the text and what the student says, provide opportunities to analyze these strategies.

Some miscues show that the student is using meaning or context clues. A student using context might substitute a word that makes sense in the context, for example, *Kleenex* for *handkerchief*. Readers bring a vast store of knowledge and competence to the reading act. When students use context clues, they are using this store of information to bring meaning to reading. The use of context clues shows a positive effort to preserve comprehension (Goodman & Gollasch, 1980–1981; Goodman, 1976; Goodman, 1965).

Other miscues show that the student is using phonics clues to recognize words. A student who uses phonics clues makes miscues that contain many of the same sounds as the words that are in the passage. However, the miscues will often not make sense in context. In fact, sometimes they are not even real words.

An exact recording of oral reading can be analyzed to see which strategies a student tends to use. We call this *miscue analysis* (Goodman, 1969). Some forms of miscue analysis are complex; others are simple. However, they all share a common purpose: to determine the reader's strategies for identifying words. Almost all try to determine whether the reader pays primary attention to letter-sound matching, to meaning, or to both as skilled readers do.

To help analyze a reader's strategies, look at a form of miscue analysis adapted from Leslie (1993) and Leslie and Caldwell (2005). Table 5.8 presents the miscue analysis worksheet.

TABLE 5.8 Miscue Analysis Work Sheet

		Sounds Alike			
Word in Text	Miscue	Begin	End	Meaning Is Retained	Corrected
_____	_____	____	____	_____	_____
_____	_____	____	____	_____	_____
_____	_____	____	____	_____	_____
_____	_____	____	____	_____	_____
_____	_____	____	____	_____	_____
_____	_____	____	____	_____	_____
_____	_____	____	____	_____	_____
_____	_____	____	____	_____	_____
_____	_____	____	____	_____	_____
_____	_____	____	____	_____	_____
_____	_____	____	____	_____	_____
_____	_____	____	____	_____	_____
_____	_____	____	____	_____	_____
_____	_____	____	____	_____	_____
_____	_____	____	____	_____	_____
Column Total	_____	____	____	_____	_____

Ask three sets of questions about each miscue:

1. Is the miscue similar in sounds to the original word?
   - Does it begin with the same sound?
   - Does it end with the same sound?

   If the answers are yes, the student is paying attention to phonics when reading. Beginning and ending similarity is sufficient to determine whether the student is paying attention to letter-sound matching. Do not consider middle sounds because these sounds are often vowels, which have highly variable sounds.
2. Does the miscue retain the author's meaning?

   If the answer is yes, the reader is paying attention to meaning and using it to help recognize words.

3. Did the reader correct the miscue?

Self-correction can indicate two things. The self-correction of an acceptable miscue, which is one that does not change meaning, suggests that the reader is paying attention to letter-sound matching. Self-correction of a miscue that changes text meaning suggests that the reader is paying attention to meaning during the reading process.

To examine reading patterns, choose about 25 miscues from the instructional-level text. Record and analyze them on the sheet provided in Table 5.8. Now you can look for patterns. Several patterns typical of students with reading problems follow:

◆ If the student has a large number of miscues that do not change the author's meaning, the student is using the meaning (or context) of a passage as a clue to recognizing words. Another indication that the student is using the meaning of the passage as a clue is the self-correction of miscues that do not make sense.

◆ If the student has a high number of miscues that are similar in sound and a small number of miscues that retain the author's meaning, the reader may be paying more attention to phonics clues than to the meaning. Some readers show a large number of miscues that are similar in sound to the beginning of the text word and a small number that are similar at the end. Examples are pronouncing *when* for *wanted*; *dog* for *don't*; *live* for *liked*; and *truck* for *teach*. In this case, instruction should focus on guiding the reader to look at all the letters in a word.

◆ If the worksheet shows a pattern of miscues that do not contain the same sounds as the text words as well as a small number of acceptable miscues or self-corrections, the reader may be a wild guesser, one who is not using either phonics or context effectively.

In the examples presented in Figure 5.4, the first student is using meaning clues and the second is using phonics.

What Is the Nature of Reading Fluency? To assess reading fluency, calculate the reading rate, or the number of words per minute, for oral and silent passages. To determine the reading rate, take the number of words in the passage, multiply by 60, and divide by the number of seconds required by the student to read the selection. This calculation yields a word-per-minute score.

$$\frac{\text{Number of words} \times 60}{\text{Number of seconds to read}} = \text{Words per minute}$$

For example, Tammie read a second-grade passage that contained 249 words in 2 minutes and 15 seconds (or 135 seconds). Two hundred and forty-nine multiplied by 60 equals 14,940. Divide this number by 135 seconds. Tammie's reading rate for that passage is 110 words per minute.

Some have argued that a words per minute score is primarily an indicator of reading speed and they suggest that measuring rate as correct words per minute

---

FIGURE 5.4   Examples of Oral Reading Patterns

Example 1.   Use of Context Clues

---

                             sea   *lots of*

Kim lives on an island far out in the <u>ocean</u>. You may think that it would be fun to live

                 unhappy

on an island. But Kim is <u>miserable</u>. Kim hasn't seen her friends in a year. There is no

one to play with or talk to. There isn't even a school!

Example 2.   Use of Phonics Clues

---

     likes   *open*

Kim <u>lives</u> on an island far out in the <u>ocean</u>. You may think that it would be fun to live

                mysterious   *family*   *Then*

on an island. But Kim is <u>miserable</u>. Kim hasn't seen her <u>friends</u> in a year. <u>There</u> is no

               Then

one to play with or talk to. <u>There</u> isn't even a school!

(CWPM) addresses both speed and accuracy (Kame'enui & Simmons, 2001; Fuchs, Fuchs, Hosp, & Jenkins, 2001). To compute CWPM, take the number of words in the passage and subtract the number of miscues to arrive at the number of words read correctly. Multiply by 60 and divide by the number of seconds the student took to read the passage. For example, Tammie made 12 miscues as she read the 249 word passage so the number of words read correctly was 237. Two hundred and thirty-seven multiplied by 60 equals 14,220. Divide this by 135 seconds and Tammie's rate is 105 corrected words per minute. See Chapter 9 for additional information on CWPM.

What is a normal rate for different levels of passages? Guidelines for reading rates, based on normal students at their instructional level, are given in Table 5.9 (Leslie & Caldwell, 2005). Notice that the ranges for reading rate at each grade level are quite wide because individuals tend to have very different rates of reading (Carver, 1990).

When you have determined a student's reading rate at a certain grade level of the IRI, use Table 5.9 to compare your student's rate with the acceptable range provided. For example, Arliss read a third-grade oral passage at 65 words per minute. This rate is within the normal range of the third-grade level: 51–97 words per minute.

However, the guidelines in Table 5.9 are only advisory. Reading rate must always be interpreted in relation to comprehension. A student who reads below the lowest reading rate given for a passage level probably needs work in reading fluency, especially if comprehension is poor. A slow reader who cannot comprehend adequately is probably concentrating all of his or her attention on recognizing the

TABLE 5.9 Reading Rates at Instructional Levels

Level	Oral WPM	Oral CWPM	Silent WPM
Preprimer	22–64	11–59	
Primer	28–66	10–52	
First	37–77	20–68	
Second	43–89	19–77	
Third	51–97	32–86	
Fourth	55–105	27–87	
Fifth	61–133	30–114	73–175
Sixth			91–235
Upper Middle School			105–233
High School			65–334

words. This situation strongly suggests a need for fluency instruction. However, fluency instruction may be less important for a student who reads slowly but comprehends well.

At times, the teacher may only need to listen to a student to determine that the need is reading fluency. Slow, hesitant, expressionless reading that is filled with pauses suggests that a student is working hard to identify words and lacks the fluency essential for making sense of the author's message.

What Is the Nature of Comprehension?   If both word recognition and comprehension levels are at the frustrational level on a passage, the comprehension problems are probably due to poor word recognition. Because of this relationship, the student needs to concentrate on improving word recognition accuracy or fluency.

However, if word recognition accuracy and fluency are good but comprehension is poor, the student probably has a comprehension problem and needs to focus on comprehension strategies. If the problem is comprehension, careful analysis of an IRI can provide some important instructional hints.

Some students have problems in comprehension because they believe that reading is "getting all the words right." These readers are often extremely accurate and tend to self-correct miscues that do not change meaning. As a result, they do not actively construct meaning as they read. For example, Susan was asked to read an IRI passage containing the following sentences: "Bill's mom saw the dog. Bill asked, 'May I keep it?' " She read, "Bill's mother saw the dog. Bill asked, 'Can I have it?' " Then she paused and went back, carefully correcting each miscue. Susan's comprehension of the total passage was poor, probably the result of her concern with accuracy. For a reader like Susan, the teacher should emphasize that reading is meaning, not just saying words.

An analysis of IRI questions may also provide insight into comprehension patterns. In the IRI presented on the website, for example, questions are divided into literal and inferential categories. Comparing the percentages correct on these two types of questions helps determine whether the reader is focused on factual information or able to draw inferences. You might also note whether a student appears to get the central focus of the passage or is more observant of details.

If you ask a student to retell a passage after reading it, you can see exactly how he or she constructs meaning. In judging a retelling, use these questions as guidelines for a narrative or story:

◆ Does the retelling contain the central events of the passage?
◆ Does the student remember the most important facts?
◆ Is the student able to retell the events in sequence?

More detailed guidelines for judging retellings are provided in Chapter 11.

The IRI can also give insights into the adequacy of the student's background information. If you begin each selection by asking the student questions to assess background, you have a good idea of the richness of a student's prior knowledge. If you find that the student has problems with the background for several passages, your comprehension instruction may concentrate on enriching background information and applying it to reading.

Finally, when students read both oral and silent passages, you can determine whether they comprehend better after oral or silent reading. Young or very disabled readers are usually able to comprehend better after they have read orally. These students need practice to increase their comfort in silent reading. More mature readers comprehend better after silent reading than after oral reading.

Most IRIs are based on narrative passages; that is, passages that tell stories. Although these passages allow you to assess comprehension, it is more appropriate to judge study strategies from informational passages. In the section that follows, we address the use of IRIs that contain informational passages.

Extending the IRI to Examine the Nature of Studying Informational Text.
Students who have problems studying can often comprehend narrative (storylike) text but have problems with informational text. Typically, IRIs focus on narrative passages. However some, like the *Qualitative Reading Inventory-4* (Leslie & Caldwell, 2005), offer both narrative and informational passages at all levels.

If the IRI you are using does not have both types of passages, use the narrative passages, which all IRIs have, to determine an instructional level for your student. Then, have your student read expository material at the instructional level to see how he or she handles material commonly used for content area instruction.

Modifying the typical IRI procedure can often answer important questions about a student's ability to study. One extension of the IRI procedure can determine whether students can locate information to answer questions. Give the student an IRI passage that was previously read so that he or she can look at it. Then ask the questions that were missed during the original administration and see whether the student can use the passage to locate the answers to these questions.

Other modifications allow a teacher to assess the student's ability to locate main ideas and take notes. To evaluate the ability to determine main ideas, give the student an instructional-level informational passage and a pencil. Then ask him or her to underline the most important parts of the selection. To investigate study strategies, ask the student to take notes on the passage as if he or she were studying for a test. A teacher can use these procedures with any text, not just an IRI.

What Is the Nature of Language and Meaning Vocabulary: Determining the Listening Level.

Because reading is a language process, people read only as well as they can understand language and word meanings. An IRI enables a teacher to determine a student's language level by *finding a student's listening level*.

To do this, the teacher reads aloud IRI passages at the reading frustrational level and asks the comprehension questions about the passage. The highest level at which the student gets 70 percent or more of the answers correct is the listening level.

The listening level provides an estimate of the student's listening, or language, comprehension level. If a student's listening level is lower than his or her grade level, that student needs to develop better language skills. Instruction should then focus on developing rich language and learning more word meanings.

In contrast, the example of Subash, the sixth grader whose IRI summary sheet is presented in Table 5.7, shows a student who has a good language base. Subash's high-listening level (6) but lower instructional reading level (4) indicate a 2-year gap between his current reading level and his language level. The fact that his listening level is equal to his grade level indicates that his language base is sufficient for reading at grade level. No language development is needed for him; instead, he needs to work on reading.

You can also use the IRI to directly assess knowledge of meaning vocabulary. After the student has read and answered the questions in a passage, ask the student to define (or use in a sentence) key vocabulary words in the passage. Remember that you may have to pronounce words that the student has not read correctly in the passage. A student who knows the meanings of difficult words in a grade-level passage has a strong vocabulary base. A student who cannot define these words or use them in a sentence needs more development of meaning vocabulary. If a student cannot define a word in isolation, you might ask him or her to reread the sentence in the passage to see if context helps the student with word meaning.

Special Issues and Options in Using IRIs

The informal nature of an IRI allows many options for administration and adaptation to the special needs of students. At times, you may face some difficult decisions. This section discusses some of these issues and, in addition, presents some alternatives for administering and interpreting the IRI.

Pronouncing Words for Students.

When reading IRI selections orally, a student may sometimes become "stuck" on a word. The teacher may be tempted to supply this word to make the student more comfortable and able to continue. However, pronouncing words for the student may inflate the student's comprehension score, because understanding the passage depends on reading the words accurately. To obtain the most accurate assessment, teachers are strongly discouraged from supplying words. Tell students to say "pass" for unknown words, and score these passes as omission errors. Also encourage students to try pronouncing a word before they give up. However, some guidelines for IRI administration permit teachers to aid students.

Alternate Administration of Oral and Silent Passages. Administer all the oral passages first to determine the oral reading levels before administering the silent passages. Then combine oral and silent reading levels into a total reading level. Some reading teachers prefer a different administrative procedure. They alternate oral and silent passages at each grade level to determine the student's reading levels.

Unclear IRI Results. When administering an IRI, you may sometimes have difficulty determining a stable level. What are some of the things that can happen? A student may score just slightly below the criteria for a specific level, for example, scoring 94 percent for word recognition accuracy on one passage, only slightly below the frustrational cutoff of 95 percent. At other times, a student may not do well on a certain topic. Should the teacher count these passages as frustrational and simply discontinue testing? If you are unsure of the correct decision, you should continue to gather information by testing at higher levels or administering another passage at the same level.

At times, however, you will not be able to come to a perfectly clear-cut decision and may have to make exceptions to some of the scoring criteria. Because the IRI is an informal instrument, you should feel free to modify criteria by using your own judgment. You should, however, note that you have made an exception to the scoring criteria and explain the reason for this exception.

Alternative Ways to Score Miscues. As stated earlier, scoring each miscue as one error is the best and most reliable way to reach an appropriate reading level for your student. This recommendation has been verified with extensive field testing.

However, miscues that do not change the author's meaning suggest that the student is comprehending the passage. For example, consider the following sentence: *The teachers divided the children into four groups.* A substitution of *put* for *divided* would not affect meaning. On the other hand, the substitution of *from* for *four* does distort meaning. Some reading teachers prefer to count miscues that retain meaning (*put* for *divided*) less severely than miscues that change meaning (*from* for *for*). If you wish to do this, count a miscue that retains the original meaning as one-half error. If a miscue changes the meaning, however, count it as one full error.

Which option should you use? Because the IRI is an informal instrument, you are free to choose the scoring system that makes you most comfortable. However, once you choose the scoring system that best fits your needs, you should use it consistently.

Alternative Norms. As with many informal measures, alternative criteria for determining reading levels have been suggested by some reading experts. Based on field testing, the criteria suggested in this chapter for word recognition accuracy and comprehension place students at appropriate reading levels. These criteria reflect the authors' experiences in developing an IRI with students who have reading difficulties.

Allowing Students to Look for Answers. Another option in administering an IRI is to use *look-backs*. After scoring the questions and determining the comprehension level, you can ask the student to look back in the text to locate or correct answers. This procedure allows you to note the difference between comprehension during reading and memory after reading. A student may read a passage and understand it fully. However, when asked questions following reading, the student may forget certain parts. Hasn't this happened to you? If a student can locate or correct answers, you can assume that he or she understood the passage. If a student is unable to successfully use the look-back strategy, perhaps the problem is one of basic comprehension during reading.

Leslie and Caldwell (2005) found that students reading at the third-grade level and above could effectively use look-backs to raise their comprehension score. This situation was most evident in upper middle school and high school passages. Students who scored at the frustrational level for comprehension often raised their scores to an instructional or independent level following look-backs. In fact, Leslie and Caldwell (2005) recommend that comprehension levels for upper level text (sixth grade and above) be determined following look-backs. Actually, the look-back strategy parallels what students are asked to do in school. Rarely are they expected to answer questions without the support of the text.

If you wish to use look-backs, first ask and score the questions to arrive at a comprehension level without look-backs. Then ask the student to look back and score the results of his or her efforts. A comprehension score with look-backs represents the total of all questions answered correctly for both procedures.

Using an IRI to Measure a Student's Growth. If you are measuring classroom growth or growth following an intervention program, decide when you wish to assess the student. Every three or four months is a realistic interval for a classroom. Intervention program intervals can be of short or long duration.

Choose an IRI passage to administer prior to instruction. Obtain a score for both word recognition and comprehension. If the student scores at an independent level, continue at higher levels until you reach the student's frustrational level. Then, when the classroom interval is over or the intervention is completed, administer the same passage as a posttest measure.

You have another option. You can administer a different IRI passage for the pretest and the posttest. This option is preferable if the duration between pretest and posttest is short and you think that memory for the initial passage may inflate the results. Of course, the two passages should be as alike as possible. They should be at the same level and have the same structure: narrative or expository. They should both be relatively familiar to the student.

Levels of Questions on IRIs. Most IRIs have two types of questions: literal (or explicit) and inferential (or implicit). However, there are multiple levels of inferential questions (Caldwell & Leslie, 2005; Ciardiello, 1998). Appplegate, Quinn, and Applegate (2002) describe three basic types: low-level inference items, high-level inference items, and response items. The answers to low-level inference items are not stated in the text, but they are relatively obvious. Some may require the reader to identify information that is stated in different words from the question. Others may require identification of simple relationships such as a causal relationship that is not marked by the signal word *because*. High-level inference items ask the reader to identify an alternative solution, offer a plausible explanation, or predict past or future actions. Response items ask the reader to defend an idea and react to the passage as a whole. Applegate, Quinn, and Applegate (2002) caution that IRIs may contain a variety of such disparate items loosely grouped under the heading of inferential, or implicit, questions. To put it simply, some inference questions are more difficult than others.

What does this variety of inferential questions mean for IRI administration? You should be aware that all questions are not the same level of difficulty and take this into account when you assess a student's comprehension. Dewitz and Dewitz (2003) carefully analyzed a student's responses on an IRI and divided them into several categories: failing to link ideas across a passage, difficulty with causal inferences, excessive elaboration or overreliance on prior knowledge, problems with vocabulary, and problems with syntax. Using these categories, they designed a program of instruction for each student based on areas of need.

We do not necessarily advise you to construct such elaborate classifications of inference difficulties. However, if you decide to further analyze a student's answers, we suggest a simpler classification scheme than those just described. You can use question answer relationships (QARs) strategy as devised by Raphael (1982, 1986) and explained in Chapter 12. This strategy provides you with two pieces of information: a system for classifying students' answers and a procedure for teaching students how to locate answers to four different kinds of questions: right there questions, think and search questions, author and me questions, and on my own questions.

Combining IRI Assessment with Think-Alouds

Assessment does not need to involve special instruments such as word lists or IRI passages. You can learn much about students' reading abilities by reading any text with them and asking pertinent questions. When students meet an unfamiliar word, you can ask how they will go about pronouncing it. If the students pronounce the word correctly but do not know its meaning, you can probe to discover what strategies they use. In talking about a selection, you can ask the students how they arrived at answers to questions. You can ask them to explain what is in their minds at that point. Basically, you are asking students to stop at various points during reading and think out loud. The *think-aloud* process has been examined by a variety of researchers who agree that it offers an interesting opportunity to observe the thinking that occurs during reading (Pressley & Afflerbach, 1995).

The think-aloud approach works only if you know exactly what you are looking for. For example, Harmon (2000) listed a variety of strategies that students might use to determine the meaning of an unfamiliar word. They could examine sentence context or the distant context of the entire selection. They could make connections to events in the text, to text and language structures, to the author's style, or to ideas beyond the text. They could use word-level strategies, such as sounding out or structural analysis, the dictionary, or other outside sources. By asking students to think aloud when they met an unfamiliar word, Harmon was able to determine the strategies they used or ignored as they attempted to determine the meaning of unfamiliar words.

The think-aloud process can also be used to examine students' comprehension. Leslie and Caldwell (2005) identified several types of think-aloud comments that suggest understanding or lack of understanding on the part of the reader. They found that think-aloud comments indicating understanding were positively and strongly related to comprehension after reading.

Think-aloud statements that indicate understanding include:

- *Paraphrasing or summarizing.* The student retells the contents of the text in his or her own words.
- *Making new meaning.* The student draws an inference, reaches a conclusion, or engages in reasoning of some sort.
- *Questioning that indicates understanding.* The student asks a question, but the question clearly indicates that he or she understood the text. For example, the student may question a character's motives or ask if the content would apply to another situation.
- *Noting understanding.* The student indicates that he or she understood what was read.
- *Reporting prior knowledge.* The student indicates that he or she knew this information before reading or thought something different.
- *Identifying personally.* The student relates the text to personal experiences in some way, such as stating agreement or disagreement, like or dislike, interest or lack of interest.

Think-aloud statements that indicate lack of understanding include:

- *Questions that indicate lack of understanding.* The student's questions indicate that the student does not understand the text. For example, the student asks about the meaning of an unfamiliar word, phrase, or sentence.
- *Noting lack of understanding.* The student states that he or she is confused or does not understand the text.

Students exhibit a variety of think-aloud patterns. Some use one comment exclusively. For example, when Jared read a selection on clouds, every comment involved a paraphrase of the text content. Some students make a variety of comments. While reading the same cloud passage, Ryan offered several paraphrases, commented on what he knew and did not know about different cloud types, and reacted quite personally to clouds that signal the possibility of severe weather, tying it to some recent tornadoes in his state. Such diverse comments certainly suggest an extremely interactive reader.

How often should you stop to ask a student to think aloud? There are no set guidelines. The text should be long enough to present enough content to think about, but you shouldn't have to stop so often that the process becomes laborious. Because there are no definitive guidelines, experiment with different text segments. Of course, segments will vary in length with the age of the reader and level of the text.

You can set up the process in different ways. One way is to mark the text with stop signals: either the word *Stop* or a colored dot. The students read orally or silently, and when they reach the signal, they stop and think aloud. You can also read orally with the students in an assisted format and stop at points of your choosing. Another way is to ask the students to read silently and stop after each paragraph or at the end of each page. You can also read to the students and use think-aloud statements to evaluate the nature of their listening comprehension processes. All methods work; choose the one that works best for you and your students.

What are you looking for? You are looking for some evidence of interaction with the text. Too many readers have difficulty thinking aloud, which suggests a lack of active comprehension processing.

Contrast the following two students who both read an article on ancient Egypt (see pages 130–131) (Leslie & Caldwell, 2005).

Using the list of think-aloud statements as a guide, you can see that John's interaction with the text is limited and minimal compared to Brittany's. John could well profit from some of the strategies outlined in Chapters 11 and 12.

Text Segment 1

Brittany: They built pyramids to bury the pharaoh and they put them there with all their possessions because they would use them in the afterlife. *Summary/ paraphrase.* Do you think they put all the pharaohs in the same pyramid? What if he died before they finished building it? Where would he go? *Questions that signal understanding.*

John: They built pyramids and used them, like tombs, they used them and they buried the kings there. *Summary/paraphrase.*

Text Segment 2

Brittany: They mummified the kings to preserve their bodies. *Summary/paraphrase.* I know all about that! They wrap them up in bandages. I saw a movie where one came to life. *Reporting prior knowledge.*

John: They made the king a mummy. *Summary/paraphrase.* Why did they do that? It seems dumb. *Question that indicates lack of understanding because the text clearly indicates the rationale for mummification.*

Text Segment 3

Brittany: Yuk, this is really gross. *Identifying personally.* They took out all the organs except the heart, rubbed the body with stuff and wrapped it. *Summary/ paraphrase.* I wonder if they took out the brain. *Question that indicates understanding,* I would think the brains should have been left in so the pharaoh could think in his afterlife. But maybe they didn't know what the brain did. *Making new meaning.*

John: It took 70 days and they rubbed oil on the body and wrapped it up like a mummy. *Summary/paraphrase.*

Text Segment 4

> Brittany: Farmers helped to build the pyramids when they couldn't work in their fields and they weren't slaves. *Summary/paraphrase*. If they didn't use slaves to build the pyramids, I wonder how much they paid the farmers. *Question that indicates understanding*.
>
> John: Farmers helped to build the pyramids. *Summary/paraphrase*. What is this word? I can't pronounce it (points to *archaeologists*). *Noting lack of understanding*.

Text Segment 5

> Brittany: They dragged all the stones with ropes and it was dangerous and a lot died. *Summary/paraphrase*. I bet sometimes the stones fell and crushed them. If they were going up hill and the rope broke, that could wipe out a bunch of workers. *Making new meaning*.
>
> John: They cut stones and worked for 8 days. *Summary/paraphrase that actually contains an error; the text states the workers worked for 10 days in a row*.

Text Segment 6

> Brittany: They were paid with food, and they had to work fast in case the pharaoh would die. *Summary/paraphrase*. Why weren't they paid with money? *Question that indicates understanding*. I would rather have money so I could buy the food I wanted. *Identifying personally*. Maybe there weren't many stores back then. *Making new meaning*.
>
> John: Nothing really, just about food and working fast. *Summary/paraphrase*. Why did they have to be courageous? They were just building something. *Question that indicates lack of understanding; the text clearly outlines the dangers*.

Summary

Assessing reading achievement involves answering two questions: How severe is the student's reading problem? and What is the general area of the reading problem?

Informal measures have not been normed on large populations as have standardized formal measures. Therefore, they may be used more flexibly and may be adapted to the needs of the student and the demands of the diagnostic situation.

The informal reading inventory (IRI) consists of a series of graded reading selections. The student reads increasingly difficult material until a frustrational level is reached. IRIs measure both oral and silent reading. Three levels of reading are obtained: independent, instructional, and frustrational. These levels are based on the student's word recognition accuracy and ability to comprehend passages. Generally, separate passages are provided for oral and silent reading.

The IRI provides information about the existence and severity of a reading problem and its general area(s). Careful analysis of the IRI can suggest whether a student is having problems with word recognition accuracy, reading fluency, comprehension, language base and meaning vocabulary, or studying. Miscue analysis, the analysis of a student's oral reading deviations, allows the reading teacher to examine the strategies that a student uses to recognize words.

Special issues and options in using IRIs involve pronouncing words for students, alternating oral and silent passages, finding unclear results, using alternative miscue scoring procedures or norms, allowing students to look back for answers, levels of questions, using an IRI to assess student growth, and employing the think-aloud procedure.

References

Applegate, M. D., Quinn, K. B., & Applegate, A. J. (2002). Levels of thinking required by comprehension questions in informal reading inventories. *The Reading Teacher, 56*, 174–180.

Caldwell, J. (1985). A new look at the old informal reading inventory. *The Reading Teacher, 39*, 168–173.

Caldwell, J., Fromm, M., & O'Connor, V. (1997–1998). Designing an intervention for poor readers: Incorporating the best of all worlds. *Wisconsin State Reading Association Journal, 41*, 7–14.

Caldwell, J. & Leslie L. (2004/2005). Does proficiency in middle school reading assure proficiency in high school reading? The possible role of think-alouds. *Journal of Adolescent and Adult Literacy, 47*, 324–335.

Carver, R. B. (1990). *Reading Rate: A Review of Research and Theory.* San Diego, CA: Academic Press.

Ciardiello, A. V. (1998). Did you ask a good question today? Alternative cognitive and metacognitive strategies. *Journal of Adolescent and Adult Literacy, 42*, 210–219.

Dewitz, P., & Dewitz, P. K. (2003). They can read the words, but they can't understand: Refining comprehension assessment. *The Reading Teacher, 56*, 422–435.

Goodman, K. S. (1969). Analysis of oral reading miscues. *Reading Research Quarterly, 5*, 9–30.

Goodman, K. S. (1965). A linguistic study of cues and miscues in reading. *Elementary English, 42*, 639–643.

Goodman, K. S., & Gollasch, F. V. (1980–1981). Word omissions: Deliberate and non-deliberate. *Reading Research Quarterly, 14*, 6–31.

Goodman, Y. M. (1976). Miscues, errors and reading comprehension. In J. Merritt (Ed.), *New Horizons in Reading.* Newark, DE: International Reading Association.

Harmon, J. M. (2000). Assessing and supporting independent word learning strategies of middle school students. *Journal of Adolescent and Adult Literacy, 43*, 518–527.

Johnson, M. J., Kress, R. A., & Pikulski, J. L. (1987). *Informal Reading Inventories* (2nd ed.). Newark, DE: International Reading Association.

Kame'nui, E. J., & Simmons, D. (2001). Introduction to this special issue: The DNA of reading fluency. *Scientific Studies of Reading, 5*, 203–210.

LaBerge, D., & Samuels, S. M. (1974). Toward a theory of automatic information processing in reading. *Cognitive Psychology, 6*, 293–323.

Leslie, L. (1993). A developmental-interactive approach to reading assessment. *Reading and Writing Quarterly, 9*, 5–30.

Leslie, L., & Allen, L. (1999). Factors that predict success in an early literacy intervention project. *Reading Research Quarterly, 34*, 404–425.

Leslie, L., & Caldwell, J. (2005). *The Qualitative Reading Inventory IV.* New York: Longman.

Lipson, M. Y., Cox, C. H., Iwankowski, S., & Simon, M. (1984). Exploration of the interactive nature of reading: Using commercial IRI's to gain insights. *Reading Psychology: An International Quarterly, 5*, 209–218.

McKenna, M. C. (1983). Informal reading inventories: A review of the issues. *The Reading Teacher, 36*, 670–679.

National Reading Panel (2000). *Teaching Children to Read: An Evidence-Based Assessment of the Scientific Research Literature on Reading and the Implications for Reading Instruction.* Washington, DC: National Institute of Child Health and Human Development. Available at www.nichd.nih.gov/publications/nrp/smallbook.htm.

Pikulski, J. J., & Shanahan, T. (1982). Informal reading inventories: A critical analysis. In J. J. Pikulski & T. Shanahan (Eds.), *Approaches to the Informal Evaluation of Reading*, pp. 94–116. Newark, DE: International Reading Association.

Pressley, M., & Afflerbach, P. (1995). *Verbal Protocols of Reading: The Nature of Constructively Responsive Reading*. Mahwah, MJ: Erlbaum.

Raphael, T. E. (1986). Teaching question-answer relationships, revisited. *The Reading Teacher, 39*, 516–522.

Raphael, T. E. (1982). Question-answering strategies for children. *The Reading Teacher, 36*, 186–190.

Spache, G. D. (1981). *Diagnosing and Correcting Reading Disabilities*. Boston: Allyn and Bacon.

Stanovich, K. E. (1993–1994). Romance and reality. Distinguished educator series. *The Reading Teacher, 47*, 280–291.

Stanovich, K. E. (1991). Word recognition: Changing perspectives. In R. Barr, M. L. Kamil, P. Mosenthal, & P. D. Pearson (eds.), *Handbook of Reading Research* (Vol. II), pp. 418–452. New York: Longman.

Stanovich, K. E. (1986). Matthew effects in reading. Some consequences of individual differences in the acquisition of literacy. *Reading Research Quarterly, 21*, 360–406.

MyEducationLab is a research-based learning tool that brings teaching to life. Go to the Jennings, Caldwell, & Lerner 6th Edition MyEducationLab for Reading Assessment site at www.myeducationlab.com to:

◆ engage in multimedia exercises to help you build a deeper and more applied understanding of chapter content;

◆ utilize extensive resources including videos from real classrooms, Praxis and licensure preparation, a lesson plan builder, and materials to help you in your teaching career.

Providing Instructional Support for Struggling Readers

CHAPTER 6

Introduction

Effective Instruction for Struggling Readers

Early Intervention Programs

Reading Recovery
Early Steps
Reading Rescue
Howard Street Tutoring Model
Book Buddies
The Boulder Project
Early Intervention in Reading
First-Grade Group Intervention
Reading Club
The Anna Plan
Literacy Booster Groups
Cross-Age Tutoring

Intervention for Older Students

Third-Grade Intervention
The Memphis Comprehension Framework
Project Success
Sixth-Grade Reading Class
Intervention Within the Classroom
Cross-Age Tutoring
Literacy Tutoring for Adolescents
Readers' Workshop

Total School or Classroom Interventions

Success for All
Four Blocks Literacy Model
Fluency-Oriented Reading Program

Guidelines for Teaching Students Struggling with Literacy

Emphasize Reading
Teach Students the Strategies that Good Readers Use
Make Assessment an Ongoing Component of Instruction
Provide a Balanced Instructional Framework
Provide a Consistent Instructional Structure and Use Time Effectively
Provide Time for Word Study and Fluency Development
Include Writing as Part of the Lesson Structure
Keep the Size of the Group as Small as Possible
Coordinate Intervention Instruction and Classroom Instruction
Application of Common Intervention Elements to Program Design

Summary

134

Introduction

Some years ago, a woman moved to the country. Her previous house in a large city had a tiny front yard and the backyard was not much bigger. She was very excited about the prospect of planting a large garden at her new home. Because she knew little about gardening, her primary question was how to begin. She bought some books and magazines on gardening. She talked to her new friends in the country and visited their gardens. When she went to the garden centers, she asked a number of questions about what she should buy, where she should plant, and how she should care for each new shrub, flower, or vegetable. In short, she did what we all do when faced with a new endeavor. She drew on the knowledge and expertise of people who had already been successful. And how did the garden grow? There were some failures, but there were many more successes, and they were due in part to her reliance on the experience of others. In preparing to teach students who are struggling with reading, it makes good sense to draw on the wisdom of those who have been successful in doing this. For this reason, we begin the chapter with a description of effective programs for helping struggling readers. Then, using these as foundations, we describe general principles or guidelines for designing and implementing instruction to help children who find reading difficult.

Effective Instruction for Struggling Readers

In recent years, a shift has occurred in the philosophy underlying the instruction of struggling readers (Klenk & Kirby, 2000). This shift has led to the development of structured intervention programs, such as Reading Recovery (Pinnell, Deford, & Lyons, 1988) and Reading Rescue (Ehri, Dreyer, Flugman, & Gross, 2007). Formerly, the term remediation was used to describe the instruction of struggling readers suggesting that, just as a physician does, a remedy could be applied to an already existing condition (Walmsley & Allington, 2007; Johnston & Allington, 1991). Unfortunately, there was little evidence that remedial programs past second grade were effective (Walmsley & Allington, 2007; Pikulski, 1994). Longitudinal research that followed children from first through third grade painted a similarly dismal picture. Poor readers in first grade still tended to be poor readers in third grade (Lyon, 2003; Juel, 1988; Juel, Griffith, & Gough, 1986).

A more optimistic picture emerges when we examine present interventions such as Reading Recovery (Pinnell, Lyons, Deford, Bryk, & Seltzer, 1994), Reading Rescue (Ehri, et al., 2007), Early Steps (Santa & Hoien, 1999), and Early Intervention in Reading (Taylor, Short, Shearer & Frye, 2007; Taylor, Strait, & Medo, 1994). The Committee on the Prevention of Reading Difficulties in Young Children, established by the U.S. Department of Education, the U.S. Department of Health and Human Services, and the National Academy of Sciences identified "a common menu of materials, strategies and environments" to support children who are at risk for learning to read (Snow, Burns, & Griffin, 1998, p. 3). The committee concluded that most reading difficulties can be prevented with early, aggressive, and excellent instruction.

But what about older children whose difficulties have not been prevented and who have not learned to read effectively? Current reading intervention programs for older students focus on engaging them in the process of reading as opposed to past reliance on completing work sheets. Literacy "is the act of accessing and communicating knowledge itself" (Walmsley & Allington, 2007, p. 31) and successful programs concentrate on modeling and explaining the strategies that children must acquire in order to read "widely and deeply" (p. 31) a variety of fiction and nonfiction genres.

In the last 10 to 15 years, a variety of intervention programs have been shown to be effective in helping children learn to read (Biggam, Teitelbaum & Willey, 2007; Hall, Prevatte, & Cunningham, 2007; Knight & Stallings, 2007; Taylor, et al., 2007; Walp & Walmsley, 2007; Winfield, 2007; Santa & Hoien, 1999; Cunningham, Hall, & Defee, 1998; Hiebert, 1994; Taylor, et al., 1994; Hiebert, Colt, Catto, & Gury, 1992; Slavin, Madden, Karweit, Dolan, & Wasik, 1992; Taylor, Frye, Short, & Shearer, 1992; Slavin, Madden, Karweit, Livermon, & Dolan, 1990; Pinnell, 1989). These programs are very different. Some focus on individuals and others on groups. Some are pullout programs and others occur in the classroom. Some move far beyond an intervention program for struggling readers and include reform of the school-wide literacy curriculum, the redesign of classroom literacy activities, implementation of collaborative staff development, and a focus on high expectations for all students. However, despite these differences, common elements exist across all programs. Note these as you read the following descriptions of representative programs. Understanding these common elements will allow you to design and implement your own instruction for students who find learning to read difficult.

Classroom teachers should also pay attention to these common elements. In the past and, unfortunately, in all too many present-day schools, the primary responsibility for teaching struggling readers falls on personnel external to the classroom: reading teachers, reading specialists, and special education teachers. However, most children with special needs still spend most of their time in the regular classroom and it is important that they are supported effectively by their classroom teacher (Lerner & Johns, 2009). The education of children who find learning to read difficult is the responsibility of all educators.

Early Intervention Programs

Reading Recovery

A variety of intervention programs have been designed to focus on first and second graders. Perhaps the most influential program has been Reading Recovery (Lyons & Beaver, 2007; Pinnell, et al., 1994; Clay, 1993; Pinnell, 1989; Pinnell, et al., 1988). The Reading Recovery program provides one-half hour per day of intensive, individual tutoring for first graders who are in the lowest 20 percent of their class. Reading Recovery lessons have a very structured format. Each day, the teacher and student engage in the same basic activities. The student reads both easy familiar and unfamiliar books. The student dictates a sentence or short story. The teacher reads it and guides the child to accurately write it. The teacher then copies the message onto a sentence strip, cuts it into individual words, and asks the child to reassemble it. The teacher and child also work with manipulating letters and saying letter sounds. Throughout the lesson, the teacher fosters the development of strategies for identifying words and comprehending text. Students are taken through 20 levels of increasingly difficult predictable books, all within the first-grade level. Typically, students stay in the program for 12 to 16 weeks. At the end of this time, most can read as well as the average student in their class. The term Reading Recovery and the method are registered trademarks. Similar programs have been developed but with different names and slightly different instructional sequences.

Early Steps

Although Early Steps is quite similar to Reading Recovery, it contains more explicit attention to letter-sound matching (Santa & Hoien, 1999; Santa, Ford, Mickley, & Parker, 1997; Morris, Shaw, & Perney, 1990). The lessons are 30 minutes in length. The child spends at least half of the instructional time reading books at his or her instructional level, and the teacher gradually moves the child through increasingly challenging selections. In addition, the child rereads familiar books to develop fluency. Daily writing is part of the lesson and takes the form of the sentence strip activity used in Reading Recovery. The word study component involves word or letter sorts. The goal of this sorting activity is to foster awareness that words share common sounds and common spelling patterns. The sorts move from a focus on letters to consonant sounds, short vowel patterns, and finally to the long vowel patterns. Throughout the lesson, the teacher helps the child to become aware of strategies for identifying words. A comparison of the achievement of children who participated in Early Steps versus a control group indicated superior growth for the Early Steps children in spelling, word recognition, and passage reading (Santa & Hoien, 1999).

Reading Rescue

Reading Rescue (Ehri, et al., 2007) is an intervention program for low-SES language minority first graders. The lessons are 30 to 40 minutes in length. Students begin each lesson by rereading familiar books to increase accuracy, fluency, and expression. Using books presented in a previous lesson, they practice word analysis and comprehension strategies. Each lesson provides systematic phonics instruction and attention to phonemic awareness using analytic and synthetic approaches as well as decoding by analogy using key words. The teacher assists the students in writing one or more sentences about the books read in class. Introduction of a new book involves an opportunity to develop oral language; students talk about the book and learn the meanings of new words. They practice strategies for comprehension. The entire tutoring sequence gradually presents more difficult concepts and materials as students develop their skills. Children who participated in Reading Rescue made significantly greater gains in reading words and comprehending text than the control group. In addition, the majority reached average reading levels at the conclusion of the tutoring sessions.

Howard Street Tutoring Model

This is a model for volunteer tutors working with second and third graders under the supervision of a reading specialist (Brown, Morris & Fields, 2005; Morris, 2005). The lessons are 45 minutes in length and occur twice a week. The tutor begins by supporting the child in reading and understanding instructional level stories using echo reading, partner reading or independent reading depending upon the skill of the child. This takes approximately 18 minutes. For the next 10 minutes, the tutor develops understanding of basic spelling patterns using games and word categorization activities. Then the child reads easy or previously read books for 10 minutes in order to build sight vocabulary, fluency, and confidence. At the end of the session, the tutor reads to the child for approximately 7 minutes using quality literature that appeals to the child's interests. Tutored children performed significantly better than the control group on both standardized and informal reading measures and tutors proved to be almost as effective as certified teachers in providing instruction.

Book Buddies

This intervention also focuses on tutors (Invernizzi, Rosemary, Juel, & Richards, 1997; Invernizzi, Juel, & Rosemary, 1996–1997). Community volunteers work with individual at-risk first graders twice a week for 45 minutes. A reading coordinator supervises and supports the tutors, writes lesson plans, provides materials, and offers feedback on instructional techniques. The tutor follows a sequence of activities that involve rereading a familiar book, engaging in word study, writing, and reading a new book. The word study component involves word cards that are used to form a word bank of known words and word sorting. The child first sorts picture cards by beginning sounds and then moves to sorting word cards by beginning sounds, consonant blends, and short vowels. Writing generally takes the form of dictation by the tutor with the tutor elongating the sounds in words to help children match letters to the sounds they hear. Yearly pretest to posttest data on this program suggest that it is both effective and practical (Invernizzi, et al., 1996–1997).

The Boulder Project

The Boulder Project focuses on first graders in groups of three (Hiebert, 1994; Hiebert, et al., 1992). In a structured daily plan, the lesson begins with oral rereading of familiar books, both individually and as a group. The teacher reviews words from the previous day's lesson and introduces a new book. The teacher and students engage in word study based on the new selection. They participate in phonemic awareness activities such as rhyming. They locate words in the text and use them in new sentences. They write the words and transform them by changing letters and letter patterns, for example, changing stop to mop. As children write on chosen topics, the teacher guides them in letter-sound matching. Like Early Steps, the Boulder Project provides explicit instruction in letter patterns as a word identification strategy. The Boulder Project also provides children with take-home book bags and emphasizes at-home reading.

Early Intervention in Reading

Early Intervention in Reading (EIR) is taught almost entirely by the classroom teacher (Taylor, et al., 2007; Taylor, et al., 1994; Taylor, et al., 1992). Each day, the classroom teacher works with five to seven of the poorest readers for an additional 20 minutes of instruction. Lesson structure revolves around a 3-day cycle. The students read short retellings of text after the teacher reads the actual book to the students. The children repeatedly read this retelling across the 3 days, both as a group and individually. The teacher supports accurate word identification by suggesting and modeling contextual clues and strategies for matching letters and sounds. On the first day, the lesson focuses on phonetically regular words from the text. The children listen for sounds and choose letters to represent sounds. On the second and third days, the children, supported by the teacher, write sentences based on the story. Gradually, students shift to longer retellings, actual books, and initial reading done independently by students.

First-Grade Group Intervention

Hedrick and Pearish (1999) describe this first-grade group intervention as "fast-paced, tightly structured and balanced" (p. 716). Daily sessions last for 30 minutes. Groups of eight students are released from their classrooms during independent reading time. The lesson structure follows a consistent sequence. First, the teacher reads aloud for 2 minutes. Then, for 6 minutes, students focus on word study and phonics. They learn and review letters and sounds, use a word wall for high-frequency words, and remake words with magnetic letters. The next lesson component is shared reading. For 2 minutes, students read sentences from the story, pointing to individual words as they do so. The 10-minute guided reading segment includes the weekly introduction of a new book and repeated reading using various formats, such as choral reading. In shared writing, students sequence and read cut-up sentences for 2 minutes. In the 3-minute guided writing section, students move from copying to independent writing. In the final component, children read independently for 5 minutes in familiar texts supported and monitored by the teacher.

Reading Club

The Reading Club (Kreuger and Townshend, 1997) is a group intervention for both first and second graders. Daily 30-minute sessions are carefully structured to include phonics, rereading, work with sentence strips, and the introduction of new reading. What is interesting about this intervention is that different individuals teach each of these components. Kreuger and Townshend lacked adequate personnel to implement the program so they used retired educators, university students, and volunteers as coaches. Having coaches teach the same daily segment simplified the training and allowed the coaches to develop expertise and confidence in their coaching ability. This effective intervention suggests a novel way to employ and retain volunteers.

The Anna Plan

The Anna Plan (Miles, Stegle, Hubbs, Henk & Mallette, 2004) is an intervention for all first and second graders, not just those who are struggling with reading. A first or second grade teacher and his or her class join three reading specialists in the "reading room" for daily 25 minute instructional periods. Students are grouped according to instructional reading levels and the teacher and three specialists each teach a group. Students rotate across the teacher and specialists spending approximately 2 weeks with each one before moving on. Students also move into and out of groups based on their progress. At midyear, kindergarten children move into the program and second graders are discontinued. Like previously described programs, the Anna Plan involves a consistent structure. On day 1, the teacher introduces a new book and the students softly read aloud at their own pace. They then discuss their performance and the book's contents. The second day focuses on reading comprehension strategies, includes a language minilesson, and involves rereading of the book introduced on the first day. Day 3 emphasizes working with words using a variety of different activities. On the fourth day, the students write in their journals aided by teacher modeling and minilessons. On day 5, one of the specialists takes over the classroom so the teacher and remaining specialists can engage in collaborative planning.

Literacy Booster Groups

Mackenzie (2001) formed Literacy Booster Groups to review and apply strategies learned in Reading Recovery. Small groups of first and second graders meet weekly. Two teachers work with the students in 30- to 45-minute sessions. In the first part of the lesson, the teacher helps the students choose four books to read during the week. While students write in their journals or read independently, the teachers meet with individuals to check their oral reading proficiency. The teachers then present a mini-lesson based on the needs of the group. Finally, the teachers support the students in practicing the minilesson strategy.

Cross-Age Tutoring

Taylor, Hanson, Justice-Swanson, and Watts (1997) designed a cross-age tutoring program for second-grade struggling readers. The children participate in a 7-week intervention class that meets daily for 45 minutes. The first 30 minutes involve activities rotated according to a 3-day cycle. On the first day, the teacher reads a selection aloud. The students participate in choral reading and discuss the selection. On the second day, the students read chorally and with a partner. They write sentences prompted by the teacher. More independent reading, partner reading, and sentence writing occur on the third day. For the last 15 minutes of the class, the teacher focuses on a variety of language-development activities, such as researching seasonal activities.

Go to MyEducationLab and select the topic *Intervention Programs*. Then, go to the Activities and Applications section, watch the video entitled "Extra Tutoring," and respond to the accompanying questions.

On 2 days, the second graders participate in a cross-age tutoring program. Fourth-grade struggling readers are their tutors. The tutors listen to the second graders read, coach them in word recognition, and read stories to them. The program for tutors also involves an entire week of activities. They spend 2 days preparing for the tutoring session, 2 days tutoring, and a day writing about their experience. Block and Dellamura (2000–2001) also promote the effectiveness of cross-age tutoring and offer numerous practical suggestions for implementation.

Intervention for Older Students

Third-Grade Intervention

The design of this intervention (McCormack, Paratore & Dahlene, 2004; McCormack & Paratore, 1999) questions the commonly held assumption that struggling readers should be taught using independent or instructional level text. Such text may allow students to read words with relative ease but it "may bar access to concepts and ideas otherwise acquired by reading grade-appropriate text" (McCormack, et al., 2004, p. 119). In other words, reliance on instructional-level text may not foster acquisition of the concepts, vocabulary, and syntactical structures needed for success in later grades. In this intervention, students read their regular classroom texts and, when they return to the classroom, they are "reintegrated into ongoing literacy instruction" as full participants (p. 123). The hour-long instruction involves the review and retelling of previously read material. The teacher introduces essential vocabulary and the students engage in word study by practicing sight words and reviewing strategies for successful decoding. The teacher and students then preview the new selection and the teacher reads it aloud using think-alouds to model comprehension strategies. The teacher and students discuss the new text and reread it several times using a variety of oral reading strategies. The intervention also includes self-selected reading on the part of the students. After approximately a year of instruction, a majority of the students performed at grade level on several assessment measures. The substitution of teacher read-alouds and student rereading for reliance on instructional level text proved to be a powerful and effective tool.

The Memphis Comprehension Framework

This purpose of this model is to improve the comprehension of expository text for middle school students (Flynt & Cooter, 2005). After assessing students' needs, the teacher chooses a comprehension skill objective to focus on for a minimum of 3 weeks. The teacher reads aloud daily for at least 10 to 15 minutes for the purpose of expanding the students' listening and speaking vocabularies. The teacher initiates active discussion of the text. Throughout the discussion, the teacher models the chosen comprehension strategy, uses graphic organizers, asks key questions, and calls attention to new vocabulary. The final step in the lesson develops students' abilities in three forms of retelling: guided oral retelling, graphic organizer retelling and written retelling. In guided oral retelling, students simply retell the text. In graphic organizer retelling, the students construct a graphic organizer. In written retelling, they use the graphic organizer as a tool for completing a written summary.

Project Success

Project Success (Cooper, 1997) is a group intervention program that emphasizes expository text. Students participate in daily lessons of approximately 45 minutes in length. The students begin by silently reading a familiar book or orally reading it with a partner. The students then discuss and review the previous day's reading by constructing a graphic organizer to illustrate the interrelationships of the ideas in the text. Before reading a new book, the teacher guides the students through prereading strategies, such as previewing the text, predicting the content, and raising questions. The students then read the text silently. Afterward, the teacher and students engage in reciprocal teaching; that is, they take turns in assuming the role of the teacher and guiding the other students through the strategies of summarizing, questioning, clarifying, and predicting. The students then complete a written response and reflect on the strategies learned and implemented during the lesson.

Sixth-Grade Reading Class

Ahrens (2005) implemented a structure for sixth-grade reading classes that grouped students according to instructional level. Students reading at or above level formed one class; those reading below level formed another. In all cases, instruction was similar with one exception. The below-level readers received approximately 10 minutes of daily instruction in systematic phonics. Both classes began with 20 to 30 minutes of independent reading of self-selected books. Following this, one student presented a 5-minute book talk. Both classes participated in spelling instruction that centered on morphemes and syllabication as opposed to memorization. Comprehension instruction focused on a single comprehension strategy for at least 2 to 3 weeks.

Intervention Within the Classroom

Short, Kane, and Peeling (2000) describe a third-grade intervention that is a regular part of the daily classroom literacy block. The teacher meets with a group of struggling readers daily for 25 minutes while other students listen to taped books, write, work on making words, or read alone or with a partner. The teacher and students follow a consistent sequence of activities. First, students reread a previously read selection. The next component is shared and guided reading, which takes about 15 minutes. The children again reread familiar text. Next the teacher introduces a new book at their instructional level. The children read the first page silently and then aloud. The teacher supports them by reinforcing cues for word identification and comprehension. Then the students read independently while the teacher works with an individual student. In the 10-minute shared writing segment, the teacher writes a sentence or several sentences about the story on chart paper and students provide input on letters, word chunks, and punctuation. The students transfer the sentence to their journals and reread the sentences pointing to each word.

Cross-Age Tutoring

Jacobson, Thrope, Fisher, Lapp, Frey, and Flood (2001) designed a cross-age tutoring program for seventh- and third-grade struggling readers. On Day 1, the teacher introduces and models the lesson that the seventh-grade tutors will use with their tutees. On the second day, the tutors form pairs and practice reading the selection and learning the meaning of five difficult words. On the next 2 days, the tutors teach the lesson to two third-grade students. On the last day, the tutors discuss the successes and challenges of the lesson and what they could do differently. As the year progressed, tutors actually began to devise their own lessons with the assistance of the teacher.

Paterson and Elliott (2006) designed a cross-age tutoring program for ninth and tenth-grade struggling readers. Their primary purpose was to improve "the attitudinal barriers of the older student by placing them in a leadership role as tutors for younger children thus implying high academic status and competence" (p. 379). The tutees were struggling second- and third-grade readers. Prior to the tutoring session, students practiced expressive reading of the books they would share. They learned some basic strategies for tutoring reading and received a lesson plan to follow involving phonics, context clues, sight words, paired and echo reading, and comprehension strategies such as prediction, questioning, and summarizing.

Similarly, Caserta-Hemy (1996) describes a successful cross-age tutoring program involving high school students and struggling first graders. Called Reading Buddies, tutors and tutees met daily for 15 minutes. Tutoring involves four basic activities: rereading an easy and predictable book each week, rereading a familiar book from the previous week, journal writing, and word study activities. The tutors receive initial and ongoing training throughout the 7-month duration of the program.

Literacy Tutoring for Adolescents

Chandler-Olcott and Hinchman (2005) suggest a framework for adolescent tutoring sessions. They believe that tutoring sessions "are most effective when sessions have a consistent structure and when tutors model the use and enjoyment of reading and writing strategies at each session" (p. 59). They recommend four different approaches to include within a single 40-minute session. This differentiation allows tutors to help their student in different ways. The first approach involves the tutor reading aloud and thinking aloud with a focus on one or two strategies. The second approach is guided practice in the strategy previously modeled by the teacher. The third approach is student engagement in independent reading or writing. The session closes with a 5-minute oral or written reflection by the student describing what was learned and what is still not understood.

Readers' Workshop

Williams (2001) adapted the readers' workshop model (Atwell, 1998) for groups of seven to eight adolescent struggling readers who meet daily. For 2 days a week, Williams uses a traditional reading workshop format. The teacher reads aloud to the students for 10 to 15 minutes, often employing a think-aloud strategy. An 8- to 10-minute minilesson focuses on strategy instruction and involves the following components: a statement of what the strategy is and why it is important; teacher modeling; group or partner practice; and reminders to use the strategy during silent reading time. Students then read silently in self-selected texts for approximately 15 minutes. Afterwards, they share what they read or what they learned. For the other 3 days, Williams structures the lessons around peer-assisted learning strategies. Student partners read and help each other with word identification and retelling. They construct short statements about the main idea and summarize each paragraph. The students predict what will come next in the text and read to check the accuracy of their predictions.

Go to MyEducationLab and select the topic *Comprehension*. Then, go to the Activities and Applications section, watch the video entitled "Think Aloud Strategy," and respond to the accompanying questions.

Taylor and Nesheim (2000–2001) used children's literature in an innovative application of the readers' workshop model with adolescents. Their goals were to present children's literature as enjoyable for readers of all ages and to provide motivation for reading children's literature. They modeled techniques for sharing reading and promoted reading as a valued activity. Minilessons focused on a variety of topics: print conventions, procedures for small group sharing, comprehension strategies, strategies for reading aloud, and techniques for fostering reader response.

Total School or Classroom Interventions

Success for All

Success for All (Borman, Slavin, Cheung, Chamberlain, Madden & Chambers, 2007; Slavin, et al., 1992, 1994; Slavin, et al., 1990) is a total school reform program. Originally implemented in low socioeconomic inner-city schools, the program has expanded to schools in suburban and rural areas. Students are grouped for reading instruction according to their reading levels. Children who are having difficulty are individually tutored in the afternoon for about 20 minutes. This tutoring is closely coordinated with the morning lessons, and whenever possible, the classroom teacher is also the child's tutor.

The tutoring session begins with oral reading of a familiar story from previous tutoring or from class instruction. A 1-minute drill of the letter sounds presented in the morning session follows this activity. The teacher and the student engage in shared oral reading. Phonetically controlled words are printed in large type, and all other words are printed in small type. The child reads the large type, and the teacher provides support by reading the small type. The teacher and student discuss the story, and the child rereads it, supported as necessary by the teacher. Like other intervention programs that have been described, a writing component is included.

Four Blocks Literacy Model

The Four Blocks Literacy Model (Hall, et al., 2007; Cunningham, Hall, & Defee, 1991, 1998) was not originally designed as an intervention program, but its success in preventing reading failure warrants its inclusion in this chapter. The focus of the project is first and second grade, but its success has prompted implementation in third grade and above. Classroom instruction is organized into four 30-minute blocks.

In the guided reading block, the teacher introduces heterogeneously grouped children to a wide array of literature selections and emphasizes comprehension instruction. The teacher models prereading strategies, guides class discussion, and supports the children in completing story maps or webs. The text is a basal anthology or multiple copies of trade books. The children read orally or silently. They read alone, with a partner, in a small group, or as an entire class.

In the self-selected reading block, students choose their own reading materials. In this block, the teacher may also read to the students. A successful self-selected reading block requires an extensive classroom library consisting of a wide variety of reading levels, genres, and topics. While most children read independently, the teacher uses the opportunity to meet with individual children.

Go to MyEducationLab and select the topic *Reading and Writing Connections*. Then, go to the Activities and Applications section, watch the video entitled "Writing Workshop Mini-Lesson in 2nd Grade," and respond to the accompanying questions.

The format of the writing block is a writers' workshop (Routman, 1995). It consists of short minilessons in which the teacher explicitly models the writing process by thinking aloud and writing in full view of the students. The children then write independently.

The working-with-words block is divided into two activities: a word wall and making words. The word wall is a display of high-frequency words arranged in alphabetical columns. The teacher reviews words written on the word wall each day and adds new words. The teacher then directs the children through the activity of making words by moving letter tiles.

Data across approximately 6 years of instruction using the Four Blocks model has demonstrated its success. The authors report that 58 to 64 percent of first-grade Winston-Salem children read above grade level at the end of the year, 22 to 28 percent read on level, and only 10 to 17 percent read below (Cunningham, et al., 1998). At the end of second grade, results improved even further.

Fluency-Oriented Reading Program

The Fluency-Oriented Reading Program (FORI) was originally designed to improve second-grade reading achievement in heterogeneous classrooms by modifying instruction modified to foster the development of reading fluency (Kuhn, Schwanenflugel, Morris, Morrow, Woo, et al., 2006; Stahl & Heubach, 2005; Stahl, Heubach, & Cramond, 1997; Stahl & Heubach, 1993).

In the lesson structure, the teacher reads the story to the class and guides discussion. Because the story is read to students, below-level readers are able to participate in discussion. Students then reread the story up to five times before the teacher moves to another selection. These repeated readings include echo reading, reading with partners, and practicing favorite parts of the story to perform. Some selections are dramatized, with individual students or small groups taking different parts. Children also take books home and share them with parents. Every day, students also read books of their choice and keep a reading log.

At the end of the year, the average gain of students in this program was 1.88 grade levels. Students at all levels of reading made substantial advances. These results meant that students beginning on grade level were now reading almost 2 years above level, and students in preprimer and primer text were now close to grade-level reading. The program showed similar success during a second year with other students. Additional research continues to demonstrate the success of FORI (Kuhn, et al., 2006; Stahl & Heubach, 2005).

Guidelines for Teaching Students Struggling with Literacy

Because students with reading problems are already behind their peers, instructional time is precious. What form should this instruction take? The intervention programs described are different, yet they all exhibit certain similarities that allow teachers to formulate some key guidelines for teaching students who struggle with literacy (Caldwell & Leslie, 2009; Horowitz, 2000; Duffy-Hester, 1999).

Emphasize Reading

A crucial component of successful literacy intervention is that students read, read, and read some more. All of the previously described interventions involved an emphasis on reading as opposed to filling out worksheets and engaging in "skill-and-drill" activities.

Why is reading important? Readers learn by doing and students must actually read if they are to learn to read well. Compare learning to read with learning to drive, skateboard, or swim. Some of you have taken swimming lessons that required you to sit at the side of a pool doing exercises for breathing, kicking, and arm strokes—yet learning these isolated skills did not make you swimmers. You became swimmers only after you learned to apply these skills as you were swimming. In the same way, students can learn to read only by applying what they learn about reading as they are actually reading a story or book. Perhaps the most important way to foster student reading is to structure lessons around reading. Teachers should read to their students and with their students and they should schedule time for students to read independently.

Reading to Students. Let's first consider teachers reading to their students. Reading to students allows students to enjoy text that they might not be able to handle independently. Reading to students is a powerful strategy for developing new concepts and grappling with unfamiliar syntactic structures. Teachers can use reading aloud to demonstrate effective comprehension strategies and students can practice these strategies during listening as well as reading. In the Third-Grade Intervention (McCormack, et al., 2004; McCormack & Paratore, 1999), teachers read classroom textbooks to the students and teach them a variety of strategies for understanding text. Many suggest following this example whenever possible. Because they cannot read these texts independently and because they often miss classroom instruction during pull-out support services, struggling readers tend to experience "curricular fragmentation" and lack "access to the rich core curriculum all children should experience" (Allington & Walmsley, 2007, pp 29–30). Reading to students is also a key component of the Memphis Comprehension Framework (Flynt & Cooter, 2005).

Reading aloud to students is a powerful tool that fosters higher level comprehension processes. It is an effective vehicle for teacher modeling of the strategies that are employed by good readers. Discussion during and after reading aloud can challenge struggling readers to higher levels of thought and encourage them to become active learners (Lane & Wright, 2007). The teacher can use open-ended questions to expand listening and speaking vocabulary and elicit greater language production on the part of the students (Beck & McKeown, 2001). Open-ended questions can also lead students to draw inferences, connect the selection to their own lives, and examine the meaning of unfamiliar words.

McGee and Schickedanz (2007) suggest reading a selection three times. At the first read-aloud, the teacher introduces the book and reads using expressive voice intonation. At the second reading, the teacher stops, asks analytic questions, models acceptable answers, and gradually draws the students into the discussion. During the second reading, the teacher can also model comprehension strategies. At the third read-aloud, the teacher only reads selected parts of the text and the students retell, reconstruct, and practice the targeted strategy.

Consider one caveat in regard to reading aloud: Use this practice primarily for text that students cannot read independently. In other words, do not do the students' work for them. If they can handle text on their own, let them. Only by reading can students truly learn to read. Many find that following a teacher read-aloud with practice in text at students' independent or instructional levels works very well.

Reading with Students. Reading with students involves using a shared reading format that supports students and ensures their success. The teacher and student can read together chorally. The teacher can read to students, and they can then reread the same text, either orally or silently. The teacher and a single student can read orally while other students listen and wait their turns. This approach is much more effective than the traditional round-robin reading, where students were expected to orally read alone and in front of their peers. Reading with students allows the teacher to model fluent and expressive reading. The teacher can also model the process of thinking during reading by stopping at certain parts and talking about the content.

Reading by Students.   Reading intervention should include both oral and silent reading on the part of the students. At different times, both of these modes are appropriate. Through silent reading, students gain control of the reading process and can pace themselves, review material, and deepen personal reactions to literature. Oral reading activities are useful for increasing fluency and comfort as well as providing an avenue for sharing text (McCormick, 1999). Beginning readers in particular are most comfortable reading orally.

Teachers need to monitor oral reading wisely. Experts strongly suggest that students should not read orally in the presence of their peers unless they have first practiced the selection. A stumbling and hesitant performance filled with miscues does not help either the reader or the listener. The reader is all too conscious of his or her limitations, and the listeners are often bored or confused. If students are orally reading a selection for the first time, employ choral reading or limit such reading to individual sessions with you. Oral reading done in the presence of peers should always be practiced or rehearsed.

Go to MyEducationLab and select the topic *Informal Assessment*. Then, go to the Activities and Applications section, watch the video entitled "Engaging in Reading," and respond to the accompanying questions.

Teachers should exercise caution when correcting miscues during oral reading. To encourage independence, teachers should limit interruptions for all students. If mistakes do not affect meaning, do not stop students. When you do interrupt, encourage students to monitor meaning and figure out words for themselves. In addition, insist that other group members not interrupt readers by calling out words. The student who is reading needs time to figure out words independently. If the student wants assistance, he or she may hold up a finger to indicate "help me." Of course, these guidelines for oral reading must be used sensibly. The teacher should assist students when they can read no further or have lost the meaning of the material.

A primary guideline for choosing text for struggling readers to read is that they should be able to handle it successfully. The text either represents an independent or instructional reading level or the teacher provides enough support that students experience success. Almost all of the described programs employ rereading familiar text and/or careful preparation for reading new selections. If children are exposed to above-level text, a variety of adaptations are used to make the text meaningful to them such as teacher read-alouds coupled with different repeated reading formats.

Encourage students to read selections several times. Rereading is a common practice in successful interventions. Repeated readings of a story or chapter improve both word recognition and comprehension (Dowhower, 1999; Samuels, 1997; Stahl & Heubach, 1993) and contribute to a sense of comfort (Gillet & Temple, 2000). Students also enjoy rehearsing material for choral reading and performing plays.

Students Reading Independently. To establish permanent reading habits, students need to read when they are not under direct supervision. Many schools and classrooms reserve 15 to 20 minutes per day when everyone in the school reads. These reading times are often called SSR (sustained silent reading) or DEAR (drop everything and read). In addition to reading in school, students need to form the habit of reading at home.

How can teachers encourage struggling readers to read? Getting students with problems to do extensive reading is a challenging task. Stanovich (1986) describes a negative cycle called the *Matthew effect*. The cycle begins when students who are not skilled readers avoid reading. Then, because they have not practiced reading, they become less skilled. In turn, because they are less skilled, they tend to further avoid reading, and so on. This pattern continues until, tragically, the students are doing almost no reading.

Teachers need to prevent the Matthew effect. Their most important job is fostering the desire to read so that students will, ultimately, make learning to read a self-sustaining process. Effective reading interventions include time for students to read as a group and individually. There are many ways to encourage students with problems to read.

Have students share their reading experiences. When students feel that others take an interest in their responses, they are more likely to read. Ganske, Monroe, and Strickland (2003) suggest that "real discussions (as opposed to the traditional teacher-ask-student-respond formula) can stimulate students' interest and involvement and enhance their understanding" (p. 124). Allington (2001) describes such sharing and discussion as the practice of thoughtful literacy.

Students with reading problems often have difficulty choosing appropriate books for independent reading. When helping students choose books, the teacher should guide them to select materials at their independent level, which is an easier level than the instructional level often used for lessons. However, reading level is not an absolute guide. Readers' backgrounds or interests can often motivate them to handle difficult material. Joshua, a star high school athlete, was able to read only fifth-grade materials unless the subject was basketball. On this topic, he could read advanced newspaper and magazine articles with greater understanding than his teacher.

Many struggling readers do not know how to browse as a way of locating something to read. Have students look at the cover, the length, and the size of the print. They can read the summaries on the back cover and ask opinions of friends who have read the book. They can read a few pages and see if it is manageable or interesting. In short, teach students to do what you do so naturally in the library or bookstore. Some students find the five-finger rule helpful. Students read one page of a book and use one finger to count each unfamiliar word. If they count past five before the end of the page, they should choose another book.

Teachers can also give short book talks that briefly describe the book. In a book talk, the teacher holds up a book and describes it in an enticing way. Next, the teacher chooses an exciting part and reads it to the students. The reading should take no more than 5 minutes, and the excerpt should be from the first third of the book. Try to choose a reading that will keep your students in suspense so they will want to read the book. The teacher should have copies of the book available after the book talk so that students can read the book for themselves.

In their efforts to match materials to students' reading levels, teachers sometimes offer reading materials intended for younger students to older students who are struggling with grade-level materials. These should be selected judiciously so that older students are not insulted by content or illustrations that are too childish. Reading does not have to be limited to books or materials provided by the school. Valuable reading and study strategies can be learned from real-life materials such as *TV Guide*, newspaper articles, baseball and football programs, popular magazines, manuals, picture captions, magazines, advertisements, and travel brochures. Using these materials demonstrates to students that reading is directly connected to their lives.

Choose materials that are interesting and personally meaningful to the students. Explore many different types of reading materials. The Internet is a wonderful source for finding reading material. A student at the reading center was fascinated with the Civil War. In particular, he wanted to know more about a Massachusetts brigade of African Americans who fought for the North. History texts mentioned the brigade but very briefly. His teacher searched the Internet and found several accounts of the brigade's activities. Needless to say, she totally captured the interest of her student as she used the text to teach comprehension strategies.

Teach Students the Strategies that Good Readers Use

A second important principle is to teach struggling readers to understand and practice the strategies of successful readers. Pressley and Afflerbach (1995) provide a comprehensive description of what good readers do as they read and comprehend text. All of the intervention programs described emphasized the reading process, in one way or another, by teaching students strategies used by successful readers. For example, Reading Recovery focuses on showing students how the semantic, syntactic, and phonological clue systems interact to aid word pronunciation. Early Steps and the Boulder Project direct the student's attention to word patterns. Project Success exposes students to the strategies of summarizing, clarifying, questioning, and predicting. In the Four Blocks literacy model, the teacher writes in front of the students and thinks aloud as he or she models the composition process.

Struggling readers must understand that the only purpose for reading is to make meaning. They must develop strategies for comprehending, for identifying unfamiliar words, and for monitoring their own comprehension. The teacher designs and implements instruction that teaches students how to read as they are actively reading. Strategy instruction thus occurs within the context of a real reading situation. It focuses on powerful thinking strategies and encourages students to use multiple approaches for identifying words and comprehending and remembering text. The teacher models the thinking process, provides the support needed to accomplish complex tasks, and makes dialogue "the central medium for teaching and learning" (Johannessen, 2004, p. 639). In short, the teacher guides students to internalize what good readers do when they meet an unfamiliar word or encounter text that is difficult to understand.

The basic activity in strategy instruction is thinking aloud "a technique in which students verbalize their thoughts as they read and thus bring into the open the strategies they are using to understand the text" (Oster, 2001, p. 64). The teacher models the process and initiates students into the practice of talking about what they read and how they read it. Thinking aloud can involve both describing a strategy and commenting about the content of the text.

Do not confuse the term strategy with a specific instructional technique that a teacher might use, such as grouping students, setting up classroom learning centers, or designing thematic units. Strategies here are about methods used by readers to comprehend and remember text. Strategies include paraphrasing, summarizing, predicting, drawing on background knowledge, inferring, determining importance, and using known words to figure out unknown ones. The term *strategy* refers to what the successful reader does as he or she reads. Strategy instruction teaches a student to think in a certain way and to apply this thinking to a variety of reading materials. Allington (2001) suggests that the following strategies provide rich opportunities to enhance students' comprehension: activating prior knowledge, summarizing, using story structure, fostering visual imagery, generating questions, and thinking aloud.

Various books and journal articles have documented the effectiveness of strategy instruction and an awareness of its importance for all students (Almasi, 2003; Barton & Sawyer, 2003; Block & Pressley, 2002; Worthy, Broaddus & Ivey, 2001; Harvey & Goudvis, 2000; Gaskins, 1998; Keene & Zimmerman, 1997). Taylor, Peterson, Pearson, and Rodriguez (2002) examined effective reading instruction and concluded that "a shift in certain teaching practices, such as higher-level questioning, style of interacting, and encouraging active pupil involvement, may be warranted" (p. 275). Sadly, such instruction is not prevalent in classrooms (Pressley, Symons, Snyder, and Cariglia-Bull, 1989). Pressley (2002) suggests that although "a good case can be made for teaching comprehension strategies" (p. 23), it does not seem to be a common practice in schools. Dougherty Stahl (2004) also noted limited use by primary teachers. Although designing effective strategy instruction is a challenging and time-consuming endeavor, it is crucial for struggling readers.

All phases of learning a strategy include talking about thinking. Basically, the teacher thinks aloud, shares his or her thoughts with students, and encourages them to do the same. Thinking is made public through discussion, teacher modeling, and practice. Paris, Lipson, and Wixson (1983) describe three types of strategy knowledge, that readers must acquire: declarative knowledge, procedural knowledge, and conditional knowledge. Declarative knowledge is knowing what a specific strategy is and why it is important. Procedural knowledge is knowing how to apply it and conditional knowledge is knowing when strategy application is appropriate.

Go to MyEducationLab and select the topic *Emergent Literacy*. Then, go to the Activities and Applications section, watch the video entitled "Guided Reading," and respond to the accompanying questions.

The popular practice of Guided Reading (Fountas & Pinnell, 1996) is an example of strategy instruction. Using text that the students can read with support, the teacher works with a small group to develop strategies "on the run" (p. 2). The ultimate goal is for students to learn how to use strategies independently and successfully in increasingly difficult text. To accomplish this goal, the teacher guides the readers in learning and using strategies for identifying unfamiliar words, dealing with confusing sentence structures, and understanding new or difficult concepts. Massengill (2004) effectively used this basic framework to teach low-literate adults.

Massey (2003) suggests the following sequence for strategy instruction. First, construct a checklist of prereading, during reading, and postreading strategies. Massey categorizes predicting content and thinking about prior knowledge as pre-reading strategies. She describes rereading, visualizing, and summarizing as during-reading strategies and checking previous predictions and developing questions as postreading strategies. After assessing a student's needs, choose one or two strategies to develop. Model the strategy several times and encourage the students to actively participate in thinking aloud. Have the students read independently and identify the strategies they used. Discuss strategy use, using the checklist as a guide.

Dowhower (1999) suggests a simple framework for strategy instruction. The framework includes three phases: prereading, active reading, and postreading. The activities in the prereading phase include eliciting prior knowledge, building back-ground, and focusing on the strategy: what it is and why it is important. The active reading phase includes reading the text in small sections. For each section, students set a purpose for reading, read, and do what Dowhower calls "working the story" (p. 673). Working the story involves discussing the effectiveness and use of the strat-egy as well as focusing on understanding the text content. The postreading phase includes a variety of independent extension activities.

A possible extension activity is to ask students to demonstrate their understand-ing of a strategy by preparing think cards (Caldwell, 1990). In this activity, students write their own understandings of a strategy on an index card, which they keep with them when they practice the strategy. The card enables students to record the features of a strategy that are most useful for them. Because a think card is the student's own creation, it is an important step in transferring control of strategic reading from the teacher to the student. In making a think card, students demonstrate how they use a strategy. Think cards are useful in many types of strategy instruction. Chapter 8 dis-cusses using them for word recognition strategies. A sample of Trina's think card for independent reading is shown in Figure 6.1. After Trina prepared her think card, she referred to it whenever she chose a book or read one independently. At first, this prac-tice took place under the direction of a teacher. Later, however, Trina was able to practice her strategies independently, using her think card to guide her. Chapters 8 through 12 include examples of various strategies and how to implement them in the intervention session.

Make Assessment an Ongoing Component of Instruction

Many of the described programs move students through increasingly difficult levels of text. In addition, they gradually expose students to more complex instructional activ-

FIGURE 6.1   Example of Trina's Think Card Strategy

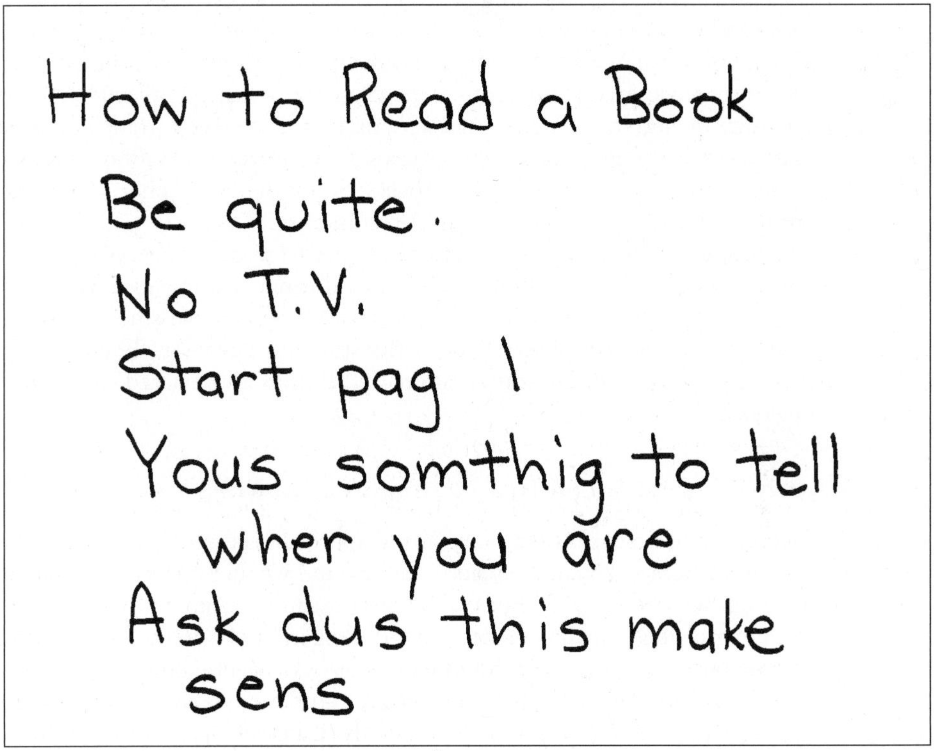

How to Read a Book
Be quite.
No T.V.
Start pag 1
Yous somthig to tell
     wher you are
Ask dus this make
   sens

ities. Assessment that occurs concurrently with instruction allows a teacher to know when to repeat a lesson and when to move on.

How does such assessment work? The teacher continually observes the student and carefully monitors what the student says and does. The teacher then uses these observations to make adjustments in instruction. If the new reading selection is too difficult, the teacher immediately substitutes a more appropriate one. If a student does not seem to understand how to sort word cards based on a specific letter-sound pattern, the teacher may amend the activity to provide more guidance, shorten it, or drop it altogether. During discussion of a story, the teacher's responses are based on what the student says. The teacher may offer a simple affirmation, provide guidance in the form of a leading question or comment, or offer specific suggestions for rereading or using a strategy. The lesson then is shaped by the assessment that occurs within it.

Perhaps an analogy will help. Consider driving home. Your ongoing assessment of traffic conditions shapes the route you will take, the lane you will stay in, and the speed you will maintain. Because of excess traffic, you may decide to move off the freeway. A detour may force you to leave the freeway. Flashing lights and an accident may prompt slower speeds. A slow-moving truck may motivate you to change lanes. In a similar way, your ongoing assessment of students shapes your instruction and acts as a catalyst for change.

This form of assessment does not result in typical forms of grading such as a letter or percent grade. Interaction between the teacher and student is the heart of instruction, and the students may seldom, if ever, receive a graded paper. If they have written something or constructed a graphic organizer, evaluation comments generally occur as they are engaged in the process. Similarly, the teacher offers praise and suggestions during the actual process of reading.

The teacher may use a variety of informal assessment methods, such as taking a running record, administering an informal reading inventory, or asking students to read a list of words. However, the heart of assessment is the lesson itself, coupled with careful observation of the student's behavior. The teacher keeps careful records of his or her observations by writing abbreviated notes throughout the lesson.

Provide a Balanced Instructional Framework

According to Spiegel (1998), a balanced approach is built on a comprehensive view of literacy. Literacy is viewed as both reading and writing. Word identification is part of reading but not the whole of it. Deriving meaning from reading and clearly writing meaningful ideas are key components. Fitzgerald (1999) looks at balance from the perspective of knowledge. Children need to learn several kinds of knowledge for reading: local knowledge, global knowledge, and affective knowledge. Local knowledge includes phonological awareness, sight-word knowledge, word-identification strategies, and understanding of word meanings. Global knowledge includes "understanding, interpretation, and response to reading; strategies for enabling understanding and response; and an awareness of strategic use" (p. 102). Affective knowledge is quite simply a love of reading.

All three forms of knowledge are equally important for struggling readers, and all should be addressed. In the past, intervention for struggling readers tended to concentrate on local knowledge. Some students received a steady diet of phonics worksheets and never read a whole piece of text! The successful interventions described in this chapter address local, global, and affective knowledge. Students learned about letter and sound correspondences as they sorted and transformed words and built word banks. Students learned strategies for understanding and remembering text. For example, Project Success emphasized the graphic organizer as a device for seeing the connections between ideas. Interventions based on the Readers' Workshop model employed minilessons to teach needed strategies. By helping struggling readers to improve in reading, interventions fostered affective knowledge. When reading is no longer a chore, students will choose to read independently.

How can you balance all three in your instruction? The answer leads into the next principle: design a structure to accommodate each one.

Provide a Consistent Instructional Structure and Use Time Effectively

Each intervention described has a clearly defined lesson structure and a series of activities that occur each day, usually in the same sequence. In the past, teacher attention often focused on the structure of the lesson: what to do next and how to do it. In these programs, once the structure becomes familiar, the teacher can shift the focus from the structure to the student.

The success of using volunteers in the Book Buddies and the Howard Street Tutoring programs was probably intertwined with the provision of preplanned and uniform lessons. Volunteers in other programs often drop out, despite initial enthusiasm, because they do not know what to do or do not feel confident enough in doing it. The uniform structure may be a factor in the high retention of volunteers in the Book Buddies program (Invernizzi, et al., 1996–1997).

Successful interventions use a basic lesson template, and the teachers adhere to it. Each day, the students participate in the same activities for approximately the same amount of time and usually in the same sequence. For example, the 30-minute Reading Recovery lesson involves the following activities: rereading familiar books; taking a running record; letter identification or word analysis; writing a story; cut-up sentences; introduction of the new book; and student reading of the new book. That is a lot of activity for one 30-minute lesson! Such a consistent and clearly defined structure allows the teacher to be very efficient, to focus on what is important, and to discourage moving off track. Structure also helps the students to know what is coming next and reduces the off-task behavior often associated with moving to a new task. A consistent lesson structure minimizes off-task behavior. Students know what is expected, and they move quite competently from task to task.

But doesn't a set lesson structure stand in the way of individualizing for students' needs? What about that ongoing assessment discussed previously? A set structure actually helps you to individualize and assess, and it makes lesson planning much easier (Caldwell & Leslie, 2009). Individualization occurs within the structure with the books you choose, the words you emphasize, and the strategies you model. It occurs within your ongoing assessment as you modify the text or the task to the needs of the students. Because you do not have to construct a lesson structure each time you prepare, you can spend more time selecting appropriate materials and refining strategies. An added bonus is that because you do not have to worry about the next step in your plan; you can focus your attention on what your students are doing!

Provide Time for Word Study and Fluency Development

Comprehension depends on the ability to accurately and fluently pronounce words and assign meanings to the pronunciations. Thus, word knowledge includes both the development of meaning vocabulary and word recognition strategies. Successful interventions focused on some form of word study. Students manipulated magnetic letters. They sorted picture or word cards. They changed letters to transform words and used letter tiles to build words. They categorized words according to meaning or structure. Although the format of the word study segments vary, systematic attention to word recognition is a major focus in all the programs. All programs also recognize the need for students to develop fluency, the automatic and expressive recognition of words and use repeated reading of easy and familiar text to develop this goal.

Include Writing as Part of the Lesson Structure

All programs include a writing component. Writing may be used to reinforce word recognition or it may include more extended and individual writing. By becoming authors themselves, low-achieving students gain dramatically in their sense of power over reading. Students who write regularly come to feel a sense of control over both reading and writing. They approach literacy with more interest. Students also enjoy expressing their opinions and showing their creativity through writing. Finally, through frequent writing experiences, students practice phonics by trying to spell words.

Students write in a wide variety of forms at the reading center. Seven-year-old Luis, who was at the beginning stages of reading, wrote "love notes" to his teacher. He usually wrote something like U AR PTE ("You are pretty"). These elaborately folded notes were given with instructions "For your eyes only." Heather, a sixth grader, wrote a variation on How Much Is a Million? (Schwartz) entitled "How Much Is My Allowance?" Alfonso, a seventh grader, composed an elaborate, multipage biography of his best friend. The student-authored books that fill the library in the reading center motivate new students to make their own contributions.

Keep the Size of the Group as Small as Possible

Students with reading problems may be instructed individually or in groups. With the exception of the classroom programs, all intervention programs provide either one-to-one or small-group instruction. The largest number in a group is seven or eight (in Project Success). Even the classroom programs make provision for small groups and individual attention. For example, during the self-selected reading and writing blocks in the Four Block model, the teacher confers individually with students.

Wasik and Slavin (1993) suggest that one-to-one tutoring is the most effective form of instruction. For students with severe difficulties in reading, individual instruction is often preferable because it allows the teacher to monitor and respond to instructional needs. In addition, highly distractible students often need an environment that protects them from irrelevant stimuli. Finally, in individual instruction, students can avoid the embarrassment of peer pressure. According to McCormick (1999), students who received individual instruction have consistently outperformed those receiving group instruction. However, because individual instruction is not always possible, teaching is often done in groups.

Group instruction often has benefits for students past the beginning stages of reading. Group instruction enables students to learn from each other. As students listen to the reactions others have to a story, their own comprehension deepens. Sometimes students can explain concepts to peers more effectively than the teacher can. Students can also share background knowledge. Group instruction also helps students to become more active. They may ask each other questions, share and discuss predictions about what will happen in their reading, and study with one another. They have opportunities to interact and to share literacy experiences.

Several successful interventions have employed cross-age tutoring where older students help younger struggling readers and peer tutoring where students of the same age work together. With careful teacher supervision, peer tutoring has proven to be worthwhile for both tutor and learner (Caldwell & Ford, 2002). In another grouping method, low-achieving students are put into pairs and asked to reread a story. Students take turns, alternating the reading by paragraphs or pages or taking parts. Richek and Glick (1991) and Stahl, Heubach, and Cramond (1997) have reported excellent results using this strategy with primary schoolchildren. Stahl, Heubach, and Cramond reported that the strategy worked best when students chose their own partners. More advanced students who are comfortable sharing may read books independently and then share their responses in a reading conference (Galda, Cullinan, & Strickland, 1997).

Coordinate Intervention Instruction and Classroom Instruction

Much intervention instruction, both in special education and reading, occurs in resource rooms by pulling out students from their regular classrooms. A major problem with this is lack of coordination between classroom instruction and intervention instruction (Walmsley & Allington, 1995, 2007). In two of the described programs (the Anna Plan and the Sixth-Grade Reading Class), intervention is carried out in the classroom by the classroom teacher and involves all students not just struggling readers. However, the majority of the programs are pull-out programs that are not coordinated with classroom objectives or activities. One exception is the Third-Grade Intervention that combined a pull-out model and close coordination with the classroom through use of classroom text.

An important goal of any supplementary reading instruction is to help students function better in regular classes. Therefore, support programs should be closely coordinated with classroom activities. Special reading teachers need to be familiar with the curriculum of the student's classroom. The classroom teacher and reading resource teacher must jointly decide how best to help the student, through collaborative planning and teaching (Walmsley & Allington, 2007). If teachers do not communicate with one another and coordinate their programs, the student may suffer greatly.

For example, three conflicting programs of reading instruction confused a first-grade student. In his regular classroom, he received instruction in a traditional reading textbook series. In his Title I class, he was taught using the Direct Instruction

Reading Program (see Chapter 15), which uses a special alphabet. In his learning disabilities resource room, he used the Orton-Gillingham method (see Chapter 15). Each teacher was unaware of what the others were doing. The student, who could barely master one method of learning to read was bombarded with three different methods every day. Walmsley and Allington (2007) suggest several important principles for literacy instruction which, if followed, will require close coordination of classroom instruction with support services: "All staff are responsible for the education of all students. Children should be educated with their peers. All children are entitled to the same literacy experience, materials and expectations" (pp. 26–29).

Application of Common Intervention Elements to Program Design

Could you design your own reading intervention program? In a small urban school, two teachers who were painfully aware that some children were not reading as well as they could did just that (Caldwell, Fromm, & O'Connor, 1997–1998). They recognized the common components of successful intervention programs: a consistent structure, an emphasis on reading, instruction in strategies, systematic word study, and writing. With these components in mind, they designed an intervention program for second- through fifth-grade students who were reading well below level.

Unfortunately, meeting the children one to one was not feasible. Instead, the teachers decided to make the groups as small as possible. They decided that seeing two children for 30 minutes was perhaps better than seeing four or five students for 45 to 50 minutes. Accordingly, they designed the lessons to fit within a 30-minute time frame, four times per week, and limited the number of students to two for each session. The lesson structure began with oral rereading of text that had been read during the preceding lesson. The children read the text at least two times using several formats: the teacher and the students read together, the two students read as partners, or they took turns reading individually. Following this supported oral reading, the teacher and students reviewed 10 words from the text. The words were printed on word cards, and the students took turns reading the words.

The next lesson component focused on learning key sight words and using the patterns in these words to decode unfamiliar words (Gaskins, Gaskins, Anderson, & Schommer, 1995; Gaskins, Gaskins, & Gaskins, 1991, 1992; Gaskins, Downer, Anderson, Cunningham, Gaskins, et al., 1988). For example, using the key words *am* and *her*, a student could decode camper. The students also played "word pickup," a form of word sorting. The teacher placed word cards in front of the students and asked them to pick up words with specific characteristics; for example, words with a certain number of letters, words that began or ended with a certain letter, words that began with a certain sound, words that rhymed with another word, and words containing specific patterns.

The fourth lesson component involved the reading of new text. First the teacher read the new text while the children followed along. Then the children were supported in their oral reading attempts using shared, group, or echo reading. The teacher guided the students' response to the content of the section by calling attention to the elements of story structure and to what good readers do when they read stories. They focused on identification and discussion of characters, settings, problems, and solutions. The children also discussed the selection from their own viewpoints or experiences.

Then the teacher presented 10 new word cards. Some words came from the text, and some included key words that could be used for decoding. The cards often included some words that had been presented previously but were still unknown. The final component involved writing. The teacher dictated a short sentence, and the students attempted to write what they heard. The teacher then guided them to correct spelling. The teachers found that the consistent plans helped. Because they were doing the same thing every day, they did not have to worry about what to do. They made lesson-plan templates that doubled as anecdotal records of students' daily progress. The children liked knowing what came next, and this consistency contributed to a saving of time. Because they knew the structure, the children exhibited little off-task behavior as they changed from one activity to the next.

The teachers used an informal reading inventory (IRI) to measure gains in achievement. A comparison of October pretests with May posttests showed a noteworthy gain of two IRI levels for both word recognition and comprehension. These results meant that, on average, children reading at the preprimer level in October were reading at a first-grade level in May; those on a second-grade level in October were reading on a fourth-grade level in May.

Daily observations validated the effectiveness of the intervention. As the year went on, teachers noted more fluent oral reading, a rise in sight vocabulary, an increasing ability to pronounce unfamiliar words, and talk about story structure as well as what good readers should do. Children also demonstrated greater self-confidence, eagerness, and participation.

Summary

A variety of successful intervention programs provide guidelines for structuring similar programs. These programs are not identical. Some are designed for individual instruction. Others focus on groups. Some are appropriate for younger readers. Others provide instruction more suited for older students. However, they all have features in common that form the basis for successful literacy instruction.

All emphasize reading. Lessons should be structured around reading as opposed to worksheets and "skill-and-drill" activities. Students need to read so they can learn by doing. Read to and with students. Employ both oral and silent reading formats. Allow time for independent reading by students and help them choose text that they can read successfully, that are interesting and personally meaningful to them and are drawn from a wide range of genres and topics. Prevent the Matthew effect by fostering a desire to read so that learning to read becomes a self-sustaining process.

All teach students the strategies that good readers use such as summarizing, predicting, inferring, employing background knowledge, and using known words to figure out the pronunciation of unfamiliar ones. Explicit strategy instruction teaches students how to read as they are reading.

All provide a balanced lesson framework. Reading is more than saying words. Students must also learn strategies for comprehending as well as a love of reading and the desire to do so.

All make assessment an ongoing and integral component of instruction. Carefully observe what your students say and do, and use these observations to individualize and shape instruction.

All provide a consistent lesson structure and use time wisely. A carefully planned and consistent lesson structure minimizes off-task behavior. It also allows the teacher to better individualize instruction by paying more attention to the students and less to what comes next in the lesson.

All provide time for word study and fluency development. Word study can take many forms, but students need to develop effective strategies for recognizing unfamiliar words.

All include writing as part of the lesson structure. Writing allows students to gain a sense of control over reading and to experience the enjoyment of expressing their opinions and showing their creativity.

All keep the size of the group as small as possible. Individual instruction is most appropriate for students with severe reading difficulties. Grouping can provide benefits in that students can learn from each other and experience opportunities for sharing literacy experiences.

Whenever possible, all coordinate intervention instruction, and classroom instruction.

References

Ahrens, B. C. (2005). Finding a new way: Reinventing a sixth-grade reading program. *Journal of Adolescent and Adult Literacy, 48*, 642–654.

Allington, R. L. (2001). *What Really Matters or Struggling Readers: Designing Research-Based Programs.* New York: Longman.

Allington, R. L. (2001). *What Really Matters for Struggling Readers: Designing Research-based Programs.* New York: Addison-Wesley.

Allington, R. L., & Walmsley, S. A. (Eds.) (2007). *No Quick Fix: Rethinking Literacy Programs in America's Elementary Schools. The RTI Edition.* Newark, DE: International Reading Association.

Almasi, J. F. (2003). *Teaching Strategic Processes in Reading.* New York: The Guilford Press.

Atwell, N. (1998). *In the Middle: New Understandings of Writing, Reading, and Learning.* Portsmouth, NH: Boynton/Cook.

Barton, J., & Sawyer, D. M. (2003). Our students are ready for this: Comprehension instruction in the elementary school. *The Reading Teacher, 57*, 334–347.

Beck, I. L., & McKeown, M. G. (2001). Text talk: Capturing the benefits of read-aloud experiences for young children. *The Reading Teacher, 55*, 10–20.

Biggam, S. C., Teitelbaum, N., & Willey, J. (2007). Improving early literacy: Vermont stories of educational change from the bottom up and the top down. In R. Allington & S. Walmsley (Eds.), *No Quick Fix: Rethinking Literacy Programs in America's Elementary Schools. The RTI Edition*, pp. 197–213. Newark, DE: International Reading Association.

Block, C. C., & Pressley, M. (Eds.). (2002). *Comprehension Instruction: Research-Based Practices.* New York: Guilford Press.

Borman, G. D., Slavin, R. E., Cheung, A. C. K., Chamberlain, A. M., Madden, N. A., & Chambers, B. (2007). Final reading outcomes of the national randomized field trial of Success for All. *American Educational Research Journal, 44*, 701–731.

Brown, K. J., Morris, D., & Fields, M. (2005). Intervention after grade 1: Serving increased numbers of struggling readers effectively. *Journal of Literacy Research, 37*, 61–94.

Caldwell, J. (1990). Using think cards to develop independent and strategic readers. *Academic Therapy, 25*, 561–566.

Caldwell, J. S., & Ford, M. P. (2002). *Where Have All the Bluebirds Gone? How to Soar with Flexible Grouping.* Portsmouth, NH: Heinemann.

Caldwell, J. S., & Leslie, L. (2009). *Intervention Strategies to Accompany Informal Reading Assessment: So What Do I Do Now?* Boston: Allyn and Bacon.

Caldwell, J. S., & Leslie, L. (2009). *Intervention strategies to follow informal reading inventory assessment: So what do I do now?* Boston: Allyn & Bacon.

Caldwell, J., & Recht, D. (1990). Using think cards to develop independent and strategic readers. *Academic Therapy, 25*, 561–566.

Caldwell, J., Fromm, M., & O'Connor, V. (1997–1998). Designing an intervention for poor readers: Incorporating the best of all worlds. *Wisconsin State Reading Association Journal, 41*, 7–14.

Caserta-Hemy, C. (1996). Reading buddies: A first grade intervention program. *The Reading Teacher, 49*, 500–503.

Chandler-Olcott, K. & Hinchman, K. A. (2005). *Tutoring Adolescent Literacy Learners: A Guide for Volunteers.* New York: The Guilford Press.

Clay, M. M. (1993). *Reading Recovery: A Guidebook for Teachers in Training.* Portsmouth, NH: Heinemann Educational Books.

Cooper, J. D. (1997). *Project Success: Literacy Intervention for Grades 3–6.* Paper presented at International Reading Association 42nd Annual Convention, Atlanta, GA.

Cooper, J. D. (1997). *Project Success: Literacy Intervention for Grades 3–6.* Paper presented at International Reading Association Convention, Atlanta, GA.

Cunningham, P. (2005). *Phonics they Use: Words for Reading and Writing.* Boston: Allyn & Bacon.

Cunningham, P. M., Hall, D. P., & Defee, M. (1998). Nonability-grouped, multilevel instruction: Eight years later. *The Reading Teacher, 51*, 652–654.

Cunningham, P. M., Hall, D. P., & Defee, M. (1991). Nonability-grouped, multilevel instruction: A year in a first grade classroom. *The Reading Teacher, 44*, 566–571.

Dougherty Stahl, K. A. (2004). Proof, practice, and promise: Comprehension strategy instruction in the primary grades. *The Reading Teacher, 57*, 598–611.

Dowhower, S. L. (1999). Supporting a strategic stance in the classroom: A comprehension framework for helping teachers help students to be strategic. *The Reading Teacher, 52*, 672–689.

Duffy-Hester, A. M. (1999). Teaching struggling readers in elementary school classrooms: A review of classroom reading programs and principles for instruction. *The Reading Teacher, 52*, 480–495.

Ehri, L. C., Dreyer, L. G., Flugman, B., & Gross, A. (2007). Reading Rescue: An effective tutoring intervention model for language-minority students who are struggling readers in first grade. *American Educational Research Journal, 44*, 414–448.

Fitzgerald, J. (1999). What is this thing called "balance"? *The Reading Teacher, 53*, 100–115.

Flynt, E. S., & Cooter, R. B. (2005). Improving middle-grades reading in urban schools: The Memphis Comprehension Framework. *The Reading Teacher, 58*, 774–780.

Fountas, L. C., & Pinnell, G. S. (1996). *Guided Reading: Good First Teaching for All Children.* Portsmouth, NH: Heinemann.

Galda, L., Cullinan, B. E., & Strickland, D. S. (1997). *Language, Literacy and the Child* (2nd ed.). Fort Worth, TX: Harcourt Brace College Publishers.

Ganske, K., Monroe, J. K., & Strickland, D. S. (2003). Questions teachers ask about struggling readers and writers. *The Reading Teacher, 57*, 118–128.

Gaskins, I. W. (1998). There's more to teaching at-risk and delayed readers than good reading instruction. *The Reading Teacher, 51*, 534–547.

Gaskins, I., Downer, M., Anderson, R., Cunningham, P., Gaskins, R., Schommer, M., & the Teachers of Benchmark School. (1988). A metacognitive approach to phonics: Using what you know to decode what you don't know. *Remedial and Special Education, 9*, 36–41.

Gaskins, R. W., Gaskins, J. C., & Gaskins, I. W. (1992). Using what you know to figure out what you don't know: An analogy approach to decoding. *Reading and Writing Quarterly, 8,* 197–221.

Gaskins, R. W., Gaskins, J. C., & Gaskins, I. W. (1991). A decoding program for poor readers—and the rest of the class too! *Language Arts, 68,* 213–225.

Gaskins, R. W., Gaskins, I. W., Anderson, R. C., & Schommer, M. (1995). The reciprocal relationship between research and development: An example involving a decoding strand for poor readers. *Journal of Reading Behavior, 27,* 337–377.

Gillet, J. W., & Temple, C. (2000). *Understanding Reading Problems: Assessment and Instruction* (5th ed.). New York: Longman.

Hall, D. P., Prevatte, C., & Cunningham, P. M. (2007). Eliminating ability grouping and reducing failure in the primary grades. In R. Allington & S. Walmsley (Eds.), *No Quick Fix: Rethinking Literacy Programs in America's Elementary Schools. The RTI Edition,* pp. 137–159. New York: Teachers College Press, and Newark, DE: International Reading Association.

Harvey, S., & Goudvis, A. (2000). *Strategies that Work: Teaching Comprehension to Enhance Understanding.* York, ME: Stenhouse Publishers.

Hedrick, W. R., & Pearish, A. B. (1999). Good reading is more important than who provides the instruction or where it takes place. *The Reading Teacher, 52,* 716–726.

Hiebert, E. H. (1994). A small-group literacy intervention with Chapter I students. In E. H. Hiebert & B. Taylor (Eds.), *Getting Reading Right from the Start: Effective Early Literacy Interventions,* pp. 85–106. Boston: Allyn & Bacon.

Hiebert, E. H., Colt, J. M., Catto, S. L., & Gury, E. C. (1992). Reading and writing of first-grade students in a restructured Chapter I program. *American Educational Research Journal, 29,* 545–572.

Horowitz, J. (2000). Teaching older nonreaders how to read. *The Reading Teacher, 54,* 24–26.

Invernizzi, M., Juel, C., & Rosemary, C. A. (1996–1997). A community volunteer tutorial that works. *The Reading Teacher, 50,* 304–311.

Invernizzi, M., Rosemary, C. A., Juel, C., & Richards H. C. (1997). At-risk readers and community volunteers: A three year perspective. *Journal of the Scientific Studies of Reading, 3,* 277–300.

Jacobson, J., Thrope, L., Fisher, D., Lapp, D., Frey, N., & Flood, J. (2001). Cross-age tutoring: A literacy improvement approach for struggling adolescent readers. *Journal of Adolescent and Adult Literacy, 44,* 528–535.

Johannessen, L. R. (2004). Helping "struggling" students achieve success. *Journal of Adolescent and Adult Literacy, 47,* 638–647.

Johnston, P. H., & Allington, R. (1991). Remediation. In R. Barr, M. L. Kamil, P. Mosenthal, & P. D. Pearson (Eds.), *Handbook of Reading Research* (Vol. II), pp. 984–1012. White Plains, NY: Longman.

Juel, C. (1988). Learning to read and write: A longitudinal study of fifty-four children from first through fourth grades. *Journal of Educational Psychology, 80,* 437–447.

Juel, C., Griffith, P. L., & Gough, P. B. (1986). Acquisition of literacy: A longitudinal study of children in first and second grade. *Journal of Educational Psychology, 78,* 243–255.

Keene, E. O., & Zimmerman, S. (1997). *Mosaic of Thought: Teaching Comprehension in a Reader's Workshop.* Portsmouth, NH: Heinemann.

Klenk, L., & Kirby, M. W. (2000). Re-mediating reading difficulties: Appraising the past, reconciling the present, constructing the future. In M. L. Kamil, P. B. Mosenthal, P. D. Pearson, & R. Barr (Eds.), *Handbook of Reading Research* (Vol. II), pp. 667–690. Mahwah, NJ: Lawrence Erlbaum Associates.

Knight, S. L. & Stallings, J. A. (2007). The implementation of the accelerated school model in an urban elementary school. In R. Allington & S. Walmsley (Eds.), *No Quick Fix: Rethinking Literacy Programs in America's Elementary Schools. The RTI Edition,* pp. 236–254. New York: Teachers College Press, and Newark, DE: International Reading Association.

Kreuger, E., & Townshend, N. (1997). Reading clubs boost second-language first graders' reading achievement. *The Reading Teacher, 51,* 122–128.

Kuhn, M. R., Schwanenflugel, P. J., Morris, R. D., Morrow, L. M., Woo, D. G., Meisinger, E. B, et al., (2006). Teaching children to become fluent and automatic readers. *Journal of Literacy Research, 38,* 357–388.

Lane, H. B., & Wright, T. L. (2007). Maximizing the effectiveness of reading aloud. *The Reading Teacher, 60,* 668–674.

Lerner, J.W., & Johns, B. (2009). *Learning Disabilities and Related Mild Disabilities*. Boston: Houghton Mifflin.

Lyons, C. A., & Beaver, J. (2007). Reducing retention and learning disability placement through Reading Recovery: An educational sound cost-effective choice. In R. L. Allington & S. A. Walmsley (Eds.), *No Quick Fix: Rethinking Literacy in America's Elementary Schools. The RTI Edition*, pp. 116–136. New York: Teachers College Press, and Newark, DE: International Reading Association.

Lyon G. R., (2001). Reading Disabilities: Why Do Some Children Have Difficulty Learning to Read? What Can Be Done About It? *Perspectives: International Dyslexia Association, 29*(2), 17–19.

Mackenzie, K. K. (2001). Using literacy booster groups to maintain and extend Reading Recovery success in the primary grades. *The Reading Teacher, 55*, 222–234.

Massengill, D. (2004). The impact of using guided reading to teach low-literacy adults. *The Journal of Adolescent and Adult Literacy, 47*, 599–602.

Massey, D. D. (2003). A comprehension checklist: What if it doesn't make sense? *The Reading Teacher, 57*, 81–84.

McCormack, R. L., & Paratore, J. R. (1999). *"What Do You Do There Anyway," Teachers Ask: A Reading Teacher's Intervention Using Grade-Level Text with Struggling Third Grade Readers*. Paper presented at the National Reading Conference, Orlando, FL.

McCormack, R. L., Paratore, J. R., & Dahlene, K. F. (2004). Establishing instructional congruence across learning settings: One path to success for struggling third grade readers. In R. L. McCormack and J. R. Paratore (Eds.). *After Early Intervention, Then What? Teaching Struggling Readers in Grades 3 and Beyond*, pp. 117–136. Newark, DE: International Reading Association.

McCormick, S. (1999). *Instructing Students Who Have Literacy Problems*. Upper Saddle River, NJ: Merrill.

McGee, L. M., & Schickedanz, J. A. (2007). Repeated interactive read-alouds in preschool and kindergarten. *The Reading Teacher, 60*, 742–751.

Miles, P. A., Stegle, K. W., Hubbs, K. G., Henk, W. A., & Mallette, M. H. (2004). A whole-class support model for early literacy: The Anna Plan. *The Reading Teacher, 58*, 318–327.

Morris, D. (2005). *The Howard Street Tutoring Manual: Teaching At-Risk Readers in the Primary Grades*. New York: The Guilford Press.

Morris, D., Shaw, B., & Perney, J. (1990). Helping low readers in grades 2 and 3: An after school volunteer tutoring program. *Elementary School Journal, 91*, 133–150.

Oster, L. (2001). Using the think-aloud for reading instruction. *The Reading Teacher, 55*, 64–69.

Paris, S. G., Lipson, M. Y., & Wixson, K. K. (1983). Becoming a strategic reader. *Contemporary Educational Psychology, 8*, 293–316.

Paterson, P. O., & Elliott, L. N. (2006). Struggling reader to struggling reader: High school students' responses to a cross-age tutoring program. *Journal of Adolescent and Adult Literacy, 49*, 378–389.

Pikulski, J. J. (1994). Preventing reading failure: A review of five effective programs. *The Reading Teacher, 48*, 30–39.

Pinnell, G. S. (1989). Reading Recovery: Helping at-risk children learn to read. *The Elementary School Journal, 90*, 161–183.

Pinnell, G. S., Deford, D. E., & Lyons, C. A. (1988). *Reading Recovery: Early Intervention for At-Risk First Graders*. Arlington, VA: Educational Research Service.

Pinnell, G. S., Lyons, C. A., Deford, D. E., Bryk, A. S., & Seltzer, M. (1994). Comparing instructional models for the literacy education of high-risk first graders. *Reading Research Quarterly, 29*, 9–30.

Pressley, M. (2002). Comprehension strategies instruction: A turn-of-the-century status report. In C. C. Block & M. Pressley (Eds.), *Comprehension Instruction: Research-Based Best Practices*, pp. 11–27. New York: The Guilford Press.

Pressley, M., & Afflerbach, P. (1995). *Verbal Protocols of Reading: The Nature of Constructively Responsive Reading*. Mahwah, MJ: Erlbaum.

Pressley, M. Symons, S., Snyder, B., & Cariglia-Bull, T. (1989). Strategy instruction research comes of age. *Learning Disability Quarterly, 12*, 16–31.

Richek, M. A., & Glick, L. C. (1991). Coordinating a literacy-support program with classroom instruction. *The Reading Teacher, 45*, 474–479.

Routman, R. (1995). *Invitations*. Portsmouth, NH: Heinemann.

Samuels, S. J. (1997). The method of repeated readings. *The Reading Teacher, 50*, 376–381.

Santa, C. M., & Hoien, T. (1999). An assessment of Early Steps: A program for early intervention. *Reading Research Quarterly, 34,* 54–79.

Santa, C. M., Ford, A., Mickley, A., & Parker, D. (1997). *Reading Intervention for Primary Students: First steps.* Paper presented at the International Reading Association Convention, Atlanta, GA.

Short, R. A., Kane, M., & Peeling, T. (2000). Retooling the reading lesson: Matching the right tools to the job. *The Reading Teacher, 54,* 284–295.

Slavin, R. E., Madden, N. A., Karweit, N. L., Dolan, L., & Wasik, B. A. (1994). Success for all: Getting reading right the first time. In E. T. Hiebert & B. Taylor (Eds.), *Getting Reading Right from the Start: Effective Early Literacy Interventions,* pp. 125–148. Boston: Allyn & Bacon.

Slavin, R. E., Madden, N. A., Karweit, N. L., Dolan, L., & Wasik, B. A. (1992). *Success for All: A Relentless Approach to Prevention and Early Intervention in Elementary Schools.* Arlington, VA: Educational Research Service.

Slavin, R. E., Madden, N. A., Karweit, N. L., Livermon, B. J., & Dolan, L. (1990). Success for All: First year outcomes of a comprehensive plan for reforming urban education. *American Educational Research Journal, 27,* 255–278.

Snow, C. E., Burns, M. S., & Griffin, P. (1998). *Preventing Reading Difficulties in Young Children.* Washington, DC: National Academy Press.

Spiegel, D. L. (1998). Silver bullets, babies, and bath water: Literature response groups in a balanced literacy program. *The Reading Teacher, 52,* 114–124.

Stahl, S. A., & Heubach, K. M. (2005) Fluency-oriented reading instruction. *Journal of Literacy Research, 37,* 25–60

Stahl, S. A., & Heubach, K. (1993). *Changing Reading Instruction in Second Grade: A Fluency Oriented Program.* University of Georgia: National Reading Research Center.

Stahl, S., Heubach, K., & Cramond, B. (1997). *Fluency-Oriented Reading Instruction.* Reading Research Report No. 79. Athens, GA, and College Park, MD: National Reading Research Center of the University of Georgia and the University of Maryland.

Stanovich, K. E. (1986). Matthew effects in reading. Some consequences of individual differences in the acquisition of literacy. *Reading Research Quarterly, 21,* 360–406.

Taylor, B. M., Strait, J., & Medo, M. A. (1994). Early intervention in reading: Supplemental instruction for groups of low-achieving students provided by first grade teachers. In E. H. Hiebert and B. M. Taylor (Eds.), *Getting Reading Right from the Start: Effective Early Literacy Interventions.* New York: Allyn & Bacon.

Taylor, B. M., Frye, B. J., Short, R., & Shearer, B. (1992). Classroom teachers prevent reading failure among low-achieving first-grade students. *The Reading Teacher, 45,* 592–597.

Taylor, B. M., Hanson, B. E., Justice-Swanson, K., & Watts, S. M. (1997). Helping struggling readers: Linking small-group intervention with cross-age tutoring. *The Reading Teacher, 51,* 196–209.

Taylor, B. M., Peterson, D. S., Pearson, P. D., & Rodriguez, M. C. (2002). Looking inside classrooms: Reflecting on the "how" as well as the "what" in effective reading instruction. *The Reading Teacher, 56,* 270–279.

Taylor, B. M., Short, R., Shearer, B., & Frye, B. J. (2007). First grade teachers provide early reading intervention in the classroom. In R. Allington & S. Walmsley (Eds.), *No Quick Fix: Rethinking Literacy Programs in America's Elementary Schools. The RTI Edition,* pp. 159–176. New York: Teachers College Press, and Newark, DE: International Reading Association.

Taylor, S. V., & Nesheim, D. W. (2000–2001). Making literacy real for "high-risk" adolescent emerging readers: An innovative application of reader's workshop. *Journal of Adolescent and Adult Literacy, 44,* 308–318.

Walmsley, S., & Allington, R. (2007). Redefining and reforming instructional support programs for at-risk readers. In R. Allington & S. Walmsley (Eds.), *No Quick Fix: Rethinking Literacy Programs in America's Elementary Schools. The RTI Edition,* pp. 19–44. Newark, DE: International Reading Association.

Walp, T. P., & Walmsley, S. A. (2007). Scoring well on tests or becoming genuinely literate: Rethinking remediation in a small rural school. In R. Allington & S. Walmsley (Eds.), *No Quick Fix: Rethinking Literacy Programs in America's Elementary Schools. The RTI Edition,* pp. 177–196. New York: Teachers College Press, and Newark, DE: International Reading Association.

Wasik, B. A., & Slavin, R. E. (1993). Preventing early reading failure with one-to-one tutoring: A review of five programs. *Reading Research Quarterly, 23*, 108–122.

Williams, M. (2001). Making connections: A workshop for adolescents who struggle with reading. *Journal of Adolescent and Adult Literacy, 44*, 588–602

Winfield, L. F. (2007). Change in urban schools with high concentrations of low-income children: Chapter I schoolwide projects. In R. Allington & S. Walmsley (Eds.), *No Quick Fix: Rethinking Literacy Programs in America's Elementary Schools. The RTI Edition*, pp. 214–235. New York: Teachers College Press, and Newark, DE: International Reading Association.

Worthy, J., Broaddus, K., & Ivey, G. (2001). *Pathways to Independence: Reading, Writing and Learning in Grades 3–8*. New York: The Guilford Press.

Wolf, M. (2007). *Proust and the Squid: The Story and Science of the Reading Brain*. New York: HarperCollins.

MyEducationLab is a research-based learning tool that brings teaching to life. Go to the Jennings, Caldwell, & Lerner 6th Edition MyEducationLab for Reading Assessment site at www.myeducationlab.com to:

◆ engage in multimedia exercises to help you build a deeper and more applied understanding of chapter content;

◆ utilize extensive resources including videos from real classrooms, Praxis and licensure preparation, a lesson plan builder, and materials to help you in your teaching career.

Early Literacy

Introduction

This chapter discusses the underlying concepts that students must develop to read and write. Early literacy comprises children's earliest awareness and use of letters through the development of fluent reading and the ability to decode basic phonics patterns. In this chapter, we will focus on the phases students go through as they develop an understanding of written language. We will include suggestions for assessment as well as instructional strategies that can be used to support students' progress through these developmental phases.

At one time, the field of reading focused on reading readiness as a set of skills students needed before they could begin reading instruction. However, research has shown that children best develop the foundation for reading as they engage in activities with print. Rather than children being "ready for reading" at one point in their lives, the basis for reading is laid gradually and involves speaking, listening, reading, and writing (Strickland, Galda, & Cullinan, 2003). In a joint position statement, the International Reading Association and the National Association for the Education of Young Children (1998) identified five stages of literacy development: awareness and exploration; experimentation; early reading and writing; transitional reading and writing; and conventional reading and writing. Ehri (2005) has proposed a phase theory to describe the processes through which early readers progress. Gentry (2007) rejects the concept of "emerging" readers and writers. He supports Ehri's phase theory and describes five phases through which students "metamorphose" into readers and writers. These phases are presented in Table 7.1.

Unfortunately, many students with reading problems have not mastered one or more of these crucial concepts. If you have students who cannot comfortably read beginning-level books, you must determine whether they have developed the foundation needed for reading. Many such students, even those in intermediate grades, lack basic concepts about print. When these concepts are developed using books, stories, letters, and words, students improve dramatically. The tasks used to assess early literacy in the reading center are based on the early reading screening instrument (ERSI), developed by Darrell Morris (1998).

This chapter focuses on the first four phases of development and the concepts that children should develop as they progress through these phases. We discuss how to assess those concepts and suggest some instructional strategies to teach them. Although most students struggling in early literacy development will progress using these techniques, some students with multiple or severe disabilities need more intensive measures as presented in Chapter 15.

Early Literacy Concepts

The National Early Literacy Panel (Strickland & Shanahan, 2004) has identified these areas that have strong research bases and are correlated with success in literacy:

◆ Oral language development and vocabulary
◆ Listening comprehension

TABLE 7.1 Phases of Becoming a Proficient Reader and Writer as Described by Gentry

Phase	Descriptor	Characteristics
0	Reads and Writes Without Letter Knowledge	Student cannot write his or her name but scribbles, sometimes using letter-like symbols
1	Reads and Writes with Letter but Without Sounds	Uses letters, but without regard to their sounds May emulate reading using picture or context cues May write words using random letter
2	Reads and Writes with Some Phonemic Awareness	Begins to match letters and sounds in writing Begins to read words using initial letters as the cues for words Begins to write words in abbreviated fashion: one or two letters may represent entire words
3	Reads and Writes with Phonemic Awareness	Matches letters and their constituent sounds in writing Matches letters and sounds in reading Spells words with one letter representing each sound
4	Reads and Writes Using Spelling Patterns	Uses phonics patterns (rimes) to write words Can apply phonics patterns, or chunking, to reading text

- ◆ Print Knowledge
- ◆ Environmental Print
- ◆ Alphabet knowledge
- ◆ Phonemic awareness
- ◆ Phonological short-term memory
- ◆ Rapid naming
- ◆ Visual memory
- ◆ Visual perceptual skills

This section discusses each of these concepts and suggests methods for assessing them.

Oral Language Development

As described in Chapter 6, reading, writing, listening, and speaking are all aspects of language. Students whose oral language is not well developed have difficulty with literacy.

Aspects of Oral Language Important for Literacy.   To read effectively, students need to be able to express and understand ideas fully. They also need to develop language skills specifically related to stories. For example, they must understand and be able to express the structure of stories. This understanding includes realizing that stories have characters and events that occur in sequence.

Questioning is also a crucial language skill. To participate fully in lessons, students must be able to respond to teachers' questions as well as ask questions to clarify their own understandings or seek information. Many students with language development problems have difficulty constructing or responding to questions.

During the "get-acquainted" activity in the reading center, it became apparent that Sean, a third grader, had language problems. When Sean's teacher asked him for a word describing himself, he could not answer. After many probes, he finally said "boy" and "brother." When he retold *Little Red Riding Hood* in his own words, he referred to the Grandmother as "Mom" and to Little Red Riding Hood as "she." Finally, despite the many problems Sean encountered, he never asked for help in reading or writing.

Assessing Oral Language Development and Vocabulary Development.

Oral language development is assessed through informal teacher observations and through narrative comprehension. As you engage students in conversations and observe their conversations with others, you should notice whether students talk about their interests and activities. When you ask students about important events in their lives, are the responses full accounts or one-word answers? Can students convey events in sequential order? When students misunderstand directions or encounter problems, can they ask for help?

If students exhibit problems in oral language development, teachers may decide to assess their language development and vocabulary more formally. The *Peabody Picture Vocabulary Test*, Third Edition (*PPVT-III*) and the *Expressive Vocabulary Test* (*EVT*) yield excellent information about students' oral language development. The *PPVT-III* measures students' receptive, or listening, vocabulary. The *EVT* measures students' abilities to provide synonyms for prompts with supporting pictures. For example, the teacher may show the student a picture of a jet and ask the student, "Can you tell me another word for *jet*?" The student would be expected to reply, "*plane*." These are norm-referenced tests that yield results as percentile ranks, age-equivalents, and stanines so that teachers can compare their students' language development to that of their peers. Also, comparing individual students' receptive language with their expressive language can provide important information for teachers in planning instruction.

Listening Comprehension

Before students become skilled readers, teachers can assess their narrative comprehension skills through story construction. Narrative comprehension is an important predictor of later reading success (Paris & Paris, 2003). One way to assess narrative comprehension is to read a story to students and ask them to retell it (Morrow, 2004). You also can use passages from an informal reading inventory as described in Chapter 4 to determine the language levels of your students. Paris and Paris (2003) have developed an assessment tool that uses wordless picture books and asks students to construct stories based on these sequential pictures. Checklists that help teachers score students' retellings and story constructions are especially useful in maintaining class records and monitoring students' progress (Walker, 2005; Gredler & Johnson, 2004).

If you need to use formal assessments to document students' progress as part of your school's RTI model, there are several instruments that you might find useful. First, you should carefully select assessments to suit your purposes; look at the actual items to see that they test the skills you want to measure. If your school has used the *KABC-2* to determine students' potential and the *KTEA-II* to determine students' achievement levels, you could use subtests from the *Kaufman Brief Intelligence Test*, Second Edition or the *Kaufman Test of Educational Achievement*, Second Edition, *Brief Form* to monitor students' progress. These provide an especially good formal assessment plan because of the co-norming across these tests.

Go to MyEducationLab and select the topic *Emergent Literacy*. Then, go to the Activities and Applications section, look at the artifact entitled "The Pet Who Came to Dinner (K-2)," and respond to the accompanying questions. What does this writing sample reveal about this student's print knowledge?

Print Knowledge

An understanding of how print works is critical to early literacy. Students must realize that print on the page is read in a certain order and that it contains individual words.

Concepts Crucial to Reading.   Students need three understandings about print:

1. Print rather than pictures carries meaning.
2. Reading is tracked, or followed, from top to bottom and left to right.
3. In print, words are separated by spaces.

Although these concepts are typically developed in the kindergarten years, some students with reading problems have not fully mastered them in the primary grades. Kelly, a first grader in the reading center, traced lines backward, from right to left, as her teacher read them. Derrick, a second-grade child, thought that every spoken syllable he heard was a printed word. These children still needed to develop fundamental concepts about print.

Assessing Concepts About Print.   In her *An Observation Survey of Early Literacy Achievement*, Marie Clay (1993) included a Concepts about Print test using two books, *Sand* and *Stone*, that were specifically designed to measure students' understanding of how print works. These books provide teachers with the opportunity to determine students' awareness of print as meaning, ability to track words and lines in text, and knowledge of what a word is. The test also measures awareness of inverted pages, transposed words, reversed letters, mismatches between pictures and text, and sentences printed out of sequence.

Many concepts about print can be measured without formal tests just by sharing a simple book with a student. Choose an 8- to 12-page book with one or two lines of text per page. The book should contain multisyllabic words and at least one return sweep. To determine awareness of print as meaning, open the book and ask the student to point to "what we read." The student should identify print, not pictures. Next, to determine tracking, point to the print and ask the student to show you "where we begin to read," and "where we go next." Notice whether the student starts at the left for each line. Finally, for word awareness, ask the student to point to and repeat words after you have read each page. From this repetition, you can see whether the student can correctly identify a multisyllabic word as one word.

Environmental Print

The first print that students recognize is environmental print. On the way to child care one morning, Andrea's 3-year-old son, Mark, starts begging for Chicken Tenders. Having just cleaned the breakfast table, Andrea is baffled until they turn the corner and Mark shouts, "MacDonald's!" Next, she hears Mark's twin sister, Anna, saying, "Slow down, Mommy, it says 'Stop.' " While Andrea would like to think her children are precocious and early readers, as a kindergarten teacher, she knows that they are in an early phase of literacy development, recognizing environmental print. This print is recognized logographically rather than orthographically; if Andrea wrote the word, *MacDonald's* on a piece of paper, Mark might recognize that it starts with the letter *M* just as his name does, but he wouldn't immediately recognize the word. Similarly, if Andrea arranged the magnetic letters, S-T-O-P, on the refrigerator Anna would not shout, "*Stop!*" when she went to the kitchen for a cup of juice. The twins are in Phase I as described by Gentry (2007). They can recognize environmental print and are moving through the natural progression of literacy development. As books, paper, and markers become a part of their world, they will make the transition from recognizing logos and signs to recognizing their names or MOM and DAD.

A child's first sight words play a critical role in literacy development, because early readers gain confidence by using their beginning sight words in reading and writing. These words also form the foundation for word analysis strategies and enable students to use known words as a basis for learning about new ones.

One way to assess early reading vocabulary is to ask students to write any words they know. This activity provides students with the opportunity to show you what they know instead of what they do not know.

Clay (1993, 2002) recommends that teachers assess beginning reading vocabulary by developing a word list using 15 high-frequency words drawn from the students' early reading materials and asking students to read these words. This method allows the teacher to discover which early reading words students know and what their strategies are for coping with unknown words. Allow 10 minutes for students to repeat this activity.

Parents and teachers can support this important phase by engaging children in "reading" as they take walks, travel, and participate in family outings to the grocery store or zoo. Reading signs and logos is an important component of early literacy development. Simple trips through the aisles of the grocery store where children recognize characters on their favorite cereal boxes provide rich learning experiences for developing readers and writers. Drawing signs as they play with their blocks and cars helps to build the foundation for literacy development.

Alphabet Knowledge

Research shows that the ability to name letters is an excellent predictor of early reading achievement (Hammill, 2004; Trieman, Tincoff, & Richmond-Welty, 1996; Walsh, Price, & Gillingham, 1988).

Knowledge Needed for Reading.   Alphabet knowledge consists of two parts: recognizing letters and writing letters. Students must identify letters automatically and must be able to name them when they are presented in random order. In addition, students must know both uppercase and lowercase letters.

Some struggling readers and writers, even in the third grade, still have problems with letter recognition. Allen, a third grader in the reading center, frequently asked the teacher how to make a *u* or a *j*.

Assessing Alphabet Knowledge.   A sample of an alphabet test is given in Figure 7.1. To administer the task, ask your student to say each letter, reading across the lines. Next, ask the student to write these same letters as you say them.

Again, if you need to use formal assessment to monitor students' progress, many of the achievement tests include an alphabet knowledge subtest.

FIGURE 7.1   Alphabet Recognition

A S D F G H J

K L P O I U Y

T R E W Q Z X

C V B N M

a s d f g h j

k l p o i u y

t r e w q z x

c v b n m

g q t a g t q

Phonemic Awareness

Phonemic, or phonological, awareness is the knowledge that speech is built from sounds. For example, the word *bed* consists of three speech sounds, or phonemes: *b*, *short e*, and *d*. The word *sleep* consists of four phonemes: *s*, *l*, *long e*, and *p*, even though it has five letters; the *ee* combination makes only one sound. Consonants can also combine to make one sound; the word *sheep*, which is five letters, consists of three phonemes: *sh*, *long e*, and *p*.

Knowledge Needed for Reading. Phonemic awareness refers to students' knowledge of individual sounds in words and their ability to manipulate those segments (Hammill, 2004; National Reading Panel, 2000; Stahl & Murray, 1994). Research shows that students' abilities to identify and manipulate these sound elements are highly related to reading achievement and spelling (Hammill, 2004; Ball & Blachman, 1991; Byrne & Fielding-Barnsley, 1991; Stanovich, 1988).

Phonemic awareness includes a variety of abilities. Students must be able to identify and separate beginning sounds of words, identify and separate ending sounds, and substitute sounds within a basic pattern. Finally, students need to be able to manipulate sounds by putting them together (or blending them), taking them apart (or segmenting them), and deleting and substituting them. All these abilities help students to master phonics in reading.

Assessing Phonemic Awareness. Phonemic awareness is assessed by asking students to blend and segment sounds, as shown in Figure 7.2. Other tasks include asking students to identify the first sound in a spoken word (e.g., "What is the first sound in *table*?") or to say a word without a sound (e.g., "Say *table* without the /t/.") (Paris, 2003; Stahl & Murray, 1994).

Most formal assessments for early literacy include subtests that measure phonemic awareness. If your school needs to use formal assessment to document students' progress for its RTI plan, you can select a comprehensive form of an achievement test, such as the *KTEA-II* and use the brief form of the test in a systematic assessment plan to document progress.

Letter-Sound Correspondence. To read successfully, students must be able to identify and manipulate sounds and associate these sounds with their corresponding letters (Morrow, 2004; International Reading Association, 1998; Trieman, et al., 1996; Ball & Blachman, 1991).

Relationship to Reading. Students' knowledge of letter-sound correspondence is highly related to later reading achievement (Morrow, 2004; Nasland & Schneider, 1996). Most important to early literacy is knowledge about beginning consonants.

Assessing Knowledge of Letter-Sound Correspondence. To assess students' knowledge of beginning consonants, the teacher gives them a word and asks them to identify the beginning sound of the word and the letter that corresponds to this sound. The words

FIGURE 7.2   Assessing Phonemic Awareness: Blending and Segmenting

Directions: I am going to say some words in a special code, and I want you to figure out the real word. If I say /s/-/a/-/t/, you say *sat*. If I say /p/-/i/-/g/, you say *pig*.

Teacher says:	Expected Response	Student's Response
/d/-/i/-/g/	Dig	
/p/-/u/-/l/	Pull	
/b/-/e/-/d/	Bed	
/f/-/a/-/s/-/t/	Fast	
/s/-/o/-/f/-/t/	Soft	

Directions: Now we will change jobs. If I say *bat*, you say /b/-/a/-/t/. If I say *feet*, you say /f/-/ee/-/t/.

Teacher says:	Expected Response	Student's Response
can	/c/-/a/-/n/	
tell	/t/-/e/-/l/	
dust	/d/-/u/-/s/-/t/	
sit	/s/-/i/-/t/	
fog	/f/-/o/-/g/	

NOTE: The use of slashes (//) indicates that you should say the letter sound.

in the sample task in Figure 7.3 are frequently found in beginning reading materials and all begin with single-letter initial consonant sounds. The task also includes some two-syllable words. Students' spelling of unfamiliar words also reveals important information about letter-sound correspondences (Gentry, 2004; Paris, 2003).

Short-Term Phonological Memory

A large body of research in early literacy has focused on the importance of short-term phonological memory in language tasks, such as reading and writing (Montgomery & Windsor, 2007; Baddeley, 2003). To understand language and respond to it, students must be able to hold a sequence of words in their short-term memory while they process their meaning. Even at the sentence level, students may be required to hold 10 to 15 words in their short-term memory while they are processing what the individual words mean, then what those words mean in relation to each other.

Research indicates that limited phonological short-term memory may be related to other language problems. For example, Gray (2004) and Ellis Weismer (1996) found that students with limited phonological short-term memory exhibited problems

FIGURE 7.3   Assessing Letter-Sound Correspondence: Beginning Letter Sounds

Practice: What is the beginning sound of mat? (Student should say /m/.) What letter makes that sound? (Student should say M. If not, model and practice another word.)

Word	*Beginning Sound*	*Beginning Letter*
fish		
little		
ride		
want		
happy		

learning new words. Further research has indicated that this limitation hinders students' sentence comprehension (Ellis Weismer & Thordardottir, 2002).

Relationship to Reading.   Consider how much of our early learning experiences rely on students' understanding the spoken word and series of spoken words—directions and instructions, story reading, even simple conversations! How can you respond to your classmate or your teacher if you can't remember a whole sentence? How can you appreciate the humor in a *Berenstain Bears* book if you can't remember a series of words that comprise a sentence? You can't even enjoy a nursery rhyme or a patterned book without an adequate memory for words.

These simple stories and rhymes provide the foundation of our reading experiences. It is through these shared reading experiences with parents and teachers in preschool and kindergarten that students develop their understanding of story structure or word families. These early language experiences provide the foundation for both word recognition and comprehension.

Assessing Phonological Short-Term Memory.   Phonological short-term memory is assessed in most studies by asking students to repeat a series of nonwords. In several formal tests of ability, students are asked to repeat a series of numbers, words, or nonwords. In other tests, they are asked to repeat sentences of varying lengths. Teachers can assess phonological short-term memory informally by asking students to repeat lines of poems or sentences. If students have problems completing this task successfully, a more structured, but still informal assessment can be conducted. Teachers can ask students to repeat short series of words or numbers. Then, if the teacher suspects limitations in a student's phonological short-term memory, screening instruments such as the *Comprehensive Test of Phonological Processing*, the *Kaufman Brief Intelligence Test*, Second Edition, or the *Slosson Intelligence Test, Revised*, Third Edition. If these screening tests indicate serious problems, the teacher can request more extensive evaluation. Then the tests just mentioned can comprise the systematic assessment plan as part of the RTI plan.

Rapid Naming

There has been extensive research in the relationships between rapid naming and early literacy development. In most studies, rapid naming tasks consist of children identifying series of numbers, letters, colors, or common objects. Others include words and pseudowords. Results have indicated that there is a relationship between students' abilities to recognize these items rapidly and accurately and early reading and spelling development (Hammill, 2004; Allor, 2002; Hammill, Mather, Allen, & Roberts, 2002).

Relationship to Reading.   While most studies in rapid naming have found a moderate-to-high correlation between rapid naming of letters and early literacy development, there is little evidence to support a lasting effect for more mature readers. There is stronger evidence that this skill is related to spelling and to fluency (Savage, Frederickson, Goodwin, Patni, Smith, & Tuersley, 2005). However, because of the strong relationship between reading and writing, especially in the early phases, this research has some important implications for reading teachers working with early literacy learners (Gentry, 2007).

Assessing Rapid Naming.   Many of the formal assessments of ability include rapid naming subtests: the *WISC-IV*, the *KABC-2*, and the *WJIII*. Some informal assessments include timed recognition of letters or words. Teachers can also construct informal assessments using flash cards or timed presentations on computer monitors.

Visual Memory

Early in the process of learning to read, students begin to store characteristics of letters in their memory. As they progress, students store aspects of words, or their spelling patterns (Ehri, 2005). As they become mature readers and writers, these aspects become more detailed and precise (Ehri, 2005). This visual memory for letters and words forms the foundation for automatic recognition, an important component for automaticity and fluency in reading as well spelling (Holmes, Malone, & Redenbach, 2008).

Relationship to Reading and Writing.   Certainly, visual memory for characteristics of individual letters is crucial to alphabet recognition, a skill highly correlated to early reading and writing. As students progress through the phases of early literacy, they begin to develop a sight vocabulary for high-frequency words (Gentry, 2007). As we mature as readers, we amass large numbers of words that become automatically recognizable. The sight vocabulary and memory for how words look supports our reading and spelling throughout literacy development.

Assessing Visual Memory.   Most early literacy assessments include spelling tests. Asking students to spell unfamiliar words reveals much about their strategies for recognizing those words. However, spelling tests measure graphophonemic knowledge; the information they yield is invaluable in planning instruction. However, if a student exhibits strong phonemic awareness but continues to struggle in spelling or reading, you may need to assess his or her visual memory. Tasks that measure visual memory are included in the *WISC-IV*, the *KABC-2*, and the *WJIII*. They are also included in the brief forms of these tests so that teachers can monitor students' progress.

Visual Perceptual Skills

An important component to storing characteristics associated with specific letters and words is the ability to distinguish individual characteristics. Students in the early phases of literacy learning are often still developing these skills. For example, a student recognizes that some letters have stems that extend upward; however, he or she may not yet distinguish between *b* or *d*, or *l* or *t*. Similarly, letters with stems that extend below the baseline may not be distinguishable so that students may identify the letter *g* as *p*, *q*, or *j*.

Relationship to Reading. The development of visual perceptual skills is a crucial component to students' ability to store letters and to associate specific letters with their constituent sounds. Reading requires the orchestration of both visual and phonological cues.

Assessing Visual Perceptual Skills. The formal assessments that include subtests for visual memory also include visual perception subtests. Often schools use the comprehensive form of one of these tests as part of the diagnostic battery of tests and use the brief forms for monitoring students' progress. In addition, teachers can construct informal measures of students' perceptual skills by engaging them in drawing specific shapes or reconstructing patterns.

Strategies to Develop Early Literacy Concepts

This section suggests activities for developing early literacy concepts. Although in assessment, we often try to separate components of literacy development, these areas are usually learned through an integrated literate environment (Morrow, 2004). In its preliminary reports, the National Early Literacy Panel (Strickland & Shanahan, 2004) has identified three broad areas for planning engaging, integrated and developmentally appropriate learning experiences for students in the early phases of literacy development:

- ◆ Oral Language
- ◆ Alphabetic Knowledge
- ◆ Print Knowledge

Suggestions in this book will focus on these three areas. Because they are presented as integrated learning experiences, one activity may foster several areas of early literacy. As previously emphasized, early literacy understandings are best taught within the context of real reading and writing in literacy-rich environments. Because literacy learning is a gradual process, the instructional activities used to support development overlap with those used for beginning reading and writing.

Oral Language Development

As stated earlier in this chapter, oral language development forms the basis for reading and writing. Three aspects of oral language development crucial to literacy are understanding and using oral language, understanding the structure of stories, and responding to and constructing questions.

Reading Aloud to Students. Reading books aloud to children is valuable for helping them to develop language skills. Many students with reading problems have not had wide experience in sharing print with an adult. Reading to students enables them to experience the rich language of books as an adult models the process of reading. Children learn to follow a story structure and to engage in conversation about books. It is important to engage students in the reading experience. In the sections that follow, additional strategies are given that may be used as the teacher reads books aloud to children.

Directed Listening-Thinking Activity. Often referred to by its initials, DL-TA, this activity is a modification of the Directed Reading-Thinking Activity (DR-TA) developed by Stauffer (1975) and discussed in Chapter 11. In DL-TA, the teacher reads the text aloud, stopping at crucial points to allow students to predict what will happen next and to confirm or revise previous predictions. These predictions and confirmations (or revisions) guide the students' understanding of the story.

After students are familiar with this strategy, the teacher can alter it by stopping before the last section of text and asking students what they think will happen in the end. Ask students to draw pictures showing what they think will happen; they may then write or dictate a sentence or two about their pictures. Next, read the author's actual ending to the story and compare it with the students' endings.

Story Structure. The structure of stories (also presented in Chapter 11) can be used to guide the discussion of books a teacher reads to children. Focusing on story elements helps students learn that (1) stories are organized in a predictable fashion; and (2) special terms, such as characters, events, and setting, are used for stories. These understandings will help children both to read and to write stories (Gillet, Temple, Crawford, & Cooney, 2003; Strickland, Cullinan, & Galda, 2003; Gillet & Temple, 2000).

After you read a story to your students, ask them, "Who is this story about?" or "Who are the main characters in this story?" Then ask the students, "Where does this story take place?" and "When does this story take place?" Next, ask students, "What is the main characters' problem?" and finally ask, "How do they solve the problem?"

In the reading center, questions are often placed on a chart. Students can answer the questions with pictures from the story or refer to the chart as they retell stories or construct their own. Learning about the language of stories provides an excellent foundation for the more complex story grammars and maps used in later comprehension instruction.

Shanahan and Shanahan (1997) have developed a related strategy called character perspective charting. In this strategy, children track the main characters in stories and identify their perspectives in relation to story events. This strategy has proved quite effective in helping students understand stories.

Shared Book Experience. In this strategy (Morrow, 2004; Holdaway, 1979), teachers imitate the "bedtime story" experience of young children. You can use the shared book experience with whole classes, in small groups, or with individuals. Students are drawn into the shared book experience by the quality of the stories shared, by the teacher's enthusiasm, and by the "sharing" format. A shared book experience may be extended over several days, as children reread and engage in several different activities. Generally, the teacher uses predictable, or patterned, books, which contain repeated words or phrases and plots simple enough for students to predict outcomes. Some favorite predictable books include *Have You Seen My Duckling?* (Tafuri), *Bears in the Night* (Berenstain & Berenstain), *Where's Spot?* (Hill), *Have You Seen Crocodile?* (West), *The Carrot Seed* (Krauss), *Titch* (Hutchins), *Ape in a Cape* (Eichenberg), *Is Your Mama a Llama?* (Guarino), *Green Eggs and Ham* (Dr. Seuss), *Too Much Noise* (McGovern), and *The Very Hungry Caterpillar* (Carle). Predictable books support students as they attempt to read on their own.

The steps in a shared book experience are:

1. Introduce the book. Ask students to predict what it will be about as you clarify any concepts that may be unknown. Show the pictures of the book.
2. Read the book aloud to students. Point to each word as you read. Read slowly but with expression rather than word by word. Position the book so that the students can see it. Then reread the book, inviting children to join you. If students do not join you in the rereading, encourage them by leaving off significant words. For example, for *I Know an Old Lady Who Swallowed a Fly*, you might read:

    > She swallowed a spider
    > That wiggled and jiggled and tickled inside her
    > She swallowed the spider to catch the fly
    > But I don't know why she swallowed the fly . . .

    Who can resist joining in with "I guess she'll die"?
3. Follow the reading with language activities. The language-related activities developed from shared book experiences can focus on letter-sound correspondences, dramatization, learning new vocabulary, or any other aspect of literacy that the teacher chooses to develop.

    For example, if you choose to focus on letter sounds, select significant words from the story and draw pictures of them on index cards. Have students group the pictures by their beginning sounds. Next, introduce the letters that correspond to those sounds. Then, you might present a picture card and ask students to write the beginning letter.

Go to MyEducationLab and select the topic Emergent Literacy. Then, go to the Activities and Applications section, watch the video entitled "Additional Sentences," and respond to the accompanying questions. How is the procedure used by this teacher similar to a language experience story? How is it different?

Language Experience Approach. The shared book experience is an excellent springboard for the language experience approach (LEA) (Allen, 1976; Morrow, 2004). In an LEA, teachers and students compose an original story or retell a story in their own words. Generally, students dictate to a teacher, who writes down their words on a chalkboard or large piece of paper.

To try this strategy, follow these procedures:

1. Brainstorm ideas for a story. Topics may include shared experiences, such as field trips, science experiments, special events, or stories read aloud. Choose one topic for your story.
2. Take dictation from students. Ask students to tell you the words you should write. At early stages, stories should be limited to four or five sentences. Write the words in large print.
3. Read each word as you write it.
4. Reread each sentence, pointing to each word as you say it. Have students reread each sentence with you.

Strategy Snapshot 7.1

A Shared Book Experience with an LEA

Ms. Burgess, a teacher in a second-grade Title I class, began with a favorite poem, "Honey, I Love" (by Greenfield), printed on chart paper. She pointed to the words and the students read along in a sing-song fashion.

Next, Ms. Burgess reread a favorite story, *Being Here with You* (Nicola-Lisa), as part of a unit on friendship. Ms. Burgess introduced the LEA saying, "Today we're going to write a story like Mr. Nicola-Lisa's, except ours is going to be about our class and how nice it is that we are all so different, but alike."

The students brainstormed ways they were alike and different. As the students talked about what they liked to do together, they recalled a picnic at which they met their seventh-grade pen pals. The students created their own story, "Pen Pals in the Park."

Next, the class divided into teams. One team played a sorting game with the letters *p* and *b*. Another group used magnetic letters to write words selected from their story. The third group sorted picture cards under the headings "Alike" and "Different." The fourth group met with Ms. Burgess to read sentences they wrote about a previous story.

After several minutes, the students reassembled for Ms. Burgess to introduce a new book, *Three Friends* (Kraus). As she read, Ms. Burgess pointed to the words in the text and stopped occasionally to ask the students how they thought the characters could solve their problems. When she came to a word that started with *b* or *p*, she asked the sorting group for help.

5. Reread the entire story with students.
6. Follow up with language activities. For example, students might select three words that they can recognize or draw pictures to go with their story. If they draw pictures, they might choose to write captions for them.

Often teachers combine the language experience activity with the shared book experience to create a cohesive lesson. One second-grade Title I teacher used this format with poetry to provide her students with rich language experiences, as seen in Strategy Snapshot 7.1.

Using Wordless Books.   Wordless books, which tell stories through pictures only and contain no text, can help students develop the skill of telling a narrative in sequence. In using a wordless book, you may wish to have students dictate a sentence for each picture. An alternative approach is to discuss the book with students, record their dictation, writing each sentence on a separate page, and have students illustrate the book. You can then bind the pages to create your own big book. Children can be encouraged to identify words that they know and to read their creation to others. Popular wordless books include *A Boy, a Dog, and a Frog* (Mayer), *What?* (Lionni), and *Apt. 3* (Keats). Each of these authors has written additional wordless books.

Print Knowledge

The activities described in the previous sections of this chapter help to develop crucial concepts about print. This section presents some additional activities to develop these understandings.

Echo Reading or Pointing.   The echo reading procedure presented earlier to evaluate concepts about print may also be used to teach these concepts. Good assessment should have much in common with instruction (Cunningham, Cunningham, Moore, & Moore, 2004).

In echo reading, teachers help students match the spoken word with the printed word. To implement this strategy, select a predictable book with limited print. First, read the entire book to the students. Next, read one sentence, pointing to each word. To echo read, students reread what you have read as they also point to words. As students become more familiar with the process, the length students repeat may be increased. Monitor students' pointing carefully; make certain that they point to each word rather than to each syllable that is read.

Uhry (2002) emphasizes that this strategy is much more complex than it appears to be. Research has shown that matching speech to print is an underlying skill for specific word learning (Morris, 1993). However, both Morris (1993) and Ehri (1992) found that students who could segment phonemes were also more successful at finger-point reading. Many children involved in finger-point reading studies have reported that they used a system of "counting words" across a line of print to help them identify specific words (Uhry, 2002).

A major implication for teachers in early grades or for teachers working with older students who are at in early literacy phases of development is that these skills are interrelated. Students need to develop one-to-one correspondence so that they can match individual words in speech and print. They need to develop the alphabetic principle in order to develop letter-sound correspondence, and they need to develop phonemic awareness to segment phonemes. The instructional strategies that follow can help you foster the development of these skills.

Counting Words.   In this activity (Cunningham, et al., 2004; Cunningham, 2008), students recognize words in speech, a skill that prepares them to recognize them later in print. To do the activity, give students objects (blocks, Popsicle sticks) to use as counters. The student listens as you say a sentence at a normal rate. Then say the sentence again, pausing after each word. Students should move a counter for each word you say. Next, have students make up their own sentences and count the words in them.

Jumbled Sentences.   In this strategy, students count words as they reorder them. Many students who develop early reading problems need this physical separation of words to develop a strong concept of word. To try this strategy, follow these procedures:

1. Begin with a story you have read or written with your students. Ask students to write a sentence about the story. Most students write summary sentences. For example, in a story about a hungry dog, Ramon wrote, "Duffy gobbled up all our food." Students often draw a picture about the story and write or dictate a sentence in a practice book.
2. Write the sentence on a large sentence strip. Have students read their sentence to you. Next, read the sentence together as you point to each word.
3. Have students rewrite their sentence on a small sentence strip. Use the large sentence strip as a model. Students then reread the sentence and point to each word as they read it.
4. Cut the large sentence strip into individual words and mix them up.
5. Have the students reassemble the sentence, using the small sentence strip as a model. Then students reread the sentence.

Being the Words.   In this activity (Cunningham, 2008), students actually "become" one word. To start, the teacher should write the sentences from a predictable book onto sentence strips. You may, of course, need to duplicate words that are used twice in a sentence, or write some words using both lowercase and uppercase first letters. However, you need not make copies of words that reappear in different sentences. Cut the words from two sentence strips into individual words and distribute each word to a student. Make a separate card for each punctuation mark.

Now tell the students they are going to be the words they are holding. Display the first two sentences of the book, and read them together. Point to the words as you read them and ask students to look at their words to see if they have any matches.

Students who have the words from those sentences come forward and arrange themselves in left-to-right order. Have the other students in the class read the sentences as you point to each "student word." Continue this activity until you have made all the sentences from the book.

For older students, write the sentences on smaller cards and deal a few (like a deck of playing cards) to each student. When you display the sentence, the students must cooperate to construct it.

Alphabetic Knowledge and Phonemic Awareness

In teaching alphabetic knowledge, the teacher combines letter names with letter sounds to help students progress more efficiently. Thus, alphabetic knowledge and phonemic awareness are integrated through instruction.

Memory Game. Sets of cards, which can be easily made or purchased, are used in this game. A set of cards is placed face down on the table. Half contain pictures (no words) of objects, and half contain the letters representing the initial consonant sounds of those objects. Students turn pairs of cards over and try to match the beginning sound of a picture card with its letter. When a match is found, students must name the object and identify the corresponding letter name.

Using Alphabet Books. A variety of beautiful alphabet books help expand children's word knowledge and appreciation of literature as they learn letters. Some favorites include *Alligators All Around* (Sendak), *ABC* (Burningham), and *I Love My Anteater with An A* (Dahlov). Research by Stahl (2003) indicates that children's alphabet books that provide words starting with a letter sound (such as *dog* for *d*) also help in developing phonemic awareness. Letters in an alphabet book should be shown in both upper and lower case (e.g., *D* and *d*).

Using Nursery Rhymes and Rhyming Books. Chanting nursery rhymes develops phonemic awareness and the ability to rhyme. Traditional poetry and songs are excellent resources to use with younger children.

Teachers can also use the many excellent books that focus on rhyming to help develop this ability. Begin by reading a rhyming book to students. Next, reread it, but this time, leave out the word that "completes the rhyme," and ask the students to provide it. For example, in the sentences "It is a nice day; I would like to play," you would omit the word play and ask the students to supply it. Students can also create their own rhymes.

Excellent books to model rhyming include *Sheep in a Jeep* and its sequels (Shaw), *The Hungry Thing* and its sequels (Slepian and Seidler), and books by Dr. Seuss, such as *One Fish*, *Two Fish* or *Green Eggs and Ham*. For older students, use collections of poetry, such as *The New Kid on the Block* (by Prelutsky) or *A Light in the Attic* (Silverstein).

As you read, children will naturally participate in the humorous rhyming words of Dr. Seuss's *There's a Wocket in my Pocket* or *The Hungry Thing's* "schmancakes."

FIGURE 7.4   Good Tongue Twisters/Alliterations

Walter Was Worried by Laura Vaccaro Seeger

Six Sick Sheep: 101 Tongue Twisters by Joanna Cole, Stephanie Calmenson, and Alan Tiegreen

Tongue Twisters to Tangle Your Tongue by Rebecca Cobb

Follow the readings with activities in which students create their own rhymes using common objects in the room. For example, you can have a "tock on the clock." You can wear a FEED ME sign and use plastic foods in a lunch bag to practice phoneme substitution and rhyming words (Cunningham, 2008; Yopp & Yopp, 2000).

Identifying Beginning Sounds.   We begin teaching beginning sounds with regular consonants and contrasting two sounds, such as /b/ and /d/ or /p/ and /t/. You might begin with a picture sort in which students categorize pictures by the beginning sounds of their names, and then add the letter cards of those beginning letter-sounds.

As children gain some understanding of beginning sounds, tongue twisters with alliterations are fun to help students understand the concept of words that "start the same." Reading books with alliterations is lots of fun. Some suggested titles are presented in Figure 7.4. You can create your own alliterations using the students' names and silly characteristics that will help support their reading. These can become posters with pictures of the children around the classroom or you can create a class book of alliterations (Cunningham, 2008).

Rhymes and Riddles.   In the rhymes and riddles activity (Cunningham, 2008), teachers select two groups of words, one to rhyme with head and the other to rhyme with feet. Next, ask students a riddle so that the answer rhymes with either head or feet. The children point to the part of their bodies that rhymes with the answer to the riddle. For example, if you ask, "When you are hungry, do you want to . . . ?" students should point to their feet, because eat rhymes with feet. You can repeat this game with other parts of the body. For example, you can ask students to answer riddles with words that rhyme with hand and knee or arm and leg.

Counting Sounds.   In this activity, students break apart words and count their sounds. To do the activity, select 10 words that contain two to four phonemes each. The words should be regular; that is, if the word has two sounds, it should have two letters. In fact, use only words with short vowels, consonants, and consonant blends (in which each consonant says a sound). Example words would be it, man, bent, stop. Students listen to you pronounce a spoken word, say it themselves, and then move one object for each sound they hear. You can use craft sticks, cubes, or counters. Try to use objects that are all the same, such as blocks of one color or similarly sized paper clips.

z

Begin by modeling the activity. Pronounce a word. Then pronounce each sound element of the word and move a counter for each sound that you say. Finally, move the counters back together and repeat the word as a whole.

Next, repeat the procedure with the same word, but this time ask students to try the game with you. Repeat this procedure with another word. Model the segmentation task. Then ask students to join you. Stop after the second phoneme and see if your students can complete the task. If practiced over a period of several weeks, this activity can produce substantial gains for students.

Deleting Phonemes. In this relatively advanced activity, students take a word apart, remove one sound, and pronounce the word without that sound. You might introduce this activity by removing parts of compound words. For example, pronounce a word, such as *playground*, and ask students to say it without *play*. Students should say *ground*. Next, tell students to say *applesauce* without the *sauce*.

Next, ask students to say words, omitting single sounds. Ask students to say *ball* without the /b/. (They should say *all*.) Try several of these, asking students to omit the beginning sounds; then ask students to omit ending sounds. When students successfully can omit beginning and ending sounds from words, ask them to say a word, omitting a medial sound. For example, you might say "Say *stack*, without the /t/." The student should say *sack*.

Segmenting and Blending. Students must be able to segment, or separate sounds in words, and to blend, or put sounds together to make words. The ability to segment sounds usually develops earlier than the ability to blend, and segmenting the onset from the rime usually develops earlier than the ability to segment individual phonemes in words. Games, songs, and chants that teachers and parents often sing and play with young children are easily adapted to help children learn to blend and segment.

You can begin with a simple riddle game: "I'm thinking of an animal that lives on a farm and is a /p/ - /ig/." Children are asked to blend the onset and rime into the correct word. As children become more skilled, you can segment the individual phonemes. You can also let the child who guesses the correct animal give the next riddle.

As students develop stronger concepts about print and the ability to identify individual sounds in spoken words, they need to connect these spoken words with printed letters and words. Start with initial consonant sounds because they are the easiest sounds for students to hear and segment and they are therefore the easiest to associate to letters.

Acting Beginning Sounds. Many students have difficulty breaking words down into their individual sounds and identifying these sounds. To develop this skill, Cunningham (2008) suggests that teachers start by working with individual sounds in words. Begin by showing a specific letter, such as *b*, and having all the students engage in an activity that begins with that sound as they repeat the sound. For /b/ students bounce; for /c/ they catch. Other actions might include dance, fall, gallop, hop, jump, kick, laugh, march, nod, paint, run, sit, talk, vacuum, walk, yawn, and zip.

Manipulating Letters and Sounds.   To use familiar words to figure out unfamiliar words, students need to be able to find familiar patterns and substitute individual phonemes. The foundation for this skill is laid in phoneme deletion (described earlier). Now we are ready to move to the next step of phoneme substitution. Cunningham (2008) has developed an activity called "Changing a Hen to a Fox" that provides practice in letter-sound manipulation. By changing one letter at a time, you can guide students to change from one word to another. For example, in Cunningham's "Changing a Hen to a Fox," you begin with the word *hen*, ask children to change *hen* to *pen*, then ask them to change *pen* to *pet*, *pet* to *pit*, *pit* to *sit*, *sit* to *six*, *six* to *fix*, and, finally, *fix* to *fox*. Magnetic letters or magnetic letter tiles are especially useful for this activity. After students practice with the magnetic letters, you can ask them to write the words. This activity is an important transition from phonemic awareness to the more advanced word analysis strategies presented in Chapter 8.

Spelling.   Allowing students to spell words they have worked with provides practice in manipulating letters and sounds in print. As students gain in their understanding of letter-sound relationships, their writing will become more conventional. Encourage students to write freely and explore their own spelling. Try not to correct them, but rather let them explore their own understandings, whether or not they are completely accurate.

Beginning Reading Vocabulary

Many activities can encourage students to develop the first sight words on which reading is built. You may make a collection of logos and children's favorite words. Some teachers prepare flash cards with words that are common in the environment. They cut out pictures from newspaper and magazine advertisements and label them. Children often enjoy bringing in and identifying food labels and wrappers. In "print walks," children and adults walk through a building and identify all the times they see a certain type of print, such as the word exit, words about weather, or 10-letter words.

Many of the activities presented earlier, such as shared book experiences and language experience stories, help children develop a fund of sight words. However, students also need to directly learn a number of important words by sight. These words, at first, might include their names, addresses, and words that they frequently see in reading or use in writing. Students might keep personal cards for each word and form them into sentences using the jumbled-sentences activity presented earlier.

Summary

In early literacy, students surrounded by reading and writing gradually develop the foundation for these activities. Students with reading problems may lack some early literacy understandings. Areas of knowledge needed for early literacy include listening comprehension, print knowledge, environmental print, alphabet knowledge, phonemic awareness, phonological short-term memory, rapid naming, visual memory, and visual perceptual skills. These should be taught in an integrated approach through oral language, knowledge about print, and alphabetic knowledge.

In oral language development, students need to express and understand ideas fully, understand how stories are organized, and develop the ability to answer and formulate questions. Instruction in oral language development includes retelling stories, composing original stories, developing questions, reading to students, the Directed Listening-Thinking Activity (DL-TA), discussing story structure, shared book activities, language experience approach (LEA), and using wordless books.

Three concepts about print are crucial to reading: understanding that print carries meaning, knowing how print is organized, and understanding what words are. Instruction includes echo reading, counting words, jumbled sentences, and "being" the word.

Alphabet knowledge is strongly related to reading. Sounds can be taught with letter names. Instruction includes the memory game and the use of alphabet books.

Phonemic awareness refers to the abilities to manipulate sounds, including segmenting, blending, rhyming, sound deletion, sound addition, and sound substitution. Activities include using nursery rhymes and rhyming books, identifying beginning sounds, guessing rhymes and riddles, identifying sounds, counting sounds, deleting phonemes, and blending.

Letter-sound correspondences, identifying a letter and its sound, can be taught by acting as beginning sounds, manipulating letters and sounds, and practicing spelling as well as several strategies mentioned above.

Students' early reading vocabulary words come from their environments. As they are exposed to more print, students start to connect environmental print with specific words. Teachers and parents help the process by reading extensively to students, labeling objects in their environments, and collecting interesting words.

References

Allen, R. V. (1976). Language experiences in communication. Boston: Houghton Mifflin.

Allor, J. H. (2002). The relationships of phonemic awareness and rapid naming to reading development. *Learning Disability Quarterly, 25*, 47–57.

Baddely, A. (2003). Working memory and language: An overview. *Journal of Communication Disorders, 36*, 189–208.

Ball, E. W., & Blachman, B. A. (1991). Does phoneme awareness training in kindergarten make a difference in early word recognition and spelling? *Reading Research Quarterly, 26*, 49–66.

Byrne, B., & Fielding-Barnsley, R. (1991). Evaluation of a program to teach phonemic awareness to young children. *Journal of Educational Psychology, 83*, 451–455.

Clay, M. M. (2002). An *Observation Survey of Early Literacy Achievement* (2nd ed.). Portsmouth, NH: Heinemann Educational Books.

Clay, M. M. (1993). *An Observation Survey of Early Literacy Achievement.* Portsmouth, NH: Heinemann Educational Books.

Cunningham, P. M. (2008). *Phonics They Use: Words for Reading and Writing* (5th ed.). Boston: Allyn & Bacon.

Cunningham, P. M., Cunningham, J. W., Moore, S. A., & Moore, D. W. (2004). *Reading and Writing in Elementary Classrooms: Research Based K-4 Instruction* (5th ed.). Boston: Allyn and Bacon.

Ehri, L. (2005). Learning to read words: Theory, findings, and issues. *Scientific Studies of Reading, 9,* 167–188.

Ehri, L. C. (1992). Reconceptualizing the development of sight word reading and its relationship to recoding. In P. B. Gough, L. C. Ehri, & R. Treiman (Eds.), *Reading Acquisition,* pp. 107–143. Mahwah, NJ: Lawrence Erlbaum Associates, Inc.

Ellis Weismer, S. (1996). Capacity limitations in working memory: The impact on lexical and morphological learning by children with language impairment. *Topics in Language Disorders, 17,* 33–44.

Ellis Weismer, S., & Thordardottir, E. (2002). Cognition and language. In P. Accardo, B. Rogers, & A. Capute (Eds.). *Disorders of Language Development.* Timonium, MD: York Press.

Gentry, J. R. (2007). *Breakthrough in Beginning Reading and Writing: The Evidence-Based Approach to Pinpointing Students' Needs and Delivering Targeted Instruction.* New York: Scholastic.

Gentry, J. R. (2004). *The Science of Spelling: The Explicit Specifics that Make Great Readers and Writers (and Spellers!).* Portsmouth, NH: Heinemann.

Gillet, J. W., & Temple, C. (2000). *Understanding Reading Problems: Assessment and Instruction* (5th ed.). New York: Longman.

Gillet, J. W., Temple, C., Crawford, A., & Cooney, B. (2003). *Understanding Reading Problems: Assessment and Instruction* (6th ed.). Upper Saddle River, NJ: Allyn and Bacon.

Gray, S. (2004). Word learning by preschoolers with specific language impairment: Predictors and poor learners. *Journal of Speech, Language, and Hearing Research, 47,* 1117–1132.

Gredler, M. E., & Johnson, R. L. (2004). *Assessment in the Literacy Classroom.* Boston: Allyn & Bacon.

Hammill, D. D. (2004). What we know about correlates of reading. *Exceptional Children, 4,* 453–468.

Hammill, D. D., Mather, N., Allen, E. A., & Roberts, R. (2002). Using semantics, grammar, phonology, and rapid naming tasks to predict word identification. *Journal of Learning Disabilities, 35,* 121–136.

Holdaway, D. (1979). *The Foundations of Literacy.* Portsmouth, NH: Heinemann.

Holmes, V. M., Malone, A. M., & Redenbach, H. (2008). Orthographic processing and visual sequential memory in unexpectedly poor spellers. *Journal of Research in Reading, 31,* 136–156.

International Reading Association & National Association for the Education of Young Children. (1998). *Learning to Read and Write: Developmentally Appropriate Practices for Young Children.* Newark, DE: International Reading Association.

Montgomery, J. W., & Windsor, J. (2007). Examining the language performances of children with and without specific language impairment: Contributions of phonological short-term memory and speed of processing. *Journal of Speech, Language and Hearing Research, 50,* 778–796.

Morris, D. (1998). Assessing printed word knowledge in beginning readers: The Early Reading Screening Instrument (ERSI). *Illinois Reading Council Journal, 26,* 30–41.

Morris, D. (1993). The relationship between children's concept of word in text and phoneme awareness in learning to read: A longitudinal study. *Research in the Teaching of English, 27,* 133–153.

Morrow, L. M. (2004). *Literacy Development in the Early Years: Helping Children Read and Write* (5th ed.). Boston: Allyn and Bacon.

Nasland, J. C., & Schneider, W. (1996). Kindergarten letter knowledge, phonological skills, and memory processes: Relative effects on early literacy. *Journal of Experimental Child Psychology, 62,* 30–59.

National Reading Panel. (2000). Teaching children to read: An evidence-based assessment of the scientific research literature on reading and its implications for reading instruction: Reports of the subgroups, (National Institute of Health Pub. No. 00-4754). Washington, DC: National Institute of Child Health and Human Development.

Paris, S. G. (2003). *What K–3 Teachers Need to Know About Assessing Children's Reading.* Naperville, IL: Learning Point Associates.

Paris, A. H., & Paris, S. G. (2003). Assessing narrative comprehension in young children. *Reading Research Quarterly, 38,* 36–76.

Savage, R. S., Frederickson, N., Goodwin, R., Patni, U., Smith, N., & Tuersley, L. (2005). *Journal of Learning Disabilities, 38,* 12–28.

Shanahan, T., & Shanahan, S. (1997). Character perspective charting: Helping children to develop a more complete conception of story. *The Reading Teacher, 50,* 668–677.

Stahl, S. A., & Murray, B. A. (1994). Defining phonological awareness and its relationship to early reading. *Journal of Educational Psychology, 86,* 221–234.

Stahl, S. A. (2003). Literature-based instruction in the early years. In S. B. Neuman & D. K. Dickinson (Eds.), *Handbook of Early Literacy Research.* New York: Guilford Press.

Stanovich, K. E. (1988). *Children's Reading and the Development of Phonological Awareness.* Detroit, MI: Wayne State University Press.

Stauffer, R. G. (1975). *Directing the Reading-Thinking Process.* New York: Harper and Row.

Strickland, D. S., & Shanahan, T. (2004). Laying the groundwork for literacy. *Educational Leadership, 61,* 74–77.

Strickland, D. S., Cullinan, B. E. & Galda, L. (2003). *Language Arts: Learning and Teaching.* Belmont, CA: Thomson/Wadsworth.

Trieman, R., Tincoff, R., & Richmond-Welty, E. D. (1996). Letter names help children to connect print and speech. *Developmental Psychology, 32,* 505–514.

Uhry, J. K. (2002). Finger-point reading in kindergarten: The role of phonemic awareness, one-to-one correspondence, and rapid serial naming. *Scientific Studies of Reading, 6,* 319–342.

Walker, B. J. (2005). Techniques for reading assessment and instruction. Upper Saddle River, NJ: Merrill/Prentice Hall.

Walsh, D. J., Price, G. G., & Gillingham, M. G. (1988). The critical but transitory importance of letter naming. *Reading Research Quarterly, 23,* 108–122.

Yopp, H. K., & Yopp, R. H. (2000). Supporting phonemic awareness development in the classroom. *The Reading Teacher, 54,* 130–143.

MyEducationLab is a research-based learning tool that brings teaching to life. Go to the Jennings, Caldwell, & Lerner 6th Edition MyEducationLab for Reading Assessment site at www.myeducationlab.com to:

◆ engage in multimedia exercises to help you build a deeper and more applied understanding of chapter content;

◆ utilize extensive resources including videos from real classrooms, Praxis and licensure preparation, a lesson plan builder, and materials to help you in your teaching career.

Improving Word Recognition Accuracy

Introduction

Reading is not a natural process (Wolf, 2008). In contrast to other developmental achievements such as learning to talk, learning to read requires careful instruction. Learning to read is also a relatively lengthy process. It takes years, and the learner must persevere over an extended period of time. Moreover, the process of recognizing words is complex; readers must use a variety of strategies to accomplish this task. Poor readers have much difficulty with word recognition. Often they must exert so much energy struggling to recognize words that they are left with little energy for concentrating on comprehending the author's message.

Word recognition strategies can be divided into those that foster reading fluency (sight words) and those that foster reading accuracy (phonics, structural analysis, and context). Sight words are words that are recognized immediately, without further analysis. Good readers identify most words easily and quickly. Right now, you are probably reading the words in this paragraph with little effort because you recognize them immediately. For fluent processing, the reader must have a large store of sight words that are recognized instantly, with no analysis. Research shows that 99 percent of the words that good readers encounter are sight words (Vacca, Vacca, & Gove, 2000). Students must be helped to build an adequate sight vocabulary, and methods for building a sight-word vocabulary are presented in Chapter 9, which discusses reading fluency.

This chapter is aimed at helping students develop accurate word recognition. First, it presents an overview of the stages of word recognition development. Then it discusses the assessment of and teaching strategies for each of the strategies that students can use to develop word recognition accuracy:

- Phonics, matching letters with their sound equivalent
- Structural analysis, ferreting out the parts of unknown words
- Context, trying to think of a word that would fit meaningfully into the passage

Stages of Word Recognition Development

The strategies to be discussed are used at different stages of reading development, as children progress from emergent reading to fluent and accurate word recognition. Normally, readers pass through these stages with relatively little effort, but students with reading problems may become "stuck" at a stage and not develop further. Understanding the stage that comes next in the reading process helps teachers to move a student with reading problems toward more mature reading development.

The first stage is called the *logographic* (Ehri, 1991, 1994), or the *visual cue reading stage* (Spear-Swerling & Sternberg, 1996). In this stage, children identify words using only visual cues. They may use an actual logo, such as golden arches to identify *McDonald's*, or they may use a few letter clues. A youngster once confided that he could recognize *dog* because the "barking" dog had its mouth open in the middle (the letter *o*). Of course, he confidently, but inaccurately, pronounced *got* and *from* as *dog* also.

Go to MyEducationLab and select the topic *Emergent Literacy*. Then, go to the Activities and Applications section, look at the artifact entitled "Phonemic (3-5)," and respond to the accompanying questions.

Children then move into the partial alphabetic (Ehri, 1991, 1994), or phonetic cue recoding stage (Spear-Swerling & Sternberg, 1996), as they begin to match letters and sounds. In this stage, they focus on the beginnings and ends of words, pronouncing, for example, *need* as *not* and *from* as *farm*. Because decoding in this stage is slow, children depend heavily on context and picture clues.

Gradually children move into full, or consolidated, alphabetic reading (Ehri, 1991, 1994; Gaskins, Ehri, Cress, O'Hara, & Donnelly, 1996) or controlled word reading (Spear-Swerling & Sternberg, 1996). They now pay attention to vowels and the patterns that contain them. For example, they might recognize *grape* as composed of *gr* and *ape*. Decoding becomes more accurate but is still slow.

Go to MyEducationLab and select the topic *Ongoing Assessments*. Then, go to the Activities and Applications section, watch the video entitled "Pre-Alphabetic Part 1 (Word Reading)," and respond to the accompanying questions.

The next stage is sight word reading (Ehri, 1991), or automatic word recognition (Spear-Swerling & Sternberg, 1996). Children begin to recognize many words automatically, without "sounding out," and develop a large store of sight words. Because word recognition takes less attention, children begin to focus on comprehension.

Strategies for Identifying Words

What do we do when we meet an unfamiliar word in print? Ehri (1997) suggests basically four ways to identify or pronounce it. The most common strategy is to identify the word from memory. Most of the words that we meet are familiar to us (words such as *the*, *girl*, *house*, *because*, etc.) and thus, we immediately pronounce them without the need to analyze letters and sounds. We refer to these words as *sight words*, and we address developing sight word vocabulary in Chapter 9.

Go to MyEducationLab and select the topic *Ongoing Assessments*. Then, go to the Activities and Applications section, watch the video entitled "Pre-Alphabetic Part 1," and respond to the accompanying questions.

A second strategy for identifying words is to match sounds to letter patterns and blend these to arrive at a pronunciation. Ehri (1997) calls this *decoding*, or word attack. However, this strategy works best with short words and often fails with long and multisyllabic words.

A third strategy is to predict a word's pronunciation from the context of the passage. This strategy is typical of beginning readers and is often overused by struggling readers. They can read *giraffe* if accompanied by a picture but are unable to read *giraffe* if printed on a word card.

Go to MyEducationLab and select the topic *Phonemic Awareness and Phonics*. Then, go to the Activities and Applications section, watch the video entitled "Word Chunking," and respond to the accompanying questions.

A final strategy, and one probably most used by good readers, is to break a word into familiar chunks and match the pronunciation of each chunk to words already known as sight words. For example, if *publisher* were an unfamiliar word, the reader might pronounce it using knowledge of *club*, *dish* and *her*. This strategy is often referred to as *decoding by analogy*, or using known words as analogues to pronounce new words. However, decoding by analogy is not foolproof; it depends on choosing the right analogue (Ehri, 1997). For example, how would you pronounce *fongue*? Would you use *tongue or fondue*? How about *disland*? Would you use *island* as your analogue or *is* and *land*? Decoding by analogy requires a large sight vocabulary of known analogues and a large listening vocabulary. Your listening vocabulary is made up of all the words you have heard. Use of analogies generally results in an approximate pronunciation: You match that approximation to your listening vocabulary, and if you have heard a similar word, you arrive at the correct pronunciation (Caldwell, 2008).

Is it important to teach sound and letter matching to struggling readers? Will instruction in sight words and use of context suffice? Probably not. Readers use all four strategies, depending on the word and the situation. However, to pronounce an unfamiliar word, and thus place it into our memory system, we must match letter patterns and sounds. In other words, we must know and use phonics (Beck, 2006).

Phonics refers to the relationship between printed letters and sounds in language. Children must learn to decode the printed language, to translate print into sounds, and to learn about the alphabetic principle of symbol-sound relationships. Much research shows that students who learn the sound-symbol system of English read better than those who have not yet mastered these critical skills (Chall, 1967, 1979; National Reading Panel, 2000).

Assessing Phonics Strategies

Miscue Analysis

As discussed in Chapter 5, miscue analysis can provide insight into a student's use of phonics. Analyzing miscues can tell you whether a student knows and applies phonics in reading and which particular letter-sound patterns the student can use. If a student's miscue contains the same sounds as the correct word, that student is using some phonics clues to read. For example, Chrissy read "the children were going on a trip" as "the chicken were going on a top." This shows that she knows, and uses, the sounds of *ch*, *short e*, *n*, *t*, and *p* but may need instruction in the sounds of *short i*, *l*, *d*, and *tr*. A teacher would need to confirm this knowledge, however, by listening to Chrissy read an entire passage.

Miscue analysis allows you to assess how students use phonics as they are actually reading, often during an informal reading inventory (IRI). In this way, you can see how their use of phonics clues interacts with their use of context and structural analysis. However, in miscue analysis, you are limited to an analysis of the words in the passage. To obtain a better overview, you can combine miscue analysis with a more systematic test of phonics patterns.

Tests of Phonics Patterns

One way to assess knowledge of phonics principles is to construct a list of *nonsense words* (or *pseudowords*) that contain important sound-symbol relationships. Because these "words" cannot be known by sight, the student must use phonics to decode them. An informal phonics test using pseudowords is given in Table 8.1. Although this assessment provides a precise assessment of phonics knowledge, you must remember that nonsense words are not an *authentic* assessment of phonics, because such words

TABLE 8.1   Words for Testing Phonics Patterns

These nonsense "words" can be used to test phonics mastery. They should be typed in a large typeface or printed neatly and presented in a list format or on individual cards. Students should be warned that they are not real words.

<table>
<tr><td colspan="3">1. Single Consonants</td><td colspan="3">5. R-Controlled Vowels</td></tr>
<tr><td>bam</td><td>fep</td><td>dif</td><td>dar</td><td colspan="2">tor</td></tr>
<tr><td>dup</td><td>jit</td><td>hak</td><td>set</td><td colspan="2">snir</td></tr>
<tr><td>sut</td><td>rez</td><td>jer</td><td colspan="3"></td></tr>
<tr><td colspan="3">2. Consonant Digraphs</td><td colspan="3">6. Vowel Combinations</td></tr>
<tr><td>shap</td><td colspan="2">chep</td><td>toat</td><td>doil</td><td>geet</td></tr>
<tr><td>thip</td><td colspan="2">quen</td><td>vay</td><td>roub</td><td>rood</td></tr>
<tr><td>nack</td><td colspan="2"></td><td>zew</td><td colspan="2"></td></tr>
<tr><td colspan="3">3. Consonant Blends</td><td colspan="3">7. Hard and Soft c and g</td></tr>
<tr><td>sput</td><td>streb</td><td>pind</td><td>cit</td><td>cam</td><td>gast</td></tr>
<tr><td>crob</td><td>plut</td><td>gart</td><td>cyle</td><td>ges</td><td></td></tr>
<tr><td>flug</td><td>grat</td><td>rupt</td><td colspan="3">8. Silent Letters</td></tr>
<tr><td>dreb</td><td colspan="2"></td><td>knas</td><td colspan="2">wret</td></tr>
<tr><td colspan="3">4. Single Vowels: Long and Short</td><td>gnip</td><td colspan="2">ghes</td></tr>
<tr><td>mab</td><td>sote</td><td>vo</td><td colspan="3"></td></tr>
<tr><td>mabe</td><td>lib</td><td>vom</td><td colspan="3"></td></tr>
<tr><td>sot</td><td>libe</td><td></td><td colspan="3"></td></tr>
</table>

do not appear in real-life reading. In addition, some young children may be reluctant to pronounce nonsense words and may simply make real words out of them. For these reasons, a nonsense-word assessment should be used together with a miscue analysis. Finally, when analyzing phonics knowledge, remember that students with reading problems are somewhat inconsistent in their knowledge. For this reason, you may need to review patterns that you thought your students had already mastered.

A short and easily administered test of phonics patterns is the names test (Duffelmeyer, Kruse, Merkeley, & Fyfe, 1999; Cunningham, 1990). This instrument avoids the use of nonsense words by providing a list of first and last names such as Dee Skidmore and Bernard Pendergraph. The names sound like their spellings, and they represent common phonics elements: initial consonants and consonant blends (*sp-, cr-, fl, dr-, st-, gr-, pl-*), consonant digraphs (*sh, ch, th, ph, wh*), short vowel sounds, long vowel sounds (*-ate, -ake, -y, -ale, -o, -ene, -ace, -oke, -ine, -ade, -ale, -ane-*) vowel digraphs (*au, oo, ay, ea, ee, oy, ay, oa, ey, ai*), r-controlled vowels (*er, ar, eu, or, ur, aw*) and the schwa sound. As the student read the names, the teacher records his or her performance and then analyzes that performance in terms of which elements were known or unknown.

Almost all early literacy assessments include tests of phonics patterns (Southwest Educational Development Laboratory, 2007; Meisels & Piker, 2001).

Teaching Phonics Strategies

Phonics can be taught in many ways, however, the one you choose should be delivered systematically. A review of the findings of the National Reading Panel (Ehri, Nunes, Stahl, & Willows, 2001) concluded that systematic phonics instruction made a more significant contribution to student growth in reading than unsystematic or no phonics instruction. Systematic phonics instruction made the biggest impact when it began in kindergarten or first grade. It was equally effective when delivered through tutoring, small group instruction, or whole class instruction. Finally, systematic phonics was significantly more effective in helping struggling readers than unsystematic or no phonics instruction.

Unfortunately, poor instruction, even if delivered systematically, may actually do more harm than good. Struggling readers often fill out numerous phonics worksheets and are skilled and drilled at the expense of reading and enjoying meaningful text. Isolated phonics drills may rob students of precious instructional time for actual reading that allows them to apply their phonics knowledge.

What makes for exemplary phonics instruction? Stahl (1992) suggested several guidelines. Exemplary phonics instruction:

1. Builds on concepts about how print functions. Students need to recognize that print is the primary source of information as opposed to pictures.
2. Builds on a foundation of phonemic awareness. This subject is addressed in Chapter 7.
3. Is clear and direct and involves teacher explanation and modeling.
4. Is integrated into a total reading program that emphasizes the use of quality children's literature.
5. Focuses on reading words, not learning rules.
6. May include word families and use of decoding by analogy.
7. May include invented spelling practice.
8. Focuses on the internal structure of words to develop independent word recognition strategies.
9. Develops automatic word recognition skills.

Letter-Sound Relationships

Phonics refers to the relationship between speech and print; that is, the relationship between letter and letter groupings and speech sounds. Knowing such relationships allows readers to pronounce unfamiliar words and match these pronunciations to word meanings. In order to understand how to teach letter-sound relationships, we need to clarify certain terminology. Most people understand the difference between consonants and vowels and can readily identify a letter as one or the other. Consonant blends or clusters are two or three adjacent consonants as *br* in *break* and *spl* in *split*. Each consonant retains its own sound; that is, you say the distinct sounds of *b* and *r* when you say *break*. Consonant digraphs are also two or more adjacent consonants but they do not retain their individual sounds. If you say the sound of *sh* in *ship*, you make a new sound.

Go to MyEducationLab and select the topic *Phonemic Awareness and Phonics*. Then, go to the Activities and Applications section, watch the video entitled "Teaching Phonics," and respond to the accompanying questions.

Vowels fall into several groups. Short vowels are those represented by the sounds of *a* as in *fat*, *e* as in *ten*, *i* as in *win*, *o* as in *hot*, and *u* as in *cut*. This pattern is often described as the consonant/vowel/consonant (CVC) pattern. Long vowels "say their own name"; that, is the sound of the vowel in a word is the same as the way the alphabet letter is pronounced. There are two main groups of long vowel sounds. The consonant/vowel/consonant final e pattern (CVCe) is represented by words where the final e is silent and the vowel makes the long sound. Examples are *cake*, *rice*, *note* and *cube*. Vowel digraphs form a second pattern. They make a long vowel sound but are represented by two adjacent vowels as in *meat*, *clay*, *seed*, and *gain*. In these words, the digraphs are *ea*, *ay*, *ee*, and *ai*. Vowel diphthongs and *r*-controlled vowels represent other common patterns. A diphthong begins with one vowel sound and moves to another as in *how*, *dew*, and *toil*. In the English language, the letter *r* often follows a vowel and influences how it is pronounced. You can differentiate *r*-controlled vowels if you read the following word pairs out loud: *fat* and *far*; *hem* and *her*; and *can* and *car*. Note how the presence of the letter *r* changes the sound of the vowel.

Go to MyEducationLab and select the topic *Emergent Literacy*. Then, go to the Activities and Applications section, watch the video entitled "Phonics Instruction," and respond to the accompanying questions.

In order for children to read words, what do they need to know? According to Beck (2006), they need to know the speech sounds that are associated with letters. They need to know how to put these sounds together to form a word and they need to do this rapidly. What they do not need to know is terminology such as digraph, diphthong, and *r*-controlled. Children must learn to match sounds and letter patterns not identify their names.

Organizing Phonics Instruction

Letter-sound patterns, the sounds represented by consonants and those represented by vowels, form the basis of phonics instruction. Consonants generally stand for dependable sounds; that is, the sound represented by the letter *b* does not change depending upon its position in a word. The sound of *b* in *back* is the same as its sound in *cab*. As just described, vowel patterns are much more variable. Vowel patterns are often presented as phonograms. A *phonogram* is a vowel and a following consonant (or consonants) such as *in* and *op*. Phonograms form the basis for syllable units in multisyllable words. Consider the word *intermittent* that contains the following phonograms: *in*, *er*, *it*, and *ent*. Knowledge of phonograms can translate into a powerful strategy for analyzing multisyllabic words.

Which pattern or phonogram should you teach and in what order? Johnson (1999, 2001) offers some general recommendations for teaching vowel patterns and matching instruction to the needs of your students. Fry (2004) describes consonant and vowel patterns in terms of their frequency in the language. Allen (1998) provides an extensive list of frequently used patterns and examples of common one syllable words that can be use as a basis for instruction. Beck (2006) arranges letter-sound patterns in the form of instructional units that move from simple to more complex patterns. These resources can be valuable tools in choosing the letters, sounds, and words to teach. Published programs (and there are many of them and more appear each day) also can offer guidelines in this respect.

Phonograms can be grouped into word families. A word family is made up of words that contain the same phonograms such as *win*, *tin*, *fin*, *bin* and *crop*, *stop*, *cop*, *hop*, and *mop*. Such words are often referred to as *onset/rimes*. The onset is the initial consonant pattern (*bl* as in *black*) and the rime is the vowel pattern (*ack* as in *black*). Children seem to learn word families easily and naturally (Caldwell & Leslie, 2009; Stahl, 1992; Adams, 1990).

The following table lists common phonogram units. Underlined phonograms represent those that occur most frequently in the English language. They either make up large word families or they are present in very frequent words.

Whether you are designing your own sequence or basing it on published material, Beck (2006) stresses the importance of several principles. First, the popular practice of teaching consonants first and then vowels needs to be reexamined. Simple vowel patterns can and should be taught in tandem with consonants. Why? It is impossible to actually pronounce a consonant by itself; it needs an accompanying vowel to make a pronounceable entity. Teaching consonants alone often leads to artificial pronunciation and later confusion on the part of students. The student pronounces the letter *b*, for example, as *buh*; however, the sound represented by *uh* is the short vowel sound. Try saying the sound of *b* without *uh*; all you get is a puff of air! For this reason, it makes sense to couple instruction in consonants with simple vowel patterns such as *at*, *an*, *en*, *it*, *op*, and *un*.

Do not just focus on consonants in the beginning position such as *t* in *tub*. Expose children to the consonant in ending positions as well as in *cut*, *wet*, and *nut*.

TABLE 8.2   Common Phonograms

ad, ag, am, an, ap, ar, at, aw, ay, ax, ack, age, ail, ain, air, ake, ale, all, alk, ame, and, ane, ang, ank, are, ash (*wash* and *smash*), ast, ate, ave, aught

e (me), ed, ee, en, et, er, ew, ear (*bear* and *dear*), eal, eat, een, eep, eet, eck, ell, end, ent, ess, est, each

id, ig, in, im, ip, it, ice, ick, ide, ife, ike, ile, ill, ine, ing, ink, ire, irt, ish, ite, ight

o (*go* and *do*), og, op, or, ot, ow (*how* and *blow*), oy, oat, ock, oil, oin, oke, old, ole, one, ong, oil, ook, ool, oom, ore, out, oast, ould, ound

ug, ue, un, up, uck, ull, ump, unk, ure, use

Poor readers are often able to decode the initial letter but falter when faced with the same letter at the end of a word. Teaching consonant letter-sound relationships in both positions can help to avoid this.

Use manipulative activities to illustrate letter-sound relationships. Having students move and exchange letters to make words can illustrate how the sound of the letter *t*, for example, remains the same in *tip* and *pot*. Having students sort words into word families or phonograms can be a very motivating activity. Letter cards should include single consonants and vowels as well as consonant blends and digraphs, vowel digraphs, vowel diphthongs, and r-controlled patterns.

Good phonics instruction involves a dual focus on words and on application in reading. You can begin with a lesson using phonograms or word families but you need to follow it with practice in a real reading situation—or you can begin with reading a book and designing your lesson around words in the book. These can include words the students knew as well as words they were not able to pronounce. For example, if the students knew the word *hill*, they can manipulate letters to make *pill*, *gill*, *silly*, *miller*, and *million*, thus extending phonics past the beginning stages and into more advanced words. If they did not know a word such as *steep*, you can use this to extend into other words with the same pattern: *stop*, *stem*, *stick* and/or *keep*, *peep*, and *weep*. It is not enough to focus on pronunciation. The lesson should also include attention to word meaning. What is a gill? What does it mean to weep? Where would we find a stem? In this way, the student recognizes that reading is not just saying words but saying words in order to make meaning. Work with letter-sound patterns must be repetitive; that is, the students must have many opportunities to interact with a specific pattern. A key role of the teacher is to point out the similarities between words relative to letter-sound patterns—that is, you need to continually demonstrate that *at*, for example, says the same sound in *hat*, *cat*, *batted*, *matter*, *fattest*, *and satisfy*.

Decoding through Analogy

Research indicates that most people (including students with reading problems) learn phonics, not by memorizing rules, but by recognizing patterns used in similar and known words (Goswami & Mead, 1992; Goswami & Bryant, 1990). In other words, people pronounce new words by using known words. This process is called *decoding by analogy*. A child learns to read *close* and *class* and thus learns how to pronounce the onset *cl*. The child learns *day* and *say* and how to pronounce *ay*. These learnings lead to the pronunciation of a new word, *clay*. Suppose you come across a word you have never seen before, such as *tergiversation*. How do you manage to pronounce it correctly? You use word elements that you know: *ter* as in *term*, the word *giver*, and *sation* as in *conversation*.

You can teach students with reading problems how to use this strategy. When they meet an unknown word, ask them to think of an analogous one. For example, if the student is unable to decode the word *bay*, you might ask, "Can you think of a word that ends like this word?" If the child can't supply an analogy, you might say, "Think of the word *day*." The use of word families helps students to recognize and use these analogies.

Allen (1998) suggests an integrated strategies approach based on the use of spelling patterns to pronounce unfamiliar words. Essential components of the program include understanding rhyme, learning to use key words and their spelling patterns to decode words by analogy, learning to cross-check to see if the word makes sense, and learning to read and spell a core of high-frequency words. Teachers choose words with frequently used spelling patterns from the literature they are using in the classroom. The teacher explicitly and frequently models strategy use and offers students many opportunities to learn and apply what they have learned by using a word wall, building words, reading new text, playing games, and writing frequently.

One instructional program for teaching word analysis through analogy is of outstanding quality. The *Benchmark Word Identification/Vocabulary Development Program* (Gaskins, Soja, Indrisano, Laurence, Eliot, 1989; Gaskins & Downer, 1986) was constructed for use at the Benchmark School, a facility for students with learning difficulties. The program stresses the use of context clues and decoding by analogy. It employs both mono- and multisyllabic words almost from the first lessons. The program, which can be purchased, is extremely detailed and provides scripts for daily lessons.

The Benchmark program teaches decoding by analogy through key spelling patterns. The teacher introduces key words for each common vowel pattern, and the students practice these words until they know them as sight words. Examples of key words for *o* patterns are *go*, *boat*, *job*, *clock*, and *long*. The students dictate language experience stories containing the key words and repeatedly read them. Students also write the key words and chant each word letter by letter. The words are displayed prominently in the classroom.

Next, the teacher shows how to use key words to identify unknown words by repeatedly modeling the process of comparing and contrasting an unknown word to a key word. For example, the teacher presents a new word in a sentence such as *Jim opened the present with joy*. Pretending not to know *joy*, the teacher thinks aloud, noting that *joy* looks like the key word *boy*. *Boy* is written below *joy*. The teacher then uses *boy* to pronounce *joy* by saying, "If b-o-y is *boy*, then j-o-y is *joy*. Does *joy* make sense in the sentence?" The teacher models by checking to see if the "unknown" word fits the context. As new key words are introduced, these same basic components are used. Other lesson activities include rhyme recognition, fitting words into cloze sentences, and sorting words into spelling patterns.

A revision of this program entitled *Word Detectives: Benchmark Word Identification Program for Beginning Readers* (Gaskins, et al., 1996) has made several research-based improvements. In the newer program, students are asked to spell and write each key word several times so that they learn each letter. In addition, the program includes more connected reading, and the pace of word introduction is slower.

The Benchmark program can be used with students at many different reading levels, and with individuals or groups. For information, visit the website, www.benchmarkschool.org/b_available_programs.htm.

Combining Phonics and Meaning

Perhaps because they have had so much difficulty recognizing words, poor readers often confuse phonics with reading. Because they think that reading is simply sounding out words, they need to learn that pronouncing words is only a step toward gaining the author's meaning. As they read, students need to constantly ask themselves, "Does this make sense?" They must remember to check whether their pronunciation efforts result in sensible meaning. Of course, this strategy involves combining context clues and phonics. Two strategies to help students use these clue systems together are *cross-checking* and the *four-step procedure*.

Cross-Checking. This variation on a cloze procedure is recommended by Cunningham (2005). The teacher writes a sentence that contains one covered word. To supply this word, students cross-check phonics clues with context clues. Teacher and students first read the sentence, saying "blank" for the covered word. Next, the students offer suggestions as to what the missing word might be. All reasonable suggestions are written down where the students can see them. (If a student offers a suggestion that does not fit, the teacher reads the sentence, inserts this word, and demonstrates how the sentence does not sound right.) The teacher then uncovers the letters, one by one. All words that do not begin with these letters are crossed out. Finally the teacher uncovers the entire word and points out that although many words might fit in the blank, the pronunciation must match the letters chosen by the author. See the example in Strategy Snapshot 8.1.

Four-Step Strategy. At a more advanced level, the four-step strategy also combines the use of several different clues to recognize words. In this sequence, students learn to use the steps that skilled readers use when they figure out unknown words. They first use context clues, then phonics, and then structural analysis clues. This sequence is successful in showing baffled readers how to integrate and apply their word recognition skills. The steps are:

1. If you don't know a word in your reading, first reread the sentence and try to figure it out. (context clues)
2. If that doesn't work, sound out the first part and reread the sentence. (phonics clues)
3. If you still don't know it, look for word endings and try to figure out the base word. (structural analysis clues)
4. If you still haven't figured it out, sound out the whole word. Remember you may have to change a few sounds to make the word make sense. (phonics clues)

Teachers should first explain the strategy and model how to use it for several words. After that, remind students to use it whenever they read. In one fifth-grade reading class, students made a list of all the words they had figured out using the four-step strategy and determined how many steps were needed to figure out each word.

Strategy Snapshot 8.1

Using Cross-Checking

Ms. Tate uses cross-checking with a small group of poor readers to stress that pronunciation should make sense. She presents them with the sentence. "Jane wanted to buy some _____" and asks what words would fit in the blank space. The children's suggestions, including *candy*, *clothes*, *cookies*, *books*, *raisins*, *flowers*, *toys*, *pets*, *shoes*, and *dolls*, are written on the board. When one child suggests *money* and another offers *friend*, Ms. Tate reads the sentence with those words inserted and asks if it makes sense. The children agree that it doesn't. Then Ms. Tate uncovers the first letter, which is a *c*. The choices narrow to *candy*, *clothes*, and *cookies*. The children agree that all three make sense; and when their teacher uncovers the entire word, they eagerly call out *candy*! Ms. Tate then gives them additional words that also start with *c* (*city*, *children*, *country*, *caps*, *cards*) and asks them if they make sense in the sentence. She reminds children that when a word is pronounced, they have to check for meaning.

Making Students Aware of Their Strategies

Several strategies to help your students figure out unknown words in print have been presented. However, to really master a strategy, your students need to become aware of what they are doing. How can you help them?

Remember that students need to see strategies modeled many times before they can use them. You must show them, over and over again, how you use these strategies to figure out unknown words.

You can also display the strategies. Put the strategies on a poster or have each student make a bookmark containing the steps in a strategy. One teacher created a bulletin board entitled "How to Read Words" and put the children's observations on the board. Another teacher placed a large tree branch in a bucket of sand and called it the "thinking tree." As students learned strategies for identifying words, they wrote them on cards and hung them on the thinking tree.

Finally, teachers can ask students to talk about how they use strategies. Helping students periodically review steps stresses the *how* of phonics instruction. Students can write down their own strategies on think cards. When students create their own versions of strategies, they personalize what you have taught them. Figure 8.1 presents examples of some student think cards.

Dealing with Exceptions

Sooner or later, students will come across words that are exceptions to the patterns that you are teaching. Rather than treating such exceptions as a problem, you can use them as an opportunity to make students aware that phonics does not always work.

FIGURE 8.1   Examples of Student Think Cards

(These retain original spelling)

Tiffany, grade 3

"When I read a book I use a strategie that strategie is to look at the pictures the pictures help me figure out what I an reading abot. When I use a strategie when I don't know a word frist I sond out the word if I get the word then I use my background knowlede of what I know abot the word."

Mark, grade 3

"If I come to a word in a sentence I don't know I think of a word with the same sounds as the word I don't know and see if it make sense. 1. kitchen, kitten, mitten 2. book, cook, hook, look, shook." (dictated to his teacher)

LaTonya, grade 2

"You think of a word you all redy now then you should get the word. Or tack the word in parts. Sound the word out a cople times. Think of a word you now in it. Does the word fit? grump jump"

For example, when you ask for words that have a *silent e*, students may suggest *have* and *love*, two words that are exceptions to the rule that the first vowel in the word takes a long sound when the second is a silent *e*. Write down such exceptions and tell the students that these words "don't play fair." Low-achieving readers often enjoy making lists of exceptions to use for sight vocabulary instruction. Exceptions also make students aware of the need to combine phonics and context clues.

Ideas for Practicing Phonics

To effectively learn phonics, students need to consistently practice letter-sound patterns. Only through extended use can low-achieving students learn to apply phonics quickly and accurately. This section gives ideas for ways to practice phonics.

Making Words.   Making words (Cunningham & Allington, 2002; Cunningham & Hall, 1994a, 1994b; Cunningham & Cunningham, 1992) involves students in actively thinking about letter-sound patterns as they use letters to make different words. This activity focuses on many different phonics patterns as children spell different words from a bigger word. By spelling, they practice creating phonics patterns. At the end of the activity, they can note similarities and differences among the words they have made.

To do the making words activity, choose a word such as *thunder* and identify *all* the words that can be made from it. Make seven cards, each containing one letter in *thunder*. Make larger squares with the same letters for your use at a chalkboard ledge. Now ask the students to make the words that you say. Begin with the shortest words, move gradually to longer words, and finally to the seven-letter word *thunder*. The sequence might look like this: *red, Ted, Ned, den, end, her, hut, herd, turn, hunt, hurt, under, hunted, turned,* and *thunder.*

Making words can be used with an individual or with a group. If you are working in a group, have individual children or pairs form each word. Then, when they have finished, have one student come to the front of the room and arrange your large letter cards into words from memory.

As each word is made, write it on a card. When all the words have been made, you will have a list of words that you can use to sort according to phonics patterns. For example, you might have students sort all of the words (made from *thunder*) that contain *ur, er,* or *ed.* You might have students sort into piles the words that contain short vowels and long vowels. Remind students that when they meet a new word or when they need to spell an unknown word, they can use these patterns to help them (Stahl, 1992).

Reading Books with Regular Phonics Patterns. Activities for practicing phonics in isolated words are enjoyable, but they will not allow students with reading problems to master phonics principles. *To master phonics, your students must read, read, read.* Only by getting practice figuring out unknown words while they are reading will students be able to *use* phonics. For this reason, this section and the next focus on materials to help students apply phonics in reading.

Students with problems can profit from using reading materials that are not only meaningful, but also present many phonetically regular words. Many books using phonetically regular words are enjoyable for children.

Caldwell and Leslie (2009) present a list of trade books that repeat different phonograms. Because poems contain many regular words, they can serve as a rich source for phonics practice. Strategy Snapshot 8.2 shows how one poem acts as a basis for a complete phonics teaching sequence.

Teaching Multisyllabic Words

As children move beyond beginning reading levels, they face the challenge of recognizing increasing numbers of multisyllabic words (words of more than one syllable). Some are relatively easy to pronounce, such as a single-syllable word joined to a common ending (*jumping, teacher*) or a compound word (*cowboy, airplane*). However, other multisyllabic words (*lilac, assisted, autograph*) are more complex. Recognizing such words is important because they often carry much of the meaning of a text.

Students with reading problems seem to have particular difficulty with multisyllabic words for several reasons:

1. Many students are simply scared by lengthy words and refuse even to try them. Some students "freeze" in front of words that contain eight or nine letters.
2. Students forget to combine phonics and context clues when they meet a long word. Unfortunately, many poor readers who have learned to use context for recognizing single-syllable words revert to only matching letters and sounds

Strategy Snapshot 8.2

Using Poetry to Teach Phonics

Mr. Lutz based a phonics lesson on the poem "Recipe for a Hippopotamus Sandwich" (by Silverstein). After he and his students read and discussed its silly story, he asked children for words that sounded alike. As they suggested *make, take, cake* and *ring, string,* he wrote each on the chalkboard under the headings -*ake* and -*ing.* Asked for more examples of these patterns, the children came up with and listed (in the proper place) *wake, sing,* and *rake.*

Mr. Lutz asked the children how knowing -*ake* and -*ing* would help them. He got them to verbalize the fact that they could use these sound patterns to figure out new words. To demonstrate, Mr. Lutz wrote "I will bring popcorn to the party." He asked them to pretend that they did not know "bring." How could they use the -*ing* in the word?

To apply this principle to other phonograms, Mr. Lutz picked out the words *slice* and *bread* from the poem and asked the children for other words that contain the sounds of -*ice* and -*ead.* They created two more lists of word families. When children offer -*led* as a rhyme for *bread,* Mr. Lutz pointed out that words that sound alike can be spelled differently or are exceptions.

Finally, Mr. Lutz copied the words from the board onto cards and handed some out to each child. As each child held up and read a word card (e.g., *nice*), another child supplied a word with the same phonogram (e.g., *twice*).

when faced with long words. Using a combination of clues is important when decoding multisyllabic words because they tend to contain irregular sound patterns; thus, students need to check what they have sounded out with the sense of the sentence.

3. Because students with reading problems often have limited meaning vocabularies, they may never have heard a particular long word before. If you have heard a word and know its meaning, being able to pronounce even a few parts may be enough to identify the entire word. However, if a word is not in your meaning vocabulary, you cannot check pronunciation against meaning. Several instructional strategies can help poor readers cope with long words.

Collecting Long Words. In this strategy, students are asked to collect long words that they can read. In doing this, they become aware that they can pronounce many long words and can use these long words to figure out words that they do not know (Cunningham, 2005). Having a collection of big words that students know also reduces the threat that such words often pose for low-achieving readers. As they become more comfortable with long words, they become eager to learn more.

To implement this strategy, ask students to note long words that they find interesting or important as they read. Don't ask them to select unknown words, because they may feel threatened. Often, however, students with reading problems will choose words that they have found difficult. To remember the targeted word, students can check them lightly with a pencil, use page markers or Post-it notes, or write the words on a separate sheet of paper.

Next, put the words on a blackboard and have students discuss them. Observe which other words they bring to mind, where to divide the syllables, and the sentence in the book that contained the word. This activity enables the students to combine context and phonics. If the students cannot figure out the word, help them work through clues, even if you must pronounce the word for them. In doing this activity, do not overwhelm students or keep them from enjoying reading. Limit students to two to three very important or interesting words per story.

After discussion, have students put each word on an index card. As the pile of cards gets larger, it becomes a visible reminder that they know many long words.

As this activity proceeds, you may want to make it more complex. For example, students can search for big words that fit into categories, such as describing words (or adjectives) like *astonished* and *overbearing*. Students can also look for synonyms. One class collected *staggered*, *evacuated*, and *advanced* for *moved* and *requested*, *communicated*, and *asserted* for *said*. Students can collect words with certain prefixes or suffixes. They can collect big words that all contain the same spelling pattern (*checkered*, *checkerboard*, *rechecked*, *checkbook*, *checkroom*). Within a short time, your students will have more than a hundred big words. As they list them, they will acquire comfort with multisyllabic words as well as a store of known words to use in figuring out unknown words.

Modeling Use of Analogies to Pronounce Long Words. Good readers often use analogies to decode multisyllabic words, just as they use them to decode one-syllable words. When they meet a multisyllabic word, they match patterns in the new word to similar patterns in a known word. A student might pronounce *publisher* by using the known words *tub*, *dish*, and *her*. However, the reader must know how to break the word into parts by looking for chunks already known.

To model the use of analogies, take a long word and explain to students the strategies you would use to pronounce it. You might write "The dark clouds portended bad weather" on the board. Then read the sentence, and when you come to *portended*, say something like, "I'm not sure I have ever seen that word before. I will read on and see if the sentence gives me a clue." After finishing the sentence, say "Well, I still don't know the word but I can figure it out. I recognize parts of it. I know *or* so *por* is easy. I know the word *tend* and I can add on the *ed* ending. So this word is *portended*. Now what does it mean?" Read the entire sentence again. "I can use context here. I know about dark clouds and rain so I bet that *portended* means the same as *signaled* or *indicated*."

You will need to model the use of analogies many, many times before students become comfortable using the strategy independently. Remember to give students opportunities to pronounce big words by making analogies to words they already know. Strategy Snapshot 8.3 focuses on modeling analogies with two third graders. To use known word parts to pronounce unknown words, students must be able to break long words into syllables. Using analogies with a multisyllabic word will not work if

Strategy Snapshot 8.3

Using Analogies to Decode Multisyllabic Words

When she came to a multisyllabic word, Deneese valiantly, but vainly, attempted to match letters and sounds, and Melanie would simply stop and say "I don't know." To help both students, Ms. Katz first identified a list of one-syllable words that each girl knew. Deneese and Melanie grouped these words according to the first vowel, putting *grab*, *black*, *snail* on the *a* list; *he*, *scream*, *treat* on the *e* list; *knife*, *pig*, *will* on the *i* list; and so on for *o* and *u*. These words were used as models for long, unknown words.

First the teacher wrote a multisyllabic word, such as *republic*, on the board. The teacher then separated the syllables, forming *re/pub/lic*. Deneese and Melanie searched their word lists for model words that had matching vowel patterns and wrote the key words underneath *republic*. The match for *re* was *he*; the match for *pub* was *club*; and the match for *ic* was *tic*. The girls first pronounced the known words (*he*, *pub*, and *tic*) and then transferred these sounds to the new word (*re*, *pub*, *lic*). Finally, Ms. Katz presented *republic* in a sentence and the girls used context to determine its meaning. Later in the semester, Ms. Katz began to ask the girls to try to divide the word into syllables for themselves by using their model words as a guide.

you do not know how to divide that word. However, teaching complex syllabication rules is often ineffective for poor readers (Johnson & Baumann, 1984). In our experience, work with phonograms and key words is much more profitable.

Assessing Structural Analysis Strategies

When readers use structural analysis clues, they break a word into meaningful parts and use these parts to help them both pronounce the word and understand its meaning. In contrast, low-achieving readers are unaware of how structural elements affect meaning. Thus, the teaching of structural analysis is an important element of teaching reading.

This section discusses basic structural analysis strategies, including compound words, contractions, and common word endings (inflectional suffixes), such as *s* (plural), *ed* (past tense), *er* and *est* (comparative), *'s* (possessive), and *ing* (gerunds and progressive tense). More advanced structural analysis strategies using prefixes, other suffixes, and roots are discussed in Chapter 10.

Students with reading problems tend not to use structural analysis strategies effectively. They are often unaware of how endings on words such as *talks*, *talking*, and *talked* signal time and number, and they often simply omit them during reading.

Miscue analysis provides information about a student's use of structural analysis clues. For example, students who repeatedly leave off word endings are demonstrating a need for analysis of word parts. In addition, informal discussion can provide much insight into the use of structural analysis clues.

For compound words, choose a few (*cowboy*, *steamboat*, *railroad*) and ask the students if there is anything unusual about them. Request that they tell you how each little word helps in knowing the meaning of the whole word. Asked about *cowboy*, Andy quickly stated that *cowboys* were boys who rode horses and shot guns in the movies, but he had no idea where cows fit into the picture.

To assess understanding of the meaning of contractions, write the base word on the board and then add the contraction. For example, write *can*; then under it, write *can't*. Ask the student if the two words are different in meaning. If the student seems unsure, place the contractions in two sentences: *I can write my name. I can't write my name.* If the student cannot verbalize the difference in meaning between the two sentences, target the contraction for instructional focus.

For inflectional endings, write both *bird* and *birds* on the board and ask your student to explain the difference in meaning. If the student is unsure, place the words in two sentences: *I have a bird. I have two birds.* Ask your student to explain the difference in meaning.

Teaching Structural Analysis Strategies

Many of the guidelines that are suggested for teaching phonics can also be used to teach basic structural analysis. To help students draw a connection between structural analysis elements and reading, ask students to collect words that contain certain word endings. Focus on meaning by telling students how adding endings changes the sense of a word but do not concentrate on spelling rules for adding endings or forming contractions.

One activity used successfully is called making words grow. Students take a one-syllable word and try to make it longer by adding inflectional endings, prefixes, or suffixes and by forming compound words. The student first writes the base word and then, directly under this word, writes a longer word. The third word is written under the second word. The base words must be written exactly under one another, for aligning them in this way allows students to see how additional structural elements change the words. Table 8.3 presents an example of making words grow.

Students enjoy trying to make lists as long as possible. They often willingly go to the dictionary to find additional words. Having students highlight the additions in color also helps to illustrate the structural analysis patterns.

One word of caution with regard to inflectional endings: They may pose a problem for speakers of nonstandard dialects and for bilingual students. Because these students may not use inflections consistently in their speech, they may have trouble reading them. When working with such students, the teacher should point out the meaning signified by the inflections but not be overly concerned about the student's pronunciation. If the student pronounces *Mary's* as *Mary* when reading orally, no corrections should be made. Rather, make sure that the student understands the meaning

TABLE 8.3   *Making Words Grow*

jump	camp	work
jumps	camps	works
jumped	camped	worked
jumping	camping	working
jumper	camper	worker
jumpy	campsite	workbook
	campout	workbench
		workman
		workshop
		workable

of the ending (Labov, 1967). Use the informal assessment procedures suggested in this chapter to determine this tendency.

Assessing Context Strategies

When readers use context strategies, they use the meaning of the passage to help them recognize a word. For example, a child might identify *elephant* because a picture of this animal appears on the page or because preceding pages were about zoo and circus animals. Thus, readers use their background knowledge and their understanding of the passage to focus on meaning. By using context clues, a student often can predict words that are left out of the text (a strategy known as *cloze*). See if you can fill in the blanks in the following story:

> We went to the zoo. We fed peanuts to the big gray *Elephant*. We watched the striped *zebra*. The *Giraffe* was funny with its long neck. The *Monkey* swung from tree to tree.
> Answers: elephant, zebra, giraffe, monkey

Because of your experiences with zoos, you probably had little difficulty supplying the missing words. You also used your understanding of how our language works. Readers know, for example, that articles such as *the* and adjectives such as *striped* tend to come before nouns. Even beginning readers use such language cues to help them identify words.

Beginning readers and those experiencing difficulties tend to be overly dependent on context. However, as they become more skilled, readers no longer use context to recognize words for three reasons (Stanovich, 1991). First, context strategies are not dependable for identifying a word. Research shows that words can be predicted from context only 10–20 percent of the time (Alexander, 1999). Second, word recognition through sight words is so rapid and automatic that context usage does not play a meaningful part. Finally, when good readers do not recognize a word automatically, they can use well-developed phonics skills. In fact, the ability to identify words accurately and quickly *out of context* is a characteristic of good readers (Perfetti, 1983, 1988; Stanovich, 1980, 1991).

In contrast, poor readers tend to overuse context precisely because they do *not* have a large sight vocabulary and cannot decode words quickly (Perfetti, 1985; Stanovich, 1986). However, context is not an effective clue for readers with difficulty. To use context to recognize some words, the reader needs to identify most of the other words accurately. Students with reading problems cannot recognize enough words to do this (Adams, 1990). In addition, a laborious focus on matching letters and sounds often demands so much attention that they lose the sense of what they are reading.

Context strategies, or meaning clues, may be assessed by using miscue analysis, through student interviews, and through comparison of words in lists and passages. Remember that students with reading difficulties have a tendency to overuse context strategies.

Miscue Analysis

As described in Chapter 4, miscue analysis, or an analysis of the errors students make during oral reading, is an excellent method for assessing the use of context clues. A student who supplies a word that makes sense in the passage is probably paying attention to context. A student whose miscue is a word that does *not* make sense in the passage is not using context clues.

Comparison of Words Recognized in Lists and Passages

Another way to assess the use of context is to contrast a student's ability to recognize a set of words in isolation (or list form) and in a passage. Students who can pronounce more words in a passage than a list are showing that they use context clues.

To construct this assessment, choose a passage at a student's instructional level and identify 20 words. First, ask the student to read these words in list form. Then ask the student to read the passage orally. For both readings, keep track of the number of targeted words read correctly. Students who recognize significantly more words in the passage than on the list are using context clues.

Teaching Context Strategies

As emphasized throughout this book, learning to recognize words is best done in the context of actual reading. If students with reading problems consistently read stories and books, they often naturally learn to make use of meaning clues. However, some students need further instruction with strategies that focus attention on using context.

Encouraging Students to Monitor for Meaning

Low-achieving students do not always demand meaning from reading. Often they continue reading long after the material has ceased to make sense to them. In fact, most of us have, from time to time, become aware that our eyes have been moving over the words, but we have no idea what they mean. What do we do? As good readers, we know that the purpose of reading is to gain meaning, so we stop and reread. Students with reading problems may finish an entire selection, proud for having "got the words right," but with no understanding of what they have read.

Thus, activities that focus on the use of context clues should reinforce the idea that reading should make sense. To encourage monitoring for meaning, have students stop periodically as they read and ask themselves four questions:

◆ Did what I just read make sense to me?
◆ Can I retell it in my own words?
◆ Are there any words that I do not understand?
◆ Are any sentences confusing to me?

Students can remind themselves to consider these questions by making bookmarks that display these questions. The teacher can also place brightly colored, removable dots in the margin at regular intervals throughout a reading as reminders for students to stop and ask themselves these questions.

Using Cloze

Cloze refers to deleting words from a passage and asking students to fill in the missing words. Students can write the missing words or supply them orally. The zoo passage presented earlier in this chapter is an example of a cloze passage. In supplying words, students practice working with context clues.

Go to MyEducationLab and select the topic *Comprehension*. Then, go to the Activities and Applications section, watch the video entitled "Word Analysis Strategy," and respond to the accompanying questions.

In constructing a cloze exercise, simply delete words from a passage. You can retype the passage or just "blacken" the words out with a magic marker. Which words should you delete? For general practice, try deleting every 10th word. Students will not be able to supply *all* the missing words, but they will get general practice in using meaning to read. Cloze can also be used to help students focus on certain types of words. For example, you might choose to delete only adjectives or connectives (*and*, *but*, *unless*). You might even choose to delete parts of words, such as word endings.

Teachers have several options for how students can respond. You may provide choices for the deleted words or ask the students to write or say the word that they think fits. Students may work alone or cooperatively to supply the words. If students write words into the passages, accept their spellings, even if they are incorrect. After students are finished filling in a cloze, go over the exercise and have them explain the reasons for their choices. Often this discussion demonstrates how class members used context clues.

Remember that as students fill in the blanks of a cloze exercise, they are not really *guessing*. Instead, they are *hypothesizing* based on their knowledge of the world around them, the content of the passage, and their knowledge of English. Remind students that they are consciously using these clues to predict words.

Summary

The stages of reading development include the logographic, partial alphabetic, full alphabetic, and sight word reading.

Readers use a variety of word recognition strategies to recognize words fluently and accurately. The use of sight words is the word recognition strategy that promotes *fluent* reading. Mature readers recognize most words as sight words.

The word recognition strategies that promote *accurate* reading include:

◆ Phonics or letter-sound patterns to help readers decode letters into sounds
◆ Structural analysis to help readers recognize compound words, word endings, contractions, and prefixes and suffixes
◆ Context, or meaning clues, to help readers decode words

Assessment of phonics can involve miscue analysis and using nonsense words that illustrate phonics patterns.

Poor readers need explicit emphasis on phonics. Teachers may organize their teaching by using phonograms (or rimes) and analogies. Decoding by analogy, or recognizing unfamiliar words by using known words, is an excellent way to approach phonics instruction. The combination of phonics and meaning clues can be promoted by cross-checking and using the four-step strategy. Students should be aware both of the strategies they use and of exceptions to the phonics pattern.

Activities for providing practice in phonics include making words to illustrate common patterns, reading books with regular phonics patterns, and most important, extensive reading. Phonics instruction should also focus on helping students deal with long words. To learn multisyllabic words, students can collect long words, use analogies, or practice breaking words into syllables using transformations.

Assessment of structural analysis strategies involves an informal evaluation method. Teaching methods include making words grow and collecting lists of words with certain endings.

Assessment of context strategies includes analyzing miscues and comparing a student's ability to read words in a list with the same words in a passage. Readers experiencing difficulties often overuse context strategies. To foster the effective use of context strategies, students should monitor for meaning as they read.

References

Adams, M. J. (1990). *Beginning to Read: Thinking and Learning About Print.* Cambridge, MA: MIT Press.
Alexander, D. (1999). *Keys to Successful Learning: A National Summit of Research on Learning Disabilities.* New York: National Center for Learning Disabilities.

Allen, L. (1998). An integrated strategies approach: Making word identification instruction work for beginning readers. *The Reading Teacher, 52*, 254–270.

Beck, I. L. (2006). *Making Sense of Phonics: The Hows and Whys.* New York: The Guilford Press.

Caldwell, J. S. (2008). *Reading Assessment: A Primer for Teachers and Coaches.* New York: The Guilford Press.

Caldwell, J. S., Leslie, L. (2009). *Intervention Strategies to Follow Informal Reading Inventory Assessment: So What Do I Do Now?* New York: Allyn and Bacon.

Chall, J. S. (1979). The great debate: Ten years later with a modest proposal for reading stages. In L. B. Resnick & P. A. Weaver (Eds.), *Theory and Practice of Early Reading* (vol. 1), pp. 29–55. Hillsdale, NJ: Erlbaum.

Chall, J. S. (1967). *Learning to Read: The Great Debate.* New York: McGraw-Hill.

Cunningham, P. M. (2005). *Phonics They Use: Words for Reading and Writing* (4th Ed.). Boston: Allyn & Bacon.

Cunningham, P. M. (1990). The names test: A quick assessment of decoding ability. *The Reading Teacher, 44*, 124–129.

Cunningham, P. M., & Allington, R. L. (2002). *Classrooms that Work: They Can All Read and Write* (3rd Ed.). New York: Allyn & Bacon.

Cunningham, P. M., & Cunningham, J. W. (1992). Making words: Enhancing the invented spelling-decoding connection. *The Reading Teacher, 46*, 106–115.

Cunningham, P. M., & Hall, D. P. (1994a). *Making Big Words.* Carthage, IL: Good Apple.

Cunningham, P. M., & Hall, D. P. (1994b). *Making Words.* Carthage, IL: Good Apple.

Duffelmeyer, F. A., Kruse, A. E., Merkeley, D. J., & Fyfe, S. A. (1999). Further validation and enhancement of the names test. In S. J. Barrentine (Ed.). *Reading Assessment: Principles and Practices for Elementary Teachers*, pp. 177–188. Newark, DE: International Reading Association.

Ehri, L. C. (1997). *The development of children's ability to read words.* Paper presented at the convention of the International Reading Association. Atlanta, GA.

Ehri, L. C. (1994). Development of the ability to read words: Update. In R. Ruddell & H. Singer (Eds.), *Theoretical Models and Processes of Reading* (4th Ed.). Newark, DE: International Reading Association.

Ehri, L. C. (1991). Development of the ability to read words. In R. Barr, M. L. Kamil, P. Mosenthal, & P. D. Pearson (Eds.), *Handbook of Reading Research* (2nd Ed.). New York: Longman.

Ehri, L. C., Nunes, S. R., Stahl, S. A., & Willows, D. M. (2001). Systematic phonics instruction helps students learn to read: Evidence from the national reading panel's meta-analysis. *Review of Educational Research, 71*, 393–447.

Fry, E. (2004). Phonics: A large phoneme-grapheme frequency count revised. *Journal of Literacy Research, 36*, 85–98.

Gaskins, I. W., & Downer, M. (1986). *Benchmark Word Identification/Vocabulary Development Program: Beginning Level.* Media, PA: Benchmark Press.

Gaskins, I. W., Cress, C., O'Hara, C., & Donnelly, K. (1996). *Overview of Word Detectives. Benchmark Extended Word Identification Program for Beginning Readers.* Media, PA: Benchmark School.

Gaskins, I. W., Ehri, L. C., Cress, C., O'Hara, C., & Donnelly, K. (1996). Procedures for word learning: Making discoveries about words. *The Reading Teacher, 50*, 312–327.

Gaskins, I. W., Soja, S., Indrisano, A., Lawrence, H., Elliot, T., Rauch, S., et al. (1986). *Benchmark School Word Identification/Vocabulary Development Program.* Media, PA: Benchmark School.

Goswami, U., & Bryant, P. (1990). *Phonological Skills in Learning to Read.* Mahwah, NJ: Erlbaum.

Goswami, U., & Mead, F. (1992). Onset and rime awareness and analogies in reading. *Reading Research Quarterly, 27*, 150–162.

Johnson, D. D., & Baumann, J. F. (1984). Word identification. In P. D. Pearson (Ed.), *Handbook of Reading Research*, pp. 583–608. White Plains, NY: Longman.

Johnston, F. P. (2001). The utility of phonics generalizations: Let's take another look at Clymer's conclusions. *The Reading Teacher, 55*, 132–153.

Johnston, F. P. (1999). The timing and teaching of word families. *The Reading Teacher, 53*, 64–75.

Meisels, S. J., & Piker, R. A. (2001). An analysis of early literacy assessments used for instruction. www.ciera.org/library/reports/inquiry-2/2-013/2-013.html.

National Reading Panel (2000). *Teaching Children to Read: An Evidence-Based Assessment of the Scientific Research Literature on Reading and Its Implications for Reading Instruction: Reports of the Subgroups*

(National Institute of Health Pub. No. 00-4754). Washington, DC: National Institute of Child Health and Human Development.

Perfetti, C. A. (1988). Verbal efficiency in reading ability. In M. Daneman, G. E. MacKinnon, & T. G. Waller (Eds.), *Reading Research: Advances in Theory and Practice* (vol. 6), pp. 109–143. New York: Academic Press.

Perfetti, C. A. (1985). *Reading Ability.* New York: Oxford University Press.

Perfetti, C. A. (1983). Discourse context, word identification, and reading ability. In J. F. Le Ny & W. Kintsch (Eds.), *Language and Comprehension.* New York: North-Holland Publishing Company.

Southwest Educational Development Laboratory. (2006). *Reading assessment database for grades K-2.* Retrieved from www.sedl.org/reading/rad/list.html.

Spear-Swerling, L., & Sternberg, R. J. (1996). *Off Track: When Poor Readers Become "Learning Disabled."* Boulder, CO: Westview Press.

Stahl, S. A. (1992). Saying the "p" word: Nine guidelines for exemplary phonics instruction. *The Reading Teacher, 45,* 618–625.

Stanovich, K. E. (1991). Word recognition: Changing perspectives. In R. Barr, M. L. Kamil, P. Mosenthal, & P. D. Pearson (Eds.), *Handbook of Reading Research* (Vol. II), pp. 418–452. New York: Longman.

Stanovich, K. E. (1986). Matthew effects in reading. Some consequences of individual differences in the acquisition of literacy. *Reading Research Quarterly, 21,* 360–406.

Stanovich, K. E. (1980). Toward an interactive-compensatory model of individual differences in the development of reading fluency. *Reading Research Quarterly, 16,* 32–71.

Vacca, J., Vacca, R., Gove, M. (2000). *Reading and Learning to Read.* New York: Longman.

Wolfe, M. (2007). *Proust and the Squid.* New York: Harper Collins.

MyEducationLab is a research-based learning tool that brings teaching to life. Go to the Jennings, Caldwell, & Lerner 6th Edition MyEducationLab for Reading Assessment site at www.myeducationlab.com to:

◆ engage in multimedia exercises to help you build a deeper and more applied understanding of chapter content;

◆ utilize extensive resources including videos from real classrooms, Praxis and licensure preparation, a lesson plan builder, and materials to help you in your teaching career.

Improving Reading Fluency

Introduction

Contrast two different oral readers. One reads a selection at an appropriate rate of speed. Tom reads smoothly, confidently, and with expression, clearly conveying the author's thoughts to an appreciative audience. Listening to this kind of reader is enjoyable, and we are sorry when he reaches the end of the text. After finishing, he talks about what he read and shows clearly that he comprehended the text. Sarah approaches the text hesitantly. She reads tentatively, skipping, repeating, and stumbling over words. This reader is uncomfortable and pauses often as if uncertain how to continue. Her voice has little expression, and when she finishes, the listener is as relieved as the performer. This reader demonstrates little understanding of what was read. These two readers are very different. One reader is fluent; the other is not, and what a difference it makes.

This chapter first defines fluency and explains its importance to the reading process. Next, it suggests methods of assessment. Most of the chapter focuses on instructional strategies for developing fluency at both a text and word level.

Role of Fluency in the Reading Process

Fluency involves three components: word identification accuracy, reading rate, and expression, often called *prosody* (Stahl, 2004; Richards, 2000). In the past, fluency was often equated solely with rate or speed of reading, or it was primarily characterized as automatic word recognition. Both of these definitions represent a limited perspective. The National Reading Panel (2000) clearly defines fluency as reading with accuracy, speed, and expression and doing so without conscious or overt attention on the part of the reader. Let us examine each of these elements.

The first component of fluency is accuracy. Fluent readers identify both familiar and unfamiliar words accurately. Unfamiliar words are words they have never before seen in print. Using decoding processes described in Chapter 8, fluent readers match letter and sound patterns and pronounce these new words almost effortlessly. Familiar words are words they have seen before. They may have initially identified them by applying the decoding process, but they have seen them so often that they can now identify them from memory. We call these familiar words *sight words*.

The second component of fluency is speed. Fluent readers identify both unfamiliar and familiar (sight) words instantaneously. They engage in the word identification process without conscious thought or overt attention. Because fluent readers identify almost all words automatically and quickly, they can devote their energies to the meaning of what they are reading (Cunningham & Allington, 2007; Cunningham, 2005).

The third component of fluency is expressiveness. Because fluent readers understand the text, they can read with suitable expression, using punctuation signals and varying voice tone to convey meaning. They read expressively by identifying cues in the structure of the text and the language that suggest the proper pitch, stress, and juncture to use (Richards, 2000). Unless readers understand what they are reading, they are not able to take advantage of such cues.

To be fluent, readers must have three things (Caldwell & Leslie, 2009). They must have effective strategies for decoding unfamiliar words (discussed in Chapter 8). Readers must also have a large number of sight words, words that are recognized immediately without any analysis. Finally, readers must understand that the purpose of reading is comprehension.

Many students with reading problems lack fluency. They have difficulty in pronouncing unfamiliar words. Because they lack an adequate sight vocabulary, they must labor to decode many of the words in their text. They read slowly, and their reading is filled with long pauses, constant repetitions, and monotonous expression. Little comprehension occurs because they focus their energies on simply recognizing words.

Struggling readers need much reading practice if they are to become fluent. Unfortunately, many low-achieving readers do not enjoy reading, find it a frustrating experience, and avoid it as much as possible (Rasinski, 2000). Because they do not read extensively, they do not develop a good sight vocabulary. In turn, lack of sight vocabulary makes reading more difficult. Thus, a vicious cycle develops (Stanovich, 1986). Teachers will find ideas in this chapter for helping their students avoid this negative cycle and for making reading an enjoyable, positive experience.

Assessing Word Recognition Fluency

Go to MyEducationLab and select the topic *Instructional Decision Making*. Then, go to the Activities and Applications section, read the case study entitled "Fluency and Word Identification," and respond to the accompanying questions.

Ways to assess fluency include listening to students read orally, determining reading rate, and timed administration of word lists. All three can be part of the administration of an informal reading inventory. However, the teacher can use these assessment procedures with any text or word list.

Listening to Students Read Orally

A teacher can determine whether students are fluent readers simply by listening to their oral reading. Three common problems with fluency are:

♦ Students stumble over individual words trying out different possible pronunciations. They repeat words. They pause. Their performance is choppy and marked by uncertainty and hesitation.
♦ Students read the text as if it were a list of disconnected words. There is little expression or variation in the rise and fall of their voices. They do not change their voices to indicate a period, an exclamation mark, or a question. They do not insert expression into segments of dialogue.
♦ Students race through the text as if the entire purpose of reading is to complete it. They ignore sentence breaks and their focus on speed causes them to make errors even on familiar words.

Many students with reading problems have a combination of these problems, because fluent reading demands that accuracy, automaticity, and expression work together.

To judge a student's fluency, simply listen to him or her read a text at an instructional or independent level. Using your own common sense and your knowledge and appreciation of what fluent reading sounds like, you can determine whether the reading is fluent. You may want to compare audiotapes of a student's reading made at different times to assess improvement. Students are often motivated by listening to their own tapes. Josh reviewed tapes of his oral reading done at the beginning and end of the semester. He frowned and actually put his head down on the desk as he listened to his first halting and choppy rendition. When he heard himself reading the same passage several months later, he broke into smiles. In his journal, he wrote, "I sounded real real REAL good!"

Determining Reading Rate

Reading rate can be measured in two ways. The most common method is to determine the number of words read per minute (WPM), discussed in Chapter 4. A second way is to determine the number of correct words read per minutes (CWPM).

Words per Minute (WPM).   Have the student read a selection at his or her instructional or independent level. Using the instructional or independent reading level is important because we are all less fluent in frustration-level text, in text on an unfamiliar topic, or in text written in an unfamiliar structure. How fluent would you be reading a mortgage agreement or directions for filling out an income tax form? As the student reads orally or silently, time the reading and then calculate words per minute (WPM). Multiply the number of words in the passage by 60 and then divide by the number of seconds it took to read the passage (Chapter 5).

A student's reading rate must be interpreted with some caution. Normal readers show a wide range of acceptable reading rates, even at the same grade level (Carver, 1990). Reading rate also varies across different selections. Most people, for example, read movie reviews faster than they read editorials. Because of this variability, do not compare the rates of individual students with one another. Table 5.9 on page 123 offers some general guidelines or ranges for students reading passages at different levels. However, remember that these levels are not absolute levels that a student should attain.

Correct Words per Minute.   Determining the number of correct words per minute (CWPM) is similar to determining words per minute, but in this case, you count only the number of words that were read correctly. Count as errors all mispronunciations, substitutions, additions, and omissions. What about errors that do not change meaning? You may choose not to count these (see Chapter 5); it is your decision. What about errors that are self-corrected? Again, you decide whether to count these. Just be consistent.

Take the number of words in the passage and subtract the number of errors. Then multiply this by 60. Finally, divide by the number of seconds it took the child to read the selection.

To contrast WPM and CWPM, let's take an example of a child who read a 346-word passage with 24 errors. The child took 3 minutes and 45 seconds to read the passage.

$$\text{WPM: } \frac{346 \text{ words} \times 60 = 20{,}760}{225 \text{ seconds}} = 92 \text{ WPM}$$

$$\text{CWPM: } \frac{346 \text{ words} - 24 \text{ errors} \times 60 = 19{,}320}{225 \text{ seconds}} = 86 \text{ CWPM}$$

Which method should you use? Both have their place. Proponents of CWPM feel that it allows you to "index both accuracy and speed" (Kame'enui & Simmons, 2001, p. 205). However, if you determine WPM in instructional or independent level text, you are also allowing for the interaction of accuracy and speed.

However, consider a word of caution regarding fluency assessment: It is often used as a proxy for comprehension or overall reading proficiency (Caldwell, 2008). A *proxy* is a form of substitute or stand-in for the real thing. Because fluency scores are highly correlated with comprehension scores on formal standardized measures and because it is much easier and faster to measure fluency than comprehension, educators often accept a fluency measure as indicative of adequate or inadequate comprehension. Almost all early literacy assessments include fluency as an important component (Southwest Educational Development Laboratory, 2006; Meisels & Piker, 2001). Fluency as a comprehension proxy is also part of a process called *curriculum-based measurement* where students orally read grade-level texts and their fluency rates are used to indicate reading proficiency (Hasbrouk & Tindal, 2006; Fuchs, Fuchs, Hosp & Jenkins, 2001; Good, Simmons & Kame'enui, 2001; Davidson & Myhre, 2000).

Experts acknowledge the importance of fluency but fluency assessment should never completely substitute for assessment of a student's comprehension—nor should teachers focus on fluency instruction and naively assume that if fluency increases, comprehension will do so as well. It may or it may not. If teachers emphasize fluency development to the detriment of comprehension instruction, teachers "may deny students what they most need, instruction in strategies for comprehension" (Caldwell, 2008, p. 152).

Timed Administration of Word Lists

Although the previous two strategies enable teachers to judge contextual fluency, the timed administration of word lists is used to judge automatic *sight word* recognition. Compare (1) *automatic* (or timed) recognition of isolated words with (2) *total* (or timed plus untimed) recognition of isolated words (both automatic words and those recognized after analysis).

To judge automaticity, give the student a list of words to recognize (such as in an informal reading inventory (IRI) or in Tables 9.1 and 9.2). As the student reads, record performance on a teacher's copy. For each word in the list, three responses are possible: (1) recognized automatically, (2) recognized after hesitation or analysis, and (3) not identified correctly. A word pronounced correctly within 1 second is marked as an automatic word. (To judge 1 second, say to yourself "one thousand." If the student pronounces the word before you are finished, count the word as automatic.) A word recognized correctly, but not automatically, is an analysis word; and of course, a word recognized incorrectly is not identified correctly.

To compare a student's instantaneous word recognition, compare automatic words and total words known (automatic words plus analysis words). If a student's total number of words is much larger than the automatic words, the student needs to practice instant recognition of sight words.

Timed administration of word lists can be helpful for assessing sight words; however, remember that reading words in lists is not real reading. In real life, we do not curl up with a good list of words! For this reason, your assessment of a student's performance should combine word-list performance with the reading of selections.

Strategies for Developing Fluency in Context

This section describes strategies for improving the ability to read passages fluently.

Promoting Wide Reading of Easy Text

A large amount of reading is critical to developing fluent reading. As students read to enjoy a story or acquire interesting information, they are unconsciously improving their reading fluency. In addition, they become comfortable with combining all word identification strategies to read in context.

Getting students with reading problems to read is a major challenge for their teachers. To get them to read, teachers must make reading enjoyable, provide regular and daily opportunities to read, and encourage reading at home. To build fluency, students need to read easy books filled with words they can recognize. Teachers should schedule time for reading. Begin by setting aside periods of about 10 minutes, because low-achieving students have difficulty concentrating during long sessions. Then these periods can be gradually increased to 20 or 25 minutes.

Low-achieving readers often have trouble choosing a book that will foster accurate and fluent word recognition. Students with problems generally select material that is too hard, or they flit from book to book without really reading any of them. To foster better choices, you can read easy books to students and then prominently display the books in your classroom. Students often choose these books to read on their own. You can also give the student several books and ask that he or she choose from among them, or you can allow the student to reread books or stories from past lessons.

Basically, you want low-achieving readers to read at their independent level. At this level, they meet few unfamiliar words, and the repetition of words they already

TABLE 9.1 Basic Sight Vocabulary Words

Preprimer	Primer	First	Second	Third
1. the	45. when	89. many	133. know	177. don't
2. of	46. who	90. before	134. while	178. does
3. and	47. will	91. must	135. last	179. got
4. to	48. more	92. through	136. might	180. united
5. a	49. no	93. back	137. us	181. left
6. in	50. if	94. years	138. great	182. number
7. that	51. out	95. where	139. old	183. course
8. is	52. so	96. much	140. year	184. war
9. was	53. said	97. your	141. off	185. until
10. he	54. what	98. may	142. come	186. always
11. for	55. up	99. well	143. since	187. away
12. it	56. its	100. down	144. against	188. something
13. with	57. about	101. should	145. go	189. fact
14. as	58. into	102. because	146. came	190. through
15. his	59. than	103. each	147. right	191. water
16. on	60. them	104. just	148. used	192. less
17. be	61. can	105. those	149. take	193. public
18. at	62. only	106. people	150. three	194. put
19. by	63. other	107. Mr.	151. states	195. thing
20. I	64. new	108. how	152. himself	196. almost
21. this	65. some	109. too	153. few	197. hand
22. had	66. could	110. little	154. house	198. enough
23. not	67. time	111. state	155. use	199. far
24. are	68. these	112. good	156. during	200. took
25. but	69. two	113. very	157. without	201. head
26. from	70. may	114. make	158. again	202. yet
27. or	71. then	115. would	159. place	203. government
28. have	72. do	116. still	160. American	204. system
29. an	73. first	117. own	161. around	205. better
30. they	74. any	118. see	162. however	206. set
31. which	75. my	119. men	163. home	207. told
32. one	76. now	120. work	164. small	208. nothing
33. you	77. such	121. long	165. found	209. night
34. were	78. like	122. get	166. Mrs.	210. end
35. her	79. our	123. here	167. thought	211. why
36. all	80. over	124. between	168. went	212. called
37. she	81. man	125. both	169. say	213. didn't
38. there	82. me	126. life	170. part	214. eyes
39. would	83. even	127. being	171. once	215. find
40. their	84. most	128. under	172. general	216. going
41. we	85. made	129. never	173. high	217. look
42. him	86. after	130. day	174. upon	218. asked
43. been	87. also	131. same	175. school	219. later
44. has	88. did	132. another	176. every	220. knew

Source: From Dale D. Johnson, "The Dolch List Reexamined," *The Reading Teacher*, *24* (February 1971), pp. 455–456. The 220 most frequent words in the Kucera-Francis corpus. Reprinted with permission of Dale D. Johnson and the International Reading Association.

TABLE 9.2 Picture Sight Words

1.	farm	23.	telephone	45.	mouth	67.	ear
2.	clothes	24.	hat	46.	nose	68.	skates
3.	money	25.	window	47.	garden	69.	sled
4.	water	26.	television	48.	hand	70.	radio
5.	grass	27.	car	49.	snow	71.	clown
6.	fence	28.	cookie	50.	rain	72.	bread
7.	stoplight	29.	apple	51.	fire	73.	tree
8.	bus	30.	school	52.	dish	74.	mirror
9.	balloon	31.	book	53.	hair	75.	bag
10.	cake	32.	chicken	54.	children	76.	pumpkin
11.	duck	33.	nurse	55.	lion	77.	flag
12.	barn	34.	store	56.	world	78.	candle
13.	street	35.	door	57.	watch	79.	castle
14.	hill	36.	doctor	58.	picture	80.	jewel
15.	man	37.	teacher	59.	shoes	81.	bicycle
16.	house	38.	egg	60.	bed	82.	baby
17.	woman	39.	rabbit	61.	chair	83.	sock
18.	airplane	40.	flower	62.	table	84.	horse
19.	train	41.	sun	63.	spoon	85.	ring
20.	boat	42.	cloud	64.	fork		
21.	dog	43.	shadow	65.	truck		
22.	cat	44.	eye	66.	bird		

Source: Compiled from a survey of widely used basal readers.

recognize fosters fluency. Administering an IRI can help you determine their independent level. Many publishers of trade books code their selections by readability level. Fountas and Pinnell (1996) present an extensive list of books that spans kindergarten through late fourth grade.

Using Patterned Books

Patterned books, which contain refrains that are repeated over and over, are an excellent source of easy books. These books are invaluable for fostering word recognition because the repeated refrains in the books provide extensive support for word recognition. Table 9.3 presents a list of patterned trade books.

How can teachers use patterned books most effectively? When introducing a patterned book, begin by paging through it with your students, reviewing pictures, and predicting the story line. Next, read the book to your children modeling fluent reading and perhaps inviting them to join in the refrains. After reading the book once, invite students to join you in rereading it. Experiences with joint readings foster confidence and fluency. Then individual students may reread the book with the teacher's help at troublesome points.

TABLE 9.3 Examples of Patterned Books

Level A

At the Zoo	Carol Kloes
Ghost	Storybox Book by the Wright Group
My Home	Literacy 2000 by Rigby
The Storm	Sunshine Book by the Wright Group

Level B

Cat on the Mat	Brian Wildsmith
Little Red Hen	Windmill-Look and Listen by the Wright Group

Level C

Brown Bear, Brown Bear	Bill Martin, Jr.
I Went Walking	Sue Williams

Level D

I Can Build a House	Shigeo Watanabe
Lizard Loses his Tail	PM Books by Rigby
School Bus	Donald Crews
Tails	Marcia Vaughn

Level E

Inside, Outside, Upside Down	Stan and Jan Berenstain
All by Myself	Mercer Mayer
Big Friend, Little Friend	Eloise Greenfield
Five Little Monkeys Jumping on the Bed	Eileen Christelow

Level F

Just Like Daddy	Frank Asch
When It Rains	Marilyn Frankford
Rosie's Walk	Pat Hutchins
Herman the Helper Lends a Hand	Robert Krauss

Level G

More Spaghetti I Say	Rita Gelman
The Bus Stop	Nancy Hellen
Titch	Pat Hutchins
Sheep in a Jeep	Nancy Shaw
Not Me, Said the Monkey	Colin West

Level H

Goodnight Moon	Margaret Wise Brown
A Picture for Harold's Room	Crockett Johnson
Whose Mouse Are You?	Robert Kraus
Toolbox	Anne Rockwell

Level I

Are You My Mother?	P.D. Eastman
Hattie and the Fox	Mem Fox
Henny Penny	Paul Galdone
Goodnight Owl	Pat Hutchins
Tidy Titch	Pat Hutchins
Leo, the Late Bloomer	Robert Kraus
Noisy Nora	Rosemary Wells

Level J

Drummer Hoff	Ed Emberley
The Doorbell Rang	Pat Hutchins
Mouse Soup	Arnold Lobel
Little Bear, Little Bear's Friend, Little Bear's Visit	Else Holmelund Minarik
Henry and Mudge Series	Cynthia Rylant
The Cat in the Hat	Dr. Seuss

Level K

A Letter to Amy	Ezra Jack Keats
Frog and Toad Are Friends, Frog and Toad Together	Arnold Lobel
If You Give a Mouse a Cookie	Laura Joffe Numeroff

Level L

Miss Nelson Is Missing	Harry Allard
The Josefina Story Quilt	Eleanor Coerr
Over in the Meadow	Paul Galdone
The Wind Blew	Pat Hutchins
George and Martha	James Marshall

Level M

Cloudy with a Chance of Meatballs	Judi Barrett
The Chalk Box Kid	Clyde Robert Bulla
Did You Carry the Flag Today, Charley?	Rebecca Caudill
Cherries and Cherry Pits	Vera B. Williams

Levels A–B	Kindergarten and Early Grade One
Levels C–H	Grade One
Level I	Late Grade One
Level J	Early Grade Two
Levels K–M	Grade Two

Source: Fountas & Pinnell (1996); Lynch-Brown & Tomlinson (1999).

A word of caution concerning patterned books: Many children easily memorize the text. When they "read," they may turn pages at appropriate places and seem to look at the page, but they are actually reciting from memory. To foster real reading, periodically ask students to read text-only copies of patterned books (Johnston, 1998) so they focus more directly on words. You can also print the words from patterned books on word cards and use them to assess if students can recognize the words.

Youngsters will probably need (and want) to review patterned books several times to foster fluency. After reading a patterned book, leave it in a conspicuous place so that students will be able to pick it up and look at it. Creating an environment rich in these books is extremely important.

In addition to their use with primary and lower intermediate-grade students, patterned books also appeal to older students who read at primary levels. To help these students, encourage them to read these books to younger children.

Assisted Oral Reading

Oral reading practice is an effective way to promote fluency (Caldwell & Leslie, 2009; Kuhn, 2007; Reutzel & Morrow, 2007; Stahl, 2004; Rasinski, 2003; Johns & Bergland, 2002) and it can take many forms. In assisted oral reading, a student or group of students and a fluent reader (usually the teacher) read material together.

Assisted reading is an excellent way to develop fluency for many reasons:

Go to MyEducationLab and select the topic *Fluency*. Then, go to the Activities and Applications section, watch the video entitled "Aesthetic Listening," and respond to the accompanying questions.

1. The teacher's support makes reading a nonthreatening activity.
2. Because word recognition efforts are supported by a fluent reader, students can pay attention to meaning and enjoy the selection.
3. Assisted reading gives a model of fluent reading. Students are exposed to the way that reading should sound and have a model to work toward. Too many poor readers are exposed to the halting, choppy reading of their peers.
4. Assisted reading provides practice reading in context. It also motivates students to read more, because after joint readings, students often read the same books independently.

Because the eventual goal of assisted reading is to promote independent reading, the teacher must gradually provide less and less support. In the beginning, teachers may simply read to the students and invite them to participate and say words when they feel comfortable—or the teacher may begin by reading an entire selection together with the students. Gradually, however, the teacher's role should be reduced so that students learn that they can read a new book on their own.

Simultaneous Assisted Reading. In this assisted reading strategy, the teacher simply reads along with the students. The teacher sets the pace and resists the temptation to slow down to the reading rate of the student, who will always lag slightly behind. When a student meets an unfamiliar word, the teacher pronounces it, and they move on. If a group is reading with the teacher, few involved in the activity will even notice that one student did not know a word. At times, you will notice a drop in volume at a certain word. You can then mark this word as a possible problem and teach it after the reading is finished.

Simultaneous reading can be changed to meet the needs and levels of your students. Sometimes, the teacher may fade out at key words and phrases to assess whether students can identify them independently. At other times, the teacher may have several students read a page together without teacher assistance. Simultaneous assisted reading is most effective when combined with repeated reading of the same book or story. To foster independence, the teacher participates less and less in each subsequent reading.

Echo Reading.   Modeling oral reading and asking the students to imitate you is another form of assisted reading. The teacher reads a few lines or a page of text to the students to model a fluent pace and effective voice expression. The students imitate the teacher's performance, or *echo* the text. Echo reading works best for short segments of text and is particularly well suited for beginning readers.

Partner Reading.   In partner reading, students read in pairs, usually by alternating pages. This type of reading provides extensive reading practice for both students. Partner reading can be an effective way to help students with reading problems develop fluency (Stahl & Heubach, 2005; Stahl, Heubach, & Cramond, 1997). However, because you want the students to experience success, you should have them read the material alone a few times before they read as partners. This practice avoids the danger of encountering too many unknown words or becoming frustrated. Often, other forms of assisted reading are used with a passage before students are asked to read with partners.

Teachers may organize students as reading partners in different ways. Sometimes, students enjoy choosing their friends as reading partners. At other times, the teacher can pair students who differ in reading abilities. Low-achieving readers of similar ability work well as partners if preliminary support has been provided. Pairing two children with reading problems helps each to realize that he or she is not the only one who has problems with words. Student self-esteem increases through the act of helping others. Danny and Peter became fast friends as a result of consistent partner reading. At one point, Danny confided, "Peter didn't know a word, and I helped him. He helps me too. When we read together, we are pretty good readers!"

Paired Reading.   Paired reading involves pairing a struggling reader with a more capable one. Originally developed by Topping (1987, 1989) as a strategy for parents and their children to read together, it can be used in a variety of other ways. The capable reader can be a parent, a tutor, an aide, or even an older student.

The student selects the material to be read, ideally at his or her instructional level. The student and tutor begin reading together, maintaining a reasonable pace. If the student mispronounces a word, the tutor says it correctly and asks the student to repeat it. When the student chooses to read independently, he or she signals the tutor using a prearranged signal such as a tap or nudge. The tutor stops reading at this point, and the student continues. If the student meets an unfamiliar word, the tutor waits approximately 5 seconds. If the student cannot pronounce the word, the tutor supplies it, and the pair resumes reading together. The paired reading continues until the student signals a desire to once again read on his or her own. Topping recommends sessions of 15 to 30 minutes in length.

Neurological Impress Method (NIM). This read-along strategy (Heckelman, 1969), often abbreviated NIM, involves the teacher and one student reading together. According to Heckelman, students learn by emulating a fluent reading model. The NIM technique is particularly effective with reading-disabled adolescents.

In NIM, the student and teacher read together orally. Begin by reading material at the student's independent level or material that has been read before. Tell your student not to be concerned about reading accuracy but to try to read fluently, without looking back.

At first, the teacher reads slightly louder and faster. As the student gains fluency and confidence, the teacher begins to read more softly and may even start to lag slightly behind the student. However, if the student encounters difficulty, the teacher should rescue the student in a firm manner. When beginning this procedure, teachers should follow the text with their fingers at the pace of the reading. As the student gains confidence, he or she can assume the responsibility for pointing to the words. The NIM strategy is a key component of the reading acceleration program (RAP), a K–8 school wide intervention aimed at low-income English language learners (Feazell, 2004).

Repeated Readings

In the repeated readings strategy, an individual student rereads a short selection until a certain level of word identification accuracy and fluency is attained (Samuels, 1979). As students read the same selection a number of times, they become more accurate, their reading speed increases, and their reading becomes more expressive (Johns & Bergland, 2002; Dowhower, 1994).

To begin repeated readings, give the student a passage of 50 to 200 words written at his or her independent or instructional level. Have the student read the selection orally. As your student reads, record the reading speed and any deviations from the text. Next, discuss any word recognition miscues with your student. Then, over a few sessions, have the student practice the selection until he or she feels capable of reading it fluently. Then have the student read the selection orally again as you record time and accuracy. The process is repeated until a certain accuracy or rate score is reached. At this point, the student moves to another reading selection.

The repeated readings strategy can be readily adapted to different student needs. To provide more extensive assistance, a teacher can read with the student until he or she feels confident enough to read alone—or students can be asked to listen to their own tapes to see if they chunked words into meaningful groups and read with expression.

In choosing material for repeated readings, remember that you need something that will hold a student's interest over several rereadings. If a student is passionately

Strategy Snapshot 9.1

Assisted Oral Reading

Ms. Bround worked with a small group of fifth-grade struggling readers. Her purpose was to prepare them for the science lesson they would experience in their regular classroom. She used their classroom textbook and focused on a four-page segment on fishes that the students' teacher had indicated would be covered the following day. All the students brought their science books to the reading resource room.

Ms. Bround began by initiating a short discussion about fishes to see what the students already knew. She then read the introduction while the students followed along. She pointed out text information about fishes that students already knew: They live in the water; there are many kinds; they have different sizes, shapes, and colors. She then asked the students to read several sentences together with her (simultaneous assisted reading) and they clarified terms such as "adapted," "fin," and "streamlined."

The next section was much longer and contained many unfamiliar terms such as *ectotherm*, *vertebrate*, *chordate*, and *parasite*. Ms. Bround read it to the students while they followed along. Then they took each sentence in turn and orally reread it. For some sentences, Ms. Bround employed assisted oral reading. For others, she asked the students to echo read. Occasionally, they read as an entire group. After each sentence, Ms. Bround modeled good reader strategies such as recognizing unknown words, raising questions, and identifying new information. She involved the students in an active discussion about what they were learning and what still confused them and, whenever possible, modeled use of context and the glossary as aids for determining the meaning of unknown words. New vocabulary words were written on chart paper. Buoyed by the model of a teacher who admitted she also had questions and did not always understand all the vocabulary in the text, students willingly shared their questions and confusions.

After taking each sentence in turn, the group then reread the entire segment orally using assisted oral reading. They also reread the list of new vocabulary. Ms. Bround repeated the process with the next three chapter segments. She added partner reading to the list of oral reading options for the single sentences. If students volunteered to read independently (and they often did), Ms. Bround allowed this and helped with gentle prompting should difficulties occur. After moving through the text sentence by sentence, the students then reread the entire segment sometimes with Ms. Bround and sometimes without her as a group or as partners.

The focus of the process was comprehension. Reading to the students and various forms of assisted oral reading allowed them to function successfully in a text that they could not handle independently. It also prepared them to participate fully in their classroom discussion and activities.

Ms. Bround kept in close contact with the teachers and built her resource room lessons around the content texts that the students were expected to read in their classroom. This increased her students' motivation as they soon realized that they could keep up with their classmates and participate in class activities with greater confidence.

interested in snakes, a selection about reptiles is a good choice. Other selections might include humor, lots of action, or sports. You can also use readings from the student's content area textbooks or novels, because in addition to improving word recognition, rereading helps the student to learn the material. Repeated reading of content text was a key component of the very successful third-grade intervention described in Chapter 6 (McCormack, Paratore, & Dahlene, 2004; McCormack & Paratore, 1999).

Experience in using repeated readings shows that students will not become bored even if they occasionally complain. Sixth-grade Gregg's tutor used repeated reading in combination with assisted reading. Gregg and his tutor worked for several months on one selection, at times reading together or taking turns on different pages. Occasionally, Gregg complained that repeated readings were "boring." But when the tutor omitted the repeated reading from the lesson one day, Gregg loudly objected. "I want to do it," he exclaimed, "because I like how I sound at the end!" As this story illustrates, pursue repeated readings on a consistent basis and not let occasional student complaints turn you away from a powerful technique for developing reading fluency.

Performance Reading

Students can develop fluency through the practice associated with preparing for a performance.

Choral Reading.   In choral reading, a group of students practices orally reading a selection together so they can perform it. The students read the entire selection together, or different groups read different parts. Because students find choral reading enjoyable, they willingly practice the word recognition that helps them to give a polished performance. Low-achieving readers enjoy this activity because it gives them the satisfaction of delivering a well-rehearsed, expressive rendition. Choral reading is particularly suited to selections, such as poetry, that contain rhythm and rhyme. Those who saw it will never forget the heartfelt rendition of "Homework Oh Homework" (by Prelutsky, in *The New Kid on the Block*) delivered by three fifth-grade boys in the reading center.

Go to MyEducationLab and select the topic *Fluency*. Then, go to the Activities and Applications section, watch the video entitled "Shared Reading—The Second Rereading in a K-3 Multilingual Classroom," and respond to the accompanying questions.

Readers Theatre.   Reader's theatre involves reading (not memorizing) a script and performing it without scenery, makeup, costumes, or props. It does not involve facial expressions, body movements, or specific acting techniques. The focus is on effective reading. Students read chorally or independently, and they practice their parts until they are ready to perform. Thus, they are engaging in repeated reading and are very motivated to do so because of the performance aspect. Worthy and Prater (2002) describe readers theatre as an "intensely meaningful, purposeful vehicle for repeated reading" (p. 295) and offer guidelines for choosing text and preparing for the performance.

Martinez, Roser, and Strecker (1998–1999) used readers theatre with second graders and noted impressive fluency gains. They offer several suggestions: provide manageable texts within the students' instructional reading level; choose books that can be easily turned into scripts; build on children's enthusiasm for series books; model effective reading by reading to the children; and provide support and feedback as students practice their parts. Roser, May, Martinez, Keehn, Harmon, and O'Neal (2004) and Rea and Mercuri (2006) recommend reader's theatre as a way of fostering the language development of English language learners. However, English language learners should not rehearse lines that have no meaning for them; the teacher should carefully assign roles based upon the student's current facility with spoken English. Roser et al. (2004) divided the class into five theatre groups. Each day included the introduction of a new text, revisiting an old one and a performance by one of the groups.

Radio Reading.   This activity is much like readers theatre but students read text as opposed to memorizing it (Johns & Berglund, 2002). A student plays the part of a radio announcer and reads a short text to an audience of peers. Only the reader and the teacher have copies of the text; the audience plays the part of active listeners. Text for radio reading is usually factual and does not necessarily involve dramatization. However, the reader must use suitable rate and expression to effectively communicate the message. Accounts of sports or news events provide motivating choices for radio reading (Caldwell & Leslie, 2009).

The Language Experience Approach

In the language experience approach, students compose personal stories, which are then used for reading instruction. Generally, students dictate their stories to a teacher, who records them in writing. Stories can also be written and edited on a computer.

Because students have actually produced these stories, they are anxious to read them. In addition, students can see the direct relationship between speech and reading, because language experience stories are *talk written down*. Although the language experience approach is used most widely with younger children, it is also effective with older students who are at a beginning reading level (Chapter 7).

Many teachers make permanent records of language experience stories. For an individual student, the stories may be printed or typed and collected in a notebook. For groups, the stories may be duplicated so that each student has a copy.

To be most effective, language experience stories should be about experiences that are exciting and of personal interest.

At times, low-achieving students may have some trouble composing stories. Many wordless picture books contain amusing stories related without words. Students can compose captions for such stories. The visual humor in comic strips can also inspire language experience stories. Teachers can eliminate the dialogue balloons of the strips or cut the words out of the strips and have students provide them.

Despite its motivational value, the language experience approach is not effective for some students. Because stories come directly from fluent oral language, words in a language experience story may accumulate faster than students can learn to read them. Alonzo, one severely disabled 13-year-old reader, had to give up learning to read by this approach because his inability to read his own experience stories eventually frustrated him.

Making Oral and Silent Reading Effective

To develop contextual fluency, readers need to have effective and enjoyable oral and silent reading experiences. This section discusses common problems and suggests guidelines for using oral and silent reading.

Difficulty Reading Silently.   Because silent reading allows students to process and think independently, it should be used as much as possible with low-achieving students. Despite this guideline, some students with reading problems often prefer to read orally. As 11-year-old Jamie often complained, "If I can't read out loud, I don't know what I am reading." Students with reading problems tend to avoid silent reading for three reasons:

1. Beginning readers link reading with oral language and thus are most comfortable when can they hear what they read. Although teachers must respect the feelings of these beginning readers, they should gently and gradually move students toward silent reading.
2. Many teachers are more comfortable with oral reading because it allows them to monitor students' word recognition skills. Although some monitoring is valuable, developing independent silent readers is even more valuable.
3. Many poor readers feel that the purpose of reading is to recognize all of the words for a teacher. For these students, reading is a performance rather than an opportunity to learn information or enjoy a story. These students must be convinced that silent reading is an important adult activity.

Students should be given direct motivation for reading silently. Stress the information or enjoyment that students will gain. If teachers follow silent reading with discussions that focus on the student's personal reactions to the text, students will start to see silent reading as meaningful.

Teachers often ask what to do when students point to words or move their lips as they read silently. Sometimes finger pointing and lip moving can act as an aid that makes halting readers more comfortable. In fact, these actions are normal for primary-grade–level readers. In addition, if the reading material is difficult, individuals of any reading level may revert to using their fingers or lips. However, because finger pointing and lip moving are often signs of frustration, check to make sure that the material your students are reading is not too difficult for them.

If you feel that students need to point or move their lips to feel comfortable, even with easy materials, then do not interfere with these habits. As students become more fluent readers, these actions usually disappear.

However, discourage students from moving their lips or pointing to the words if you sense they are just doing so from force of habit. First, and most effective, the student should be made aware of these habits, told how they slow readers down, and asked, respectfully, to eliminate them. This simple procedure, plus an occasional reminder, often solves the problem. Finger pointing can also be eliminated by providing a marker to replace a finger and gradually eliminating the use of the marker. For lip moving, students may be asked to consciously close their lips while reading.

Making Oral Reading Comfortable.   Although silent reading is the preferred mode of reading, oral reading can be an effective way for students to gain reading experience and for the teacher to see how students are dealing with material.

However, students—even those without reading problems—often see oral reading as a negative, performance-oriented experience. College students often single out oral reading as being stressful and humiliating. They remember quite vividly their feelings of anxiety and shame when they missed a word. One student rather poignantly remarked, "It was only when I did not have to read out loud that I actually began to enjoy reading. Did it have to be that way?" If successful college students have had these experiences, what must such experiences be like for children with reading problems?

Individual oral reading can be made into a more positive, meaning-focused experience in several ways:

- Students can practice a selection before being asked to read it in front of their peers. The only reason for reading orally to someone without practice is an assessment session that involves only two people: the student and a supportive teacher.
- The amount of oral reading should be limited. It is helpful if oral reading serves only a specific purpose, such as finding information, proving a point, or reading a favorite part.
- Teachers should remember not to treat oral reading time as a chance to teach phonics. When a student attempts to pronounce an unknown word (and poor readers meet many unfamiliar words), try not to interrupt the reading by saying, "Sound it out." The student's repeated attempts to decode the word make him or her, and everyone else reading, lose the meaning of the story. Furthermore, the experience is humiliating.

What should a teacher do if a student doesn't know a word? If readers pause or stumble on an important word, the teacher should simply tell them the word and move on, at the same time marking the unknown word for later teaching.

Not all mistakes are worth correcting. If a reading mistake involves only a small function word (such as *it* or *the*) that does not greatly affect meaning, it should simply be forgotten.

At times, if a student struggles with a word, a peer will laugh or simply call out the correct term. These unkind responses are all too common for low-achieving readers. In fact, poor readers tend to laugh at the errors of other poor readers. You can prevent this situation by taking a few simple precautions:

1. Never ask children to read alone in front of their peers without practicing first or without providing some support.

2. Teach students to signal when they meet an unfamiliar word. They can tap the book or raise a finger (rather than looking up).
3. Stress that group members must always be respectful of one another.

By using these guidelines, teachers emphasize that reading is an enjoyable and meaningful experience. This understanding is crucial for struggling students.

Fluency Development Lesson

The fluency development lesson (Rasinski 2003; Rasinski, Padak, Linek, & Sturtevant, 1994) involves a 10- to 15-minute lesson incorporating five steps. Teachers use a different text each day but they also use previously practiced selections. Content, predictability, and rhythm are important consideration in choosing the daily selection.

1. The teacher reads a short text of 50 to 150 words to the students while they follow along silently with their own copies.
2. The teacher and students discuss what the text is about. They also discuss the teacher's use of expression during the reading.
3. The teacher and class read the text chorally several times.
4. The students then practice reading the selection in pairs. Each partner takes a turn reading and receives help if needed from his or her partner. The partner also provides positive feedback.
5. Volunteers perform the text for the entire class. This performance can be done individually, in pairs, or in groups of four.

Strategies for Developing Sight Words in Isolation

A *sight word* is a word recognized instantly, without analysis. How do words become sight words? Each time a reader sees the word *dog* and correctly identifies it, the next recognition of *dog* becomes a little easier and faster. Think of something you learned to do, such as knitting or driving. The early stages were difficult, time-consuming, and often frustrating. As you practiced, the action became easier and easier; and now you can do it almost automatically, even while thinking about other things. Similarly, each time you accurately identify a word, it becomes easier and easier, and eventually, the word becomes a sight word.

Students with reading problems can best learn to recognize words by reading them in context. However, they may also need additional practice with words in isolation to reinforce automaticity and give them a sense of progress. Practicing individual words is useful for readers at many different levels. A core of sight words enables beginning readers to read easy books and serves as a basis for learning phonics. Reinforcement of sight vocabulary also enables more advanced students to identify the difficult words in their classroom textbooks.

This section first discusses which words should receive additional practice in isolation. Then it suggests some guidelines and strategies for teaching these words.

Choosing Words for Instructional Focus

Lists of frequently used words can help the teacher select words for instructional focus. Table 9.1 provides high-frequency words based on a study of the Dolch Basic Sight Vocabulary, as updated by Johnson (1971). Table 9.2 lists some nouns that can be easily pictured.

Many high-frequency words are *function words*, such as *the*, *of*, and *to*. These words, usually articles, prepositions, and pronouns, have little meaning of their own and take on meaning only by acting as connectors for other words. Six-year-old Scott, working on the function words *when* and *then*, sighed and muttered, "These sure aren't fun words like *brontosaurus*!"

Function words are difficult to learn for several reasons:

1. They have abstract meanings.
2. They tend to look alike. Words such as *then*, *than*, *when*, *what*, *where*, and *were* are easily confused.
3. Because they tend to have irregular sound-spelling relationships, they often must be mastered as sight words.

Because recognition of function words may be particularly troublesome for poor readers, such words deserve special attention. Function words appear so frequently that if they are not recognized instantly, reading will become uncomfortable and disfluent.

In addition to choosing high-frequency words for teaching, select words that are important to your students. At times, these words will appear in a novel your students are reading or be used in social studies and science texts. At other times, students may want to select words that are important in their lives. Peter, a fourth grader, insisted on learning *Pokemon*, *tae kwon do*, and *karate*.

Guidelines for Teaching Sight Words

Several guidelines will make learning sight words more effective.

Associate Sight Words with Meaning.   This association is particularly critical for function words. When readers are simply given word cards and expected to memorize them, learning becomes a rote task that is meaningless. To make this learning more meaningful, have your students write phrases for words on their word cards. For example, they might remember *in* by thinking of the phrase *in the garbage*. Pictures can be cut out, labeled, and placed around the room to illustrate other function words: a can *of* Coke; a fish *in* water; a cat *on* the fence. The students can then be guided to think of, for example, the contents of other cans, what else can be *in* water, or what could be *on* a fence.

Practice Sight Words Frequently.   As already emphasized, words are recognized automatically only after repeated exposures. Practice should include activities both with single words and with reading connected text. Frequent writing, reading, word games, and other word-centered activities all provide practice that develops sight word recognition. Poor readers need daily opportunities to read, write, and play with words.

Keep Records of Progress. Students with reading problems are motivated by their improvement. Students can keep records or journals of words they have learned. Word banks also can record progress. The one pictured in Figure 9.1 was made from a shoe box and was used as an alphabetical file for new words. Students can refer to a word bank when they review words or when they write.

Teachers can also demonstrate progress by sorting word cards into three piles: sight words, words that need to be analyzed, and unknown words. Fourth-grade Pat eagerly looked forward to going through his word cards at each lesson. His goal was to get rid of that third pile: unknown words. After each session, Pat filed his three piles separately in a shoe box and took them home for practice. Each time Pat and his teacher went through the cards, he watched the third pile get smaller, giving him visible proof of his improvement. Finally, Pat's third pile disappeared entirely.

Strategies for Focusing on Words

Several strategies provide motivating and important practice in recognizing words. These strategies include word cards, collecting words, word sorts, and word walls.

Word Cards. Word cards provide one way to practice sight words. Either the teacher or the student can construct the cards. Word recognition clues, such as a sentence containing the word or a picture illustrating the word, can be placed on the back of the card. Placing words on cards is motivating for students. As the number of word cards increases, they have a concrete reminder of how many words they are learning.

FIGURE 9.1   Word Bank to Record Student Progress

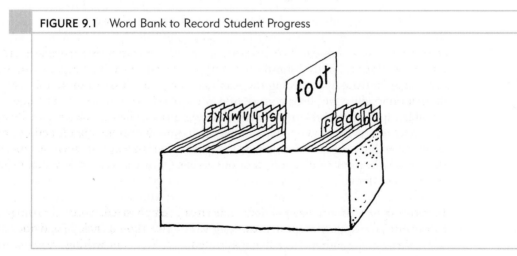

Use word cards in a variety of ways. Many students enjoy forming sentences from the cards. They can also select the word card that correctly fits a missing word in a sentence. Students can collect personal cards to practice at home with a parent or friend.

Flashcards.   Nicholson (1998) describes how to effectively use flashcards to increase fluency. He suggests that short sessions of flashcard training prior to reading a selection helps low-achieving readers and prepares them for a positive reading experience. He lists several guidelines to follow:

1. Choose words from the story that will be read.
2. Make certain that the students understand the meanings of the words. There seems to be little point in training children to quickly read words that they do not understand.
3. Use single-word flashcards or short-sentence flashcards. Write an explanatory phrase on the back of the single word flashcards as a cue to meaning.
4. If the word is unfamiliar, help the students to decode it. This way you can teach word recognition strategies for words the students will actually meet while reading the story.
5. After the flashcard session, ask the children to predict what the story will be about based on the words they have just learned.

Collecting Words.   Collecting words that follow certain patterns is another way to practice sight vocabulary. The patterns can emphasize the spelling of a word, its pronunciation, or its meaning. Students can collect words that contain the same letter pattern, such as *cat*, *bat*, *sat*, and so on. They can collect words about a favorite topic, such as snake words: *boa*, *slither*, *bite*, etc. The collected words are kept in a personal file.

Word Sorts.   In word sorting, students are presented with several words to sort according to different categories. The words are on cards, and the student is asked to sort the words into piles and to give reasons for placing each word in a certain pile.

The words used for word sorts can come from many sources: words collected by the students, words the students have found difficult, words from textbooks, or spelling words. Words can be sorted according to sound or spelling patterns (Bear, Invernizzi, Templeton, & Johnston, 2004; Bear, 1994), according to the presence of prefixes or suffixes, or according to meaning. Word sorts are enjoyable and give students with reading problems a sense of control over their language. They also offer valuable experience with letter patterns, sounds, and meanings.

Word sorts are of two different types. In a *closed sort*, the teacher tells the student how to sort the words. For example, you might tell students to sort the words *tree*, *run*, *sit*, and *table* by parts of speech (nouns and verbs). Closed sorts are often used to practice phonics, because teachers have patterns in mind that they want the students to notice. For example, they might ask students to sort words into *long a* and *short a* piles. In a second type of sort, an *open sort*, students are free to choose their own categories for sorting. Thus, they might choose long words and short words, happy words and sad words, or a phonics pattern. After sorting in one way, students may often want to repeat the sort using other categories. Strategy Snapshot 9.2 describes how a second-grade teacher used the same words for two different kinds of word sorts.

Sorting words provides many opportunities for students to look at a word and pronounce it accurately. Because low-achieving readers find this game-like activity both enjoyable and motivating, word sorts can help to increase a student's fund of sight words.

Word Walls. A word wall is an effective device (Cunningham & Allington, 2007; Cunningham, 2005) for displaying high-frequency words and making them easily accessible to the students. A word wall can be placed on a bulletin board or a classroom wall. It is divided into sections for each letter of the alphabet (*a, b, c . . .*). As words are selected for special emphasis, they are placed on the word wall according to their initial letter. These words may be suggested by the teacher or by students. Sometimes they are displayed with a picture or sentence clue; sometimes they are displayed alone. Five or so new words are added each week, and sometimes, when a space becomes full, they are taken down. To ensure that you can change words, either put them on cards or laminate each section for individual letters (the *a* section, the *b* section) and use erasable magic marker to write the words.

Go to MyEducationLab and select the topic *Vocabulary*. Then, go to the Activities and Applications section, watch the video entitled "Creating Word Walls," and respond to the accompanying questions.

Students can find, write, spell, and say words from their word wall. The teacher can devise riddles and games using the words. Students or the teacher can compose sentences from words found on the wall. If teachers dictate such a sentence, students then find the missing word. Students can also find all the words on the wall that, for

Strategy Snapshot 9.2

Sorting Words

To start a word sort, Ms. Lessiter gave a group of low-achieving second graders cards containing the words: *sat, mitt, rat, tin, pin, fan,* and *fin*. This sort was an open one, and the children chose to sort words by spelling patterns. They first placed the words into four piles: (1) *mitt,* (2) *tin, pin, fin,* (3) *fan,* and (4) *sat, rat*. This sort put the words into the word families *it, in, an, at*. Ms. Lessiter then asked the students to sort into only two piles. The children sorted on the basis of a single vowel: Group 1 had words with an *i* (*mitt, tin, pin, fin*), and Group 2 had words with an *a* (*fan, sat, rat*).

Ms. Lessiter then asked the children to sort the words by using the meaning. First, the children sorted according to what could be bought. They agreed that a *mitt,* a *pin,* a *fan,* and a *rat* could be bought, and the other words could not. Next they sorted according to what was in their houses. They first decided that all except *sat, fin,* and *rat* could be found in their homes. One of the group members then asked if pet goldfish have *fins*. The children decided they do and placed *fin* in the "home" pile. The group finally sorted according to what they actually owned. The children grouped *mitt* and *pin* together until one student informed the group that she had a *pet rat*. Word sorting was abandoned as the children discussed the joys of such an exciting pet.

example, have seven letters, are verbs, or contain an *r*-controlled vowel. In the "I'm thinking of" game, one student gives hints about a particular word on the wall, and the others try to guess it. For example, a student thinking of the word *beautiful* might give the hints that it is an adjective meaning very pretty.

An important use of word walls is that they serve as resources for students who have difficulty spelling words. Instead of asking a teacher or struggling for themselves, they simply find the word on the wall. This process also reinforces the learning of alphabetical order.

Word walls are an easy way to remind students of important words. A picture of a fourth-grade word wall is shown in Figure 9.2.

Go to MyEducationLab and select the topic *Vocabulary*. Then, go to the Activities and Applications section, watch the video entitled "Word Walls," and respond to the accompanying questions.

Mastering Function Words

Function words, such as *in*, *when*, and *there*, may be particularly troublesome for students with reading problems. The teacher needs to emphasize that context clues can help students to recognize function words. The cloze strategy described in Chapter 8 can help call attention to using context clues. In preparing a cloze passage for function words, simply delete one of every four *function* words from a passage and challenge students to provide these "little" words.

Highlighting function words in text can also help students learn them. Teachers can underline words or use highlighters to mark them. Then ask students to read the text, first silently and then aloud. Several passages should be used to give students extended practice in recognizing function words over a period of time.

An occasional student with reading problems needs intensive instruction in function words. Remember that, in this instruction, each function word should be accompanied by a phrase or sentence, because function words contain little meaning by themselves.

FIGURE 9.2   Part of a Word Wall from a Fourth Grade Class

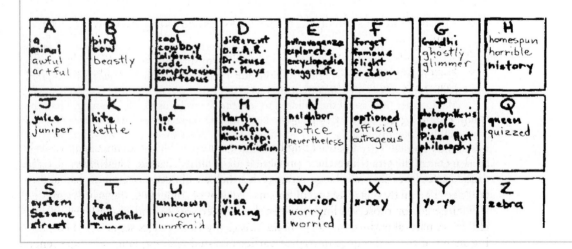

Dealing with Reversals

Students with reading problems who are achieving on the first- and second-grade levels tend to reverse certain letters and words while reading. Commonly, they substitute *b* for *d*, *no* for *on*, or *saw* for *was*. In fact, emergent and beginning readers commonly produce backward "mirror writing." Reversals have sometimes been interpreted as a symptom of deep-seated reading problems or even brain dysfunction. However, in most cases, reversals simply indicate a lack of experience with literacy. They are seen often in normally achieving children reading at primary-grade levels. In fact, learning-disabled students have been found to make no more reversals than normal readers when both groups of students are reading equally comfortable material (Adams, 1991). Reversals also may occur with teenagers and adults who are just learning to read.

One reason that students make reversals is that reading and writing are the only processes in which symbols change because of their directional orientation. Thus, the only difference between the letters *b* and *d* is that one faces right and the other left. On the other hand, a real-life object, such as a *chair* or *dog*, maintains its identity regardless of its orientation in space. A student beginning to read may not yet realize that the orientation of letters and words makes a difference.

When a student with reading problems exhibits reversals, the teacher must decide whether to provide special instruction to eliminate them. If the reversal is only occasional, no special instruction is warranted. If reversals are frequent and interfere with effective reading, special instruction is needed.

To correct reversals of single letters, concentrate on one letter at a time. For example, to correct a *b-d* reversal, first concentrate on *d*. Teachers can make a large chart containing the letter *d*, a memory word (e.g., *dog*), and pictures of words that start with *d*. One teacher cut out a 2 ft. by 3 ft. felt *d* and pasted it on a board. The student reinforced the *d* concept by tracing over the letter with a finger. After the concept of *d* has been mastered thoroughly, wait a week before introducing the letter *b*. This *divide and conquer* method is effective for students with problems. Other methods are:

◆ Making flashcards containing confusing words and having students practice recognizing them.
◆ Underlining the first letter of a confusable word in a bright color, such as red.
◆ Having students manipulate letters on a felt or magnetic board to form words that are frequently reversed.

The *Curious George* Strategy

The interest created by a captivating book sometimes enables students to successfully read material that is above their previously determined instructional level. A technique called the *Curious George* strategy has helped children overcome barriers to reading. The method is most useful for small groups of students in the primary grades; it is targeted for those reading between the primer and second-grade levels. Using children's natural enthusiasm for *Curious George* (by Rey) and its sequels and employing many of the techniques described earlier (assisted reading, language experience, and focus on individual words), many teachers have been able to achieve dramatic gains in reading level and enthusiasm.

The *Curious George* strategy has been used informally many times (Richek, 1999; Richek, McTague, Anderson, Baker, Luchitz et al., 1989). A documented field study was reported by Richek and McTague (1988). At the end of an 18-day period, the experimental *Curious George* group had, when compared to a control group, increased comprehension by 25 percent and decreased miscues by 65 percent on passages from an IRI. These differences were statistically significant, and teachers also noticed an increase in enthusiasm for reading and in the ability to write independently. A description of the strategy in action is given in Strategy Snapshot 9.3.

Strategy Snapshot 9.3

The *Curious George* Strategy

Instruction was divided into four-day segments of about 30 minutes each. On the *first* day of instruction, the teacher enthusiastically read *Curious George* to the children while holding the only copy of the book (Figure 9.3). Next, asking the students to help in reading the book, the teacher and students read together the first 16 pages in an assisted fashion. Generally, the context enabled students to supply many words and to read with some fluency. Next, the focus was on individual words. Each child chose five words, and the teacher wrote them on pieces of construction paper. Each child was given a different color. Finally, each child was handed a paperback copy of *Curious George* to take home along with his or her five cards and told to bring the cards and book back the next day.

On the *second* day of instruction, children "showed off" their cards to others and read them if they could. The teacher then continued with the assisted reading of *Curious George*, pages 17–32. Because they had had the book overnight, the children had generally gained considerable fluency. Next, the children chose five more words, and the teacher wrote them down on individual cards. They again took their personal cards and words home and were instructed to return them the next day.

On the *third* day of instruction, the procedures of the second day were repeated, but the children completed the assisted reading of the book, reading pages 32–48.

On the *fourth* day of instruction, the teacher presented a "book" made from yellow construction paper. Each page contained a picture cut out from a page of *Curious George*. Children took turns dictating the words to accompany the pictures, thus making their own Curious George book.

After completing four days of *Curious George* instruction, the children read sequels, including *Curious George Goes to the Hospital*, *Curious George Flies a Kite*, and *Curious George Takes a Job*, in the same manner. At first, the process of completing a book took 4 days, but as children became more confident, they took less time.

Children should be allowed to control their own reading process. For example, at a certain point, some tired of word cards and preferred to spend their time simply reading books. As children moved toward more independent reading, the teacher supplied additional books about Curious George (more than 30 are available). Children also enjoyed writing letters to Curious George or writing such personal books as "Curious George and Charita."

FIGURE 9.3 The *Curious George* Strategy The teacher starts instruction using the *Curious George* strategy by reading the story aloud to the students.

In addition to using this strategy with the *Curious George* series, you can use it with the *Clifford the Big Red Dog* (by Bridwell), the *Harry the Dirty Dog* (by Zion), and other picture book series. The use of a connected series of books is critical to the strategy. A book series consists of several books that involve the same character or situation. Each book introduces new words but, more important, also repeats words from previous books. The repetition of words, characters, and situations provides the student with a growing sense of control over reading.

Summary

A fluent reader reads accurately, quickly, and expressively. Fluency is an important component of successful reading. Readers who can recognize words automatically and without analysis can pay attention to meaning.

Fluent reading can be assessed in three ways: listening to students read orally, determining student reading rate, and timed administration of word lists.

Fluency is best developed as students read connected text. Therefore, teachers must promote wide reading of easy text. The use of predictable books and assisted reading is also effective. In assisted reading, students read material with a fluent reader, who is often the teacher. The various forms of assisted reading are simultaneous assisted reading, echo reading, choral reading, paired reading, partner reading, simultaneous listening-reading, and the Neurological Impress Method. Repeated reading is another effective technique for developing fluency. Students repeatedly read a text until a desired level of accuracy and fluency is reached. Performance reading using choral reading, Readers theatre and radio reading can also be used to develop fluency.

In the language experience approach, students compose and dictate personal stories, which are then used for reading instruction. Students repeatedly read these stories and develop fluency as they do so.

Fluency can also be developed by focusing on words in isolation to develop sight vocabulary. This is particularly important for helping students master high-frequency function words. Students can make word cards, collect words, engage in word sorts, and construct word walls. Reversals of letters and words are common in all beginning readers and do not signal neurological problems. The *Curious George* strategy promotes the development of fluency within contextual reading.

References

Adams, A. (1991). The oral reading of learning-disabled readers: Variations produced within the instructional and frustration ranges. *Remedial and Special Education, 12*, 48–52, 62.

Bear, D. (1994). Word sort: An alternative to phonics, spelling, and vocabulary. (Paper presented at the National Reading Conference, San Diego, CA.)

Bear, D., Invernizzi, M., Templeton, S., & Johnston, F. (2008). *Words their way* (3rd ed.). New York: Macmilan/Merrill.

Caldwell, J. S., & Leslie, L. (2009). *Intervention Strategies to Follow Informal Reading Inventory Assessment: So What Do I Do Now?* Boston: Allyn & Bacon.

Caldwell, J. S. (2008). *Comprehension Assessment: A Classroom Guide.* New York: The Guilford Press.

Carver, R. B. (1990). *Reading Rate: A Review of Research and Theory.* San Diego, CA: Academic.

Cunningham, P. (2005). *Phonics They Use: Words for Reading and Writing* (4th ed.). Boston: Pearson.

Cunningham, P., & Allington, R. (2007). *Classroom that Work: They Can All Read and Write.* Boston: Pearson.

Davidson, M., & Myhre, O. (2000). Measuring reading at grade level. *Educational Leadership, 57*, 25–28.

Dowhower, S. L. (194). Repeated reading revisited: Research into practice. *Reading and writing quarterly: Overcoming learning difficulties, 10*, 389–406.

Feazell, V. S. (2004). Reading Acceleration Program: A schoolwide intervention. *The Reading Teacher, 58*, 66–72.

Fountas, I. C., & Pinnell, G. S. (1996). *Guided reading: Good first teaching for all children.* Portsmouth, NH: Heinemann.

Fuchs, L. S., Fuchs, D., Hosp, M. K., & Jenkins, J. R. (2001). Oral reading fluency as an indicator of reading competence: A theoretical, empirical, and historical analysis. *Scientific Studies of Reading, 5*, 239–257.

Good, R. H., Simmons, D. C., & Kame'enui, E. J. (2001). The importance and decision-making utility of a continuum of fluency-based indicators of foundational reading skills for third-grade high-stakes outcomes. *Scientific Studies of Reading, 5*, 257–289.

Hasbrouck, J. & Tindal, G. A. (2006). Oral reading fluency norms: A valuable assessment tool for reading teachers. *The Reading Teacher, 59*, 636–643.

Hasbrouck, J. E., & Tindal, G. (1992). Curriculum-based oral reading fluency norms for students in grades 2 through 5. *Teaching Exceptional Children*, Spring, 41–44.

Heckelman, R. G. (1969). The neurological impress method of remedial reading instruction. *Academic Therapy, 4,* 277–282.

Johns, J. L., & Berglund, R. L. (2002). *Fluency: Questions, Answers, Evidence-Based Strategies.* Dubuque, IA: Kendall/Hunt Publishing Company.

Johnson, D. D. (1971). The Dolch list reexamined. *The Reading Teacher, 24,* 449–457.

Johnston, F. R. (1998). The reader, the text, and the task: Learning words in first grade. *The Reading Teacher, 51,* 666–675.

Kame'enui, E. J., & Simmons, D. C. (2001). Introduction to this special issue: The DNA of reading fluency. *Scientific Studies of Reading, 5,* 203–210.

Kuhn, M. R. (2007). Effective oral reading assessment (or why round robin reading doesn't cut it). In J. R. Paratore & R. L. McCormack (Eds.), *Classroom Literacy Assessment: Making Sense of What Students Know and Do,* pp. 101–112. New York: The Guilford Press.

Martinez, M., Roser, N. L., & Strecker. S. (1998–1999). "I never thought I could be a star": A reader's theatre ticket to fluency. *The Reading Teacher, 52,* 326–337.

McCormack, R. L., & Paratore, J. R. (1999). *"What Do You Do There Anyway," Teachers Ask: A Reading Teacher's Intervention Using Grade-Level Text with Struggling Third Grade Readers.* Paper presented at the National Reading Conference, Orlando, FL.

McCormack, R. L., Paratore, J. R., & Dahlene, K. F. (2004). Establishing instructional congruence across learning settings: One path to success for struggling third grade readers. In R. L. McCormack & J. R. Paratore (Eds.), *After Early Intervention, Then What? Teaching Struggling Readers in Grades 3 and Beyond,* pp. 117–137. Newark, DE: International Reading Association.

Meisels, S. J., & Piker, R. A. (2001). An analysis of early literacy assessments used for instruction. www.ciera.org/library/reports/inquiry-2/2-013/2-013.html.

National Reading Panel. (2000). *Teaching Children to Read: An Evidence-Based Assessment of the Scientific Research Literature on Reading and Its Implications for Reading Instruction: Reports of the Subgroups* (National Institute of Health Pub. No. 00-4754). Washington, DC: National Institute of Child Health and Human Development.

Nicholson, T. (1998). The flashcard strikes back. *The Reading Teacher, 52,* 188–193.

Rasinski, T. V. (2000). Speed does matter in reading. *The Reading Teacher, 54,* 146–151.

Rasinski, T. V. (2003). *The Fluent Reader: Oral Reading Strategies for Building Word Recognition, Fluency, and Comprehension.* New York: Scholastic Professional Books, Inc.

Rasinski, T. V., Padak, N. D., Linek, W. L., & Sturdevant, E. (1994). Effects of fluency development on urban second graders. *Journal of Educational Research, 87,* 158–165.

Rea, D. M., & Mercuri, S. P. (2006). *Research-Based Strategies for English Language Learners.* Portsmouth, NH: Heinemann.

Reutzel, D. R., & Morrow, L. M. (2007). Promoting and assessing effective literacy learning classroom environments. In. J. R. Paratore & R. L. McCormack (Eds.), *Classroom Literacy Assessment: Making Sense of What Students Know and Do,* pp. 33–49. New York: The Guilford Press.

Richards, M. (2000). Be a good detective: Solve the case of oral reading fluency. *The Reading Teacher, 53,* 534–539.

Richek, M. A. (1999). *Reading Success for At-Risk Children: Ideas that Work.* Bellevue, WA: Bureau of Education and Research.

Richek, M. A., & McTague, B. (1988). The "Curious George" strategy for students with reading problems. *The Reading Teacher, 42,* 220–225.

Richek, M. A., McTague, B. K., Anderson, C. A., Baker, K. S., Luchitz, M. M., Hendler, L. W., et al. (1989). The "Curious George" strategy: Experiences of nine teachers. *Reading: Issues and Practices, Maryland Reading Journal of the International Reading Association, 6,* 36–44.

Roser, N. L., May, L. A., Martinez, M., Keehn, S., Harmon, J. M., & O'Neal, S. (2004). Stepping into character(s): Using reader's theatre with bilingual fourth graders. In R. L. McCormack & J. R. Paratore (Eds.), *After Early Intervention, Then What? Teaching Struggling Readers in Grades 3 and Beyond,* pp. 40–69. Newark, DE: International Reading Association.

Samuels, S. J. (1979). The method of repeated readings. *The Reading Teacher, 32,* 403–408.

Southwest Educational Development Laboratory. (2006). Reading assessment database for grades K-2. Retrieved from www.sedl.org/reading/rad/list.html.

Stahl, S. A. (2004). What do we know about fluency? Findings of the National Reading Panel. In P. McCardle & V. Chhabra (Eds.), *The Voice of Evidence in Reading Research*, pp. 213–234. Baltimore, MD: Paul H. Brookes Publishing Co.

Stahl, S. A., & Heubach, K. (1993). *Changing Reading Instruction in Second Grade: A Fluency-Oriented Program.* Athens, GA: National Reading Research Center.

Stahl, S. A., & Heubach, K. M. (2005). Fluency-oriented reading instruction. *Journal of Literacy Research, 37,* 25–60.

Stahl, S., Heubach, K., & Cramond, B. (1997). *Fluency-Oriented Reading Instruction.* Reading Research Report No. 79. Athens, GA, and College Park, MD: National Reading Research Center of the University of Georgia and the University of Maryland.

Stanovich, K. E. (1986). Matthew effects in reading. Some consequences of individual differences in the acquisition of literacy. *Reading Research Quarterly, 21,* 360–406.

Topping, K. (1987). Paired reading: A powerful technique for parent use. *The Reading Teacher, 40,* 608–614.

Topping, K. (1989). Peer tutoring and paired reading: Combining two powerful techniques. *The Reading Teacher, 42,* 499–494.

Worthy, J., & Prater, K. (2002). "I thought about it all night": Reader's theatre for reading fluency and motivation. *The Reading Teacher, 56,* 294–297.

PEARSON
myeducationlab
Where the Classroom Comes to Life

MyEducationLab is a research-based learning tool that brings teaching to life. Go to the Jennings, Caldwell, & Lerner 6th Edition MyEducationLab for Reading Assessment site at www.myeducationlab.com to:

◆ engage in multimedia exercises to help you build a deeper and more applied understanding of chapter content;

◆ utilize extensive resources including videos from real classrooms, Praxis and licensure preparation, a lesson plan builder, and materials to help you in your teaching career.

Improving Vocabulary Development and Listening Comprehension

Introduction

This chapter discusses two important facets of language—listening comprehension and meaning vocabulary—and suggests strategies that help students with reading problems improve their language abilities. Because reading is language, students cannot read material that is above their language level. Thus, the richer a student's language is, the better he or she will read.

Importance of Language to Reading

Language abilities are critical to success in reading, particularly after the primary grades. Although the greatest challenge to young children in the early phases of learning to read is to recognize, in print, words that they use in everyday speech, the language background that is developed throughout the preschool years provides the foundation for continued success in literacy (Strickland & Shanahan, 2004). As students progress beyond the primary grades, high-level words and concepts are introduced in school reading. Those students who have a rich language background cope well with this new challenge; many who lack higher-level language begin to struggle. Many of the students in the reading center have developed problems as the material they have to read becomes more complex.

The relationship between vocabulary and the ability to understand text was one of the earliest lines of research in literacy (Thorndike, 1973; Davis, 1944, 1968). Correlational studies continue to support the strong connections among meaning vocabulary, listening comprehension, listening vocabulary, and reading comprehension (Joshi, 2005; Carver & David, 2001).

Causes of Problems with Language

Many low-achieving students lack a solid language base for building reading achievement. Three major causes of problems with language are language disability and delay, lack of reading, and lack of a rich-language environment.

Language Disability and Delay

A problem with language may severely affect reading abilities. Dawn, an A pupil in first and second grades, could read words accurately and fluently. She had a highly supportive family that promoted literacy. In third grade, however, she began to fail science and social studies tests. She could not remember new terms, and her parents began to notice that she had difficulty expressing herself. At the reading center, Dawn's teacher orally read her social studies text to her. Not surprisingly, Dawn could not summarize, answer questions, or understand key words from the text. These responses indicated that Dawn's reading problem was related to a language problem.

In some cases, language problems are severe enough to be noticed early, and they affect beginning reading skills. In other cases, like that of Dawn, problems are noticed only as children meet the complex demands of intermediate-grade material. Chall (1983) referred to this situation as the "fourth-grade slump." Language disabilities and related problems, such as speech impediments, are further discussed in Chapter 15.

Lack of Reading

Of course, other students with reading problems have had problems recognizing words from the beginning of their reading instruction. Interestingly, these students also tend to have problems developing rich language. In these cases, language problems are related to a lack of wide reading. How does this happen?

Many difficult words and complex syntactic structures are met only in reading. Therefore, students who read extensively have opportunities to build their meaning vocabularies and learn complex sentence structures. Unfortunately, students who have difficulties recognizing words do very little reading and, therefore, are not exposed to these rich language structures. Thus, many readers who start out with only word recognition problems may also eventually develop deficiencies in language (Stanovich, 1986, 1988).

Lack of a Rich Language Environment

Some students are not exposed to rich language in the home and in other everyday environments. Activities done in a nurturing home, such as reading books, listening to stories, and engaging in the free exchange of ideas, form an important basis for language skills. However, not all families can provide such advantages. Some parents lack the reading skills to foster literacy, others lack time, and others are not aware of the value of such experiences.

Thomas, a 10-year-old in the reading center, had been taught to be quiet and respectful. Before each session, his mother warned him to obey his teacher, and afterward, she asked if he had been a good boy. Thomas's mother was at first baffled by the teacher's request that she read to him, because to her, reading was the responsibility of the child. After a few months and attendance at our weekly parent program, Thomas and his mother became comfortable with the noise and excitement generated as Thomas talked freely and expressively to improve his language.

Assessing Language Abilities

Language abilities can be assessed using both informal and formal measures.

Informal Measures

Informal observations while students are interacting with one another or with you can provide many insights into students' language levels and comfort levels in expressing their thoughts. You can learn much from conducting student interviews or talking with students about their interests and experiences. The normal classroom discourse about text can also provide valuable information about students' language levels as they respond to text and classroom discussions. However, this interactive assessment is difficult to document unless you are diligent with anecdotal record keeping. To document students' progress, a more systematic approach is needed.

Reading stories to students and asking them to retell the stories in their own words is another way to measure students' language levels (Morrow, 2004). Many checklists are available to record students' abilities to retell stories (Walker, 2005; Gredler & Johnson, 2004; Morrow, 2004; Clay, 2002). Paris and Paris (2003) have developed an assessment tool for measuring students' abilities to retell stories. Systematic use of retelling checklists can provide excellent documentation of students' abilities to retell stories. Retelling checklists are included for the silent reading passages in the informal reading inventory that accompanies this text. These materials are provided on the website for this text.

Teachers can determine how well-developed students' language is by reading orally to them and asking them comprehension questions. If students can comprehend the material, it is within their language levels. This procedure is described in Chapter 5. Using an informal reading inventory, read passages orally to a student and ask comprehension questions to determine a listening level—then compare this level with the student's reading level. Teachers can also read content area materials to students and ask questions. This procedure was used with Dawn when her teacher read from her social studies textbook to determine whether she had a language problem. When Dawn could not answer questions about the text, her teacher concluded that she needed further language development to support her reading school materials successfully. Using the listening comprehension component of an informal reading inventory as part of a systematic assessment plan is another good way to document students' progress.

A good way to determine whether students have the necessary vocabulary and concept knowledge to understand a specific selection is to use a cloze procedure. Using the cloze procedure can help teachers assess the ability of students to process the language of the reading selection, construct meaning from that selection, and make connections between ideas encountered in text. This is especially helpful in content areas where the specialized vocabulary is crucial to students' understanding of the text. Students' abilities to supply a word where one has been deleted indicate how familiar the readers are with the language and content of a passage. It is also a measure of how closely the language and background knowledge of the author and readers are matched.

Directions for constructing a cloze test are presented in Figure 10.1.

Classroom teachers and reading teachers often use informal measures to determine whether (1) a student's language abilities are more advanced than reading skills or (2) language abilities and reading are at the same level. If a student's language abilities are more advanced than reading, the student needs word recognition instruction so that the student can learn to read at the language level that he or she can understand. If a student's reading and language are at the same low level, additional devel-

FIGURE 10.1   Constructing a Cloze Test

1.	Select a passage from the book students will be expected to read.	
	Primary Grades	100 words
	Intermediate and Middle-level Grades	250–300 words
2.	Reproduce the passage, leaving the first and last sentences intact.	
3.	Delete every fifth word.	
	From 15 to 20 deletions are recommended.	
	Replace the deleted words with blanks of equal length.	
4.	Ask students to fill in each blank with a word that makes sense.	
5.	Estimate the student's "level" for this text:	
	>60 % accuracy	Independent Level	Students can read the text on their own
	40–60% accuracy	Instructional Level	Students can read the text with guidance
	<40% accuracy	Frustrational Level	Students cannot read the text successfully

opment of language abilities is needed to improve reading. To determine which is the case, a teacher must determine whether a reading problem is due to poor word recognition (part of reading) or a low listening level (part of language).

Teachers can select words from students' miscue analyses and present those words orally to see if students know the words' meanings if the word recognition component is removed. This analysis provides valuable information about whether students' abilities to understand words are higher than their abilities to identify those words.

An informal probe of a standardized test also allows you to compare reading and language. First, administer a standardized reading test in the regular manner. Then, administer the same test by reading it to the student (an informal probe). If the student scores about the same on both the reading and listening versions, a need for language development is indicated. If the student scores better on the listening version than the reading version, the student needs to develop more word recognition abilities. To summarize:

> Reading and listening equal language development needed
> Listening better than reading: word recognition needed

You may choose to probe only specific subtests of a standardized test. Eric's sixth-grade teacher was interested in whether his difficulties stemmed from poor word recognition or poor language. To find out, Eric was first given the vocabulary subtest of the *Gates-MacGinitie Reading Test*, Level 4. In this subtest, he read words and chose synonyms for them. After Eric had taken the vocabulary subtest using this standard administration, the teacher orally read the same subtest to Eric and had him give his answers aloud. If Eric's ability to recognize words had been interfering with his original score, he would have improved his score when the subtest was read to him. Because Eric did not improve his score, the teacher concluded that his problem was with language rather than with recognizing words. Using the same procedure for the comprehension subtest of the *Gates-MacGinitie Reading Test*, Eric again failed to improve his score. This result further confirmed Eric's need for language development.

Formal Measures

Many formal tests include subtests that measure language skills. The *Peabody Picture Vocabulary Test*, Third Edition (*PPVT-III*) and the *Expressive Vocabulary Test* (*EVT*) are designed specifically for this purpose. The *PPVT-III* assesses listening vocabulary. In this test, an examiner reads a word, and the student chooses one of four pictures that represent the word. The examiner might say "Point to pencil," and the four picture choices might be paper, a pencil, pen, and crayon. No reading is involved. In addition, because the student is not required to say any words, the *PPVT-III* is a measure of understanding, or receptive vocabulary, rather than expressive vocabulary. The test covers ages 2.5 to adult, has norms enabling comparison to a reference group, and comes in two alternative forms.

The *EVT* is an individual, norm-referenced test used to measure expressive vocabulary using two types of items: labeling and providing synonyms. In the first portion of the test, the examiner points to a picture or part of the body and asks the student a question requiring a one-word response. In the second portion of the test, the examiner shows the student a picture and provides a stimulus word. The student responds with a one-word answer. The *EVT* was co-normed with the *PPVT-III*. By comparing the difference between a student's standard scores in receptive and expressive vocabulary, the examiner may evaluate the student's word retrieval abilities.

Conditions that Foster Language Learning

Although research has established a strong relationship between vocabulary knowledge and reading comprehension, little has been done to identify what constitutes "good vocabulary instruction." In fact, research indicates that programs specifically designed to teach vocabulary have had little effect on reading achievement (Stahl & Fairbanks, 1986). Further, Nagy, Anderson, and Herman (1987) found that explicit instruction in word learning results in approximately 300 words per year being learned. In contrast, Anderson, Wilson, and Fielding (1988) found that students engaged in reading self-selected, less difficult material learn about 2,000 words per year. What can teachers do to foster students' growth in language?

First, incorporate vocabulary instruction into literacy curriculum. Despite a history of research indicating that vocabulary is related to reading achievement, recent research has shown that little attention in classrooms is focused on vocabulary development (Blachowicz, Fisher, Ogle, & Watts-Taffe, 2006; Scott, Jamieson-Noel, & Asseling, 2003).

Second, decide which words to teach. Beck, McKeown, and Omanson (1987) suggested a "tiered" approach to making this decision:

- Tier I words are comprised of the basic, familiar words that are part of everyday oral vocabulary
- Tier II words are not commonly used by most people in their everyday oral vocabulary, but are considered highly useful in a literate environment
- Tier III words are rarely used or are used in specific content areas.

Tier II words should be the focus of vocabulary instruction because they will have the greatest impact across texts (Beck, McKeown, & Kucan, 2002, 2008).

Third, address the issue of how to teach vocabulary. Blachowicz and Fisher (2002) suggest that teachers follow some specific guidelines to ensure effective practice in vocabulary instruction:

- Create a word-rich environment that provides for both incidental and explicit learning of words
- Support students' independent word learning
- Use instructional strategies that model good word-learning behaviors
- Use assessment that matches instructional goals

Teachers' sharing the richness of language and their love of the beauty of language with their students allows them to enjoy themselves while building an invaluable base for reading.

Exposure to Rich Language

The most valuable tools teachers have for increasing students' vocabulary are books. Books can help teachers bring rich language to their students (Anderson, et al., 1988). While all children hear commands and requests in their everyday lives, they may not all have the rich experiences of listening to detailed verbal descriptions, explaining their own reasoning, or hearing a variety of uncommon words. Similarly, all children study their school texts, but not all get to listen to language-rich books, such as *Tikki Tikki Tembo* (by Mosel) or *To Think that I Saw It on Mulberry Street* (by Dr. Seuss).

The language found in books is richer than that contained in oral language, both in vocabulary (Cunningham & Stanovich, 1998) and in grammatical structures (Purcell-Gates, 1986). Books also tend to contain knowledge that is well reasoned and transcends the limits of personal information (Stanovich & Cunningham, 1993). Therefore, in working with students who have reading problems, teachers should use the language of books.

You will need patience to foster an appreciation of language-rich books in a student with reading problems, but you will be well rewarded. There is a special magic in seeing a child enjoy rich language for the first time.

Active Participation

To gain full control over language, students with reading problems must be comfortable not only listening to and reading language, but also using it expressively in their own speech and writing. "Doing something" with language gives students a stake in their own learning and helps them overcome the passivity that is a problem for so many low-achieving readers. Language that has been processed deeply, through many different activities, is learned well and used often (Stahl & Fairbanks, 1986).

Planning for Vocabulary and Language Learning

Much language learning occurs through incidental learning by absorbing meaning vocabulary, grammatical structures, and concepts from being exposed to rich language. Struggling readers and writers may lack this language-rich background or may need more explicit help to benefit from exposure to rich language and literacy experiences. While we know that isolated vocabulary instruction is less effective than developing meaning vocabulary through exposure to rich literature, as reading specialists working with struggling readers and writers and with their classroom teachers, we need to restructure instruction so that we provide explicit instruction *through* rich literacy experiences (Anderson, et al., 1988; Nagy, et al., 1987). Further, we need to plan our instruction so that students have multiple opportunities to use new vocabulary so that it becomes part of their own oral or written language (Stahl & Fairbanks, 1986). Dale (1965) found that vocabulary knowledge could be described in four stages of gradual learning:

1. Never saw or heard this word
2. Saw or heard it but don't know it
3. Know it in a sentence; know the meaning vaguely
4. Know it well

How do teachers bring students to the "know-it-well" stage of vocabulary learning? Nagy and Scott (2000) found that students need perhaps 20 or more exposures and opportunities to use words in context and over an extended time for full mastery. Students must also learn how to learn vocabulary. Such concepts as word parts, the use of context to infer meaning, and the relationship of a definition to the word it defines are learned gradually and often require teacher intervention. These concepts are called the *metalinguistic awareness of vocabulary* (Nagy & Scott, 2000).

Students with reading problems often must master unknown words and concepts unique to specific content areas to support them as they read their school assignments. Many interesting and exciting strategies are available to give these pupils the explicit instruction that enables them to have successful reading and studying experiences.

Making Connections

As mature readers, when we encounter an unfamiliar word, we are comfortable with incomplete images of word meanings as we continue to read and gather clues about the new word's meaning. We automatically start trying to solve the puzzle of the word's meanings as we categorize it with similar known words and construct a more complete meaning. Teachers may need to help students connect new words to information they already know. Blachowicz and Fisher (2002, 2005) suggest a framework for connecting unfamiliar words to known information. As presented in Figure 10.2, students reading the sentence, "When I awoke, I saw a huge *schalamel* outside my window" can start to build a framework for *schalamel*.

Throughout each step of the process, students "fine-tune" their perceptions of the *schalamel* until they have an image of a funny, furry animal with long ears and big eyes.

FIGURE 10.2   Framework for Connecting Unfamiliar Words to Known Information

Sentence:		When I awoke, I saw a huge *schalamel* outside my window.	
Unfamiliar word		*Schalamel*	
	Class	visible object	
		A schalamel	can be seen
			can be big
Students continue to read and add to framework:		Its furry face was staring at me.	
	Class	living creature	
		A schalamel	can be seen
			can be big
			has a face
			has fur
Students read further and fill in framework.		His huge eyes and long ears gave him a comical look, and I knew I had nothing to fear.	
	Class	living creature	
		A schalamel	can be seen
			can be big
			has a face
			has fur
			looks funny
			is not scary

Strategies for Fostering Language:
Listening Comprehension

Many strategies foster students' language development through listening. These listening activities are nonthreatening and time efficient and pay handsome dividends in enjoyment and language growth.

Reading Books to Students

Reading books aloud to students is a powerful way to provide a text-based discussion of concepts and words from books written above the students' reading levels (Edwards Santoro, Chard, Howard, & Baker, 2008; Biemiller, 2001). Through listening to reading material containing sophisticated language and structures, students acquire the language proficiency that later enables them to read at a high level. We highly recommend reading to low-achieving students at least a few times per week.

Listening to a teacher read is beneficial for students with reading problems for three reasons: (1) Students absorb rich language, build background knowledge, and learn story organization; (2) Students are motivated to learn to read as they become aware of the many interesting things that can be read; and (3) Listening to a teacher read is a relaxing activity.

Materials that are above students' reading level, and on the cutting edge of their language level, are most effective in fostering language growth. These materials should contain language that is challenging, but not overwhelming, for students. Read-alouds can be used for enjoyment to enrich students' language development and to share the rich, sophisticated language found in books as well as to build background knowledge for content areas (Edwards Santoro, et al., 2008). Teachers should try to read both short stories and longer books. Reading full-length novels to students helps them to develop comprehension strategies for longer material. Teachers should also include varied genres: fantasy, poetry, historical fiction, and informational books.

A few suggestions for language-rich books suitable for teacher read-alouds for primary grades include *Amos and Boris* (Steig), *Many Moons* (Thurber), and *To Think that I Saw It on Mulberry Street* (Dr. Seuss). For intermediate and upper grades, try *Mrs. Frisby and the Rats of NIMH* (O'Brien), *Ben and Me* (Lawson), *North to Freedom* (Holm), *Sarah Plain and Tall* (MacLachlan), *In the Year of the Boar and Jackie Robinson* (Lord), and *The Indian in the Cupboard* (Banks). Short stories by Edgar Allan Poe, Jack London, and Mark Twain, are filled with sophisticated concepts and vocabulary. Books using figurative language, such as *Amelia Bedelia* (Parish), help enrich students' language. Reading informational texts aloud to students is enjoyable and provides important background information so that students with reading problems can benefit more from content area instruction. One group of Title I fourth graders was kept enthralled as, using the book *Fabulous Facts about the 50 States* (Ross), they covered one state each session.

When reading to students, do not be alarmed if they don't know the meanings of all the words. If, however, you feel that students are uncomfortable or someone asks a question, stop and explain concepts and words. Young children often like to hear

Go to MyEducationLab and select the topic *Comprehension*. Then, go to the Activities and Applications section, watch the video entitled "Listening," and respond to the accompanying questions. How does this teacher help his students understand vocabulary in the story? How does he foster comprehension?

favorites reread. Such rereading enables them to get more from the story and to develop a sense of security.

With all the content that teachers are expected to address, it is easy to feel rushed and overwhelmed. Read-aloud time is often the item that is omitted from our busy schedules. It is important to find time for this beneficial component to language development! Try to use times when students may not be at peak energy, such as after lunch or at the end of the day. Read for 10 to 15 minutes at one time. Don't be surprised, however, when your students become so involved in a book, that they beg you to read longer. Try to stop at meaningful points, such as the end of a chapter. This whets your students' appetites for the next reading and provides you the opportunity to model reflecting about what you just read and predicting what will happen next.

Paired Story Reading

Some teachers are concerned that their students may not be able to grasp the literary style of classic fairy and folktales, yet recognize that these stories are valuable listening experiences. Paired story reading provides a way to share the rich-language and cultural experiences of the classic tales while providing background experiences needed to understand the stories (Richek, 1989).

For this strategy, find two versions of the same fairy tale or folk tale: an easier version and a more difficult version. Many fairy tales and folktales are available in beautifully illustrated picture books that readily engage students. Some publishers offer adapted versions of many folk tales and fairy tales to meet guidelines for primary levels. To implement the strategy, follow the guidelines presented in Figure 10.3.

Directed Listening-Thinking Activity

The Directed Listening-Thinking Activity (DL-TA) parallels the Directed Reading-Thinking Activity (DR-TA, Stauffer, 1975) presented in Chapter 11. The DL-TA is

FIGURE 10.3 Paired Story Reading Strategy

1.	Find two versions of the same fairy tale or folk tale: an easier version and the more traditional, classic version.
2.	On the first day, read the easy adaptation of the story to students. Discuss the story so that students learn and enjoy the basic plot.
3.	The next day, read the more difficult version of the same story. Having the background from the easier version allows students to enjoy the rich language of the more difficult version and to grasp more of the details.
4.	Provide opportunities for students to compare the differences between the two stories.

recommended for primary children who need to develop a sense of story structure and for students of any age who need to improve their language abilities.

In DL-TA, students listen to a story being read and predict what will happen next. When reading the story, the teacher stops at several critical points and asks students to predict (Richek, 1987). Freed from the constraints of having to recognize words, students can apply all of their energies to thinking about the story. Implementation suggestions for DL-TA are presented in Figure 10.4.

Formalizing the thinking process is just as important in DL-TA as in DR-TA. Thus, when using DL-TA, carefully write down all of the students' predictions on the board. This activity encourages a reading response, because students want to read their own language as written on the board. (Adaptations of DL-TA suitable for early literacy are discussed in Chapter 7.)

Sentence Stretchers

Students with reading problems often have difficulty with sentence comprehension. Their verbal expression may be limited as reflected in their conversations as well as their writing. The sentence building strategy (Richek, 1999) is a creative way to give students practice in constructing their own long sentences. Although best suited to a group situation, this strategy, presented in Figure 10.5, can also be used individually.

The object is to create a long sentence. Because students will usually add to the end of a sentence, the teacher should also require that they make additions to the beginning and the middle. After a sentence has been finished, discuss appropriate capitalization and punctuation with the students. Finally, young children in a large class often enjoy each holding a word card. Then, as the sentence grows, they can move to different places.

Encouraging Verbal Expression

How do we address the fact that students with reading problems often fear expressing their thoughts and opinions when we know that active use of language is essential to building language skills? A few principles, if practiced consistently by teachers, can make pupils feel more comfortable with expressing themselves.

FIGURE 10.4   Directed Listening-Thinking Activity

	Share the title and pictures with the students so that they can predict the content of the text.
	Read the text aloud, stopping at crucial points to allow student to predict what will happen next and confirm or revise previous predictions.
	Write students' predictions on the board or on chart paper so that you can refer to them when confirming or revising.
	Summarize the story.

FIGURE 10.5 Sentence Stretchers

Instructions	Examples
1. Write the words from a simple sentence on word cards or sentence strips. Do not include punctuation or capitalization. Attach the word cards to the board.	the boy walked the dog
2. Tell the students you want them to stretch the sentence. Each student takes a turn making the sentence longer. Each student must read the entire sentence, including the addition.	First student: "the boy walked the dog to the park" Second student: "Johnny and the new boy walked the dog through the alley to the park" Third student: "Johnny and the new boy walked the dog through the alley until they came to the park" Fourth student: "Johnny and the new boy walked the dog through the alley in the pouring rain until they came to the park" Fifth student: "Johnny and the new boy walked the lost dog through the alley in the pouring rain until they came to the park"
3. Continue until the sentence is too long to read in one breath.	Final sentence constructed by fourth-grade students: "Johnny and the muscle-bound new boy walked the lost dog through the alley in the pouring rain until they came to the park and found a little girl calling, 'Samson, where are you?' " Final sentence constructed by sixth-grade students: "Who was the dumb ugly boy with a holey shirt and holey pants who walked the dog all the way home and gave him a bone and gave him some food with water?"

- Never interrupt students who are speaking or allow others to interrupt them. Cultivate your own personal patience and insist on respectful behavior of students toward each other.
- Genuinely value students' points of view. This attitude is fostered when you ask students for their opinions. You can model how to express opinions by using phrases such as "I think that . . . " and "It's my opinion that. . . . " Often, if you express your opinions in long sentences, students will be inspired to follow your example.
- Do not judge the quality of what pupils say. Instead, respond to what students say and try not to judge how they express themselves. This attitude gives students confidence to express themselves more fully. Students who feel that their

language is being judged will be intimidated. In contrast, students who feel that their opinions are valued will be more comfortable talking.

Strategies for Fostering Language: Meaning Vocabulary

The first decision teachers must make about vocabulary instruction is "Which words should I teach?" This decision is difficult when each story introduced may include 25 to 30 "vocabulary words" and each unit or chapter in each content area presents its own list of new "Words to Learn"! The decision becomes even more difficult when working with struggling readers or ELLs whose English-meaning vocabularies may be so limited. Cunningham (2009) offers some suggestions for selecting which words to use for vocabulary instruction:

◆ Select words that are unfamiliar to your students, words for which they do not have rich meanings
◆ Select words your students need to know, words that they could use in speaking and writing, or that you think they will encounter in reading again
◆ Select words that are essential to your students' understanding of the passage or topic to be read
◆ Select words that have word parts that you want to focus on, selecting root words with multiple derivatives is an efficient way to help students learn many words

The next decision is to select the best instructional strategies. Although research has shown that students learn more words through wide reading than through isolated vocabulary instruction, students with reading problems often need more explicit strategy instruction within the context of wide reading (Anderson, et al., 1988).

Students with reading problems need extensive work in developing strategies to learn word meanings. Meaning vocabulary is highly correlated with a student's ability to comprehend, and words themselves embody important concepts that students will meet in reading (Anderson & Freebody, 1981).

In a wide-ranging review of the literature, Blachowicz and Fisher (2000, 2002) stress the need for active, personalized, and rich vocabulary instruction. Graves (2000, 2006) states that the four components of a vocabulary program should be extensive language experiences in reading and writing, teaching individual words, word consciousness, and teaching strategies for word learning. Bauman, Ware, and Carr Edwards (2007) report that a comprehensive vocabulary program grounded in Graves' model proved successful for a classroom of fifth-grade students in a diverse, low-income setting; using these principles, teachers reported increases in their students' receptive and expressive vocabulary levels as well as an increase in their use of rich, sophisticated language; the students wrote longer samples and included more low-frequency words in their writing; and students expressed greater interest and aptitude for learning new words.

This section discusses explicit instructional strategies for introducing and practicing words, ways to encourage vocabulary learning, and helping students to figure out words independently. These topics address three of the four components identified by Graves (2000). Suggestions to foster wide reading are found in Chapter 6.

Introducing Words Before Reading

Go to MyEducationLab and select the topic *Vocabulary*. Then, go to the Activities and Applications section, watch the video entitled "Creating Word Walls," and respond to the accompanying questions. How does this teacher use a word wall to help students build background knowledge prior to reading?

Knowing key words in a story or book helps students read more effectively. Even a short introduction of a word helps, because a large part of learning a word is simply noticing that it exists. Have you ever noticed how often you hear a word after you learn it? This phenomenon occurs because you have become conscious of the word. The strategies presented here are not meant to give students a complete mastery of words before reading, because they will understand the words better after they have read (or listened to) them in a text. Rather, these strategies focus on getting words into use so that students are comfortable enough to read.

Knowledge Rating. The knowledge rating strategy fosters an awareness of words and gives students control over their own knowledge. The teacher lists the new words for a story or passage and students think about how well they know them. Each student checks one of four categories for each word; the categories are based on Dale's (1965) four stages of vocabulary knowledge.

1. Never saw or heard this word
2. Saw or heard it but don't know it
3. Know it in a sentence; know the meaning vaguely
4. Know it well

Students then read the selection, keeping the words in mind. After reading, the chart is reviewed again (Blachowicz, 1986). Students are delighted to find that they know many words better after they have read them in a story or passage (Blachowicz & Fisher, 2002, 2005; Blachowicz, 1986).

In Strategy Snapshot 10.1, Ms. Laskey, a second-grade teacher combines several strategies in a science lesson about magnetism.

Go to MyEducationLab and select the topic *Vocabulary*. Then, go to the Activities and Applications section, watch the video entitled "Vocabulary Instruction," and respond to the accompanying questions. How does the first teacher help his students learn new vocabulary?

Classifying. When students classify words into categories, they are actively engaged in using higher-level skills to learn vocabulary (Blachowicz & Fisher, 2002, 2005). To ensure that students are successful, however, the teacher may have to go over some of the words with the students before they classify. To prepare third-grade children to read the story *Dragon Stew* (by McGowen), words were classified into three categories: (1) king words, (2) cook words, and (3) dragon words. The words were *stew, royal, castle, throne, palace, fellow, rare, fellow, ordinary, stirred, pork, lit, fiery breath, banquet hall, majesty, proclamations, drawbridge, roast, applesauce, sliced, bubbling, vinegar, simmer, onions, gravy-stained, assistant, fanciful*. While doing this activity, the students' lively discussions about the words helped them deepen vocabulary learning.

Strategy Snapshot 10.1

Combining Multiple Strategies for Effective Instruction

For a unit on Magnetism, Ms. Laskey included the following words on a Topic Board for her second-grade class:

magnet
pole
opposite
attract
repel
like
metal

First, she read the words as her students completed a Knowledge Rating Chart. The only word her students indicated that they didn't know was *repel*. To help them figure out the new word, Ms. Laskey made a transparency of a paragraph from the science book and covered the word *repel* with masking tape:

> Magnets have two poles: a positive pole and a negative pole. While opposite poles attract each other, like poles   each other.

Ms. Laskey asked her students to read the sentence with the missing word. The students immediately encountered a problem because they had never heard the word *like* used as an adjective. Ms. Laskey connected their knowledge of the words *like* and *alike* to explain this new use. The students reasoned that if something is *attractive*, you want it. So opposite poles must pull toward each other. So poles that are *alike* must push each other away. By the process of elimination, Josh suggested the word *repel* because that was the only word they hadn't used in their discussion. Josh "zipped" off the tape to discover his choice matched the author's!

Predict-o-gram.   By classifying words into story grammar categories (see Chapter 11) before they read a story, students become actively involved in learning meanings and predicting story content. To do a Predict-o-gram, list the new words in a story, and then ask students to predict whether each word will be used to describe the setting, the characters, the actions, or the ending. Next, as they read, students can see if these words are used in the way that was predicted (Blachowicz, 1986). If the words are written on Post-it–style notes, students can move them after reading if the words need to be reclassified.

Possible Sentences.   This strategy can be used to introduce new vocabulary in areas such as social studies and science texts (Blachowicz & Fisher, 2002, 2005; Moore & Arthur, 1981). First give the title of a chapter that the students are about to read, then write the new words on the board (e.g., *molecule, proton, atom, electron, neutron*). Next have students construct sentences that might possibly be true using at least two target words in each sentence. An example would be "A molecule could contain two atoms." Students develop expectations of the chapter as they go through this activity. Then have students read the chapter. After reading, students evaluate the possibly true sentences they have written to see if they are indeed true. They change sentences that are inaccurate and add other sentences reflecting their new knowledge. This simple strategy combines learning vocabulary with the learning of content material.

Practicing and Reinforcing Meaning Vocabulary

After words have been introduced, several strategies can be used to reinforce word meaning by keeping students actively engaged with words: display and vocabulary picture cards, multiple-sentence game, and automaticity.

Display and Vocabulary Picture Cards. Displaying words they have learned helps students feel a sense of accomplishment and informs others of their achievements. Public displays of words can also help students remember them. A group of eighth-grade students created the web presented in Figure 10.6 as part of their unit study of U.S. government.

Students can become "word experts." In a seventh-grade classroom a teacher working with a group of students with learning disabilities placed the study words from a book on individual small cards, which could be flipped up. Each student was given two words and was asked to construct cards for them. On the front, the student wrote his or her name to establish ownership. Inside, the student wrote a definition and a sentence for the word, both of which had to be approved by the teacher. The student who had signed his or her name to the word was an "expert consultant" on

FIGURE 10.6 Vocabulary Web for the U.S. Government

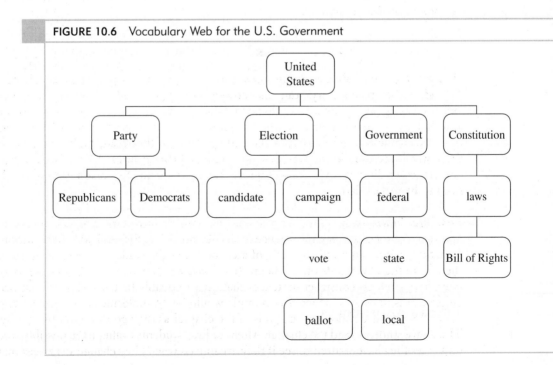

that word. All word cards were put on display on the bulletin board. When students wanted to review the words, they went to the board, read the word, and flipped up the word card to check the definition.

Vocabulary cards featuring picture clues are often effective in reminding students of word meanings. Lansdown (1991) effectively combined picture clue word cards and the "expert consultant" strategies, as shown in Strategy Snapshot 10.2.

Multiple-Sentence Game.   Students enjoy trying to put a number of their new words into one sentence (Richek, Caldwell, Jennings, & Lerner, 2002; Jennings, Caldwell, & Lerner, 2006). This difficult (but exciting) strategy is recommended for upper-elementary and secondary students. To do this activity in a group, prepare a list of target words. Next divide students into small groups and have each group select three new words. Groups now exchange words with one another. When each group gets its new list, they must put the words in the least number of sentences.

> For a sentence with 1 word, they get 1 point.
>
> For a sentence with 2 words, they get 3 points.
>
> For a sentence with 3 words, they get 6 points.

As the teacher, you judge the correctness and sense of a sentence before giving credit. Students are allowed to change the form of the word (for example, *slow* to *slowly*). Formerly unmotivated students have worked on this activity with extraordinary interest and have even asked to do it for homework.

Automaticity.   To fully master words, students need to recognize them quickly. Spending a few minutes a week having students say words quickly, rapidly supply definitions, or quickly compose sentences is a good way to foster automaticity.

A game of "Beat the Clock" can be readily adapted to help students access meanings quickly so that they maintain comprehension when reading in context (Beck, et al., 2002; Beck, Perfetti, & McKeown, 1982).

Students can be given statements like the following:

A paleontologist studies space.	True	False
An anthropologist studies humans.	True	False
An archeologist studies buildings.	True	False

They have to understand the meaning of the words to respond correctly.

Some teachers in our reading center used two different sounds to represent true and false: a bell and a buzzer. Students enjoyed racing each other to push the right button and show off their word knowledge.

Fostering Vocabulary Learning through Rich Literate Experiences

Most meaning vocabulary is learned through listening and reading in the context of a rich literate environment. This section focuses on strategies that help students learn

Strategy Snapshot 10.2

Picture Cards and Word Learning

To prepare her 20 at-risk sixth graders to read the difficult novel *Rascal* (by North), Ms. Lansdown chose 100 *difficult and important* words from the novel and assigned five to each student. The individual student became a "word expert" in these words by preparing cards for each one. The word appeared on the outside along with a picture representing it. On the inside was a definition (in the student's own language) and a sentence. The words stayed up on the bulletin board unless the students were using them. When working with the words, the students were put in pairs. For 10 minutes, each "word expert" drilled a partner on his or her five words and was drilled on the partner's words in return. Students changed partners for each drill session.

After a week, the students started to read the novel. As they went along, they noticed the words they had been studying. Ms. Lansdown began to give points, cumulative for the entire class, for finding the words either in the book, other reading materials, or nonprint sources (radio, TV, speech). In three weeks, the class had almost 1,000 points.

The excitement of learning these words was matched by the enthusiasm students felt in being able to read *Rascal* with considerable proficiency. As an ending project, Ms. Lansdown tested the students on all 100 words, and this class of low-level readers averaged 97 percent. A month later, their proficiency had not slipped. A student word card for *perpetually* is shown below.

| Outside of Word Card | Inside of Word Card |

words from their environment. Such activities foster word consciousness, through both knowledge and interest in words (Graves, 2000).

Modeling Difficult Words in Speech.   If teachers consciously try to use "million-dollar words," students will unconsciously absorb them. Use words that challenge students to expand their vocabularies. Encourage them to ask the meanings of these words and thus to take control of their own learning. For example, in a noisy fourth-grade Title I class, the teacher said, "I find this noise *onerous* and *burdensome*." Fascinated by the words, the pupils immediately quieted down and requested the meaning of this intriguing statement. The teacher wrote the words on the board and discussed them. Teacher use of challenging vocabulary takes a little additional time yet exposes students to many words. Million-dollar words also can become an ongoing game. Teachers can identify a couple of especially challenging words from their vocabulary lists and award points to students when they "catch" a teacher or another student using the word or double points for using the word correctly themselves. One middle school team has turned this game into a competition among classrooms. They count the points until one room has earned a hundred points, enough to trade in for a pizza or taco party.

Word Collections.   Collecting different types of words increases students' interest in meaning vocabulary. A class of low-achieving fifth graders collected soft words (*whisper*, *slipper*), green words (*grass*, *lime*), and happy words (*ecstatic*, *birthday*) and placed them in individual canisters.

Semantic Gradients.   Students also collect synonyms for overused words such as *say*, *went*, *big*, *little*, *sad*, *happy*. Then the students arrange the words in order of degree (Blachowicz & Fisher, 2002, 2006). One third-grade class created a list of synonyms for *bad* after a read-aloud of *Alexander and the Terrible, Horrible, No Good, Very Bad Day* (by Judith Viorst and Ray Cruz) and arranged them by degrees of "badness" as presented in Figure 10.7.

The students were surprised to find that *bad* was the least bad word they could think of! After the semantic gradient for *bad* was completed, the group created one for *good* and wrote their own story about the best day of their lives. As the group read and wrote more stories, they continued to create semantic gradient posters and placed them in the writing center to remind them to use million-dollar words.

Collected Expressions.   Other students have collected expressions. One intermediate class's collection of expressions containing the words *gold*, *green*, and *black*, included several figures of speech, like "golden years," "golden egg," "green-eyed," "green thumb," "black belt," and "black hole." Your students will become quite creative in thinking up categories they would like to pursue. These word collections are especially helpful in enriching students' vocabulary in their writing.

Relating Words to Students' Environments.   Words become interesting when they relate to the lives of students (Richek, 1987). Students can look up the meanings

FIGURE 10.7 Semantic Gradient for *bad*

Brainstormed List	*Ranked from Best to Worst*
bad	bad
disastrous	awful
awful	worst
icky	sorry
horrible	blah
terrible	icky
horrendous	nasty
sorry	stinky
blah	depressing
rotten	rotten
nasty	terrible
depressing	horrible
stinky	disastrous
worst	horrendous

of their names in How to Name Your Baby books. Car names often intrigue older students. For example, Chevrolet was a famous car racer, Cadillac was the French explorer who founded Detroit, Seville and Granada are names of cities, and Mustang and Pinto are types of horses. Other students enjoy discussing the reasoning behind the names of common household products, such as Tide, Wisk, Mr. Clean, Cheer, and Vanish. Common foods, such as *hamburger*, *frankfurter*, *tomato*, *banana*, and *tea* have origins in other languages. Students may use them to practice dictionary skills as well as to gain geographical knowledge.

Using Strategies to Figure Out Unknown Words

This section describes some strategies to teach students to figure out word meanings.

Go to MyEducationLab and select the topic *Vocabulary*. Then, go to the Activities and Applications section, watch the video entitled "Vocabulary Strategies," and respond to the accompanying questions.

Using Context Clues. Instruction in context clues is an effective way to help students learn word meanings (Blachowicz & Fisher, 2002, 2006). Although the context will not always define a word thoroughly, it is effective in giving many clues to meaning (Cunningham, Cunningham, Moore, & Moore, 2004). However, the process of gaining meaning from context is not easy for many students with reading problems. To build vocabulary in this way, they must be encouraged to take risks and to make "intelligent hypotheses" (we often use these exact words to encourage our students).

Blachowicz and Fisher (2002, 2006) recommend a four-step process to guide students' use of context clues:

1. Look at the unfamiliar word—then read the sentence before and after the word.
2. Connect what you know with the text.
3. Predict a meaning.

4. Confirm or revise your prediction. Reread the sentence using your prediction. Are you satisfied with your prediction, or do you need to read further back or forward in the text to see if the author provides more clues? Do you need to use a resource beyond the text? If so, try a dictionary or ask someone.

Using word detective posters with these steps on them or giving students word detective bookmarks reminds them to follow these steps as they are reading.

Josel (1988) dramatically demonstrated to low-achieving eighth graders that they used context clues to determine meaning. First, she gave them a list of words taken from a novel and asked them to match the words with their definitions. Because the list contained words such as *etesian* and *clamorous*, few students could match any correctly. Next, she presented sentences from the book that contained these words, such as "We are sailing before the *etesian*, which blows from the northwest," and asked students to define the words. Students found they were able to define the majority of the words. This activity demonstrated the helpfulness of context clues in determining word meanings.

After students have become comfortable with context clues, ask them to use these clues consciously as they are reading. First, list new words from a selection students are about to read, then have students read the selection. When they finish reading, go back to the words and ask students what meanings they hypothesized from the context. The teacher should write down the location of the words in the text so that the class can easily find the words for discussion. If questions remain, the class can consult a dictionary to clarify meanings. This procedure models the way that good readers combine context clues and dictionary skills.

Students with reading problems can also be taught that when they come to a word they don't know, they should substitute a word or phrase that makes sense. The substitution is likely to be the definition of the unknown word. For example, in the sentence, "Because prices were going up, we decided to defer buying a car until next year," many students would substitute the phrase *put off* or the word *delay* for the word *defer*. These words are, in fact, approximate definitions of *defer*.

After choosing the new words for a selection, display them on a topic board, bulletin board, word wall, or overhead. To teach students to use context clues effectively, select a word from the passage that is contextually explained. Display the passage with the target word omitted. A good technique is to cover the target word. Tell students to read the words before and after the omitted word. If the sentence containing the word is not helpful, have students read the previous and following sentences. Guide students to connect what they know with the text. Predict a possible meaning for the target word. Select the word from your display that best matches the prediction. You may need to reach consensus on a prediction. Decide whether they are satisfied with their prediction or need to read further. Remove the tape to reveal the author's choice. Discuss to reconcile differences, and use references as needed.

Cloze Procedure.   The cloze procedure is an excellent way to help students learn to use context clues to figure out word meanings. Instead of deleting every fifth word as you would when using a cloze procedure for assessment purposes, delete the words you want your students to learn from the passage. The cloze procedure can be modified for multiple instructional purposes.

Oral Cloze.   In an oral cloze, teachers read the passage to students, omitting key words as they read. Students provide possible words to fill in the blanks. As students select the "best possible fit" for each blank, they engage in rich discussions about word meanings and relationships.

Zip Cloze.   In this adaptation of the cloze procedure, Blachowicz and Fisher (2002, 2006) recommend creating a transparency of the text and using masking tape to cover the target words. As students suggest possible words to complete the sentences, they can "zip" off the masking tape to immediately compare their predictions with the author's choices.

Maze Cloze.   In another adaptation of the cloze procedure, Blachowicz and Fisher (2002, 2006) suggest that teachers provide choices for the students when filling in the blanks:

	rock	
Mr. and Mrs. Parker lived in the biggest	*book*	on our block.
	house	

Synonym Cloze   For students who need further support, Blachowicz and Fisher (2002, 2006) recommend providing a synonym or synonym phrase under the space where the target word is deleted:

The mother cat purred when she found her kitten.

_____

[baby cat]

Using Prefixes, Suffixes, and Roots.   The structural parts of words—prefixes, suffixes, and roots—are helpful in giving students with reading problems effective clues to meaning (Cunningham, 2009).

Suffixes, or word endings, are common in written English, and they provide valuable clues to recognizing long words. However, students with reading problems often ignore word endings and need to practice focusing on them. Because suffixes are relatively easy to teach, a small amount of effort can dramatically increase the ability to recognize long words. Chapter 8 gives guidelines for teaching the easiest suffixes (*s*, *ed*); this section gives strategies for more advanced suffixes.

Many suffixes change the part of speech of a word. Examples of this are *identify-identification* (verb becomes a noun) and *comfort-comfortable* (noun or verb becomes an adjective). Table 10.1 lists some of the most common suffixes in English and their approximate grade levels (Richek, 1969). Because almost all students have some familiarity with suffixes, you do not have to teach them one at a time. Instead, simply teach students to be aware of suffixes as they read in context.

TABLE 10.1   Graded List of Suffixes

First Grade		Second Grade	
er, est*	bigger, biggest	able	serviceable
s, es (plural)*	ponies	al	seasonal
s (possessive)*	Jane's	ing	singing
s (third person)*	she dances	ly	slowly
ed (past)*	waited	ness	bigness

Third Grade		Fourth Grade		Fifth Grade	
y	cheery	ish	childish	ance	insurance
tion	relation	ive	impulsive	ity	serenity
ist	violist	ful	beautiful	ent	excellent
ic	angelic	ency	presidency	age	postage
ize	idolize	ery	slavery	an	musician
ment	contentment	ous	famous		
		ate	activate		

*Inflectional suffixes. Other suffixes are derivational.

Three activities are especially useful for helping students to use suffixes:

1. Select a short text and ask students to underline each suffix that they find. Provide the hint that some words contain two or even three suffixes. (Words like *illness-es* and *publish-er-s* are found in third- and fourth-grade materials.) Once students have completed this task, review it with them. Few students catch all of the suffixes, and they enjoy finding out about the less-obvious ones, such as *hurry-hurried*.

2. In a slightly more difficult task, students listen to a text read by the teacher. Each time they hear a suffix, they tap a table. For some words, they must tap two or three times. Because this activity requires intense attention, it deepens students' understanding of suffixes. Older students often enjoy listening to newspaper articles.

3. Select one word and see how many different words students can make from it by using suffixes. For example, from the word *sleep*, students made *sleeping*, *sleepily*, *sleepless*, *sleepy*, and *sleeper*.

Students can also increase their facility with suffixes by collecting words with suffixes and keeping notebooks of suffixed words that they encounter in reading. Have students put a different suffix on the top of each page of a blank notebook. As they encounter words with this suffix, they simply enter them in the book. Figure 10.8 shows a list developed by Ramiro, a 15-year-old student reading on a sixth-grade level.

FIGURE 10.8   Ramiro's Suffix List

In addition to suffixes, difficult words include many *prefixes* (word beginnings) and *root words* (the main part of the word). Many English prefixes and roots descend from Greek and Latin. Because both prefixes and roots contribute basic meaning to the words they form, students can use them for vocabulary building. Examples of prefixes that affect word meaning are *pre-* (before) and *trans-* (across). Examples of roots that affect meaning are *port* (to carry) and *script* (to write). Students who know the meaning of a root such as *script* have valuable hints to the meanings of such words as *postscript*, *prescription*, *scribe*, and *inscription*. A list of useful roots and prefixes (Richek, 1969) is given in Table 10.2.

Word history adds variety to the study of word parts. For example, the word part *uni* is descended from Greek, and the many words that incorporate *uni*, such as *unicycle*, *universe*, *unity*, and *unicorn* are derived from Greek. The word *astronaut*, formed in the 1950s, is derived from the Greek elements *astro* (or star) and *naut* (or sailor). More mature students can use the dictionary to learn about word histories as related to content area reading.

TABLE 10.2 Useful Prefixes and Roots

Prefixes			Roots		
ante	antedate	before	aque	aqueduct	water
anti	antifreeze	against	astro	astrology	stars, heavens
aqua	aquarium	water	auto	automation	self
endo	endoderm	inner	micro	microscope	small
ex	exoderm	outer	bio	biosphere	life
ex	ex-president	former	dent	dentist	teeth
geo	geography	earth	dict	dictate	word
im	impossible	not	equi	equivalent	equal
non	nonparallel	not	graph	biography	write
post	posttest	after	itis	bronchitis	illness
pre	pretest	before	ling	linguistics	language
re	rewind	again	mid	amid	middle
semi	semisweet	sort of	ortho	orthodontist	straight
sub	subterranean	below	phobia	claustrophobia	fear
tele	television	far	phon	phonics	sound
trans	transistor	across	polit	political	politics
un	undo	not	script	scripture	writing
			sonic	resonant	sound
			spec	spectator	sight
			therm	thermometer	heat
			viv	vivid	life

Numbers

mono, uni	1	oct	8
di, bi	2	non	9
tri	3	dec	10
quadr, tetr	4	cent	100
quint, penta	5	milli	1/1000
hex, sex	6	kilo	1000
hept, sept	7	hemi	1/2

Using the Dictionary.   The dictionary gives students independence in learning word meanings; however, it should not be overused as an instructional tool. Students with reading problems find looking up word meanings tedious, and if they can learn words through other means, they should be encouraged to do so. Interrupting the reading process to look up a word in the dictionary is disruptive to the reading. Furthermore, dictionary definitions are often more difficult than the word itself. Finally, because dictionaries do not teach correct usage, sentences using words and discussions of words should accompany dictionary study.

Research has shown that dictionary definitions, even those from children's dictionaries, are difficult to understand (Beck, et al., 2002, 2008). For this reason, when students ask what a word means, guide them through the most efficient strategy for that particular word. You might begin with the word detective process, or you might need to help students break the word into its root and affixes. Then use the dictionary to confirm the meaning they derive.

Even though the dictionary is not the best way to develop word meanings, it does have many uses. It provides definitions, offers a means to distinguish among definitions, gives a key for pronunciation, and supplies the different forms of a base word. Dictionary skills, organized from less to more advanced are:

1. Alphabetizing words. To alphabetize, teach children to use the first letter in a word and then the second letter, third letter, and so on.
2. Locating words. Opening the dictionary to the correct half or quarter to locate a word and using key words to determine if a word is on a page.
3. Using the dictionary pronunciation key.
4. Determining the correct dictionary entry for different word forms. For example, the word *slowly* should be looked up under the word *slow*.
5. Determining which of several definitions should be used in a particular context.
6. Determining the historical origin of a word. Usually only advanced dictionaries provide this information.

Games can help students to learn effective dictionary use:

1. Making dictionary sentences. Students can open the dictionary to a given page and try to construct the longest sentence possible using words from that page (Moffett & Wagner, 1991). Words such as *the*, *and*, *is*, *if*, and *I* may have to be added.
2. Drawing pictures of words found in dictionaries. Students can record the page where they found a word and draw a picture of it. Other pupils must then find the word in the dictionary.
3. Seeing who can locate a word in the dictionary using the fewest opening "cuts." This exercise helps students to locate words quickly.

Remember that different dictionaries are helpful for students at different levels. Young students struggling with reading and writing may need a primary-level or intermediate dictionary. Older students can profit from college- or adult-level dictionaries.

Using Poetry to Develop Language

Using language in playful, imaginative ways helps students with reading problems enjoy and appreciate it. Poetry is an effective language form because in this medium, sounds and word arrangements assume a special importance. Many teachers have had enormous success using poetry to foster language and personal growth. Because poetry invites students to memorize and recite it, it is an excellent way to build expressive language skills.

Simply reading and allowing students to react to the work of outstanding children's poets helps them to explore language and ideas. Kutiper and Wilson (1993) found that narrative poetry, which tells a story, is most popular. Students like poems that contain strong rhyme, rhythm, and humor. Familiar experiences and animals are popular poetry topics. Some popular children's poetry books are:

The New Kid on the Block by Prelutsky

Where the Sidewalk Ends by Silverstein

A Light in the Attic by Silverstein

If I Were in Charge of the World by Viorst

Honey I Love by Greenfield

Of course, you may have your own personal choices. For example, *Hailstones and Halibut Bones* (by O'Neill), a book of nonrhyming poems that each reflect a color, became a favorite of several classes of low-achieving third graders. In reading *The Giving Tree* (by Silverstein), a short book with a poetic story, one teacher cried along with her fourth-grade students. When working with poetry, read poems that you enjoy.

Shapiro (1994) suggests many easy ways to encourage students to explore poetry. She urges teachers to make poetry books and poems readily available on a poetry shelf or in a poetry corner. Poetry is an oral medium, and it is meant to be read aloud. To set a mood, poetry can be read at a certain time, perhaps at the beginning of an instructional session. Have a poetry reading once a week. Students can also form a group poetry circle.

Poetry can be effectively shared during read-aloud time. Make sure that you practice beforehand so that you read smoothly and with interpretation. Students will often want to read the poem aloud after you finish it. As you will see, a poem takes on a different interpretation with every individual who reads it.

Students also enjoy reacting to poetry. They can share experiences that the poem reminds them of. They can discuss what they liked or disliked in the poem. They can also discuss their favorite parts, rhymes, or words.

Shapiro (1994) has invited students to copy favorite poems into a poetry journal. This is an educational experience, because as they copy poems into a journal, students realize that poets use lines and spaces for a variety of effects. They also begin to learn how poets use rhyme, rhythm, and repetition.

Students who become involved in poetry may wish to give readings of favorite poems. They can perform in choral readings, with partners, or individually. Students should always have the option of memorizing the poem or reading it. Some poetry is particularly useful for performing. For example, *Joyful Noise: Poems for Two Voices* (by Fleishman) contains parts for two voices in rhythmic, nonrhyming poetry. Of course, because fluent, expressive oral reading is the essence of reading poetry, this activity helps improve reading fluency. Remember that students with reading problems may need much practice before they become comfortable performing.

Art and writing are also effective mediums for responding to poetry. After a teacher in a low-achieving fourth-grade classroom shared "Homework Oh Homework" (from *The New Kid on the Block* by Prelutsky), each child drew a response to the unpopular topic.

Summary

Language is the basis of all reading, and you cannot read language that you cannot understand. Language development is important throughout the grades. Causes of problems with language include language disability and delay, a lack of reading (because reading is the source of much language growth), and a lack of exposure to rich language in the environment.

Teachers usually assess students' language abilities through informal measures, such as observations or conversations. They can also obtain a listening level from an informal reading inventory. Language abilities can also be assessed through formal measures, such as the *Peabody Picture Vocabulary Test*, Third Edition and the *Expressive Vocabulary Test*.

Conditions that foster language include exposure to high-level language, active responses in learning, and explicit teaching as well as incidental exposure to rich language in listening and reading.

Strategies for fostering listening comprehension include reading books to students; paired reading of easy and harder versions of one story; the Directed Listening-Thinking Activity, in which students listen to a story and predict what will happen; building sentences on the board from a short sentence; and encouraging students to employ advanced verbal styles.

Explicit instructional strategies for fostering meaning vocabulary before reading include noticing words that appear in text; classifying words into categories; Predict-o-gram, or classifying how words will be used in a story; knowledge rating, or rating one's knowledge of words; and possible sentences, or composing possibly true sentences before reading. Strategies for reinforcing meaning vocabulary include making word cards with pictures, fitting a multiple number of words into one sentence, and practicing responding to words quickly. Vocabulary growth can be fostered by the teacher's modeling of difficult words in speech, collecting words of different types, relating words to students' environments, and noticing words as the teacher reads them in a story.

To learn how to figure out unknown words, students can use context clues; structural analysis, such as prefixes, suffixes, and roots; and the dictionary. Because dictionary definitions are difficult for students, this tool should be used for limited purposes.

References

Anderson, R. C., & Freebody, P. (1981). Vocabulary knowledge. In J. Guthrie (Ed.), *Comprehension and Teaching: Research Views*, pp. 77–117. Newark, DE: International Reading Association.

Anderson, R. C., Wilson, P., & Fielding, L. (1988). Growth in reading and how children spend their time outside of school. *Reading Research Quarterly, 23*, 285–303.

Bauman, J. F., Ware, D., & Carr Edwards, E. (2007). "Bumping into spicy, tasty words that catch your tongue": A formative experiment on vocabulary instruction. *The Reading Teacher, 61*, 108–122.

Beck, I. L., McKeown, M. G., & Kucan, L. (2008). *Creating Robust Vocabulary: Frequently Asked Questions and Extended Examples*. New York: Guilford Press.

Beck, I. L., McKeown, M. G., & Kucan, L. (2002). *Bringing Words to Life: Robust Vocabulary Instruction.* New York: Guilford Press.

Beck, I. L., McKeown, M. G., & Omanson, R. (1987). The effects and uses of diverse vocabulary instructional techniques. In M. G. McKeown & M. E. Curtis (Eds.), *The Nature of Vocabulary Acquisition.* Hillsdale, NJ: Erlbaum.

Beck, I. L., Perfetti, C. A., & McKeown, M. G. (1982). The effects of long-term vocabulary instruction on lexical access and reading comprehension. *Journal of Educational Psychology, 74,* 506–521.

Biemiller, A. (2001). Teaching vocabulary: Early, direct, and sequential. *American Educator, 25,* 24–28, 47.

Blachowicz, C. L. Z., & Fisher, P. J. (2006). *Teaching Vocabulary in All Classrooms* (3rd ed.). Upper Saddle River, NJ: Pearson Education, Inc.

Blachowicz, C. L. Z., & Fisher, P. J. (2002). *Teaching Vocabulary in All Classrooms* (2nd ed.). Upper Saddle River, NJ: Pearson Education, Inc.

Blachowicz, C. L. Z., & Fisher, P. (2000). Vocabulary instruction. In R. Barr, M. L. Kamil, P. Mosenthal, & P. D. Pearson (eds.), *Handbook of Reading Research* (Vol. III), pp. 503–523. Mahwah, NJ: Lawrence Erlbaum Associates.

Blachowicz, C. L. Z., Fisher, P. J. L., Ogle, D., & Watts-Taffe, S. (2006). Vocabulary: Questions from the classroom. *Reading Research Quarterly, 41*(4), 524–539.

Carver, R. P., & David, A. H. (2001). Investigating reading achievement using a causal model. *Scientific Studies of Reading, 5,* 107–140.

Chall, J. S. (1983). *Stages of Reading Development.* New York: McGraw-Hill.

Clay, M. M. (2002). *An Observation Survey of Early Literacy Achievement* (2nd ed.). Portsmouth, NH: Heinemann Educational Books.

Cunningham, A., & Stanovich, K. (1998). What reading does for the mind. *American Educator, 22,* 8–17.

Cunningham, P.M. (2009). *What Really Matters in Vocabulary: Research-Based Practices across the Curriculum.* Boston: Pearson.

Cunningham, P. M., Cunningham, J. W., Moore, S. A., & Moore, D. W. (2004). *Reading and Writing in Elementary Classrooms: Research-Based K-4 Instruction* (5th ed.). Boston: Allyn & Bacon.

Dale, E. (1965). Vocabulary measurement: Techniques and major findings. *Elementary English, 42,* 895–901, 948.

Davis, F. B. (1968). Research in comprehension in reading. *Reading Research Quarterly, 3,* 499–545.

Davis, F. B. (1944). Fundamental factors of comprehension in reading. *Psychometrika, 9,* 185–197.

Edwards Santoro, L., Chard, D. J., Howard, L., & Baker, S. K. (2008). Making the *very* most of classroom read-alouds to promote comprehension and vocabulary. *The Reading Teacher, 6,* 396–408.

Graves, M. (2000). A vocabulary program to complement and bolster a middle-grade comprehension program. In B. M. Taylor, M. F. Graves, & P. Van Der Brock (Eds.), Reading for Meaning, pp. 116–135. Newark, DE: International Reading Association, and New York: Teachers College Press.

Graves, M. F. (2006). *The Vocabulary Book.* Newark, DE: International Reading Association.

Gredler, M. E., & Johnson, R. L. (2004). *Assessment in the Literacy Classroom.* Boston: Allyn & Bacon.

Jennings, J. H., Caldwell, J., & Lerner, J. W. (2006). *Reading Problems: Assessment and Teaching Strategies* (5th Ed.). Boston: Allyn & Bacon.

Josel, C. A. (1988). In a different context. *Journal of Reading, 31,* 374–377.

Joshi, R. M. (2005). Vocabulary: A critical component of comprehension. *Reading and Writing Quarterly, 21,* 209–219.

Kutiper, K., & Wilson, P. (1993). Updating poetry preferences: A look at the poetry children really like. *The Reading Teacher, 47,* 28–34.

Lansdown, S. (1991). Increasing vocabulary knowledge using direct instruction, cooperative grouping, and reading in junior high school. *Illinois Reading Council Journal, 19,* 15–21.

Moffett, J., & Wagner, B. J. (1991). *Student-Centered Language Arts, K–12* (4th ed.). Portsmouth, NH: Heinemann-Boynton/Cook.

Moore, D., & Arthur, S. V. (1981). Possible sentences. In E. D. Dishner, T. W. Bean, & J. E. Readence (Eds.), *Reading in the Content Areas: Improving Classroom Instruction* (pp. 138–142). Dubuque, IA: Kendall/Hunt.

Morrow, L. M. (2004). *Literacy Development in the Early Years: Helping Children Read and Write* (5th ed.). Boston: Allyn and Bacon.

Nagy, W., Anderson R., & Herman, P. (1987). Learning word meanings from context during normal reading. *American Educational Research Journal, 24,* 237–270.

Nagy, W. E., & Scott, J. A. (2000). Vocabulary processes. In R. Barr, M. L. Kamil, P. Mosenthal, & P. D. Pearson (Eds.), *Handbook of Reading Research* (Vol. III, pp. 269–284). Mahwah, NJ: Lawrence Erlbaum Associates.

Paris, A. H., & Paris, S. G. (2003). Assessing narrative comprehension in young children. *Reading Research Quarterly, 38,* 36–76.

Purcell-Gates, V. (1986). Lexical and syntactic knowledge of written narrative held by well-read-to kindergarteners and second graders. *Research in the Teaching of English, 22,* 128–157.

Richek, M. A. (1999). *Reading Success for At-Risk Children: Ideas that Work.* Bellevue, WA: Bureau of Education and Research.

Richek, M., Jennings, J., Caldwell, J., & Lerner, J. (2002). *Reading Problems: Assessment and Teaching Strategies.* Boston: Allyn & Bacon.

Richek, M. A. (1989). *Increasing the Achievement of Your Remedial Reading Students.* Paso Robles, CA: Bureau of Education and Research.

Richek, M. A. (1987). DRTA: 5 variations that facilitate independence in reading narratives. *Journal of Reading, 30,* 632–636.

Richek, M. A. (1969). A study of the affix structure of English: Affix frequency and teaching methods. Unpublished paper, University of Chicago.

Richek, M. A., Caldwell, J. S., Jennings, J. H., & Lerner, J. W. (2002). *Reading Problems: Assessment and Teaching Strategies* (4th ed.). Boston: Allyn & Bacon.

Scott, J. A., Jamieson-Noel, D., & Asselin, M. (2003). Vocabulary instruction throughout the day in twenty-three Canadian upper-elementary classrooms. *Elementary School Journal, 103,* 269–312.

Shapiro, S. (1994). From reading poetry to poetry reading in the classroom. *Illinois Reading Council Journal, 21,* 67–71.

Stahl, S. A., & Fairbanks, M. (1986). The effects of vocabulary instruction: A model-based meta-analysis. *Review of Educational Research, 56,* 72–110.

Stanovich, K. E. (1988). *Children's reading and the Development of Phonological Awareness.* Detroit: Wayne State University Press.

Stanovich, K. E. (1986). Matthew effects in reading. Some consequences of individual differences in the acquisition of literacy. *Reading Research Quarterly, 21,* 360–406.

Stanovich, K. E., & Cunningham, A. E. (1993). Where does knowledge come from? Specific associations between print exposure and information acquisition. *Journal of Educational Psychology, 85,* 211–229.

Stauffer, R. G. (1975). *Directing the Reading-Thinking Process.* New York: Harper and Row.

Strickland, D. S., & Shanahan, T. (2004). Laying the groundwork for literacy. *Educational Leadership, 61,* 74–77.

Thorndike, R. L. (1973). *Reading Comprehension Education in Fifteen Countries.* New York: Wiley.

Walker, B. J. (2005). *Techniques for Reading Assessment and Instruction.* Upper Saddle River, NJ: Merrill Prentice Hall.

Improving Comprehension of Narrative Text

Introduction

Comprehension is the essence of reading—indeed, it is the only purpose for reading—yet, many low-achieving students are unable to read effectively because they lack critical elements of comprehension. They need to develop strategies that help them become active, competent readers who demand meaning from text.

Focusing on reading comprehension is important even when a student's primary area of difficulty is word recognition. When students understand what they read, they enjoy it and are motivated to read more. This increased reading results in additional practice in recognizing words. In addition, students who are focused on meaning can use their general understanding of a story to help them recognize difficult words.

This chapter describes the general nature of comprehension—then the chapter discusses the comprehension of narrative (or storylike) text, including what it is, how to assess it, and what strategies to use for instruction. The comprehension of informational text is addressed in Chapter 12.

Effective Reading Comprehension

Good readers share subconscious knowledge and attitudes about four important aspects of comprehension:

1. The purpose of reading is comprehension.
2. Comprehension is an active and accurate process.
3. Readers use their background knowledge to comprehend.
4. Comprehension requires higher-level thinking.

The Purpose of Reading Is Comprehension

Good readers know that the purpose of reading is to understand, enjoy, and learn from material. In contrast, students with reading problems often think that reading means recognizing words. Some feel that once they have read all of the words orally, they are finished. To help students with reading problems understand that reading is comprehension, you can:

◆ Always ask students for a comprehension response after they read material. You can use questions, story retellings, or some of the more detailed strategies in this chapter. You can also use the think-aloud strategy described in Chapter 12.
◆ Encourage silent reading. Students who read only orally come to think of reading as a performance. Silent reading helps them to understand that reading is a personal, meaning-focused activity.

Comprehension Is an Active and Accurate Process

As discussed in Chapter 1, reading is the active construction of meaning. Good readers construct a text in their minds as they read. This text is similar to the text that the author has written, but good readers use their background knowledge to supply details and draw conclusions not stated explicitly in the text. In contrast, problem readers often focus on remembering small details rather than constructing their own meaning. As a result, low-achieving readers tend not to monitor their comprehension (Pressley, 2000; Van Der Broek & Kremer, 2000); that is, when they lose the meaning of the material, they do not go back in the text and try to understand. In fact, disabled readers are often unaware that something is wrong. The ability to monitor one's own comprehension and employ fix-up strategies is called *metacognition*.

Reading should be accurate as well as active. Sometimes, when struggling readers come across unfamiliar words, they abandon the actual text and substitute words that have little relation to the text's meaning. Some simply construct a story based on just a few words. Teachers can use these strategies to encourage active, yet accurate, reading:

1. Interest students in the material before they begin. Tell them what is good or exciting about a story or topic. Discuss the author to show students that stories are written by real people. Draw parallels between the students' lives and the events in a story.
2. Remind students to be aware of their own comprehension. If they are lost, they should stop, reread, look at pictures, ask themselves questions, retell what they have read so far, or ask for help.

Comprehension Uses Background Knowledge

The ability to comprehend is highly dependent on the background knowledge, or *schema*, that readers bring to reading (Goldman & Rakestraw, 2000). When students understand concepts important to the story, their comprehension increases (Beck, Omanson, & McKeown, 1982).

Unfortunately, students with reading problems often lack the background knowledge that ensures comprehension. Mike, a fifth grader, read a story about a boy who found a skunk, which later turned out to be a mink. Unfortunately, because Mike did not know what minks were, he could not understand that most people had different attitudes toward the two animals. In short, Mike lacked the background information to understand the story.

Because print often deals with more sophisticated concepts than conversation, reading itself helps to build background information needed in school. For example, most of you learned about ancient Greece through school and leisure reading rather than at the family dinner table. However, because students with reading problems do not read much, they do not learn the many sophisticated concepts needed for success in school (Cunningham & Stanovich, 1993; Snider & Tarver, 1987).

Even when students with reading problems do have background knowledge, they may not use it effectively (Pace, Marshall, Horowitz, Lipson, & Lucido, 1989). Some readers underuse their background knowledge and do not summon it to consciousness when they read. Other low-achieving readers overuse their background knowledge (Williams, 1993) and let their personal points of view intrude into their comprehension. To illustrate, Angel, a fourth grader, read a selection about a football game in which the star player was a girl. Unfortunately, Angel's schema that only boys played football was so strong that she overlooked the information in the text and consistently insisted that *she* was a *he*.

Research shows that increasing students' prior knowledge of a topic improves their reading (Paris, Wasik, & Turner, 1991). Many techniques help students to build and use background knowledge:

◆ Help students build background before they read; gently correct misperceptions.
◆ If you are teaching in a resource setting, discuss the background knowledge students need to comprehend their regular classroom material.
◆ Encourage students to modify their own ideas when the text presents new information.

Comprehension Requires Higher-Level Thinking

Higher-level thinking processes are important to story comprehension. Good readers combine their own background information with the information in the text to draw inferences. As they read, they make predictions, which are confirmed or disproved later in the text (Allbritton, 2004). Unfortunately, students with reading problems are often literal readers who do not connect and reason from text in a logical manner. Teachers can foster higher-level comprehension in several ways:

1. Ask students inferential and prediction questions and limit the number of factual questions asked. When teachers simply ask more inference questions, students improve in their abilities to draw inferences (Sundbye, 1987; Wixson, 1983; Hansen, 1981).
2. Model higher-level thinking skills for students. Low-achieving readers need to see the thought processes underlying skilled comprehension.

Comprehending Narrative Materials

Narrative text is one popular and common form of writing. In narratives, stories are told and plots unfold. Narratives have characters and a plot with a sequence of events. Although most stories are fiction (e.g., *Charlotte's Web* by White, the Harry Potter books by Rowling, *The Cat in the Hat* by Dr. Seuss, *The Three Little Pigs*) some chronicle real-life events (*My Side of the Mountain*, by George). Narrative materials inspire personal responses and are organized in certain ways.

Narratives Inspire Imaginative Personal Responses

Narratives are written to inspire personal responses (Pearson & Fielding, 1991). Through stories, children and adults leave the limits of their everyday lives and "travel" to a boarding school for wizards with Harry Potter (Rowling) or to rural

Wisconsin in the 1800s in *Little House on the Prairie* (Wilder). In this way, children learn to represent people, objects, and events in their imagination (Graesser, Golding, & Long, 1991). Thus, cognitive growth is fostered by an enjoyable experience.

Good readers become involved in the narratives they read. They put themselves in the character's place and ask themselves, "What would I do if I were in this situation?" Students who identify with a character comprehend better and read more (Thomson, 1987; Golden & Guthrie, 1986).

Sadly, some struggling readers have limited experience using their own imaginations and lack these responses to narratives. One group of low-achieving third graders responded negatively to all types of fiction and anything that seemed unreal. Only after several months of reading and listening to fantasies in books, poems, and stories did they begin to feel comfortable.

To foster personal responses, students must share their reactions to reading. Adults often do this naturally. Typically, if you tell a friend that you saw a movie, the first question is "Did you like it?" Most children also have strong personal responses to stories, yet teachers rarely ask for their reactions (Gambrell, 1986). When you ask students for personal reactions, you honor their opinions, focus on enjoyment, and raise their self-esteem.

To focus on students' personal responses, ask students to rate their enjoyment of a story (e.g., I disliked it. It was OK. I liked it. I loved it.). Ask them if they have anything in common with the story characters or with the situations in a story. When students share responses, they come to realize that others may have differing opinions and experiences.

Narratives Have Story Organization

Narratives are written according to a specific form, called a *story grammar* and include different types, or *genres*, of literature.

Story Grammar.   A story grammar includes specific elements. If you recall a story you read recently, it had characters, a setting, events, and a conclusion. In addition, the characters probably had problems to solve. Students need to be able to:

- Identify important characters.
- Identify the setting: time and place.
- Recall the major events in proper sequence and separate important events from less-important ones.
- Identify the problem that the character(s) had to solve and explain how that problem was resolved.

Shanahan and Shanahan (1997) have shown that students who use story grammar and analyze the different perspectives of the characters improve their comprehension of the story. Readers must track the characters and events, remembering relevant information and ignoring irrelevant information, to read and comprehend narrative text (Gernsbacher, Robertson, Palladino, & Werner, 2004).

Narratives have themes or main points; many narratives, such as fables, have morals. Skilled readers not only understand the characters and events, they also grasp the overall meaning or theme of the story (Zhang & Hoosain, 2005). As most students mature, they grow in the ability to understand themes and morals. Struggling readers may have problems keeping track of the characters and events to construct a coherent understanding of the theme of the story. They may not be able to determine the relevance of information presented in the story.

Good readers implicitly identify story features and use them as a road map to guide their comprehension. In contrast, struggling readers are often unaware of story structure. Research shows that low-achieving students benefit from explicit instruction in story grammar (Goldman & Rakestraw, 2000).

Genres of Narrative Text. Different varieties of reading materials are called genres. Narrative genres include:

◆ Realistic fiction
◆ Fantasy, including books with talking animals, science fiction, and horror stories
◆ Fairy tales, folktales, and tall tales
◆ Fables
◆ Mysteries
◆ Humor, language play
◆ Historical fiction, set in a period in the past
◆ Plays
◆ Narrative poetry: poems that tell stories
◆ Real-life adventures
◆ Biographies and autobiographies

To become good readers, students need to gain experience reading many different genres.

Assessing Abilities with Narrative Text

This section provides guidelines for measuring general comprehension abilities. These guidelines are followed by techniques to help you judge students' comprehension of a specific story or book.

Measuring General Comprehension Ability

Many standardized tests of reading contain at least one subtest measuring comprehension. These tests include the *Woodcock Reading Mastery Tests–Revised*, the *WJIII Diagnostic Reading Battery*, the *Gates-MacGinitie Reading Test*, Fourth Edition, and the *Iowa Tests of Basic Skills*. In interpreting these subtests, be aware that a low score on a comprehension subtest does not always indicate a comprehension problem. First, a low score on a comprehension subtest may be due to problems with recognizing words in the passage. If the general test has a vocabulary subtest, you can compare that score with the student's comprehension score. You can also present the vocabulary test as a probe, reading the words and answer choices to the student. If the student scores high on the probed vocabulary test, his or her problems probably lie in the area of word recognition. If the student's score on the probed presentation of the vocabulary test are also low, then the problem probably lies in the area of comprehension.

Second, the actual tasks students are asked to do on comprehension subtests may not reflect what they do in classrooms. For example, in the *WJIII Reading Mastery Battery Comprehension Subtest*, students read a paragraph orally and fill in a missing word. In school, however, students must read long stories and answer questions after silent reading. Thus, to interpret test information correctly, look at the actual items on the test.

Certainly, comprehension should be included in a systematic assessment plan. Initial measures of comprehension usually occur within the context of a school-wide standardized achievement test. If a student's performance raises concerns, diagnostic tests may be administered to determine specific issues. If a student is diagnosed with reading problems or a learning disability, an instructional intervention plan is developed, and a systematic assessment plan should be part of the instructional plan. In some states, informal measures can be used to document student progress; in others, a brief form of a standardized test must be used.

Judging the Comprehension of Specific Materials

Can a student effectively comprehend a specific story? This section gives two strategies to determine how well a student has comprehended a story: retelling and questioning. It also describes how these strategies can be used to improve comprehension as well as assess it.

Retelling.   When students retell a story, the teacher gains insight into the text they have constructed in their minds. Retelling shows how a student has mentally organized a selection and what information the student considers important enough to remember. Thus, the teacher observes and analyzes comprehension in action.

To elicit a retelling, begin by informing the student that he or she will retell a story to you after it is read. Next, ask the student to read the story. When the student has finished, say, "Tell me about the story as if you were telling it to a person who had never read it." To avoid undue emphasis on details in a longer story, older students can be asked to summarize rather than to retell.

Do not interrupt as the story is told. When the student has finished, however, you may ask the student to tell more about certain things. This prompting is important for low-achieving readers, because they often know more about a story than they will tell in free recall (Bridge & Tierney, 1981).

Leslie and Caldwell (2001) and Caldwell and Leslie (2005) offer guidelines for evaluating the quality of a retelling. Generally, retellings should include:

◆ The presence of the major character(s)
◆ The defining characteristics of the characters (good, bad, curious)

◆ The problem presented by the story
◆ The solution to that problem (or the end)
◆ Events presented in sequential order
◆ The ability to include only those events important to the story and exclude unimportant events

Teachers should be aware of some indications that a retelling may be immature:

◆ Referring to all characters as "him," "her," or "they"
◆ Giving a detailed description only of the first page or story segment

When judging retellings, remember that a student's concept of story structure may not fully mature until the teen years. Thus, young students often produce unsophisticated retellings.

Evidence suggests that students who retell stories improve their comprehension (Koskinen, Gambrell, Kapinus, & Heathington, 1988; Morrow, Gambrell, Kapinus, Koskinen, Marshall, & Mitchell, 1986; Gambrell, Pfeiffer, & Wilson, 1985). When teachers give students feedback about their retellings, improvement in comprehension increases, especially for young students.

Questioning. Although questioning is perhaps the most common way to assess comprehension, it does have several drawbacks. First, it does not demand an active response from children. Questions enable teachers to determine whether the student knows what adults consider important to the story. They do not provide information about whether students were able to construct the main events in their own minds. Second, formulating good questions is difficult. Third, all questions are not similar (Ciardiello, 1998). A question can be literal or inferential, and each kind can represent various levels of difficulty. For example, answering a literal question may involve a short answer found in one section of the text, or it may involve stringing together several elements spread throughout the text. Teachers need to be aware of the variation in the difficulty level of questions, particularly those provided in teacher manuals. If you are going to ask questions, remember the following guidelines:

◆ Don't have students spend too much time. Students should not spend more time answering questions than they spent reading a selection. When using questions from a teacher's manual, feel free to eliminate some.
◆ Do not provide answers to questions as you ask other questions.
◆ Try to avoid yes-no questions or either-or questions. Students have a 50 percent chance of a right answer just by guessing.
◆ Focus on some questions that require long answers. Encourage students to explain the reasons for their answers.
◆ Focus on asking higher-level questions, such as those calling for inferences and predictions.
◆ When one student gives an incorrect answer to a question, work with that student to correct that answer rather than redirecting the question to another student (Crawford, 1989).

◆ To increase comprehension, students can be encouraged to formulate their own questions (Caldwell & Leslie, 2005; Van Der Broek & Kremer, 2000).
◆ Teach students to look back in the text to find answers.

A Strategic Approach to Teaching Reading Comprehension

Good comprehension is an important reading skill. Students need to learn strategic approaches to reading to develop this skill. Teachers can support students in learning effective strategies to improve comprehension. Shanahan (2005) suggests that the reciprocal teaching strategy developed by Palinscar and Brown (1984) is actually an instructional approach to teaching comprised of multiple strategies. The premise of reciprocal teaching is that teachers should gradually release the responsibility for learning to their students.

The reciprocal teaching approach includes:

1. Summarize
2. Question
3. Clarify
4. Predict

The cycle begins with predicting content based on the title and pictures. Students read a segment of text, then summarize the text in one sentence. Next students ask a question about the segment of text. We usually tell our students to ask a question they think we would ask about the whole section if we were constructing a question for a test. Next, students clarify any concepts or words that presented problems. Finally, they predict what will happen next. In implementing the reciprocal teaching strategy, as developed by Brown and Palinscar, teachers divide text into one- to two-paragraph segments. This breaks the chore of comprehension into a manageable task for struggling readers.

Shanahan (2005) identifies the components of this mega-strategy as individual strategies integrated into a highly effective approach for teaching. Teachers model each component and explain its purpose. Students have multiple opportunities to practice these components as teachers guide them to gradually assume responsibility for each component. Reciprocal teaching has a strong research base that has shown dramatic increases in students' comprehension of text. One word of caution: Some teachers have relinquished responsibility too soon; students' comprehension of text tends to increase quickly. However, this does not mean they have learned the components of the strategy well enough to implement them independently.

Reciprocal teaching begins with teachers modeling the strategy and explaining its components. Then students are given opportunities to "take turns" being the teacher for each component of the strategy as the teacher monitors their progress. Gradually, students assume all of the roles and become self-sufficient in implementing the strategy.

Strategies for Improving Comprehension before Reading

The remainder of this chapter focuses on strategies to develop comprehension in narrative text. These strategies are divided according to whether they are used before, during, or after reading.

This section describes strategies to use before students read. In a classic study, Durkin (1978–1979) found that the first part of a reading lesson is the most crucial and yet the most neglected. This section describes three specific activities: building background knowledge, prediction, and reading a selection to students before they read it for themselves.

Building Background Knowledge

Because background knowledge greatly influences comprehension, it is essential to build knowledge of specific concepts in a story before students read it. How can you do this?

Before students read, teachers can provide factual information about key concepts they will meet in a story (Richek & Glick, 1991). Often, teachers can simply read informational material to students. Factual books, such as *The Kids' Question and Answer Book* (edited by Owl Magazine), *Mammoth Book of Trivia* (Meyers), and a children's encyclopedia are good sources for these read-aloud selections. When you read factual material to low-achieving students, you remind them of what they know about a topic and supply them with new facts. You also increase vocabulary because factual articles mention new vocabulary words that children will meet later in the story they read. Finally, you model the process of summoning up background information before reading.

In one example, before children read a story about a heroic horse, a third-grade teacher read aloud a children's encyclopedia article on horses. The article contained unfamiliar facts, and it used words, such as mare and foal, that the children later found in their story.

Objects and displays can also help children absorb background knowledge. In preparation for reading a folk tale about Russia, teachers of at-risk fourth graders brought in Russian nesting dolls, ruble currency, postcards, and books written in Russian.

Students can be actively involved in building their own background knowledge. Rather than simply supplying information, begin your lesson by asking them what they know about a subject or topic. Before low-achieving third graders read a story about two child detectives, they listed all of the different detectives they knew about. This activity dramatically increased their involvement in the story.

Students can also respond actively to information that the teacher presents. For example, to prepare first graders to read a story about a "sleep out," the teacher read A New True Book: *Sleeping and Dreaming* (Milios) to them (Richek & Glick, 1991). Then the students dictated their favorite facts as the teacher listed them on the board:

You grow when you sleep.

Your eyelids flutter when you sleep.

When you sleep, you dream.

Making Predictions about Text

Predicting what a story will be about before reading it gives students an active orientation toward learning and encourages them to use background knowledge. Struggling readers often don't predict what stories will be about (Beers, 2003). Teachers can help students predict by using specific strategies that support predicting.

Predicting.   To help students predict, write the title of a book or selection on the board and ask students what they think it will be about or what kind of story it will be. "The Skates of Uncle Richard" will probably involve sports. "How the Duck Learned to Talk to the Pig" probably involves some fantasy.

Students can also predict what a story is about from a list of important story words. For example, after you list the words *witch*, *invisible*, and *wand*, students might hypothesize that the story is about magic.

You can also read a story in segments, stopping and asking students to predict what will happen next. As you read the subsequent material, allow students to revise or confirm their predictions.

We must offer one word of caution regarding prediction. Often students misinterpret the purpose of predicting and look on it as they do teacher questions. They want to provide the right answer. They do not understand that all readers make predictions as they read, and they do not comprehend the fun of being surprised when the story turns out quite differently from what they predicted. Sometimes, when teachers ask students to predict, some students peek ahead in the text to find out what really happened, thus allowing them to make the "right" prediction. Teachers modeling the excitement of predicting and the fun of being surprised is therefore extremely important.

Semantic Impressions.   This predictive strategy (McGinley & Denner, 1987) enables students to create their own story by using words that they will later meet in a published story. By writing or dictating their own story, they are actively employing story grammar, using specific vocabulary, and drawing on their own background knowledge. Students may write individual stories, or a class can write a group story. In some classes, students have become so fond of their stories that they have bound them into class books. The teacher should use the following procedure presented in Figure 11.1 when using the semantic impressions strategy. Two excellent books to use with this strategy are *The Paper Bag Princess* (Munsch) and, for young children, *Harriet and the Roller Coaster* (Carlson). Strategy Snapshot 11.1 shows how semantic impressions was used with *The Paper Bag Princess*.

The semantic impressions strategy has been shown to improve comprehension across a wide variety of grade levels and is particularly effective with low-achieving readers (Pearson & Fielding, 1991; McGinley & Denner, 1987). This valuable

FIGURE 11.1   Semantic Impress... Strategy

1. Before students read a story, ... important words fr...m ...t on the board. The words should be written in the ord... ...ey appear in the story.
2. Have students use the word... ...he order they appear on the board to compose their own story. Words can be re... You may have the students dictate their story or they can write their own.
3. After the students have wr... their story, have them read the published version, and then compare the two ver... Often, intermediate and middle-level students like to write about which story t... fer.

method, which can be u... ...ith any story or book, encourages students to think like authors and fosters com... ...on, a higher-level skill.

Predicted or Prol... Passages.   Predicted or probable passages is a strategy that combines eler... ...of semantic impressions and story structure. In predicted passages, the teach... ...s students a list of words from the text to be read, and the students categori... words as they might be used in the story. Figure 11.2 presents a predicted p... amework completed by a group of seventh-grade students preparing to re... ...ks by Fleischman. A reproducible copy of the predicted passage

Strategy Snapshot 11.1

Semantic Impressions

The Paper Bag Princess (by Munsch) is an excellent story to use with the semantic impressions strategy. In this "twisted" fairy tale, a princess refuses to marry a less-than-gallant prince. Begin by putting the following words from the book on the board:

princess
prince
dragon
carried off
chase
bag
forests
fiery breath
meatball
sleep
mess
bum
marry

Continued

Strategy Snapshot 11.1 *(Continued)*

Ms. Walega's second-grade class, which included several struggling readers children, dictated this story:

There once was a princess and a prince. The prince went to fight the dragon. The dragon got past the prince and carried off the princess to his cave. The prince chased the dragon. The dragon caught the prince in a bag. The dragon went into the forest with the prince in a bag. The dragon his fiery breath and made a fire. He ate a magic meatball. Then the dragon fell asleep. The dragon made a mess of his cave because he was real mad. The prince called the dragon a bum! The prince married the princess and then he killed the dragon.

After they finished, each struggling reader the class was paired with an on-level student and assigned one sentence to illustrate jointly. The resulting book, entitled "The Horrible Dragon," became part of the classroom library.

Ms. Smith's low-level fourth-grade class (Room 204) produced a somewhat more sophisticated story, which they entitled "The Fire-Breathing Dragon." After reading the published story, students wrote comparisons:

KEVIN: I like 204's story better because it had a happy ending.
CRYSTAL: I like *The Paper Bag Princess* because I hate the prince and the book has a real author.
MICHEL: I like "Fire Breathing Dragon" because it is longer, and we made it.
KATRINA: I like "Fire Breathing Dragon" because it had a lot of activities, and a dragon can't fly, and the prince saved the princess. And boys are supposed to save girls.

framework is available on the website for this text. When one teacher started using the predicted passage strategy, she used a photocopied paper and students wrote the words into the boxes for the categories. Then, as they read, if they changed their minds about where words belonged, they erased those words and rewrote them into new cells. This erasing or scratching out proved to be frustrating and messy. Now the teacher laminates a small poster or large cardstock and either gives the students words on removable labels or has them write the words on small Post-It–style notes so that they can move the words to their appropriate cells as they read. Students enjoy the strategy much more this way.

Reading a Story to Students

When a story is long or difficult, teachers can read it to students before the students read it for themselves. This strategy enables them to learn the story format, sequence of events, and many words in the story before they attempt to read it independently. Prereading stories to students is particularly effective if they are asked to predict what will happen next as they listen. However, prereading should be followed by opportunities for students to read the stories on their own.

FIGURE 11.2   Predicted Passage Framework for *Seedfolks* Completed with a Group of Seventh-Grade Students

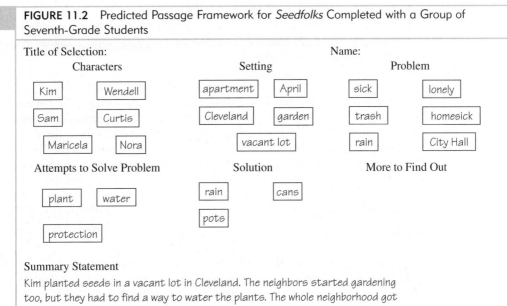

Title of Selection: Name:

Characters	Setting	Problem
Kim Wendell	apartment April	sick lonely
Sam Curtis	Cleveland garden	trash homesick
Maricela Nora	vacant lot	rain City Hall

Attempts to Solve Problem	Solution	More to Find Out
plant water	rain cans	
protection	pots	

Summary Statement

Kim planted seeds in a vacant lot in Cleveland. The neighbors started gardening too, but they had to find a way to water the plants. The whole neighborhood got to know each other better because of the garden.

Sometimes, simply reading part of a story to students is useful. One middle-school teacher reads the first couple of paragraphs of exciting short stories to her students. After their interest has been sparked, students continue to read these stories independently for homework.

Strategies for Improving Comprehension during Reading

Many strategies encourage understanding and enjoyment while students read. This section discusses the Directed Reading-Thinking Activity (DR-TA), using imagery, Post-it–style note reactions, constructing content-free questions, and using discussion cards.

The Directed Reading-Thinking Activity

A basic predictive comprehension strategy is the DR-TA. This strategy, developed by Stauffer (1975, 1980), models the processes good readers use to comprehend text. DR-TA has provided a strong foundation for other predictive comprehension strategies to build on.

- ◆ Using the title and pictures to predict what the story will be about
- ◆ Reading a section and stopping to confirm initial predictions or revise them to suit the content

◆ Predicting what the next section will be about
◆ Reading to a crucial point and revising or confirming previous predictions
◆ Following a cyclical pattern of predicting/reading/confirming or revising predictions to the end of the story
◆ Reflecting about the entire story after reading

For maximum benefit, DR-TA should be used on a long-term basis so that students' reading processes can mature and they can internalize the components of a good comprehension strategy so that they can apply it independently.

The DR-TA should be used with stories that students have not yet read. To implement the DR-TA, teachers should follow the procedures presented in Figure 11.3.

While working with a group of fourth-grade students in a resource room, the reading specialist used the DR-TA to guide the reading of "Nate the Great and the Sticky Case" (Sharmat). The students predicted "Something will be stolen," "It's about glue," and "Nate will be stuck somewhere."

The teacher wrote the individual students' predictions on the board. As each prediction was stated, he asked the student his or her reason for making that prediction. The student who predicted that "Something will be stolen" gave as his reason that "the title says 'case' and that means a crime, and that's stealing."

After several predictions were written and explained, the teacher read the first two paragraphs to the students and asked them to review their earlier predictions. He

---

FIGURE 11.3   The Directed Reading-Thinking Activity

Before introducing the story to students, read the story and decide on the theme. Then divide the story into four to five segments that help guide the student to the theme. Construct questions that help students predict content, then reflect on their predictions as they relate to the actual events in the story. Finally, construct a summative question that will tie the segments of the story together.

1. Introduce the story to students. Write the title on the board and ask students what they think the story will be about based on the title and any pictures.
2. Write students' predictions on the board. Ask them why they made that prediction. Develop the habit of substantiating predictions.
3. Ask students to read the first segment. When they have finished, ask them if what they predicted actually happened. Give them opportunities to confirm or revise their predictions by referring to the text. For example, ask, "What in the story made you change your mind?" or "What in the story shows that your prediction is what happened?" Then ask them what they think will happen next and why.
4. Continue in the predict-read-revise/confirm-predict-read cycle to the end of the story.
5. Ask students a summative question at the end of the story so that they can tie all the segments together.

asked which ones had actually happened in the story. He put a check by each prediction that had happened, then asked which might still happen. He left those predictions on the board. The group then decided which predictions should be revised or completely erased. Finally the teacher asked if they would like to add any new predictions.

Students read the next section of the story silently, and after reading, they again revised their hypotheses. This sequence continued until they had completed the story. The teacher asked how the case was finally solved, and if that is how they would have solved the case. Some students liked Sharmat's ending of the story; others preferred their own endings.

The DR-TA and other predictive strategies are extremely motivating. Asking students to make predictions, especially if they write those predictions, draws them into the story. They become actively engaged and participate in the events of the story as they unfold. Predictive strategies often stimulate students to read longer selections and to read silently. In their predictions, students naturally combine background information with the clues in the story to anticipate the ending before they actually read it. Readers also begin to use story structure to form predictions. After much practice, students can implement the strategy independently as they read longer selections, making predictions at the beginning of each chapter and confirming/revising those predictions at the end of each chapter.

Using DR-TA is no more time consuming than reading stories in a traditional manner. Almost any narrative story can be used with this strategy. However, students with reading problems do not always participate freely in a DR-TA. Some read so passively that they have trouble making predictions. In a group situation, shy students can be encouraged to participate by voting "yes" or "no" on some hypotheses. Allowing "abstentions" ensures that even the most passive students will take part. When using DR-TA in an individual situation, a teacher can model involvement by making hypotheses along with the student.

When using DR-TA, students should be told to not look ahead into a following section in the story. The occasional student who looks ahead should be pulled from a group DR-TA and asked to sit on the side without making comments. Of course, such students are unconsciously demonstrating that they see reading as "showing off" the right answer rather than thinking about the material. After using DR-TA several times, even these students will come to value the role of their own thinking in reading stories.

When low-achieving readers do their first DR-TA, their predictions are often highly implausible. Strategy Snapshot 11.2 presents a description of a teacher using DR-TA with low-achieving students. As they continue using the process, predictions will improve. In addition, as a group of students approaches the end of a story, individuals will start to agree on plausible endings. These reactions are important signs of progress in reading narrative text.

The DR-TA is a versatile strategy that can be done in many different ways. At times, you may want to write predictions on the board, and at other times, you may want students simply to give them verbally. Sometimes students who disagree with the author's ending for a story enjoy writing and illustrating their own endings.

Strategy Snapshot 11.2

DR-TA in a Low-Achieving Fifth-Grade Class

The 31 students in this room used the DR-TA process with the stories in their fourth-grade reading series. The first story described the adventures of a misbehaving boy who interfered with a class experiment on feeding rats.

We first put the title on the board and asked for hypotheses about the story. The four hypotheses focused on a laboratory with a scientist. We then passed out the story and asked children to read the first page silently and reformulate their hypotheses. After reading page one, students correctly refocused their predictions on the boy, Otis, and a classroom. However, the students identified the animal as a mouse rather than a rat, so they were asked to go back and reread. We finished two more sets of predictions on the first day, for pages 2–3 and 4–5 of the story.

As we proceeded, student excitement mounted. More students made predictions, and the predictions became more plausible. We ended the day by taking a vote on the weights of the rats in the story. At the conclusion of the lesson, one student, Perry, copied the predictions from the board for use the next day. In fact, three other students also copied them, just to ensure accuracy.

On the second day, Perry recopied the predictions onto the board, and the class did two more prediction segments. Students continued to increase their hypotheses, until we had so many that we were unable to call on all students who wanted to contribute. As the story progressed, students began to agree on their hypothesis for the ending. Thomas, who had been making the others wait because of his slow silent reading, started to speed up his reading rate.

On the third day, the children realized that the story would end. Keana and Ryan met us in the hall before school and asked us whether we could reveal the ending if they wouldn't tell the others. We declined to do this. In class, the ending was finally revealed, to the delight of the children. After the reading was completed, the class had an in-depth discussion of the clues the author gave about the conclusion and of other stories that had similar plots.

DR-TA without Justification. In this activity (Richek, 1987), readers give predictions but are not asked to supply reasons for them. We began to use DR-TA without justification when we found that many of our students were able to predict but could not give reasons for their predictions. In fact, when asked for justification, some became quite uncomfortable. Some low-achieving students may need to use the DR-TA without justification for a brief time before moving on to the more challenging step of supplying reasons. However, you want students to substantiate their answers early in the process.

Silent DR-TA. In this strategy, students are each given a story with prearranged, written stopping points. Each student reads the selection individually and silently until he or she comes to the first stopping point. Students then write their predictions at their desks without discussing them. They then read until they come to another stopping point and write that prediction. In the last part of the story, the ending is, of course, revealed, and each student can see how close he or she has come to predicting the author's ending.

Silent DR-TA helps older students take responsibility for their own reading and avoids the embarrassment of public discussions (Richek, 1987; Josel, 1986). In addition, making written records of their predictions helps students to monitor their own comprehension. Silent DR-TA motivates students to read silently and respond in writing. After they have completed the story, students look back at their predictions to see how well they caught the clues given in the story.

Monitoring Responses to Reading

The Post-it note strategy (Caldwell, 1993) gives students the opportunity to "talk back" to authors as they are reading silently. The Post-it notes, pieces of paper with one sticky edge, can be easily placed on text, removed, and reused. Using small notes helps students to pinpoint the precise part of the reading to which they are reacting.

The Post-it notes contain three graphic messages: Each reader is given three of each type of note per story or chapter. They can have more if needed.

!   indicates that a reader has been surprised by something.

☺   shows that the reader likes something that happened in the story.

?   notes that the reader has a question about something in the story.

As students read silently, they place a Post-it note wherever they meet something in the story that surprises, delights, or baffles them. In this way, they are recording their own reactions to the text. After they read, the Post-it notes make an excellent starting point for discussing a story. For low-achieving students, start by discussing the question-mark Post-it notes and then moving to surprising and well-liked parts. Students enjoy seeing that others have the same questions and appreciate the same parts as they do. Sharing responses to reading helps students build confidence, self-esteem, and a sense of participation. Alvermann (2000) has found that middle-school students have particularly positive views toward such participation.

Making Mental Images

Developing mental imagery in response to reading is an effective way to improve comprehension and interest for students with reading problems (Gernsbacher, et al., 2004; Pressley, 2000; Gambrell & Bales, 1986). When students form mental images as they read, they combine their background information with the text. Reading becomes more personal and relevant as students construct their unique images. In focusing on their own internal responses to text, students become more willing to read silently. Finally, mental imagery helps students to become comfortable reading text without pictures because they create pictures in their own minds.

Comparing their mental images is both enjoyable and instructive for students. When students realize that no two people see precisely the same thing, they learn to value personal response in reading (Sadowski, 1985).

Laying the Foundation for Mental Imagery.   To prepare students for reading activities, first develop the students' abilities to form images while listening by doing one of the following activities:

◆ Ask students to close their eyes and imagine that they are seeing their mother, father, or other adult. Each student, in turn, describes what he or she sees.
◆ Instruct students to imagine a hot-fudge sundae as you, verbally, build it, giving such clues as "I put in two scoops of vanilla ice cream, I slowly pour hot fudge over the top. . . ." Ask students to describe the colors they see. Then, without describing the container, ask students the types of containers they imagine. By imagining something that is not directly described, students develop the ability to build a complete mental picture from partial clues, precisely what readers do when they make mental images during reading.
◆ Read short stories to students and ask them to describe their mental images of the characters.
◆ The book *Hurricane* (Weisner) is excellent for developing imagery. In this book, a hurricane knocks over a tree. Two brothers use their imagination to incorporate this tree into imaginary scenes, such as a safari and a space ship. After reading it, ask students to individually tell you what else they could imagine the tree to be. Responses have included a submarine, gym, airplane, raft, tank, and limousine. One fifth grader saw the tree as a castle and reported seeing dragons, a princess, and birds (because she was up high).

Mental Imagery in Reading.   After forming mental images while listening, students are ready to apply imagery to reading. Ask students to read something silently and then focus on their own mental images.

Imagery can be used at several points in a story. Asking for a mental image after the students have read the first few paragraphs of a story helps them to make the rest of the story more vivid. Teachers may also ask for images at places in the story where students would normally be stopped for questions. You can ask students to stop at crucial points in the story and ask them to draw what they see or write a brief description of what they see. Finally, if students have read a story independently, imagery can be used as a follow-up strategy.

When working with imagery, ask students to focus on the most important or exciting part of a story and describe it. Focusing on only one image helps students to organize their thoughts and avoids confusing or conflicting responses. You might have students close their eyes immediately after reading to hold their images in their minds. Despite the value of imagery, some students with reading problems find the strategy difficult to use at first. Teachers need to be patient with a student who reports seeing "nothing" on the first day of instruction. Within a week, such readers will often start to construct images. If students simply list a sequence of events in the story, special attempts should be made to focus on exciting story parts so that they will become personally involved enough to form an image. You can also focus students on imagining what a character looks like.

If students report seeing images that do not match the text, they have probably misread something. Encourage them to reread the material silently and see if their images change. If students consistently misread, break up stories into shorter segments and follow silent reading with oral reading. This strategy focuses the students' attention on the need to read more carefully.

Mental imagery was used to help Bobby, a fourth grader who had poor comprehension and found silent reading difficult. Bobby silently read the first two paragraphs in a story about a snowstorm. When he was finished, he was asked to describe his image. At first, Bobby could not report anything, but after rereading the paragraphs, Bobby said he saw snow on the lawn, children building a snowman outside, and a car up the street. This imagery activity made him interact with the text, and his comprehension of the story improved dramatically.

Constructing Content-Free Questions

Teaching students content-free questions can show them how to approach reading strategically and foster independence. What are content-free questions? Consider the following two questions: "At the beginning of the story, what was Simon's problem?" and "What was the problem of the main character?" Text content or the character's name is embedded in one question but absent in the other. Caldwell and Leslie (2005) describe content-free questions as general questions that students can ask about any narrative selection. They are questions that are based on the elements of story structure previously discussed. They are questions that a reader can ask about any narrative, and they help to set expectations for reading.

Students tend to regard questions as content-specific; that is, questions about one story are different from those about another story. In reality, questions about narrative selections may be very similar in their focus on characters, settings, problems, and solutions. However, because they contain text-specific names such as Simon, students do not see their similarity. Students need to be taught the value of general questions that can be asked of any narrative selection and to model how such questions help them to comprehend.

Caldwell and Leslie (2005) list possible content-free questions for narratives based on narrative structure and the typical reactions of readers to any narrative text:

- ◆ Who is the main character? Why do I think so?
- ◆ Who are other important characters? Why are they important?
- ◆ What is the character's problem?
- ◆ How is the character trying to solve his or her problem?
- ◆ How is the setting important to the story?
- ◆ What do I predict will happen next? Why do I think so?
- ◆ Do I agree or disagree with what the character did? Why?

◆ Do I like or dislike this part of the story? Why?
◆ Is this story true to life? Why or why not?
◆ How did the story end?
◆ Is there anything I don't understand?
◆ What surprised me about this story?
◆ If I were going to write to the author, what would I say?

You want students to read with questions in mind. Questions build expectations in the mind of the reader, and these expectations, in turn, improve comprehension (Geiger & Millis, 2004). After all, if you know what you are looking for, you have a better chance of finding it. Use content-free questions to set up expectations prior to and during reading. Place the questions in a prominent place so that students can refer to them during reading. Model the process of asking content-free questions and finding answers to them. Occasionally stop during reading and discuss if the questions were answered and what new ones might be generated. However, learning to read with content-free questions in mind is not a quick fix. It takes a long time and a lot of practice, but it can be a very motivating experience. Struggling readers often find answering questions an intimidating process, and they enjoy the experience of forming their own questions and reading to find the answers.

Using Discussion Cards

Discussing a story is a common activity in literacy classrooms, but it is very often an ineffective and poorly handled procedure. The teacher asks questions, and the students answer them—or at least some students do. Often the same students participate each day, while others slide down in their seats and try to make themselves as unobtrusive as possible. Discussion questions are often relatively low level and focus on identification of literal elements in the text as opposed to higher-level thinking. All readers must learn to generate specific and thoughtful reactions to what they read or practice thoughtful literacy (Allington, 2001, 2006). Discussion cards can help students engage with what they are reading (Caldwell & Leslie, 2005).

Discussion cards provide suggestions as to possible comments that a reader might make. This activity can be an effective lesson on how readers should react during reading. Each student should have a set of cards labeled with possible topics, such as character, setting, or problem. You can make them or have the students construct their own pack. Always have additional sets available because card packets can easily become lost or misplaced.

The student chooses a card to indicate what he or she wishes to talk about and holds it up. If the student holds up the character card, he or she must talk about the character. If he or she holds up the problem card, then he or she must comment about a character's problem. The students can make any comment as long as it is tied to the card they hold up. During discussion, students sometimes make observations that are unrelated to the text. Having students select a specific discussion card and limiting responses to the topic on the card tends to prevent students from digressing. The cards actually play two roles: They suggest topics for comments, and they focus the discussion on the text as opposed to unrelated items.

Caldwell and Leslie (2005) suggest the following topics for narrative discussion cards:

- ◆ Character: The student may identify a main character or another important character, comment on a character's actions, suggest a motivation for a character's actions, predict what might happen to the character, or note a similarity between a character and a character in another selection.
- ◆ Setting: The student may indicate where and when the action occurs and comment on the importance of the setting.
- ◆ Problem: The student may identify a problem of the main character or other characters, predict a problem that might occur later, relate the problem to his or her own life or to another selection, or offer suggestions for solving the problem.
- ◆ Solution: The student may identify or predict the solution, question the solution in some way, indicate another solution, or comment on the steps that led to the solution.
- ◆ Question: The student may ask a question about something that was not understood, ask a question about a character's actions, or ask why an author wrote what he or she did.
- ◆ My Idea: The student may relate the text to his or her life, make a judgment about a character's actions, indicate like or dislike for the entire selection or for specific parts, or indicate how he or she might write it differently.

In addition to these basic topics, teachers may want to add others, such as *Prediction* and *Vocabulary*. If a student wishes to make a prediction or comment on a previous one, he or she holds up the *Prediction* card. If the student wants to comment on a new word or a new meaning for a familiar word, he or she holds up the *Vocabulary* card. Another possible card is *Author's Purpose* where the students comment on why the author wrote what he or she did. Choose four of five cards to use in each discussion so that you don't overwhelm students with too many choices. Select the cards that match your goals for the discussion.

Some card topics overlap. A student could hold up a *Character* card to offer an opinion about a character's actions. The *My Idea* card could signal the same intention. The key issue is that the student can justify his or her choice of card if questioned. Pictures or icons on the cards can be very appealing especially for younger readers. Caldwell and Leslie (2005) suggest the following: a simple stick figure for the *Character* card, a picture of a house and tree for *Setting*, a frown face for *Problem*, and a lightbulb for *Solution*. One clever teacher pasted pictures of her students on their *My Idea* card. What happens if a student holds up the same card time after time? This student was probably successful with one topic and is not willing to risk possible failure with a different card. Gently nudge him or her to other cards. Have the students spread out their cards face up. When they have held up a specific card and offered an appropriate comment, they must place that card face down. They cannot select it again until all cards have been used.

How much text should you read before asking the students to hold up their cards? That will vary with the type of text and the age of the students. Discussion cards work well for an individual student, a small group, or an entire class. You can also pair students to decide on the card and the comment. One interesting benefit of discussion cards is forcing teachers to wait longer before calling on a student. Generally, teachers tend to not wait long enough for a response.

Strategies for Improving Comprehension after Reading

Comprehension strategies that can be used after reading include those that develop a sense of story grammar, encourage a personal response, and connect the literacy experience.

Comprehension Strategies that Develop an Understanding of Story Structure

Go to MyEducationLab and select the topic *Comprehension*. Then, go to the Activities and Applications section, watch the video entitled "Checking Comprehension," and respond to the accompanying questions. How are these teachers using story structure to support students' understanding of text?

As discussed earlier, narratives are usually written according to certain forms, called story grammars. Most narratives contain the elements of characters, setting (time and place), and plot. The plot is generally further broken into a problem that a character must solve and different events (or episodes) that take place in the story. The end of the story has a solution or resolution to the problem. When students recognize these common elements of narratives, they read with more understanding and are better able to make sense of a narrative.

You can begin with simple story structures for young children and increase the complexity as students mature.

Go to MyEducationLab and select the topic *Comprehension*. Then, go to the Activities and Applications section, watch the video entitled "Mapping," and respond to the accompanying questions.

Story Maps.   Story maps are visual diagrams that show students the elements that all stories contain. When students use these maps, they learn to identify the common elements of narrative text. Story maps are suitable for both shorter stories and novels. A common story frame map contains (1) characters, (2) setting, (3) problem, and (4) solution. Figure 11.4 presents a story map that has been filled out for the story "Catalog Cats" in the book *The Stories Julian Tells* (Cameron). In "Catalog Cats," Julian tells his brother, Huey, about special kinds of cats that work in the garden. More complex story maps suitable for older students contain episodes to link the problem and solution (or resolution) and goals for the characters.

Teachers can introduce story maps before students read and ask them to fill in the frame either during or after reading. They can also give the map to the students after a story has been read and ask them to identify story elements. Students with reading problems often enjoy working on maps in pairs.

FIGURE 11.4 Story Map "Catalog Cats" from *The Stories Julian Tells*

Title of Story:	Name:
Characters	**Setting**
Julian Huey Father	In Julian and Huey's house
Problem	**Solution**
Julian tricks Huey into believing that you can order cats from a catalog to do all the work in a garden.	Father tells Huey that catalog cats exist, but they are invisible and don't do all the work. Also, you have to request them, not order them.

Shanahan and Shanahan (1997) and Emery (1996) suggest using character perspective charts. Students make separate charts for the story elements as seen from the perspective of different important characters. For example, for the folk tale *The Three Little Pigs*, students make two charts: one for the three little pigs and one for the wolf. Each chart contains the setting, problem, goal, attempts to solve the problem, outcome, reaction, and theme from the point of view of the character it charts—in this case, the pigs or the wolf.

Struggling readers often need teacher modeling before they can successfully generalize the features of story grammar. Patient teacher demonstration followed by discussion will lead students to using story grammar independently. Remember that story structure is learned gradually and must be practiced consistently over an extended period of time.

At times, you will find that students focus on only one part of the story, usually the first part or the most exciting part. To help them refocus on the story as a whole, place a story grammar frame on the board or on an overhead projector and read a short story to them. As they listen to the story, students should try to fill in the story grammar frame. Then reread the story and have them confirm or revise their story grammars.

As students become more comfortable with story grammar, they will become independent of visual maps. At that point, simply use a story grammar framework to guide comprehension by asking such questions as "Who was the main character?" and "What was the central problem in the story?" Students might also enjoy asking one another these questions.

Somebody Wanted but So.   A related strategy that helps students focus on characters and their goals is the somebody-wanted-but-so (SWBS) strategy developed by MacOn, Beweel, and Vogt (1991). In this strategy, students focus on a character, that character's goal(s), what happened when that character tried to accomplish his or her goal, and the outcome. Figure 11.5 presents a framework for SWBS based on

FIGURE 11.5   Somebody-Wanted-but-So Strategy for *Breadwinner* Used with a Group of Sixth-Grade Students

Title of Story:

Somebody	Wanted	But	So
Parvana	to work to help her family	The Taliban forbade girls to go out in public	Parvana dressed like a boy and got a job
Mother	wants Parvana to go to Nooria's wedding	Parvana wants to wait for Father to get out of prison	Mrs. Weera stays in the apartment with Parvana

Breadwinner by Ellis. Identifying a specific character and following that character through the text helps students to make personal connections to the story and improves comprehension (Roser, Martinez, Fuhrken, & McDonald, 2007).

Problem-Solution Identification.   The identification of the problem and the solution to that problem in a story is a shortened form of story grammar that is useful for intermediate and secondary students. To encourage long-term learning, students can make charts showing the problem of the story in one column and the solution in another. Because the ability to identify the problem and solution is a sophisticated skill, it requires careful teacher guidance. At first, students may confuse the main problem of the story with the first event. When this situation occurs, teachers should carefully review story structure.

Story Pyramids.   Students often enjoy creating their own, personal "pyramids" of stories they have read. In pyramids, students are allowed only eight lines and may only use a certain number of words per line. Each line must describe something different. The form of a pyramid is:

- One word naming the main character
- Two words describing the main character (for students in grades three and above, encourage the use of adjectives)
- Three words describing the setting (time and place)
- Four words describing the problem (for students in primary grades who have difficulty with problem identification, ask them for four words describing the first thing that happened)
- Five words describing the next important event
- Six words describing another important event
- Seven words describing another important event
- Eight words describing the ending

If used in a group, the teacher should write the class pyramid on the board for all to see. If used individually, students often like to decorate and illustrate their personal constructions. Pyramids can be used by at-risk readers from kindergarten through high school.

Students with reading problems have made many creative constructions using the pyramid format. Of course, because a pyramid is a personal response, each pyramid will be a little different. Here are two pyramids from third-grade Title I classes in response to reading *Cinderella*:

Cinderella
cute   nice
palace   house   backyard
her mother was dead
stepmother made her sweep floor
She went to the palace ball.
She danced with the prince and ran.
They got married and lived happily ever after.

Cinderella
nice person
past   palace   house
had mean stepmother
had two mean stepsisters
She could not go to the ball.
prince found the glass slipper for Cinderella
After they got married they lived very happily.*

*Full sentences are given capital letters and periods.

In constructing these pyramids, the children chose the characters, descriptions, and events that were most important to them. However, because a set number of words was needed, they had to manipulate words and combine them creatively. At times, they had to leave out words. This format encourages creative responses; and in fact, a group of boys in one class insisted on writing an alternative version, using the prince as the major character.

Story pyramids develop many important skills. If students work in groups, they naturally tend to discuss the story, an activity that fosters active comprehension. Pyramids give students practice with the major elements of a story (characters, setting, events). Students learn to separate important events from unimportant ones. Students develop language by manipulating and elaborating words to fit into a specified format. Students review vocabulary and concepts mentioned in the story. Building a pyramid is fun. Youngsters look forward to building and displaying their creations.

In intermediate and upper grades, pyramids make excellent alternatives to traditional book reports. Used as a response to independent reading, the pyramid activity does not require much writing, but it enables students to respond actively to their reading. Furthermore, you will always be able to tell if students have read the book.

Comprehension Strategies that Nurture Personal Response

Readers experiencing difficulties often have problems reacting fully to reading. This section describes strategies that foster creativity, engagement, and enjoyment, so that low-achieving students can see that reading belongs to them.

Drama.   Acting out a story immediately involves readers. As they experience story events from the character's point of view, students with reading problems deepen and improve comprehension (Wolf, 1998; Sebesta, 1993). Drama encourages discussion of a story and fosters cooperation and other social skills in at-risk students.

The tableaux strategy is one way to dramatize a story (Purves, Rogers, & Soter, 1995). It has been used effectively at elementary- and secondary-grade levels. In tableaux, students form still lifes, or *tableaux*, to dramatize story events. To illustrate the scenes, they assume appropriate expressions and body postures. Figure 11.6 shows one scene from the play "The Little Pine Tree" (in *Carousels*, 1989) demonstrated by two second graders in front of appreciative classmates. If possible, capture the tableaux on film.

In tableaux, students put themselves physically into the story. They discuss events as they decide which scenes they will act out. Furthermore, because tableaux involve the students "freezing" the scene, events acquire a permanence that they do not

FIGURE 11.6   Tableau of "The Little Pine Tree"

always have in the ongoing action of the story. Because these still lifes are silent, at-risk children are able to focus on the story without the distraction of movement and noise.

Tableaux can be done in many formats. In a large class, students can be divided into several groups. After the class lists the important events, the teacher can assign one event to each group. If more students are in the group than there are story characters, some can play houses and trees. For young children, playing a noncharacter role helps establish the difference between characters and scenery. More advanced students often enjoy deciding secretly on the scene they will dramatize and asking classmates who watch the tableau to identify it. Secondary students, who are often reading longer material, should be encouraged to pick the most crucial and exciting events to dramatize.

Character Webs. In this activity, the name or picture of a story character is placed in the center of a page and surrounded by the traits of that character. Then, incidents from the story that illustrate each character trait are listed. A character web done by a third grader reading the story *Clifford, the Big Red Dog* (Bridwell) is presented in Figure 11.7.

Skinny Books. This strategy, which is most useful for primary children, combines the review of a story with a chance to create a personal version of it. To make a skinny book (Richek, 1999), the teacher needs to obtain two extra copies of the children's reading series. Illustrations are cut from a story that the children have just completed reading and pasted into a skinny book. (Two copies are needed because many illustrations are on the back sides of facing pages.) A front page should be left for a cover.

Now the students have an opportunity to become "authors" of the story they have just read by dictating their own text to match the story pictures. Generally, students take turns dictating pages. Individuals may want to sign each page that they have dictated. One group of Title I third graders made a skinny book of the book *Miss Nelson Is Missing* (Marshall). Authors Robert, Sherri, Travis, and Chris entitled their skinny book "Where Is Ms. Schultz?" Each student dictated a separate page as the teacher recorded their responses in magic marker. As they summarized the story, they changed it into their own words. These four students proudly carried their skinny book back to their regular class and read it to their peers.

Connecting the Literacy Experience

Students deepen their comprehension as they compare different texts and share their literacy experiences with one another. This section discusses two strategies that help students connect literacy experiences: conceptually connected instruction (themes) and genre studies.

Conceptually Connected Instruction Using Themes

Thematic instruction is really an approach to providing learning experiences rather than a specific strategy. However, concentrating on one interesting topic and focusing all literacy activities around it offers teachers an opportunity to use students' interests

FIGURE 11.7 Character Web of *Clifford, the Big Red Dog* by Norman Bridwell © 1985, published by Scholastic, Inc.

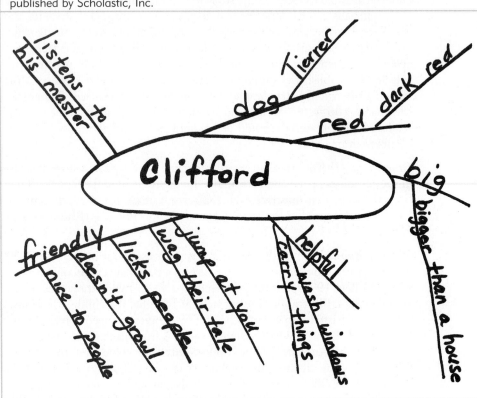

for instruction. It also helps students relate associations from known to unknown material. Thus, a student's interest in football may lead to understanding the business concept of negotiating contracts, bringing lawsuits, and judging profit margins.

A theme can also lead students to varied types of reading materials. Students may explore football through stories, newspaper activities, score sheets, encyclopedias, books, and manuals. They will be better able to grasp the structure of sophisticated types of text if they deal with familiar topics. The theme approach is particularly successful with students who are quite far behind in reading and need highly motivating instruction. Elizabeth, a 17-year-old reading on a fifth-grade level, decided to research successful women who had, in her words, "made it." Role models were chosen from entertainment, sports, and business. Elizabeth read books, collected newspaper articles, watched TV programs, and listened to audiotapes and compact discs. Her teacher brought in technical terms from the three fields. At the end of three months, Elizabeth had dramatically improved her reading skills.

Edmund, a fifth grader reading on a second-grade level, became interested in Hawaii and volcanoes and collected many vivid pictures. For homework, his reading teacher asked him to find all the ways pineapples were sold in the supermarket. His results became a written essay featuring 15 different types of pineapples. Edmund also read travel brochures, maps, and social studies textbooks. At the end of the semester, he gave his teacher a fresh pineapple as a gift.

Twelve-year-old Eugene, who was reading on a third-grade level, was intrigued by the escape artist Houdini. After starting with some easy books, he read through all the books in the school and local libraries. Before another hero replaced Houdini, Eugene had made several trips to the central New York City Public Library to read about him.

Sometimes teachers must suggest a topic for a passive student. In the case of Oneka, a 14-year-old student, her tutor chose food. She explored the history of popcorn, the taste of egg rolls, and how to eat gyros and incidentally gathered much information about the world.

The theme approach motivates low-achieving students to read a wide variety of reading materials. At the same time, teachers can focus on specific comprehension strategies.

Studying Different Genres

Studying a genre, such as mystery stories or fairy tales, allows disabled readers to connect and compare their readings. Students should read many examples of one genre and then compare their common features. For example, Marcus, a sixth grader who loved watching mysteries on TV, was motivated to read several with his tutor. Marcus made a chart listing how each story contained the crime, the detective, the clues to solve the mystery, and the solution.

Students with reading problems also love to explore fairy and folktales. Students can chart the features of magic, hero, villain, beginning words (such as "once upon a time"), and ending for each tale.

Students can also compare different versions of one tale. The Cinderella Story has been told in many versions. For instance, in *Prince Cinders* (by B. Cole), the lead is cast as a picked-on boy. The story of the three little pigs has been published as *The True Story of the Three Little Pigs* (by Szieska), a hilarious revisionist version told from the wolf's point of view, and *The Three Little Wolves and the Big Bad Pig* (by Trivizas), which reverses the usual roles. Hans Christian Andersen's tale "The Emperor's New Clothes" has been recast in a school as *The Principal's New Clothes* (by Calmenson).

Students can compare two versions of a tale using a Venn diagram, or two partially overlapping circles. The common portions contain the things that are alike about the two tales. The unique portions list things that appear in only a single tale. Figure 11.8 shows a Venn diagram that Sheila and her tutor constructed for two versions of Cinderella. In exploring and recording differences between these different versions, students gain flexibility in thinking.

Summary

The purpose of reading is comprehension. General features of effective comprehension include (1) realizing that you read to comprehend, (2) realizing that comprehension requires the reader to actively construct a text in his or her mind, a process that

FIGURE 11.3   Venn Diagram for Cinderella

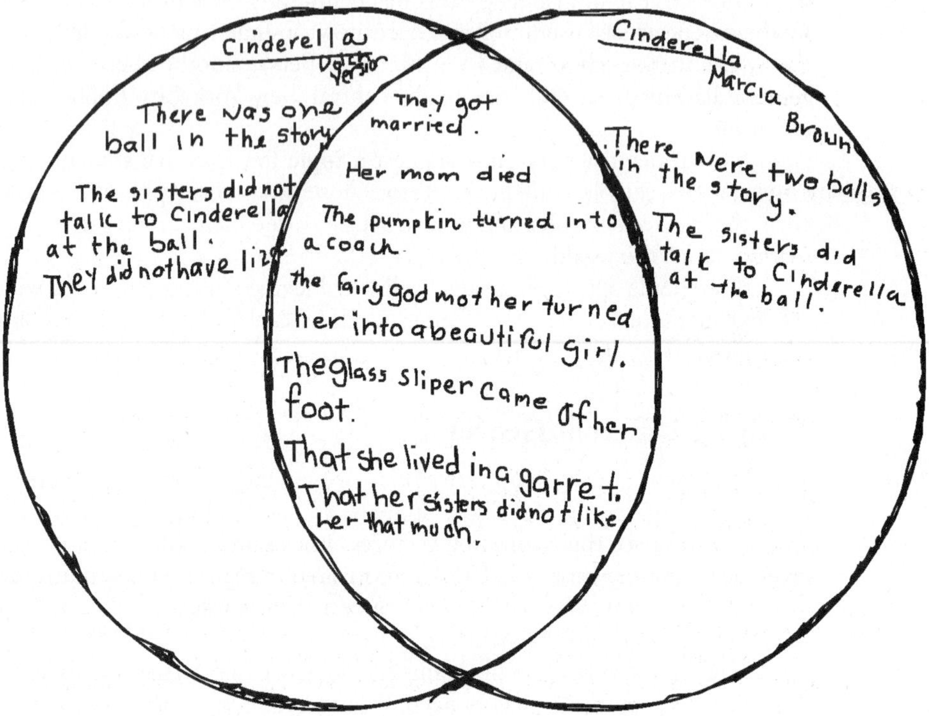

Cinderella Disney Version

There was one ball in the story.

The sisters did not talk to Cinderella at the ball. They did not have li...

They got married.

Her mom died

The pumpkin turned into a coach.

the fairy god mother turned her into a beautiful girl.

The glass sliper came of her foot.

That she lived in a garret. That her sisters did not like her that much.

Cinderella Marcia Brown

There were two balls in the story.

The sisters did talk to Cinderella at the ball.

accurately reflects the material that the author has written, (3) applying personal background knowledge appropriately to text, and (4) employing higher-level thinking to understand text. Too much teacher questioning discourages active responses to stories.

Narratives, or texts that tell stories, inspire imaginative personal responses. They also have certain organizational factors, including story grammars (characters, setting, plot). They include many different genres, such as adventure, fantasy, and science fiction. To assess abilities with narrative text, you can use the comprehension tests from general standardized tests. In addition, you can judge whether a student has comprehended a specific text well by using story retelling and questioning.

Reciprocal teaching is a highly effective way to teach comprehension strategies. Strategies for improving comprehension before reading include building background knowledge, predicting what will happen in a story, having students build a semantic impressions story from selected story words, and reading students the story to support comprehension.

Strategies for improving comprehension during reading include using the Directed Reading-Thinking Activity, a prediction strategy used while reading; using Post-it notes to mark pleasing, surprising, and puzzling parts of text; responding with mental images; constructing content-free questions; and using discussion cards.

Strategies for improving comprehension after reading can develop an understanding of story structure through story maps and identifying the problem and solution. Ways to nurture a personal response after reading include drama, art, character webs, and skinny books that rewrite stories in students' own words. Finally, the literacy experience may be connected through the study of one theme or doing genre studies.

References

Allbritton, D. (2004). Strategic production of predictive inferences during comprehension. *Discourse Processes, 38*, 309–322.

Allington, R. L. (2006). *What Really Matters for Struggling Readers: Designing Research-Based Programs* (2nd ed.). New York: Longman.

Allington, R. L. (2001). *What Really Matters for Struggling Readers: Designing Research-Based Programs.* New York: Longman.

Alvermann, E. (2000). Classroom talk about texts: Is it dear, cheap, or a bargain at any price? In B. M. Taylor, M. F. Graves, & P. Van Der Brock (Eds.), *Reading for Meaning*, pp. 136–151. Newark, DE: International Reading Association, and New York: Teachers College Press.

Beck, I. L., Omanson, R. C., & McKeown, M. G. (1982). An instructional redesign of reading lessons: Effects on comprehension. *Reading Research Quarterly, 17*, 462–481.

Beers, K. (2003). *When Kids Can't Read: What Teachers Can Do.* Portsmouth, NH: Heinemann.

Bridge, C. A., & Tierney, R. J. (1981). The inferential operations of children across text with narrative and expository tendencies. *Journal of Reading Behavior, 31*, 210–214.

Caldwell, J. (1993). *Developing a Metacognitive Strategy for Comprehension Monitoring for Narrative Text.* Milwaukee, WI: Cardinal Stritch College. Unpublished strategy.

Caldwell, J. S., & Leslie, L. (2005). *Intervention Strategies to Accompany Informal Reading Assessment: So What do I do Now?* Boston: Allyn and Bacon.

Ciardiello, A. V. (1998). Did you ask a good question today? Alternative cognitive and metacognitive strategies. *Journal of Adolescent and Adult Literacy, 42*, 210–219.

Crawford, J. (1989). Instructional activities related to achievement gains in Chapter I classes. In R. E. Slavin, N. L. Karweit, & N. A. Madden (Eds.), Effective Programs for Students at Risk, pp. 264–290. Boston: Allyn & Bacon/Simon and Schuster.

Cunningham, A. E., & Stanovich, K. E. (1993). Children's literacy environments and early recognition subskills. *Reading and Writing: An Interdisciplinary Journal, 5*, 193–204.

Cunningham, A., & Stanovich, K. (1998). What reading does for the mind. *American Educator, 22*, 8–17.

Durkin, D. (1978–1979). What classroom observations reveal about reading comprehension instruction. *Reading Research Quarterly, 14*, 481–533.

Emery, D. W. (1996). Helping readers comprehend stories from the characters' perspectives. *The Reading Teacher, 49*, 534–541.

Gambrell, L. B. (1986). *Functions of Children's Oral Language During Reading Instruction.* Paper presented at the 36th annual meeting of the National Reading Conference, Austin, TX.

Gambrell, L. B., & Bales, R. J. (1986). Mental imagery and the comprehension-monitoring performance of fourth- and fifth-grade poor readers. *Reading Research Quarterly, 21*, 454–464.

Gambrell, L. B., Pfeiffer, W., & Wilson, R. (1985). The effects of retelling upon reading comprehension and recall of text information. *Journal of Educational Research, 78*, 216–220.

Geiger, J. F., & Millis, K. K. (2004). Assessing the impact of reading goals and text structures on comprehension. *Reading Psychology, 25*, 93–110.

Gernsbacher, M. A., Robertson, R. R. W., Palladino, P., & Werner, N. K. (2004). Managing mental representations during narrative comprehension. *Discourse Processes, 37*, 145–164.

Golden, J., & Guthrie, J. (1986). Convergence and divergence in reader response to literature. *Reading Research Quarterly, 21*, 408–421.

Goldman, S. R., & Rakestraw, J. A., Jr. (2000). Structural aspects of constructing meaning from text. In R. Barr, M. L. Kamil, P. Mosenthal, & P. D. Pearson (Eds.), *Handbook of Reading Research* (Vol. III), pp. 311–335. Mahwah, NJ: Lawrence Erlbaum Associates.

Graesser, A., Golding, J. M., & Long, D. L. (1991). Narrative representation and comprehension. In R. Barr, M. L. Kamil, P. Mosenthal, & P. D. Pearson (Eds.), *Handbook of Reading Research* (Vol. II), pp. 171–205. White Plains, NY: Longman.

Hansen, J. (1981). The effects of inference training and practice on young children's reading comprehension. *Reading Research Quarterly, 16,* 391–417.

Josel, C. A. (1986). A silent DRTA for remedial eighth graders. *Journal of Reading, 29,* 434–439.

Koskinen, P. S., Gambrell, L. B., Kapinus, B. A., & Heathington, B. S. (1988). Retelling: A strategy for enhancing students' reading comprehension. *The Reading Teacher, 41,* 892–896.

Leslie, L., & Caldwell, J. (2001). *The Qualitative Reading Inventory III.* New York: Longman.

MacOn, J., Bewell, D., & Vogt, M. (1991). *Responses to Literature.* Newark, DE: International Reading Association.

McGinley, W. J., & Denner, P. R. (1987). Story impressions: A prereading/writing activity. *Journal of Reading,* 31, 248–253.

Morrow, L. M., Gambrell, L., Kapinus, B., Koskinen, P., Marshall, N., & Mitchell, J. N. (1986). Retelling: A strategy for reading instruction and assessment. In J. A. Niles & R. Lalik (Eds.), *Solving Problems in Literacy: Learners, Teachers, and Researchers: Thirty-Fifth Yearbook of the National Reading Conference,* pp. 73–80. Rochester, NY: National Reading Conference.

Pace, A. J., Marshall, N., Horowitz, R., Lipson, M. Y., & Lucido, P. (1989). When prior knowledge doesn't facilitate some text comprehension: An examination of some of the issues. In S. McCormick & J. Zutell (Eds.), *Cognitive and Social Perspectives for Literacy Research and Instruction: Thirty-Eighth Yearbook of the National Reading Conference,* pp. 213–224. Chicago: National Reading Conference.

Palincsar, A., & Brown, A. L. (1984). Reciprocal teaching of comprehension: Fostering and comprehension-monitoring activities. *Cognition and Instruction, 1,* 117–175.

Paris, S. G., Wasik, B. A., & Turner, J. C. (1991). The development of strategic readers. In R. Barr, M. L. Kamil, P. Mosenthal, & P. D. Pearson (Eds.), *Handbook of Reading Research* (Vol. II), pp. 609–640. White Plains, NY: Longman.

Pearson, P. D., & Fielding L. (1991). Comprehension instruction. In R. Barr, M. L. Kamil, P. Mosenthal, & P. D. Pearson (Eds.), *Handbook of Reading Research* (Vol. II), pp. 815–860. White Plains, NY: Longman.

Pressley, M., (2000). What should comprehension instruction be the instruction of? In R. Barr, M. L. Kamil, P. Mosenthal, & P. D. Pearson (eds.), Handbook of Reading Research (Vol. III), pp. 545–561. Mahwah, NJ: Lawrence Erlbaum Associates.

Purves, A. C., Rogers, T., & Soter, A. O. (1995). *How Porcupines Make Love: Readers, Texts and Cultures in the Response Based Literature Classroom.* White Plains, NY: Longman.

Richek, M. A. (1987). DRTA: 5 variations that facilitate independence in reading narratives. *Journal of Reading, 30,* 632–636.

Richek, M. A. (1999). *Reading Success for At-Risk Children: Ideas that Work.* Bellevue, WA: Bureau of Education and Research.

Richek, M. A., & Glick, L. C. (1991). Coordinating a literacy-support program with classroom instruction. *The Reading Teacher, 45,* 474–479.

Roser, N., Martinez, M., Fuhrken, C., & McDonald, K. (2007). Characters as guides to meaning. *The Reading Teacher, 60,* 548–556.

Sadowski, M. (1985). The natural use of imagery in story comprehension and recall. *Reading Research Quarterly, 20,* 658–667.

Sebesta, S. (1993). Creative drama and language arts. In B. E. Cullinan (Ed.), Children's Voices

Shanahan, T. (2005). *The National Reading Panel Report: Practical Advice for Teachers.* Naperville, IL: Learning Point Associates.

Shanahan, T., & Shanahan, S. (1997). Character perspective charting: Helping children to develop a more complete conception of story. *The Reading Teacher, 50,* 668–677.

Stauffer, R. G. (1980). *The Language Experience Approach to the Teaching of Reading* (2nd ed.). New York: Harper and Row.

Stauffer, R. G. (1975). *Directing the Reading-Thinking Process.* New York: Harper and Row.

Sundbye, N. (1987). Text explicitness and inferential questioning: Effects on story understanding and recall. *Reading Research Quarterly, 22,* 82–98.

Van Der Broek, P., & Kremer, K. E. (2000). The mind in action: What it means to comprehend during reading. In B. M. Taylor, M. F. Graves, & P. Van Der Broek (Eds.), Reading for Meaning: Fostering Comprehension in the Middle Grades, pp. 1–31. Newark, DE: International Reading Association, and New York: Teachers College Press.

Williams, J. P. (1993). Comprehension of students with and without learning disabilities: Identification of narrative themes and idiosyncratic text representations. *Journal of Educational Psychology, 93,* 631–641.

Wixson, K. (1983). Questions about a text: What you ask about is what children learn. *The Reading Teacher, 37,* 287–293.

Wolf, S. A. (1998). The flight of reading: Shifts in instruction, orchestration, and attitudes through classroom theater. *Reading Research Quarterly, 33,* 382–415.

Zhang, H., & Hoosain, R. (2005). Activation of themes during narrative reading. *Discourse Processes, 40,* 57–82.

MyEducationLab is a research-based learning tool that brings teaching to life. Go to the Jennings, Caldwell, & Lerner 6th Edition MyEducationLab for Reading Assessment site at www.myeducationlab.com to:

◆ engage in multimedia exercises to help you build a deeper and more applied understanding of chapter content;

◆ utilize extensive resources including videos from real classrooms, Praxis and licensure preparation, a lesson plan builder, and materials to help you in your teaching career.

Improving Comprehension of Informational Text

Introduction

As students move through the grades, the reading tasks that confront them change dramatically. Stories become less important, and work with informational, or expository, text increases.

Students are often assigned to read science and social studies textbooks independently. Thus, without any help, students are expected to read a chapter, complete a written assignment, and participate in class discussion. Not surprisingly, many low-achieving readers cannot do these tasks.

This chapter first describes the nature and importance of informational material and discusses why it tends to be more difficult to read than stories and novels. Next, it describes strategies for assessing the abilities of students to read and study from informational text. Finally, it discusses three kinds of strategies for helping students with reading problems deal with informational material: using background knowledge, monitoring comprehension, and reorganizing or transforming informational text. The focus is on developing independent readers who eventually apply these strategies in the absence of a teacher.

Nature of Informational Text

Informational, or *expository text*, conveys information, explains ideas, or presents a point of view.

Types of Informational Text

Informational material is usually organized in one of five ways (Caldwell, 2008; Moss, 2004).

Sequence or *time order* is often used to present events such as the French and Indian War (in history class) or cell division (in biology class). Signal words for the sequence structure include *first, second, third, next, last, before, after, during, while,* and *finally*.

Listing or *description* is used to explain the features of an object or event. Biology textbooks list the features of reptiles, giving their body temperature, reproductive habits, eating habits, and so forth. No specific signal words are associated with the listing pattern.

Compare and contrast involves discussing similarities and differences. A social studies text might compare a congressional system of government with a parliamentary system; a science text might contrast several planets in the solar system. Signal words include *alike, similar to, same as, resembles, is compared to, unlike, different from, both, but,* and *yet*.

A *cause-effect* pattern outlines reasons for events. The author describes an event (such as the fall of Fort Sumter) and explains what caused the event and the effects that followed from it. Signal words are *if, so, so that, because, as a result of, in order to, since, therefore, cause,* and *effect*.

Authors using the *problem-solution* pattern discuss a problem and then suggest possible solutions. A history author might discuss the events in a U.S. president's life in terms of the problems he faced and how he solved them. Signal words include *problem, solution, because, so that,* and *as a result.*

Skilled adult readers recognize these organizational patterns and use them to facilitate comprehension. However, recognizing such patterns is not always easy. The ability to recognize and remember these patterns depends to a large degree on the reader's sensitivity to organizational patterns. In addition, informational materials often do not conform precisely to the patterns described. Authors may combine two patterns. For example, a listing or description of the battle of Vicksburg may be intertwined with the cause-effect pattern. Also, two readers may see different patterns in the same text. An account of how trade goods in the Middle Ages were brought from Asia to Europe could be interpreted as description, problem-solution, or sequence. Informational text also requires readers to understand main ideas and supporting details.

Difficulties Presented by Informational Text

Informational text presents difficulties for many able readers not just students with reading problems. Caldwell and Leslie (2003–2004) found that proficient middle school readers differed significantly in their ability to read and understand narrative and informational text. They were more successful retelling and answering questions on a narrative selection as opposed to social studies and science selections. Part of this difficulty may be due to a lack of familiarity with informational text; students tend to read more narratives than informational selections, especially in elementary school (Goldman & Rakestraw, 2000). However, even if exposure to both types of text was equal, informational text tends to be more difficult. Why is this?

- ◆ Recognizing and using the author's organizational patterns is a complex task. Such patterns are not always explicitly signaled.
- ◆ Informational text is less personal than narrative text.
- ◆ In reading informational text, students are often required to demonstrate their understanding by taking tests, which can be very stressful for any student.
- ◆ Informational text usually contains more difficult vocabulary and technical terms than narrative text.
- ◆ Informational text tends to be extremely concept dense. Four to five new ideas may be included in a single paragraph. For example, a sixth-grade paragraph on weather includes the following concepts: humidity, water vapor, evaporation, relative humidity, condensation, and dew point.
- ◆ Reading informational text often requires extensive background information. If that background is lacking, comprehension becomes more difficult.
- ◆ Informational text tends to be longer than narrative text. This length may simply overwhelm students with reading problems.
- ◆ The reading level of school textbooks is often well above the frustrational level of students with reading problems.

Importance of Informational Text

Students must be taught effective strategies for understanding and remembering expository material (Moss, 2004; Pearson and Duke, 2002; Rhoder, 2002; Goldman & Rakestraw, 2000; Yopp & Yopp, 2000). We live in what has been called the Information Age. Being literate in this age demands that students be familiar with and understand informational text. Ours is also a technological society, and students must be able "to read and write not only in the print world but also in the digital world" (Moss, 2004, p. 711). Schmar-Dobler (2003) emphasizes that the ability to effectively use the Internet to access, select, and synthesize information is critical to academic success as well as to success in the workplace. Most of the text on Internet websites is informational in nature; therefore, it is crucial that all readers become somewhat comfortable reading informational text.

An additional reason for teaching students to read informational text is the increasing importance being placed on standardized tests (Moss, 2004). Performance on such measures is used to evaluate students for promotion and for acceptance into various programs and educational institutions. Informational text represents a large portion of standardized test content (Daniels, 2002).

Assessing Abilities with Informational Text

This section presents strategies for judging how well students can handle informational materials. To successfully read and remember informational text, students must do three things: use background knowledge, monitor their own comprehension, and reorganize or transform the text to remember it. The assessment and teaching of informational text is organized around these three components.

Focusing the Informal Reading Inventory on Informational Text

Some informal reading inventories like *Qualitative Reading Inventory-4* (Leslie & Caldwell, 2005) have both narrative and expository selections. You can evaluate a student's ability to read informational text by choosing appropriate selections from the inventory.

You can also adapt the informal reading inventory procedure to the student's own textbook. Choose a passage of 200 to 400 words that has a clearly defined beginning, middle, and end. Duplicate the passage so you will have a copy to write on but have the student read from the book. Prepare 10 questions to ask the student that focus on important ideas in the passage. A reader cannot realistically be expected to remember insignificant details after one reading.

Have the student read the selection silently and allow him or her to reread the passage or study it for a short time before responding to the questions. When the student is ready, ask the questions. If the student scores below 70 percent, have the student look back in the text to find the answers to the missed questions. If a student can raise his or her score to an instructional level, the initial low score was probably due to memory problems rather than lack of comprehension. The ability to look back and find answers to incorrect questions also indicates that the student is monitoring his or her comprehension. If the student is unsuccessful when looking back, have the student reread the passage orally to help you determine if word recognition difficulties are interfering with comprehension.

To judge the level of the passage, use the comprehension score and, if the student reads orally, the word recognition accuracy score. The guidelines in Chapter 5 can help you determine whether this passage is at an independent, instructional, or frustrational level.

If the student is at a frustrational level for word recognition, do not pursue further assessment or instruction in this textbook. If the student scores at the instructional level for word recognition but at a frustrational level for comprehension, you will need to probe further by using the procedures that follow.

Assessing the Use of Background Knowledge

Good readers use what they know about a topic to help them understand informational text. One way to determine whether a student uses prior knowledge is to compare performance on familiar and unfamiliar informational texts. Again, use the IRI procedure but choose selections that you think may be familiar to the student and ones that you believe are relatively unfamiliar. Ask the student to tell you what he or she knows about the topic of the passage. For example, if the passage is about Roosevelt's New Deal, ask the student for information on Franklin Roosevelt or the New Deal.

Next, have the student silently read a familiar passage and an unfamiliar one. You can expect that students who use their background knowledge as they read will perform better with familiar text. If a student performs equally well in both passages, you should teach the strategies for using background information that are presented later in this chapter.

Assessing Comprehension Monitoring

Skilled readers are continually aware of their own comprehension as they read informational text. In contrast, students with reading problems are often not aware of their comprehension processes and therefore do not take steps to solve problems that they may encounter in reading.

One way to assess comprehension monitoring is to ask the student to find answers to questions that were answered incorrectly. You can have the student underline the answers to literal questions. However, inferential questions demand that the reader combine background knowledge with the author's clues. For these questions, ask the student to identify anything in the selection that gives clues for answering higher-level questions. If the student cannot identify anything, provide the clue and see if he or she can use it to arrive at a correct answer. Going back into the text to correct questions requires active comprehension monitoring. In fact, you will actually be teaching as you assess comprehension.

Assessing Ability to Transform Text for Studying

Many students understand a text while they are reading but quickly forget it afterward. As a result, they perform poorly on tests. To study effectively, students must transform the text in some way so that they can remember it. For example, they must reorganize the text to identify and set apart important ideas. Students often use the tools of underlining and note-taking to help in this transformation.

To assess the student's ability to study from text, choose an informational passage and ask the student to take notes as if he or she were studying for a test. You can ask the student to underline or to choose the form of note-taking that he or she prefers. Either method enables you to identify the student who cannot pick out important main ideas, take effective notes, or reorganize the text.

Strategies for Helping Students Read Informational Text

Go to
MyEducationLab
and select the
topic *Content Area Literacy*.
Then, go to the Activities
and Applications section,
watch the video entitled
"Content Area Literacy,"
and respond to the accompanying questions.

This section focuses on strategies that can lead students to read and study informational text independently. The strategies presented are learned slowly and must be used on a long-term basis. As a teacher, you will need to model them repeatedly. You must encourage students to verbalize what they are doing, why they are doing it, and how they are proceeding. After choosing a strategy, stay with it for some length of time. Having students construct bookmarks containing the steps of a strategy also helps. They can tuck these into their content area textbooks.

When teaching students with reading difficulties to deal with informational text, try to use textbooks written at their instructional level. If you must deal with textbooks above their level, you should read the text to the students in four- or five-paragraph chunks while they follow along in their books. You can also combine some form of assisted or repeated reading with the lesson. McCormack and Paratore (1999, 2004) and McCormack, Paratore, & Dahlene, (2003) found that teacher reading in combination with various forms of assisted and repeated reading effectively compensated for having to use a frustrational-level text.

All students, including younger primary students, need extensive exposure to informational text. Narrative text predominates in primary classrooms, suggesting that teachers believe informational text is inappropriate for younger readers. Nothing could be farther from the truth! Yopp and Yopp (2000) stress that depriving younger students of many and varied experiences with informational text may actually contribute to future problems with such materials in the upper grades. They emphasize that informational texts expose students to a variety of text structures and features, to specialized vocabulary, and, more important, to new concepts. Tower (2000) believes in the importance of preparing elementary students for the inquiry process by focusing on informational text.

Rhoder (2002) suggests the following three-step framework for teaching strategies for comprehending informational text. First, present a minilesson to the class or group. Describe the strategy, and tell why it is helpful. Provide short and simple segments of text, and model how the strategy works. Rhoder suggests that such texts should be curriculum free. Have the students work with the texts and the strategy in a nonthreatening and enjoyable atmosphere. The second step involves individual and group practice with longer segments of text on familiar topics. The third step is small-group and whole-class work, using selections from the students' textbooks.

Strategies for Combining Prior Knowledge with Informational Text

Go to MyEducationLab and select the topic *Comprehension*. Then, go to the Activities and Applications section, watch the video entitled "Before and During Reading Strategies," and respond to the accompanying questions.

Even if you possess only a small amount of knowledge about a topic, you can use this knowledge to read more effectively. When you use your knowledge of a topic as you read, you look for familiar *landmarks*, or background knowledge. For example, in reading about Theodore Roosevelt, summon up your landmarks. You might remember when he lived and that he was a soldier, a president, and an environmentalist. You use these landmarks to organize your reading by mentally categorizing information you read in the text under these general topics.

Students with reading problems have two difficulties with background knowledge: (1) They generally have less background knowledge than good readers because they do not read as much, and (2) They often do not apply the background knowledge they *do* have to their reading. In fact, they are so used to regarding themselves negatively that they often are not even aware of the knowledge and abilities they can bring to text. These problems are intensified because often content area teachers assign chapters without preparing students for what they will be reading.

Two strategies, the expectation grid and K-W-L, are effective in teaching students to combine their prior knowledge with informational text. The expectation grid begins with general categories and moves to specific items of information. In contrast, K-W-L begins with specific bits of knowledge and moves to the general categories. With careful guidance, both can be used independently and mentally by students.

The Expectation Grid.   Constructing an expectation grid is a strategy that students can use independently to prepare for reading informational material (Caldwell & Leslie, 2009; Caldwell, 1993a). Students first learn how to construct an expectation grid in written form. Eventually, however, the formation of the grid becomes a mental exercise that students do before reading.

As a good reader, you probably construct mental expectation grids without even being aware of them. For example, suppose you are about to read an article on a new bill before Congress. Even if you know nothing about the bill, you have certain expectations about the categories of information that you will read in the article. You expect the author to explain the purpose of the bill and describe who is supporting and opposing it. These expectations come from your knowledge of how government works. They are the landmarks that allow you to organize your reading.

Students with reading problems can be taught to approach reading with similar expectations. They may know little about the French and Indian War that they are studying, but they often know a lot about wars. Even if this knowledge comes from war movies and the *Star Trek* TV series, it can help them to form expectations about the categories discussed in their textbook.

To make an expectation grid, students create an organized visual representation of their knowledge before they read. A general topic (war, animals, important people, etc.) is placed in the center of the page and, around this topic, students write categories of information they expect to read about. For example, if the topic is an animal, you can expect that the author will describe the animal's appearance, behavior (movement, noise, temperament, etc.), habitat, and mating habits. Perhaps they will learn about the animal's relationship to people. Do people use it for food or clothing? Is it dangerous? Figure 12.1 is an example of an expectation grid on the topic of *animal*.

Suppose you are reading about the *ratel*. We suspect that you do not know much about this animal. However, as a skilled reader, you expect the categories of information previously described, and you use them to organize your thoughts as you read and recall information.

To teach students the use of expectation grids, choose part of a chapter and help students preview it by reading headings and looking at maps, graphs, or pictures. This preview helps students choose a topic for the center of the grid. Remember that the topic must be a general one such as animal, war, or country. Write the topic on the grid and then model how your knowledge of this general topic allows you to form expectations for the categories of information that will be in the reading.

Suppose that your text is an account of the French and Indian War. Put the general topic, *war*, in the center of the grid. Next, ask the students what they know about wars, perhaps from movies, television, or stories of others. Guide them to recognize such categories as who fought the war, where it was fought, causes of the war, effects of the war, who won it, and what weapons were used. Write these categories on the grid.

After you have determined your general categories of information, write *French and Indian War* under *war*. Ask the students what they know about the French and Indian War. Perhaps they saw some hints in the text during their preview. The students might have information from their own background to add to information obtained from the preview. As students offer what they know about the French and Indian War, have them identify the proper category and write the information on the grid.

Fill in the grid as long as the students have information to offer but always have them indicate which category their information goes under. You may need to add new categories to accommodate some information.

FIGURE 12.1 Expectation Grid for Animal

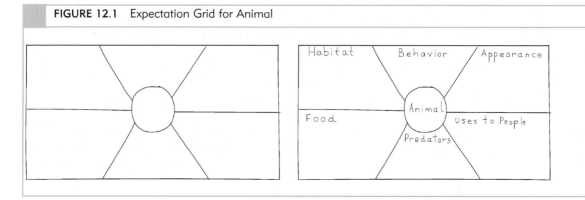

What if a student offers something that you know is not true? Perhaps a student says that the French and Indian War was between the French and the Indians. If other students question this comment, put a question mark next to the item and indicate that effective learners read to answer questions. However, if no one questions it, simply let it be. You will return to the grid after reading, and at that point, erroneous information can be corrected. Students often can identify incorrect information as they read, and they are eager to correct their grid after they finish. This opportunity for correction is one of the most valuable features of an expectation grid. Students can also use the grid to take notes as they read by adding items to each category.

As you and the students construct an expectation grid, repeatedly explain that this activity is something they should do by themselves before they read. Tell students that a grid does not need to be written. In fact, the most efficient expectation grid is one that is done mentally.

Go to MyEducationLab and select the topic *Content Area Literacy*. Then, go to the Activities and Applications section, watch the video entitled "Building Background Knowledge," and respond to the accompanying questions.

Table 12.1 presents some general topics with expected categories of information. This table is merely meant as a guide, and you should feel free to modify these categories as you and your students see fit. For students in the primary and intermediate grades, use only two or three categories. Always have a category titled "other" for items of information that do not fit into your chosen categories.

Strategy Snapshot 12.1 and Figure 12.2 present an example of a class constructing an expectation grid.

TABLE 12.1   Topics and Categories for an Expectation Grid

Animal: appearance; behavior; habitat; mating habits; life cycle; food; predators; uses to people.

Plant: type; appearance; habitat; uses; life cycle; enemies.

Important person: achievements, obstacles, personal characteristics; sequence of life; friends or associates; enemies.

Important event: causes; why important; description; people involved; countries involved; sequence; effects.

Country, city, or state: location; size, geographical features; government; industry; culture; landmarks.

War: location; time; causes; effects; countries involved; significant events or battles; important people; methods of warfare.

Process: who carries it out; needed organisms; needed materials; end products; possible problems; usefulness.

Government: form of government; structure of government; when established; problems; current status.

Strategy Snapshot 12.1

Constructing an Expectation Grid

Ms. Scanlon works with a small group of high school students who are using an expectation grid for their world history text. She helps them preview five pages on how Spanish colonies in the New World gained independence. The students decide that the topic is an important event.

She then asks them to describe some important events. Students describe a murder charge brought against a city official, an earthquake, a famine in Africa, a local train wreck, the Super Bowl, and a destructive blizzard. Ms. Scanlon asks them to imagine that they were writing about these events to someone who had never heard about them. What information would they include?

As the students offer information about their chosen event, Ms. Scanlon guides them to see how descriptions of important events are similar: they involve people, list specific places, tell why the event was important, describe causes and effects, and list events in order of time (first this happened, next this, etc.). Ms. Scanlon writes the categories: people, location, cause, effects, sequence, why important. She then writes Spanish colonies gain independence under important event and asks the students what they know about the Spanish colonies' fight for independence.

Using the headings from their book preview, students offer the expected information that the colonies had grievances, they were influenced by the American and French revolutions, Haiti gained independence early, and Father Hidalgo began Mexico's struggle. Using pictures, the students add Toussaint L'Ouverture to their grid.

When they run out of preview information, Ms. Scanlon suggests that they think of the American Revolution and leads them to offer the information that war was probably involved, people might have died, and Spain probably fought the colonies. They decide that Spain acted toward its colonies like England did toward the United States: taxing people and depriving them of rights. Finally, they suggest that colonies formed new governments when they became independent. Ms. Scanlon asks students to identify the category where each piece of information fits.

When the expectation grid is complete, Ms. Scanlon reminds the students to look for these categories as they read. One student comments that she knew more about the topic than she thought. Ms. Scanlon gives each student a blank grid and suggests using it for notes during reading. After reading, the students compare their notes and add information to the grid on the board.

Figure 12.2 shows the expectation grid that the students completed before they began reading their text.

The K-W-L Strategy.   This strategy activates prior knowledge before reading informational text and facilitates retention. Like the expectation grid, students can use K-W-L independently. The initials of K-W-L (Ogle, 1986) represent:

K—What I know
W—What I want to find out
L—What I learned

FIGURE 12.2   Expectation Grid on Spanish Colonies Gaining Their Independence

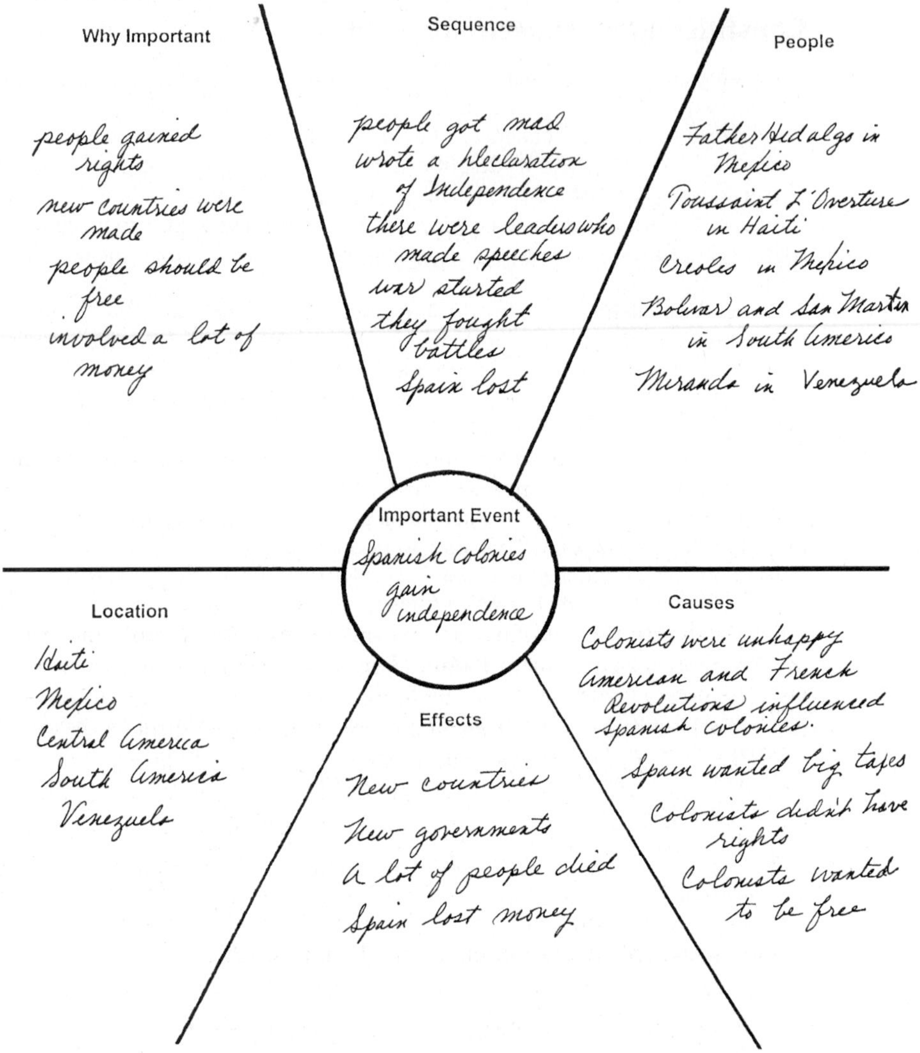

Why Important

people gained rights

new countries were made

people should be free

involved a lot of money

Sequence

people got mad wrote a Declaration of Independence

there were leaders who made speeches

war started

they fought battles

Spain lost

People

Father Hidalgo in Mexico

Toussaint L'Overture in Haiti

Creoles in Mexico

Bolivar and San Martin in South America

Miranda in Venezuela

Important Event

Spanish colonies gain independence

Location

Haiti

Mexico

Central America

South America

Venezuela

Effects

New countries

New governments

A lot of people died

Spain lost money

Causes

Colonists were unhappy

American and French Revolutions influenced Spanish colonies.

Spain wanted big taxes

Colonists didn't have rights

Colonists wanted to be free

K—What I Know. Ask students to preview part of an informational selection. Then have them think of everything that they know about the topic. List their responses on the board.

Pupils may present some misinformation. For example, a group of low-achieving fourth graders studying the state of Washington said that "the President lives there." If they offer such misinformation, you may simply list it, as with the expectation grid, and wait for students to read and make corrections. For students who have many misperceptions, you might want to use the category "What I Think I

Know" (instead of "What I Know"). This category naturally leads students to correct any misinformation after reading.

After they give information, ask students to examine their pooled information and classify it into categories. The fourth-grade class just described found this direction quite confusing at first. To begin the classification, the teacher suggested the category of mountains. The students were then able to suggest items to fit under this category. Stimulated by this hint the students were then able to add categories such as work, weather, and visiting.

W—What I Want to Find Out.   Ask each student to write down the things that he or she wants to find out or expects to learn. The W step is often difficult for low-achieving readers, because they do not have well-developed expectations of informational material. One fourth-grade boy wanted to learn, "Do nice people live in Washington?" a question he would be unlikely to learn from his text. As he experienced K-W-L over a period of several weeks, however, his expectations of text began to mature. Other children wanted to learn things that were not answered in the text but could be answered from other sources. One girl wondered how many people had been injured or killed in the eruption of Mt. St. Helens. Such questions help students realize that learning does not stop with a single textbook, and several learners began to bring in other resources. Often teachers use these unanswered questions as the basis for research projects to extend students' learning.

L—What I Learned.   Ask students to read a section of the chapter. If the text is at their instructional level, they should read silently. If it is too difficult for them, use assisted reading or read it to them. Then, have each student write down what he or she learned from reading. After recording their learning, students are usually eager to share new knowledge with others. Continue this process throughout the chapter.

Before beginning the text chapter, the fourth graders listed all that they knew or wanted to know about Washington. Then daily, as they read each of the four sections of the text, they did a K-W-L sheet for each section. To conclude the unit, the students listed all of the things that they learned about Washington and wrote a composition. Working with K-W-L, the students became more adept at understanding and remembering informational text. The K-W-L strategy can also be used to write responses that enhance comprehension (Jennings, 1991).

Strategies for Monitoring the Comprehension of Informational Text

Good readers constantly monitor their comprehension as they read. They make predictions, ask questions, and look for prior knowledge landmarks. If their comprehension falters, they stop reading and attempt to make sense of the text by rereading, identifying what confused them, and possibly using context to identify word meanings. The awareness of one's own mental activities and the ability to direct them is called *metacognition*.

Students with reading problems generally lack metacognition in reading. Because they often do not expect reading to make sense, they let their eyes move over the text and proceed on, unconcerned that they understand

Go to MyEducationLab and select the topic *Comprehension*. Then, go to the Activities and Applications section, watch the video entitled "During Reading," and respond to the accompanying questions.

almost nothing. This passive orientation toward reading is one reason why low-achieving students have comprehension problems. By developing an awareness of monitoring strategies, low-achieving readers can increase their learning. The strategies of content-free questions, text coding, topic-detail-main idea, think-aloud, reciprocal teaching, and question-answer relationships (QARs) strategies help students both to demand and to obtain meaning from text.

Content-Free Questions

For many struggling readers, questions come after reading. The teacher asks them, and the students provide answers or attempt to. Many suggest that this represents an extremely limited view. Good readers ask themselves questions before they read and *as* they read, and they read to find the answers. Questions are what keep you up past your normal bedtime as you attempt to find out how the chapter or novel ends. We also read informational text with questions in mind. What is the senator's point of view, and do I agree with it? Why is the movie so successful, and do I want to see it? How is the stock market behaving, and will its behavior affect my portfolio? What caused the team to lose the game? These kinds of questions are clearly related to general expectations for text content as described in the previous section on expectation grids. However, struggling readers need explicit guidance in using questions to monitor their comprehension. Content-free questions are a strategy for providing such guidance (Caldwell & Leslie, 2009).

Content-free questions are general questions that can be asked of any selection. They are not specifically tied to content. Consider the following examples. *How did the Egyptians mummify their pharaohs? What process is the author describing, and what are its steps?* Both deal with a process, but the content elements of *Egypt*, *mummify*, and *pharaoh* are part of one question and missing in the other. Let's look at another example. *What new nations were formed after the Treaty of Paris? What important information is the author sharing?* The first question is specifically tied to components of content, *nations* and *Treaty of Paris*; the second is not. If students learn examples of content-free questions, they can use these to guide and monitor their comprehension.

Questioning the author (Beck, McKeown, Hamilton, & Kucan, 1997) is a similar strategy. Content-free questions are called queries, and their purpose is "to assist students in grappling with text ideas as they construct meaning" (p. 23). Queries take two forms: initiating queries and follow-up queries. Initiating queries focus on the author's purpose, and follow-up queries emphasize integration of ideas. For example, an initiating querie might be "What is the author talking about?" A follow-up querie might be "Does this connect with what we read before?"

Teach students to read with content-free questions in mind. Decide on specific questions as a prereading exercise. During reading, stop periodically and decide if the questions were answered. Place the questions in a prominent place in the classroom or construct bookmarks for students. Guide students to monitor their understanding of the text by asking and answering content-free questions as they read.

The following are content-free questions for informational text (Caldwell & Leslie, 2009):

- ◆ What is the topic of this section?
- ◆ What is the author's purpose in writing this selection?

- ◆ What are the most important ideas?
- ◆ What is most interesting to me?
- ◆ What did I learn?
- ◆ What do I already know about this?
- ◆ How is this different from what I already knew?
- ◆ What surprised me?
- ◆ How could I explain this in my own words?
- ◆ What are some words that I do not know the meaning of?
- ◆ What don't I understand?

Text Coding.   Text coding (used by Caldwell, 1993b) teaches students with reading problems to recognize and remember known information, newly learned information, and remaining questions. Teaching students with reading problems to recognize these three things is an important first step in teaching them to monitor their comprehension. To make this activity short and concrete, teach them to use symbols to code text: Use a plus sign (+) to indicate something the reader already knows. Mark new information with an exclamation mark (!). Mark questions with a question mark (?). To avoid defacing books, place these symbols on small Post-it–style notes.

Teacher modeling is the best way to show students how to code text. Remember that you are teaching a *mental* process, one that you would like students eventually to do in their heads without the aid of written codes. At first, the coding symbols help to make the thinking process visible and bring it to the student's attention. Later, however, you will want the students to do this mentally.

When you teach students to use text coding, begin by getting an oral response. First, read an informational selection to them and model the coding process by stopping periodically to report information that you already knew, information you just learned, and questions you have. Invite the students to join you in talking about what they already knew or something they just learned. Do they have any questions? As you proceed, stop at specific pieces of information in the text and ask students to respond to them.

Low-achieving students tend to say they already knew an item of information when, in fact, they didn't. Refrain from criticizing them in this first stage; as the strategy proceeds, they will become more comfortable identifying new information. If students continue to say that everything was known, you might want to simplify the process by using only two categories: unknown facts and questions. In addition, students just beginning this process will have difficulties framing questions. Again, their abilities to ask good questions will increase as you model and guide their efforts.

If some students simply echo what their peers say, you might require each student to make a personal decision about text by constructing individual coding cards. Take index cards or Post-it–style notes and print the coding symbols (+, !, ?) on each one. After giving each student one for each coding symbol, read a segment of expository text to them. Ask them to hold up one of the cards to indicate whether they already knew this information, had just learned it, or had a question. When doing this activity, you may ask for a student's explanation.

After students have grasped the idea of identifying what they already knew, what they just learned, and what questions they have, move on to a written format. Choose a short segment of informational text and show it to the students. For a large group, you might want to code the text on an overhead. Students in a small group can sit around you and watch as you write the coding symbols on the page. As you read the text, think aloud about what you already knew, what you just learned, and what questions you have. At each item, mark the coding symbols on the text. (You can lightly pencil them in on the page or attach Post-it–style notes containing !, +, ?) The use of written symbols is an important step that makes a mental strategy visible for the students.

As a next step, students should each receive an individual copy of a short text (no more than one page) to read silently and code for themselves in the margins or above a line of print. Before students read, the teacher should decide how often they need to react. In the early stages of strategy instruction, or with easy text, you should code each sentence. However, as text becomes more difficult, many different items of information can be included in a single sentence, so one sentence could have several different codes. For example, Kenneth coded one sentence by indicating already known (+) for the fact that cicada eggs hatched but just learned (!) for the fact that the animals from hatched eggs are called nymphs. He also had a question (?) because he wondered why they were called nymphs. Figure 12.3 shows Josh's coding of a paragraph about the cicada.

Coding is a flexible strategy that can be used orally or in writing to guide the understanding of any type of expository text. However, teaching this strategy requires a generous amount of teacher modeling and student response. Students need to verbalize what they are doing, why they are doing it, and how it should be done.

FIGURE 12.3 Josh's Text Coding

The female cicada lays$^+$her eggs in tree$^!$branches. She makes tiny$^+$holes in the wood and lays$^?$her eggs in these holes. The cicada eggs hatch$^+$into nymphs. Nymphs are very small$^!$and they look like$^!$worms. The nymphs crawl down the trees and bury$^!$themselves in the ground. They stay in the$^!$ground for 17$^?$years! They feed on tree$^!$roots. During the 17 years, the nymph slowly$^!$turns into a cicada. It finally comes out of the ground and climbs into a tree. After it sheds its$^!$skin, it can$^+$fly. The cicada lives on tree$^?$leaves and other plants but only lives for 6$^!$more weeks.

Josh's questions, each corresponding to a mark on the paper, were:

How many eggs does she lay?

Why do they call them nymphs?

Why don't they freeze in winter?

Do they hurt the trees?

Twelve-year-old Tischa wrote that she used the coding strategy in this way:

1. If you already knew something put a plus and skip it when you review.
2. If its [*sic*] new info and you understand it circle a key word and put an exclamation point.
3. If its [*sic*] confusing put a question mark and reread it or ask somebody.
4. This can help when you read new, hard, and long things.

Nine-year-old Justin explained the coding strategy by writing:

When I read I THINK

◆ about what I already know
◆ about what I will learn
◆ about what questions to be ansed [*sic*]

I Love to think!

The Topic-Detail-Main Idea Strategy.   As they read informational text, competent readers consciously try to determine the main ideas and supporting facts. They effectively interrelate facts by forming a core of main ideas and a cluster of facts around those ideas. Interrelating information reduces memory load and allows more effective study.

However, constructing main ideas is a complex ability that requires many component skills (Goldman & Rakestraw, 2000). Because they are often not stated directly in the text, learning to identify main ideas requires careful and systematic teaching over an extended period of time. Students with reading problems tend to remember interesting, rather than important, information. Often these intriguing details obscure the more important main points (Alexander & Jetton, 2000).

In addition, low-achieving students often have formed misconceptions about main ideas, sometimes based on previous instruction. They believe that every paragraph contains a main idea, which is stated in a topic sentence. However, the reality is much more complex. An analysis of social studies texts in grades two, four, six, and eight found that only 44 percent of the paragraphs contained topic sentences. The same study discovered that only 27 percent of short passages in the social studies texts had topic sentences stating the main ideas (Baumann & Serra, 1984).

Students with reading problems also believe that the first sentence in the paragraph is the topic sentence. Asked to take notes on main ideas, Allison cheerfully underlined the first sentence in every paragraph. She then put down her pencil and announced, "I'm all done. It was real easy." In reality, finding the main idea requires hard work and careful monitoring of one's comprehension. As you read, you need to be aware of the topic of the paragraph, what you are learning about the topic, and what is the most important statement that the author has made to explain the topic.

The topic-detail-main idea strategy is based on the strategies used by mature readers to construct main ideas and recognize the organizational patterns of text. As with all informational text strategies, you will need to model the topic-detail-main idea strategy on a regular basis. In this strategy, students identify the topic of a paragraph, the details of a paragraph, and the main ideas of a paragraph. The main idea often must be *constructed* by the student.

The steps of the strategy are as follows:

1. Read the entire selection.
2. Reread the first paragraph and identify the topic of the paragraph. (The topic is what the paragraph is about.) State the topic in one or two words. You can figure out a topic by asking yourself what each sentence is talking about.
3. Now, underline, in your paragraph, each thing that the author tells you about the topic. These ideas are the details.
4. Now that you have the topic and details, check to see if there is a main idea sentence (a topic sentence). Remember that each detail should be connected to this sentence.
5. If you don't find a main idea sentence, and you probably won't, construct one. Asking yourself these questions helps:

   ◆ Is the author describing something: a person, a thing, a process, or an event?
   ◆ Is the author comparing or contrasting two or more things?
   ◆ Is the author explaining a problem or a solution?
   ◆ Is the author explaining a cause and effect?

As students begin to construct their own main idea sentences, they often use statements such as "The author is describing the cicada's life cycle" or "The author is listing problems with the way we get rid of garbage." These main idea statements provide a good framework for clustering facts.

In modeling the topic-detail-main idea strategy, duplicate a section of the students' textbook and write directly on the page or use an overhead transparency. You might write the topic in one color and underline the details in a second color. If the paragraph contains a topic sentence, underline it in a third color or use this color to write your constructed main idea sentence. The different colors help students to visualize a strategy that, like the other strategies discussed, should eventually be done mentally.

Share with students that not every paragraph contains a main idea. Often several small paragraphs can be joined together to form one main idea unit, or long paragraphs can be split into two main idea units. A selection may also include introductory, transition, and summary paragraphs that do not really contain main ideas. Students often call these paragraphs "get going" paragraphs, "glue" paragraphs, and "bye-bye" paragraphs. Strategy Snapshot 12.2 illustrates the topic-detail-main idea procedure.

Lubliner (2004) used a *questioning cue card* to help struggling readers generate questions about main ideas in informational text. The cards reminded the students to think, build, summarize, question, and ask: They think about what the author is saying; they build by putting ideas together; they summarize the main ideas; they construct a question about the main idea; and finally, they ask the main idea question and find an answer to it. Again, the topic-detail-main idea strategy can be incorporated in the think, build, and summarize segments.

Strategy Snapshot 12.2

Topic-Detail-Main Idea Strategy

Ms. Gillman and a small group of fifth-grade low-achieving readers used this selection:

> The elephant is the largest living animal and one of the most intelligent, and yet elephants are rather easily captured. They are very nearsighted, and so they cannot see anything distinctly unless it is close to them. Hunters take advantage of this to get near to elephants they wish to capture. Even if discovered, a person can escape an angry elephant by getting out of its line of vision.
>
> There are two kinds of elephants, the Asian (or Indian) elephant and the African elephant. Next time you are at the zoo, look at each kind, especially at their ears and sizes. See if you can tell the difference.
>
> Both the Asian and African elephants roam about in herds. The leader is usually an older female elephant. When grass becomes scarce in one valley, she will decide when and where to go next. The younger elephants follow her in single file to better grazing land.
>
> Members of the herd will often help one another. Once when an elephant was wounded by a hunter, others of the herd helped it to escape. Two large elephants walked on either side of the wounded animal to keep it from falling.

Students first read the entire selection orally together and then reread the first paragraph. Ms. Gillman guided the students to see that each sentence was about elephants so this topic was written in the margin by the first paragraph. They then underlined information about the elephants and looked for a main idea sentence. When one student suggested that the first sentence was the main idea, Ms. Gillman asked if all the sentences talked about the elephant as large, intelligent, and easily captured. They agreed that none of the other sentences mentioned size or intelligence and only the third sentence talked about capture. The group decided that they had to make up their own main idea sentence. They used step 5 of the strategy and decided that the main idea sentence was "The author is describing elephants." Ms. Gillman asked if the author was describing a particular thing about the elephant. After some lively discussion, the group changed their original main idea sentence to "The author is describing the elephant's eyesight."

The second paragraph puzzled the students. Ms. Gillman suggested that they skip this paragraph and move on to the next one. She explained that not all paragraphs have main ideas.

The students reread the third paragraph and decided that the topic was elephant herds and they underlined what they learned. However, the students disagreed upon the main idea sentence. Two thought the first sentence a fine main idea sentence because each sentence talked about what the elephants did in herds. Three other students wrote: "The author is describing how the herd acts." Ms. Gillman assured them that both were fine main idea sentences.

The students chose *herd* as the topic of the last paragraph. After underlining what they learned, they all agreed that the first sentence was a good main idea sentence.

Source: Excerpt from "One of the Smartest," *New Practice Readers, Book E,* 2nd ed., Phoenix Learning Resources, 1988, by permission of publishers.

Think-Aloud Strategy.   In this strategy, the teacher thinks out loud and models the way that a skilled reader makes sense of text. Pressley and Afflerbach (1995) provide an extensive summary of the cognitive behaviors that readers engage in as they read. The think-aloud strategy has the potential to be used effectively as an instructional activity (Wilhelm, 2001). Think-aloud procedures have been studied with readers of all ages, and with appropriate modeling, most ages can engage in think-alouds.

To use the think-aloud strategy, select a short passage that contains unknown words and other points of difficulty. Give the passage to each student and retain one copy for yourself. Read the passage aloud, stopping after each paragraph. Verbalize the thought processes you used in trying to make sense of the passage and ask students to do the same. Leslie and Caldwell (2009) modeled the following activities and guided students to do the same:

- Paraphrase or summarize the text in your own words. For example, say "This is all about how the war started with the assassination of the archduke. It describes the countries on both sides."

Go to
MyEducationLab
and select the
topic *Content Area Literacy*.
Then, go to the Activities
and Applications section,
watch the video entitled
"Reading for Information," and respond to the
accompanying questions.

- Create new meaning. Predict what might come next. Make an inference. Form a visual image. For example, say "I bet the Allies really wanted to hurt Germany for starting the war. A lot of times, winners really try to get back at the losers." or "I suppose the next paragraph will tell why Germany didn't want to sign the treaty."
- Ask questions about the topic or events and offer probable answers. For example, say "Why didn't Britain and France think the League of Nations would work? Maybe they figured it was unrealistic to think nations would never go to war again."
- Mention that you understand what you have read. For example, say, "This makes a lot of sense to me. A new leader wouldn't want to carry on a war that he didn't believe in, so I can understand why Lenin offered to make peace."
- Mention that you did not understand what you read and point out the confusing word or concept. Model a possible fix-up strategy. For example, say, "I was not sure what *stalemate* means, but I reread the sentence, and if neither side is winning, then it could mean a draw or equal positions."
- Talk about your prior knowledge and indicate how the information in the text matches with what you previously knew. Explain what you have learned. For example, say, "I knew they carved up all these little countries after the war, but I didn't know that they mixed up the languages and nationalities when they did it."
- Identify personally with the text. For example, say, "I'll bet Wilson felt bad that people didn't believe in the League of Nations. It reminds me of a time when I suggested that we all go camping and no one in the family agreed. In fact, they weren't really polite in telling me so."

As you model the think-aloud process, encourage students to share their own thoughts. This process tends to be nonthreatening to poor readers, who are often asked to respond to questions for which they do not know the answers. In the think-aloud process, *no answer is wrong*, and students soon grasp this point. In the beginning stages, students often copy what the teacher said, saying "I thought that too" or "I didn't understand that either." As they begin to feel more comfortable with think-alouds, they offer more original thoughts. They take on more and more ownership, and the need for modeling will diminish.

Throughout the process, constantly stress that the comments made during think-alouds are what good readers do as they read. In the initial stages, when a student shares a comment, identify the type of strategy that he or she used: for example, say "Alan just tied the text to his own personal experience" or "Kelsey described what she did not understand" or "Perry made a great inference." Students should understand exactly what they are doing when they offer comments. You can also stress what they are doing by having the students make a bookmark that lists the strategies.

If you are helping poor readers prepare for their content area classes, the think-aloud strategy has an added bonus. As students share their thoughts and listen to the thoughts of their peers, they actually learn the content of the text.

Go to MyEducationLab and select the topic *Content Area Literacy*. Then, go to the Activities and Applications section, watch the video entitled "Reciprocal Teaching," and respond to the accompanying questions.

Reciprocal Teaching. Reciprocal teaching, designed by Palincsar and Brown (1984), is similar to think-alouds. It employs teacher modeling, focuses on what good readers do as they read, and engages students in sharing their thoughts during the reading process. Reciprocal teaching stresses four reader strategies: summarizing, raising questions, clarifying vocabulary and concepts, and predicting subsequent content. Much instruction of poor readers is in a small-group format, and reciprocal teaching lends itself to this situation.

Reciprocal teaching begins with the teacher modeling the four comprehension strategies—summarizing, questioning, clarifying, and predicting—and drawing the students into the discussion. Gradually as students begin to feel comfortable with the strategies, they take over the teaching role and model strategy use for their peers. The names of the four steps need to be used often and perhaps prominently displayed in the classroom or on a bookmark. If a student encounters difficulty, the teacher steps in to provide necessary support. The teacher then allows the student to continue.

Herrmann (1988) offers a possible sequence for a reciprocal teaching lesson:

1. Read the title, preview the pictures, and ask the students to predict possible content.
2. Read the text aloud paragraph by paragraph.
3. After each paragraph, ask questions about the content and invite students to share possible answers. Ask the students to offer additional questions.
4. At appropriate places, summarize what was read and share with students how you arrived at the summary. Did you use a topic sentence? Did the author offer any clues about important segments?
5. Discuss any words or concepts that are confusing and help the students clarify these. As in think-alouds, the students must have names for what they are doing.

Go to MyEducationLab and select the topic *Comprehension*. Then, go to the Activities and Applications section, watch the video entitled "After Reading," and respond to the accompanying questions.

Question Answer Relationships

The ability to answer questions is an important one for academic success. Teachers ask questions, worksheets contain questions, and tests consist of questions. Struggling readers often experience difficulty in finding acceptable answers. Sometimes, they have not understood the text. Sometimes, forgetting what they read and understood in the culprit. Often they just do not understand the structure of the question and lack strategies for locating an answer.

Raphael (Raphael, Highfield & Au, 2006; Raphael & Au, 2005; Raphael, 1982, 1986) devised a user-friendly framework called question answer relationships (QARs) for teaching students how to answer questions by learning where to find the answers. Answers are either in the text or in the mind of the reader. Raphael calls these *In the Book* and *In My Head* questions.

There are two kinds of *In the Book* questions: *Right There* questions and *Think and Search* questions. The answer to a *Right There* question is explicitly stated in the text, usually in a single sentence. The words in the questions and the words in the text are extremely similar. Question: *What were the most important crops in ancient Egypt?* Answer: *The most important crops were wheat and barley.*

The answers to *Think and Search* questions are also explicitly stated, but the reader finds the answers in several sentences often interspersed throughout the text. The reader has to pull different parts of the text together to arrive at an answer. Question: *How did the ancient Egyptians prepare their pharaohs for the afterlife?* Answer: *They built pyramids, mummified the body, and placed it in the tomb with all the pharaoh's possessions.* This answer is drawn from three separate paragraphs.

In My Head questions take two forms: *Author and Me* and *On My Own*. *Author and Me* questions are basically inference questions. The reader must locate clues in the text and construct an inference to answer the question. Question: *Why did Egyptian civilization begin along the Nile River?* Answer: *The rich land that resulted from flooding allowed people to stay in one place and have enough to eat.* To arrive at this answer, the reader must identify the text clues that explain the life-giving properties of the Nile flooding and connect this fact with knowledge of how civilizations develop.

Answers to *On My Own* questions are not in the text. Sometimes, such questions can be answered without even reading the selection. Question: *Why would someone build an elaborate tomb?* Answer: *To impress people; to make themselves feel better about death.*

Teach QARs by moving from easy to difficult. *In the Book* questions are easier. When students have mastered these, move on to *In My Head* questions. An effective way of helping students deal with QARs is to begin by asking the question, giving the answer, providing the QAR label, and explaining the rationale for the label. Gradually, drop the rationale, and ask the students to supply it. Then present the question and the label. Have the students find the answer and provide the rationale. Finally, ask the question and support the students in finding the answer, providing the QAR label, and explaining the rationale. Start with short segments of text and gradually move to longer selections. Mesmer and Hutchins (2002) suggest using the QAR process to help students answer questions involving charts and graphs.

Caldwell and Leslie (2009) suggest using visuals to illustrate the four question types. A picture of an open book with a single bolded line on one page is an effective way to describe a *Right There* question. Several bolded lines across two pages can indicate a *Think and Search* question. Pictures of a book and a person's head or a brain indicate an *Author and Me* question. An *On My Own* question is effectively illustrated by a picture of a person's head or a brain.

Strategies for Transforming Informational Text

In addition to understanding informational text, students must also study and remember what they read so that they can discuss it and pass tests. Effective studying requires students to do two things: recognize important information and actively process, or *transform*, it (Anderson & Armbruster, 1984). Taking notes and reconstructing the text in a visual fashion are ways of transforming the text.

One college student took a course in neuropsychology that involved remembering many details about brain structure and function. To master this difficult information, the student transformed it by creating labeled pictures of the brain and making diagrams relating the brain to body parts. She underlined the text, took notes on the underlined parts, and rewrote the notes. Finally, she mastered the course content. As this example shows, effective studying involves transforming text and changing it into a form that can be remembered.

Teachers generally expect students to study on their own, yet it is difficult to develop the self-guidance and systematic approaches necessary for this independence. Students with reading difficulties need direct instruction in transforming the text so that they can remember it.

The strategies discussed in the earlier parts of this chapter aid in understanding text and recognizing important information. This section discusses different ways of transforming text content into visual diagrams. Constructing these diagrams involves the student in actively processing the information. The diagrams can also be used as study aids and can be extremely effective in helping students understand and remember text.

The Main Idea Grid.   The main idea grid can be used as a diagram for taking notes as students work through the topic-detail-main idea strategy (presented earlier in this chapter). After students read and analyze a paragraph, the grid is used to record the *topic*, *details*, and *main idea sentence*. A guide is given in Figure 12.4.

The main idea grid serves several purposes: (1) It acts as a reminder of the comprehension strategy students should be using as they read; (2) it involves students in actively transforming the text; (3) it helps students take brief notes in their own words. Because space for notes is limited, students must often shorten their writing; and (4) it provides a simplified and transformed summary from which students can study. Give the students copies of the grid to fill in or they can draw their own grids as they go along.

Idea-Mapping.   Idea-mapping (Armbruster, 1986) visually demonstrates the organizational patterns of informational text and helps students recognize how ideas in a textbook are linked together. Idea-mapping is based on the different patterns of infor-

FIGURE 12.4 Main Idea Grid

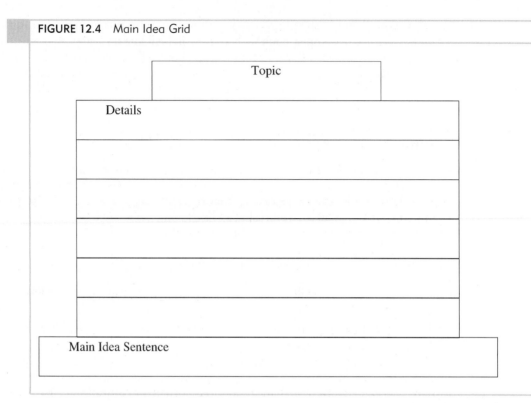

mational text described earlier in the chapter: sequence or time order, listing or description, comparison-contrast, cause-effect, and problem-solution. Each text structure is represented by a unique idea-map form. The students fill in the map with information from the text. We have simplified and adapted the original idea-maps of Armbruster (1986) and used them successfully with low-achieving readers. Idea-maps remind students to identify patterns of informational organization.

In the early stages of using idea-mapping, identify an organizational pattern for the students and give them the appropriate map to fill in. The next step involves giving them two idea-map choices. The students read the text and decide which organizational pattern best fits, then they fill in the map. Finally, students independently choose which idea-map to use.

The compare-contrast is an effective map to present first. The items that are to be compared are written in the top spaces. The characteristics of each are written next. If the characteristics are similar or identical, the equals symbol (=) is written between them. If the characteristics differ, the symbol is the equals sign with a line drawn through it (≠). An idea-map for comparing and contrasting deciduous and coniferous trees might look like Figure 12.5.

You can also present the idea-map for the description or listing pattern in the early stages of teaching the strategy. The item to be described is written in the top

FIGURE 12.5   Compare-Contrast Idea-Map

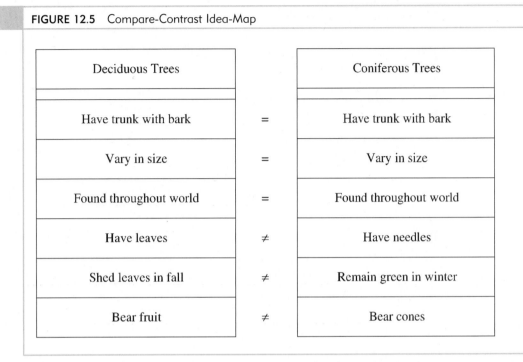

Deciduous Trees		Coniferous Trees
Have trunk with bark	=	Have trunk with bark
Vary in size	=	Vary in size
Found throughout world	=	Found throughout world
Have leaves	≠	Have needles
Shed leaves in fall	≠	Remain green in winter
Bear fruit	≠	Bear cones

space, and the descriptive characteristics are listed underneath. An idea-map for describing poison ivy might look like Figure 12.6.

Three other idea-maps represent the informational patterns of sequence, problem-solution and cause-effect. The first box of the sequence idea-map contains the title of the process that is being described. Numbered rectangles connected by arrows indicate that the events placed in each box occur in a set order (Figure 12.7).

The problem-solution idea-map has a rectangle for the problem connected by an arrow to another rectangle for the solution. Characteristics or comments about the problem or solution are written underneath each. A problem-solution idea-map might look like Figure 12.8.

The cause-effect idea-map is similar. The cause is written in one rectangle, and the effect is written in another. They are connected by an arrow indicating that the cause precedes or leads into the effect. Again, description or comments about the cause or effect can be written underneath. An example of a cause-effect idea-map is given in Figure 12.9.

Idea-maps, like most of the strategies presented in this chapter, take time for students to learn and apply independently. As mentioned earlier, these informational patterns are not always clear. Two students may choose different idea-maps to represent the same text. Kelly and Amy were reading about the early years of Franklin Delano Roosevelt's presidency. Kelly chose the sequence idea-map to represent Roosevelt's actions. Amy chose the problem-solution idea-map and

FIGURE 12.6 Description Idea-Map

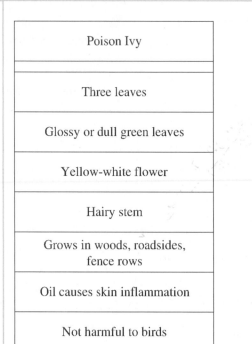

organized her notes around the many problems faced by Roosevelt and his attempts to solve them.

Of course, students cannot choose just any idea-map. They must choose an appropriate one that fits the text, but variation in choices will occur. Your role is to encourage the students to verbalize why they chose a particular map. Students enjoy sharing their choices with their peers, and lively discussion often occurs as students defend these decisions.

In the early stages of instruction, use short segments of text to illustrate idea-maps. Gradually increase the length of the text. As students move into longer text, they often have to use multiple idea-maps. Amy used several problem-solution maps to summarize the problems faced by Roosevelt. Kelly divided Roosevelt's early presidency into two sequence idea-maps, one for each of his first two terms.

Summary

Informational material refers to informational materials such as school textbooks. Informational material is organized around five basic patterns: sequence, listing, compare-contrast, cause-effect, and problem-solution. Comprehension of the main ideas in a passage is heavily dependent on recognition of these patterns.

FIGURE 12.7 Sequence Idea-Map

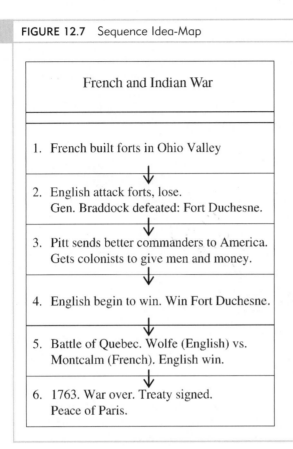

French and Indian War

1. French built forts in Ohio Valley

2. English attack forts, lose.
   Gen. Braddock defeated: Fort Duchesne.

3. Pitt sends better commanders to America.
   Gets colonists to give men and money.

4. English begin to win. Win Fort Duchesne.

5. Battle of Quebec. Wolfe (English) vs.
   Montcalm (French). English win.

6. 1763. War over. Treaty signed.
   Peace of Paris.

Informational text tends to be difficult, especially for poor readers. Text organization is often unclear. Informational text is less personal than narratives and contains more difficult vocabulary. Students must both understand and remember the content of their textbooks. Poor readers often lack the background knowledge needed to successfully comprehend informational selections.

Successful reading of informational text requires that students activate their prior knowledge before they read, monitor their own comprehension, and develop strategies for reorganizing or transforming text so they can remember it.

Several strategies can be used to assess a student's ability to read informational material. The teacher can adapt the informal reading inventory procedure for use with textbooks. The teacher can assess the use of background knowledge by comparing a student's performance on familiar and unfamiliar text. The teacher can assess comprehension monitoring by having the student identify troublesome parts of the text. Finally, the teacher can assess students' ability to reorganize text by watching them take notes.

Strategies for helping students read informational text should be student-centered; that is, the student should be able to use the strategies independently. Such

FIGURE 12.8   Problem-Solution Idea Map

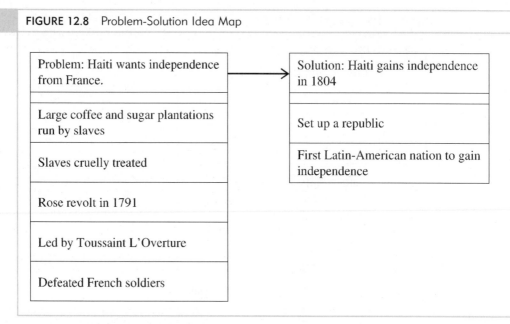

strategies take a long time to learn and apply. Teachers need to focus on a single strategy over a long period of time. Teachers should model the strategy and repeatedly ask students to verbalize what they are doing, why they are doing it, and what procedures they are using.

Students can activate their own knowledge of a topic by using the expectation grid and the K-W-L strategy. They can monitor their own comprehension by using

FIGURE 12.9   Cause-Effect Idea-Map

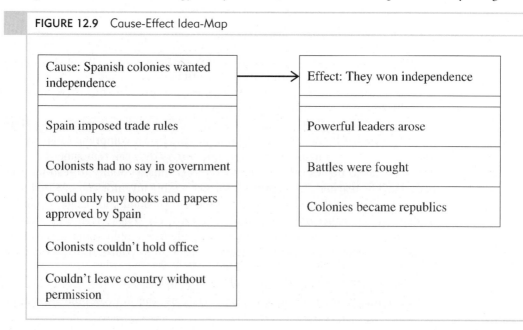

content-free questions, text coding, the topic-detail-main idea strategy, the think-aloud strategy, the reciprocal teaching strategy, or question answer relationships. They can transform the text to remember it by using the main-idea grid and idea-mapping.

References

Alexander, P. A., & Jetton, T. L. (2000). Learning from text: A multidimensional and developmental perspective. In R. Barr, M. L. Kamil, P. Mosenthal, & P. D. Pearson (Eds.), *Handbook of Reading Research* (Vol. III), pp. 285–310. New York: Longman.

Anderson, T. H., & Armbruster, B. B. (1984). Content area textbooks. In R. C. Anderson, J. Osborn, & R. J. Tierney (Eds.), *Learning to Read in American Schools: Basal Readers and Content Texts*, pp. 193–226. Hillsdale, NJ: Erlbaum.

Armbruster, B. B. (1986). *Using Frames to Organize Expository Text.* Paper presented at National Reading Conference, Austin, TX.

Baumann, J. F., & Serra, K. K. (1984). The frequency and placement of main ideas in children's social studies textbooks: A modified replication of Braddock's research on topic sentences. *Journal of Reading Behavior, 16*, 27–40.

Beck, I. L., McKeown, M. G., Hamilton, R. L., & Kucan, L. (1997). *Questioning the Author: An Approach for Enhancing Student Engagement with Text.* Newark, DE: International Reading Association.

Caldwell, J. (1993a). *Developing an Expectation Grid for Understanding Expository Text.* Milwaukee, WI: Cardinal Stritch University. Unpublished strategy.

Caldwell, J. (1993b). *Developing a Text Coding Strategy for Understanding Expository Text.* Milwaukee, WI: Cardinal Stritch University. Unpublished strategy.

Caldwell, J. S. (2008). *Comprehension Assessment: A Classroom Guide.* New York: Guilford Press.

Caldwell, J., & Leslie, L. (2003–2004). Does proficiency in middle school reading assure proficiency in high school reading? The possible role of think-alouds. *Journal of Adolescent and Adult Literacy, 47*, 324–335.

Caldwell, J. S., & Leslie, L. (2009). *Intervention Strategies to Follow Informal Inventory Assessment: So What Do I Do Now?* Boston: Allyn & Bacon.

Daniels, H. (2002). Expository text in literature circles. *Voices from the Middle, 9*, 7–14.

Goldman, S. R., & Rakestraw, J. A., Jr. (2000). Structural aspects of constructing meaning from text. In R. Barr, M. L. Kamil, P. Mosenthal, & P. D. Pearson (eds.), *Handbook of Reading Research* (Vol. III), pp. 311–335. Mahwah, NJ: Lawrence Erlbaum Associates.

Herrmann, B. A. (1988). Two approaches for helping poor readers become more strategic. *The reading teacher, 42*, 24–48.

Jennings, J. H. (1991). A comparison of summary and journal writing as components of an interactive comprehension model in social studies. In *The Fortieth Yearbook of the National Reading Conference*, pp. 67–82. Chicago: National Reading Conference.

Leslie, L., & Caldwell, J. (2005). *Qualitative reading inventory 4.* New York: Longman.

Lubliner, S. (2004). Help for struggling upper-grade elementary readers. *The Reading Teacher, 57*, 430–438.

McCormack, R. L., & Paratore, J. R. (1999). *"What Do You Do There Anyway," Teachers Ask: A Reading Teacher's Intervention Using Grade-Level Text with Struggling Third Grade Readers.* Paper presented at the National Reading Conference, Orlando, FL.

McCormack, R. L., Paratore, J. R., & Dahlene, K. F. (2003). Establishing instructional congruence across learning settings: One path to success for struggling third grade readers. In R. L. McCormack & J. R. Paratore. (Eds.) *After Early Intervention, Then What: Teaching Struggling Readers in Grades 3 and Beyond* (pp. 117–136). Newark, DE: International Reading Association.

McCormack, R. L., Paratore, J. R., & Dahlene, K. F. (2004). Establishing instructional congruence across learning settings: One path to success for struggling third grade readers. In R. L. McCormack and J. R. Paratore (Eds.). *After Early Intervention, Then What? Teaching Struggling Readers in Grades 3 and Beyond*, pp. 117–136. Newark, DE: International Reading Association.

Moss, B. (2004). Teaching expository text structures through information trade book retellings. *The Reading Teacher, 57*, 710–718.

Ogle, D. (1986). KWL: A teaching model that develops active reading of expository text. *The Reading Teacher, 39*, 564–570.

Palincsar, A., & Brown, A. L. (1984). Reciprocal teaching of comprehension: Fostering and comprehension-monitoring activities. *Cognition and Instruction, 1*, 117–175.

Pearson, P. D., & Duke, N. K. (2002). Comprehension instruction in the primary grades. In C. C. Block and M. Pressley (Eds.), *Comprehension Instruction: Research-Based Best Practice*, pp. 247–258. New York: Guilford.

Pressley, M., & Afflerbach, P. (1995). *Verbal Protocols of Reading: The Nature of Constructively Responsive Reading*. Mahwah, NJ: Erlbaum.

Raphael, T. E. (1986). Teaching question-answer relationships, revisited. *The Reading Teacher, 39*, 516–522.

Raphael, T. E. (1982). Question-answering strategies for children. *The Reading Teacher, 36*, 186–190.

Raphael, T. E., & Au, K. (2005). QAR: Enhancing comprehension and test taking across grades and content areas. *The Reading Teacher, 59*, 206–221.

Raphael, T. E., Highfield, K., & Au, K. (2006). *QAR Now: Question Answer Relationships*. New York: Scholastic.

Rhoder, C. (2002). Mindful reading: Strategy training that facilitates transfer. *Journal of Adolescent and Adult Literacy, 45*, 498–513.

Schmar-Dobler, E. (2003). Reading on the Internet: The link between literacy and technology. *Journal of Adolescent and Adult Literacy, 47*, 80–85.

Tower, C. (2000). Questions that matter: Preparing elementary students for the inquiry process. *The Reading Teacher, 53*, 550–557.

Wilhelm, J. D. (2001). *Improving Comprehension with Think-Aloud Strategies*. Jefferson City, MO: Scholastic, Inc.

Yopp, R. H., & Yopp, H. K. (2000). Sharing informational text with young children. *The Reading Teacher, 53*, 410–423.

PEARSON
myeducationlab
Where the Classroom Comes to Life

MyEducationLab is a research-based learning tool that brings teaching to life. Go to the Jennings, Caldwell, & Lerner 6th Edition MyEducationLab for Reading Assessment site at www.myeducationlab.com to:

◆ engage in multimedia exercises to help you build a deeper and more applied understanding of chapter content;

◆ utilize extensive resources including videos from real classrooms, Praxis and licensure preparation, a lesson plan builder, and materials to help you in your teaching career.

Reading and Writing

Introduction

Research has consistently shown that strong ties exist between reading and writing (Johnston, 1997; Tierney, 1990). Of particular interest to those who work with students with reading problems is the support that writing provides for reading development and the influence of reading on students' writing. This chapter discusses the writing process and how it relates to reading and gives many strategies to foster the development of writing. Some instructional strategies that help students connect reading and writing are included. Finally, suggestions are presented for teaching spelling and handwriting.

Importance of Teaching Writing

Why should a reading teacher focus on writing? The process of writing is highly related to the process of reading because readers and writers are both constructing—or composing—meaning. Readers construct meaning from the author's text; writers compose or construct meaning as they create text.

The reading-writing relationship begins in early literacy and continues throughout a student's literacy development (Richgels, 2003; Jacobs, 2002; Greene, 1995). In early literacy, the relationship focuses on sound-symbol relationships and concepts about print (Gentry, 2007; Dyson, 2003; Goswami, 2003; Richgels, 2003; Castle, Riach, & Nicholson, 1994). As students mature, the relationship between reading and writing becomes more complex. As students read a wider variety of texts, the influence of those texts can be observed in their writing (Calkins, 2004; Fletcher & Portalupi, 2001; Lancia, 1997; Sitler, 1995; Wollman-Bonilla & Werchadlo, 1995). Sharing good models of writing through reading provides the support students need to improve their writing (Saddler & Graham, 2008). As students engage in more mature writing, they begin to relate to authors' perspectives, and this relationship leads to a deeper understanding of text (Greene, 1995; White, 1995; Calkins, 1994, 2000; Weech, 1994). Students who perceive themselves to be writers are motivated to improve their writing, and they want to use models of written text to help them; thus, students' efforts to improve their writing foster improvement in the reading (Glenn, 2007).

In early literacy, writing helps students understand that print progresses from left to right and from the top of the page to the bottom. In beginning reading, writing provides students with the practice they need to pay attention to individual words and helps them match letters and sounds in words (Gentry, 2007; Richgels, 2003; Clay, 1998, 2002).

Throughout the phases of literacy development, practice in writing increases the understanding of how authors compose text (Olness, 2005; Calkins, 2004). Tierney (1990) interviewed students and found that those who identified themselves as authors viewed reading in a new light. These students expressed more enthusiasm for both reading and writing, and they read more critically. They viewed reading as a resource for new ideas and information for their writing.

Students also use writing to clarify their understanding of what they read. When they make written responses to reading, they increase comprehension (Freeman, 2003; Jacobs, 2002; White, 1995; Weech, 1994; Wells, 1992–1993; Jennings, 1991; Wittrock, 1984). Writing can help students master information in science, social studies, and other subjects (Jacobs, 2002; Cawley & Parmar, 2001; Button & Welton, 1997; Mayher, Lester, & Pradl, 1983). Writing can be a powerful tool in supporting students' learning (Unrau, 2008).

Using writing in instruction offers important sources of success and motivation for struggling readers. Students just learning to read may write or dictate messages and read their own words. Freed from the burden of trying to determine what another author meant, these students now have an opportunity to create, read, and display their own meanings.

For more advanced students with reading problems, writing can be used to deepen comprehension responses and to stimulate more reading. These students enjoy the permanence of responding in writing to books they have read, and their responses can be referred to later and shared with others. In addition, students who identify a topic to write about are often motivated to use reading as a way to find information.

Assessing Writing

Go to MyEducationLab and select the topic *Assessing Reading and Writing*. Then, go to the Activities and Applications section, watch the video entitled "Writing Assessment," and respond to the accompanying questions. How can a teacher use a student's writing to gain information about that student's reading?

In their preliminary diagnosis of students, teachers in our reading center collect five or six writing samples and analyze the students' writing across those samples. They try to collect different genres of writing to measure students' abilities to match genres to purposes for writing: description, informational, expository, and a personal narrative of an event. For students in the early phases of literacy development, they include at least one piece of dictation, using an adapted language experience approach (LEA). The LEA provides the opportunity to compare students' abilities to compose and effectively convey meaning through print when the constraints of physically producing letters and sounds are removed. This helps the teachers focus their attention on what students already know about using written language and how to support their continued development (Johnston & Rogers, 2003).

First, the teachers collect background information about students as described in Chapter 3; then they determine students' reading levels using an informal reading inventory as described in Chapter 5 and analyze the results. As they are collecting this information, the teachers ask students to write for several different purposes, and then evaluate the writing samples based on the students reading levels. Thus, the writing samples from an eighth-grade student reading at a fourth-grade level would be evaluated using the criteria for a student at the intermediate level.

In the early phases of literacy development, reading teachers examine students' writing for conventions of print: left-to-right progression, top-to-bottom arrangement on the page, separation of individual words, and phonological representations of words. They also examine students' use of print versus drawing or scribbling. Examples of the forms used to analyze students' writing are included on the website for this text.

For students reading at a primer level through level 2, examine their abilities to present ideas in sequential order or in logical sequence. Also, consider their abilities to organize words into sentences and beginning paragraph organization, including appropriate punctuation.

For students reading at levels 3 through 5, examine their abilities to select appropriate genres of writing for different purposes. Also, consider paragraph organization, including topic sentences and supporting details. At these levels, teachers should expect conventional representation of spelling patterns and varied punctuation.

For students reading at levels 6 through 12, expect appropriate genre selection, conventional spelling, varied sentence structure, and correct punctuation. Also, expect paragraphs to include topic sentences and supporting details. Teachers should expect students to provide main ideas with subordinate sentences and to present a logical argument with supportive positions.

Interactive assessment should occur throughout instruction to monitor students' progress and to provide guidance for instructional decisions (Johnston & Rogers, 2003). Thus, as students write summaries of what they have read, write new endings to stories, or write their own stories, periodically compare their writing to their previous samples to ensure that instruction is meeting their needs and resulting in progress commensurate with their progress in reading.

Writing Instruction

Many instructional strategies can be used successfully with students who have reading problems. Students learn that a person writes for different purposes and for different audiences. For example, you use lists to organize your life and letters, email, or text messages to communicate with friends and family and you use reports to convey information.

This section first describes the writing process that students may use as they develop thoughts into finished written pieces. It then explores three more specific types of personal writing: written conversations, personal correspondence, and personal journals.

Writing Process

Teachers use the writing process to help students become joyful, proficient composers of text. This process has several stages, which range from a first idea to the creation of a formal product. In completing these stages, students in the reading center have come to write more easily and naturally. They have also become proud authors of written pieces that are now part of our library.

Selecting Topics.   Topic selection is a key feature of good writing. Students are more willing to write if they choose what to write about. In shaping their content, they also think about the audience who will listen to or read their pieces.

At first, students tend to do personal writing about their own experiences. Topics may include someone they know, a special event, or themselves. Ideally, students should select their own topics; however, struggling readers often have little confidence in themselves as writers. Teachers can help these students by asking them to make lists of people who are special to them. While students were creating their lists, Ms. Grant, a third-grade teacher wrote her own list on the board:

Special People
Granddaddy

Mother

Betty, my sister

Dad

Next, Ms. Grant shared her list with the students and explained briefly why she chose these people. Finally, she encouraged students to share their lists. Then, she asked students to choose one person to write about. While students wrote about their topic, she wrote about hers. When beginning the writing process, you may want to stop periodically to support students in their efforts.

Of course, some students may wish to write reports or letters rather than doing personal writing. Because topic selection is important, you should honor these choices.

Writing Drafts.   After topic selection, students begin writing drafts. Encourage your students to write what comes to mind about their topics. Students need not worry about spelling, punctuation, or the other mechanical aspects of writing as they draft their thoughts.

Next, give students opportunities to share their writing with a few of their classmates. Remind the classmates that they should only tell their friends what they like about their writing at this point.

You may devote several writing sessions to topic selection, drafting, and responding positively to students' writing. This procedure helps students develop the habit of writing on a regular basis and builds their confidence in an accepting environment.

Making Revisions.   As ideas become clearer, writers revise their pieces. Mature writers do this constantly, making many insertions, deletions, and other changes. However, students with problems in reading and writing are often reluctant to revise. Sometimes, just writing a draft has required extensive effort and making revisions seems overwhelming.

Teachers can use several strategies to encourage revision. First, teachers can model revision in dictated stories and in their own work so that students view revision as a natural part of the writing process. Share one of your unfinished pieces and ask students for suggestions. Use their responses to make changes in your own writing and share the revised version with students in the next lesson.

When students meet to share their drafts, revision is often fostered through suggestions. Writers may find that others have questions about things that are unclear or suggestions for improvement. However, sharing drafts should also be a positive experience. First, have students identify something they like about the draft that is being shared. Only then should they ask questions and make suggestions. To model the concept that it is acceptable to question each others' writing and to make suggestions, have students ask questions of an author of a book you have read to them.

For your more reluctant revisers, try transforming an existing text into another genre. For example, you might alter a fairy tale from its narrative version to create a play. In this process, students must revise the text to create a script. After trying this activity with well-known stories, students are usually better able to write their own stories and are more willing to make revisions.

Editing.   When students are satisfied with the content, they are ready to focus on mechanics (spelling, punctuation, and grammar), which are important so that someone else can easily read their pieces. Do not overburden students with changes. Guidelines that foster editing include:

 ◆ Focus on items that can be changed immediately.
 ◆ Limit suggestions to items that have been presented in instruction.
 ◆ Make no more than three suggestions to younger students and no more than five to older students.

Make notes about items that cannot be changed easily and save these for later instruction. Explicit instruction that addresses revision or editing concerns can be given as short minilessons during writing time.

Publishing.   When the editing process is complete, the writing is ready to be shared with a wider audience. Graves (1994) refers to this as "publishing." Publishing is not limited to binding a book and sharing it with the class or placing it in a classroom library. Publishing may consist of a presentation, a bulletin board display, a play, or even a puppet show. Opportunities to publish for audiences beyond the classroom are especially motivating for many students. School-wide or cross-school poetry slams and readers' theater can provide students with opportunities to share their writing as well as enhance their reading and reading fluency. District-wide writing fairs can be held for students to share their best writing. As students write throughout the year, they are aware that they may select one of their pieces to represent their best writing as part of the writing fair (Strickland, Ganske, & Monroe, 2002). As the writing process develops, students' contributions will fill your literacy environment.

Evaluation of Writing.   In guiding students to improve their writing, teachers must be able to evaluate their pieces. The evaluation of writing should focus on several levels, including content, organization of ideas, structure, and mechanics. By evaluating each, they gain a broad overview of a student's writing capabilities. To permit organized evaluation, start with the most general level—the content—and work toward the most specific—mechanics.

As a teacher, first, focus on content, the ability of the student to communicate thought. Ask two questions about the student's piece: "Does this student have an understanding that writing is a means of communication?" and "Does this student use writing effectively to express his or her ideas?"

Second, focus on the student's ability to organize ideas. For students in the beginning stages of writing, organization may consist of the ability to write information in sentences. Later, evaluate primary students' ability to present ideas in sequential order. For intermediate-level writers, evaluate abilities to organize related ideas into paragraphs. For more mature writers, evaluate the ability to organize paragraphs and sections of papers by related ideas.

Third, evaluate structure—the ability to use different writing forms, or genres, appropriately. For older students, focus on the characteristics of specific formats, such as an essay or thesis. For students in the beginning stages of writing, focus on sentences and grammatical structure. For intermediate students, judge paragraph structure as well.

Finally, after a selection of writing has been evaluated for content, organization, and structure, focus on the mechanics. Mechanics include spelling, punctuation, and proper use of capitalization.

From this evaluation, you can make decisions about a student's instructional needs on several different levels. For example, students may need help on aspects of writing as broad as how to write a letter or as narrow as using an apostrophe.

Evaluation leads you to two instructional decisions. First, decide what the student should correct to make his or her writing more easily read by others. This decision depends on the level of the student's reading ability. In addition, limit your corrections to areas that the student has been taught previously. The second decision is what the student needs to learn next in instruction. From the second decision, formulate instructional plans and present minilessons, short lessons focused on specific aspects of writing.

Supporting Students' Writing

In the early phases of literacy development, much of students' writing focuses on developing concepts about print, phonological awareness, and word identification. However, teachers know that the concurrent development of students' understandings about stories and story grammar is also important (see Chapter 7). Thus, in early literacy development, teachers provide extensive support for the physical act of writing by assuming the role of scribe while students engage in composing texts. As students become more proficient in letter production and sound representation, teachers gradually release responsibility for more of the writing process to students. This approach to writing instruction and the gradual release of responsibility to students parallels the reciprocal teaching approach advocated in comprehension instruction (Shanahan, 2005; Palinscar & Brown, 1984). Teachers must constantly assess students' writing to determine levels of expectations and how much responsibility to relinquish. In other words, teachers want to make sure they are guiding students within their zones of proximal development (Vanderburg, 2006). The next section provides descriptions of varying levels of scaffolding provided in writing instruction.

Modeled Writing.   We begin with modeled writing, often in the form of the morning message. In primary classrooms, teachers often start the day with a morning message to preview the day and to build background knowledge for the day's learning experiences. As students become more experienced, this activity shifts to incorporate more student input (Mariage, 2001).

Interactive Writing.   As students gain experience and develop an understanding of the teacher's expectations for morning message as well as the day's routines, they begin to contribute to the content of the morning message (Figure 13.1). Although the process shifts to look more like language experience activity, with students dictating the content and teachers assuming the role of scribe, it differs in that the teacher knows some components of the morning message that the students don't yet know. For example, the students may contribute to the "news" portion of the morning message while the teacher introduces the story and other learning experiences.

In this example, the teacher began the procedure with the first paragraph already written on the board as the students entered the room. She began the second paragraph, and Luis contributed the fact that his grandfather planned to read a story from Puerto Rico. The teacher asked the students if they could remember what she had told them they would begin studying in math, and the teacher and students constructed the first sentence together. The children added the sentence about needing their counters based on their experience with learning new concepts. The teacher contributed the first sentence of the paragraph about science, and one of the children added the sentence about hoping to see pictures of lava based on a television show he had seen. Then the teacher asked if the students had any news to add, and Carol added the information about her new brother.

FIGURE 13.1   Morning Message

Today is Wednesday, April, 16 2008. This morning, we will read a story about a girl named Madlenka, who wants to tell all of her neighbors that she has a loose tooth.

Luis's grandfather will visit during story time today. He will read a story about his country, Puerto Rico.

In math, we will learn about adding numbers between 10 and 20. We will need our counters.

In science, we will read about volcanoes. We hope we will see pictures of red lava.

Carol has some news. Last week, Carol's mother had a baby. Carol has a new brother named Josh.

Thus, the responsibility for composing the morning message flowed back and forth between the teacher and the students. Because this particular morning message occurred late in the year, the teacher carried the process a little further to "share the pen" (Rubadue, 2002). As the teacher was writing, she invited individual children to come to the board and write parts of the message. Luis wrote his own name. David used labels from bins in the classroom to help him write *counters*. Carol not only contributed the news paragraph, but she also wrote her own name as well as the word *baby* and the beginning letter of *Josh*.

Guided Writing.   As students gain understanding and confidence, more of the responsibility for writing is relinquished to them. Guided writing may occur in whole group, small group, or individual instruction. In guided writing, the students do the actual writing, but the teacher provides support as needed. Teachers may model topic selection or offer "limited choice" topic selection. Especially when relating reading and writing, teachers may guide the prewriting component of organizing by providing a graphic organizer to help students plan their writing. Teachers also establish classroom routines for sharing, responding to peers, revising, and editing. Guided writing occurs with all kinds of writing: stories, letters, journal entries, or reports. It is a gradual release of responsibility to foster students' independent writing (Olness, 2005).

Independent Writing.   As with reading, the goal of writing instruction is independence. In independent writing, students initiate writing, provide their own structures for moving through the process, and engage writing as a natural part of the learning process as well as an avenue for reflection and pleasure. Students may reach independence in writing for some purposes while needing guidance in writing for other purposes. Often, students who are struggling in reading continue to need support in writing throughout their school years (Olness, 2005; Strickland, et al., 2002).

Personal Communication

Writing provides a means of sharing information about our personal lives with each other. As mature writers, we text, email, send cards and letters, and leave notes for family members. Students should emulate the purposes for written communication.

Written Conversations

In the written conversations strategy, developed by Carolyn Burke (Anderson, 1984), two students, or a student and a teacher, sit beside each other and communicate. The partners cannot speak; writing is the only communication allowed. If one person's message is unclear, the partner must ask for clarification in writing. Using this activity on a regular basis helps students learn to record their thoughts in writing.

This strategy is often used in the reading center as a way of "catching up on the news" with students. Instead of asking how things are going, the teacher writes a greeting and question to the student; the student, in turn, responds in writing. You can use different colored pens or pencils and date each page.

Some teachers like to have both partners writing at the same time. Other teachers prefer to have participants use one paper and take turns writing. Each session can include two or three exchanges.

If a teacher and a student form a partnership, the teacher can model correct spellings and grammatical structures in his or her responses. Over several weeks, you often notice significant improvements in a student's writing. Figure 13.2 presents an example of a written conversation between a teacher and her student in the reading center.

Of course, students also enjoy forming partnerships with one another. When two students are paired, they may form friendships and share interests and everyday experiences with their partners.

In a variation of written conversations called *personal correspondence*, students are assigned a pen pal to communicate with over a longer period of time. Partners may be in the same school, but they should not be in the same class. This activity is especially nice for establishing cross-grade partnerships. The older students' writing models the patterns the younger students need to learn, and older students become more aware

FIGURE 13.2   A Written Conversation

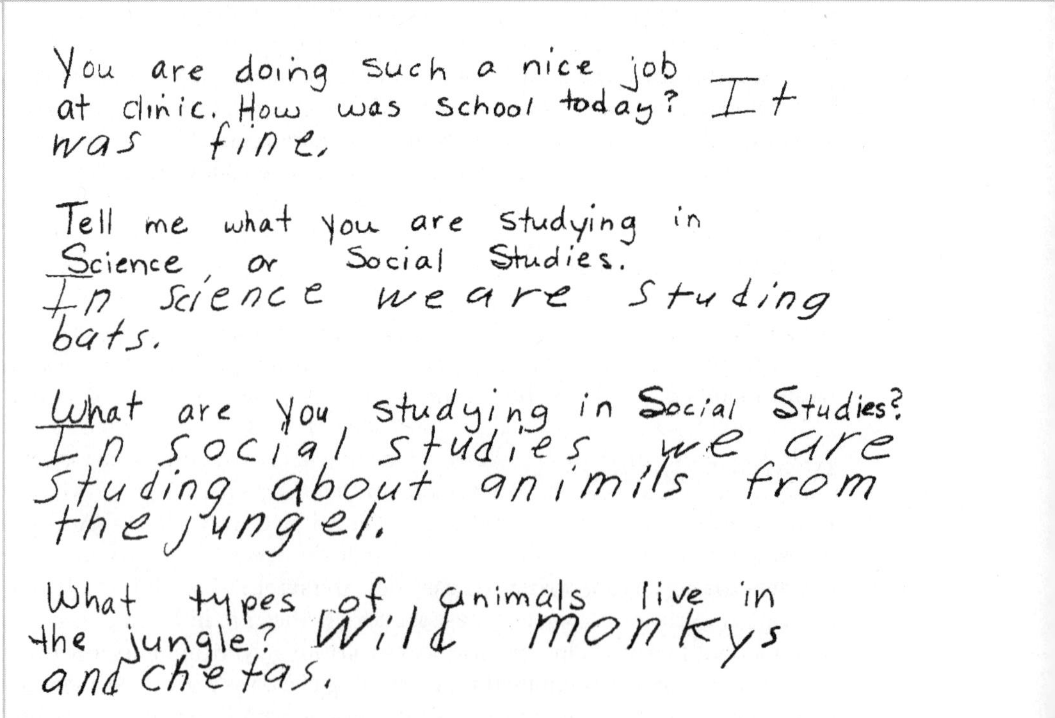

You are doing such a nice job at clinic. How was school today? It was fine.

Tell me what you are studying in Science, or Social Studies. In science we are studing bats.

What are you studying in Social Studies? In social studies we are studing about animils from the jungel.

What types of animals live in the jungle? Wild monkys and chetas.

of making their writing clear for their younger pen pals. The teacher can serve as the "mail carrier," or a student can be assigned the job.

Personal Journals

In personal journals, students reflect on events or experiences as is done in diaries; they practice recording personal experiences in writing. Usually, journals provide day-to-day records of events in their lives and how they felt about them.

When students maintain personal journals, they create a record of their own thoughts and feelings, which they can later read. To begin, each student needs a personal journal, usually a notebook of lined paper. Students may want to include titles for their journals or decorate them. Time is set aside, usually three or four periods a week, to record personal thoughts in journals. Ask students to write only on one side of a page.

After writing, a few students may choose to read their reflections to their classmates and ask for their responses. In addition, the teacher can collect journals, read them, and write responses. However, students may not want to share all of their journal entries. To preserve privacy, students can simply fold a page in half, lengthwise, to cover it; the teacher should not read folded pages. In responding to journals, teachers should be careful not to correct grammatical and spelling errors, because this practice undermines the student's confidence and may lessen the amount of writing. Instead, try to respond personally to the content of the student's message. Try to use words the student originally misspelled in your responses so that the student can see the words spelled correctly.

Sometimes, students with reading problems have such low self-esteem that they lack the confidence to maintain journals. They often feel that their lives are not important enough to deserve recording. Teachers can help students overcome this problem by modeling journal writing about everyday issues they address.

Students with reading problems sometimes have difficulty thinking of journal topics. To help them, supply one category for each of the first six journal writing sessions and ask them to brainstorm a list within this category. Then, they choose one idea from their list and write about it. Topics might include favorite places, special people, favorite stories, things I like to do, things I don't like to do, things that make me angry, and things I do well. To help them keep a record of these ideas, students create an "Ideas to Write About" page in their journals.

After engaging in journal writing using this technique six times, students are ready to choose their own topics without guidance. Then, if students have trouble thinking of a topic, suggest they use one of the topics from their "ideas" page.

Strategies for Integrating Reading and Writing

This section discusses ways to incorporate writing into reading instruction. Included are strategies for responding to narrative and informational text. Students need opportunities to reflect about their reading and to respond to it thoughtfully. Writing their thoughts about materials they are reading helps students to organize the ideas presented in the text and increases their comprehension (Fletcher & Portalupi, 2001; Calkins, 1994, 2000). As they formulate these responses, they also improve their writing skills.

Writing and Reading Narrative Text

Many motivating formats can be used to help students with reading problems. These formats include writing as a prereading experience, scripted stories, rewritten stories, and reader response journals.

Writing as a Prereading Experience.   Teachers often use writing prior to reading stories to provide support for students' reading. In the story impressions strategy (Blachowicz & Fisher, 2002; Fisher, 1998; McGinley & Denner, 1987), teachers present students with a list of words and phrases from a story and have the students construct sentences that predict the plot. Semantic impressions, a strategy similar to story impressions, is presented in Chapter 11 for story comprehension. A teacher in the reading center presented the following list of words from *The Knight Who Was Afraid of the Dark* (by Hazen) to her student:

> Dark Ages
> Sir Fred
> knight
> afraid
> darkness
> bully
> Melvin the Miffed
> spy
> Lady Wendylyn
> love
> banner
> secret meeting

The student wrote the following possible sentences:

> Long ago in the Dark Ages, there lived a knight named Sir Fred.
> Sir Fred was the bravest knight in the land, but he was afraid of one thing—darkness.
> One day a big bully came to the village, Melvin the Miffed.
> Melvin was mad because he wanted to marry Lady Wendylyn, but she said no.
> One night Melvin decided to spy on Lady Wendylyn.
> He wanted to see if she was in love with someone else.
> Melvin saw Lady Wendylyn making a banner for the village fair.
> The banner had a picture of Sir Fred on his horse.
> Melvin went to Sir Fred and told him that Lady Wendylyn wanted to meet him.
> But they had to have a secret meeting at the castle at midnight.
> Sir Fred was afraid, but he loved Lady Wendylyn.
> Would he be brave enough to meet her?

Two other strategies that have proved successful in supporting students' understanding of narrative text include writing the story before reading and autobiographical prewriting. Using these two strategies has helped engage students in their reading and has deepened their appreciation for and understanding of text (Weech, 1994; White, 1995).

White (1995) used writing to help ninth-grade students relate to stories to be read. Students were asked to respond to questions that were designed to help them activate background knowledge and personal experiences relevant to the stories to be read. White found this strategy to be highly effective in increasing students' engagement in the story, identification with characters, and understanding of the concepts presented.

Weech (1994) uses another kind of prereading strategy in which she has students write the story before reading it. She presents the students with scenarios, actions they must assume to have committed. These scenarios are related to events in the story to be read. For example, in preparing students to read *The Rime of the Ancient Mariner* (by Coleridge), Ms. Weech had students respond to three different situations: (1) Some were friends who revealed a secret they had promised to keep; (2) some were to assume they had lost a precious family heirloom but were to pretend they hadn't; and (3) some were to assume they had accidentally killed a mother bird leaving the babies in the nest. Having students assume these roles and substantiate or defend their actions helped them relate to literature that sometimes seems irrelevant to contemporary adolescents.

Scripted Stories. Patterned, or scripted, writing is a good strategy for beginning readers. In this strategy, the teacher shares a predictable book or poem with students. Then the students write their own version, altering the author's version slightly. This activity gives them the security of a writing frame that they can use to form their own, personalized response. Children love to substitute people and objects from their own experiences in response to Bill Martin's *Brown Bear, Brown Bear, What Do You See?*

Scripted writing encourages students to use their imaginations and practice words they meet in reading as they build their own confidence as writers. Good books to use for scripted writing include *Goodnight, Mr. Fly* (Jacobs), *Polar Bear, Polar Bear* (Martin), and *Alligator Pie* and *Jump Frog, Jump* (Lee). Useful poems are contained in *Beneath a Blue Umbrella, Poems by A. Nonny Mouse, Zoo Doings*, and *Laughing Out Loud* (Prelutsky); *Honey, I Love* (Greenfield); *The Pocketbook Book of Ogden Nash* (Nash); *Sing a Soft Black Song* (Giovanni); and *The Big O, The Missing Piece, Where the Sidewalk Ends*, and *A Light in the Attic* (Silverstein).

A group of kindergarten children dictated their own version of *Alligator Pie* presented in Figure 13.3.

Following the dictation, the teacher wrote each line on a page, and the students chose their favorites and illustrated them. Then the teacher bound the book and it became a favorite in the classroom library.

Rewritten Stories. Having students rewrite stories is invaluable in providing a model for story structure, enhancing language development, and comprehending text. This activity can be used along with comprehension strategies, such as the directed reading-thinking activity or story grammar (see Chapter 10).

After your students have read a story, ask them to recreate it in their own words. Young children who have difficulty with the mechanics of writing may prefer to

---

FIGURE 13.3   Scripted Story in Response to *Alligator Pie*

Alligator sandwich, alligator sandwich

If I don't get some, I think I'm gonna itch

Alligator drink, alligator drink

If I don't get some, I might turn pink

Alligator ice cream, Alligator ice cream

It's so good, it's like a happy dream

Source: Adapted from *Alligator Pie* by Lee (2008).

---

dictate a story version to the teacher. Older students are usually able to write their own versions. In creating their own rewritten versions of stories, students need to reflect upon the structure of the story they have read. You can provide guidance for this activity in several ways:

◆ Use a story grammar and have students identify a character, setting, problem, and events. Then have students make sure they include these elements as they reconstruct the story. Thus, they become familiar with the story grammar elements and begin to use them as they create their own stories.

◆ Students can tell or write about a story they have read but take another point of view. As an example, you might use *The True Story of the Three Little Pigs* (by Sciesza), which retells the classic fairy tale from the wolf's point of view. Then students can create their own versions of classics, for example, rewriting *Snow White* from the stepmother's perspective.

◆ Students can rewrite by assuming a role within a story they have read. Lauren, a sixth grader in the reading center, read the book *If You Grew Up with George Washington* (Fritz) and then rewrote it, casting herself as the main character. A selection from the resulting book, "If You Grew Up with Lauren Lang," is shown in Figure 13.4.

We've all read stories with disappointing or surprising endings. Students may be asked to write their own endings to such stories. After reading "The Garden Party" (Mansfield), Karen, a high school student, wanted to change the ending (see Figure 13.5).

Reader Response Journals.   A reading journal is used to write personal reactions to reading. Reading journals provide students with opportunities to connect reading to their own experiences.

These journals can also provide teachers with valuable feedback about students' understanding of ideas presented in text. When students respond to a story in writing, the teacher can tell whether they understood the story (Cahill, 2004; Farr, Lewis, Fasholz, Pinsky, Towle, Lipschutz, & Faulds, 1990).

FIGURE 13.4 A Rewritten Story of "If You Grew Up with Lauren Lang"

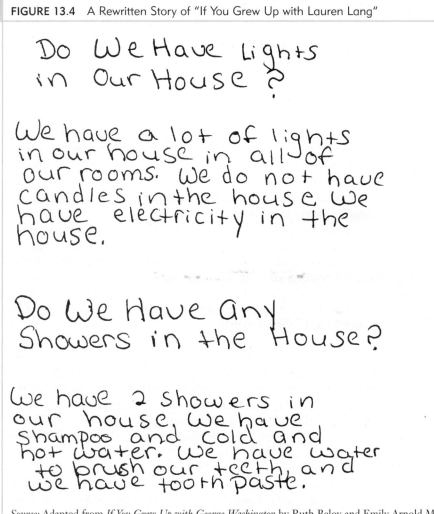

Do We Have Lights in Our House?

We have a lot of lights in our house in all of our rooms. We do not have candles in the house We have electricity in the house.

Do We Have any Showers in the House?

We have 2 showers in our house, We have shampoo and cold and hot water. We have water to brush our teeth, and we have tooth paste.

Source: Adapted from *If You Grew Up with George Washington* by Ruth Belov and Emily Arnold McCully © (1993), published by Scholastic, Inc.

To introduce reading journals, start by writing about something you and your students have read together, such as a short story. Try to connect the story to the students' own experiences. Students also like to use reading journals as opportunities to critique stories. At times, you can ask students to give "stars" in their journals to something they have read, ranging from one ("I hated it") to four ("I loved it"). Then, beneath the stars, ask them to explain why a chapter or story received this rating.

Teachers may also ask students to write about their favorite characters. Asking students to write about why they think the author had a character act in a certain way helps to make them more aware of how authors create stories. This awareness helps students when they write their own stories. Keeping a record of their own reactions to a character's development in a reading journal fosters students' literary appreciation.

FIGURE 13.5   Karen's Ending to "The Garden Party" by Mansfield

I think Laura would have said, "Isn't life a learning experience?" The reason why I think Laura would have said this is because Laura has learned that life isn't always joy and happiness, but pain and sorrowful.

Karen's new ending caused her to reflect more on the story, and she gained further insight into the story and wrote more:

I think Laura also learned about her own life. She has lived a sheltered life. Now she realizes that people don't have to dress nicely to be good. She realizes this when she apologizes for her hat.

Some teachers write responses to students' reading journals, thus making them into reading dialogue journals. Through these written responses, teachers can enhance a student's understanding, correct misunderstandings, offer a different perspective, or simply share a mutual appreciation for a story.

A special kind of response journal, the dialogue journal, provides an excellent opportunity for students and teachers to interact about text. In dialogue journals, students use a letter format to respond to materials read. Teachers can initiate the interaction by writing a letter to a student asking about a particular character or about the student's favorite event in the story.

When using dialogue journals, students should have opportunities to write not only to teachers but to one another as well. Students write differently to different audiences. When writing to teachers, students usually provide more thorough retellings, perhaps to show the teacher they have actually read the story. However, when writing to classmates, students usually write abstracts of the stories and focus more attention on evaluating and recommending books they have read (Wells, 1992–1993).

We have used an adaptation of the dialogue journal with students in book clubs. First, we established book clubs at the primary, intermediate, and middle-level grades. At the first meeting of each club, we collected information about the students, including email addresses. Then we established a listserv for each book club. After the second meeting, when students were engaged in conversations about the books, we initiated a discussion thread for students' responses. These discussion threads have maintained active participation between book club meetings and provided an avenue for ongoing support as students read outside of meeting time.

Writing and Reading Informational Text

This section presents strategies for responding to informational texts that students read. In using these written responses, students are able to absorb, organize, and reflect on information more effectively and fully.

Learning Journals.   In a learning journal or log, teachers ask students to write the most important things that they learned from a content area, such as social studies or science. Students may respond to a chapter in a textbook, an article, or a lesson. Students are also free to ask questions in their journals, and if a teacher notices a misunderstanding, he or she may clarify it for the student. Learning journals are especially helpful in content areas (Strickland, et al., 2002; Giacobbe, 1986). By asking students to describe what they have learned, teachers can see which concepts need reteaching. In this way, writing can help content-area teachers teach diagnostically. Unrau (2008) found that his responses to students' logs and his sharing of good examples precipitated improved writing as well as improved comprehension. Figure 13.6 presents a sample of a learning journal entry by a student in the reading center. This entry was written in response to a science article about peccaries.

RAFT.   This strategy helps students to develop imaginative responses by assuming different roles and tasks in writing (Santa, Havens, & Harrison, 1989). RAFT stands for:

    Role—who is writing

    Audience—who is being written to

    Format—the type of writing being done

    Topic—what is being written about

FIGURE 13.6   Robin's Learning Journal Entry

THE PECCARY

Today I read about a peccary. I read that peccaries eat thorns, weeds, roots, cactus, and nuts. They live in Arizona, Texas, New Mexico, North America, South America, and Central America. The paper said they make sounds like a dog. They look like a pig and on their neck it is white and then it turns brown.

Each of these four parts of writing can vary. For example, a role may include any character or object that has been studied. Students may write from the point of view of a participant in a historical event or of a cell in a biological function. In addition, any other character or object can form an audience. A student may write to another cell or to a historical figure on the opposing side. Formats can also vary. Students can write a letter, poetry, an invitation, a television script, a telegram, or a complaint. Finally, students can choose any one of a number of topics to write about.

One middle school teacher of struggling students was having difficulty teaching the scientific concepts of matter. To enliven this subject, she asked each student to choose one of three roles: a solid water molecule, a liquid water molecule, or a gas molecule. Students were also free to choose their audiences, formats, and topics. One student, for example, chose to be a liquid water molecule writing to the cloud from which he had come. His format was a letter, and the topic concerned what it felt like to be in a raindrop. The RAFT activity dramatically increased learning and enthusiasm in this science classroom.

Teachers may assign RAFT tasks or let the students choose them. The more varied the RAFT choices, the more students will develop an appreciation for other points of view and possibilities. Santa, Havens, and Harrison (1989) suggest that teachers avoid the word write and instead use more precise words, such as describe, convince, or explain, in assignments. These terms encourage students to be more precise in their writing and to develop the ability to write persuasively.

Figure 13.7 shows a RAFT written by a fifth-grade student during a unit on the fight for independence. In this RAFT, the student has assumed the role of an American officer. The audience was not specified because the format was a personal journal entry. However, the student indicated that he thought the officer would like to keep a journal to give to his children after the war. The topic as provided by the section of the chapter being studied: "Winning the War."

Writing with Poetry

When students write poetry, they use language actively and express themselves in imaginative ways. However, students with reading problems have difficulty writing poetry that rhymes because imposing rhyming patterns on your thoughts requires almost professional-level skill. For this reason, you should encourage students to write poetry that doesn't rhyme.

To be effective in teaching students to write poetry, teachers must be willing to become poets as well. They should write their own poetry and write collaboratively with their students. Parr and Campbell (2006) offer these suggestions for teaching poetry in your classrooms:

1. Look at any preconceived notions that you and your students may have about poetry.
2. Develop a poetry-rich environment to share your love and respect for poetry.
3. Discover poetry in everyday experiences.

FIGURE 13.7 Murray's RAFT about "Winning the War"

> Part 3 Winning the War/Journal of an American Officer
>
> December 19th, 1778 Valley Forge We are having a very hard winter here in Valley Forge. While the British are in Philidelpheia in people's homes, we are starving and freezing to death. Even in my cabin its cold. We are suffering heavy losses. My favorite soldier, Robert Price has died. Not only he died 2,999 others died too. We are having very hard time. But we are getting better. Baron Von Steuben of Prussia is helping us in many ways. He is turning our group of poorly trained men into a well-trained Prussian army!

4. Focus on process rather than product; this will foster students' enjoyment.
5. Be a poet and engage your students in writing poetry; accept your current level and move forward.
6. Support students' writing and move them forward gradually. Take risks yourself and encourage your students to do so.
7. Create a comfortable environment for sharing poetry.
8. Keep it fun!

FIGURE 13.8   Character Poem

Format for Character Poem	Jennifer's Character Poem
First name	Jennifer
Three words describing yourself	Shopper, athlete, pretty
Sister/brother/daughter/son of . . .	Sister of Steven
Who likes . . .	Who likes birds and basketball
Who fears . . .	Who fears the dark
Lives in . . .	Lives in Chicago
Last Name	Smithers

Students with reading problems often feel more comfortable creating poetry from structured formats. Character poems provide a high comfort level as well as an opportunity for getting acquainted. One of the formats the reading center students enjoy is presented in Figure 13.8.

In Strategy Snapshot 13.1, teacher Mary Welch uses the poetic formats of haiku and rap to help Eddie, a disabled high school student, record his interests.

A third-grade class with many low-achieving students read "Sarah Cynthia Sylvia Stout Would Not Take the Garbage Out," a poem by Shel Silverstein in *Where the Sidewalk Ends*, about the fate that befell a child who refused to take out garbage. Students were asked to use each of their five senses to describe what they thought the garbage would be like. The class created a book consisting of five pages, one for each sense.

Examples of what the garbage felt like included:

It's gooey around you.

Gook

Mashed potatoes

Mud

Yuck

Nasty stuff

A soft chicken

The class book was decorated with illustrations by several students and placed in the classroom library.

Developing the Ability to Spell

To make their writing more easily read by others, students need to learn to spell. Spelling is best developed by practice; daily writing experiences develop good spelling

Strategy Snapshot 13.1

Eddie Writes Poetry

Mary Welch (Shapiro & Welch, 1991) used poetry to motivate and instruct Eddie, a 15-year-old boy classified as severely learning disabled and reading five years below his grade level. He wrote poems with different forms. Eddie extended his expertise into haiku, a poem of three lines, using the following format:

> Line 1: What or who (5 syllables)
> Line 2: Feeling, action, or description (7 syllables)
> Line 3: A summative phrase (5 syllables)

Eddie wrote about his favorite motorcycle:

> Harley Davidson
> Ride into the setting sun
> Stay with their design.

Eddie also wrote raps:

> Harleys are cool, especially when they're blue
> They look so fine, all of the time
> When I go for a ride, everybody wants a ride
> If I say no, you'll say go!
> So bye-bye, it's time to fly

To help Eddie use his interest in music to improve his reading, Mary used *The Poetry of Rock* (Goldstein, 1969), which features the lyrics to popular songs. One of the best outcomes of Eddie's program was his growing sense of power as he taught Ms. Welch important facts about cars and motorcycles.

abilities. This writing should be done for genuine purposes and specific audiences rather than just being writing "exercises" (Gentry & Gillet, 1993). In addition to writing, however, many students with reading problems need more explicit instruction in spelling.

Spelling is challenging for many people, even some who read well. Students who have reading problems are almost always poor spellers. Spelling is certainly more difficult than reading. The context, structural analysis, and meaning clues that help you to read a written word are not present when you want to spell it. In reading, you can sometimes substitute a word for an unfamiliar one and maintain meaning for the text. In spelling, only one pattern of letters is accepted as correct; no substitutions are allowed. Finally, the correspondence between spoken sounds and written forms in English is not always consistent.

Reading, writing, and spelling are closely related. Learning letter-sound associations in reading helps you use them in spelling. As children read, they repeatedly see words spelled correctly. As their reading and writing develop, students learn regular sound-letter patterns, which they use to read new words and to spell (Gentry, 2004; Ehri, 2000; Wong, 1986; Henderson, 1985).

Spelling Development

Just as children go through stages when learning to talk, they go through stages in learning to communicate in print. Much research has focused on the concept of invented spelling. For example, Read (1971, 1975) has documented that preschool children use the sounds of letter names to write words before formal instruction. Children follow similar sequences as they learn to spell, although they may go through phases at different rates (Gentry, 2004; Morrow, 2004; Gentry & Gillet, 1993; Henderson, 1981).

Drawing and Scribbling.   Children in early stages of literacy may draw pictures to communicate ideas. As they become aware that adults communicate through lines and squiggles on paper, they begin to do so too.

Precommunicative Stage.   When children become aware that writing uses letters, they begin to make strings of letters. They may make no connection between letter sounds and names. Instead, children simply write letters they have seen in their environment, such as a cursive K made the way it appears on a cereal box. Adults usually cannot read what children have written at this stage. In fact, children themselves often cannot reread what they have written unless they read it immediately.

Semiphonetic Stage.   When children become aware that letters are associated with sounds, they begin to use letter names to help them in their writing. They may write only one letter (usually the first sound) to represent an entire word. Frequently, one string of letters, without spaces, represents an entire sentence or several sentences. Although children can often immediately reread what they write, teachers seldom can. Thus, having the child read the message to you is important so that you are aware of instructional needs.

Phonetic Stage.   Once children understand what words are, they can identify sounds within them. At the phonetic stage, students write all the sounds they hear in words. Although these "invented" spellings may not look like the English spellings, they are systematic and phonetically correct. Students at this stage still use letter names to determine which letters to write, but each sound is represented, and adults can often read them.

Transitional Stage.   As students receive reading and writing instruction, they become aware that print represents visual characteristics of words as well as sounds. For example, rather than writing the *r* that they hear for the last syllable in letter, they now begin to use the conventional English *er* to represent this final syllable. Frequently, students will overgeneralize patterns. After students learn the word *enough*, they may overuse the letters *gh* to represent the *f* sound in other words. Most students now separate words by spaces. Often students in the transitional stage become reluctant to take risks in writing and use only words they know how to spell.

Conventional Stage.   In this stage, students use all aspects of print to represent words. They know that letters represent specific sound patterns. They are also aware that some patterns differ from the typical English letter-sound correspondence.

Based on research by Ehri (1997, 2004), Gentry (2007) espouses a phase theory to describe early literacy development. Gentry (2004) describes five levels of early writing as presented in Figure 13.9. The terms for the levels are attributed to Ehri (1997).

Spelling Assessment

Teachers can learn a great deal about students' word knowledge by analyzing samples of their writing. However, students with reading problems often choose only familiar words in their writing. For this reason, spelling tests provide valuable tools for analyzing students' word knowledge.

Spelling, writing, and reading develop concurrently and provide support for each other as students engage in literacy experiences. Thus, in the early stages of spelling, instruction should provide connections between phonemic awareness and spelling. As students advance in reading and writing, their spelling instruction should reflect the morphophonemic aspects of word knowledge as they learn base words and affixes. Finally, the focus should be bases and derivatives.

FIGURE 13.9   Gentry's Writing Scale Levels of Early Spelling

Level	*Characteristics*
Non-Alphabetic	Writer may scribble in letter-like forms but does not use real alphabetic letters.
Pre-Alphabetic	Writes random letters with no letter-sound correspondence
Partial Alphabetic	Uses letters to represent sounds
	Sometimes uses vowels, but not consistently
	May mix some memorized conventional spelling with developmental spelling
Full Alphabetic	Almost all sounds in words are represented by letters, but some may be represented by letter sounds rather than conventional patterns. For example, the letter *r* may represent an entire syllable: the student may write *batr* for the word *batter*.
	Quite a few sight words (from reading) may be mixed with developmental spelling
Consolidated Alphabetic	Begins to use patterns, syllables, and chunks of letters to represent sounds. Can spell most *consonant-vowel-consonant* patterns conventionally. Uses known words to represent unfamiliar chunks of words. For example, may use the word *you* to represent the long *u* sound.

To assess students' abilities to apply phonics skills, ask them to write unfamiliar words. In *Teaching Kids to Spell* Gentry and Gillet (1993) designed a developmental spelling test for primary children that includes 10 words:

monster	human
united	eagle
dress	closed
bottom	bumped
hiked	type

Gentry says to pronounce each word, give a sentence using that word, and repeat the word. Teachers should tell their students that the words are too difficult for most first and second graders to spell but that they are to write their best guesses. In analyzing the spellings, teachers should classify the students' responses and analyze specific patterns to determine instructional needs (Gentry & Gillet, 1993).

Gillet and Temple (2000) have more recently designed two spelling inventories to analyze students' spelling and document progress. Developmental Spelling Inventory I is for use with Grades K through 2. This test consists of 16 words, presented in two sessions. In the first session, teachers present eight words:

fish	learned
bend	shove
jumped	witch
yell	piece

At the second session, the teacher presents eight additional words:

late	chirped
bench	neck
drive	trained
wet	tick

The directions for administration and analysis are similar to those presented by Gentry and Gillet (1993). The analysis provides the basis for planning for word study instruction. Using the pretest as the baseline, teachers can develop a systematic assessment plan to monitor students' progress as part of their school's response-to-intervention plan.

There are many published spelling assessments so it is recommended that you select one that aligns well with your reading instruction. There are spelling tests and directions for analysis in *Words Their Way* by Bear, Invernizzi, Templeton, and Johnston (2004) and in *Word Matters: Teaching Phonics and Spelling in the Reading/Writing Classroom*, by Pinnell and Fountas (1998). Both of these books provide suggestions for analyzing the results, placing students along a developmental continuum, and providing developmentally appropriate instruction. For young children, teachers in the reading center use the spelling portion of the Early Literacy Assessment available on the website for this text.

Spelling Instruction

Many different formats and strategies can be used for spelling instruction. Gentry (2004) provides guidelines for successful word knowledge instruction:

1. Follow a specific curriculum to provide consistency and continuity.
2. Use techniques that are grounded in research.
3. Select developmentally appropriate words and patterns for instruction. Remember that spelling levels lag behind reading levels. Students can read words before they can spell them. Indeed, much of our learning and visual memory for spelling is derived from our reading.
4. Provide differentiated instruction. Just as teachers differentiate their reading instruction, they should differentiate spelling instruction so that they can provide developmentally appropriate instruction as described in number three above.
5. Make connections between spelling and word study and reading/writing. While struggling readers and writers may need intensive, explicit instruction in word analysis and spelling, teachers should take every opportunity to demonstrate the connections between recognizing words and spelling and how those skills are applied in reading and writing. Words that have been learned in reading provide patterns for spelling instruction. Writing provides opportunities to practice newly learned words. Good spelling helps to make writing more readily accessible to audiences.

Spelling Workshop. Gentry and Gillet (1993) recommend a workshop approach to teaching spelling similar to that used in teaching the writing process. This approach includes several steps:

1. To foster ownership, students select their own words to study for a week. These words may be selected from their writing folders, or they may be words from stories or topics being studied. Young children should select only four or five new words. Older children may choose 10 or more. In addition, teachers may add words for study based on student needs. Sometimes, the class may decide to focus on a specific pattern, such as a word ending.
2. Students keep their own records as they progress through the week's activities. They may also monitor their progress on end-of-week tests and select missed words for another week's study. They may keep a spelling log to record their new words.
3. Students work together to learn their words. They may play games, work on common patterns, practice with one another to improve visual memory, and help provide feedback for one another.

Visual Memory. In spelling, students need to visualize patterns in words. This visualization becomes even more important in later spelling development, because they must visualize root words to help them in spelling derivatives (e.g., *nation, nationality, nationalize*). Visual memory can be developed in many ways. Visualizing words and writing them allows students to learn words independently. It also avoids the useless step of merely having students copy words.

In tactile writing, students use their fingers to trace words cut from felt, sandpaper, or other textured paper. This technique is a good way to help very disabled students remember words and patterns. Using these aids, ask students to trace words within one word family (*rate, mate, skate*).

Look-Cover-Write-Check.   The look-cover-write-check strategy has been used successfully for years. The steps include:

1. Look at a spelling word.
2. Cover the spelling word.
3. Visualize the covered word in your mind.
4. Write the spelling word from memory.
5. Check your writing with the uncovered spelling word.

Word Walls.   Cunningham (2000, 2005) suggests the use of word walls to support students' spelling and writing. Teachers can write the words being studied on word cards, order them according to their beginning letter, and attach them to the wall. Word walls are helpful both in giving students ideas for writing and in supporting their spelling. Encourage students to visualize words and try to write them before they look at the wall. For a more complete discussion of word walls, see Chapter 8.

Structural Patterns.   Students need to develop an awareness of root words and combining affixes to create more complex words. Compound words provide a good introduction to structural patterns.

Gentry and Gillet (1993) suggest beginning with a compound word from a story or content area lesson. For example, reading the book *Snow* (Keats) can serve as a springboard to a lesson on such compound words as *snowfall*; then brainstorm words to combine with snow to create other compound words (*snowbank, snowmobile*).

Students can also study root words and the prefixes and suffixes that can be added to create derived words. To explore such spelling patterns, students can create lists of words that end with *-tion, -ic,* or *-ence* or begin with *anti-* or *pre-*.

A variation of the game Concentration can help students focus on root words and derivatives (Gentry and Gillet, 1993). To play this game, write sets of derived words on cards. One set might include *confide, confidence, confidential, confidante*. Another set could be *remind, remember, memory, reminisce*. To play the game, students try to make pairs of related words (for example, *remind* and *reminisce*).

Handwriting

Despite the growing popularity of computers, the physical act of handwriting remains basic to many school and life activities. A student with difficulties in handwriting is greatly hampered. Many students who do not read well also suffer from problems that result in poor handwriting. These problems include poor eye-hand coordination, deficient motor development, and limited spatial judgment (Lerner & Kline, 2006; Lerner & Johns, 2009). Because the writing system is adapted to right-handed students, those who are left-handed often have difficulties.

Most children begin writing in manuscript (or printing), which is relatively easy to construct and similar to the typeface in printed material. Students learn cursive writing in second or third grade. Even students without reading problems sometimes have difficulty making the transition from manuscript to cursive writing. Cursive letters are complex and require a greater variety of lines, curves, loops, and transitions.

Many teachers report easier transitions from manuscript to cursive writing if the D'Nealian method is used in beginning writing instruction. In this method, students are taught to write in manuscript, but the manuscript letters are written at a slant and the end strokes end in upward curves rather than straight lines. However, in D'Nealian, the difference between the appearance of their written words and the printed words in books is greater.

Some simple suggestions, if practiced regularly, may help improve handwriting.

◆ Have students practice on the chalkboard before using paper. They can make large circles, lines, geometric shapes, letters, and numbers with large, free movements using the muscles of arms, hands, and fingers.
◆ Some students need to trace printing and writing. Make heavy black letters on white paper and clip a sheet of onionskin (thin) paper over the letters. Have students trace letters with crayons or felt-tip pen.
◆ Put letters on transparencies and use an overhead projector to project the image on a chalkboard or large sheet of paper. The student can then trace over the image.
◆ Guide students verbally as they write. For example, say "down, up, and, around" as children form letters.
◆ Because writing is a matter of habit, monitor proper posture and ways to hold writing implements. Students may need lines on a desk to show them how to position paper.

Summary

Reading and writing are related processes that involve constructing, or composing, meaning. Writing strengthens reading by giving insight into spelling for early readers, by helping students to understand how text is organized, and by serving as a springboard to reading as students need to collect information about the pieces they compose.

Writing instruction should incorporate the writing process: selecting topics, writing drafts, making revisions, editing, and publishing. In this process, students choose and develop their own topics and are not evaluated on mechanics until near the end of the process. To evaluate writing, focus, in this order, on content, organization, format (the ability to use genre properly), and mechanics. Some writing strategies include written conversations (or conversing in writing), personal correspondence with another student, and journals that record personal reactions.

Teachers can help students to integrate reading and writing by using writing to support students' reading. Several ways to integrate writing and reading are to use writing as a prereading activity, to organize information during reading, and to respond to reading. Students can explore imaginative aspects of writing by composing poetry.

Spelling development occurs in stages beginning with the precommunicative stage and moving through the semiphonetic, phonetic, transitional, and conventional stages. Students' writing throughout these stages should be viewed as a natural developmental process. Spelling assessment instruments can provide insight into students' abilities to apply phonics principles and enable teachers to plan for instruction as well as to monitor progress. Spelling instruction should include connections between phonics and visual memory as well as the derivational aspects of structural patterns in more complex words.

References

Anderson, S. (1984). *A Whole-Language Approach to Reading.* Landham, MD: University Press of America.

Bear, D. R., Invernizzi, M., Templeton, S., & Johnston, F. (2004). *Words Their Way: Word Study for Phonics, Vocabulary, and Spelling Instruction* 3rd ed. Upper Saddle River, NJ: Pearson Education.

Blachowicz, C. L. Z., & Fisher, P. J. (2002). *Teaching Vocabulary in All Classrooms* (2nd ed.). Upper Saddle River, NJ: Pearson Education, Inc.

Borman, G. D., & D'Agostino, J. V. (1996). Title I and student achievement: A meta-analysis of federal evaluation results. *Educational Evaluation and Policy Analysis, 4,* 309–326.

Brown, A. L., & Palincsar, A. S. (1982). Inducing strategic learning from texts by means of informed, self-control training. Technical Report No. 262. Champaign: Center for the Study of Reading, University of Illinois.

Button, K., & Welton, D. (1997). Integrating literacy activities and social studies in the primary grades. *Social Studies and the Young Learner, 9,* 15–18.

Cahill, B. (2004). Return to sender: Stories in letters. *Writing,* November, 24–27.

Calkins, L. M. (2004). *The Art of Teaching Writing.* Portsmouth, NH: Heinemann.

Castle, J. M., Riach, J., & Nicholson, T. (1994). Getting off to a better start in reading and spelling: The effects of phonemic awareness instruction within a whole language program. *Journal of Educational Psychology, 86,* 350–359.

Cawley, J. F., & Parmar, R. S. (2001). Literacy proficiency and science for students with learning disabilities. *Reading and Writing Quarterly, 17,* 105–125.

Clay, M. M. (1998). *By Different Paths to Common Outcomes.* York, ME: Stenhouse Publishers.

Clay, M. M. (2002). *An Observation Survey of Early Literacy Achievement* (2nd ed.). Portsmouth, NH: Heinemann Educational Books.

Cunningham, P. M. (2000). *Phonics They Use: Words for Reading and Writing* (3rd ed.). New York: Longman.

Cunningham, P. M. (2005). *Phonics They Use: Words for Reading and Writing* (4th ed.). Boston: Allyn & Bacon.

Dyson, A. H. (2003). Writing and children's symbolic repertoires: Development unhinged. In S. B. Neuman & D. K. Dickinson (Eds.), *Handbook of Early Literacy Research.* New York: Guilford Press.

Ehri, L. C. (2000). Learning to read and learning to spell: Two sides of a coin. *Topics in Language Disorders, 20,* 19–36.

Ehri, L. C. (1997). *The Development of Children's Ability to Read Words.* Paper presented at the convention of the International Reading Association, Atlanta, GA.

Farr, R., Lewis, M., Fasholz, J., Pinsky, E., Towle, S., Lipschutz, J., & Faulds, B. P. (1990). Writing in response to reading. *Educational Leadership, 47,* 66–69.

Fisher, P. J. (1998). Teaching vocabulary in linguistically diverse classrooms. *Illinois Reading Council Journal*, *26*, 16–21.

Fletcher, R., & Portalupi, J. (2001). *Nonfiction Craft Lessons: Teaching Information Writing K–8*. Portland, ME: Stenhouse Publishers.

Freeman, M. S. (2003). Using writing to assess student understanding of informational text. *New England Reading Association Journal*, *39*, 21–28.

Gentry, J. R. (2004). *The Science of Spelling: The Explicit Specifics that Make Great Readers and Writers (and Spellers!)*. Portsmouth, NH: Heinemann.

Gentry, J. R. (2007). *Breakthrough in Beginning Reading and Writing: The Evidence-Based Approach to Pinpointing Students' Needs and Delivering Targeted Instruction*. New York: Scholastic.

Gentry, J. R., & Gillet, J. W. (1993). *Teaching Kids to Spell*. Portsmouth, NH: Heinemann.

Giacobbe, M. E. (1986). Learning to write and writing to learn in the elementary school. In A. R. Petrosky & D. Bartholomae (Eds.), *The Teaching of Writing: Eighty-Fifth Yearbook of the National Society for the Study of Education*, pp. 131–147. Chicago: University of Chicago.

Gillet, J. W., & Temple, C. (2000). *Understanding Reading Problems: Assessment and Instruction* (5th ed.). New York: Longman.

Glenn, W. J. (2007). Real writers as aware readers: Writing creatively as a means to develop reading skills. *Journal of Adolescent & Adult Literacy*, *51*, 10–20.

Goswami, U. (2003). Early phonological development and the acquisition of literacy. In S. B. Neuman & D. K. Dickinson (Eds.), *Handbook of Early Literacy Research*. New York: Guilford Press.

Graves, D. H. (1994). *A Fresh Look at Writing*. Portsmouth, NH: Heinemann.

Greene, B. G. (1995). Exploring the reading-writing relationship. *Reading Psychology: An International Quarterly*, *16*, 261–268.

Henderson, E. H. (1985). *Teaching Spelling*. Geneva, IL: Houghton Mifflin.

Jacobs, V. A. (2002). Reading, writing, and understanding. *Educational Leadership*, *60*, (3), 58–61.

Jennings, J. H. (1991). A comparison of summary and journal writing as components of an interactive comprehension model in social studies. In *The Fortieth Yearbook of the National Reading Conference*, pp. 67–82. Chicago: National Reading Conference.

Johnston, P. H. (1997). *Knowing Literacy: Constructive Literacy Assessment*. York, ME: Stenhouse Publishers.

Johnston, P. H., & Rogers, R. (2003). Early literacy development: The case for "informed assessment." In S. B. Neuman & D. K. Dickinson (Eds.), *Handbook of Early Literacy Research*. New York: Guilford Press.

Lancia, P. (1997). Literacy borrowing: The effects of literature on children's writing. *The Reading Teacher*, *50*, 470–475.

Lerner, J. W. & Johns, B. (2009). *Learning Disabilities: Theories, Diagnosis, and Teaching Strategies*. Boston: Houghton Mifflin Co.

Lerner, J. W. & Kline, F. (2006). *Learning Disabilities and Related Disorders: Characteristics and Teaching Strategies*. Boston: Houghton-Mifflin Co.

Mayher, J. S., Lester, N. B., & Pradl, G. M. (1983). *Learning to Write/Writing to Learn*. Upper Montclair, NJ: Boynton/Cook.

McGinley, W. J., & Denner, P. R. (1987). Story impressions: A prereading/writing activity. *Journal of Reading*, *31*, 248–253.

Morrow, L. M. (2004). *Literacy Development in the Early Years: Helping Children Read and Write* (5th ed.). Boston: Allyn & Bacon.

Olness, R. (2005). Using literature to enhance writing instruction: A guide for K–5 teachers. Newark, DE: International Reading Association.

Palincsar, A., & Brown, A. L. (1984). Reciprocal teaching of comprehension: Fostering and comprehension-monitoring activities. *Cognition and Instruction*, *1*, 117–175.

Parr, M., & Campbell, T. (2006). Poets in practice. *The Reading Teacher*, *60*, 36–46.

Pinnell, G. S., & Fountas, I. C. (1998). *Word Matters: Teaching Phonics and Spelling in the Reading/Writing Classroom*. Portsmouth, NH: Heinemann.

Read, C. (1971). Preschool children's knowledge of English phonology. *Harvard Educational Review*, *41*, 1–34.

Read, C. (1975). Children's categorization of speech sounds in English. NCTE Research Reports, No. 17. Urbana, IL: National Council of Teachers of English.

Richgels, D. J. (2003). Phonemic awareness, and reading and writing instruction. In S. B. Neuman & D. K. Dickinson (Eds.), *Handbook of Early Literacy Research*. New York: Guilford Press.

Rubadue, M. (2002). Sharing the pen. www.TeachingK-8.com.

Saddler, B., & Graham, S. (2008). The relationship between writing knowledge and writing performance among more and less skilled writers. *Reading and Writing Quarterly, 23,* 231–247.

Santa, C., Havens, L., & Harrison, S. (1989). Teaching secondary science through reading, writing, studying, and problem solving. In D. Lapp, J. Flood, & N. Farnan (Eds.), *Content Area Reading and Learning: Instructional Strategies*. Upper Saddle River, NJ: Prentice Hall.

Shanahan, T. (2005). *The National Reading Panel: Practical Advise for Teachers*. Naperville, IL: Learning Point Associates.

Shapiro, S., & Welch, M. (1991). Using poetry with adolescents in a remedial reading program: A case study. *Reading Horizons, 31,* 318–331.

Sitler, H. (1995). Letters from Emily: Writing-reading connection. *Language Arts, 72,* 360–365.

Strickland, D. S., Ganske, K., & Monroe, J. K. (2002). *Supporting Struggling Readers and Writers: Strategies for Classroom Intervention 3–6*. Newark, DE: International Reading Association.

Tierney, R. J. (1990). Redefining reading comprehension. *Educational Leadership, 47,* 37–42.

Unrau, N. (2008). *Content Area Reading and Writing: Fostering Literacies in Middle and High School 2nd ed.* Upper Saddle River, NJ: Pearson.

Vanderburg, R. M. (2006). Reviewing research on teaching writing based on Vygotsky's theories: What we can learn. *Reading and Writing Quarterly, 22,* 375–393.

Weech, J. (1994). Writing the story before reading it. *Journal of Reading, 37,* 364–367.

Wells, M. C. (1992–1993). At the junction of reading and writing: How dialogue journals contribute to students' reading development. *Journal of Reading, 36,* 294–302.

White, B. F. (1995). Effects of autobiographical writing before reading on students' responses to short stories. *Journal of Educational Research, 88,* 173–184.

Wittrock, M. C. (1984). Writing and the teaching of reading. In J. M. Jensen (ed.), *Composing and Comprehending,* pp. 77–83. Urbana, IL: ERIC Clearinghouse on Reading and Communication Skills.

Wollman-Bonilla, J. E., & Werchadlo, B. (1995). Literature response journals in a first-grade classroom. *Language Arts, 72,* 562–570.

Wong, B. Y. (1986). A cognitive approach to teaching spelling. *Exceptional Children, 53,* 169–172.

PEARSON
myeducationlab
Where the Classroom Comes to Life

MyEducationLab is a research-based learning tool that brings teaching to life. Go to the Jennings, Caldwell, & Lerner 6th Edition MyEducationLab for Reading Assessment site at www.myeducationlab.com to:

◆ engage in multimedia exercises to help you

build a deeper and more applied understanding of chapter content;

◆ utilize extensive resources including videos from real classrooms, Praxis and licensure preparation, a lesson plan builder, and materials to help you in your teaching career.

Literacy Instruction for Diverse Populations

Multicultural Diversity, English Language Learners, Parents and Families, Adolescents, and Adults with Reading Problems

Introduction

In this chapter, we look at literacy instruction for several different populations. We review literacy in today's diverse multicultural society, examine English Language Learners (ELLs), analyze the important role of the family and parents in developing literacy, and discuss adolescents and adults with reading problems.

Literacy in a Multicultural Society

The value of diverse cultures and the benefits of linguistic and cultural diversity are well recognized in today's society. Each cultural, racial, and linguistic population makes unique and immeasurable contributions to the U.S. society. The term *cultural pluralism* reflects this philosophy. Today's society appreciates the values that stem from different cultural populations.

Society is becoming increasingly pluralistic and diverse. As immigrant groups come to North America with their own languages, cultures, and traditions, the U.S. society increasingly appreciates it's rich cultural resources. Schools are called on to meet the challenges of increasing diversity and to respond vigorously and flexibly to these new challenges. Teachers have the responsibility to offer the best instruction they can to all students.

Diverse Cultural Views about Reading

Diverse cultures may hold different views about many issues that affect reading and literacy learning. For example, a student's family may view reading very differently than the school or the teacher. Schools traditionally expect children to have the kinds of literacy background experiences that middle-class, English-speaking parents traditionally provide. For example, middle-class parents frequently read and discuss stories with their children (often at bedtime) and discuss them. Through these literacy experiences, children become aware of what a book is, how to handle books, how print and speech match, and how a story is constructed. Middle-class parents frequently ask their children questions for which the parents already know the answer. Such literary activities are also are common school experiences in kindergarten and first grade. This practice is, again, an experience frequently repeated in school, when a teacher questions children about material they have read (Armbruster, Lehr, & Osborn, 2006; Lerner, Lowenthal, & Egan, 2003; Jiménez, 2002).

However, these types of early literacy experiences may not occur within all cultures and families. For example, in some cultures, storybook reading to children is uncommon; in others, parents read stories to their children but do not follow up with the adult-child interactions that foster the ability to handle books or talk about stories. Thus, children come to school with different kinds of background experiences with books and with reading. Teachers must honor the experiences that children already have while providing experiences that children do not have.

Cultural differences also are seen in children's oral language and styles of verbal interactions. In some cultures, children are not encouraged to speak in an extended fashion until they develop enough competence to "hold their own" on a topic (Cazden, 1988). The child may conclude that a good child is a quiet child. If children are not encouraged to display extended language use at home, they may be fearful of offering opinions or engaging in conversations in class.

Teachers should realize that some children from diverse cultures may be reluctant to express themselves in class. Teachers should not underestimate the extent of children's knowledge about a subject, even though they are reluctant to speak in class. It is important that children be encouraged to talk to build language and reading skills.

Decades of research shows that children in all cultures need to have the following building blocks of reading and writing (Armbruster, et al., 2006). All children need to:

- have many experiences in talking and listening
- learn about print and books
- become aware of sounds in spoken language, such as rhyming words and individual sounds in word and language
- have knowledge about the letters of the alphabet
- have many experiences of parents and others reading stories aloud
- have opportunities to expand their vocabulary and knowledge of words

Teaching Children from Diverse Cultures

There are many ways for teachers to encourage children to share their linguistic and cultural heritage. Some activities include:

- **Use volunteers from the child's culture.**   Ask grandparents, other relatives, or community members to visit or donate time to a school. Community volunteers can relate successfully to the children.
- **Explain expectations.**   Fully explain the expectations and routines when working with all students. For example, provide explicit instruction in how to choose a book, what happens during quiet time, how to take turns, and how to listen as the teacher reads a story.
- **Have students make and share contributions from their own cultures.** One teacher had children write raps that summarize their learning in U.S. history and science as well as novels (Spinelli, 2006).
- **Have children from a diverse culture and the mainstream culture teach each other.**   For example, in one school Hispanic children in a bilingual class were paired with children from a mainstream class. Each child taught five words on different topics such as sports or food from their culture. English-speaking children learned Spanish words, and Spanish-speaking children learned English words. This activity culminated in the second grade's participation in the annual bilingual celebration of the school as well as the communal breaking of a stubborn piñata to celebrate the holiday Cinco de Mayo.

◆ **Have families from different cultures share experiences.** Families from different cultures often can share experiences and feelings orally or in writing. In one classroom, the children's older brothers and sisters were asked to write the story of how their families came to the United States. The following story was written by an older brother:

My Family's Trip to America

This story all began when my family was in the war suffering. Lots of people were pushing and shoving. They pushed and shoved because they wanted to escape from the Communists. If they were caught, they would die or would be their prisoner and would be put in jail. Thee jail is a cark, damp. dreary dungeon. Most were killed by gun shots. My family cam to America. My mom and dad came from Vietnam. Freedom is what my father and mother came for. They chose the right place, America. They were glad they made it.

◆ **Display pictures that show people from diverse backgrounds and communities.** Include people from culturally diverse backgrounds at work, at home, and in leisure activities.

◆ **Use seating arrangements and class organization to encourage students to try new ways of interacting and learning.** Students from different cultural groups enjoy sharing ideas and experiences. This environment is best fostered if students have a variety of opportunities in which to sit, talk, and work with others.

◆ **Use books about cultural traditions.** Books representing the child's cultural traditions can contribute to a rich and accepting atmosphere. Table 14.1 provides some book titles to foster multicultural understanding.

Table 14.2 provides some principles for teachers to support cultural diversity in the classroom.

TABLE 14.1 Multicultural Children's Books

African and African American

A Is for Africa by I. Onyefufo. Photographs in alphabet book provide a stunning view of life in a Nigerian village.

Afrobets series by S. Willis Hudson. Preschool concepts (colors, shapes, numbers) presented with African animals, artifacts, and everyday objects.

Amazing Grace by M. Hoffman. Can an African English girl play Peter Pan in a school play? This story concerns racial awareness and self-esteem.

Mary Had a Little Lamb by S. Hale (illus. by B. McMillan). Photographs of an African American Mary offer a unique interpretation of this classic nursery rhyme.

The People Could Fly by V. Hamilton. Anthology of 24 folktales focus on the black experience in the southern United States.

Pink and Say by P. Polacco. In this true story, a black Union soldier nurses a wounded Confederate soldier.

Continued

TABLE 14.1 (CONTINUED)

Native American

Dancing with the Indians by A. S. Medearis. An African American author tells of her ancestors' participation in a Seminole Indian celebration.

Encounter by J. Yolen. Set in 1492, a Taino Indian child recounts the visit of Columbus, highlighting differences between Native Americans and Europeans.

Ikomi and the Boulder by P. Goble. Lively trickster tale explains why the Great Plains are covered with rocks and bats and have flat faces.

Knots on a Counting Rope by B. Martin, Jr., & J. Archambault. Wise grandfather helps a Native American boy to face his blindness.

Maii and Cousin Horned Toad by S. Begay. This Navaho fable explains why coyotes stay away from horned toads.

Momma Do You Love Me? by B. Joosse. An Eskimo child questions mother about "What if I . . . ?" Many Eskimo terms are explained.

Sunpainters by Baje Whitethorne. According to Navajo legend, the sun must be repainted after an eclipse.

Hispanic

Diego by J. Winter. The life of the famous muralist Diego Rivera is depicted in simple bilingual text with artwork that mirrors his own.

Everybody Has Feelings by C. Abery. A bilingual (Spanish-English) exploration of people and their feelings.

First Day of School by M. Deru. Young foxes hunting for chickens make friends with them instead.

Gathering the Sun by A. F. Ada. A poem for each letter of the Spanish alphabet celebrates farmworkers and their products. Poems are translated into English.

Let's Go (Vamos) by E. Emberley. This book explores the four seasons in bilingual text.

Moon Rope by L. Elhert. This Peruvian folktale (Spanish-English) about why there is a moon features a fox.

Radio Man by A. Dorros. A child of a migrant worker family sends a message to his friend by radio. Text is bilingual.

Un Cuento de Queztalcoatl by M. Parke & S. Panik. Part of the Mexican and Central American legends series in which each of several tales is told (in separate short books) in English and Spanish. This tale tells of a game among the Aztec gods.

Asian

Baseball Saved Us by K. Mochizuki. A Japanese-American boy interned during World War II finds solace in baseball.

The Dragon's Robe by D. Nourse. A Chinese girl weaves a beautiful silk robe to save her father's life.

Grandmother's Path, Grandfather's Way by L. Vang & J. Lewis. Lore and legends of the Hmong Southeast Asian tribe (Hmong-English).

Jar of Dreams by Y. Uchida. Rinko, a Japanese-American girl, tells about her family life in California.

The Little Weaver of Thai-Yen Village by Tran-Khanh-Yuyet. One of the Fifth World Tales series, in Vietnamese and English. A Vietnamese girl comes to the United States for an operation. Other books in this series feature different Asian groups.

Source: This list was compiled by Susan Ali.

> **TABLE 14.2**   Strategies to Support Cultural Diversity
>
> ◆ Be responsive to cultural and individual diversity.
> ◆ Create an open, accepting classroom environment to ensure all students from all cultural and linguistic backgrounds feel comfortable in class.
> ◆ Include books and stories in the curriculum to enhance understanding of other cultures.
> ◆ Teach about sensitivity and acceptance issues.
> ◆ Share personal experiences about cultural issues.

English Language Learners

Go to MyEducationLab and select the topic *English Language Learners*. Then, go to the Activities and Applications section, watch the video entitled "An ESL Vocabulary Lesson," and respond to the accompanying questions.

English Language Learners (ELLs) are students whose first language is not English and who are not yet proficient in English. Understandably, ELL students may experience difficulty in understanding or speaking English or in reading or writing in English.

Who Are ELLs?

In today's diverse society, the number of students who come from homes in which a language other than English is spoken is rapidly increasing. Today, one in five students speaks a language other than English in his or her home (International Reading Association, 2007). The number of English Language Learners rose to three-quarters of a million in the year 2000 (Jiménez, 2002). The Hispanic population increased to 44.3 million in 2006, making it the largest language group in the United States (U.S. Census Bureau, 2006). Spanish speakers represent 76 percent of the non-English language population, However, there are more than 100 distinct language groups served in U.S. schools (Jiménez, 2002). Common languages of ELL students include Spanish, Russian, Vietnamese, Hmong, Creole, Korean, Cantonese, Chinese, and Arabic. To make the task of teaching ELL students even more challenging, some ELL students also have a basic learning disability in addition to their limited English proficiency. If a language disorder is present in the primary language, it also will be present in the secondary language (McCardle, 2005). Over 15 percent of the students with learning disabilities are identified as Hispanic (U.S. Department of Education, 2006).

Several federal laws affect ELL students. The No Child Left Behind (NCLB) Act of 2001 requires that ELL students take the state standards tests taken by all students in U.S. schools. Further, the scores of ELL students are grouped and reported separately. Understandably, many ELL students have difficulty with these tests and their low scores can negatively impact the standing of their school.

The second law that can impact ELL students is the Individual with Disabilities Education Improvement Act of 2004 (IDEA-2004). This law requires that all students with disabilities take the state standards tests. The scores of students with disabilities also are grouped and reported separately. Individualized education programs (IEPs) must consider their language needs. IDEA-2004 also requires that states report the number of children with disabilities served by race or ethnicity (Lerner & Johns, 2009; Klingner, Artiles, & Barletta, 2006).

Methods for Teaching ELLs

Several different methods are used for teaching students who are ELLs. These methods include:

- **English as a second language (ESL).** This method is used in classes that have students who come from many different language backgrounds. Students learn through carefully controlled oral repetitions of English language patterns. This approach often is used in schools where children come from many different language backgrounds and providing instruction in all native languages is not feasible.
- **Bilingual instruction.** This method is used when all of the students in the class are from one language background. Instruction is provided in two languages. Students use their native language for part of the school day and use the second language (English) for the other portion of the school day. Academic subjects are often taught in the student's native language and the student receives oral practice in English. The objective of bilingual instruction is to strengthen school learning through the native language and gradually to add the secondary language.
- **Instruction through immersion.** In this method, students are immersed in, or receive extensive exposure to, the second language. In fact, where no formal instruction is available for a person learning a second language, immersion is usually what occurs naturally. Individuals simply learn English as they live in the mainstream of an English-speaking society. Immersion is widely employed with schoolchildren in Canada, where it is used to teach French to English-speaking children by enrolling them in French-speaking schools.

Teaching Reading to ELLs

Students who are ELLs often have difficulty in learning to read in English. They are not yet proficient in English, yet must learn to read in English. The following methods can help build reading skills for ESL students (August & Shanaham, 2006; Jiménez, 2002; Hudson & Smith, 2002; Ortiz, 2001):

- **Provide abundant oral language practice.** Reading is connected to listening and speaking. By providing opportunities for students to speak in English and to converse with one another, students can improve their oral language skills in English, which helps provide a basis for reading in English.
- **Use easy-to-read English language books.** Practice with English language books offers opportunities to strengthen abilities in English. When ESL students read high-interest, easy-to-read storybooks in English, they improve in reading and in reading comprehension.
- **Build reading fluency.** Reading fluency refers to the ability of students to read easily quickly, without labored hesitancy. The strategy of repeated reading is a useful method for building fluency in reading. Have students re-read orally

from books they have previously read. (See Chapter 9 for more suggestions for developing reading fluency.)

◆ **Incorporate writing into the lesson.** Have students write a story about a selection that they have just read. Reading and writing are strongly connected, and the process of writing can strengthen reading. (See Chapter 13 for more strategies for integrating reading and writing.)

Strategies for Teaching Reading to ELL Students

The school settings in which students spend so much time should reflect their language backgrounds. The following strategies are examples of ways to make classrooms and materials reflect their language backgrounds:

◆ **Encourage ELL students to use their first language around the school.** For example, books in the classroom and library, bulletin boards, and signs can be in the students' native language. Students can also help each other. For example, Jerzy, a child whose native language was Polish, was paired with Irena, a child who had just immigrated from Warsaw. This pairing increased the self-esteem and language skills of both students.

◆ **Help students to understand that reading is based on language.** They should understand that to read in English, they must understand the English words and sentence structures they meet in books. ELL students should be free to learn sophisticated information and concepts in the language they are most comfortable using. Information and abilities can be learned first in any language and then transferred to another language.

◆ **Build oral language skills.** At noted, reading is connected to listening and speaking. Reading in English can strengthen all language abilities in English. If students have some proficiency in English, reading English books will further all English language skills.

◆ **Use English books.** Reading books in English can be an excellent way to improve general mastery of English. When students learning English are given an abundance of high-interest storybooks in English, their progress in reading and listening comprehension increases. Use books that have repetition in language structures. For example, predictable books, which repeat refrains over and over, are excellent for learning English. Well-known folktales and fairy tales with familiar plots are also useful. Fairy tales typically have repeated phrases that children enjoy hearing and saying. Also, attractively illustrated books, in which pictures support the text, are excellent for ELL students. Some good books to use for developing concepts include *The Toolbox* (Rockwell); *Circles, Triangles, and Squares; Over, Under, Through, and Other Spatial Concepts*; and *Push-Pull, Empty-Full: A Book of Opposites* (Hoban); *Bread, Bread, Bread* (Morris); *People* (Spier); and *Growing Vegetable Soup* (Ehlers). Books that invite talk include *A Taste of Blackberries* (Smith) and *The Biggest House in the World* (Lionni); *Nana Upstairs, Nana Downstairs* (De Paola); *The Keeping Quilt* (Polacco); and *The Story of Ferdinand* (Leaf).

◆ **Use books that focus on language use.** ELL students who are more advanced in English language skills profit from using books focusing on language use, such as *Amelia Bedelia* and its sequels (Parish), which feature common idioms in amusing situations, and *Many Luscious Lollipops* and its sequels (Heller), which focus on parts of speech, such as adjectives, nouns, and adverbs. Finally, the increasing number of books written in two languages allows students to match their native language patterns with corresponding English ones.

♦ **Provide numerous opportunities to use English.** ELL students must be given many opportunities to move from learning and producing limited word translations and fragmented concepts to using longer sentences and expressing more complex ideas and feelings. Engage students in increasingly complex reading and writing experiences; check to make sure that they understand the concepts.

♦ **Find opportunities to use more complex English.** These situations will vary according to the level of students. In one kindergarten class of Russian-speaking children, a game of "Simon Says," complete with gestures, provided an active response to English. At a more advanced level, a third-grade bilingual Spanish class listened to the hilarious "twisted" fairy tale, *The True Story of the Three Little Pigs* (Scieszka) in both English and Spanish, and then acted it out. Later that year, the class listened to *Charlotte's Web* (White) read in English, chose their favorite words, and then matched these words in Spanish.

♦ **Use conversation about books to foster natural language usage.** In fostering a discussion of a story, the teacher can ask such questions as the following: "What do you think this story will be about?", "What do you think will happen next?", "Why do you think that?", "Tell me more about . . .", "What do you mean by . . . ?" Encourage students by giving them time to respond. In addition, students may respond in pairs to make the activity less threatening. Conversation about personal reactions to stories is excellent for giving meaning-based practice in using English. Students enjoy discussing their favorite characters and the best parts of a story. To aid them, the teacher may list helpful English adjectives on the board.

♦ **Foster home-school collaboration.** Establishing communication with the parents and other family members such as siblings is important. More can be accomplished when the school and home work together. Parents should be contacted frequently to communicate students' successes as well as the problems their children encounter. Remember that parents often have valuable information and insights that can be useful in the teaching process. Families can also make valuable contributions to school programs. In one fourth-grade bilingual room, two mothers sewed all the costumes for 36 fifth-grade children who sang Venezuelan songs. In helping the school's celebration, parents, school staff, and students gained a sense of community involvement (Spinelli, 2006).

♦ **Develop units for reading and language arts that use literature from a variety of linguistic and cultural backgrounds to reflect the diversity in U.S. society.** Table 14.1 lists books suitable for students from many different backgrounds. Students of all backgrounds enjoy reading them but, of course, they are especially important for the self-esteem of students in the groups they feature.

The Important Role of Families and Parents in Fostering Literacy

Learning to read starts at home, long before the child goes to school. Parents and family members play a key role in early literacy and preparing the child for reading. Children begin to understand the nature of written language when parents read stories to them (Armbruster, et al., 2006).

When the child fails to learn to read, the parents react with feelings of frustration and anxiety. It is important for teachers to talk regularly to parents of children with reading problems. Devoting time to understanding the needs of these families is important because it shows the teacher's willingness to help. When parents realize how hard the teacher is trying, the parents will often match the teacher's efforts by reading with their children at home or buying books for them. Of course, during these encounters with parents, teachers must be respectful of parents' perspectives. In fact, by listening to the parents' experiences with their children, teachers often gain information that is important for instruction (Spinelli, 2006).

One useful strategy that parents can use is the "You Read to Me, I'll Read to You" strategy described in Table 14.3.

Parent Workshops

Being the parent of a child with a reading problem can be frustrating and discouraging. Workshops for parents provide a way to involve parents. Parents need to share their feelings and experiences with others and perhaps get useful ideas from them. They also need information about the best placement for their child and their rights under the law. Perhaps most important, parents need to share positive literacy experiences they have had with their children.

TABLE 14.3   You Read to Me, I'll Read to You Strategy

In the You Read to Me, I'll Read to You Strategy, a child places two books in a large bag. One is to be read by the parent to the child; the other is to be read by the child to the parent. Primary children are expected to engage in 15 minutes of personal reading and to listen to a parent read for an additional 15 minutes. For older children, the times are extended to 20 minutes. To verify that the reading has occurred, parents use a form to list the books read and the number of minutes spent reading and then initial the form.

In this strategy, parents become participants in the reading process. This also acquaints parents with a variety of reading formats. Parents may read a high-level book to their children to provide language development. Parents and children may read different books at the same time, silently, so each enjoys a private reading experience, or parents and children may read the same book and then discuss it after reading. Parents may read a book to a child, and the child can "echo read" each page that the parent has read. Parents and children can also take turns reading the same book or read a book as a play by taking the parts of different characters. Easy books and tapes can be provided to parents who are uncertain of their own reading abilities.

The parent workshops typically meet once per week for about 10 sessions. During the workshop sessions, parents share experiences and ideas with one another and often develop close relationships with other parents. Parents often ask for information concerning laws on special education and educational placement. They also seek ways to foster reading in their children.

One activity is to ask parents to bring a favorite book that they remember reading as a child. The books they bring are usually easy and entertaining and fun to share at the parent workshops. Parents can also be asked to relate the affectionate experiences that they and their own parents shared during reading. Parents can discuss ways to foster similar warm experiences with their own children.

One activity for the parent workshop is to encourage parents to write. A writing activity deepens the parents' own understanding of literacy and helps them understand how difficult writing can be for children. Parents come to understand the nature of the writing process and how spelling and punctuation should be a last step in writing rather than the first step.

At the end of the series of workshops, a piece of writing from each child and participating parent can be bound into a book and read at a final celebration. Each parent and child can receive a copy of this joint book as a memento of a positive experience.

Additional activities that can be used during the parent workshops are listed in Table 14.4.

Adolescents with Reading Problems

Go to MyEducationLab and select the topic *Comprehension*. Then, go to the Activities and Applications section, watch the video entitled "Think Aloud Strategy," and respond to the accompanying questions.

Adolescence (the 13- to 20-year-old age range) is a well-documented period of social, emotional, and physical change. Adolescents must resolve conflicts between their desires for freedom and security, as they are torn between wishing for independence and yet not being ready for the responsibilities of full adulthood. Adolescents must cope with rapid physical changes in growth, appearance, and sexual drive. Peer pressure greatly affects adolescents; they seek group acceptance and are increasingly aware of how their peers are doing. All these characteristics of adolescence present challenges that may negatively affect learning.

TABLE 14.4 Activities for Parents

- Make family message boards to encourage literacy.
- Read a favorite book over again.
- Display books in theme baskets (e.g., Halloween, spring).
- Provide suggestions on how to choose books at libraries and bookstores.
- Model thinking about what you learned after reading a book.
- Suggest ways to purchase discount or used children's books.

Characteristics of Adolescents with Reading Problems

Teenagers with reading problems not only have difficulty in school, but they must also cope with the normal challenges and adjustments presented by adolescence. Trying to deal with this combination creates special burdens for teenagers, such as:

◆ **Passive learning.** Adolescents with reading and learning problems often develop an attitude of *learned helplessness* and dependence. They wait for teacher direction instead of active learning (Deshler, Schumaker, Lenz, Bulgren, Hock, Knight, et al., 2001).

◆ **Poor self-concept.** Low self-esteem and other emotional problems result from years of failure (Smith, 1992).

◆ **Poor social skills.** Adolescents with academic problems often have difficulty making and keeping friends during a period when friendships and peer approval are important (Bryan, 1991; Vaughn, 1991).

◆ **Difficulty with attention.** Poor attention and concentration are common in teenagers who read poorly (Lerner, Lowenthal, & Lerner, 1995). Because long periods of concentration are required for high school work, attention problems can be quite serious.

◆ **Lack of motivation.** After years of failure, many teenagers feel that they are dumb and that their efforts to learn are useless. Adolescents can learn only if they are motivated and can attribute success to their own efforts (Lenz & Deshler, 2003).

Special Considerations at the Secondary Level

Adolescents who have reading problems face many challenges in the secondary school. Secondary schools require all students to pass statewide performance tests, and adolescents with reading problems often have difficulty taking these statewide tests. Poor performance on these statewide tests can jeopardize their graduation from high school. States now require that high school students pass state standards tests to receive their diplomas. Only 57 percent of students with learning disabilities (many of whom have reading problems) receive high school diplomas (U.S. Department of Education, 2006). Many of these students drop out of school and often face grim futures in the streets. Unless students with reading problems are given opportunities to learn, holding them to higher standards will only victimize these students (Lerner & Johns, 2009).

In addition, many content-area secondary teachers are not oriented to working with low-achieving readers. The training and orientation of secondary teachers is typically in their area of specializations (history, science, English literature, etc.). Content-area secondary teachers may not have not been trained to adjust their teaching for poor readers.

There are many strategies to help adolescents with reading problems. If the student has a severe reading problem, the teacher might be able to tape lessons. Books recorded for the blind can be made accessible to low-achieving readers. During examinations, students might be allowed to give answers orally, to tape answers, or to dictate answers to someone else. Students who do write could be allowed additional time.

Components of Effective Secondary Programs

Effective components for poor readers in the secondary schools include (Zigmond, 1997):

- **Intensive instruction in reading.**   Students with reading problems need rigorous individualized instruction.
- **Direct instruction in high school "survival" skills.**   Training may be needed for successful functioning in a high school. For example, training in behavior control helps students learn how to stay out of trouble in school. Training students in teacher-pleasing behaviors allows students to acquire behavior patterns (look interested, volunteer responses) that make teachers view them more positively. Strategies such as organizing time, previewing textbooks, taking notes from a lecture or text, organizing information, and taking tests are needed for academic success.
- **Successful completion of courses.**   Students with reading problems may cut classes, come late, and not complete assignments. Empathetic, caring teachers and counselors can foster course completion. Success in the ninth grade is particularly critical for high school.
- **Planning for life after high school.**   Adolescents with reading problems need to prepare for a successful transition to higher education or the world of work.

Adults with Reading Problems

For many individuals, a reading disability is a lifelong problem, a problem that does not disappear when schooling has been completed.

Adult literacy presents an ever-growing challenge. Some adults with problems in reading have dropped out of school and now find themselves blocked from employment. Others may be employed but want to advance in their jobs or enhance their personal skills. Some adults have been denied opportunities because they lived in countries that did not provide a free education. Still other adults are concerned with learning to speak and write in English.

Postsecondary and College Programs

Postsecondary education includes community colleges, vocational-technical training, and colleges. Programs in a variety of settings at a growing number of colleges and other postsecondary institutions serve adult learners with reading problems.

Accommodations for students with disabilities for colleges have been triggered by Section 504 of the Rehabilitation Act (1973). This law requires educational institutions that receive federal funds to make reasonable accommodations for students who are identified as having a disability. Many such individuals suffer from reading problems.

Some strategies for helping adult students in postsecondary education cope with academic demands are:

◆ Give students course syllabi 4 to 6 weeks before class begins and provide time to discuss them personally with students.
◆ Begin lectures and discussions with systematic overviews of the topic.
◆ Use a chalkboard or overhead projector to outline lecture material and orally read what is written on the board or transparencies.
◆ Use a chalkboard or overhead projector to highlight key concepts, unusual terminology, or foreign words.
◆ Clearly identify important points, main ideas, and key concepts orally in lectures.
◆ Give assignments in writing and orally; be available for further clarification.
◆ Provide opportunities for student participation, question periods, and discussion.
◆ Provide time for individual discussion of assignments and questions about lectures and readings.
◆ Provide study guides for the text, study questions, and review sessions to prepare for exams.
◆ Allow oral presentations or tape-recorded assignments instead of requiring students to use a written format.
◆ Modify evaluation procedures: Include untimed tests, wide-lined paper for tests, and alternatives to computer-scored answer sheets.

Needs of Adults with Reading Problems

Although some adults are lucky enough to get higher education, many adults with reading problems have great difficulty finding their niche in the world. They have trouble working, socializing, and even coping with daily tasks. Many adults with reading problems have ingenious strategies for avoiding, hiding, and dealing with their problems.

One story of an adult with significant problems in reading was a man whose wife had died a few years before and was caught in a social dating whirl. He coped with his poor reading by routinely entering a restaurant with his lady friend, putting down the menu, and saying, "Why don't you order for both of us, dear? Your selections are always perfect." This man hired professionals to handle all of his personal matters, including his checkbook. His friends attributed his actions to wealth and never suspected his inability to read.

Instructional Programs for Adults

Adults who seek help with their reading problems are likely to be highly motivated to learn and to demand an explanation of the goals and purposes of their programs. This commitment enables them to succeed.

More and more adults seek help that goes beyond the basic stages of literacy. As a result, the field of adult literacy has expanded its original responsibilities from basic functional literacy to a high-technical level (approximately twelfth-grade reading level). Some instructional options for adult reading programs include the following:

◆ Adult Basic Education (ABE) and General Education Development (GED) programs provide adult basic education (from elementary levels through eighth grade) and a high school level education with a general education diploma. Both the ABE and GED are funded by the federal government and require group instruction. Approximately two-and-a-half-million adults are enrolled in these programs (Gottesman, 1994).

◆ Literacy Volunteers of America, (www.proliteracy.org) a private organization training volunteers to work with adults, serves the needs of more than 52,000 people. Instruction is individual, and programs are aimed at the illiterate and semiliterate adult. A component for teaching English as a second language is available.

◆ Laubach Literacy Action is the U.S. division of Laubach Literacy International. Frank Laubach, a missionary, developed a program to teach literacy to people worldwide. This program uses volunteers and currently serves more than 150,000 adults. Materials, including initial instruction in a pictorial alphabet, are available through New Readers' Press.

◆ ELL adult literacy programs concentrate on English as a second language. Federal funding comes from the Adult Education and Family Literacy Act (1998). These programs currently serve more than one million limited-English-proficient adults. As more immigrants enter the U.S. workforce, ESL services are expected to increase (Newman, 1994).

Adults with reading problems express their wishes for a wide variety of life skills. They express needs for improving social skills, career counseling, developing self-esteem and confidence, overcoming dependence, survival skills, vocational training, job procurement and retention, reading, spelling, management of personal finances, and organizational skills. They often express a particular need for help in coping with jobs.

Summary

The diversity of U.S. culture is one of the country's most important strengths. As new immigrant groups continue to come to the United States with their own languages, cultures, and traditions, U.S. society is increasingly enriched in cultural resources. Although cultures differ in their views about literacy and language, teachers can make school a welcome place where all children can share their linguistic and cultural backgrounds.

English Language Learners (ELL) are students whose native language is not English. ELL students may have limited proficiency in English. The number of ELL students is increasing in U.S. schools. About 80 percent of ELL students speak Spanish.

The No Child Left Behind Act of 2001 and the Individual with Disabilities Education Improvement Act of 2004 are two laws that are impacting ELL students. Models for teaching English as a second language include the bilingual or native language model, the English as a second language (ESL) model, sheltered English, and immersion. Several research projects are currently under way to determine the most effective ways to teach reading to ELL students, especially Spanish-speaking students. Currently, recommended strategies for teaching reading to ELL students include using literature from various linguistic and cultural backgrounds, using interactive seating arrangements, using language-based instruction, building oral language skills, using predictable, repetitive books, using conversations about books, and using cooperative learning.

Parents and families play an important role in fostering literacy. Early reading begins in the home.

Many adolescents have reading problems. Secondary programs should focus on content-area reading.

Many individuals have reading problems that continue into adulthood. Programs for adults in postsecondary and college programs include ABE and GED classes, Literacy Volunteers of America, Laubach Literacy Action, and ELL programs for adults.

References

Armbruster, B., Lehr, F., & Osborn, J. (2006). *A Child Becomes a Reader: Proven Ideas from Research for Parents.* Washington, DC: National Institute for Literacy.

August, D., & Shanaham, T. (Eds). (2006). *Developing Literacy in Second-Language Learners: Report of the National Literacy Panel on Language-Minority Children and Youth.* Mahwah, NJ: Lawrence Erlbaum Associates.

Bryan, T. (1991). Social problems and learning disabilities. In B. Wong, (Ed.) *Learning about Learning Disabilities* (pp. 195–231). San Diego: Academic Press.

Cazden, C. (1988). *Classroom Discourse: The Language of Teaching and Learning.* Portsmouth, NH: Heinemann.

Deshler, D., Schumaker, J., Lenz, B., Bulgren, J., Hock, M., Knight, J., et al. (2001). Ensuing content learning by secondary students with learning disabilities *Learning Disabilities Research and Practice, 16*(2), 96–108.

Gottesman, R. (1994). The adult with learning disabilities: An overview. *Learning Disabilities: A Multidisciplinary Journal, 5*(1), 1–13.

Hudson, R., & Smith, S. (2002). Effective reading instruction for struggling Spanish-speaking readers: A combination of two literatures. Available at www.ldonline.org.

International Reading Association. (2007). *Key Issues and Questions in English Language Learners Literacy research.* Newark, DE: International Reading Association and Washington, DC: International Institute of Child Health and Human Development.

Jiménez, R. (2002). Fostering literacy development of Latino students. *Focus on Exceptional Children, 34*(6), 1–10.

Klingner, J., Artiles, A., & Barletta, L. (2006). English language learners who struggle with reading: Language acquisition or LD? *Journal of Learning Disabilities, 39,* 2, 108–128.

Lenz, B., & Deshler, D. (2003). *Teaching Content to All: Evidence-Based Inclusive Practice in Middle and Secondary Schools.* Boston: Pearson.

Lerner, J. W., Lowenthal, B., & Lerner, S. (1995). *Attention Deficit Disorders: Assessment and Teaching.* Pacific Grove, CA: Brooks/Cole.

Lerner, J. W., & Johns, B. (2009). *Learning Disabilities and Related Mild Disabilities: Characteristics, Teaching Strategies, and New Directions.* Boston: Houghton Mifflin.

Lerner, J., Lowenthal, B., & Egan, R. (2003). *Preschool Children with Special NeEds: Children At-Risk and Children with Disabilities.* Boston: Allyn & Bacon.

McCardle, R. (2006). Bilingual literacy research. The DELSS Research Network and beyond. *The International Dyslexia Association Perspectives, 32*(2), 1–5.

Newman, A. P. (1994). Adult literacy programs: an overview. *Learning Disabilities: A Multidisciplinary Journal, 5*(1), 51–61.

Ortiz, A. (2001). English language learners with special needs: Effective instructional strategies. Available at www.ldohline.org/aticle/5622.

Spinelli, C. (2006). *Classroom Assessment for Students in Special and General Education.* Columbus, OH: Pearson Merrill/Prentice Hall.

U.S. Census Bureau. (2006). Washington, DC: U.S. Department of Congress, Bureau of the Census.

U.S. Department of Education. (2006*). To assure the free appropriate public education of all children with disabilities.* Twenty-fifth Annual Report to Congress on the Implementation of the Individuals with Disabilities Education Act. Washington, DC: U.S. Department of Education.

Vaughn, S. (1991). Social skills enhancement in students with learning disabilities. In B. Wong, (Ed.). *Learning about Learning Disabilities* (pp. 408–440). San Diego: Academic Press.

Zigmond, N. (1990). Rethinking secondary school programs for students with learning disabilities. *Focus on Exceptional Children, 23*, 1–22.

Zigmond, N. (1997). Educating students with disabilities: The future of special education. In. J. Lloyd, E. Kame euni., & D. Chard (Eds.). *Issues in Educating Students with Disabilities* (pp. 275–304, 377–391). Mahwah, NJ: Erlbaum.

MyEducationLab is a research-based learning tool that brings teaching to life. Go to the Jennings, Caldwell, & Lerner 6th Edition MyEducationLab for Reading Assessment site at www.myeducationlab.com to:

◆ engage in multimedia exercises to help you build a deeper and more applied understanding of chapter content;

◆ utilize extensive resources including videos from real classrooms, Praxis and licensure preparation, a lesson plan builder, and materials to help you in your teaching career.

Literacy Instruction for Students with Special Needs

Introduction

This chapter examines reading instruction for students with special needs. Students with special needs include at least three different groups of students: (1) students who have disabilities, (2) students who are English Language Learners (ELLs), and (2) students who are at-risk for learning failure. In this chapter, we discuss students who have disabilities and students who are at risk. Chapter 14 discussed ELLs.

In this chapter, we also examine programs for teaching reading to students with special needs. Most children with special needs encounter problems in reading. Further, most of these children today receive their instruction in the general education class. Classroom teachers at the elementary and secondary levels are typically responsible for teaching students with special needs.

Students with Disabilities

Go to MyEducationLab and select the topic *Special Needs*. Then, go to the Activities and Applications section, watch the video entitled "Lily," and respond to the accompanying questions.

Students with disabilities are recognized under the special education law of the Individuals with Disabilities Education Improvement Act-2004 (Public Law 108-446) (U.S. Department of Education, 2004). The law indicates that students with disabilities need "specially designed instruction." There are 13 categories of disabilities recognized in this law and these categories are shown in Table 15.1. They are divided by high-incidence disabilities (those categories of disabilities that have a large number of children) and low-incidence disabilities (those categories with a smaller number of children).

The Individuals with Disabilities Education Improvement Act of 2004

IDEA-2004 is a reauthorization of an earlier law that was passed in 1997. This special education law has undergone versions. Table 15.2 shows the versions of the special education law as well as the history and the sequence of the special education laws.

TABLE 15.1   Categories of Disabilities in the Special Education Law (P.L. 108-446)

High-Incidence Disabilities	*Low-Incidence Disabilities*	
Learning disabilities	Orthopedic impairment	Traumatic brain injury
Language impairment	Hearing impairment	Blind-deaf
Mental retardation	Visual impairment	Multiple disabilities
Emotional disturbance	Autism	Developmental delay
Other health impairment		

Source: Adapted from Lerner & Johns (2009).

FIGURE 15.1   Percentage of Children With All Disabilities, Ages 6–17

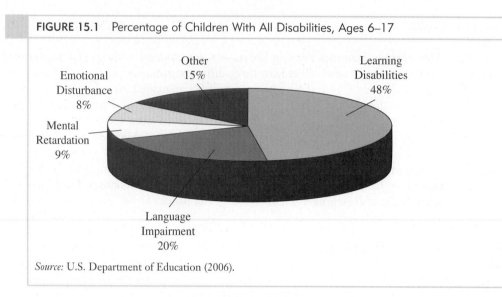

Source: U.S. Department of Education (2006).

The changes in the law affect the assessment and instruction of students with disabilities. Several of the highlights of the 2004 law are described later. A useful website describing key features of IDEA-2004 is www.ideapractices.org.

Response to Intervention.   One feature of IDEA-2004 is that it presents a major shift in the procedures for teaching and evaluating all students with a procedure called response-to-intervention (RTI). RTI is discussed in greater detail in Chapter 1. Briefly, instead of identifying students with disabilities using an evaluation of the students to diagnose the student's problem, the RTI procedure begins with general education instruction. RTI uses an evidenced-based or research-based method to instruct

TABLE 15.2   The History of the Special Education Laws

Date	Title of the Law	Number of the Law
1975	The Education of All Handicapped Children Act	PL 94-142
1990	IDEA Individuals with Disabilities Education Act	PL 101-475
1997	IDEA-1997 Individuals with Disabilities Education Act of 1997	PL 105-17
2004	IDEA-2004 Individuals with Disabilities Education Improvement Act of 2004	PL 108-446

students. The student receives instruction through several tiers or levels of instruction. Students who do not respond successfully in one tier of instruction, go to the next tier where the student receives more intense intervention. After the student does not respond successfully to several tiers of intervention, the student then may receive an evaluation for special education (Fuchs & Deshler, 2007; Hollenbeck, 2007; Fletcher, Coulter, Reshley, & Vaughn, 2004).

The Individualized Education Program

Another feature of IDEA-2004 is that it requires that an individualized education program (IEP) be written for each student with a disability. An IEP is a written statement for each child with a disability that is developed, reviewed, and revised annually in accordance with the law.

In addition, IDEA-2004 requires that IEPs designate annual goals for each student. Formerly, these goals were required to include objectives or benchmarks needed to meet these goals. In an effort to reduce the burden of paperwork for teachers and schools, the new law no longer requires that objectives and benchmarks be included. However, the law does require specific indicators of progress and how they will be measured.

Contents of the IEP. The contents of the IEP must include the following components (IDEA, 2004):

1. Statement of the child's present levels of achievement
2. Statement of measurable annual goals, including academic and functional goals
3. Description of how the child's progress toward meeting the annual goals will be measured
4. Statement of the special education services, related services, and supplementary aids based on peer-reviewed research to the extent practical
5. Explanation of the extent to which the student will not participate with nondisabled children in the regular class
6. Projected date for the beginning of the services and modifications and the anticipated frequency, location, and duration of those services and modifications

Participants at IEP Meetings. According to IDEA-2004, IEP meetings must include the following participants:

◆ Parents of the child with a disability
◆ At least one regular education teacher
◆ At least one special education teacher
◆ A representative of the school district who is qualified to provide or supervise the provision of specially designed instruction to meet the unique needs of children with disabilities, is knowledgeable about the general education curriculum, and is knowledgeable about the resources of the school
◆ An individual who can interpret the instructional implications of the IEP

◆ Other individuals who have knowledge about the child are invited at the discretion of the parent or the school

Transition Services

Transition planning is required in IDEA-2004. *Transition* refers to the process of preparing a student to move from the school environment to the adult world. Transition settings include postsecondary education, vocational education, integrated employment, supported employment, independent living, and community participation. IDEA-2004 requires that transition plans be included in the student's IEP beginning, with the first IEP to be in effect when the student is 16 and that they be updated annually.

Procedural Safeguards

Procedural safeguards are protections for the student and the student's family that are part of the law. Parents who disagree with the recommendations of the IEP team have several options. They can ask for a mediation meeting, at no cost to them, to try to reach an agreement. The school can then ask for a dispute resolution meeting to find agreement. Parents also have the option of calling for a due-process hearing.

Learning Disabilities

Two categories of students with disabilities are discussed: learning disabilities and attention deficit hyperactivity disorder (ADHD). Many of students with learning disabilities and students with ADHD have reading problems. Moreover, they are often in general education classes and teaching them is the responsibility of the general education teacher.

Learning disability is one of the special education categories that is recognized in IDEA-2004. Almost one-half of all students who have disabilities are identified with learning disabilities. Further, 5 percent of all children with disabilities have learning disabilities. About 80 percent of the students with learning disabilities have reading problems (Lerner & Johns, 2009).

The definition of specific learning disabilities in IDEA-2004 is:

a disorder in one or more of basic psychological processes involved in using language, spoken or written, which may manifest itself in an imperfect ability to listen, think, speak, read, write, spell, or to do mathematical calculations. The term includes such conditions as perceptual handicaps, brain injury, minimum brain dysfunction, dyslexia, and developmental aphasia. The term does not include children who have learning problems that are primarily the result of visual, hearing, or motor handicaps, of mental retardation or emotional disturbance, or of environmental, cultural, or economic disadvantage.

Characteristics of Learning Disabilities

Although many different characteristics are associated with learning disabilities, each individual is unique and will present only some of these characteristics. For example, some students with learning disabilities have serious difficulty in mathematics, whereas others excel in mathematics. Attentional problems are symptomatic for many students with learning disabilities but not all. Further, certain kinds of characteristics are more likely to be exhibited at certain age levels. For example, preschool children are more likely than adolescents to be hyperactive. In addition, deficits are manifested in different ways at different age levels. For example, an underlying language disorder may appear as delayed speech in the preschool child, as a reading disorder in the elementary pupil, and as a writing disorder in the secondary student (Lerner & Johns, 2009).

Additional information about learning disabilities can be found on the website www.ideaamerica.org. Table 15.3 shows the common learning and behavioral characteristics displayed by students with learning disabilities.

Educational Settings for Students with Learning Disabilities

Many students with learning disabilities receive instruction in general education inclusion classrooms About 85 percent of the students with learning disabilities are in the general education class for at least part of the day. IDEA-2004 requires that students with disabilities be placed in the least-restrictive environment (LRE) for

TABLE 15.3 Common Learning and Behavioral Characteristics of Learning Disabilities

Poor motor skills	Exhibits general motor awkwardness and clumsiness. Difficulty with gross-motor and fine-motor skills
Poor attention abilities	Difficulty focusing when a lesson is presented. Easily distracted, poor concentration
Problems with cognitive processing	Difficulty in interpreting visual or auditory stimuli, memory problems
Poor strategies for learning	Passive learning style, lacks organization skills, cannot direct his or her own learning
Oral language problems	Problems in language development, listening, speaking, vocabulary, difficulty in recognizing language sounds (phonological awareness)
Reading difficulties	Problems in decoding words, basic word recognition skills, problems with reading comprehension
Writing difficulties	Performs poorly in tasks requiring written expression, spelling, and handwriting
Mathematics difficulties	Difficulty with quantitative thinking, arithmetic facts, time, space, and calculation
Poor social skills	Does poorly with social interactions

Source: Adapted from Lerner & Johns (2007).

instruction. This requirement means that students with disabilities are to be included with students who do not have disabilities (Lerner & Johns, 2009).

A challenge for the classroom teacher is to make accommodations for children with learning disabilities in the general education classroom setting. To provide effective instruction for these children, the classroom teacher, reading specialist, and special education teacher can collaborate to develop instructional plans.

Eligibility of Learning Disabilities for Special Education

As noted earlier, IDEA-2004 has created major changes in the procedure for determining the eligibility of students for learning disabilities services. The law describes two pathways for determining whether a student is eligible for learning disabilities services:

1. *Discrepancy between achievement and intellectual ability.* IDEA-2004 states that in determining whether a student is eligible for learning disabilities services, the school shall not be required to take into consideration whether a child has a severe discrepancy between achievement and intellectual ability in oral expression, listening comprehension, written expression, basic reading skill, reading comprehension, mathematics calculation, or mathematics reasoning.
2. *Response-to-intervention.* IDEA-2004 also states that in determining whether a student is eligible for learning disabilities services, the school may use a process that determines if the child responds to scientific, research-based intervention as part of the evaluation process.

The implications of having two methods of identification for eligibility are far-reaching. In the past, schools have used the discrepancy between achievement and intellectual ability procedure to identify students with learning disabilities. The discrepancy process for determining reading disabilities is described in Chapter 5. The RTI method is relatively new and discussed in Chapter 1.

Dyslexia

Dyslexia is a type of learning disability in which the person exhibits severe difficulty in learning to read. For individuals with dyslexia, recognizing letters and words and interpreting information that is presented in print form is extremely challenging.

The severe, persistent, and baffling condition of dyslexia has puzzled the educational and medical communities for many years. For many years, scholars strongly suspected that dyslexia had a neurobiological basis, but until recently they lacked the scientific evidence to support this belief. A major tool for the new brain research is functional magnetic resonance imaging (fMRI). This new, noninvasive functional MRI method can study the human brain as it is working or in the process of reading. The fMRI brain research shows measurable differences in brain activity between dyslexic and nondyslexic subjects (Shaywitz, 2003; Sousa, 2001). The neurological factors associated with dyslexia are discussed in greater detail in Chapter 2.

Individuals with dyslexia are often intelligent in other ways and even excel in areas such as mathematics and art. Dyslexic adults often recall the anguish of trying to cope with this mysterious condition in a world that requires people to read. Even though many people with dyslexia become successful adults, their reading problem often continues throughout their lives. A follow-up study of children who were identified with dyslexia in the early grades showed that they continued to display symptoms of dyslexia as adolescents (Shaywitz, Fletcher, Holahan, Shneider, Marchione, Steubing, et al., 1999). Charles Schwab, the founder of the successful and innovative stock brokerage firm, struggled with severe reading problems throughout his life. Schwab says he coped by developing other abilities, such as the ability to envision, to anticipate where things are going, and to conceive solutions to business problems. Schwab believes that his reading problem forced him to develop these skills at a higher level than people for whom reading came easily (Kantrowitz & Underwood, 1999; West, 1997).

Attention Deficit Hyperactivity Disorder

Another area of disability in which children often display problems in reading is ADHD. In IDEA-2004, ADHD is a component within the larger disability category called Other Health Impaired (OHI). ADHD is a condition of the brain that makes it difficult for children to control their behavior in school and in social settings. It affects between 4 percent and 12 percent of all school-age children (American Academy of Pediatrics, 2001). Children with ADHD have difficulty staying on task, focusing attention, and completing their work.

Characteristics of ADHD

Three characteristics associated with ADHD are (Barkley, 2006; Silver, 2006):

◆ **Inattention.**   The child cannot concentrate on a task and has developmentally inappropriate attention skills.
◆ **Impulsiveness.**   The child has a tendency to respond quickly without thinking through the consequences of an action.
◆ **Hyperactivity.**   The child's behavior is described as a constant driving motor activity, in which the child races from one endeavor or interest to another. Some children may have ADHD without hyperactivity.

Three subtypes of ADHD are designated by the *Diagnosis and Statistical Manual of Mental Disorders*, 4th edition (DSM-IV) from 2006. They are

1. *ADHD-IA: Primarily inattentive.*   The ADHD-IA subtype refers to children who have problems primarily with inattention.

2. *ADHD-HI: Primarily hyperactive and impulsive.*   Individuals who display behaviors of hyperactivity and impulsivity but not inattention.
3. *ADHD-C: Combination of ADHD-IA and ADHD-HI.*   Individuals who have both attention problems and also display symptoms of impulsivity and hyperactivity.

Educational Settings for Students with ADHD

Most students with ADHD receive their instruction in the general education class. The U.S. Department of Education (2006) reports that educational settings for students in the category of OHI are: general education class (50%), resource room (31%), separate class (15%), and other placements (4%).

Medication for Students with ADHD

Many students with ADHD receive medication to improve their attention and to control their hyperactive behavior. The most commonly used types of medication for treating ADHD are psychostimulant medications. About 75 to 85 percent of students with ADHD show general improvement with psychostimulant medication. The most widely used psychostimulant medications for ADD are Ritalin, Dexedrine, Cylert, Adderall, Concerta, and Vyvanse. A nonpsychostimulant medication that appears to be effective is Strattera (Lerner & Johns, 2009; Silver, 2006; Froehlich, Lanpher, Epstein, et al. 2004; www.help4adhd.org/ (National Resource Center on ADHD: a program of CHADD).

Students Who Are at Risk for School Failure

Some children with special needs are at risk for school failure; for learning and learning to read. Many of these students live in poverty, are born into single-parent homes, and have other factors of risk factors. These factors can include fetal alcohol syndrome, drug dependence at birth, exposure to malnutrition and smoking during mother's pregnancy, lead exposure, premature birth, child abuse, and lack of early cognitive and language stimulation. An estimated one-third of the nation's children are at risk for school failure before they enter kindergarten (Lerner & Johns, 2009).

Many at-risk students receive instruction through supplementary instructional programs supported through Title I of the Elementary and Secondary Education Act (U.S. Department of Education, 2002). The purpose of Title I legislation is to provide education to at-risk students from low-income homes.

Title I grants, which are distributed through school districts, serve students whose academic performance is below grade-level criteria (as determined by the state or local education agency) and who attend a school that has enough low-income children to warrant funding. Schools that are eligible for Title I funds provide supplementary instruction oriented to achieving high standards.

Providing Reading Instruction for Students with Special Needs

Go to MyEducationLab and select the topic *Special Needs*. Then, go to the Activities and Applications section, watch the video entitled "Accommodations for Heather," and respond to the accompanying questions.

This section discusses ways to teach reading to students with special needs who have serious reading problems. Teachers may need to adapt or modify strategies that are used to teach reading to other students. Children with special needs require more intensive, explicit instruction and they may need frequent monitoring of progress.

Students with special needs may acquire skills at a slower pace, particularly at the beginning phases of instruction. For example, Ronnie spent 10 weeks learning eight sight words. Although this progress seems extremely slow, it was a remarkable achievement for Ronnie. In fact, these words were the first that he had been able to learn and retain. Because progress may be painstaking, highlighting every success by charting or graphing progress on the road to reading is especially important.

Adapting Standard Reading Methods for Students with Severe Reading Disabilities

Methods or materials designed for teaching reading in the regular classroom can often be modified for use with students with special needs who have severe reading disabilities. These modifications require a few specialized materials, but they allow for flexibility in instruction. It is important that all teachers working with an individual student use similar strategies and terminology with the student.

Teachers often adapt word knowledge instruction to meet individual students' needs. One diagnostic word-learning lesson can help to determine whether a student learns better through a sight word or phonics approach. In this task, a student learns two sets of words: five words are presented as sight words and five words that are presented as phonics words. By comparing performance on these two tasks, the teacher can judge the student's learning strengths. A sample word learning task with directions is presented in Figure 15.2. Once teachers determine which approach is more effective for the student, they can plan accordingly. Students who learn better through the sight word task might be instructed using a sight or language experience method. Students who perform better on the phonics test can be instructed using a phonics teaching strategy first. In addition to learning about achievement on the two tasks, the process of watching students learn by different methods provides many diagnostic insights.

Adapting a Sight Word Method.   The sight word method involves teaching students to recognize the visual forms of words instantly, without further analysis. In using this approach with students with special needs, words should be selected with care. In general, long words are harder to learn than short words, although an occasional long word adds interest. Concrete words are easier to learn than abstract words.

FIGURE 15.2 Example of a Diagnostic Word Learning Task

Sight word task	Words are *house, children, boy, farm, wagon*
	1. Use a word processer to print each word on a card.
	2. Take each word; read it aloud to the student, use it in a sentence, point out visual features of the word (the children has the *ch* sound; the word, the word *boy* has an *oy* sound)
	3. Mix up the cards. Present five trials of each word, mixing the words after each trial.
	a. For the first three trials, pronounce incorrect words for the student and use the word in a sentence.
	b. For the last two trials, do not correct incorrect responses.
Phonics word task	Words are *at, bat, cat, rat, fat*
	1. Use a word processer to print each word on a card.
	2. Show students each *at* word card; say each word as the student looks at the card.
	3. Mix up the cards. Present five trials of the word, mixing the words after each trial.
	a. For the first three trials, pronounce incorrect words after each trial.
	b. For the last two trials, do not correct incorrect responses.

Response form: Mark correct or incorrect. Compare responses with the *sight word task trial* and the *phonics task trial*.

Sight word task trial

	1	2	3	4	5
house					
children					
boy					
farm					
wagon					

Phonics Task Trial

	1	2	3	4	5
at					
bat					
cat					
rat					
fat					

For example, the student's name, parts of the body, the name of the school, and so on are easier to learn than function words, such as *the*, *when*, or *to*.

The words selected for instruction should also be varied in shape or configuration and in length to avoid visual confusion. Move carefully from words to sentences to books. Words should also be reviewed many times to firmly establish them in the student memory. Be careful to use standard manuscript writing or a word processor for all teacher-made materials. Because severely disabled readers may focus on small differences, they may be confused by a letter d with a "tail" attached.

Adapting a Phonics Method. Children need developmentally appropriate, systematic instruction in phonics (National Reading Panel, 2000). However, no one approach to phonics instruction has been found to be more effective than other approaches (Stahl, Duffy-Hester, & Stahl, 1998). Cunningham (2005) identified three major approaches to phonics instruction: synthetic, analytic, and analogic. All three approaches can be adapted for use with special needs.

Synthetic Phonics In synthetic phonics, students first learn individual letter sounds and then learn how to blend letter sounds or groups of letter sounds into a whole word. For example, children learn the short *a* sound and the sounds for *b* and *t*. Then they learn the words *at*, *bat*, and *tab*. As they learn additional sounds, such as the sound for *m* and *r*, they can add *mat*, *rat*, *ram*, and *bam*. As more sounds are added, more decodable words can be read. Although the teacher usually reads "real" stories aloud to the children, all the early stories that the children read are comprised of the sounds they have been taught and a few high-frequency sight words such as *a*, *the*, *is*, and *on*. Similarly, the children' writing consists of words that contain the sounds they have been taught (Cunningham, 2005).

The concept of synthetic phonics is often difficult for students with severe reading disabilities to grasp at first. Before using a synthetic approach, teachers should make sure the student possesses needed prerequisite skills, such as phonemic awareness. However, once basic phonics concepts are mastered, the student often gains rapidly in reading performance.

Although intense effort is required, this method works for some severely disabled readers. Betty, an intelligent 13-year-old, had a long history of reading failure, but she was anxious to learn. Her teacher taught her the sounds of the consonants followed by the short *a* and long *a* sounds and rules for using them in a process that took several months. Once these initial steps were mastered, however, progress was much faster. In fact, she learned the other vowels quite easily, and in her second 6 months of instruction, Betty demonstrated gains of more than 2 years.

Analytic Phonics In analytic phonics, children are taught some words and are then taught to construct generalizations about the words based on similarities and differences. Most basal reading series use an analytic approach to phonics instruction, and children learn to apply their phonics generalizations along with sight words, context, and predictions to read stories. Children are encouraged to read a wide variety of texts and to engage in a wide variety of writing. Although the stories and writing may be more engaging, analytic phonics approaches require a longer period of time to cover the basic phonics patterns than synthetic phonics (Cunningham, 2005).

Ten-year-old Billy was a nonreader who was taught analytic phonics for several months. His initial learning rate was one word family per week for 4 weeks and two families a week thereafter. Billy's teacher controlled the word families carefully so that they would not be too similar. After each word family was learned, it was presented in a story. The words from the word family were at first color coded (for example, one family was written in yellow and another in red). Billy's independent reading was done with books containing rhyming words, such as Dr. Seuss's *Hop on Pop* and *Green Eggs and Ham*. Billy also created his own book of word families that featured one word family (e.g., -ight, -ake) with many example words on each page.

Analogic Phonics   Analogic phonics instruction also begins with words children have learned, but instead of teaching rules or generalizations, teachers guide students to notice patterns in words and to use the words they know to figure out new words. For example, if you know the word *man*, you can figure out the words *ran*, *pan*, and *fan*. As in analytic phonics instruction, children are encouraged to read a variety of stories and write about various topics (Cunningham, 2005).

Differentiated Instruction

Not all people learn in the same way. Differences in temperamental styles are observed even in infants (Thomas & Chess, 1977). Some babies are alert and responsive; others are irritable or passive. Teachers should not assume that everyone learns in the same way. Students with special needs may not respond to a standard curriculum (or a one-size-fits-all curriculum) if it is not geared to their learning differences. These students require teaching that is responsive to their personal talents, interests, and proclivities. The concept of *differentiated instruction* suggests that teachers find the special approach that can be successful for the individual student (Bender, 2006; Tomlison, 2001).

Differences in Cognitive Processing

Cognitive processing refers to the different ways that students process information within the brain (Sousa, 2001). With the understanding that learning occurs in the brain, many psychologists and educators recognize that that individuals have different ways of learning. For example, Howard Gardner (1999) proposes a theory of "multiple intelligences," and Mel Levine (2002) proposes a theory called "all kinds of minds." Both theories emphasize that children have different ways of learning. Differentiated instruction means that teachers must adjust instruction to the learning styles of individual students.

A basic concept underlying the field learning disabilities is that individuals have strengths in different modes of processing information. For example, students with strong visual processing skills may be visual learners and learn better through sight word or language experience methods and that students with strong auditory processing skills may be auditory learners and learn better through phonics methods (Lerner & Johns, 2009).

Although the concept of differences in modes of processing is appealing to our common sense, research has not found that they predict reading success (Allington, 1982). Caldwell (1991) found that the amount of reading done by disabled students rather than their auditory or visual aptitude determines reading progress.

Students can also be described active or passive learners. Efficient learning requires an active and dynamic involvement in the learning process. Active learners organize information, ask themselves questions about the material, and compare new information to what they already know. They are motivated and have a desire to learn. Students with passive learning styles lack interest in learning, possibly because of frustrating past experiences (Lerner & Johns, 2009). Believing that they cannot learn, these students become passive and dependent, a style that is often called learned helplessness. Passive learners wait for the teacher to do something to lead them to the learning instead of taking the initiative. In effect, they expect to be spoon fed, step-by-step.

As teachers, focus on planning learning experiences that tap students' diverse strengths and afford them opportunities to approach learning from their strengths. For example, in planning a unit of instruction, provide learning experiences that include listening, speaking, reading, writing, organizing, and categorizing information, and responding to text through art or movement.

Multisensory Methods for Teaching Reading

Multisensory methods are built on the premise that stimulation of several sensory avenues reinforces learning. For example, multisensory methods uses visual, auditory, kinesthetic, and tactile sensory avenues for teaching reading. *Multisensory methods* are a collection of programs that are based on the use of multisensory teaching (Birsh, 2005). Some of the multisensory methods are the Orton-Gillingham method, Project Read, the Wilson method, Alphabetic Phonics, S.P.I.R.E., the Herman method, the Spalding method, and the SLANT reading program.

The multisensory concept is indicated in the abbreviation VAKT (visual, auditory, kinesthetic, tactile). To stimulate all of these senses, children might hear the teacher say a word, say the word to themselves, hear themselves say the word, feel the muscle movement as they trace the word, feel the tactile surface under their fingertips, see their hands move as they trace the word, and hear themselves say the word as they trace it.

The VAKT method emphasizes the tracing process. Children may trace the word by having their fingers in contact with the paper. To increase the tactile and kinesthetic sensation, sandpaper letters, sand or clay trays, and finger paints are sometimes used. The Orton-Gillingham method (described later in this chapter) was the first multisensory program and is considered the basis for the other programs (Birsh, 2005).

Orton-Gillingham Method. The Orton-Gillingham method, a multisensory approach for teaching reading, is an outgrowth of Samuel Orton's neurological theory of language disorders (Orton, 1937). More than 70 years ago, Orton, a physician who specialized in children with language disorders, worked with a teacher, Anna Gillingham, to develop a multisensory, synthetic phonics approach using direct instruction. The approach is associated with the International Dyslexia Society, which is an organization dedicated to finding causes and treatments for dyslexia.

The original Orton-Gillingham method (Gillingham & Stillman, 1970) is a highly structured approach requiring five lessons a week for a minimum of 2 years. The initial activities include learning letters and sounds, learning words, and using words in sentences.

Letter names and sounds are learned through six sensory associations. These are visual-auditory (V-A), auditory-visual (A-V), auditory-kinesthetic (A-K), kinesthetic-auditory (K-A), visual-kinesthetic (V-K), and kinesthetic-visual (K-V). Instruction takes place in three phases:

1. Phase I:
   A. The teacher establishes a V-A association with the letter name by showing a card with a letter on it and saying the letter name. The student repeats the letter name, making an A-K association. This step is the foundation for oral reading.
   B. When the student has mastered the letter name, the teacher develops a V-A association with the letter sound by saying the sound while exposing the card. The student repeats the sound, making both V-A and A-K associations.

2. Phase II:
   The student develops the ability to relate the sound to the letter name. The teacher, without showing the card, makes the letter sound, and the pupil tells the name of the letter. This step is the basis for oral spelling.

3. Phase III:
   A. The teacher prints the letter and explains its construction. The student then traces over the original, copies it, and finally writes the letter from memory while averting eyes from the paper; this makes a V-K and K-V association.
   B. The teacher says the sound and the pupil writes the letter that has that sound, thereby developing the A-K association.

After learning letter-sound associations, the student learns to read words. This learning starts by blending letter sounds and spelling the words. The initial words taught contain two vowels, *a* and *i*, and eight consonants, *b, g, h, j, k, m, p,* and *t*. The blended words follow a consonant-vowel-consonant (CVC) pattern, and blending occurs by pronouncing the first consonant and vowel together (rǎ) and then adding the final consonant (rat). These words are written on colored cards, which are called the student's "jewel case." Sample jewel case words are bat, hip, bib, and job. After these words are mastered, words containing other letters are added.

After the student learns a basic set of words, the words are combined into sentences and stories, and the student learns to read these. Reading continues to be taught by a phonics method and combines spelling and dictation exercises.

Fernald Method. More than 50 years ago, Grace Fernald (1943–1998) developed a multisensory approach for extremely poor readers that simultaneously involves four sensory avenues—visual, auditory, kinesthetic, and tactile. Because progress with this method a word as a total pattern by tracing the entire word and thereby strengthening the memory and visualization of the entire word. The words to be learned are selected by the student. The method consists of four stages:

1. Stage One

   A. The student dictates a story to the teacher and chooses a word from the story to learn. The teacher writes the word on a card with a crayon, using print about the size of blackboard script.
   B. The student finger-traces over the word written by the teacher. While tracing each letter, the student says the name of that letter. This step is repeated until the student can successfully write and spell the entire word while looking at it.
   C. The student repeats Step B without looking at the word. When the student can write the word without looking at it, it is filed alphabetically in a word bank to be used when the student writes stories. Students should read stories from typed, rather than handwritten, copies.

2. Stage Two: This stage does not include tracing every new word. In this stage, the student looks at a copy of the word written by the teacher and says the word while writing it. Students add learned words to their individual word banks and continue to write stories.
3. Stage Three: During Stage Three, students may begin to read from books. Students learn a new word by looking at the printed word, saying it to themselves, and then writing it. The teacher should continuously check for retention of words in the word bank.
4. Stage Four: In the final stage, students can recognize new words by finding similarities to previously learned words or part of words.

S.P.I.R.E.. Another multisensory reading program designed for struggling readers is S.P.I.R.E. (Educators Publishing Service). This program addresses the skills of phonological awareness, phonics, fluency, vocabulary, and comprehension. It uses a step-by-step multisensory approach to teaching reading. For further information, visit the EPS website at www.epsbooks.com.

Lindamood Phoneme Sequencing Program

The Lindamood Phoneme Sequencing (LIPS) program is a phonemic awareness and phonics program for children with severe reading problems. It focuses on the conscious processing of sensory information, particularly involving the mouth and speech mechanism. The program develops metacognitive phoneme awareness of the lip, tongue, and mouth actions that produce the sounds students hear in words. It strives to teach students to use sensory information from feeling, seeing, and hearing to develop a feedback system that promotes self-correction in speech, reading, and spelling (Lindamood & Lindamood, 1998; Lindamood-Bell Learning Process).

Direct Instruction Reading Program

Direct Instruction reading has been shown to be highly effective with children who are considered at risk because of poverty (Carnine, Silbert, Kame'enui, & Tarver, 2004). This program is a revision of the former DISTAR reading program (Engelmann & Bruner, 1974, 1995).

This highly structured reading program consists of lessons based on carefully sequenced skill hierarchies. Based on principles of behavioral psychology, the program contains drills and instructional reading as well as repetition and practice. Students progress in small planned steps, and teacher praise is used as reinforcement. Teachers are guided in specific procedures and oral instructions through each step of the program. The program uses a synthetic phonics approach, and students are first taught the prerequisite skill of auditory blending to help them combine isolated sounds into words. In addition, the shapes of some alphabet letters are modified to provide clues to the letter sounds. The special alphabet is gradually phased out as children progress.

In this program, the teacher presents fully scripted lessons. The direct instruction reading program prescribes what the teacher says and does. The students (individually and in unison as a group) provide the anticipated response. The teacher evaluates the degree of mastery of individuals and of the group on criterion-referenced tasks and tests.

The corrective reading program (Engelmann, Becker, Hanner, & Johnson, 1995) is designed for the older student (Grades 4 through 12). It consists of two strands: decoding, which follows the regular direct instruction format, and comprehension, which uses text materials of interest to the older student. The web address for the direct instruction programs is www.sra-4kids.com.

Fast ForWord

Fast ForWord is an Internet- and CD-ROM–based training program for children with language and reading problems. It is designed for children who have trouble processing sounds quickly enough to distinguish rapid acoustical change in speech. This program alters the acoustics of speech by drawing out sounds and then gradually speeding them up; that is, stretching out certain speech sounds and emphasizing rapidly changing speech components by making them slower and louder. In an intensive series of adaptive interactive exercises using acoustically modified speech sounds, the Fast ForWord program stimulates rapid language skill development as children learn to distinguish the various components of speech (Miller, DeVivo, LaRossa, Pycha, Peterson, et al., 1998).

Fast ForWord Two is an advanced program that uses the Internet and a CD-ROM training program to help students develop the language and reading skills critical for reading or becoming a better reader using adaptive technology. The program uses interactive exercises to cross-train the brain on a number of skills that improve listening, thinking, and reading skills. The Fast ForWord program is used with children ages 5–12 (Miller, et al., 1998). The website for Fast ForWord is www .scientificlearning.com.

Summary

Students with special needs may have severe difficulties in learning to read due to environmental problems, neurological problems, or a lack of proficiency in English.

The Individuals with Disabilities Education Improvement Act of 2004 (IDEA-2004) contains many features that apply to reading and to students with reading problems. There are 13 categories of disabilities recognized in IDEA-2004. Each student with a disability is required to have an individual education program (IEP). Transition is the process of preparing a student to move from the high school environment to the adult world. Procedural safeguards are protections for the student and the student's family built into the law.

Learning disability is one of the special education categories that is recognized in the special education law, IDEA-2004. About 80 percent of students with learning disabilities display reading problems. Students with learning disabilities are covered by IDEA-2004 and may receive services through special education. Most students with learning disabilities are in general education settings.

Dyslexia is one type of learning disability, which is a serious reading disability. Many students with attention deficit hyperactivity disorder (ADD) have reading problems. Services in the schools for these students are covered under the IDEA-2004 category "Other Health Impaired." A number of instructional methods are used to teach reading to students with severe reading problems. Standard reading methods can be adapted for use with students who have severe reading disabilities. Multisensory methods use visual, auditory, tactile, and kinesthetic sensory pathways to reinforce learning. Multisensory methods include the Orton-Gillingham Methods, the Fernald Method. Other methods for students with special needs are the Lindamood Phoneme Sequencing Program, Direct Instruction Reading Programs, and Fast ForWord.

References

Allington, R. L. (1982). The persistence of teacher beliefs in the perceptual deficit hypothesis. *Elementary School Journal, 82*, 351–359.

American Academy of Pediatrics. (2001). Clinical practice guideline: Treatment of the child with attention deficit hyperactivity disorder. *Pediatrics, 108*(4), 1033–1044.

Barkley, R. (2006). *Attention Deficit Hyperactivity Disorder: A Handbook for Diagnosis and Treatment.* New York: Guilford Press.

Bender, W. (2006). *Differentiating Instruction for Students with Learning Disabilities.* Arlington, VA: Council for Exceptional Children.

Birsh, J. (2005). *Multisensory Teaching of Basic Skills.* Baltimore, MD: Brookes.

Caldwell, J. (1991). *Subtypes of Reading/Learning Disabilities: Do They Have Instructional Relevance?* Paper presented at the Learning Disabilities Association of America,

Carnine, D., Silbert, J., Kame'enui, E., & Tarver, S. (2004). *Direct Instruction in Reading. Instruction Reading* (4th ed.). Upper Saddle River, NJ: Pearson Education.

Cunningham, A. E. (2005). Vocabulary growth through independent reading and reading aloud to children. In E. H. Hiebert & M. L. Kamil (Eds.), *Teaching and Learning Vocabulary: Research and Practice*, (pp. 45–68). Mahwah NJ.: Lawrence Erlbaum.

Engelmann S. & Bruner, E. (1974). *Reading Mastery Series.* Worthington, OH: SRA Macmillan/McGraw-Hill.

Engelmann, S., & Bruner, E. (1995). *Reading Mastery Series.* Worthington, OH: SRA Macmillan/McGraw-Hill.

Engelmann, S., Becker, W., Hanner, S., & Johnson, G. (1995). *Corrective Reading Series Guide.* Chicago: Science Research Associates.

Fletcher, J., Coulter, W., Reschley, D., & Vaughn. S. (2004). Alternative approaches to the definition and identification of learning disabilities: Some questions and answer. *Annals of Dyslexia, 54*(2), 304–331.

Froehlich, T., Lanpher, B., Epstein, J., et al. (2007). Prevalence, recognition, and treatment of attention-deficit/hyperactivity disorder in a national sample of U.S. children. *Archives of Pediatric and Adolescent Medicine, 161,* 857–864.

Fuchs, D, & Deshler, D. (2007). What we need to know about responsiveness to intervention (and shouldn't be afraid to ask). *Learning Disabilities Research and Practice, 22*(2), 129–136.

Gardner, H. (1999). *Intelligence Reformed: Multiple Intelligences for the Twenty-First Century.* New York: Basic Books.

Gillingham, A. & Stillman, B. (1970). *Remedial Training for Children with Specific Disability in Reading, Spelling, and Penmanship.* Cambridge, MA: Educators Publishing Service.

Hollenbeck, A. (2007). From IDEA to implementation: A discussion of the foundational and future response-to-intervention research. *Learning Disabilities Research and Practice, 22*(2), 86–118.

IDEA 2004. Individuals with Disabilities Education Improvement Act of 2004. Public Law 108-446, 108th Cong. 2nd sess. (December 3, 2004).

Kantrowitz, B., & Underwood, A. (1999). Dyslexia and the new science of reading. *Newsweek, 123,* 71–80.

Lerner, J., & Johns, B. (2009). *Learning Disabilities and Related Mild Disabilities: Characteristics, Teaching Strategies, and New Directions.* Boston: Houghton Mifflin.

Levine, M. (2002). *A Mind at a Time.* New York: Simon & Schuster.

Lindamood-Bell Learning Process. Available at www.lindamoodbell.com.

Miller, S., DeVivo, K., LaRosa, A., Pycha, A., Peterson, B., Tallal, P., et al. (1998). *Acoustically Modified Speech and Language Training Reduces Risk for Academic Difficulties.* Paper presented at the Society for Neuroscience, Los Angeles, CA.

National Reading Panel. (2000). Teaching children to read: An evidenced-based assessment of the scientific research literature on reading and implication for reading instruction. www.nichd.nih.gov/publications/nrp/smallbook.htm.

National Resource Center on AD/HD: A Program of CHADD. Available at www.help4adhd.org.

Orton, S. (1937). *Reading, Writing, and Speech Problems of Children.* New York: Norton.

Shaywitz, S. (2003). *Overcoming Dyslexia: A New and Complete Science-Based Program for Reading Problems at Any Level.* New York: Alfred A. Knopf.

Shaywitz, B., & Shaywitz, S. (1999). Brain research and reading: Lectures at Schwab Learning. www.schwablearning.com.

Shaywitz, S., Fletcher, J., Holahan, J., Shneider, A., Marchione, K., Steubing, K., et al. (1999). Persistence of dyslexia: The Connecticut longitudinal study at adolescence. *Pediatrics, 104,* 1351–1360.

Silver, L. (2006). *The Misunderstood Child.* New York: Three Rivers Press.

Sousa, D. (2001). *How the Brain Learns.* Thousand Oaks, CA: Corwin Press.

Stahl, S., Duffy-Hester, A., & Stahl, K. (1998). Everything you wanted to know about phonics (but were afraid to ask). *Reading Research Quarterly, 33,* 338–355.

Thomas, A., & Chess, S. (1977). *Temperament and Development.* New York: Bruner/Mazel.

Tomlison, C. (2001). *How to Differentiate Instruction in Mixed Ability Classrooms.* Alexandria, VA: Association for Curriculum and Development.

U.S. Department of Education. (2002). *To assure the free appropriate education of all children with disabilities.* Twenty-fourth Annual Report to Congress on the Implementation of the Individuals with Disabilities Education Act. Washington, DC: U.S. Department of Education.

U.S. Department of Education. (2004). The Individuals with Disabilities Education Improvement Act of 2004. Washington, DC: U.S. Department of Education.

U.S. Department of Education. (2006). *To assure the free appropriate public education of all children with disabilities.* Twenty-fifth Annual Report to Congress on the Implementation of the Individuals with Disabilities Education Act. Washington, DC: U.S. Department of Education.

West, T. (1997). *In the Mind's Eye: Visual Thinkers, Dyslexia, and Other Learning Difficulties, Computer Imaging and the Ironies of Creativity.* New York: Prometheus Books.

PEARSON
myeducationlab
Where the Classroom Comes to Life

MyEducationLab is a research-based learning tool that brings teaching to life. Go to the Jennings, Caldwell, & Lerner 6th Edition MyEducationLab for Reading Assessment site at www.myeducationlab.com to:

◆ engage in multimedia exercises to help you build a deeper and more applied understanding of chapter content;

◆ utilize extensive resources including videos from real classrooms, Praxis and licensure preparation, a lesson plan builder, and materials to help you in your teaching career.

CHAPTER

Collaborative Assessment and Instruction

16

Introduction

Reading specialists must collaborate with classroom teachers, teachers of special education, students, parents, administrators, psychologists, other professionals, and paraprofessionals to provide the most effective instruction possible. From the initial contact, the assessment process involves a multitude of teachers, schedules, program considerations, and student needs. This chapter presents the collaborative nature of assessing students' literacy needs and providing for their continuing instruction.

Changing Roles of Reading Specialists

In recent years, the roles of reading specialists have changed dramatically. Previously, these teachers received their specialist degrees and certification, gathered their assessment instruments and instructional materials, and set up shop in a small room near the furnace, in a nurse's office, or even under the stairwell! Teachers sent their lowest-achieving students, and the reading specialist diagnosed the problems and taught remedial reading classes in small groups throughout the day. Sometimes, teachers were not even involved in the student selection process; it was based solely on achievement test results. Most of the communication that occurred between the reading specialist and the teacher involved scheduling. Some carved out more collaborative efforts to support children in classrooms when they weren't in the intervention class, but that was truly dependent on personal relationships with classroom teachers.

Research conducted in the late 1980s and early 1990s revealed significant problems with this model. Allington (1986) reported that reading specialists were often unaware of the instruction students received in their classrooms, and classroom teachers were not aware of the instruction students received in their remedial reading classes. Further, so much time was lost in traveling from classroom to classroom, gathering the appropriate materials, and settling down to work that the very students who needed more reading instructional time were actually engaged in fewer minutes of reading!

Possibly related to the loss of instructional time was the students' reluctance to leave their regular classrooms: They didn't want to be labeled as dumb or different. This stigma of being different or dumb often led to low self-esteem for students assigned to remedial reading classes (Bean, 2004). Allington (1986) also questioned the cost effectiveness of these pullout programs. Was the instruction provided different enough and extensive enough to outweigh the loss of time, instruction, and self-esteem?

Title I Programs

Finally, although the Title I funding legislation for most of these programs clearly identified remedial programs as supplemental to classroom instruction, most classroom teachers viewed the reading specialists as the person responsible for teaching these students to read (Bean, 2004; U.S. Department of Education, 1997; Bean,

Cooley, Eichelberger, Lazar, & Zigmond, 1991; Allington & McGill-Franzen, 1989). Many of us can remember the difficulties of scheduling students when all the teachers wanted their students to come to reading classes during their first period "reading time"! The specialists tried to explain the concept of supplemental instruction, but they could hardly blame teachers for feeling overwhelmed trying to juggle reading groups and independent work with their limited time and resources for students who need extraordinary amounts of attention and different materials than they have available on a regular basis!

Evaluating the effectiveness of Title I programs is difficult because Title I is a funding source rather than an actual set of guidelines for instruction. Individual states and, indeed, individual districts and schools have developed diverse programs designed to best meet the needs of their student populations.

Borman (2003) has conducted extensive, long-term research in the area of the effectiveness of compensatory programs, such as Title I. His analyses have led him to conclude that an achievement gap exists between children entering kindergarten in high-poverty schools and those entering kindergarten in affluent schools, and that this gap increases as these students progress through school. Thus, the achievement gap is a chronic, preexisting condition that continues and worsens throughout students' early, elementary, middle, and secondary educational experiences!

In fact, a national evaluation of Title I programs conducted in the early 1990s resulted in some policymakers suggesting that the program be eliminated (Borman, 2003; Puma, Karweit, Price, Ricciuti, Thompson, & Vaden-Kierman, 1997). However, in their meta-analysis of Title I programs, Borman and D'Agostino (1996, 2001) concluded that students served by Title I programs were better off academically than they would have been without the programs and that, based on data from the National Assessment of Educational Progress, funding and policies could have a positive impact over a relatively short period of time in overcoming educational inequality (Borman, 2003). Borman (2003) reminds us that although individual districts and schools utilize the funds in diverse ways, Title I has provided extra resources, materials, and personnel that have helped children: "Whenever an inner-city or poor rural school produces an exemplary program that helps its students achieve notable results, Title I funding almost invariably made it possible" (p. 49).

In an examination of evaluations of Title I since 1965, McDill and Natriello (1998) found that some characteristics were common across the most effective programs funded through Title I. Effective programs included:

◆ Clear, specific goals for student achievement
◆ Alignment between those goals and the methods and materials used
◆ Ongoing assessment of student performance
◆ Coordination and integration with the regular instructional program
◆ Additional instructional time through before-school, after-school, or summer programs
◆ Intensive, high-quality professional development

No Child Left Behind Act

Thus, in 2001, the U.S. Congress approved the reauthorization of Title I funds along with the No Child Left Behind Act (2001). This legislation included some specific guidelines:

◆ To narrow the achievement gap between weak and gifted students, all students should be integrated into a classroom. This means that the use of pullout programs is minimized so that students can receive individualized instruction within the classroom to support them in the subjects with which they are struggling.
◆ Beginning in academic year 2005–2006, all states will implement reading and math assessments in Grades 3 through 8 as well as at least once during Grades 10 through 12.
◆ Beginning in academic year 2007–2008, all students will be assessed in science at least once in elementary school, once in middle school, and once in high school.
◆ Teachers must attend seminars and workshops to advance their knowledge and skills.
◆ Teachers' assistants must have 2 years of college or participate in classes and pass a paraprofessional examination.
◆ Teachers are to be held accountable for student progress.
◆ Teachers must pass written examinations in their subject areas and in general education.
◆ By the end of the 2013–2014 academic year, all students in public schools must be at or above proficiency levels in reading, math, and science.

Teachers and other educators have expressed skepticism about some aspects of the legislation. First, how will all students ever achieve proficiency as it is currently measured? How can teachers be held accountable for all learning, both in and out of school? How can teachers overcome the preexisting gaps in achievement so that all children receive an equitable opportunity for learning (Birdwell, 2003)?

Narrowing the Achievement Gap

Borman (2003) offers some specific suggestions for continuing to narrow the achievement gap. First, emphasize early intervention. If the gap exists as students enter kindergarten, start programs with children and parents through preschool programs. Second, provide for the acceleration of learning throughout the school year by reducing class size and offering before- and after-school programs. Third, extend learning into summer programs. Fourth, provide for systemic changes rather than school-by-school implementation. Concerns about fade-out as students progress into the middle and high school years can be addressed by planning for ongoing support (McDill & Natriello, 1998).

What are the implications for reading teachers and reading specialists in the current climate? In its position statement, the International Reading Association recommends a new educational model in which "teachers and reading specialists work collaboratively to provide effective instruction for all students" (International Reading Association, 2000, p. 1). The position statement identifies three primary roles for reading specialists: instruction, assessment, and leadership (IRA, 2000). Each of these roles requires that the reading specialist collaborate with teachers, administrators, other professionals, and members of the community.

Role of the Reading Specialist in Assessment

Assessment includes evaluation of student performance as an integral part of instruction, evaluating student achievement through formal measures, and assessing student needs for diagnostic purposes. Throughout this book, we have presented suggestions for assessing literacy that require collaboration between the classroom teacher and reading specialist as well as with the student and parents.

Evaluation of Student Performance

Throughout instruction, teachers assess student performance. As reading specialists have become more involved in classroom instruction, they are often given the role of ensuring that state and local standards are implemented. These standards may require the development of special rubrics or alternative forms of assessment. Reading specialists often work with teachers to develop and implement these instruments, both at the individual classroom level and at the school level.

At the conclusion of a topic of study, curricular materials often provide tests to evaluate student performance. This is especially true of commercial reading series. Sometimes, teachers need help analyzing or interpreting the results of these tests. Reading specialists should be familiar enough with the programs used in their schools and with the analysis and interpretation of results to help teachers make diagnostic teaching decisions based on the results of these tests. As coordinators of school literacy programs, reading specialists are involved in the school-wide evaluation plan. They should be involved in planning for program evaluation as well as interpreting the results. However, most public school-wide evaluation plans operate under the constraints of district, state, and federal guidelines. Thus, individual public schools often have little input into designing all aspects of their evaluation plans. Reading specialists in these settings can be most helpful in helping administrators interpret overall results and in using those results to plan for instruction and professional development, based on patterns and trends in test results. Reading specialists may be involved in documenting a student's response to intervention. Schools are expected to develop RTI plans as part of their assessment plan. Classroom teachers may need help in selecting, implementing, and documenting appropriate measures of student progress, once an initial achievement level is established.

Individual Diagnostic Procedures

In a school setting, the classroom teacher usually initiates the assessment and intervention process. In a reading center setting, classroom teachers, reading specialists, or parents may initiate the process. We will focus on the school setting because that is where most reading specialists function. Most teachers base their concerns about students' academic performance on problems students encounter as they complete class assignments. This informal assessment often prompts them to contact other professionals for advice and support.

Working with Classroom Teachers. If students are struggling to read and write at a level similar to that of the majority of their classmates in reading or other subject areas, teachers usually contact the reading specialist. Teachers share their concerns through anecdotal records of observed behaviors as well as samples of student work. Sometimes, the student's performance on the school-wide standardized general achievement test raises concerns, and a more thorough diagnosis is initiated. Reading specialists should begin by visiting the classroom to observe the student firsthand. These visits should occur both during reading instructional time and during subject area instructional time. As reading specialists, we must remember that even if students receive supplemental reading instruction, the majority of their instructional time is spent in the general education classroom. Become familiar with the context of the student's learning to provide effective support for the teacher who will be primarily responsible for instruction. Sometimes, students function well in literacy instruction but struggle when reading content area materials and responding to informational text in writing. Often, the reading specialist can offer some concrete suggestions to meet the students' needs within the context of the classroom. Sometimes, these suggestions include providing additional time to complete assignments, pairing the student with a buddy for reading, reorganizing seating arrangements, or making minor adjustments in the way information is presented.

More often, if a teacher has sought help, the issue is more complex and will require more extensive support. The individual assessment process may begin with a few visits and a consultation. Then the reading specialist may ask the teacher to administer some screening instruments to confirm their concerns. These instruments may include a fluency snapshot, an informal assessment to determine reading level, and a writing sample. If these measures confirm the teacher's and reading specialist's concerns, more in-depth assessment is needed.

To begin an individual diagnostic process, the reading specialist should elicit the help and support of parents, any other teachers or educational professionals working with the student, any other professionals, such as doctors, social workers, or therapists who have worked with the student, and, of course, the student.

Working with Parents. If the teacher and reading specialist determine that an individual student needs a complete literacy diagnosis, they need to contact the student's parents. After consulting with the parents and explaining their concerns and plans to address those concerns, the reading specialist or teacher should conduct a thorough parent interview such as the one provided on the website for this text. Parent cooperation and support will be needed throughout the assessment process, decision making, and instructional planning.

Working with Other Professionals.   The reading specialist should contact any other teachers who work with the student, explain that an assessment procedure has begun, and ask for any insight they can provide into the students' performance in their classes. They should be asked to provide information as indicated in the school information form, also provided on the website.

Other resource personnel who have worked with the child should be involved in the assessment and decision-making process. Most schools have school-based problem-solving teams, assessment teams, or student services teams. The student's case should be presented to these teams early in the process so that any information these professionals have can be accessed. The professionals comprising these teams often include social workers, school nurses, speech and language therapists, and psychologists. Any of these professionals who have worked with the student can provide valuable information to the reading specialist and teacher. As the diagnostic procedures progress, the reading specialist may need the services of one or more of these professionals to complete the diagnosis. For example, the student may need a current vision or hearing screening.

Administering the Literacy Diagnosis.   The reading specialist should begin with a diagnostic administration and analysis of an informal reading inventory. A diagnostic administration and analysis is more in depth than the leveling information gained through most informal reading inventories. Using the informal reading inventory for diagnostic purposes is described in Chapter 4.

After the reading specialist has determined whether the student's major area of instructional need is in the area of comprehension or word recognition, more in-depth diagnosis can begin. If the student is having problems in word recognition, administer a spelling or phonological test. If the student is having problems in comprehension, a language development or vocabulary test should be administered (see Chapter 13). Based on the analysis of the results of these measures, the reading specialist and classroom teacher can develop an instructional plan to meet the student's needs.

However, if the student's language level is significantly lower than grade level, the reading specialist may decide to measure the student's academic potential. Usually, the reading specialist administers a screening instrument, such as the *Kaufman Brief Intelligence Test*, Second Edition or the *Slosson Intelligence Test-Revised*, Third Edition (see Chapter 4). If the results of these screening instruments indicate a significant problem, the reading specialist and teacher return to the assessment team with a recommendation for a full psychological evaluation and consideration for services for students with special needs.

Role of the Reading Specialist in Instruction

Once the in-depth diagnosis is complete, instructional intervention can begin. The reading specialist's role in instruction has changed dramatically in recent years. Previously, students were evaluated for reading services or for special education services. If students qualified for reading support, they were placed in pullout remedial reading classes. If they qualified for special education services, they were placed in pullout special education classes. Now both services are provided in more inclusive settings so that students remain in their regular classrooms, and special education teachers or reading specialists provide in-class support or instructional support to the general education classroom teacher as the primary person responsible for providing instruction.

Working with Classroom Teachers

To provide in-class instructional support, reading specialists must coordinate carefully with classroom teachers to plan effective intervention. Sometimes, the reading specialist works with a small group of students who need additional support to read text during literacy instruction. The reading specialist often provides similar support in content area classes. Such support requires extensive collaboration among teams of teachers. To accomplish this, reading specialists need to know the curricular content and expectations of the classroom teacher, and classroom teachers need to know how reading specialists plan to adapt instruction to meet the needs of struggling students.

Often reading specialists in these coaching roles provide demonstration lessons in classrooms to model highly effective literacy instruction. They may model differentiated instruction, and they may help teachers organize their classrooms and their schedules to provide differentiated instruction (Toll, 2006).

Working with Other Professionals

Under the No Child Left Behind guidelines, a major instructional goal is to keep students in their regular classrooms for instruction, whether they qualify for special education services or for reading interventional instruction. Thus, students who would have previously left their classrooms for instruction to address specific needs now remain in their classrooms, and specialists in learning disabilities and reading may both come into the classrooms to support the classroom teacher. In these settings, reading specialists working with small groups of students may be involved with students with diverse learning needs. Thus, extensive coordination and collaboration among teams of teachers is needed to provide effective, appropriate intervention. Because most schools have only one or two reading specialists or literacy coaches, they cannot be available as often as teachers may need them to be throughout the day or week. One solution to this problem is for reading specialists to provide classroom teachers with professional development in adapting instruction to support struggling students (Moxley & Taylor, 2006).

Reading Specialists as Literacy Leaders

The greatest change in reading specialists' roles has been in the area of leadership. In its position statement about reading specialists, the International Reading Association (2000) describes the leadership role of reading specialists as "multidimensional," serving as a resource to other educators, parents, and the community. Their roles include:

- Suggesting ideas, strategies, or materials to teachers to support instruction for struggling readers or to provide enrichment experiences for students reading above grade level
- Enhancing teachers' and administrators' knowledge about reading instruction
- Leading professional development workshops
- Modeling strategies or techniques for teachers
- Conducting demonstration and collaborative instructional experiences
- Serving as a resource to other educational personnel
- Serving on student services teams
- Working with parents and helping teachers to learn how to work effectively with parents
- Providing professional development for paraprofessionals or aides
- Providing instructional guidance for school volunteers

To be effective in all of these roles, reading specialists must have excellent interpersonal skills. They must have a strong knowledge of adults as learners and know how to shift roles from supporting other professionals to assuming instructional leadership (IRA, 2000).

Providing Support for Teachers

As reading specialists assume more of the responsibility for providing professional development for teachers and other resource personnel, they sometimes need additional support themselves. We have worked closely with a group of reading specialists for several years now as they have worked to make the shift from pullout remedial reading teachers to assuming the role of literacy leadership for their schools. We have provided support behind the scenes to help them plan for professional development as well as opportunities to practice demonstration classes for individual teachers. Creating their own support group has helped these reading specialists gain confidence and brainstorm ideas for their own continued professional growth.

In developing a professional development plan, begin by gathering and analyzing data from multiple sources. Students' performance on a school-wide standardized achievement test can provide a good starting point. By analyzing the results of these tests, you may identify some general strengths and needs. You should also conduct a needs assessment with the teachers. This can be accomplished through informal interactions, or you may want to ask teachers to complete a brief survey. Once you have obtained the results, work with the teachers to design a professional development plan (Casey, 2006). We typically develop 3-year plans that provide for school-wide, grade cluster, and individual professional growth opportunities.

In helping reading specialists prepare for professional development, we have also helped them find ways to integrate underlying theory with hands-on experiences for teachers learning new strategies. We suggest they provide teachers with strategy "cheat sheets"—one-page summaries of the procedures needed to implement the strategies they present. An outline for developing these cheat sheets is provided in Figure 16.1. Include a brief connection to the theoretical perspective that provides the foundation for strategies so that teachers see how different strategies are related. Also include original sources of the strategies so that teachers can access more in-depth information about the strategy and its development.

Reading specialists have described their new roles as literacy leaders in their schools. They are expected to direct the literacy instructional program for the entire school. They guide teachers in making curricular decisions and selecting appropriate materials. They work as change agents to foster school improvement. This leadership role affords reading specialists the opportunity to exert a strong positive influence on students' reading achievement (Klein, Monti, Mulcahy-Ernt, & Spock, 1997).

Providing Support for Paraprofessionals

Reading specialists also design professional development for paraprofessionals. First, develop an instructional plan for students. As you develop these plans, think through sets of strategies that work well with struggling students—then consider ways to help adults who may have limited professional education use the strategies to provide effective instructional support for struggling students. A format used for instructional plans for paraprofessionals is included in Figure 16.2.

Serving as Liaison between Teachers and Administrators

Leadership roles often place reading specialists or literacy coaches in the position of liaison between the administration and teachers. Reading specialists are often responsible for conveying administrative decisions to teachers and for helping

---

FIGURE 16.1 Template for Strategy Guide

Name of Strategy:

Originator of Strategy:

Theory Underlying Strategy Development:

Purpose of Strategy:

Procedures to Implement Strategy:

Adaptation of Strategy for Struggling Students:

Suggestions for Student Evaluation:

Reference Information for Original Source:

FIGURE 16.2 Paraprofessional Instructional Plan

Paraprofessional Instructional Plan

Student: Grade Level:

Age: Reading Specialist:

READING ASSESSMENT

Results of Assessment		
	Independent Level	**Instructional Level**
Oral Reading		
Silent Reading		
Language Level		
Student's Area of Strength		
Student's Major Area of Instructional Need		

INSTRUCTIONAL NEEDS

Guided Reading

Level:
Suggested Materials:
Recommended Strategies:

Writing

Kinds of Writing Needed:
Skills to Emphasize:
Suggested Strategies and Tools:

Word Knowledge

Vocabulary Development Needs:
Sight Word Development Needs:
Word Analysis Needs:

Independent/Shared Reading

Suggestions for Reading with An Adult or Skilled Reader:
Suggestions for Independent Reading:

RELATED FACTORS TO CONSIDER

teachers implement these decisions in their classrooms. As teacher advocates with the administration, reading specialists lobby for additional resources or organizational changes to support teachers' instructional needs. In this role, reading specialists must stay informed about current materials and funding sources to help teachers obtain appropriate materials. Reading specialists often search for grants and write proposals or help teachers in writing grant proposals to obtain supplemental books and other materials.

Although reading specialists are usually not responsible for teacher evaluation, they may be involved in providing support for teachers whose instructional practices present concerns to principals. Principals often ask reading specialists to provide support for teachers who need to improve their practices. In these circumstances, reading specialists' interpersonal skills may be put to the test. They may need to model best practices through demonstration lessons, conduct collaborative lessons as they co-teach, and suggest quality professional development opportunities or continuing educational opportunities (Rodgers & Rodgers, 2007). After each demonstration lesson or co-teaching experience, the literacy coach and classroom teacher should debrief, analyze the experience, and plan for subsequent instruction and necessary support (Puig & Froelich, 2007).

Serving on Student Services Teams

Reading specialists or literacy coaches usually participate in their schools' assessment teams or school-based problem-solving teams to determine the best instructional intervention for struggling students. The reading specialist is often the first person classroom teachers approach when they encounter a problem with a student. After the reading specialist observes the student in the classroom, the teacher and reading specialist agree on a follow-up plan. If the reading specialist and teacher agree that the student needs more in-depth diagnosis, they try to determine whether the student's problems are specific to language and literacy, a broader learning disability, or other factors, such as physical or environmental issues. This decision is based on data collected through assessment procedures.

The reading specialist and teacher should present the student's case to the student services team as they begin their collaboration. If other professionals are needed in the diagnostic phase of the process, this initial presentation will have provided the background information they need to assist in the process.

Usually, the reading specialist proceeds with a diagnostic informal reading assessment, an analysis of writing samples collected from the classroom teacher, any formal assessments needed, and a more in-depth diagnostic instrument to evaluate the student's language development or word analysis abilities. These findings should be presented to the student services team to decide the most appropriate instructional intervention. Figure 16.3 includes a form reading specialists can use to present their findings to their student services teams.

Although the information presented on the form should be limited to a summary of the results, the reading specialist should be prepared to provide more detailed information if requested by any member of the team.

FIGURE 16.3 Form for Presentation to Staffing Team

Northeastern Illinois University Reading Center

Staffing Information

Student's Name: Grade Level: Date of Birth:

Reading Specialist Intern:

INFORMAL READING ASSESSMENT

Informal Reading Assessment Administered:

Results of Informal Reading Assessment		
Mode of Reading	**Independent Level**	**Instructional Level**
Oral Reading		
Silent Reading		
Combined Reading Levels		
Student's Language Level		
Student's Area of Strength		
Student's Major Area of Instructional Need		

FORMAL READING ASSESSMENT

Formal Reading Assessment Administered:

Results of Formal Reading Assessment				
Subtests	**Total # of Items Correct of Possible Items**	**Percentile Rank**	**Grade Equivalent**	**Stanine**

Continued

Interpretation of Results

IN-DEPTH ANALYSIS

Additional Tests Administered:

Provide a table if you administered *PPVT-III* and/or *EVT*.
Provide a chart of strengths and instructional needs if you administered a phonics or spelling test (Title).

Interpretation of Results

Related Factors

Introduce any additional professionals needed to support your findings regarding factors.

Recommendations for Appropriate Instruction

Include instructional recommendations to provide a balanced approach to literacy instruction as well as recommendations for placement if necessary.

Parents should be invited to the student services meeting to provide input when the instructional intervention decisions are made for their children. At this point, they should receive a copy of the assessment summary.

Serving on the Instructional Intervention Team

After the intervention decision is made, the reading specialist, classroom teachers, and any other resource professionals who may be needed develop an instructional plan. Figure 16.4 presents a framework for helping the instructional team as they develop their plans.

As the reading specialist continues to work with the classroom teachers, the team should meet on a regular basis to review their plan and make necessary adjustments. After the team has worked with the student for 9 to 10 weeks, or the equivalent of a grading period, the reading specialist should prepare a written report to share with the parents at a conference. Guidelines for preparing a written report for parents are presented on the website.

The initial report to parents is usually quite detailed and lengthy. Remember that you are reporting extensive test results, sometimes from several professionals, as well as the initial intervention plan and implementation.

Brief progress reports should be prepared for each grading period. Try to limit progress instructional progress reports to the front and back of a single page. Some reading specialists prefer to use a form for these reports similar to the form used (in the staffing), but most seem to prefer a less-constrictive format. Present the reports in the context of a parent conference so that you can talk with the parents about the contents and explain any terms that might be unfamiliar to them. An example of a framework used for progress reports is provided on the website.

FIGURE 16.4   Framework for Instructional Planning

INSTRUCTIONAL PLAN

Student: Teacher:

Age: Grade: Date:

Student's Reading Levels		
Areas Evaluated	**Independent Levels**	**Instructional Levels**
Oral Reading		
Silent Reading		
Combined Reading		
Language Level		
Major Area of Strength		
Major Area of Instructional Need		

Areas of Emphasis

   Specific instructional needs

Strengths that can be used to address needs

What are some topics of interest to the student that you can use for motivating literate behaviors?

Based on your analysis of the student's reading and writing performance, what are your objectives in the following areas? Identify one to two strategies that you can use with your student to help you achieve these objectives.

Guided Reading

1.

2.

3.

Strategies:

Writing

1.

2.

3.

Continued

Strategies:

Word Knowledge/Word Recognition

1.

2.

3.

Strategies:

Word Knowledge/Vocabulary Development

1.

2.

3.

Strategies:

Independent Reading

1.

2.

3.

Possible Titles:

Do you need to administer any additional assessment instruments? If so, please list and identify your purpose for administering that instrument. This may change after you meet the student.

Instrument	Purpose for Administration

Go to MyEducationLab and select the topic *Involving Parents*. Then, go to the Activities and Applications section, watch the video entitled "A Teacher's Experience in Involving Parents in Their Children's Reading and Writing," and respond to the accompanying questions.

A systematic assessment plan should be incorporated into the student's instructional intervention. This assessment plan should provide documentation of the student's response to intervention. General education classroom teachers may need help designing the assessment plan and documenting progress. Careful records should be maintained so that if the student services team questions the student's progress and decides to consider referral for further evaluation, documentation can be provided.

Working with Parents

As coordinators of the literacy program, reading specialists serve as advocates of the literacy program with parents. Parent support is a crucial component to the success of

FIGURE 16.5   Family Literacy Suggestions for Primary Students

FAMILY LITERACY SUGGESTIONS

Primary Students   Student:

                                                    Teacher:

                                                    Date:

The most important thing you can do at home is to share books with your children. You should read with your child every day for at least 15–20 minutes. This should include time you read to your child or listen to a taped book together and follow the text. It should also include time you listen to your child read.

As you read, you should stop at critical points in the book and ask your child to predict what will happen next. For example, when the main character is faced with a dilemma, ask your child what he or she thinks the character will do. Also ask why your child thinks the character will take that action. You should also predict. After you read further, ask your child if the character did what she or he had expected. If not, what did the character do instead? How would the story have been different if the character had done what you and your child predicted?

When you read books to *Student's Name*, please select books at the 00 grade level or lower.

When *Student's Name* is reading books to you, please select books at the 00 grade level or lower.

Student's Name especially likes to read books about animals.

You can also support what we are doing in the reading center by giving your child additional practice in skill development.

These are our instructional goals for this term:

> *Include four to five bulleted goals*

You can help at home by having *Student's Name* practice:

> *Include four to five bulleted ideas*

Go to MyEducationLab and select the topic *Involving Parents*. Then, go to the Activities and Applications section, watch the video entitled "Working with Parents and Families," and respond to the accompanying questions.

literacy programs as well as student achievement. Children's early literacy development is highly correlated to their literacy experiences at home. Research has shown that shared reading experiences that occur through storybook reading enhance children's language development and listening comprehension. When parents engage in explicit teaching of literacy skills, they support children's development of phonemic and phonological awareness (Sénéchal & LeFevre, 2002).

Parents can model fluent reading, guide children's listening through effective questioning techniques, and play learning games to develop specific literacy skills. In the reading center, teachers share guidelines for selecting reading materials as well as games and learning experiences for families to enhance children's literacy development. Parents also provide a captive audience for children to practice their early reading skills. After teachers introduce a book in school, children can take copies of the book home to read to family members. Figure 16.5 provides an example of a family literacy plan that may be distributed to parents of primary-age students.

Reading specialists also design home reading projects to support instruction and develop reading incentive programs for the entire school. As students mature, parents' roles in their literacy development change. Older students usually prefer to read on their own. However, they still need literacy role models. Parents need to model reading and writing for different purposes. Reading specialists and teachers should encourage parents to read magazines, newspapers, and books while their children are reading. Then they can share items of interest from their reading and ask their children to share interesting items with them. If parents ask their children to substantiate their answers by reading part of the text, children have opportunities to practice fluent reading. Figure 16.6 is an example of a family literacy plan developed for intermediate- and middle school-age students.

Reading specialists are often included in parent conferences. If they are involved in the student's instruction, they meet with teachers during parent conferences to describe collaborative instructional intervention for their children.

Reading specialists need to communicate with parents and classroom teachers about how parents can support students as they complete homework assignments. Parents of students who are in special education classes or in instructional intervention programs frequently report that classroom teachers are often unaware of their children's limitations and special needs (Munk, Bursuck, Epstein, Jayanthi, Nelson, & Polloway, 2001). Reading specialists need to serve as liaisons in these situations. They need to provide support for classroom teachers and collaborate with them so that they have a strong understanding of students' needs and adaptive instructional strategies to support their literacy development. They can also initiate teacher-parent communication to ensure good home-school relations to best support students' learning.

If students are administered a complete literacy assessment, reading specialists should remain in contact with parents during and after the assessment to keep them apprised of the procedures and instructional intervention plans for their children. As discussed previously, this contact begins with a conference with the parents and classroom teachers working with the student as well as any resource professionals who work with the student. The initial conference is followed with a parent interview as part of the assessment process.

Go to MyEducationLab and select the topic *English Language Learners*. Then, go to the Activities and Applications section, watch the video entitled "Incorporating the Home Experiences of Culturally Diverse Students into the Classroom – Part 4," and respond to the accompanying questions.

Literacy Advocates in the Community

As leaders of the literacy program for their schools, reading specialists also serve as literacy advocates in the community. This means they must be able to articulate the program to parents, volunteers, school board members, community agencies, and members of the community at large (Moxley & Taylor, 2006).

Reading specialists can arrange for community members to volunteer in schools. Often, schools can foster partnerships with community businesses

FIGURE 16.6 Family Literacy Suggestions for Intermediate and Middle School Students

FAMILY LITERACY SUGGESTIONS

Middle School and High Schools Students

Student:

Teacher:

Date:

The most important thing you can do at home is to share books with your children. However, most students at this age read silently, and they need to practice silent reading. While *Student's Name* is reading, read your own book, a favorite section of the newspaper, or a magazine article. After 20–30 minutes of reading, share an interesting part of what you read with *Student's Name* and ask her or him something about his or her reading. If you read an excerpt aloud, you are more likely to encourage *Student's Name* to read a short piece of text aloud to you.
Possible questions include:

For fiction:

Who is/are the most important character(s) in your book?
What problem is the character trying to solve?
What is your favorite part so far?
How do you think the character will try to solve the problem?
Does the character remind you of someone you know or have read about before?
Could something like this happen?

For nonfiction:

What is the most important thing that has happened?
Who are the people involved? What are they trying to accomplish?
Does this remind you of anything else you have read about or learned?

Student's Name should be reading books independently at the 00 grade level.

You can also support what we are doing in the reading center by giving your child additional practice in skill development.

Our instructional goals for this term have been:

Include four to five bulleted goals

You can help at home by having *Student's Name* practice:

Include four to five bulleted ideas

or agencies to provide people to share books with students. Community agencies provide small grants for individual classrooms or schools. Sometimes, businesses will provide incentive programs to support students' reading or writing.

Summary

The roles of reading specialists have evolved from pullout remedial reading teachers to leaders of literacy instruction at the school, district, and community levels. Their responsibilities include instructional support, coaching, assessment, planning for instructional intervention, professional development, and coordination of literacy programs.

Reading specialists must collaborate with teachers and other professionals to provide effective instruction for struggling readers. They often work with teachers in their classrooms to provide adaptive instruction for small groups of students. They work with student services teams to ensure appropriate placement and intervention for students with special leaning needs. They often bring together the appropriate professionals to provide services to meet students' needs. Reading specialists provide training for paraprofessionals so that they can provide instructional support for students.

Communication with parents and facilitating communication between classroom teachers and parents are important parts of a reading specialist's responsibilities. Specialists may also conduct parent workshops or participate in parent-teacher conferences to foster students' literacy development.

Reading specialists often serve as liaisons between administrators and teachers. They may convey administrative decisions to teachers or serve as advocates for teachers to obtain resources needed to support instruction.

References

Allington, R. L. (1986). Policy constraints and effective compensatory reading instruction: A review. In J. B. Hoffman (Ed.), *Effective Teaching of Reading: Research and Practice*, p. 261–289. Newark, DE: International Reading Association.

Allington, R. L., & McGill-Franzen, A. (1989). School response to reading failure: Instruction for Chapter 1 and special education students in grades 2, 4, and 8. *Elementary School Journal*, 89, 529–542.

Bean, R. M. (2004). *The Reading Specialist: Leadership for the Classroom, School, and Community*. New York: Guilford Press.

Bean, R. M., Cooley, W., Eichelberger, R. T., Lazar, M., & Zigmond, N. (1991). In-class or pullout: Effects of setting on the remedial reading program. *Journal of Reading Behavior*, 23, 445–464.

Birdwell, J. (2003). High hopes: The 2001 reauthorization of Title I. www.Sewanee.edu/Education/nclb_paper.pdf.

Borman, G. D., & D'Agostino, J. V. (1996). Title I and student achievement: A meta-analysis of federal evaluation results. *Educational Evaluation and Policy Analysis*, 4, 309–326.

Borman, G. D. (2003). How can Title I improve achievement? *Educational Leadership*, 60, 49–53.

Borman, G. D., & D'Agostino, J. V. (2001). Title I and student achievement: A quantitative synthesis. In G. D. Borman, S. Stringfield, & R. E. Slavin (Eds.), *Title I: Compensatory Education at the Crossroads*, pp. 25–57. Mahwah, NJ: Lawrence Erlbaum Associates.

Casey, K. (2006). *Literacy Coaching: The Essentials.* Porstmouth, NH: Heinemann.

International Reading Association. (2000). *Teaching All Children to Read: The Roles of the Reading Specialist—A Position Statement of the International Reading Association.* Newark, DE: International Reading Association.

Klein, J., Monti, D., Mulcahy-Ernt, P., & Spock, A. (1997). *Literacy for All: Reading/Language Arts Programs and Personnel in Connecticut Schools.* Connecticut Association for Reading Research.

McDill, E. L., & Natriello, G. (1998). The effectiveness of the Title I compensatory education program: 1965–1997. *Journal of Education for Students Placed at Risk, 3,* 317–335.

Moxley, D. E., & Taylor, R. T. (2006). *Literacy Coaching: A Handbook for School Leaders.* Thousand Oaks, CA: Corwin Press.

Munk, D. D., Bursuck, W. D., Epstein, M. H., Jayanthi, M., Nelson, J., & Polloway, E. A. (2001). Homework communication problems: Perspectives of special and general education parents. *Reading and Writing Quarterly, 17,* 189–203.

No Child Left Behind Act of 2001. Public Law 110, 107th Cong. 2nd sess. (January 8, 2002).

Puig, E. A., & Froelich, K. S. (2007). *The Literacy Coach: Guiding in the Right Direction.* Boston: Allyn & Bacon.

Puma, M. J., Karweit, N., Price, C., Ricciuti, A., Thompson, W., & Vaden-Kiernan, M. (1997). *Prospects: Final Report on Student Outcomes.* Bethesda, MD: Abt Associates.

Rodgers, A., & Rodgers, E. M. (2007). *The Effective Literacy Coach: Using Inquiry to Support Teaching and Learning.* New York: Teachers College Press.

Sénéchal, M., & LeFerre, J. A. (2002). Parental involvement in the development of children's reading skill: A five-year longitudinal study. *Child Development, 73,* 445–460.

Toll, C. A. (2006). *The Literacy Coach's Desk Reference: Processes and Perspectives for Effective Coaching.* Urbana, IL: National Council of Teachers of English.

U.S. Department of Education. (1997). *Reauthorization of the Elementary and Secondary Education Act.* Washington, DC: U.S. Department of Education.

PEARSON
myeducationlab
Where the Classroom Comes to Life

MyEducationLab is a research-based learning tool that brings teaching to life. Go to the Jennings, Caldwell, & Lerner 6th Edition MyEducationLab for Reading Assessment site at www.myeducationlab.com to:

◆ engage in multimedia exercises to help you

build a deeper and more applied understanding of chapter content;

◆ utilize extensive resources including videos from real classrooms, Praxis and licensure preparation, a lesson plan builder, and materials to help you in your teaching career.

Materials for Obtaining Background Information

parent interview

~K-6

middle School

↓ *previous or current teacher*

NORTHEASTERN ILLINOIS UNIVERSITY READING CENTER

Parent Interview

New Student

Student's Name: _____ Age: ____ Grade: ____ Birth Date: _____

Person Being Interviewed: _____ Relationship to Student: _____

Person Conducting Interview: _____ Date of Interview: _____

Can you tell me three positive things about your child?

1. _____

2. _____

3. _____

Environmental Information

Home Environment

Members of Family Present in Home:

Name	Relationship to Student	Age	Birthplace	Occupation

Family Members not Living in Home:

Name	Relationship to Student	Age	Birthplace	Occupation

Describe any reading or learning problems experienced by family members.

_____

_____

What reading activities, including reading to or with your child, are done at home?

_____

_____

Describe your child's TV viewing.

_____

_____

What are your child's responsibilities at home?

_____

_____

What are the attitudes of family members toward reading?

_____

_____

School Environment

Describe your child's preschool and kindergarten experiences.

_____

_____

At what age did your child enter first grade?

_____

Describe your child's reading experiences in first grade.

_____

_____

Has your child repeated any grade? If so, why?

_____

_____

Describe your child's current school and classes, including any special placements, such as special education or bilingual instruction.

_____

_____

Describe the homework your child is assigned.

_____

_____

How does your child do in areas other than reading, such as math, spelling, hand-writing, social studies, science?

_____

_____

Has your child's school attendance been regular?

_____

Describe any extended absences from school.

_____

_____

Describe your child's reading instruction, including grouping within the class, if any.

_____

_____

Does your child receive any special help in school? If so, please describe.

_____

_____

Please describe any testing your child has experienced.

_____

_____

Please describe any help your child has received outside of school, such as summer school or outside tutoring.

_____

_____

When did you first become concerned about your child's reading?

_____

_____

Can you think of anything that might have contributed to your child's reading problem?

_____

_____

Social and Cultural Environment

Describe your child's relationship with other family members.

_____

_____

What are your child's interests and leisure activities?

_____

_____

Describe your child's friends and social group.

_____

_____

Information about the Individual

Physical Information

How would you compare your child's physical development with that of other children of the same age?

_____

_____

Please describe pregnancy, delivery, and early history of your child.

_____

_____

Please describe your child's general health.

_____

_____

Please describe any specific illnesses, allergies, or accidents.

_____

_____

Is your child taking any medications? If so, please list and describe.

_____

_____

_____

_____

Has your child ever been unconscious? If so, please describe the circumstances.

_____

_____

Does your child seem to have any difficulty maintaining attention?

_____

_____

When is the last time your child's hearing was tested?

_____

_____

Who tested his/her hearing, and what were the recommendations?

_____

_____

Has your child ever experienced a hearing loss?

_____

_____

When is the last time your child's vision was tested?

_____

_____

Who tested his/her vision, and what were the results?

_____

_____

Emotional Information

Does your child seem to be happy?

_____

_____

Does your child exhibit any signs of emotional tension or lack of self-confidence? If so, please describe.

_____

_____

What is your child's attitude toward reading?

_____

_____

_____

Language Development

What languages are spoken in your home?

_____

_____

What languages does your child speak?

_____

_____

How did your child's early language development compare to that of others?

_____

_____

Has your child received any bilingual or ESL services?

_____

_____

Has your child received any speech or language therapy?

_____

_____

Comments and Suggestions

Is there anything else we should know about in working with your child? Does s/he have any special needs that we should take into consideration?

_____

_____

_____

_____

ALL ABOUT ME

Student's Name: _____ Age: _____ Grade: _____

Teacher's Name: _____ Date: _____

Who lives at home with you?

_____

_____

What are some things that you and your family do together?

_____

_____

What are some of your favorite books?

_____

_____

Do you read at home?

_____

Do you get books from the library or store?

_____

_____

What are some of your favorite TV shows?

_____

_____

What are some of your favorite movies and videos?

_____

_____

What kinds of music do you like?

_____

_____

What are some of your favorite songs?

_____

_____

Who are your favorite actors?

_____

_____

Singers?

_____

_____

Do you like sports?

_____

If yes:

What is your favorite sport?

_____

What is your favorite team?

_____

Who is your favorite athlete?

_____

What sports do you play?

_____

_____

Do you have any pets? What kinds?

_____

_____

Do you have any chores to do at home?

_____

_____

What is your favorite subject in school?

_____

_____

What are some subjects you don't like?

_____

_____

Do you have reading groups, or does the whole class read together?

_____

_____

What are the names of some books you are reading in school?

_____

_____

What happens in your class during reading time?

_____

_____

Do you like learning to read?

_____

_____

If you could change one thing about your reading class, what would it be?

_____

_____

What kind of homework do you have?

_____

_____

Who are your best friends?

_____

_____

Who are your friends in school?

_____

_____

What do you like to do with your friends?

_____

_____

Do you ever have trouble hearing things?

_____

Do your eyes ever hurt?

_____

Do you ever have trouble seeing the board in school?

_____

Do you ever have trouble seeing the print in books?

_____

What clubs do you belong to?

_____

_____

What kinds of lessons do you take?

_____

_____

What are you interested in?

_____

_____

What do you want to do when you grow up and finish school?

_____

_____

Why do people read?

_____

_____

What do you do when you come to something you don't know while you are reading?

_____

_____

Who is the best reader you know?

_____

_____

What makes this person such a good reader?

_____

_____

NORTHEASTERN ILLINOIS UNIVERSITY
READING CENTER

Interest/Attitude Interview for Adolescents

Student Name: _____ Age: ____ Grade in School: _____

Person Conducting Interview: _____ Date of Interview: _____

Home Life

How many people are there in your family?

Names	Relationship to You

Do you have your own room or do you share a room?

_____

_____

Do your parent(s) work?

_____

What kinds of jobs do they have?

_____

_____

Do you have jobs around the house? What are they?

_____

_____

What do you usually do after school?

_____

_____

Do you have a TV in your room?

_____

How much time would you say you spend watching TV a day?

_____

Do you have a certain time to go to bed during the week?

_____

What time do you usually go to bed on a school night?

_____

Do you belong to any clubs at school or outside school?

_____

What are they?

_____

_____

What are some things you like to do with your family?

_____

_____

School Environment

Do you like school?

_____

_____

What is your favorite class?

_____

_____

What classes do you not like?

_____

_____

How much homework do you usually have on a school night?

_____

_____

What kinds of homework do you usually have?

_____

_____

Do you have a special place to study at home?

_____

_____

Does anyone help you with your homework?   Who?

_____

_____

What kind of reader do you consider yourself? [*Good, not so good*]

_____

If good: What do you think has helped you most to become a good reader?

_____

_____

If not so good: What do you think causes someone to not be a good reader?

_____

_____

Is there anything you can think of that would help you get better at reading?

_____

_____

Do you like to write?

_____

What kinds of writing do you like to do?

_____

_____

Do you do much writing at school?

_____

_____

What kinds of writing do you do at school?

_____

_____

What kinds of writing assignments do you like?

_____

_____

What kinds do you dislike?

_____

_____

If you went to a new school, what is one thing you would like the teachers to know about you?

_____

_____

If you were helping someone learn to read, what would be the most important thing you could do to help that person?

_____

_____

How does knowing how to read help people?

_____

_____

Social Life

What do you like to do after school and on weekends?

_____

_____

Who are your best friends?

_____

_____

Does your best friend go to your school?

_____

_____

What do you like to do with your friends?

_____

_____

_____

Do you like music?

_____

What kinds?

_____

_____

Who are your favorite performers?

_____

_____

What are your favorite TV shows?

_____

_____

Who are your favorite TV stars?

_____

_____

Do you like movies or videos?

_____

What kinds of movies do you like?

_____

_____

Who are your favorite stars?

_____

_____

Do you like sports?

_____

What kinds of sports do you play?

_____

_____

What kinds of sports do you like to watch?

_____

_____

What is your favorite team?

_____

Who are your favorite athletes?

_____

_____

If you could read a book about anything, what would you choose?

_____

_____

What is the best book you've ever read?

_____

Do you have any favorite magazines?

_____

Do you ever read the newspaper?

_____

What parts do you usually read?

_____

_____

SCHOOL INFORMATION FORM

Student's Name: _____ Grade: ____ Date: _____

School or Organization Name: _____

Teacher Requesting Information: _____

Person Providing Information: _____ Position or Title: _____

School Attendance

How long has this student attended this school?

_____

Describe regularity of attendance.

_____

_____

Reading Performance

Is this student having problems in reading?

_____

Please describe these problems.

_____

_____

When were these problems first noticed?

_____

Describe this student's areas of strength in reading.

_____

_____

Describe this student's areas of weakness in reading.

_____

_____

Please describe the reading instruction provided, including whether reading is taught as a separate subject, whether students are grouped and which group this student is in, whether students change classes for reading, whether a reading series or separate reading book is used for instruction, and what supplementary materials are used.

_____

_____

_____

_____

_____

List some books this student is reading.

_____

_____

Describe this student's progress in other areas, such as spelling, writing, math, science, social studies, and gym.

_____

_____

Describe any help this student receives in addition to regular classroom instruction.

_____

_____

Describe the student's independence, ability to complete tasks, follow directions, and pay attention.

_____

_____

What kinds of homework is this student given? Is it usually completed?

_____

_____

Does this student read for pleasure?

_____

Does this student seem tired at school?

_____

Does this student seem to have any vision or hearing problems?

_____

How does this student's physical development compare with that of others?

_____

_____

How does this student's oral language compare with that of other students?

_____

_____

Has any testing been done at school? If so, please provide a summary below or attach information with returned form.

_____

_____

_____

_____

_____

_____

_____

_____

_____

_____

_____

Student Informal Reading Assessment

Accompanying teacher protocols and administration guide can be found in the Instructor's Manual.

Word List A

play	run	day	she	a	this
with	and	make	yes	pet	is
they	jump	in	it	he	home
like	ride	said	good	dog	the
to					

Word List B

his	sat	saw	made	green	mother
dad	next	duck	fast	frog	got
animals	still	swim	why	tree	bed
went	then	rock	over	house	box
lake					

Word List C

other	family	brother	noise	best	hurt
children	clean	baked	sounded	doctor	leg
stay	chairs	cake	bark	tiger	soon
grandma	watch	heard	stuck	zoo	again
coming					

Word List D

camp	packed	teeth	seemed	shirts	world
year	clothes	kitchen	forever	tent	playground
spend	dressed	eggs	hundreds	knew	classroom
whole	brushed	toast	shorts	teacher	card
week					

Word List E

miserable	discovered	underwater	accident	underneath	bandage
chosen	unusual	camera	maple	screeched	reporters
parents	seaweed	capture	excitement	rescue	information
study	dusk	film	dangerous	arrived	passengers
harbor					

Word List F

champion	performance	athlete	permit	mountainside
skater	junior	confidence	slopes	challenger
instruction	competes	countless	convince	gear
ladybug	article	represent	daybreak	sunrise
approval	brilliant	national	icicles	disappointment

Word List G

placid	nightfall	cramped	destruction	injured
surroundings	rainfall	rampaging	woodpile	mechanic
spectacular	belongings	roused	restore	frontier
adventurous	continuous	thrashed	ranger	reassured
refreshing	tensions	thunderbolts	camper	civilization

Word List H

sunup	parallel	acknowledged	veterinarian	observation
perspiration	effective	midafternoon	biology	orangutan
embarrassment	downpour	inspection	recommended	specialize
frustration	alternate	enterprising	zookeeper	equipped
drainage	rainwater	declined	placement	surgery

Word List I

algebra	bolstered	appreciative	tolerated	contempt
comical	mistrust	perceived	coordination	gymnastics
bifocals	expectation	confront	acrobatic	cartwheel
desperation	quizzical	ample	inseparable	unison
computation	cartoonist	alternative	enthusiastically	elegance

Word List J

excelled	overpowering	corrugated	journalist	devastated
biological	hysteria	innermost	correspondent	phenomenal
dissecting	preserved	administrator	southeastern	inclination
agonizing	contemplation	disheartened	eroded	prestigious
envision	dismantled	extensive	seacoasts	ambassadors

ORAL READING PASSAGES

Jill and Pat Make a Cake

Jill likes to play with Pat. They like to run and jump. They like to ride bikes, too.

One day, they wanted to make a cake. Jill asked her mom if they could make a cake in her house. Jill's mom said no. She did not have time to help.

Jill and Pat went to Pat's house. Pat asked her mom if they could make a cake in her house. Pat's mom said yes.

Jill and Pat made a cake. Pat's mom helped. It was good.

Nick's Trip to the Lake

Nick and his dad like animals. One day, Nick and his dad went to the lake. They went to see the animals. They sat next to the lake. They were very still.

Then Nick saw a big duck. He saw the duck swim to a big rock in the lake. Something made the duck fly away fast.

Nick asked his dad, "Why did the duck fly away?"

Nick's dad said, "Look over there." He showed Nick something in the lake. Nick thought he would see something big.

What a surprise to see a little green frog!

Ben Helps his Mom

Ben was sad. He wanted to go to the park with the other children. But his mom said he had to stay home.

Ben's grandma was coming to see his family. He had to help clean the house.

Ben had to put away his toys. He had to make his bed. He had to move the chairs. Then Mom cleaned the floor.

Then he had to watch his baby brother while Mom baked a cake.

At last, Grandma's car was coming down the road! She got out of the car. She had a big box. Ben heard a noise. It came from the box. It sounded like a bark!

Danny Goes to Camp

Danny is very happy this morning! This is the first day of camp. Last year, Danny went to day camp. This year, he can spend nights at camp. He is going to stay a whole week, just like his brother.

Last night, Danny packed his clothes. This morning, he dressed and brushed his teeth. Then he went to the kitchen. Danny's dad gave him some eggs and toast. But Danny was too happy to eat!

Danny's dad drove him to camp. The trip seemed like it would take forever. Finally, they came to the camp. There were hundreds of boys and girls all dressed in blue shorts and yellow shirts. As soon as the car stopped, Danny saw his friend Joe. Joe told him they would be sleeping in the same tent. Danny knew this would be a great week!

Kay's Island Home

Kay lives on an island far out in the ocean. You may think that it would be fun to live on an island. But Kay is miserable. Kay hasn't seen her friends in a year. There is no one to play with or talk to. There isn't even a school!

Why has Kay's family chosen such a lonely life? Kay's parents study animals that only live in the harbor of this island. But Kay's dad knows how unhappy Kay is. He wants to do something to make her happy.

Kay's dad discovered a new kind of fish. It has bright orange fins and a blue tail. Dad named this unusual fish after Kay. He calls it the Kayfish. It hides in the seaweed. It only comes out in the morning and at dusk.

Kay's dad takes his underwater camera to the harbor every day. He hopes to capture the Kayfish on film. Maybe someday her dad will learn enough about the Kayfish. Then Kay can go back to her old school. Then she can see all her old friends again. Kay hopes that day will come soon.

Jessie, Champion Skater

More than anything, Jessie wants to be a champion skater! She can't remember a time she didn't want to skate or a time she didn't want to be the best.

Jessie began skating instruction when she was three years old. In her first ice show, she played the part of a ladybug. She still remembers her red and black spotted costume. Most of all, Jessie remembers the audience clapping their approval of her first performance.

Jessie doesn't have much time for ice shows anymore. Now she must practice jumps and turns. When Jessie was six, she started skating in contests for ages six to twelve. By the time she was eight, Jessie was the junior state champion. Now that she is thirteen, Jessie competes with adults. She is the state champion in ice skating.

Last week, a sports writer wrote an article about Jessie's performance. It said she was a "brilliant young athlete." It said her skating showed "confidence and grace." Jessie thought about the countless falls she had taken to make each jump look perfect. She didn't feel very graceful or confident!

Next week, Jessie will represent her state in a national meet. This will be the first time she has skated at this level. She hopes all her practice and hard work will pay off. Jessie hopes that her confidence and grace will help her win.

Ted's Camping Trip

Ted's family was taking one last camping trip before school started. They found the perfect campsite! It was just where a clear stream trickled into placid Green Lake. The surroundings were ideal. Ted and his brothers could swim to their hearts' content. They could row into hidden coves along the shore. It was a perfect place to fish or relax.

The first two days were great, with spectacular sunrises and adventurous days. The nights were cool and refreshing. Just before nightfall on the third day, a rainfall began. Everyone joked and laughed as they packed their belongings. But, by the second day of continuous rain, tensions rose. The four boys grew tired of sharing their cramped tent. Late that night, Ted was awakened by a loud crash. He realized he was floating! Their quiet stream had become a rampaging river and their tent had been washed into it! Ted roused his brothers and they thrashed about in the darkness as they struggled to pull themselves onto the riverbank. Streaks of lightning flashed across the sky. Thunderbolts shook the earth. The storm raged through the night.

Near daybreak, the lightning and thunder ceased. The brothers could see the path of destruction left by the storm. The huge oak across the stream had been struck down. Now it was no more than a jumbled woodpile. Their canoes had been tossed about the shore like toys. They worked hard all morning to restore their campsite. During lunch, a park ranger came by to see if they were okay. He told them a camper had been injured when a tree was hit by lightning and fell on his tent. Ted and his brothers were lucky to have escaped with only scratches and bruises.

Mike's New Bike

Mike squinted at the midday sky. He had been working since sunup and needed a break. Wiping the perspiration from his face, he continued his exhausting work.

Mike had been working all summer to earn enough money for a new bike. His ancient, beaten up bike was a total embarrassment. But his mom said they couldn't afford a new one. Even though Mike knew she was right, in his frustration, he shouted back at her, "You never give me anything!"

He only needed fifty more dollars. Mr. Painter had offered him forty dollars to dig a new drainage ditch. He wanted to stop the flooding in his rose garden. Mr. Painter wanted the new ditch to run parallel to the old one. Mike didn't think that would be effective in a downpour. So he suggested an alternate plan to direct the rainwater away from the house.

Mike noticed Mr. Painter watching him from behind a curtain. Knowing the old grouch, he'd deduct that little brow-wiping break from his pay. As he returned to his work, Mike waved. Mr. Painter acknowledged the wave and disappeared.

Mike worked steadily until midafternoon. Then Mr. Painter came out for an inspection. "Why don't you lay off for today and get a fresh start tomorrow?"

"I'd rather finish up," replied Mike. "It's supposed to rain tonight, and I'd like to have this operational before the next storm."

About six-thirty, Mike laid the last pipe in place. As he was returning the tools to the shed, Mr. Painter walked up, "Mike, you're an enterprising young man. You don't see many young people these days who care about their work." He handed Mike an envelope and went to inspect his roses.

When Mike opened the envelope, he counted three twenty-dollar bills. He ran to catch Mr. Painter and started to hand one back to him. Mr. Painter declined the offer, "Take it as thanks for keeping an old man from making the same mistake twice."

In Trouble Again

I knew I shouldn't be drawing in algebra class, but I just couldn't resist. Mr. Galvin had such a comical look as he peered over his bifocals at Jamie's futile attempt to solve the problem on the board. Maybe I could call this brilliant work of art "Galvin-eyes" or something equally insulting.

I suddenly realized Mr. Galvin was calling my name, "Peter, what is your solution to this problem?" Oh no, Mr. Galvin was walking in my direction! If I got in trouble again, I could be suspended. In desperation, I tried to adjust my book to cover the drawing, but it was too late. "Peter, have you completed the computation for problem number seven?"

Even though I hadn't even started the problem, I replied in my most respectful tone, "Not quite, sir." When he stopped at the front of the row, it bolstered my confidence. "I'll have it done in just a couple of minutes." Why did I always have to open my big mouth, instead of leaving well-enough alone? Now he was coming directly toward my desk.

Mr. Galvin, in a tone of total mistrust, suggested, "Why don't you come to the board and show us how far you've gotten, and perhaps your classmates can help you complete the problem?"

As I fumbled for an answer, Mr. Galvin reached my desk. He lifted my book with the expectation of finding a partially solved algebra problem. Instead, he found a drawing of himself, bifocals and all, glaring at Jamie with a quizzical look on his face. At least I hadn't had time to write the caption!

"Peter!" boomed Mr. Galvin, "just what do you expect to make of yourself with this kind of behavior?"

Without thinking how it might be taken, I replied, "A cartoonist."

Wrong answer! The class gave an appreciative round of applause. But Mr. Galvin perceived this as yet another attempt on my part to confront him. Once again, I had tried to undermine his authority with the class.

I had ample opportunity to think of alternative replies while I waited in the assistant principal's office.

Biology Woes

James had always excelled in science, winning every science fair and making straight As. But this year, he would be taking Biological Studies, and he knew that meant dissecting animals. He was agonizing over the thought of cutting up a creature that had been alive. He couldn't even envision cutting into a cockroach—and he hated those! James started the summer with an overpowering fear of embarrassing himself. By July, he had worked himself into a state of near hysteria.

To solve his problem, James bought a dissecting kit to practice. Inside the kit, he found an address to order preserved animals. After some contemplation, James chose an earthworm, a crawfish, a frog, and a snake.

When the animals arrived, James carefully dismantled the corrugated box so he wouldn't damage the contents. When he reached the innermost container, he was shocked beyond words! There must have been a mistake. Not only were these animals not preserved, they weren't even dead! James looked at the order form and discovered his mistake. He had marked the wrong code!

Suddenly, James was the proud owner of four creatures who were very much alive. He had no idea what to feed any of these animals nor any desire to find out. Deciding to dispose of them as quickly as possible, he biked to the nearest pet shop to sell the animals. The manager told him they only bought from licensed dealers. He tried the administrator of the zoo, but she didn't have room for any more animals just now. James was disheartened. He realized he would have to accept responsibility for the animals himself.

First, James went to the library. There he learned that the animals would have to be housed in separate containers. He went back to the pet store and bought four small aquariums. By the end of the summer, James had learned an extensive amount of information about his new pets. What had started as a dissection project had turned into a valuable study of live animals.

SILENT READING PASSAGES

Bill Wants a Pet

Bill wanted a pet. He asked his mom for a pet. She said he had to wait.

One day, Bill saw a little dog. The dog was crying.

Bill said, "This dog is lost." Bill took the dog home.

Bill's mom saw the dog. Bill asked, "May I keep it?"

Bill's mom said he could keep the dog.

Bill had a pet!

Jane and Meg's House

Jane and Meg are friends. One day, Meg went to Jane's house to play.

They went outside. Jane showed Meg a big tree. Jane said, "I want to make a house next to this tree."

Meg said, "I know! Come to my house! My mother just got a new bed. It came in a very big box. Maybe we can have the box for our house."

Meg and Jane went to Meg's house. They asked Meg's mother if they could have the box. Meg's mother said yes.

Jane and Meg took the box to make a house. They had fun.

Jan's Favorite Book

Jan loves to read books!

Most of all, Jan loves books about animals. She likes books about dogs that help put out fires. She likes books about cats that get stuck in trees.

The best book is about a doctor. The doctor in the book takes care of animals. Jan loves to read about him.

In the book, a tiger at the zoo was hurt. The doctor came to the zoo. He put something on the tiger's leg. Soon the tiger was well again. When Jan grows up, she wants to be a doctor. She will take care of animals, too.

Sarah's New Teacher

Today is the first day of school. But Sarah doesn't want to go. This year, Sarah was supposed to have Mrs. Black for her teacher. But last June, Mrs. Black told the class she wouldn't be back this year. She told them their new teacher would be very nice.

Mrs. Black is the best teacher in the world! Last year, sometimes the big girls on the playground wouldn't let Sarah and her friends jump rope. Then Mrs. Black would come out to turn the rope just for them. Sarah doesn't think a new teacher will do that.

Sarah was surprised when she got to her classroom. The new teacher's name was Mr. Black. He said, "Good morning, boys and girls. My name is Mr. Black. I am married to Mrs. Black. I will be your new teacher. Mrs. Black asked me to tell you that she had a baby on Friday. I brought a picture of Mrs. Black and the baby." Sarah and her friends made a card for Mrs. Black and the baby. Maybe the new teacher wouldn't be so bad after all.

The Accident

Yesterday, Bill's dad ran into the kitchen, shouting, "There has been an accident!" He told Bill to call the police. He said to tell them a bus had hit a car at the corner of Oak and Maple Streets.

Bill wanted to go back to the corner with his dad. He wanted to join the excitement. But his dad said it was too dangerous. Bill watched out the window as his dad ran back out to the street. He hoped his dad wouldn't go on the bus. It was leaning against a wall. The car was underneath the bus and gas was all over the ground.

But his dad did go back on the bus. Bill watched as his dad carried people from the bus to the grass. Bill saw his dad carry a little girl from the bus. She was clinging to a teddy bear. He said, "Thank goodness, that's the last one!" Just then, a truck screeched to a stop as the rescue workers arrived. The rescue workers rushed to care for the people who were hurt. They even put a bandage on the little girl's bear! Then the news reporters arrived. They wanted information about Bill's dad. This morning there was a picture of Bill's dad in the paper. Under the picture, in big print, it said, "LOCAL HERO SAVES PASSENGERS".

Josh's Ski Trip

At daybreak, Josh looked out the window of the cabin. He looked through the icicles to the snow-covered mountainside. He couldn't wait to get out on the slopes! This year he would get to go on the Challenger Slope. He wanted to feel the wind rushing past his face as he raced down the hill.

When Josh's family came to Bear Mountain last year, Josh was the best skier in his class. But he was too short, and the ski patrol wouldn't permit him on the more difficult slopes. He tried to convince the captains of the ski patrol. He knew he was good enough to go on the tougher slopes, but they wouldn't bend the rules for anyone.

But during the long summer months, Josh had grown to five feet, seven inches, and nobody could stop him now! It was the first ski trip of the new season. The mountain was just outside the window, but everyone else was still sleeping peacefully. Josh couldn't stand it any longer! In silence, he picked up his boots and goggles and crept downstairs. He quietly lifted his gear down from the rack and slipped out the door.

The morning was perfect! The air was crisp, and the snow sparkled in the sunrise like silver as Josh made his way to the ski lift. He was anxious to feel the wind in his face. What a disappointment when he saw the new sign: "No children under fifteen without an adult!"

Grandpa's Farm

Sometimes Beth hated towns and cities! They were taking over, and the farms and open land were disappearing. Beth wished she could live on a farm, but her dad was a mechanic. He repaired machinery for a mill in town.

Beth's favorite times were spent with Grandpa on his farm. Beth spent almost all her weekends with Grandpa. On cool evenings, Grandpa would light a fire. Beth loved to read by the firelight, just like girls did when this was the frontier.

On Saturday mornings, Grandpa was always up early, ready for his long day of chores. First, the pigs had to be fed, and the chicken coop had to be cleaned. Then the stallion had to be brushed. When Beth was little, Grandpa let her help milk the cows, but now he used milking machines.

In the afternoon, Beth and Grandpa walked the horses. This was Beth's favorite chore. Grandpa's favorite place to walk the horses was Bear Mountain. It took most of the afternoon to ride all the way out to the mountain and back. Grandpa and Beth always packed a snack to eat on the mountaintop. As they shared their fruit and milk, they talked. Grandpa told her how much he liked to look out over the farms and towns for miles. These trips to the mountain reassured Beth. They showed her that there was still enough land and open spaces. They helped her to feel less closed in by civilization.

Pam's New Job

More than anything, Pam wanted to be a veterinarian. She was great with animals. For the last two years, Pam had volunteered at the zoo. But this summer, she was going to be paid. Pam's biology teacher had recommended her to work in a special science program.

Pam was disappointed when she found out she was assigned to the zoo nursery. Pam didn't want to feed a bunch of baby animals. She had hoped for something more exciting, like reptiles. Pam decided to talk to the zoo's vet, Dr. Mack. Maybe she would understand how Pam felt, and Pam could ask her to convince the zookeeper to change her placement.

When Pam arrived at the zoo, Dr. Mack was in the nursery. There had been an emergency, and Dr. Mack had been called to help. The nurse asked Pam to wait for Dr. Mack in the observation room. She was surprised to find that the observation room overlooked a small operating room. There she saw Dr. Mack, working frantically to save a baby orangutan. After several minutes, the tiny ape started to breathe on its own, and Dr. Mack came out to greet Pam, "I thought we were going to lose her! Since we rescued her from a fire, we've been trying to bottle-feed her, but suddenly she stopped breathing. The nurse called me because I specialize in great apes. Now that I'm sure she'll be all right, how can I help you?"

"I'm glad she's going to be okay," replied Pam. "I didn't know you were equipped for surgery."

"That's why we need someone like you. We just added the hospital last winter. We had it built in the nursery because it had separate rooms to house sick or injured animals. We need someone who can handle frightened animals and comfort them while they wait for surgery and while they recover. Now, what was it you wanted to discuss?"

Pam replied, "I think you've answered all my questions. When can I start?"

Gym Class

Sometimes, Debbie wondered how she and Kim even tolerated each other, much less remained best friends. While Debbie was outgoing, Kim was quiet and shy. While Debbie was famous for her total lack of coordination, Kim was the most acrobatic person in the entire school. Yet the girls were inseparable, best friends since kindergarten. They were thrilled to find out they would be in gym class together. But as usual, they had opposite opinions about actually taking gym. Kim greeted the class enthusiastically, and Debbie had nothing but contempt for it.

Today, they began the gymnastics unit, and Debbie wished she could crawl into a deep hole and disappear. Down the hall came the new gymnastics teacher, Ms. Bain. She announced that today they would be tumbling. Then Ms. Bain described some of the moves the girls would be doing, the forward roll, the backward roll, and the cartwheel.

Ms. Bain asked if anyone could demonstrate any of the moves for the class. The whole class sang out in unison, "Kim!" Then Ms. Bain asked Kim if she had taken lessons, and she nodded shyly. When Ms. Bain asked if Kim had gotten far enough along to demonstrate any of these moves, the class giggled. Debbie realized that Kim was too modest to tell Ms. Bain the truth, so she spoke up proudly, "Ms. Bain, Kim is the state champion in gymnastics. She's a competitor at the national level."

Ms. Bain smiled at Kim and said, "Maybe you could give us a demonstration of the routine you performed at the state meet." With some encouragement from her classmates, Kim agreed to show the class part of her tumbling routine.

As Debbie watched in admiration, Kim stepped onto the floor mat. As soon as she started to perform, her whole personality changed. Usually, Kim was awkward in front of people, but when she stepped onto the gym floor, her body became elegance in motion. Kim's normal shyness disappeared, and she seemed to be an actress playing the part of a gymnast. Even Ms. Bain was taken aback! She applauded approvingly and said she hoped Kim would invite her to the next meet.

Kate Becomes a Journalist

Kate's greatest ambition is to be a journalist. Throughout her high school years, she has been a photographer on the school newspaper. Now she is the senior editor of the school paper, but her goal is to be a foreign correspondent. Kate is taking a class in photography and learning how to use pictures to tell a story. Kate would like to find a way to combine writing about international relations and photography, perhaps writing for a news magazine or for a TV news show but using her own photographs.

Two years ago, Kate's history class took a trip to the southeastern states. She took her camera and photographed the eroded seacoasts. When Kate's pictures were published in the local newspaper, there were many letters to the editor praising her work.

Last year, when Kate was a junior, her class went to Mexico. Kate took pictures of how the recent earthquake had devastated the entire region. When Kate showed her pictures to the editor of the town newspaper, he asked her to write an article to go with her pictures. He told Kate that she had a unique talent for capturing people's attention with a profound photograph. He said if she wrote an article go with the pictures, people would understand the message in the photographs better. This time, public reaction was phenomenal! Kate could finally see a way to combine her ability to write with her interest in photography.

Now in her senior year, Kate is deciding where to go to college. Kate's inclination is to go to a prestigious college in Washington, DC or New York. She wants to be near the ambassadors and diplomats. Kate has never abandoned her goal to be a foreign correspondent. She keeps that in mind through all her decisions.

Test Index

Name Index

Subject Index

Photo Credits